Designing Security for a Microsoft®
Windows Server™ 2003 Network (70-298)

Textbook

Tony Northrup

PUBLISHED BY
Microsoft Press
A Division of Microsoft Corporation
One Microsoft Way
Redmond, Washington 98052-6399

Library of Congress Control Number 2005920970

Printed and bound in the United States of America.

1 2 3 4 5 6 7 8 9   QWT   9 8 7 6 5

Distributed in Canada by H.B. Fenn and Company Ltd.

A CIP catalogue record for this book is available from the British Library.

Microsoft Press books are available through booksellers and distributors worldwide. For further information about international editions, contact your local Microsoft Corporation office or contact Microsoft Press International directly at fax (425) 936-7329. Visit our Web site at www.microsoft.com/learning/. Send comments to *moac@microsoft.com*.

Acquisitions Editor: Lori Oviatt
Project Editor: Laura Sackerman

ISBN 13: 978-0-470-76745-0

SubAssy Part No. X11-15626
Body Part No. X11-15615

CONTENTS AT A GLANCE

CONTENTS

ABOUT THIS BOOK

Welcome to *Designing Security for a Microsoft Windows Server 2003 Network (70-298)*, a part of the Microsoft Official Academic Course (MOAC) series. Through lectures, discussions, demonstrations, textbook exercises, and classroom labs, this course teaches students the skills and knowledge necessary to protect networks running Windows Server 2003 in a corporate environment. The 13 chapters in this textbook walk you through key concepts of network security, including analyzing risk, distributing updates, designing a management infrastructure, hardening client and server platforms, designing a Public Key Infrastructure (PKI), and protecting remote access.

TARGET AUDIENCE

This textbook was developed for beginning information technology (IT) students who want to learn to design hardened networks with the most recent Microsoft operating systems and server applications. The target audience will provide network design services for enterprises, or they will use their knowledge to work in their own security consulting businesses.

PREREQUISITES

This textbook requires students meet the following prerequisites:

- One year of experience implementing and administering a network operating system in an enterprise environment

- A working knowledge of how to configure security on client and server computers running a Windows operating system

- Prerequisite knowledge and coursework as defined by the learning institution and the instructor

THE TEXTBOOK

The textbook content has been crafted to provide a meaningful learning experience to students in an academic classroom setting.

Key features of the MOAC textbooks include the following:

- Learning objectives for each chapter that prepare the student for the topic areas covered in that chapter.

- Chapter introductions that explain why the information is important.

- An inviting design with screen shots, diagrams, tables, bulleted lists, and other graphical formats that makes the book easy to comprehend and supports a number of different learning styles.

- Clear explanations of concepts and principles, and frequent exposition of step-by-step procedures.

- A variety of reader aids that highlight a wealth of additional information, including the following:

  - Note—Real-world application tips and alternative procedures, and explanations of complex procedures and concepts

  - Caution—Warnings about mistakes that can result in loss of data or are difficult to resolve

  - Important—Explanations of essential setup steps before a procedure and other critical instructions

  - More Info—Additional resources for students

- End-of-chapter review questions that assess knowledge and can serve as homework, quizzes, and review activities before or after lectures. (Answers to the textbook questions are available from the instructor.)

- Chapter summaries that distill the main ideas in a chapter and reinforce learning.

- Case scenarios (usually two per chapter) that provide students with an opportunity to evaluate, analyze, synthesize, and apply information learned in the chapter.

- A comprehensive glossary that defines key terms introduced in the book.

THE SUPPLEMENTAL COURSE MATERIALS STUDENT CD

This book comes with a Supplemental Course Materials CD, which contains a variety of informational aids to complement the book content:

- An electronic version of this textbook (eBook). For information about using the eBook, see the section titled "eBook Setup Instructions" later in this introduction.

- The Microsoft Press Readiness Review Suite built by MeasureUp. This suite of practice tests and objective reviews contains questions of varying complexity and offers multiple testing modes. Students can assess their understanding of the concepts presented in this book and use the results to develop a learning plan that meets their needs.

- An eBook of the *Microsoft Encyclopedia of Networking*, Second Edition.

- Microsoft PowerPoint slides based on textbook chapters, for note taking.

- Microsoft Word Viewer and Microsoft PowerPoint Viewer.

A second CD contains a 180-day evaluation edition of Windows Server 2003, Enterprise Edition.

> **NOTE**   The 180-day evaluation edition of Windows Server 2003 provided with this book is not the full retail product; it is provided only for the purposes of training and evaluation. Microsoft Technical Support does not support evaluation editions.

Readiness Review Suite Setup Instructions

The Readiness Review Suite includes a practice test of 300 sample exam questions and an objective review with an additional 125 questions. Use these tools to reinforce your learning and to identify areas in which you need to gain more experience before taking your final exam for the course, or the certification exam if you choose to do so.

▶ **Installing the Practice Test**

1. Insert the Supplemental Course Materials CD into your CD-ROM drive.

    NOTE If AutoRun is disabled on your machine, refer to the Readme.txt file on the Supplemental Course Materials CD.

2. On the user interface menu, select Readiness Review Suite and follow the prompts.

eBook Setup Instructions

The eBook is in Portable Document Format (PDF) and must be viewed using Adobe Acrobat Reader.

▶ **Using the eBook**

1. Insert the Supplemental Course Materials Student CD into your CD-ROM drive.

    NOTE If AutoRun is disabled on your machine, refer to the Readme.txt file on the CD.

2. On the user interface menu, select Textbook eBook and follow the prompts. You also can review any of the other eBooks provided for your use.

    NOTE You must have the Supplemental Course Materials Student CD in your CD-ROM drive to run the eBook.

THE LAB MANUAL

The lab manual is designed for use in either a combined or separate lecture and lab. The exercises in the lab manual correspond to textbook chapters and are for use in a classroom setting supervised by an instructor.

The lab manual presents a rich, hands-on learning experience that encourages practical solutions and strengthens critical problem-solving skills:

- Lab exercises teach procedures by using a step-by-step format. Questions interspersed throughout lab exercises encourage reflection and critical thinking about the lab activity.

- Lab review questions appear at the end of each lab and ask questions about the lab. They are designed to promote critical reflection.

- Lab challenges are review activities that ask students to perform a variation on a task they performed in the lab exercises, but without detailed instructions.

- Labs are based on realistic business settings and include an opening scenario and a list of learning objectives.

Students who successfully complete the lab exercises, lab review questions, and lab challenges in the lab manual will have a richer learning experience and deeper understanding of the concepts and methods covered in the course. They will be better able to answer and understand the testbank questions, especially the knowledge application and knowledge synthesis questions. They will also be much better prepared to pass the associated certification exams if they choose to do so.

NOTATIONAL CONVENTIONS

The following conventions are used throughout this textbook and the lab manual:

- Characters or commands that you type appear in **bold** type.

- Terms that appear in the glossary also appear in **bold** type.

- *Italic* in syntax statements indicates placeholders for variable information. *Italic* is also used for book titles and terms defined in the text.

- Names of files and folders appear in Title Caps, except when you are to type them directly. Unless otherwise indicated, you can use all lowercase letters when you type a file name in a dialog box or at a command prompt.

- File name extensions appear in all lowercase.

- Acronyms appear in all uppercase.

- **Monospace** type represents code samples, examples of screen text, or entries that you might type at a command prompt or in initialization files.

- Square brackets [ ] are used in syntax statements to enclose optional items. For example, [*filename*] in command syntax indicates that you can type a file name with the command. Type only the information within the brackets, not the brackets themselves.

- Braces { } are used in syntax statements to enclose required items. Type only the information within the braces, not the braces themselves.

KEYBOARD CONVENTIONS

- A plus sign (+) between two key names means that you must press those keys at the same time. For example, "Press ALT+TAB" means that you hold down ALT while you press TAB.

- A comma (,) between two or more key names means that you must press the keys consecutively, not at the same time. For example, "Press ALT, F, X" means that you press and release each key in sequence. "Press ALT+W, L" means that you first press ALT and W at the same time, and then you release them and press L.

COVERAGE OF EXAM OBJECTIVES

This book is intended to support a course that is structured around concepts and practical knowledge fundamental to this topic area, as well as the tasks that are covered in the objectives for the MCSE 70-298 exam. The following table correlates the exam objectives with the textbook chapters and labs. You may also find this table useful if you decide to take the certification exam.

> **NOTE**   The Microsoft Learning Web site, *http://www.microsoft.com/ learning*, describes the various Microsoft Certified Professional (MCP) certification exams and their corresponding courses. It provides up-to-date certification information and explains the certification process and the course options for MCP, as well as specific certifications offered by Microsoft.

Textbook and Lab Manual Coverage of Exam Objectives for MCSE Exam 70-298

Objective	Textbook	Lab Manual
Creating the Conceptual Design for Network Infrastructure Security by Gathering and Analyzing Business and Technical Requirements		
Analyze business requirements for designing security. Considerations include existing policies and procedures, sensitivity of data, cost, legal requirements, end-user impact, interoperability, maintainability, scalability, and risk.	Chapter 2	Labs 1 and 2
■ Analyze existing security policies and procedures.		Lab 2
■ Analyze the organizational requirements for securing data.		Labs 1 and 2
■ Analyze the security requirements of different types of data.		Lab 2
■ Analyze risks to security within the current IT administration structure and security practices.		Lab 1
Design a framework for designing and implementing security. The framework should include prevention, detection, isolation, and recovery.	Chapters 2, 10, and 13	Labs 1, 2, 10, and 13
■ Predict threats to your network from internal and external sources.	Chapter 2	Labs 1 and 2
■ Design a process for responding to incidents.	Chapter 2	
■ Design segmented networks.	Chapter 10	Lab 10
■ Design a process for recovering services.	Chapter 13	Lab 13
Analyze technical constraints when designing security.	Chapter 2	Lab 2
■ Identify capabilities of the existing infrastructure.		
■ Identify technology limitations.		
■ Analyze interoperability constraints.		

Textbook and Lab Manual Coverage of Exam Objectives for MCSE Exam 70-298

Objective	Textbook	Lab Manual
Creating the Logical Design for Network Infrastructure Security		
Design a public key infrastructure (PKI) that uses Certificate Services.	Chapter 9	Lab 9
■ Design a certification authority (CA) hierarchy implementation. Types include geographical, organizational, and trusted.		
■ Design enrollment and distribution processes.		
■ Establish renewal, revocation and auditing processes.		
■ Design security for CA servers.		
Design a logical authentication strategy	Chapters 5 and 9	Labs 5 and 9
■ Design certificate distribution.	Chapter 9	Lab 9
■ Design forest and domain trust models.	Chapter 5	Lab 5
■ Design security that meets interoperability requirements.	Chapter 5	Lab 5
■ Establish account and password requirements for security.	Chapter 5	Lab 5
Design security for network management.	Chapter 4	Lab 4
■ Manage the risk of managing networks.		
■ Design the administration of servers by using common administration tools. Tools include Microsoft Management Console (MMC), Terminal Server, Remote Desktop for Administration, Remote Assistance, and Telnet.		
■ Design security for Emergency Management Services (EMS).		
Design a security update infrastructure.	Chapter 3	Lab 3
■ Design a Software Update Services (SUS) infrastructure.		
■ Design Group Policy to deploy software updates.		
■ Design a strategy for identifying computers that are not at the current patch level.		

Textbook and Lab Manual Coverage of Exam Objectives for MCSE Exam 70-298

Objective	Textbook	Lab Manual
Creating the Physical Design for Network Infrastructure Security		
Design network infrastructure security.	Chapter 10	Lab 10
■ Specify the required protocols for a firewall configuration.		
■ Design Internet Protocol (IP) filtering.		Lab 10
■ Design an Internet Protocol Security (IPSec) policy.		Lab 10
■ Secure a Domain Name System (DNS) implementation.		Labs 7 and 10
■ Design security for data transmission.		Lab 10
Design security for wireless networks.	Chapter 10	Lab 10
■ Design public and private wireless local area networks (LANs).		
■ Design 802.1x authentication for wireless networks		
Design user authentication for Microsoft Internet Information Services (IIS).	Chapter 12	Lab 12
■ Design user authentication for a Web site by using certificates.		
■ Design user authentication for a Web site by using IIS authentication.		
■ Design user authentication for a Web site by using Remote Authentication Dial-In User Service (RADIUS) for IIS authentication.		
Design security for Internet Information Services (IIS).	Chapter 12	Lab 12
■ Design security for Web sites that have different technical requirements by enabling only the minimum required services.		
■ Design a monitoring strategy for IIS.		
■ Design an IIS baseline that is based on business requirements.		
■ Design a content management strategy for updating an IIS server.		

Textbook and Lab Manual Coverage of Exam Objectives for MCSE Exam 70-298

Objective	Textbook	Lab Manual
Design security for communication between networks.	Chapter 11	Lab 11
■ Select protocols for virtual private network (VPN) access.		
■ Design VPN connectivity.		
■ Design demand-dial routing between internal networks.		
Design security for communication with external organizations.	Chapters 9 and 11	Labs 9 and 11
■ Design an extranet infrastructure.	Chapter 11	
■ Design a strategy for cross-certification of Certificate Services.	Chapter 9	
Design security for servers that have specific roles. Roles include domain controller, network infrastructure server, file server, IIS server, terminal server, and Post Office Protocol 3 (POP3) mail server.	Chapter 7	Lab 7
■ Define a baseline security template for all systems.		
■ Create a plan to modify baseline security templates according to role.		
Designing an Access Control Strategy for Data		
Design an access control strategy for directory services.	Chapter 6	Lab 6
■ Create a delegation strategy.		
■ Analyze auditing requirements.		
■ Design the appropriate group strategy for accessing resources.		
■ Design a permission structure for directory service objects.		

Textbook and Lab Manual Coverage of Exam Objectives for MCSE Exam 70-298

Objective	Textbook	Lab Manual
Design an access control strategy for files and folders.	Chapters 6 and 13	Labs 6 and 13
■ Design a strategy for the encryption and decryption of files and folders.	Chapter 6	Lab 6
■ Design a permission structure for files and folders.	Chapter 6	Lab 6
■ Design security for a backup and recovery strategy.	Chapter 13	Lab 13
■ Analyze auditing requirements.	Chapter 6	Lab 6
Design an access control strategy for the registry.	Chapter 6	
■ Design a permission structure for registry objects.		
■ Analyze auditing requirements.		
Creating the Physical Design for Client Infrastructure Security		
Design a client authentication strategy.	Chapter 5	Lab 5
■ Analyze authentication requirements.		
■ Establish account and password security requirements.		
Design a security strategy for client remote access.	Chapters 10 and 11	Lab 11 Lab 11
■ Design remote access policies.	Chapter 11	
■ Design access to internal resources.	Chapter 1	Lab 11
■ Design an authentication provider and accounting strategy for remote network access by using Internet Authentication Service (IAS).	Chapter 10	
Design a strategy for securing client computers. Considerations include desktop and portable computers.	Chapter 8	Lab 8
■ Design a strategy for hardening client operating systems.		
■ Design a strategy for restricting user access to operating system features.		

THE MICROSOFT CERTIFIED PROFESSIONAL PROGRAM (MCP)

The MCP program is one way to prove your proficiency with current Microsoft products and technologies. These exams and corresponding certifications are developed to validate your mastery of critical competencies as you design and develop, or implement and support, solutions using Microsoft products and technologies. Computer professionals who become Microsoft-certified are recognized as experts and are sought after industry-wide. Certification brings a variety of benefits to the individual and to employers and organizations.

> **MORE INFO**   For a full list of MCP benefits, go to http://www.microsoft.com/learning/itpro/default.asp.

Certifications

The MCP program offers multiple certifications, based on specific areas of technical expertise.

- **Microsoft Certified Professional (MCP)**   In-depth knowledge of at least one Windows operating system or architecturally significant platform. An MCP is qualified to implement a Microsoft product or technology as part of a business solution for an organization.

- **Microsoft Certified Systems Engineer (MCSE)**   Qualified to effectively analyze the business requirements for business solutions and design and implement the infrastructure based on the Windows and Windows Server 2003 operating systems.

- **Microsoft Certified Systems Administrator (MCSA)**   Qualified to manage and troubleshoot existing network and system environments based on the Windows and Windows Server 2003 operating systems.

- **Microsoft Certified Database Administrator (MCDBA)**   Qualified to design, implement, and administer Microsoft SQL Server databases.

- **Microsoft Certified Desktop Support Technician (MCDST)** Qualified to support end users and to troubleshoot desktop environments on the Windows operating system.

MCP Requirements

Requirements differ for each certification and are specific to the products and job functions addressed by the certification. To become an MCP, you must pass rigorous certification exams that provide a valid and reliable measure of technical proficiency and expertise. These exams are designed to test your expertise and ability to perform a role or task with a product, and they are developed with the input of industry professionals. Exam questions reflect how Microsoft products are used in actual organizations, giving them real-world relevance.

■ Microsoft Certified Professional (MCP) candidates are required to pass one current Microsoft certification exam. Candidates can pass additional Microsoft certification exams to validate their skills with other Microsoft products, development tools, or desktop applications.

■ Microsoft Certified Systems Engineer (MCSE) candidates are required to pass five core exams and two elective exams.

■ Microsoft Certified Systems Administrator (MCSA) candidates are required to pass three core exams and one elective exam.

■ Microsoft Certified Database Administrator (MCDBA) candidates are required to pass three core exams and one elective exam.

■ Microsoft Certified Desktop Support Technician (MCDST) candidates are required to pass two core exams.

ABOUT THE AUTHORS

The textbook, lab manual, pretest, testbank, and PowerPoint slides were written by instructors and developed exclusively for an instructor-led classroom environment.

Tony Northrup, CISPP, MCSE, and MVP, is the author of the textbook and slides and is a consultant and author living in the Boston, Massachusetts, area. During his seven years as Principal Systems Architect at BBN/Genuity, he was ultimately responsible for the reliability and security of hundreds of Windows servers and dozens of Windows domains—all connected directly to the Internet. Needless to say, Tony learned the hard way how to keep Windows systems safe in a hostile environment. Tony has authored and co-authored many books on Windows and networking, from *NT Network Plumbing* in 1998 to the *MCSA/MCSE Self-Paced Training Kit (Exam 70-299): Implementing and Administering Security in a Microsoft Windows Server 2003 Network*. Tony has also written many papers for Microsoft TechNet covering firewalls, ASP.NET, and other security topics.

Martin Grasdal, CISSP, MCSE, and MCT, is the author of the lab manual and is a collaborating writer and technical editor of several technical manuals, books, and publications. His credits include books and articles on Windows Internet Security and Acceleration Server 2000 and 2004, Windows XP, Windows Server 2003, and Microsoft SharePoint Portal Server 2003. He is the author of the *Microsoft Press Academic Learning Series Security + Lab Manual*. A professional educator with more than 20 years experience in adult education, he has been a Microsoft Certified Trainer since 1995 and has delivered training on a wide range of Microsoft products and technologies. Based in Edmonton, Alberta, Canada, he is currently a self-employed consultant, trainer, and author who assists organizations with network design and implementation as well as providing training, skills evaluation, and courseware development. He wishes to thank his family for their patience and understanding during the writing of the lab manual. He also wishes to thank the technical editor, Rozanne Whalen, for her close reading, attention to detail, and the many improvements she suggested.

Ed De Simone, the primary testbank author, is an MCP and the Network Operations Manager for a venture capital firm in northern New Jersey. The firm specializes in supporting startup technology companies from concept to market, providing management, financial backing, and IT services ranging from Help Desk to Hosting and comprising just about everything in between. Ed, who holds a Bachelor's Degree from Upsala College, is married and lives in Montclair, New Jersey, with his wife, Kim, a personal trainer, and their three children.

Robert Dean, the author of the pretest, is a Senior Systems Engineer who has been working as an IT professional for about nine years. He has also been working on authoring and technical editing projects for the last four years.

FOR MICROSOFT OFFICIAL ACADEMIC COURSE SUPPORT

Every effort has been made to ensure the accuracy of the material in this book and the contents of the companion CD.

Contact Wiley Technical Support at *http://higheredwiley.custhelp.com* where you can view our Knowledge Base of frequent questions, Chat live with an Agent, or submit a question.

Please note that product support is not offered through the above addresses.

CHAPTER 1
ASSESSING THE NEED FOR SECURITY

Upon completion of this chapter, you will be able to:

- Describe fundamental security design concepts, including why businesses need security, the three pillars of information security, and defense-in-depth.

- List the components of an attack, and analyze attacks to identify each component.

- Relate historical security compromises, and describe how each could have been prevented.

Designing security is a serious responsibility and a difficult job. To do your job well, you need to understand potential attackers, outsmart them by designing countermeasures to defend your assets, justify the cost of those countermeasures to your management, and oversee the implementation and maintenance of your design. Unfortunately, you do not have the luxury of learning from your own mistakes, because each mistake can be devastating for you and your organization. If you can learn from the mistakes of other security designers, however, you can protect your assets from serious harm.

To understand this book, you should already know how to implement security on a Microsoft Windows network. Many people who know how to implement security assume they automatically know the best way to design security, but *implementing* security and *designing* it are very different skills.

For example, if you know how to implement security on a Windows network, you should know how to configure operating systems and Group Policy to accomplish the following tasks:

- Allow users in an Active Directory directory service domain to run only approved applications

- Configure auditing to record evidence of attempted attacks

- Deploy security updates to all computers on a network

- Configure and troubleshoot encryption for files and network communications

Designing security covers these same topics, but takes them to the next level. Implementation answers the question, "How do I do this?" and design answers the question, "Why, and when, should I do this?" This book explores many of the same topics you covered while learning to implement security, but from a different angle. After you have read this book, you will know how to accomplish these similar, but different, tasks:

- Determine whether restricting users from running unapproved applications will reduce the risk of a security compromise significantly enough to offset the cost of inconveniencing users

- Determine how long you need to retain auditing records, based on balancing the following requirements:

  - Legal requirements specific to your organization's business and region

  - Law enforcement needs for gathering evidence

  - Computer forensics requirements for reconstructing attacks after the fact

  - Costs associated with storing and managing log files

- Weigh the benefits of deploying security updates against the costs associated with testing and deploying the update, and troubleshooting any problems caused by the update

- Identify where encryption is necessary to reduce the risk of compromising confidential data, and where the risk is not significant enough to justify the performance overhead and the higher cost of managing encrypted data

SECURITY DESIGN CONCEPTS

Security design requires many skills beyond those required when implementing security. First, you must have well-rounded business skills (although this book will not teach these skills). Next, you must have a solid understanding of why businesses invest, and do not invest, in security. You must know the fundamental goals of information security: confidentiality, integrity, and availability. To protect against human errors, including your own, you must understand the **defense-in-depth** security design approach. Finally, because threats appear in many different forms, you must know the ten security domains and the importance of considering each when designing security.

Why Security Designers Need Well-Rounded Skills

Security designers make the most serious design mistakes in the first year after their promotion from a hands-on position. At this point in their career, they have a very detailed knowledge of how to manage Active Directory networks, how network protocols function, and what does not work as well as it is supposed to. That is important knowledge, but being an effective security designer requires you to have many non-technical skills, too. Security designers also require knowledge of law, finance, accounting, human resources, sales, marketing, and strategy.

Usually, a new security designer does not appreciate the importance of these non-technical skills, and believes the most important knowledge is a detailed understanding of the technologies being used. This leads some security designers to create networks that meet security requirements, but fail to meet legal requirements; they should have spent more time with the company's legal team. As an alternative, a security architect might design an auditing system that can detect many types of attacks, but unknowingly violates the privacy of employees; they need to get to know the human resources team.

For example, knowledge of a company's finances and long-term business strategy might lead a security designer to enable Active Directory to merge more easily with another company. Knowledge of a public company's ready access to capital, and investors' desire to see positive EBITDA (Earnings Before Interest, Taxes, Depreciation, and Amortization) figures, might cause a security designer to recommend investing in a costly new intrusion detection system rather than adding operations staff to review audit logs regularly. On the other hand, a private company focused on improving cash flow might be better off adding staff to meet the security auditing requirements because the initial expense would be lower.

Why Businesses Need Security

Most people would answer the question, "Why harden a network?" with the obvious answer, "So I don't get hacked." That is a good enough reason to turn on encryption at your home's wireless network, but businesses need more justification. Specifically, businesses need cost justification. Businesses see security as an investment and, to a business, there must always be a return on investment (ROI).

Most chief executive officers (CEOs) would answer the question, "Why harden a network?" with the answer, "To keep my costs predictable by controlling my business's exposure to risk." That is not as easy to understand as, "So I don't get hacked," but it makes sense when you consider that most businesses exist to produce a product and make a profit. Dedicating personnel time to improving the security of a network diverts energy from producing a product, and spending money on security reduces the business's profit margins. For these very valid reasons, many businesses choose not to spend money on security.

To a business, network security makes sense only when you consider the cost of not adding security. A business can function with absolutely no network security. However, there is a good chance that an attacker will notice the lack of security and compromise the network. The losses could be small, and perhaps even insignificant. For example, if the attacker simply uses the business's bandwidth to trade files on the Internet, the business might incur no cost at all.

The losses from a successful attack can also be tremendous, however. If the attacker publishes a list of the business's customers' credit card numbers, the business will lose many customers. For larger businesses, this could become front-page news and cost them millions of dollars. Certainly, a business that suffers such a huge loss would have been wise to spend at least a fraction of the earnings lost on network security that could have prevented a successful attack.

To a CEO, network security is a form of insurance. Consider homeowner's insurance: you pay for the insurance every month, whether you need it or not. In fact, you might never need it, in which case, paying for the insurance has been a huge waste of money, and a terrible investment. However, there is a chance that fire or a flood might damage your house, which confirms that the money you spent on insurance was an excellent investment.

Security, like insurance, is a way to manage risk. Businesses pay a security designer to harden their network to reduce the likelihood that they will have an unpredictable expense in the future, when an attacker might compromise the network.

> **NOTE   Security as a Business Priority**   Businesses do not spend money and time just for the sake of improving security. Security must save businesses money by reducing risk.

The Three Pillars of Information Security

There are three pillars of information security, known as the *CIA (Confidentiality, Integrity, and Availability) triad*:

- **Confidentiality**   Let people who should see your data access it, but nobody else.

- **Integrity**   Know who has created, viewed, and modified your data, and prevent unauthorized changes and impersonations of legitimate users.

■ **Availability**   Allow users to access data when they need it, even when attacks and natural disasters occur.

You should constantly think about each of the three pillars when designing security. Depending on business priorities, one pillar might be more important than the others. Figure 1-1 visually illustrates the CIA triad.

THE CIA TRIAD

Confidentiality   Integrity

Availability

Confidentiality: Ensuring that only those who are supposed to see the information see it.

Integrity: Ensuring that the information has not been altered or corrupted.

Availability: Ensuring that the information is easily and readily accessible to those who need it.

Figure 1-1   CIA triad of confidentiality, integrity, and availability

> **NOTE   CIA Triad**   The CIA triad is well known in the security community, and is not specific to Microsoft technologies.

Confidentiality is the easiest to understand of the three pillars. Most children have used a secret decoder ring to send a secret message to a friend. This is a primitive form of encryption, one of the most useful technologies for improving confidentiality. Even children understand the need for confidentiality—someone else might read that secret message. Naturally, businesses have much more important data to protect. Plans and financial data can have a devastating effect on a business if they fall into the wrong hands. If a military organization has a breach of confidentiality, the effects can be devastating to an entire country.

Integrity is not as easy to understand as confidentiality, but it is equally important. The Internet's e-mail system is an excellent example of the importance of data integrity, because it does not have any. How many times have you received a message sent by someone other than the address shown in the From box? Most Internet e-mail systems accept mail without validating the sender at all, which means you cannot trust that the sender actually sent you a message. In addition, because Internet e-mail does not have any way to prevent tampering, an attacker with access to an e-mail server can modify messages without the sender or recipient noticing. Although most people overlook e-mail's lack of integrity, one should consider the potential benefits of an e-mail system with data integrity:

- You will receive little or no spam.

- If you do receive an unwanted e-mail, you can block the sender without worrying about him or her using a different sending address in the future.

- E-mail messages can be used for legal agreements such as business contracts.

Availability is the third pillar of information security. Many people disregard availability as being an aspect of information security because hardware failures, software problems, or network faults cause most availability problems. Although traditional attackers cause none of these most common availability problems, many of the most serious attacks do target availability. For example, denial-of-service (DoS) attacks that take a Web site offline affect the availability of that site. In a similar way, a virus that formats a user's hard drive denies the user access to the data. Therefore, you must consider availability when designing an information security strategy.

Do not place more importance on one pillar than on another. If you have ever known someone who encrypted a file but did not back it up, you have seen this phenomenon in action. Confidentiality can protect you from an attacker with a network sniffer, but it will not protect you from hard drive failure, fire, or data theft. Confidentiality can also protect against an attacker reading a business's private financial data. You will need data integrity, however, to protect against a human resources employee who modifies a database to give himself a raise.

Principles of Information Security Design

Much of a security designer's energy will be spent designing countermeasures to limit the risk of a compromise. There are several well-known and accepted security principles that you can use to protect almost any kind of system. Future chapters discuss how you can apply each of these principles to protect specific types of assets:

- **Reduce the attack surface** Any application might contain vulnerabilities. The more applications you add to your network, the greater the risk of a vulnerability being exploited. You can minimize risk by keeping the number of running computers, applications, and services to a minimum by uninstalling unnecessary components and disabling unused services.

- **Assign least privilege** Give users and services only the privileges they absolutely need. For example, users should not have administrator permissions on their desktop computer because a virus or Trojan horse could misuse those permissions.

- **Patch** Systems change, and new bugs and insecure practices are discovered all the time. Systems must be patched, and administrators need to be knowledgeable about the latest defense mechanisms. Make sure administrative staff has sufficient time available to test and deploy patches in a timely manner, and have another group audit the delivery of those patches.

- **Secure by default** Computers should be at their most secure when initially configured because most users will not go out of their way to improve the security of a system. For example, ports on firewalls should always be closed by default, and you should only open those for which you want to provide access. Antivirus software should run on all of your users' computers automatically, rather than requiring the user to manually enable it.

- **Leverage diversity of mechanism** If you have five firewalls protecting your network, but they are all running the same software, an attacker could bypass all the firewalls by exploiting a single vulnerability. However, if you use two different types of firewalls, you have made the attackers' job more difficult because they will have to identify two separate vulnerabilities to **exploit**. Using a variety of defense mechanisms from different vendors increases your management costs, but decreases the risk of multiple systems being exploited because of a single vulnerability.

- **Enforce separation of duties** Whenever possible, assign different parts of important operations to different people. For example, programmers should not have network administration privileges; those with backup rights should not have restore rights; and auditors should not be able to modify systems. When you separate two aspects of a task that might be abused by an attacker, you require the attacker to work with another person to compromise your systems—an act called collusion. Collusion greatly increases the attacker's risk of being caught, which will make compromise less likely to occur.

- **Keep it simple** If a countermeasure is too complex, your users will find ways to simplify it—reducing the effectiveness of your countermeasure. For example, instead of requiring users to carry a badge to enter their building and a separate smart card to authenticate on their computer, issue badges with built-in smart cards.

■ **Consider psychological acceptability**   Avoid countermeasures that make your users uncomfortable. For example, one reason retinal scans are not widely used for authentication is because users are not comfortable with a computer scanning their eyes. Even though there is no real danger, many users are frightened by retinal scanning devices, which might lead them to find ways to bypass it. For the same reason, avoid defense mechanisms that invade your users' privacy, such as randomly reading e-mails. Even if you warn users about the policy beforehand, they are liable to be uncomfortable with it and find other ways to communicate besides the corporate e-mail system.

■ **Trust but audit**   Users and administrators must have the privileges they need to do their jobs, but no one is completely and permanently above suspicion. Remember that people change, temptation can be great, and anger can make some people overstep their usual reluctance to break the rules. As a result, all systems should have auditing enabled and configured, and those audit logs should be reviewed on a regular basis. For example, you can match computer restarts with approved maintenance requests. Investigate the discrepancies and determine who rebooted and why. In addition, you should monitor the use of administrative functions such as group and user management. Make people aware of your auditing policies beforehand. When you discover discrepancies, do your best to avoid making people feel like you are accusing them of a crime; rather, assume that there is a legitimate reason for the activity but seek to identify that reason for your own peace of mind.

What Is Defense-In-Depth?

Defense-in-depth is a proven technique for reducing the exposure of vulnerabilities. Network engineers use defense-in-depth to protect computers on a network by providing multiple layers of protection from potential attackers. For example, an engineer might design a network (such as the one shown in Figure 1-2) with three layers of packet filtering: a packet-filtering router, a hardware firewall, and software firewalls on each of the hosts (such as Internet Connection Firewall). If an attacker manages to bypass one or two of the layers of protection, the hosts are still protected from communications that have not specifically been allowed. For more information about firewalls, refer to Chapter 10, "Protecting Intranet Communications."

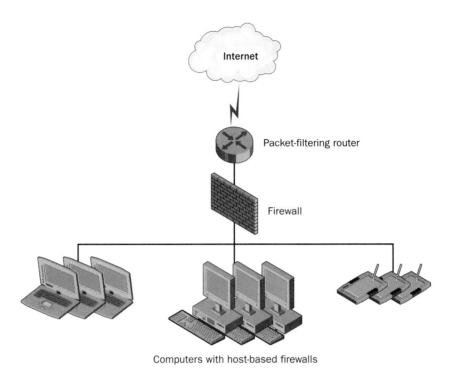

Figure 1-2   Defense-in-depth used to protect a network

The real benefit to defense-in-depth is its ability to protect against human error. Human error is, ultimately, the root cause of most successfully exploited vulnerabilities. Imagine a network, such as that shown in Figure 1-3, that provided packet filtering with only a perimeter firewall at the connection to the Internet. This configuration is extremely common today, and many security designers feel perimeter firewalls provide sufficient security.

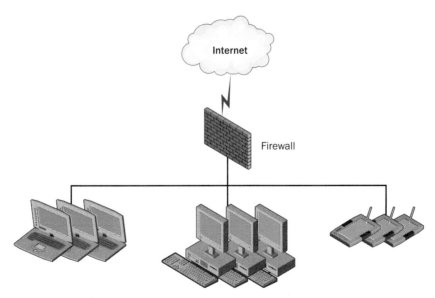

Figure 1-3   Networks without defense-in-depth can become vulnerable after a single administrator mistake.

A single layer of defense might be sufficient under normal circumstances. However, imagine that the firewall vendor releases a software upgrade and, during the upgrade process, erases the firewall rules, leaving the internal network unprotected. Attacks from the thousands of computers on the Internet infected with worms and viruses would immediately bombard the computers on the internal network. If a worm infected a salesperson's laptop while he or she was traveling, that worm could spread to the other computers on the internal network as soon as the salesperson returned to the office.

Human error is much less likely to neutralize multiple layers of defense, however. If a misconfiguration removes the filtering rules from the firewall shown in Figure 1-2, the packet filtering on the router would still provide some level of protection for the internal network. If a worm were introduced to the internal network, host-based firewalls would protect most of the computers.

> **NOTE Defense-in-Depth**   You should always use defense-in-depth to protect important assets.

Although Figure 1-2 shows three layers of defense, many environments would require additional layers. A monitoring system verifying that the firewall was filtering traffic would enable you to quickly detect and correct a misconfiguration. An intrusion detection system capable of detecting traffic generated by worms, viruses, or other attackers could alert you to a worm that bypassed your network's perimeter defenses. Finally, backups would be critical if the other layers of defense failed, because you could restore any data lost during a successful attack. For more information about mitigating software risks, refer to Chapter 3, "Reducing the Risk of Software Vulnerabilities."

The 10 Security Domains

One of the worst, and most common, mistakes a security designer can make is to focus too much attention on a single aspect of security. For example, if a security designer who has recently attended a firewall training class is asked to review an organization's network infrastructure, there is a strong likelihood that the designer will point out weaknesses in the organization's firewall design. Firewalls are an important part of network security, but they are not the only important part.

The International Information Systems Security Certifications Consortium, Inc. (ISC2) is a nonprofit organization dedicated to educating information security professionals. ISC2 classifies security knowledge in 10 different security domains. Each of these domains deserves an equal amount of attention from most security designers. Many security designers, unfortunately, focus only on a single domain, which can cause them to overlook significant vulnerabilities in other domains. The 10 domains are as follows:

- **Access Control Systems and Methodology** Techniques for controlling access to resources. This domain includes everything from user groups and access control lists in Microsoft Windows Server 2003 to security guards who allow only authorized personnel into a datacenter.

- **Applications and Systems Development** If you have ever been attacked by a virus or worm that infected someone else's system, you know that applications and operating systems contain security vulnerabilities. Proper application and systems development techniques can reduce these vulnerabilities. Access control systems, such as firewalls, can also help protect against such vulnerabilities, but they cannot substitute for using secure application development techniques.

- **Business Continuity Planning** After you design a Windows Server 2003 infrastructure, the organization will depend on its functioning correctly. Many things can interfere with that functioning, however, including worms, viruses, sophisticated attackers, and natural disasters such as earthquakes, fires, and hurricanes. Business continuity planning is a critical security concept that plans to keep critical systems running, even in a degraded state, when such a disaster strikes. Business continuity planning must be considered when designing any critical infrastructure. For more information about business continuity planning, refer to Chapter 13, "Creating a Disaster Recovery Plan."

> **NOTE** Sophisticated Attackers and Script Kiddies Throughout this book, the term "sophisticated attacker" refers to a motivated individual with networking, computer, and security skills. Sophisticated attackers are very different from "script kiddies," who typically use tools developed by sophisticated attackers and are therefore much more predictable and easier to defend against.

- **Cryptography** Data is vulnerable when it is stored and transmitted. Cryptography can protect data when communications are captured during transmission or when storage systems are separated from the computers and access control systems that protect them. Cryptography, the science of making data difficult for unauthorized users to interpret, is one of the most challenging domains to understand completely. However, Windows Server 2003 makes cryptography simple to design and implement. For more information about cryptography and encryption, refer to Chapter 6, "Protecting Data," and Chapter 9, "Designing a Public Key Infrastructure."

- **Law, Investigation, and Ethics**   If you spend more than a few years in the security field, you will probably become friends with several lawyers and law enforcement officials. Understanding laws, investigations, and ethics has a significant impact on how you design a Windows Server 2003 infrastructure. For example, you need to gather auditing information in very specific ways to enable law enforcement officials to use that auditing information as evidence when prosecuting an attacker. In addition, you might have to warn both authorized and unauthorized users that their actions on your computer systems are being monitored. Depending on regional laws, the information you can collect might be restricted. To be ethical, you must never use your security knowledge to invade someone's privacy or to probe a computer system without the owner's permission. You must also avoid using fear, uncertainty, and doubt to motivate people to follow security guidelines.

- **Operations Security**   Personnel are often the weakest link in a security architecture. Many famous security compromises took advantage of vulnerabilities in operations security. For example, an attacker might use **social engineering**: the attacker would place a phone call impersonating a legitimate staff member attempting to work from home who cannot get access, and have the user's password reset. To protect against this type of attack, you must implement procedures that protect the security of your infrastructure, including proper security training and background checks for operations staff. Although you can never eliminate the possibility that personnel will maliciously bypass your procedures, you can greatly reduce the risk caused by personnel by implementing proper methodologies.

- **Physical Security**   Attacks across a network are extremely common because of the convenience; the attacker does not have to leave his or her chair to launch an attack, and network attacks provide a wide variety of options for evading detection. However, sophisticated attackers will also seek out vulnerabilities in physical security. An attacker who can physically touch a computer can bypass any network access control system. Examples of physical security mechanisms include video cameras (for both detecting intrusion and gathering evidence), security guards, and identification cards.

> **MORE INFO**   **Further Study: Physical Security**   If you are interested in physical security but do not want to read another textbook, read the first half of *Confessions of a Master Jewel Thief* by Bill Mason (Villard, 2004). Also, read *The Art of Deception: Controlling the Human Element of Security* by Kevin Mitnick, William Simon, and Steve Wozniak (Wiley, 2002).

- **Security Architecture and Models**   You are probably already familiar with the Windows Server 2003 role-based security model. However, this security model is not the only model. Even Windows Server 2003 includes a different security model, because it includes the Microsoft .NET Framework, which features code-access security. Other computer systems, especially those designed for government and military use, have very different designs that might physically separate information at different confidentiality levels. Whereas studying other security models is interesting, this book will focus on only the security models provided by Windows Server 2003.

- **Security Management Practices**   This domain covers risk management, one of the concepts discussed throughout this chapter. Security is, inherently, a technique for managing risk associated with attacks and natural disasters. Calculating this risk, and determining the security techniques to offset the most expensive risks, is both an art and a science.

- **Telecommunications, Network, and Internet Security**   Much of protecting network communications occurs at the *Physical Layer*, the *Data Link Layer*, and the *Network Layer* of the Open Systems Interconnection (OSI) model. Mastering this security domain will require you to understand, for example, the different security levels provided by dedicated circuits such as T1s and T3s, and virtual private networks. When designing a Windows Server 2003 infrastructure, you identify different security, performance, and cost requirements for links. To choose the correct link, you must have a solid understanding of low-level network security risks and countermeasures.

For more information about network security, refer to Chapter 10 and Chapter 11, "Protecting Extranet Communications."

Understanding these domains is extremely important to create a balanced security infrastructure without any significant weak links. However, this book focuses on software and network security. Though such topics as physical security, hiring practices, and legal requirements are briefly discussed, they are not covered in depth because they are not within the scope of this book. They are extremely important, however, and you will not be capable of designing a complex security infrastructure without a thorough understanding of all 10 domains.

> **MORE INFO** *CISSP Certification Program*   ISC2 offers the Certified Information Systems Security Professional (CISSP) certification program that allows you to demonstrate a degree of mastery over each of the 10 security domains. For more information, visit *http://www.isc2.org.*

THE COMPONENTS OF AN ATTACK

Attacks, whether successful or unsuccessful, have several different components. In this section, you dissect attacks and study each of the individual components to better understand how the components fit together. This section describes the following attack components:

- Asset
- Threat agent
- Threat
- Vulnerability
- Compromise
- Countermeasure

You might already be familiar with these terms. However, security engineers assign very specific meanings to these terms that are slightly different from the commonly used definitions.

What Is an Asset?

An **asset** is anything in your organization's environment that might require some level of protection. This could include items that you have purchased outright, such as software, hardware, and facilities. Assets can also be data, people, and information.

A key aspect of security risk management is determining the value of each primary asset in your organization, the value of the information that each asset contains, and how each asset relates to others in your environment. For example, if your company's biggest asset is the design of a proprietary microchip technology, the loss of that critical data will substantially reduce your company's value. In a similar way, if that data falls into a competitor's hands, it could undermine the company's business plan.

The overall associated value of each asset will determine the time, effort, and cost you put into protecting them. To make this more complicated, keep in mind that assets might depend on each other. For example, if you determine that having access to a specific database is critical for your business to function, you must protect not only the database, but also the routers and other network hardware that connect the database to the client computers.

Consider, also, how users accessing these resources are authenticated and how users are authorized to gain access to each asset and the data that it exposes. For example, weak authentication can expose confidential files if the laptop of a chief information officer (CIO) is protected by a weak password. In a similar way, if an application queries your Active Directory to determine if a user has authorization to perform a specific task, an attacker who can take the Active Directory servers offline can also successfully bring down your application. In this example, you must protect Active Directory to protect the application.

What Is a Threat Agent?

A **threat agent** is a person, place, or thing that has the potential to access resources without proper authorization and cause harm. Threats can originate from four primary sources: malicious attackers, non-malicious attackers, mechanical failures, and catastrophic events. The sections that follow provide more detailed descriptions of each of the different threat agent categories, as well as information specific to each category that you will need to take into account when performing security risk management. For more information about security risk management, refer to Chapter 2.

Catastrophic Events

Any event relating to extreme weather, naturally occurring phenomena, or a catastrophic event might cause severe damage to your organization's infrastructure. Information can be lost, hardware can be damaged, and a loss of productivity can occur along with the disruption of other essential services. Although catastrophic events are not very common, the damage can be severe. A hurricane might destroy communication lines, disrupting phone and network communications for days or weeks. Fires or acts of war can destroy buildings completely, and might even result in loss of human life.

You must plan that some employees will not be available during catastrophic incidents. Closed roads might prevent employees from commuting. Communication lines might be unavailable, preventing employees from telecommuting. If schools close because of the event, employees might need to care for their children. Employees might also be injured, or be required to care for other injured people.

To enable your organization to accomplish its business goals when faced with these missing resources, assign disaster recovery roles to multiple individuals, so that if one person is unavailable, another person can assume that person's responsibilities. Whenever possible, assign redundant roles to individuals in other locations. Be sure to include yourself in this planning—you should not have any knowledge in your head that is not well documented, so that others can assume your job in the event of a catastrophe.

Few preventive measures, unfortunately, can be implemented to mitigate the potential for catastrophic incidents. The best you can do to reduce the likelihood of a catastrophic event is to select a location for your organization's facilities that is less likely to be affected by severe weather, fire, acts of war, and other catastrophic events. Because few organizations can change location to reduce the risk of a catastrophe, the best approach for these types of **threats** is to have disaster recovery and contingency plans in place to help minimize the effects of a loss. Having these plans in place and ready to go will help your organization resume close-to-normal business operations as quickly as possible.

Mechanical Failures

Mechanical threats include power outages, hardware failures, and network outages. Proper planning can often prevent vulnerabilities that might arise from these threats. Hardware clustering, redundant power connections, and robust network designs can help eliminate single points of failure that might cause mechanical failures in your organization. However, implementing these countermeasures can be extremely expensive and should be evaluated carefully to ensure that the value of the asset warrants using such methods.

As a practical example, consider an organization that requires Internet access for its business to function with a single, nonredundant T3 connection to an Internet service provider (ISP). If the wires that compose its T3 connection or any of the network hardware between its facility and the ISP's facility fail, the company loses its critical Internet access.

There are several ways to mitigate this risk. The best, and most expensive, solution would be to procure a second T3 connection to a different ISP and ensure that the two circuits do not follow the same physical path. If one of the T3s failed, traffic could be rerouted to the second ISP with minimal impact. A less expensive solution would be to procure a lower-bandwidth T1 connection for use when the primary T3 connection fails. Although this dramatically reduces bandwidth, some level of Internet access would still be available.

A third way to mitigate the risk does not involve redundancy at all. Instead, the organization could choose an ISP that offers service-level guarantees (SLGs). Although SLGs vary, they generally provide a rebate to the customer if the service provider has a significant failure. In this example, if the organization's T3 failed for an extended time, the ISP might reduce the monthly service fee by 1/30th (essentially giving the organization a free day of service). This reduced cost helps offset the organization's losses from the outage, and ensures that the ISP is motivated to repair the failed circuit quickly. Although the rebate helps, it cannot completely compensate for the cost of the outage.

Malicious Attacks

Malicious threats consist of attacks by disgruntled employees or malicious people from outside the organization. Insiders are likely to have specific goals and objectives and usually have some level of legitimate access to systems in the environment. Employees are the group most familiar with your company's network, applications, and security procedures, including having knowledge of what compromises and vulnerabilities might cause the most damage to your organization. This type of attack can be extremely difficult to detect or prevent.

> **NOTE**   **The Danger of Casually Revealing Vulnerabilities**   Be careful not to reveal security weaknesses to other employees during casual conversation. Even offhand comments such as "I can't believe they wouldn't fund an intrusion detection system—now we'll never know if we're being attacked" can be used against you in the future if a coworker becomes disgruntled.

Often, having a standard user account enables an attacker to gain administrative-level privileges easier than an attacker who has no user account. Insiders might also have knowledge of your intrusion detection systems that can enable them to avoid detection. A malicious insider attack can affect all components of your computer security or applications.

Other types of security crimes instigated by malicious insiders might involve bribery or social engineering. Social engineering is the process of tricking people into revealing their passwords or some form of security information. Often these actions go undetected because audit trails are inadequate or they fail to be reviewed. A malicious attacker can also use social engineering to deceive employees and gain entry to your environment. For example, an attacker could masquerade as an administrator and ask for passwords and user names. Employees who are not well trained and are not security conscious can fall for this deception.

To anticipate the types of malicious attackers you might encounter, start by considering possible motives. The following list suggests some common motivations.

- **Motivated by ego**   Today, threat agents who are motivated by ego initiate most attacks. Many of the worms and viruses that have infected millions of computers were created by threat agents attempting to create the most efficient and widespread threat ever. That worms and viruses often have taunting messages written from one threat agent to another demonstrates this fact. For example, in March 2004, the authors of the widespread NetSky and Bagle worms released several new variations of their worms in an effort to outdo the other. One NetSky variation included a message that said they would not stop releasing worms until Bagle did. These threat agents are often identified after the fact because they eagerly take credit for the attack.

- **Intellectually motivated**   Curiosity motivates the classic hacker. Intellectually motivated attackers do not usually intend to damage a network, but strive to understand how a network works. Intellectually motivated attackers might even notify you that they identified a vulnerability in your network. Although these threat agents often feel that they are not doing anything wrong, their actions are considered crimes, and law enforcement officials offer very little leniency in consideration of their nondestructive motivations.

- **Personally motivated**   Few organizations become successful without irritating at least a few people. Often, personally motivated attackers are disgruntled employees, unsatisfied customers, or angry investors seeking revenge. Because these attackers are emotionally driven, they tend to be destructive and careless about avoiding detection, as Shakuntla Singla demonstrated in July 1997. Shakuntla used her inside knowledge of the U.S. Coast Guard's personnel system to destroy a great deal of valuable data. The Coast Guard had to reenter the data manually into the system, which took almost 2000 hours.

- **Socially or politically motivated**   So-called "cyber-activists" or "hacktivists" attempt to rectify what they deem an injustice. Socially motivated attackers frequently target government organizations; however, any organization that others feel performs unethical actions might be targeted. For example, in March 2003, a DoS attack took a United Kingdom government Web site offline. The attackers claimed the attack was an act of political protest against that organization's actions. You might be targeted by socially or politically motivated attackers if your organization, or any organization you do business with, becomes the subject of controversy. These attackers are very likely to deface Web sites or use DoS attacks because of the similarity to traditional physical protests.

- **Financially motivated** Although financially motivated attacks are relatively uncommon, they tend to be well publicized. Financially motivated threat agents might attempt to steal information from which they can profit. Many threat agents have attacked, successfully and unsuccessfully, bank networks to redirect funds into their own bank accounts. For example, in 1994, an attacker named Vladimir Levin stole Citibank customer IDs and passwords and successfully withdrew about $400,000. Financial organizations that deal directly with money are the most likely targets by financially motivated attackers; however, any organization with valuable assets is a potential target. Above all, these attackers wish to avoid detection. Therefore, they will not destroy data except for log files that could be used to identify them or uncover their actions.

Non-Malicious Attacks

Malicious attackers are not the only ones who can harm an organization. One of the most significant threats to data integrity comes from authorized users who are not aware of the actions they are performing. Errors and omissions can cause your organization to lose, damage, or alter valuable data. Errors and omissions are important threats to data integrity. Errors are caused not only by data entry clerks processing hundreds of transactions per day, but also by all users who create and edit data. Many programs, especially those designed by users for personal computers, are lacking in appropriate quality-control measures. However, even the most sophisticated programs cannot protect against all types of input errors or omissions.

Programming and development errors (bugs) range in severity from irritating to catastrophic. Improved software quality has reduced but not eliminated this threat. Installation and maintenance errors can also cause security problems. Many organizations address errors and omissions in their computer security, software quality, and data quality programs by implementing security policies.

In July 2004, a programming bug crashed the Chicago *Tribune*'s newspaper production system. According to the *Tribune*'s president, Scott C. Smith, lost advertising revenue, the expense of resolving the problem, and providing credits to subscribers who missed deliveries cost the *Tribune* "under $1 million." In this case, the team that developed and tested the software were non-malicious attackers. As a security architect, it is not your job to prevent this type of attack;

however, you should identify the possibility that such a bug could stop a company's workflow, essentially a denial-of-service attack. Identifying the threat would allow you to create a business continuance plan that provides a backup plan to carry out daily activities in the event something did go wrong.

What Is a Threat?

A threat is the method of attack; a threat agent is the individual responsible. Therefore, if your coworker, Eric, tries to guess your password using a password-guessing tool, Eric is a malicious threat agent. The act of password guessing is the threat. In a similar way, a farmer with a backhoe could be a non-malicious threat agent; the threat is damage to a communication line that prevents your employees from accessing remote networks. A single threat agent might give rise to multiple threats if the attacker tries different techniques.

There are dozens of ways to categorize threats. Microsoft developed the STRIDE method of categorizing the following malicious threat types:

- **Spoofing identity** Anything done to illegally obtain, or access and use, another person's authentication information, such as a user name or password, is a spoofing identity threat. Any time an attacker impersonates a legitimate user, it is a spoofing identity attack. Examples include an attacker who spoofs an Internet Protocol (IP) address to bypass a firewall, and an attacker who calls your help desk pretending to be an employee to reset a password. Another common spoofing attack is the man-in-the-middle attack, in which an attacker impersonates a server. The server transparently forwards all communications to the legitimate server while capturing the user's credentials and other private information, as shown in Figure 1-4.

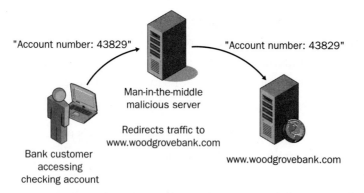

Figure 1-4   Spoofing the identity of both the client and the server to gain access to private information is a man-in-the-middle attack.

- **Tampering with data**   Tampering-with-data threats involve making malicious changes to data. Examples include unauthorized modifications made to persistent data, such as defacing a Web site, altering information held in a database, or changing data as it flows between two computers over an open network. Actual occurrences of this type of attack include an attacker who modified a public business's press release to profit from the resulting changes in the company's stock price, and students who modified classroom grades.

- **Repudiation**   Repudiation threats are associated with users who deny performing an action with other parties having no way to prove otherwise. For example, an attacker might order a product from a retail store for delivery at his home. After delivery of the item, the attacker pretends that he or she never received it. Non-repudiation is the ability of a system to counter repudiation threats by proving that a particular user took an action. An example of this would be a delivery service that requires a signature to accept a package. The delivery service can then use the signature as evidence that it delivered the package.

- **Information disclosure**   Information disclosure threats involve the exposure of information to individuals who are not supposed to have access to it. Examples include the ability of users to read files that they were not granted access to, or the ability of an intruder to read data in transit between two computers. This type of attack has been used by employment firms to gain access to internal employee directories, and then to contact the individual employees with job offers from outside firms. The military often performs this type of attack to gain access to confidential enemy plans.

> **NOTE How Communications Are Compromised**   Communications between a client and a server occur across a network. If an attacker can gain control of network hardware, he or she might be able to capture the communications. At a minimum, this capture will reveal important information about how the application works; it can also reveal private information—such as user names and passwords—that the attacker can use to gain elevated privileges.
>
> Only the most sophisticated attackers are capable of cracking encrypted **ciphertext**. Ciphertext is the encrypted form of data, and resembles random data. Even with the proper skills and tools, it can take years (or even thousands of years) for an attacker to identify the unencrypted data given in an encrypted message. However, many cryptographic techniques have flaws that allow the attacker to crack the cryptography much faster. In addition, a developer who does not follow best practices for implementing encryption might introduce weaknesses into an otherwise strong encryption method.

For example, an application that uses a strong encryption method but stores the private key in a location that is publicly accessible to an attacker might allow an attacker to gain access to private, encrypted communications.

- **Denial of service**   Denial-of-service (DoS) attacks disrupt service to legitimate users. Any time an attacker can send a request that uses more legitimate resources than it does of the attacker's resources, a DoS vulnerability exists. DoS attacks often target Web servers because Web servers accept requests from the public Internet, and processing requests is more resource intensive for the Web server than for the Web client. Protection against certain types of DoS threats can help improve system availability and reliability. DoS attackers have protested an organization's actions by taking the organization's Web site offline. DoS attackers also commonly target individual home users' Internet connections after a user irritates an attacker. Only highly distributed, very expensive computer systems can prevent DoS attacks, especially the more serious distributed denial-of-service (DDoS) attacks. Most organizations cannot justify the cost of building a highly distributed system and choose to reactively detect and respond to DoS attacks as quickly as possible. Generally, they resolve DoS attacks by identifying the threat agents and working with Internet service providers to block the malicious requests.

- **Elevation of privilege**   In this type of threat, an unprivileged user gains privileged access that enables him or her to take actions not normally allowed. In a common example of this attack, an attacker exploits a known vulnerability on a computer to gain administrative privileges and then to install remote-control software. The attacker can then use the software and elevated privileges to launch attacks against other computers while disguising the attacker's identity.

Threats are a concern only if you have a vulnerability. As the next section discusses, however, vulnerabilities are numerous and unavoidable.

What Is a Vulnerability?

A **vulnerability**, often called a *weakness* or a security **compromise**, is an opportunity for an attacker to launch a successful attack. In other words, a vulnerability is a point at which an asset is susceptible to a threat. Vulnerabilities can originate from technology, people, or processes. Most often, they are viewed as technological flaws in the implementation of software or hardware, or in how a system is designed. Poorly defined and communicated organizational policies and procedures are also vulnerabilities. In addition, vulnerabilities can be weak points or loopholes in security that a malicious attacker exploits to gain access to the network or to resources on the network. The key point to understand is that the vulnerability is not the attack itself, but rather the exploitable weak point in the system or network.

Table 1-1 shows a list of common types of vulnerabilities, with real-world examples of each. These represent just a few of the many vulnerabilities that exist and include examples in the areas of physical, data, and network security.

Table 1-1   **Common Types of Vulnerabilities**

Vulnerability Type	Examples
Physical	Unlocked doors or windows
	Unmonitored doors or windows
	Combination locks with easily guessed combinations
Natural	Buildings without fire-suppression systems
	Facilities built on fault lines or other areas prone to natural disasters
Hardware and software	Operating systems missing security updates
	Computers without locking screensavers
Media	Communications circuits subject to interference or breakage
Communications	Unencrypted protocols
	Wireless networks
Human	Sleeping security guard
	Security guard who is willing to participate in an attack
	Users with easily guessed passwords
	Users who tell an attacker their password

Table 1-1 shows examples of common, significant vulnerabilities, but there are additional vulnerabilities that might be significant to your organization, depending on the security requirements. For example, although unencrypted protocols are very vulnerable to **sniffing**, encrypted protocols are also a vulnerability, because it is possible for the attacker with both the encryption key and access to the encrypted traffic to decrypt the communications. In Chapter 2, you will explore how to assess the risk posed by different kinds of vulnerabilities so that you can focus your energy on eliminating the most important vulnerabilities.

What Is a Compromise?

A compromise is a successful attack. As a security designer, you must strive to prevent compromises. This is an important distinction; preventing vulnerabilities is not your ultimate goal. Although you will often mitigate, or reduce the effect of, vulnerabilities to reduce the risk of a compromise, you might also choose to address the threat or threat agent directly to reduce the risk of a compromise. The compromise *is* the problem.

> **TIP** **Security Lingo** If a threat attacks you but does not penetrate your defenses, you should say that you were attacked. If the threat successfully penetrates your defenses, you should say that you were compromised.

What Is a Countermeasure?

Countermeasures, or safeguards, reduce the likelihood of a compromise by making it more difficult for a threat to take advantage of a vulnerability. In other words, countermeasures help mitigate the potential risk of an asset being compromised. A countermeasure is designed to eliminate a vulnerability or reduce the risk of a threat compromising a vulnerability in a computer environment. Examples of countermeasures include strong password management, a security guard, access control mechanisms within an operating system, the implementation of basic input/output system (BIOS) passwords, and security awareness training.

Computer software is always a vulnerability, because it could contain a weakness that an attacker could exploit. Not all software contains security weaknesses; however, there is no way to know for sure if a piece of software has a weakness. Therefore, software always carries some level of risk.

One type of countermeasure to this type of vulnerability is to apply updates issued by Microsoft and other software organizations. One of the more effective ways to implement this type of countermeasure is to use Automatic Updates to install security updates and service packs rapidly and automatically on all computers in your organization.

> **MORE INFO** For more information about Automatic Updates, refer to Chapter 3.

Another type of countermeasure for software vulnerabilities is to block unwanted network traffic that might be part of an effort to exploit a vulnerability. Enabling a host-based firewall such as Internet Connection Firewall or Windows Firewall on all computers is another countermeasure for this same risk, because the Windows Firewall can block many types of attacks. In a similar way, you could also use a network firewall as a countermeasure for this risk.

Depending on your needs and budget, you might choose to implement all three countermeasures for the same risk: a network firewall, host-based firewalls, and Automatic Updates. You still will not entirely eliminate the risk, however. Countermeasures never eliminate risk; they just reduce it.

Firewalls and software updates are **preventive countermeasures**. They are designed to prevent a threat from exploiting a vulnerability. Naturally, you should prevent compromises whenever possible. However, it is impossible to prevent all compromises. Therefore, you also need **detective countermeasures** and **reactive countermeasures**.

Detective countermeasures detect a compromise and alert you to the problem so that you can immediately respond. Because detective countermeasures enable you to respond quickly, they reduce downtime, which reduces the damage caused by the compromise. Examples of detective countermeasures include intrusion detection systems, fault monitoring software, and file integrity checking. Reactive countermeasures enable you to respond to and recover from a compromise. Although preventive and detective countermeasures are always in use, reactive countermeasures are used only after a compromise has occurred.

Backups are the most important reactive countermeasure. If you do not have backups and a threat bypasses your countermeasures and destroys your data, you will have no way to recover that important asset. If an attacker copies data but does not destroy it, you might never discover the theft unless you have a reactive countermeasure such as an intrusion detection system. Disaster recovery and business continuance plans are reactive countermeasures to catastrophic events.

Table 1-2 shows common threats and the preventive, detective, and reactive countermeasures typically used for each.

Table 1-2 **Countermeasures for Common Threats**

Threat	Preventive Countermeasures	Detective Countermeasures	Reactive Countermeasures
Destruction of data by worm or virus	Firewalls, antivirus software, security updates	File integrity checking software, intrusion detection software	On-site backups

Table 1-2   **Countermeasures for Common Threats**

Threat	Preventive Countermeasures	Detective Countermeasures	Reactive Countermeasures
Spoofing identity	Authentication systems, employee security training, complex password requirements	Security auditing, intrusion detection systems	Contacting law enforcement agencies
Denial-of-service attack	Generic packet filtering	Fault monitoring software	Packet filtering designed to block the specific attack, coordination between Internet service providers, law enforcement
Destruction of assets by fire	Fire-suppression systems, fire-resistant building construction	Fire alarms	Off-site backups, geographically distributed redundancy, disaster recovery plans, insurance
Physical theft	Door locks, security guards	Alarm systems, security guards	Law enforcement, security cameras, off-site backups, geographically distributed redundancy, disaster recovery, insurance

How the Components Fit Together

If a threat agent gives rise to a threat and exploits a vulnerability, the attack leads to a potential security compromise. The attack can then damage the asset by degrading its confidentiality, integrity, or availability. Therefore, the attack causes an exposure to potential company losses; however, countermeasures can minimize these exposures.

For example, operating systems are susceptible to viruses that may cause the loss or corruption of data—a vulnerability. You can minimize this vulnerability with antivirus software (a countermeasure), but the presence of such a countermeasure does not eliminate the risk because virus signatures used to detect viruses are released only after the virus is found in the wild. Other risk factors include outdated virus signatures or an undetected failure of the antivirus software. Although this particular countermeasure does not completely eliminate the risk, it is probably still worthwhile because it does reduce the risk. Very few counter-measures are perfect. Therefore, some level of risk usually exists.

Figure 1-5 visually demonstrates how threats, exposures, vulnerabilities, counter-measures, and assets fit together. Threat agents use a simple, logical path to com-promise assets. First, they have motives and goals to achieve. For sophisticated attackers, the goal might be financial gain. Other attackers are motivated by fame and glory. The threat agent uses tools, techniques, and methods to exploit assets' vulnerabilities.

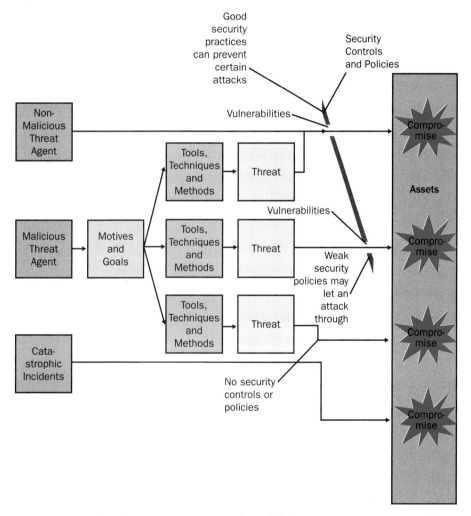

Figure 1-5 Fitting threats, exposures, vulnerabilities, countermeasures, and assets together when a compromise occurs

HISTORICAL COMPROMISES

The following list shows historical examples of attacks and each of the components used in the attack. As you read them, think about how assets, threats, threat agents, vulnerabilities, compromises, and countermeasures connect. Each of these compromises was preventable, so think about countermeasures that might have prevented the attacks. Your organization expects you, as a security architect, to prevent similar attacks.

1938: Poles Break Nazi Encryption

Both before and after World War II, the Nazis used radio communications extensively to communicate with military units. Like today's wireless networks, radio communications have a vulnerability: anyone with a receiver can intercept them. The Nazis relied on encryption as a countermeasure, using very similar technologies to those used by many of today's wireless networks. The encryption countermeasure dramatically reduced the risk of their enemies intercepting and interpreting their communications; however, it did not eliminate the risk.

The Poles (the threat agent) were able capture radio communications (a threat), capture a Nazi Enigma decryption device (another threat), and identify encryption keys by using cryptanalysis (a third threat). The Poles combined these three threats to decrypt Nazi communications (an information disclosure exploit). The Nazi cryptography expert's biggest mistake was to trust people to generate random encryption keys. Human error ultimately exposed too much of the Nazis' encryption scheme.

1972: John Draper Uses a Cap'n Crunch Whistle to Avoid Long-Distance Phone Charges

John Draper, an engineer (and threat agent), noticed that several blind children had discovered that a whistle (a threat), included free with Cap'n Crunch breakfast cereal, produced a pure 2600-Hz tone identical to that recognized by telephone equipment. The telephone equipment would remove any long distance charges that applied to a call when this tone was present (a vulnerability). Draper used the whistle repeatedly to bypass long-distance charges (the compromise). Preventive countermeasures obviously failed, but reactive countermeasures were successful.

By monitoring usage logs, the telephone company detected the compromise and used the evidence to identify and prosecute the threat agent. The telephone company later reduced the vulnerability by switching to more complex signaling techniques. The biggest mistake by the telephone company's equipment designer was relying on **security-by-obscurity**. The only thing preventing people from abusing the system was their lack of knowledge of the specific tone used.

1988: Kevin Mitnick Steals Source Code from DEC (Digital Equipment Corporation)

Kevin Mitnick (threat agent) poses as an authorized user (threat: spoofing identity) to gain access to DEC computer systems (compromise). In this example, the vulnerability was in DEC's authentication system, because Mitnick was able to gain access to a legitimate user's credentials. The authentication system (a countermeasure) failed to prevent Mitnick's access.

Whereas preventive countermeasures failed to prevent the compromise, reactive countermeasures were successful. The Federal Bureau of Investigation was able to monitor Mitnick's computer usage to gather evidence that was later used to convict Mitnick of multiple counts of computer crime.

2000: An Attacker Steals Confidential Microsoft Source Code

Although the specific details are unknown, experts believe attackers (threat agents) gained access to Microsoft's private network by e-mailing a Trojan horse (threat) called QAZ Trojan to a Microsoft employee. The employee ran the Trojan horse, successfully enabling the attackers to exploit the vulnerability that allowed e-mailing malicious applications to internal staff (compromise). The QAZ Trojan software gave the attackers access to the computer (elevated privilege). The attackers then used this access to collect employee passwords and pose as employees (threat: spoofing identity) to gain access to source code (information disclosure).

Microsoft could have used several countermeasures to prevent this compromise, including security training and filtering of executable attachments. Preventive countermeasures failed but reactive countermeasures were successful. Microsoft security personnel detected passwords being e-mailed from Microsoft's internal network and engaged the FBI to assist in identifying the attackers.

Each of these examples is a successful compromise that was discovered after the fact. However, the vast majority of successful compromises go undiscovered because of poor intrusion detection mechanisms. Later in this course, you will learn how to use preventive countermeasures to reduce the risk of a compromise and reactive countermeasures to reduce the damage caused by a compromise and to prevent future compromises.

> **NOTE**   **The Security Architect's Pledge of Modesty**   Say these to yourself at the start of every workday and you will keep yourself humble and well-rounded:
>
> - "I will never make anything secure. I can only hope to make my networks *more* secure."
> - "I am personally responsible for every compromise of my network. I cannot blame others for making mistakes that lead to vulnerabilities. I must anticipate and plan for human error."
> - "I will be hacked. I must plan to detect it, recover from it, and learn from it."
> - "My technical skills are a small part of what I need to know to design security. I must have well-rounded business skills to make security design decisions."

SUMMARY

- Businesses use security to control unexpected costs. Like insurance, the purpose of security is risk management. Most security requirements involve three goals: confidentiality, integrity, and availability. The most effective way to meet these goals is to provide multiple layers of countermeasures, a technique called defense-in-depth.

- A threat agent initiates an attack on an asset by using a threat to compromise an asset's vulnerability. The role of a security architect is to identify these threats and use countermeasures to reduce the risk of compromised assets.

- People have made the same security mistakes repeatedly in history. Although the technologies have changed over time, the concepts remain the same. In particular, history can teach you the following security design lessons:

  - ❏ You must plan for human error.

  - ❏ You must use both preventive and reactive countermeasures.

  - ❏ You cannot rely on a single layer of defense to protect an important asset.

  - ❏ Most vulnerabilities will never be compromised, which can cause people to think implementing countermeasures is not worth the effort. However, attacks are frequent enough that most networks will be compromised at some point in the future. The cost of a single compromise can be huge, which makes the gamble of dedicating energy to security worthwhile.

REVIEW QUESTIONS

1. Michael Zeman creates a worm that he names M3gaW0rm. The worm infects a known vulnerability in Microsoft Internet Information Services (IIS) on your Windows Server 2003 computer. Because users access the server from the public Internet, you had allowed Hypertext Transfer Protocol (HTTP) traffic through the firewall. The worm then replicates itself to other computers on the Internet and generates so much traffic that it takes your Internet connection offline, preventing your users from accessing Internet resources. What are the asset, threat agent, and threat?

    a. Your firewall, Michael Zeman, M3gaW0rm

    b. Michael Zeman, M3gaW0rm, the Internet connection

    c. The Internet connection, Michael Zeman, M3gaW0rm

    d. Windows Server 2003, IIS, M3gaW0rm

2. You have identified your company's financial records, stored as files on a computer running Windows Server 2003, as critical assets. Which of the following countermeasures would you recommend using to protect vulnerabilities on the server? (Choose all that apply.)

    a. Automatic Updates

    b. A network firewall

    c. A host-based firewall

    d. Security log auditing

    e. Backups

    f. Network encryption

    g. File encryption

3. You are a security architect at a medium-sized firm. You have taken great care to harden your network. Early one morning, you discover that a virus transferred as an attachment in e-mail has infected several users' computers. How could you have prevented the problem? (Choose all that apply.)

    a. Added antivirus software to the mail servers.

    b. Added antivirus software to the mail clients.

    c. Configured your network firewall to block TCP port 25, which the Simple Mail Transfer Protocol (SMTP) uses.

    d. Configured host-based firewalls on each computer to block TCP port 25, which the SMTP uses.

    e. Trained users not to open unexpected attachments.

    f. You could not have prevented the problem. It is the users' fault.

4. You are a security engineer at Fourth Coffee, a national retail coffee outlet. Several human rights organizations recently have pointed out that several of the growers your organization purchases supplies from use questionable labor practices. Which of the following malicious attack motivations poses the greatest threat to your organization?

    a. Intellectually motivated

    b. Personally motivated

      c. Politically motivated

      d. Financially motivated

5. Which of the following types of malicious threats is most likely to delete important data from a database?

      a. Intellectually motivated

      b. Personally motivated

      c. Politically motivated

      d. Financially motivated

6. Which are the three pillars of information security? (Choose all that apply.)

      a. Authentication

      b. Integrity

      c. Encryption

      d. Availability

      e. Redundancy

      f. Confidentiality

      g. Authorization

7. Which of the following are threat agents? (Choose all that apply.)

      a. A tornado

      b. A destructive worm

      c. A developer who creates a bug that causes critical systems to crash

      d. A port-scanning tool

      e. An employee who gives a user name and password to an attacker posing as a systems administrator

CASE SCENARIOS

Case Scenario 1-1: Responding to a Newly Discovered Vulnerability

You are a security engineer in the information technology group of an enterprise software company with about 50,000 employees. During a weekly meeting, you listen to a summary of a newly discovered vulnerability:

"...and in the database area, we've got a couple buffer overflows in SQL Server that could be abused by an attacker to gain elevation of privileges. The vulnerability affects Microsoft SQL Server 2000 and MSDE. There are no known tools that can exploit it, and our firewalls block the network protocols a threat would need to use, so we're probably okay. The SQL Server developers are putting a patch together. After we get the patch, we should roll it out to all our database servers just to be safe. SQL patches are tough, though, because the database administrator really needs to take the database offline, run the patch manually, and then make sure the database starts back up okay. That'll mean scheduling some downtime with users... And you know what that means: working late. Oh, and if anyone is using MSDE, you'd better install the patch, too."

The purpose of this case scenario is to exercise your ability to understand and analyze new types of threats. This chapter has not provided a technical background about the type of vulnerability that was described (though future chapters will). Leverage your own personal experiences, and the knowledge of your classmates, to answer the questions that follow to the best of your ability.

1. What skills would a threat agent need to exploit this vulnerability?

2. List possible motivations for a threat agent to exploit this vulnerability.

3. List possible forms the threat could take.

4. Considering the time required to test the update for compatibility with internal applications and to schedule downtime for the database, how long do you estimate it would take to patch all vulnerable computers?

5. Your firewalls block the network protocols that a threat would need to use to exploit the vulnerability. Is it worth the cost and energy to deploy the update to remove the newly discovered vulnerability?

6. Many users install MSDE without realizing that they have SQL Server installed. Besides the existing firewalls, how can you protect these users from exploitation of the vulnerability?

This case scenario is a fictional account based on actual historical events that occurred within the Microsoft internal IT group around July 2002. About six months later, on January 25, 2003, the SQL Slammer worm made its first appearance on the Internet. Within 10 minutes, it had infected 75,000 computers. The SQL Slammer worm exploited a known vulnerability in the SQL Server 2000 database application. After infecting a computer running SQL Server, the SQL Slammer worm looks for other hosts to infect so that it can replicate itself. Whereas SQL Slammer did not directly damage the computers it infected, it generated large amounts of network traffic while searching for other vulnerable computers. This increase in network traffic resulted in a widespread DoS attack that affected hundreds of private networks and the Internet.

The SQL Slammer worm is interesting because it exploited a vulnerability for which Microsoft had released an update six months prior to the SQL Slammer's first appearance. No customers who downloaded and installed the patch were vulnerable to the SQL Slammer threat. Firewalls that blocked SQL communications also protected customers from the threat. Yet, hundreds of thousands of computers were infected.

On January 28, 2003, the media reported that the SQL Slammer worm had infected many computers within Microsoft's private network. Microsoft's own internal IT department was not successful in thoroughly deploying the patch. The compromise had a significant cost to Microsoft:

- The worm's traffic slowed network traffic for several days, reducing the productivity of Microsoft employees.

- Many employees were dedicated to removing the worm after the successful compromise, wasting personnel time that would have otherwise been focused on more productive tasks.

- The media coverage tarnished Microsoft's reputation.

In hindsight, Microsoft should have put more energy into identifying vulnerable computers that required the update and verifying that they were quickly patched. In addition, Microsoft should have configured host-based firewalls on all computers to provide defense-in-depth protection. The perimeter firewalls that protected Microsoft's internal network were not sufficient to protect against the SQL Slammer worm because the worm only needed to infect a single computer on the internal network to replicate freely. SQL Slammer may have compromised the Microsoft internal network by infecting a laptop computer that an employee had taken home, and then propagating across the internal network after the employee returned to work.

Case Scenario 1-2: Helping a Friend Choose Security for a Small Network

Your friend, David Jaffe, runs a 1,000-acre vineyard called Coho Vineyard. He helped you move, and now he is asking you to return the favor by making some security recommendations. He describes his network to you over lunch.

"First, let me say that I'm no computer guy. I read the manual and I do okay, though. I bought a computer that runs Microsoft Small Business Server 2003. It has wizards that helped me set up a domain and a mail server. Then I've got my laptop, Jenny's desktop, and Chris's desktop. We're all running Windows XP Professional. We're all networked together by this router with 4 Ethernet ports and 802.11g. I use the wireless connection because I spend a lot of time in different parts of the building. Besides setting up Internet access and e-mail, everything is set to the default. I wasn't too worried about it, but when I talked to you the other day you made me think I might get attacked across the Internet. What should I do to protect myself? Oh, I should add that I have almost no money to spend. In fact, can you get lunch?"

Based on this information, answer the following questions.

1. List, in order of priority, which of the following preventive countermeasures David should add to his network:

   ❑ Enable wireless encryption

   ❑ Configure Automatic Updates

   ❑ Buy a dedicated network firewall

   ❑ Configure host-based firewalls

   ❑ Configure antivirus software

   a. Enable wireless encryption, configure Automatic Updates, buy a dedicated network firewall, configure host-based firewalls, configure antivirus software

   b. Configure Automatic Updates, configure host-based firewalls, configure antivirus software, enable wireless encryption, buy a dedicated network firewall

   c. Configure Automatic Updates, buy a dedicated network firewall, configure host-based firewalls, enable wireless encryption, configure antivirus software

   d. Buy a dedicated network firewall, configure host-based firewalls, enable wireless encryption, configure Automatic Updates, configure antivirus software

2. List, in order of priority, which of the following reactive countermeasures David should add to his network:

   ❑ On-site backups

   ❑ Off-site backups

❏ Intrusion detection system

❏ Periodic auditing of the security event log

a. On-site backups, off-site backups, intrusion detection system,
    periodic auditing of the security event log

b. On-site backups, intrusion detection system, off-site backups,
    periodic auditing of the security event log

c. On-site backups, intrusion detection system, periodic auditing of
    the security event log, off-site backups

d. On-site backups, off-site backups, periodic auditing of the secu-
    rity event log, intrusion detection system

CHAPTER 2
ANALYZING RISK

Upon completion of this chapter, you will be able to:

- Initiate the security risk management process by finding an executive sponsor, assemble a security risk management team, and schedule time for the team to complete the process.

- Complete phase 1 of the security risk management process by identifying potential threats to your organization and assessing the risk level each threat poses to your critical assets.

- Complete phase 2 of the security risk management process by comparing multiple countermeasures to find the countermeasure that most effectively reduces the risk of a security compromise.

- Complete phase 3 of the security risk management process by maintaining your organization's security on an ongoing basis.

Too often, an organization's security architecture is determined casually, rather than analytically. For example, an executive might meet a salesperson at a party and decide to buy a $10,000 intrusion detection system (IDS). Although the IDS could improve the organization's security, it might not be the best way to spend $10,000. The organization might be better served by spending $3,000 on a firewall and $7,000 on employee security training. Identifying the best ways to improve security is complicated, especially in large organizations. Fortunately, you can use the security risk management process to identify the most efficient way to improve an organization's security.

This chapter describes how to start the security risk management process at your organization, and then it describes each of the three phases in detail.

> **MORE INFO** The process described here is loosely based on the Microsoft security risk management discipline. For more information, refer to *http://www.microsoft.com/technet/security/guidance/secmod134.mspx*.

STARTING THE SECURITY RISK MANAGEMENT PROCESS

If your organization hasn't gone through the security risk management process, there's a good chance that you have significant, unknown vulnerabilities. Anyone can initiate the security risk management process, and you'll have the best chance of success if you follow these steps:

1. Find an executive sponsor.

2. Assemble a security risk management team.

3. Schedule time for the security risk management team to complete the process.

The following sections discuss each of these three steps.

Find an Executive Sponsor

Most security efforts start with a bottom-up approach. For example, an engineer might notice some security vulnerabilities and ask his boss for some time to put together a security plan; however, the chances of the engineer making a difference without support from executive management are slim. It's difficult to make changes that affect multiple groups in an organization because one group might not have the time or desire to cooperate. In addition, you need to consult people from many different groups to assess and implement a security risk management plan.

An executive sponsor enables you to successfully cooperate with many different groups within your organization and increase your chances of getting the budget you need. If you don't have a relationship with your executive management, ask your manager to raise the topic at the next staff meeting. Your first choice should be your company's Chief Security Officer (CSO), followed by the Chief Information Officer (CIO), Chief Technology Officer (CTO), Chief Operations Officer (COO), and Chief Legal Officer (CLO). If none of these executives are available, or your organization does not have these roles, ask your manager for guidance.

Assemble a Security Risk Management Team

After you identify an executive sponsor for the security risk management project, you need to create a security risk management team. The charter of this team is to determine the objectives, scope, policies, priorities, standards, and strategies for security within your organization. The first members of the team should be senior executives within the company. It's important to use senior executives because they are the most effective at assigning personnel and resources, and a top-down approach will make it easier for the team to acquire additional funding and other resources that they determine are necessary to meet the organization's security requirements. In addition, executives are often the only people at an organization who understand the long-term direction, and long-term direction can have a significant impact on how you design security. These executives then assign the middle-level managers, who can further delegate responsibilities to subject-matter experts.

Senior management should begin creating the security team by assigning roles and responsibilities within the organization that are necessary to launch the security risk management process. The involvement of senior management keeps the project strong and evolving as the business and technical environments change. Creating roles within a security program validates that the organization recognizes security as a cohesive part of its business rather than as just a concern.

At a minimum, your team needs people to fill the following roles:

- **Project manager**   Project managers are critical to ensuring that the project continues to move forward. Project managers are skilled at coordinating different resources, finding ways to solve problems that block your progress—such as uncooperative coworkers—and ensuring that resources such as people and conference rooms are available. The project manager should attend every meeting to ensure that each meeting's goals are accomplished.

- **Security subject-matter expert (SME)**   Security SMEs are familiar with security design concepts and the security risk management process. These people would, ideally, also be familiar with the company's critical assets and strategic direction.

- **IT manager**   IT managers are familiar with the company's critical assets and network connections. Large organizations with distributed responsibilities need to have multiple IT managers on the team to ensure that someone familiar with every critical resource participates. Every IT manager does not need to attend every meeting. However, he or she needs to provide detailed information about each asset, including its use, value, vulnerabilities, and existing countermeasures. IT managers are the most likely to object to your designs because new countermeasures might impact their ability to do their jobs. Therefore, it is important to have their support and guidance throughout the process.

In addition, the security risk management team needs regular input from members outside the team. For example, someone in your organization's strategy group should review the plans to ensure that the team's assessment of the value of different assets is consistent with the company's long-term plans. IT managers in an enterprise might be unaware that a particular asset will not be needed in the near future, or that a seemingly unimportant asset will soon become critical.

Of course, not all organizations have people to fill all these roles. In small businesses, you may be acting as the project manager, SME, and IT manager. If you find yourself in this situation, do your best to think about both the business and technical perspectives.

Schedule Time for the Security Risk Management Team to Complete the Process

After your team is assembled, the project manager has an extremely important task: creating the project schedule. You need to work with the project manager to describe the different phases of the project and estimate the amount of time required by each phase. There are three phases to the security risk management process: assessment, implementation, and operations.

- **Assessment**   This phase involves gathering relevant information from the company's environment to perform a security assessment. First, you must gather existing security policies and assess the importance of each of your organization's assets. Then, you must determine which threats are likely to attack those assets, and create a Security Action Plan that identifies countermeasures to use to reduce risk in the Implementation phase.

- **Implementation**   This phase focuses on developing, testing, and deploying countermeasures identified in the Security Action Plan. You also assemble an **incident response** team and draft security policies.

- **Operations**   This phase involves making modifications and updates to your environment as needed to keep it secure. Contingency plans are carried out as needed during this phase. You use auditing and monitoring to keep the infrastructure intact and secure. You can also add new countermeasures when you discover new threats or vulnerabilities. Because network infrastructure, threats, and vulnerabilities change regularly, the Operations phase is ongoing.

Figure 2-1 shows the three phases and the steps within each phase.

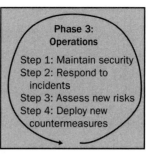

Figure 2-1 Follow the security risk management process to optimize your organization's security.

The project manager should make sure that each team member has enough time in his or her schedule to dedicate to the project. At the outset, you will be able only to create an accurate schedule for the assessment phase. During that phase, you determine how much work will be required in phases 2 and 3.

PHASE 1: ASSESSMENT

In the assessment phase, you determine what your assets are worth, identify risks, and calculate the potential damage if an asset is exploited. The five steps in this phase are the following:

1. Inventory security policies

2. Assess assets

3. Assess threats

4. Assess risks

5. Create a Security Action Plan

Step 1: Inventory Security Policies

The first step of the security risk management process is to create an inventory of existing security policies and controls. During your review, make note of areas in which security policies are obviously lacking. During the implementation phase, you review these policies more thoroughly and make changes where necessary. Ask a member of your legal team to review the security policies to verify that they comply with the company's legal policy.

For convenience, obtain printed copies of each policy and bind them together. You need to refer to these documents frequently.

Step 2: Assess Assets

In this step, you create a list of every significant asset in your organization. As discussed in Chapter 1, "Assessing the Need for Security," an **asset** is anything in your organization's environment that might require some level of protection. This could include items that you've purchased outright, such as software, hardware, and facilities. Assets also can be data, people, and information.

For each asset, you must assess its value and its relationship to other assets. The sections that follow discuss this in more detail. If you are part of a large organization, divide the assets into multiple lists. For example, create a separate list for each regional office or create separate lists for servers, network hardware, and organizational roles. Table 2-1 shows a simplified example of the information to gather.

Table 2-1   **Asset Inventory**

Asset	Description	Dependencies	Value
File server	Used to store and share internal documents	Router, Switch1, domain controller	3
Domain controller	Authenticates users, distributes Group Policy objects	Router, Switch1	2
Router	Forwards packets between Switch1 and Switch2		2
Switch1	Forwards frames to computers on Subnet1		3
Switch2	Forwards frames to computers on Subnet2		3
Firewall	Forwards traffic from router to Internet connection		3
Product designs	Designs used by manufacturing to create core products	File server	1

The sections that follow describe how to qualitatively and quantitatively assess value. When you use a qualitative approach to valuing assets, you assign each asset a rough estimate of its value. When you use a quantitative approach, you attempt to identify a dollar value for the asset. For reasons you will understand when you study the quantitative approach later in this chapter, most successful security risk management efforts use a qualitative approach rather than a quantitative approach.

Qualitatively Valuing Assets

During this step, you assign a value to each asset. **Asset valuation** is how much it costs to maintain an asset, what it would cost if it were lost or destroyed, and what benefit would be gained if another party obtained this information. The value of an asset should reflect all identifiable costs that would arise if the asset were completely destroyed. Asset valuation is used to summarize the following aspects of an asset:

- The profits for which the asset is responsible

- The value the asset would have to the competition

- The cost expended to acquire or develop the asset

- The cost required to re-create or recover the asset

- The potential future value of the asset

Although different organizations use different qualitative scales to assess the importance of each asset, the following four levels, based on the impact on the company if the asset is compromised, are generally sufficient.

- **1: Catastrophic**   If the asset is lost or damaged, it would have a catastrophic effect on the organization. The organization would not be able to recover.

- **2: Very serious**   Damage to this asset would severely affect the organization's ability to do business or would cost the organization a significant amount of money.

- **3: Moderately serious**   If this asset were compromised, the organization would be affected and would need to spend money and employee time to recover. However, day-to-day business would continue as normal.

- **4: Not serious**   A successful attack on this asset would have minimal impact on the organization.

> **NOTE   Six of One, a Half-Dozen of the Other**   Some security designers use a scale of 1–3; others use a scale of 1–10. Any scale will work, but keep in mind that too many levels can lead to team members bickering about the importance of an asset. Using too few levels doesn't allow you to adequately distinguish assets that deserve more protection. Using four levels is a good compromise. You will also see scales that refer to the value of an asset (Critical, Important, Not Important) rather than the cost if the asset is lost. Regardless of the terminology used, the concept is the same.

Consider a fictional organization named Tailspin Toys that manufactures parts that other companies use to build toys. Tailspin Toys has a public Web site that contains only a brief overview of the company and contact information. They have an e-mail server that employees often use to communicate with vendors and customers, although no highly confidential communications occur through e-mail. The database server contains the designs and manufacturing instructions for each of the parts that they sell. During this step of the security risk management process, you might value the assets as shown in Table 2-2.

Table 2-2 **Example of Qualitative Asset Valuation**

Asset	Value	Explanation
Web site	4: Not serious	If the Web site were to go offline, be maliciously modified, or otherwise be compromised, it would not significantly impact business and it could be restored easily.
E-mail server	3: Moderately serious	If the e-mail server is taken offline by a successful attack, customers and vendors can fall back on using the phone or fax systems. However, it would be an inconvenience and might hurt relations with customers and vendors.
Database server	1: Catastrophic	The database server contains the designs for all the company's products. If that information were lost, the company would not be able to continue business. If the information were to fall into a competitor's hands, the company would lose a great deal of its market advantage.

Later in this process, you consider both the asset's value and the potential damage a threat could do to an asset to weigh your risk and determine the countermeasures required.

Quantitatively Valuing Assets

Some organizations prefer to value assets quantitatively. Quantitative analysis has the advantage of being more precise than qualitative analysis. However, it has a significant disadvantage: accurately assessing the value of assets is extremely time-consuming. Generally, your time is better spent in other phases of the security risk management process because qualitative analysis does a good job of estimating the same results you would get from a quantitative analysis. This section describes quantitative asset valuation because it is an important theory to understand. In practice, qualitative techniques are usually more efficient.

To assign a value to an asset appropriately, calculate the annual value, direct impact, and the annual indirect impact.

- **Value**   This is the overall value of the asset to your organization. Calculate or estimate the asset's value in direct financial terms. For example, if you have an e-commerce Web site that normally runs seven days a week, 24 hours a day, and it generates an average of $2,000 per hour in revenue from customer orders, you can state with confidence that the annual value of the Web site in terms of sales revenue is $17,520,000. You might also need to factor in the potential value of the asset. For example, some assets such as trade secrets and chemical formulas can dramatically and suddenly increase in value because of world events. In a similar way, some assets can suddenly lose their value if a competitor releases a superior product or if a substantial flaw in the asset is discovered.

- **Direct impact**   This is the immediate financial impact of losing the asset, including the cost of replacement if the asset is entirely destroyed. For physical assets, base the direct-impact value on the cost of a catastrophic event such as a fire and reduce the amount to accommodate insurance. Include the cost of the labor of rebuilding, replacing, and reconfiguring the asset.

- **Indirect impact**   This is the indirect business impact of losing the asset. For example, if your organization sells Web-hosting services and a security compromise causes your Web server to fail, your reputation will be tarnished and some customers will switch to a competitor. In this example, the indirect impact would be an estimate of the long-term lost revenue. On the other hand, if advertising is required to restore your reputation or to rebuild lost business, you could base the indirect impact value on the cost of advertising.

> **NOTE** *Value vs. Cost*   Remember, the value of an asset is not just the cost of the hardware. A backup tape is inexpensive, but if you needed to restore data from the tape and you discovered that it had been damaged, the loss could be significant.

Table 2-3 shows an example of a quantitative asset valuation.

Table 2-3 **Quantitative Asset Valuation**

Asset	Value	Direct Impact	Indirect Impact
Web site	$520,000	$12,000	$28,000
E-mail server	$125,000	$17,000	$35,000
Database server	$1,200,000	$500,000	$75,000

In the real world, most people make very rough estimates to arrive at quantitative asset valuations, which reduce the value of the quantitative analysis in the short run, but become more accurate over time.

Step 3: Assess Threats

In this step, you perform **threat modeling** to brainstorm for potential security threats to each asset in step 2. When you perform threat modeling, you ask the questions "What type of attacks do I need to defend against?" and "What conditions might lead to an attacker successfully compromising my network?" Just evaluating and protecting against well-known threats assumes that every network is the same, that every attacker will attempt the same types of access, and that every attacker has the same skill set.

Threat modeling uses the security administrator's intimate knowledge of specific networks and applications as well as logical and chaotic thinking to come up with potential scenarios. What, for example, could a knowledgeable insider who developed your accounting systems do with that knowledge—both as an employee and after leaving the company? How about contractors to whom security management is outsourced? What practices need to be implemented to make the code in your internal applications more secure against both the insertion of backdoors and immature coding practices?

> **MORE INFO** *Writing Secure Code*, 2nd Edition, by Michael Howard and David LeBlanc (Microsoft Press, 2002), includes additional information about threat modeling with respect to the development process. Although the book deals with writing secure code, it embodies principles and practices that can easily be applied to designing secure networks.

Many threats, especially those involving legacy systems and interoperability constraints, can be identified only with thorough analysis. In particular, you should consider that software often defaults to a less-secure state when communicating with a client that does not support a more secure communications protocol.

For example, if your organization currently uses the Extensible Authentication Protocol (EAP) to authenticate remote-access users with a smart card, your remote-access server might be configured to allow less-secure authentication protocols based on a user name and password if the client does not support EAP. If a threat agent installed keyboard logging software onto a computer that did not support EAP, and therefore used a user name and password to log on, the keyboard logging software could capture the user's credentials and bypass the countermeasure provided by the smart cards. You might be required to accept this risk to continue support for the legacy system, but it is important that you list and acknowledge the vulnerability.

> **MORE INFO**   An excellent way to identify vulnerabilities caused by software configuration in computers running Windows is to use the Microsoft Baseline Security Analyzer (MBSA). For more information about MBSA, refer to Chapter 3, "Reducing the Risk of Software Vulnerabilities."

Although most organizations have other threats, the following partial list of common threat agents and threats will get you started.

Threat agents
- Script kiddies
- Sophisticated attackers with financial motivation
- Employees
- Competitors

Threats
- Viruses
- Worms
- Fire
- Natural disaster
- Acts of war
- Hardware failure
- Network failure
- Software failure

Where you name a threat agent rather than a threat, think of what would motivate an attacker to target your organization. Understanding motivations leads you to better understand your threats, as well as the assets they are likely to target. For example, if your organization uses suppliers who use controversial labor techniques, an attacker would be likely to launch a denial-of-service (DoS) attack against your Web site to protest these techniques. If your organization handles financial transactions for other businesses, a financially motivated attacker is more likely to target you and attempt to compromise confidential data without being detected. You must use different countermeasures to protect against each of these types of attacks. These threats can change over time, so it is important that someone on your security team stay up to date on threats. New methods, tools, and techniques for circumventing security measures are being devised constantly.

After you identify potential threats for each asset, you must assess the vulnerability level for each asset-and-threat pair. If you used a qualitative approach during asset valuation, you also will use a qualitative approach here. If you are using the more detailed quantitative approach, you will use the values generated during the asset assessment phase to estimate the damage, in dollars, threats could do to your assets.

Possible damage to assets in your environment can range from minor computer glitches to catastrophic data loss. The damage caused to the system depends on the type of attack. If possible, use a test or lab environment to clarify damage resulting from different types of attacks. This enables security personnel to accurately assess the physical damage. Not all attacks cause the same type or amount of damage. Tests that could be run include the following:

- A simulation of an e-mail virus attack on a lab system followed by an analysis to determine the damage caused and potential recovery procedures required.

- A test to determine whether employees are susceptible to social engineering attacks by attempting to acquire user names and passwords from several unsuspecting employees.

- A drill or a simulation of a data center disaster. Measure the production time lost and the time taken to bring services online in a different facility.

- A simulation of a malicious virus attack. Measure the time required to recover one computer. This time factor can then be multiplied by the number of computers infected in the system to ascertain the amount of downtime or loss of productivity.

It is also a good idea to involve an incident response team in this process because a team is more likely than an individual to spot all of the different types of damage that have occurred. An incident response team manages the prioritization of security incidents and the escalation paths to resolve them. The sections that follow discuss the qualitative and quantitative approaches.

Qualitatively Assessing Threats and Vulnerabilities

Now you must assess the vulnerability each threat poses to your assets given your current security policies and countermeasures. To determine the vulnerability, consider both the likelihood of a successful compromise and the potential damage to the asset. For example, it's very likely that a Web server will be compromised by a worm in a given year. However, the worm is not likely to do irreversible damage, so the total risk posed by worms is relatively small.

Different organizations use different qualitative scales to assess the vulnerability of each asset to a particular threat. You should use the same number of levels to assess both value and vulnerability. The following four levels are usually sufficient:

- **A. Extremely high**   If left unprotected, it is almost certain that the asset will be compromised by the threat, and the damage will be severe. For example, if you discovered a public Web server and the default Administrator account had no assigned password, there is an extremely high chance that a threat will compromise and abuse the server.

- **B. Very high**   It is very likely that the threat will compromise the asset in the next year if no countermeasures are added and that the threat will cause significant damage.

- **C. Moderately high**   The asset probably will not be exploited by the threat in the next year, or the threat is not capable of causing significant damage. However, the risk exists.

- **D. Low**   The asset is not likely to be compromised and damaged by the threat.

For example, consider a database server that contains valuable, confidential information in an enterprise environment with thousands of employees. Table 2-4 shows a typical database server's vulnerability to several different threats.

Table 2-4   **Typical Database Server Vulnerabilities**

Threat	Vulnerability Level	Description
Worms	B	Database servers must listen for network communications from clients, making worms a threat. Historically, database servers have had several vulnerabilities that allowed them to be compromised by worms. Therefore, the risk is very high. This risk is somewhat offset by existing perimeter firewalls; however, the server could still be compromised by a worm on the internal network.
Employees	C	Employees have detailed knowledge of the data on the database. Because of the large number of employees who have some level of access to the database, there is a strong likelihood that an employee will attempt to abuse the data. However, the employee would need knowledge of the SQL query language to extract data directly from the database, reducing the risk.
Fire	D	The threat of fire always exists. However, this particular database server is located in a server room with fire suppression systems. Therefore, the risk of damage to the server is minimal.
Hardware failure	A	During the inventory process, the team discovered that this computer has nonredundant hard disks. In addition, although there are file backups, the database itself was not being backed up.

Quantitatively Assessing Threats and Vulnerabilities

To quantitatively assess an asset's vulnerability to a threat, you must determine the **exposure factor** (EF). The EF is the amount of damage (expressed in terms of percents) a threat could cause to an asset if the asset is compromised. For example, you need to assess the vulnerability of fire damage to data stored on a server that has never been backed up. The EF is 100 percent because the fire would permanently destroy the data. On the other hand, if the data had recently been backed up and stored offsite, a lower EF of 5 percent would account for lost data that had not been backed up and for the energy required to restore the data.

Calculating the EF is one of the most challenging aspects of quantitative analysis because there is no set formula. Rather, you must work with your team to collectively create the most accurate estimate.

Step 4: Assess Risks

Security risk analysis has three main goals: prioritize risks, quantify the impact of potential threats, and provide an economic balance between the impact of the risk and the cost of the countermeasure. You use information created in previous steps to estimate the level of risk of each threat. This analysis is then used to prioritize threats and enable your team to commit resources to address the most critical security issues.

Security risk analysis helps integrate the security program objectives with the company's business objectives and requirements. The more your business and security objectives are in alignment, the more support you'll get from upper management. If you don't clearly establish a relationship between security expenditures and business objectives, there's a good chance that management will, at some point, question whether your security expenses are necessary. When that happens, you might lose budget, personnel, or other resources, and not be able to successfully complete the project.

The analysis also helps your company draft a proper budget for a security program. Once you know how much your company's assets are worth, and you understand the possible threats they are exposed to, you can make intelligent decisions on how much money to spend toward protecting those assets. You'll never get management to agree to spend large amounts of money on security if you simply tell them that security is worth a lot of money. However, you just might get your budget if you tell them what it will cost if they *don't* spend money on security.

Qualitatively Assessing Risk

You can combine the qualitative assessment of your assets' value and the qualitative assessment of their vulnerabilities to determine which threats pose the greatest risk to your organization. Figure 2-2 illustrates how a typical organization could combine the value and vulnerability to determine whether the risk is high, medium, or low.

	1. Catastrophic	2. Very Serious	3. Moderately Serious	4. Not Serious
A. Extremely High	1A	2A	3A	4A
B. Very High	1B	2B	3B	4B
C. Moderately High	1C	2C	3C	4C
D. Low	1D	2D	3D	4D

Figure 2-2   Assess risk by combining value and vulnerability assessments.

Now you have grouped your threats into three manageable groups, which is critical to properly prioritizing your security risk management efforts. In the next step, you focus your energy on identifying countermeasures for the high-risk threats. After those threats have been adequately addressed, you can design countermeasures for medium-risk threats. If security is a high priority and you have the man-hours and budget available, you can continue to address the low-risk threats.

Quantitatively Assessing Risk

To quantitatively assess the risk of any given threat, determine the average annual damage the threat will do to the asset. For example, if a database server (the asset) is worth $250,000 and a particular threat would cost $100,000, and there is a 10 percent chance of a compromise occurring in the next year, the risk is $10,000—10 percent of the damage the threat would do.

Follow these steps to perform a quantitative security risk analysis:

1. Determine the **single loss expectancy** (SLE). The SLE is the total amount of revenue that is lost from a single security compromise. Calculate the SLE by multiplying the **asset value** (AV) determined in step 2 of the assessment phase by the exposure factor (EF) determined in step 3:

    $SLE = AV \times EF$

    For example, if an asset has a value of $100,000 and a security compromise would destroy half the asset's value, the SLE is $50,000:

    $\$50,000 = \$100,000 \times .5$

2. Determine the **annual rate of occurrence** (ARO). The ARO, expressed in terms of percents, is the chance of a security compromise in any given year. To estimate the ARO, draw on your past experience and consult risk management experts as well as security and business consultants.

The ARO range typically extends from 0 percent (never) to 100 percent (once per year). You can use a value greater than 100 percent if the compromise would occur more than once per year, when analyzing worm or virus threats.

3. Determine the **annual loss expectancy** (ALE). The ALE is the average amount of money that your organization will lose in one year if nothing is done to mitigate the risk. Calculate this value by multiplying the SLE and the ARO. The ALE is similar to the relative rank of a qualitative risk analysis. Determine the ALE by using the following equation:

ALE = SLE x ARO

For example, if you have identified an SLE of $50,000 and the ARO is 15 percent, the ALE would be $7,500:

$7,500 = $50,000 × .15

In the next step in the process, you evaluate the effectiveness of different counter-measures by recalculating the ALE with the decreased damage or risk that the countermeasure provides. As you can probably tell, quantitative analysis is much more involved. Depending on the accuracy of your data, it might not be considerably more effective than the qualitative approach.

Step 5: Create a Security Action Plan

In this step, you first use the information obtained from the previous steps to create a Security Action Plan for implementing your defenses. Table 2-5 shows a simplified example of a Security Action Plan, and the sections that follow describe how to create it. In the real world, it is most efficient to create a spreadsheet that contains all of the information that you have created about each risk throughout this process.

Table 2-5   **Sample Security Action Plan**

Asset	Threat	Response	Countermeasures
Database server	Worm	Mitigate	Network firewall
			Host-based firewall
			Antivirus software
		React to	On-site backups
Database server	Employees	Mitigate	Host-based firewall
			Least privilege permissions
			Signed computer use policies

Table 2-5 **Sample Security Action Plan**

Asset	Threat	Response	Countermeasures
		React to	On-site backups
			Security auditing
			Legal prosecution
Database server	Fire	Mitigate	Fire suppression system
		React to	Off-site backups
		Transfer	Fire insurance
Database server	Hardware failure	Mitigate	Disk redundancy
		React to	On-site backups

After the plans are created, you and the project manager produce an implementation schedule for the proposed changes. Finally, you and your organization's management assign team members to carry out the plan.

The sections that follow describe how to categorize your responses and then design preventive countermeasures and create contingency plans for risks you must respond to.

Responding to Risks

Before you begin this step, you should create a list of risks ordered from greatest risk to least risk. For each risk, you need to identify one or more responses. There are five basic responses:

- Mitigate
- React
- Transfer
- Research
- Accept

Depending on the responses you choose, you might have more work to do. For example, if you choose to mitigate a risk, you need to design a countermeasure; if you choose to transfer the risk, you need to research the cost and coverage of insurance policies. You will not actually implement these changes until phase 2, however.

The sections that follow discuss each of these responses in more detail.

Mitigate   Security risk mitigation involves adding a preventive countermeasure to either reduce the chances of a compromise occurring or reduce the impact to an acceptable level. For example, you could mitigate the risk of a threat guessing a user name and password to access your payroll system by implementing complex password policies, or you could reduce the impact of a similar attack by using the principle of least privilege to reduce the access a compromised user account would have to the payroll system. For serious risks, you should implement multiple countermeasures to reduce the risk to an acceptable level.

In this step, you identify the best countermeasures, but you do not deploy them yet. In the case of configuration-based countermeasures such as Group Policy objects, it is not necessary to develop the Group Policy object until phase 2 of the security risk management process. For more information about evaluating countermeasures to mitigate risk, refer to the sections titled, "Qualitatively Planning Countermeasures" and "Quantitatively Planning Countermeasures" later in this chapter.

React   Use the mitigate response when you choose to implement a preventive countermeasure, and use the react response when you choose to implement a **contingency plan** as a reactive countermeasure. A contingency plan is a process that can be activated in case efforts to prevent an attack fail.

A contingency plan starts with trigger values that describe the circumstances in which the plan should be executed. Typical trigger values might be detecting a security compromise of a critical asset, a natural disaster that makes a facility unusable, or the failure of a hardware device. An alert from an intrusion detection system also could be a trigger value. The result of your contingency plan should always be to control the threat and restore the damaged asset.

It is good practice to create contingency plans for all serious risks, including those that have preventive countermeasures. The reason for this is simple: no matter how effective your countermeasure, an unknown threat, exploit, or vulnerability can still exist that can harm an asset.

For more information about reacting to risk, refer to the section titled "Guidelines for Creating a Contingency Plan" later in this chapter.

> **NOTE Comparing Mitigate to React**   When you choose to mitigate, you reduce the possibility of a compromise. When you choose to react, you reduce the damage caused by a compromise. Both involve proactive planning and investment before the attack occurs. Other security risk management models include the concept of creating a response plan to react to a compromise as part of the mitigate response.

Transfer Insurance allows you to transfer a fraction of a risk to an insurance company. Insurance is most commonly used to transfer the risk of catastrophic events and theft. Transferring the security risk does not mean that a risk has been eliminated. In general, a transfer strategy generates new security risks that still require proactive management, but transferring the risk reduces the threat to a more acceptable level.

For instance, purchasing fire insurance reduces the financial damage a fire causes because the insurance company reimburses you for some of your expenses in the event of a fire. However, the insurance company will probably reimburse you only for the cost of the physical assets that have been destroyed. You still need to absorb the cost of the time required to restore your assets.

Research The security risk management process itself carries some risk. For example, if you incorrectly estimate the value of an asset or the risk posed by a threat, you might spend too much money on countermeasures. On the other hand, if you underestimate the value or risk, you might not spend enough and will expose your organization to more risk than you expected.

You can't eliminate the risk of making a mistake during this process. However, security risks that are related to a lack of knowledge might be resolved or managed effectively by learning more about the threat, exploit, vulnerabilities, or the asset itself before proceeding. For example, a team might choose to pursue a vulnerability assessment or conduct a security drill to learn more about the environment or the team's skills in reacting to a security breach before completing the security implementation plan.

Ideally, research would be accomplished before this step. However, the active discussion that occurs during this phase often highlights the need for additional information. If the decision by the team is to perform research, then the Security Action Plan should include an appropriate research proposal including the areas to be tested and the issues to be answered, including staffing and any required equipment.

> **NOTE** **Research as a Response** Other Security Risk Management Process models that you might encounter do not include Research as a separate response. Instead, the Security Risk Management team would be required to do further research before adding an official response. However, in practice, it's useful to specify this response in a meeting to ensure the additional work is performed and the risk is addressed at a later date. Once you have the information you need, you will need to change the Research response to one of the other responses. In this way, Research is more of a placeholder than an actual response.

Accept You will probably not have the time and budget to develop a response to every risk. If there are risks you simply cannot address, you must choose to accept them. Accepting a risk is important because it ensures that everyone on the security risk management team is aware the risk is, and will continue to be, present. You should include on your Security Action Plan a documented rationale for why the team has elected to accept the risk.

> **NOTE** *Cover Yourself* Senior management must be aware of risks that you choose to accept. In fact, you should have senior management physically sign a document showing the risks that are being accepted. If an accepted risk becomes a compromise and senior management acknowledged that the risk was accepted, the compromise is senior management's responsibility. If you choose to accept a risk without support from senior management, however, that compromise is entirely your responsibility.

Qualitatively Planning Countermeasures

If you are using the qualitative approach to security risk management, you now specify countermeasures for each risk that you chose to mitigate. To select an appropriate countermeasure, you must have a deep technical understanding of the asset's vulnerability and how the threat would exploit that vulnerability. If you do not have a detailed technical understanding of the risk, you should consult a subject-matter expert. Later chapters in this book provide a great deal of information about common vulnerabilities and countermeasures on Windows networks.

The qualitative approach does not provide you with detailed information about the monetary cost of each risk. However, keep in mind that you should almost never spend more on a countermeasure than what might be lost in the event of a compromise. Instead, you should strive to spend just enough to reduce the risk to an acceptable level. One exception to this is when you are required by law to implement specific countermeasures. If the law requires you to implement a countermeasure, you will need to implement it regardless of the risk level.

Quantitatively Planning Countermeasures

Although the quantitative security risk management process is much more time consuming, you will appreciate the detailed information the process produces when you are evaluating different countermeasures. You can use the monetary values you assigned to the risks to identify the countermeasure that provides the best value. This also reduces the chance of spending too much on a countermeasure.

For each risk, you should identify multiple countermeasures. Imagine that you have implemented each countermeasure, and calculate the ALE of the risk with the countermeasure in place (ALE_2). It should be lower than the original ALE (ALE_1). The difference between the old and new ALEs, minus the annual cost of the countermeasure (C), is the value (V) of the countermeasure. The following formula illustrates this:

$$V = ALE_1 - ALE_2 - C$$

Note that the formula requires the *annual* cost of the countermeasure. This is not what you pay for the countermeasure but, rather, the total cost of the counter-measure—including purchase price and maintenance—spread across the lifetime of the countermeasure. For example, consider that a firewall initially costs you $15,000 and requires 5 hours per week for a $100,000-per-year employee to man-age. If you expect to use it for three years, the annual cost of the purchase would be $5,000 and the annual cost of maintenance would be $12,500. Therefore, the total annual cost would be $17,500. If the firewall reduces your ALE from $100,000 to $20,000, you would calculate the firewall's value to be $62,500:

$$\$62,500 = \$100,000 - \$20,000 - \$17,500$$

You must also factor reduced productivity into the cost of a countermeasure. If you are evaluating the use of fingerprint scanners to replace user name and password credentials and some users initially experience problems with the fin-gerprint scanners, that will cause them to lose productive working hours. You must estimate the cost of this lost productivity and include it in the cost of the countermeasure.

Table 2-6 shows the value of three different countermeasures for protecting con-fidential data contained in a database server against the risk of compromise by a sophisticated attacker. Before each countermeasure, the data had an ALE of $100,000.

Table 2-6   **Sample Countermeasure Values**

Countermeasure	ALE_2	Annual Cost	Value
Network firewall	$85,000	$17,500	−$2,500
Host-based firewall	$40,000	$1,000	$59,000
Harden database security configuration	$15,000	$45,000	$40,000

Based on Table 2-6, the host-based firewall would be the most effective counter-measure for the imaginary database. If you determine that all countermeasures have a negative value (in other words, they cost more money than they save), then you are better off choosing to react to or accept the risk.

Guidelines for Creating a Contingency Plan

If you decide to react to a security compromise of an asset, you must create a contingency plan. Contingency plans should have five steps:

- **1. Limit the damage**   Containing the damage caused during the attack limits the amount of further damage. For example, if you get a virus in your environment, you try to limit the damage as soon as possible by disconnecting the servers from the network, even before you determine how many servers are affected. This should be done as swiftly as possible.

- **2. Assess the damage**   To assess the damage, you must determine what resources were compromised. Was a single computer compromised, or did the attacker gain privileges that enabled him or her to access other computers on your network? You must also identify critical resources that are offline as a result of the attack. Step 3, determining the cause of the damage, will also help to identify resources that might have been affected.

   > **NOTE Gathering Evidence**   If you need to gather legal evidence about the attack, it is important to take computers offline and back up their hard disks and other storage before analyzing the logs. A sophisticated attacker might install software to delete log files if the attack is discovered. This requires you to keep computers offline longer than if you focused on recovering from the damage, so you need to weigh the importance of gathering evidence against the cost of downtime.

- **3. Determine the cause of the damage**   To determine the cause of the damage, it is necessary to understand at what resources the attack was aimed and what vulnerabilities were exploited to gain access to or disrupt services. Review system logs, audit logs, and audit trails. These reviews often help in discovering where the attack originated in the system and what other resources were affected.

- **4. Repair the damage**   It is very important that the damage be repaired as quickly as possible to restore normal business operations and any data lost during the attack. The incident response team also should be available to handle the restore-and-recovery process, and to provide guidance on the recovery process. During this process, contingency procedures are executed to limit further spread of the damage and to isolate it.

■ **5. Perform a postmortem review**   After a compromise, you must review the cause of the compromise and, hopefully, identify a counter-measure to prevent the compromise in the future. During the postmortem review, you also should examine the success of the contingency plan and make any adjustments necessary to better prepare yourself for the next compromise.

To carry out a contingency plan for a compromised computer system, you need to ensure that you have auditing logs, backups, and an out-of-band method of managing the compromised asset (such as physically connecting a keyboard to a server after disconnecting it from the network). Contingency plans for physical assets, such as buildings, require the development of a disaster recovery plan. Disaster recovery planning is an interesting and immense topic that is outside the scope of this book.

You must practice contingency plans before a compromise occurs. Otherwise, there is an excellent chance that you will discover a problem with your plan, and it will take you longer than expected to restore the services. Even worse, you might discover that your backup process hasn't been working correctly, resulting in data loss.

Guidelines for Integrating Legacy Infrastructure in Security Designs

Very few security designers get to choose hardware, operating system software, security devices, and processes from scratch. Instead, they must ensure that security designs consider legacy computers, operating systems, network devices, or other infrastructure components. These considerations are often a large part of security design work. This section describes what a legacy system is and then provides guidelines for integrating legacy infrastructure in security designs.

What Is a Legacy System?   A **legacy system** is any infrastructure component such as hardware, operating system software, network device, or application that is technically outdated and cannot be upgraded. Because legacy systems are out-dated, they cannot support the same security features as other systems. Often, legacy systems cannot be replaced because of technical or budgetary constraints.

Integration Guidelines   To successfully integrate legacy systems into your security design, you must recognize their capabilities and then work within those constraints. Some legacy systems are not able to meet your security requirements because they were developed before modern security best practices. Other legacy systems can negatively impact the security of your entire organization by preventing you from implementing infrastructure security. For example, the presence of Windows 2000 Active Directory directory service domain controllers prevents you from upgrading from a Windows 2000 native mode domain, which has known security weaknesses that are resolved in pure Microsoft Windows Server 2003 domains.

Use the following guidelines to integrate legacy systems into security designs:

- **Add clauses to security policies to provide different requirements for legacy systems**   If you require 10-character passwords but a legacy system only supports 8-character passwords, you should add a clause to your security policy that permits legacy systems to use shorter passwords. You should then formally accept the additional risk this compromise introduces by making management aware of the risk.

- **Maintain a separate infrastructure for legacy systems**   Rather than enabling interoperability features in your Active Directory domain to enable legacy clients to join the domain, create a separate domain for legacy systems. After the legacy systems are upgraded, move them to the more secure Active Directory domain. Although the legacy domain contains security weaknesses that are not present in the new domain, you will be more secure with a separate domain because the damage from a compromise would be restricted to the legacy systems. Note, however, that trusts required to share resources between domains could also enable an attacker to gain access to resources in a more secure domain.

- **Use network security to reduce risks associated with legacy systems**   While you might not be able to add a host-based firewall to a legacy system, you could provide much of the same security by placing the legacy system on a separate network segment and adding a separate network firewall.

- **Create a plan to migrate away from the legacy system**   Although you might not immediately be able to remove the legacy system, you should explain the risks the legacy systems introduce to your security plans to management, and request they put together a plan to migrate to a more up-to-date platform.

Guidelines for Planning Around Interoperability Constraints

Most organizations have operating systems and applications from different vendors. These complex networks can be the result of natural growth, consolidation, or mergers. Specifically, many organizations have computers running both UNIX-based and Windows-based systems.

Computers running UNIX-based and Windows-based systems often have different security capabilities and might use entirely different infrastructures for security configuration management and patch management. You will almost certainly use operating system–specific security features as countermeasures in your Security Action Plan, which means you are required to design multiple techniques to accomplish the same security goals.

To reduce interoperability problems when designing security, rely on network security as much as possible. Network firewalls are essential in heterogeneous environments because it is extremely challenging to ensure that every computer provides sufficient host-based network security. In a similar way, if you plan to implement an intrusion detection system, choose a network-based intrusion detection system that does not require software to be installed on individual hosts.

Choose security configuration management and patch management solutions that support every platform your organization uses. Although Active Directory Group Policy and Software Update Services provide excellent solutions for managing security configurations and security updates on computers running Windows, neither can be extended to UNIX systems. However, non-Microsoft cross-platform management tools can enable you to manage and update multiple platforms.

PHASE 2: IMPLEMENTATION

During the assessment phase, you identified assets, threats, and risks, and then created a plan to deploy countermeasures to improve your security. In this phase, you deploy those countermeasures. The three steps in this phase are as follows:

1. Develop countermeasures
2. Test countermeasures
3. Implement countermeasures

Step 1: Develop Countermeasures

Security risk remediation development is the process of taking the plans that you created in the assessment phase and using them to create the actual tools, documentation, and procedures that improve your organization's security. This is a lengthy task, but it should be straightforward because you completed the planning during the assessment phase.

The sections that follow describe how to develop the countermeasures you identified in the assessment phase, assemble an incident response team, and develop operational policies and procedures.

Developing Countermeasures

Whereas the specific tasks you need to do depend on the countermeasures you plan to use, most organizations need to perform the following tasks:

- **Specify security configuration policies for networks and computers**   On Windows networks, this task almost always involves developing Group Policy objects to enforce configuration settings on computers running Windows-based client and server systems. For example, if during the assessment phase you specified that desktop computers would be hardened to restrict what applications users can run, in this phase you would create Group Policy objects for enforcing that countermeasure. You will not deploy these settings until step 3 of this phase. However, you must also determine configuration policies for other network hosts. If you determined that you would use packet filtering on your routers as a countermeasure in the assessment phase, in this phase you specify which routers have what packet filtering.

- **Design a patch management solution**   Assets running software, such as servers, laptops, routers, and firewalls, require regular updates. In this phase, you must develop a patch management solution that ensures discovery and deployment of new updates. On Windows networks, this often requires you to design a Windows Update Services (WUS) infrastructure. You need to develop other procedures for patching hosts that do not run Windows. For more information about developing a patch management solution, refer to Chapter 3.

- **Develop a system-monitoring solution**   If you determined in the assessment phase that your current monitoring solution does not provide you sufficient fault detection or intrusion detection capabilities, you should now design a new system-monitoring solution. On Windows networks, this often involves using Microsoft Systems Management Server (SMS), Microsoft Operations Manager (MOM), and, possibly, the Microsoft Baseline Security Analyzer (MBSA) tool.

> **NOTE** *Effective Application Monitoring*   *Although SMS, MOM, and MBSA might meet your security monitoring requirements, the most effective way to monitor applications is to have developers create tools that check application functionality and report an error to your monitoring system in the event of a problem. For example, if a public Web site that accepts orders from your customer is a critical asset, the Web developers should create a tool that simulates a customer submitting an order and verifies that the order is processed successfully. This is the most effective way to determine if a critical asset has failed.*

- **Specify detailed auditing requirements**   During the assessment phase, you probably identified several requirements related to auditing, such as regularly verifying important aspects of computer configuration and reviewing security audit logs. In this phase, you turn those high-level requirements into detailed specifications. Define which security configuration settings must be verified, and how often. If an employee is to review the Security event logs, specify how often and what types of occurrences need to be reported. If you need to create automated auditing tools, you should specify the configuration of those tools.

- **Create an incident response team**   One of the most important tasks is to create an incident response team that is responsible for both responding to incidents and proactively addressing new security developments. For more information about creating an incident response team, refer to the section "Assemble the Incident Response Team" later in this chapter.

- **Develop operational policies and procedures**   Human error is one of the most significant causes of security-related problems, and one of the best ways to reduce the likelihood of human error is to create well-defined operational policies and procedures. You need to document practices for day-to-day tasks such as resetting user passwords, as well as processes for responding to infrequent occurrences such as security compromises.

For more information about developing operational policies and procedures, refer to the section "Developing Operational Policies and Procedures" later in this chapter.

Assemble the Incident Response Team

Regardless of the assets, threats, and countermeasures you identified during the assessment phase, your organization needs an incident response team to deal with threats that you discover, whether before or after a successful compromise. Small organizations need an incident response team, too, even if it's just you and your manager.

Besides responding to incidents, the team should be involved in the proactive efforts to ensure system security, including the following tasks:

- Developing incident handling guidelines

- Preparing paths and procedures of escalation to law enforcement for computer crimes

- Identifying software tools for responding to incidents and events

- Researching and developing other computer security tools

- Conducting training and awareness activities

- Performing research on viruses

- Conducting system-attack studies

These efforts provide knowledge that the organization can use to address issues before and during incidents. It's important that at least one individual be dedicated to the security role, even in smaller organizations. If a single person is responsible for both supporting and securing systems, there's a very good chance that security will become the lower priority. In many organizations, system administration can consume administrators full time (or even longer). Whereas administrators might be willing to work late to fix a failed server, they're not likely to work late to carry out a security audit. Most organizations without dedicated security staff don't successfully maintain a level of security that meets their requirements.

Developing Operational Policies and Procedures

You can't rely on individual employees to make security decisions for themselves because they don't have the training you do. The average employee can't be expected to choose an encryption algorithm, determine which e-mail attachments might have a virus, or identify applications that might have security vulnerabilities. You can use technology to prevent employees from having to make some of these decisions, but not all security problems can be resolved with technology. Use operational policies and procedures to define what employees can and should do to protect your organization's security.

All organizations should have, at a minimum, the following security policies:

- **Acceptable-use policy**   Defines what users can and cannot do with the computers that are assigned to them. It is critical to have employees acknowledge an acceptable-use policy because it enables you to punish employees who use their computers for unethical or illegal purposes. Otherwise, employees could claim they were not aware that they could not use the computer for those purposes.

- **Business continuance and disaster recovery plans and tests**   Business continuance and disaster recovery (BC/DR) plans provide steps for recovering critical services after catastrophic events. If you have never been through a catastrophic event, it is impossible to anticipate what will happen during a disaster. Therefore, you should consult with an experienced BC/DR planner.

■ **E-mail policy**   E-mail is one of the most common ways for employees to communicate with those outside their organization. Because e-mail is written and easily duplicated, casual communications should be treated very seriously. For example, an employee might send an e-mail to a friend discussing a project they're working on. Within a few hours, the e-mail might be quoted in a news story discussing the company's confidential plans. An e-mail policy can ensure that employees understand what they can and can't write in e-mails and reduce the risk of your organization's confidential information falling into the wrong hands. In addition, an e-mail policy can reduce the organization's liability for offensive e-mail communications sent by an employee.

■ **Password policy**   Password policy defines your organization's requirements for password complexity and how often passwords need to be changed. Although you can enforce these requirements by using Group Policy settings, a written policy can be extended beyond just the Active Directory. Most organizations have multiple password databases for different applications and platforms, and they should all use a single password-protection policy.

■ **Physical computer security policies that define physical access controls**   This type of security policy might require that employees lock their docking stations when away from their computers and that all data centers have locking doors that require an employee ID badge to open.

■ **Remote-access policy**   Remote-access policy defines the requirements for remotely connecting to the network. In particular, define the protocols that employees can use, and the security requirements placed on the remote computer. Without a remote-access policy, employees could take remote access into their own hands by circumventing your network controls. This has the potential to add vulnerabilities that you are not aware of to your network.

> **NOTE   The Importance of Policy**   It is obvious that having a remote-access policy doesn't prevent employees from setting up their own dial-in server or VPN tunnel. However, it does prevent them from doing it innocently. If an employee sets up remote access after acknowledging your remote-access policy, it will be much easier for your human resources team to discipline him or her than if you hadn't created a remote-access policy.

- **Router security policy**   Router security policy defines standards for router configurations. In general, this documents router-based packet filtering rules. In addition, you should require that routers block traffic not originating from a valid Internet Protocol (IP) address on a particular subnet to reduce the likelihood of IP spoofing.

- **Server security policy**   Server security policy defines security configuration requirements for servers. These security policies should be applicable to all of your servers, including computers running both Windows and non-Windows systems.

- **Wireless communication policy**   Wireless communication policy specifies wireless security requirements. Even if you do not currently allow wireless networks, it's important to create a wireless communication policy. Otherwise, employees could set up their own wireless networks without your permission, exposing your network to vulnerabilities that you are not aware of.

> **MORE INFO**   For more information about security policies and procedures, visit the SANS (SysAdmin, Audit, Network, Security) Institute's Security Policy Project page at *http://www.sans.org/resources/policies/*.

Step 2: Test Countermeasures

Testing occurs after you've developed your remediation strategies, documented configuration changes, created Group Policy objects, and purchased any countermeasures to determine their effectiveness and compatibility. The testing process enables the team to determine how these changes affect the production environment and verify that the countermeasure improves security. You also use the testing phase to identify any deployment challenges and determine if the countermeasure impacts end users. If end users need training to work with a new countermeasure, you will discover it in this step.

Most large organizations have their own procedures for testing changes. In general, follow these four steps:

1. Test the deployment method for the countermeasures by deploying them in a test environment. Pay particular attention to security measures that have an impact on critical production systems. A problem during production deployment could take the critical system offline for hours longer than you expect.

2. Verify that the countermeasure does not prevent any important applications from running. Countermeasures often restrict user access or block unexpected network communications, either of which can cause applications to fail.

3. Assess end-user impact, if any. If you are adding countermeasures that affect users, such as replacing user name and password credentials with smart cards, find volunteers to test the new security measures. Determine what level of training they need and document common problems so that you can distribute help files with the production deployment.

4. Verify that the countermeasure provides the security benefit you anticipated. If possible, all attack scenarios should be physically tested and documented to determine the best possible security policies and controls to be implemented.

Testing should not be performed on a live production system because the outcome could be disastrous. After all, if your test successfully compromises a system, you might bring it offline. Yet, not everyone has the budget to build a lab that accurately simulates the production network. To find the necessary funds for testing, it is important that management is aware of the risks and consequences of an attack, as well as the security measures that might need to be taken to protect the system, including testing procedures. If it's not possible to test in a lab environment, make sure that management understands they are making a choice that increases the chance of an exploit.

Certain attacks, such as natural disasters, cannot be initiated at will, but they can be simulated. For example, you could simulate a fire in a datacenter by taking all the servers temporarily offline (preferably after hours). This disaster scenario can be useful for testing the responsiveness of administrators and security personnel, and for ascertaining how long it will take to get the organization running again.

> **NOTE Security Lingo** Simulating disasters is commonly known as a "fire drill."

If your test is an accurate simulation, you can probably identify several problems. Don't be discouraged when some people don't know what to do during a simulated disaster. That's the purpose of testing: to identify weaknesses. Adjusting security policies and controls based on the test results is an iterative process. The process is never finished and should be evaluated and revised periodically so that improvements can be implemented.

Step 3: Implement Countermeasures

Finally, follow your organization's change management procedures to deploy your countermeasures. In large environments, use a staged deployment. Deploy client-based countermeasures to a single technology-oriented division, such as the internal IT group. Use this production experience to refine the deployment process before deploying the countermeasures to the rest of the organization. With server-based countermeasures, deploy them to low-priority servers first.

When deploying security measures in a production environment, have rollback procedures prepared. If you discover a problem with a countermeasure, you can use the rollback procedure to return the network to its previous state. This reduces the impact on production systems. Then you can resolve the problems in a testing environment and attempt the deployment again.

PHASE 3: OPERATIONS

At some point, your planning will pay off and you complete the implementation of your security plan. Although the hardest part is over, there's a great deal of ongoing work to do to maintain the level of security reached during the deployment and implementation phase. The four steps in this phase are as follows:

1. Maintain security

2. Respond to incidents

3. Assess new risks

4. Deploy new countermeasures

Step 1: Maintain Security

Over time, security configurations degrade without auditing and maintenance, primarily because modifying security configuration is a common troubleshooting task. For example, if a user is having trouble running an application, the help desk technician might make the user a member of the local Administrators group. If this solves the problem, they might choose to leave the user in the Administrators group. Whereas this does solve the user's problem, it reduces security by granting the user excessive privileges. In large environments with dozens or hundreds of administrators capable of changing security configuration, these changes significantly degrade network security over a period of months.

The Security Configuration and Analysis Tool, the Resultant Set of Policy, the Group Policy Management Console, and GPResult tools, described in the following list, are extremely useful for maintaining security. The MBSA tool, described in Chapter 3, is also useful for security configuration auditing.

- **Security Configuration and Analysis Tool**   The Security Configuration and Analysis snap-in gives you an immediate, detailed list of security settings on a computer that do not meet the security requirements you have defined in a security template. Recommendations are presented alongside current system settings, and icons or remarks are used to highlight any areas where the current settings do not match the proposed level of security. Security Configuration and Analysis uses a database to perform analysis and configuration functions. Using a database gives you the ability to compare the current security settings against custom databases that are created by importing one or more security templates.

- **Resultant Set of Policy**   The Security Configuration and Analysis tool is useful for determining differences between a computer's configuration and an existing security template; the Resultant Set of Policy tool is easier to use to manually audit specific security settings. Manually auditing configuration settings is important to ensure that they are consistent with the settings specified in your Security Action Plan. It is difficult to determine effective security settings in an Active Directory environment, however, because settings can be specified in many different locations. The Resultant Set of Policy tool enables you to determine a computer or user's effective settings, automatically taking into account the priorities of multiple Group Policy objects.

- **Group Policy Management Console (GPMC)**   The GPMC is a free download from Microsoft.com that simplifies editing, modeling, and analyzing group police in an Active Directory domain. With the Group Policy Results node, you can perform analysis similar to that provided by the Resultant Set of Policy tool, but with additional information including a list of errors that have occurred while applying policy settings. With the Group Policy Modeling node, you can simulate the effect of settings before applying a Group Policy object.

- **GPResult**   GPResult is a command-line tool that displays detailed information about user and computer policies. Although many administrators shy away from command-line tools, GPResult is the best way to quickly determine what Group Policy objects were applied, in which order they were applied, and what security group memberships might have influenced which Group Policy objects the computer or user has permissions to access. Administrators or developers familiar with scripting tools can even use the text output from GPResult to detect unexpected changes to effective security settings. Unlike other tools, GPResult displays policies that were filtered, and why they were filtered.

Step 2: Respond to Incidents

When you detect a security compromise, the incident response team should execute the contingency plan to limit, assess, and repair the damage. After the attack has been controlled, the incident response team should perform a postmortem review to learn from the incident. The review should include details on loss in productivity, lost data or hardware, and the time taken to recover from the attack.

If policies exist for defending against an attack that has taken place, they should be reviewed and checked for effectiveness. If your organization didn't react efficiently to the attack, think about what could have been done better and modify the policies. If no policies exist, new ones must be drawn up to minimize or prevent future attacks.

Step 3: Assess New Risks

When new threats, vulnerabilities, and corresponding countermeasures are identified, you don't need to repeat the entire security risk analysis process. Most organizations rely on the system administration, security administration, and network administration teams to identify new assets, threats, and vulnerabilities. As these teams learn about new vulnerabilities and countermeasures, the knowledge must be captured and redeployed to continually optimize the effectiveness of the security protecting company assets. In addition, business communities should be educated via training or security awareness bulletins.

To identify new assets, especially those that might attract new threats or have new vulnerabilities, work with teams that are involved in the purchase and configuration of new hardware. Depending on how a business is organized, the provisioning, purchasing, inventory, accounting, or IT teams might need to be instructed to inform a security administration team when new equipment is to be configured.

Step 4: Deploy New Countermeasures

After you identify a new significant threat and vulnerability, you must also identify a countermeasure. You can usually adjust existing security mechanisms without significant impact. Changes might be as simple as adjusting firewall rules, which does not require purchasing new equipment and can be changed to its previous state easily if problems arise. More complex countermeasures might require changes to the network architecture or purchasing new equipment. Think through how these changes should be handled and develop a process for gaining approval from any parts of your organization that might be affected by the change.

For example, if a new threat requires that you begin filtering remote procedure call (RPC) traffic at all perimeter firewalls in your organization, notify all members of your technical staff prior to making the change. Some users might require RPC traffic. These requirements could be accommodated by filtering all RPC traffic except traffic destined for specific IP addresses.

It's important to notify people before making the change because unexpected changes can cause downtime. Changes during the operations phase can still cause unexpected problems, but the technical team will be able to more quickly identify the source of the problem if it has been notified in advance that the change was going to be made.

ITNW

management process by finding an executive

our security risk management team, and work-

ager to schedule time to see the project through

risk management process is the assessment

se, you work through five steps:

ry of your security policies.

f the assets in your organization.

t types of threats that pose a risk to your assets.

e of your assets and the danger posed by the

he different security risks you need to address.

Action Plan that identifies whether to mitigate,

research, or accept each risk that you identified.

ntation phase. During this phase, you identify

asures to use to mitigate your security risks;

countermeasures.

- Phase 3 is the operations phase. This phase is the day-to-day task of maintaining security in your organization.

REVIEW QUESTIONS

1. You are in the process of putting together a team to perform threat modeling of a Web server that runs a number of critical Web-based applications. Who should you *not* invite to participate in the threat modeling?

    a. The Web developer who wrote the code and created the database connection strings

    b. Management

    c. Anyone with appropriate technical expertise who can think creatively

    d. Informed outsiders

    e. Users

2. Which of the following are goals of the security risk management process? (Choose all that apply.)

   a. Ensure that every network is protected by a firewall.

   b. Deploy patches to computers immediately after being released by a vendor.

   c. Allocate the security budget as efficiently as possible.

   d. Eliminate legacy systems that cannot meet security requirements.

   e. Identify currently unknown risks.

   f. Migrate to a homogeneous computing platform.

3. Which of the following are advantages of quantitative analysis over qualitative analysis? (Choose all that apply.)

   a. Greater accuracy

   b. Less time required

   c. Fewer people required

   d. Known monetary value of countermeasures

   e. Greater flexibility for accommodating legacy systems

   f. Compatible with computers running both UNIX-based and Windows-based systems

4. What is the best way to accommodate legacy systems in a Security Action Plan?

   a. Migrate all systems to newer operating systems.

   b. Use virtual machines to run legacy systems on a modern operating system.

   c. Provide special clauses in security policies for legacy systems.

   d. Place legacy systems on a separate network that is not accessible from any other network.

5. What is the formula to determine the single loss expectancy (SLE) of a compromise?

   a. $SLE = ALE_1 - ALE_2 - C$

   b. $SLE = AV \times EF$

   c. $SLE = ARO - C$

   d. $SLE = EF \times ARO$

6. What is the formula to determine the annual loss expectancy (ALE) of a risk?

   a. ALE = SLE – AV

   b. ALE = AV × EF

   c. ALE = SLE – C

   d. ALE = SLE x ARO

7. What is the formula to determine the quantitative value (V) of a countermeasure?

   a. $V = ALE_1 - ALE_2 - C$

   b. $V = AV \times EF$

   c. $V = SLE - C$

   d. $V = SLE \text{ x } ARO$

8. Which of the following are valid responses to a risk in a Security Action Plan? (Choose all that apply.)

   a. Mitigate

   b. Ignore

   c. Accept

   d. Magnify

   e. Eliminate

   f. Contain

   g. Divide

9. Which of the following are valid responses to limit the risk of an earthquake destroying data? (Choose all that apply.)

   a. Mitigate

   b. React to

   c. Transfer

   d. Research

   e. Accept

10. Which of the following tools are useful for auditing the security configurations of Active Directory domain member computers? (Choose all that apply.)

   a. Performance logs and alerts

   b. Security templates

   c. GPResult

   d. Resultant Set of Policy

   e. Disk management

   f. Security Configuration and Analysis

CASE SCENARIOS

Case Scenario 2-1: Evaluating Countermeasures Quantitatively

You are a security consultant who has been hired by Lucerne Publishing to evaluate several different countermeasures to reduce the risk associated with network attacks. Lucerne is specifically concerned that an attacker could gain elevated privileges to its 250 Windows XP client computers by exploiting a currently undiscovered vulnerability in Windows or in an application. All computers are currently running Windows XP Professional with Service Pack 1. Internet Connection Firewall (ICF) is not enabled.

Lucerne has completed phase 1 of the security risk management process using quantitative analysis. The ALE of a network attack against one of its client computers is $100 per computer. The company has evaluated a perimeter firewall that reduces the risk of a compromise by 65 percent. The number would be higher, but many of Lucerne's users travel with their laptops and connect to unprotected networks at hotels, airports, and other wireless hot spots. The firewall costs $5,000 to purchase and $2,000 per year to maintain. They expect to use the firewall for three years.

Lucerne also has considered host-based firewalls. They think some users might disable the firewall, so it doesn't provide absolute protection. They think host-based firewalls on every computer would reduce the risk of a compromise by 70 percent. They estimate that using ICF would cost $2,500 in administrative time initially to deploy, and then $10,000 per year for the next three years to maintain and troubleshoot. As an alternative, they could deploy Windows Firewall with Service Pack 2, which would cost them $12,500 to deploy. However, Service Pack 2 mitigates other risks as well, so they plan to attribute only $2,500 of the cost to Windows Firewall. Because it's easier for users to configure exceptions and they can use Group Policy settings to configure Windows Firewall, the maintenance and troubleshooting costs would be only $1,000 per year.

Consider this information and answer the following questions.

1. What is the value of the perimeter firewall? Show your work as you calculate the value.

2. What is the value of ICF? Show your work as you calculate the value.

3. What is the value of Windows Firewall? Show your work as you calculate the value.

4. Which of the three firewall solutions provides the greatest value?

5. Calculate the value of using both a perimeter firewall and Windows Firewall simultaneously. Based on the quantitative risk analysis, should Lucerne Publishing implement both a perimeter firewall and a host-based firewall? Show your work as you calculate the value.

Case Scenario 2-2: Creating a Security Action Plan

You are a security designer for A. Datum Corporation. For the past week, you and the security risk management team have been meeting with different managers to create a list of your organization's assets and to qualitatively assess the vulnerability of each. Now you are ready to move on to step 3 of the assessment phase of the security risk management process and list possible threats.

Today, you are meeting with the security risk management team to identify threats to the assets in the downtown Boston region, your smallest remote sales office. Figure 2-3 shows the region's network diagram, and Table 2-7 shows just the region's assets.

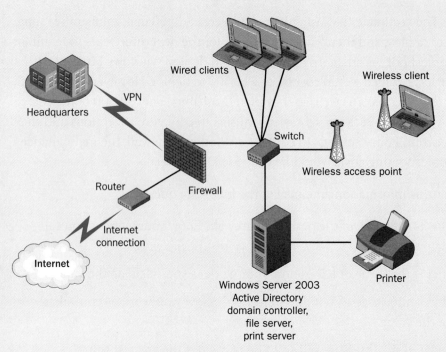

Figure 2-3 You have created a network diagram showing the relationships between your Boston region network assets.

Table 2-7 **Boston Asset Inventory**

Asset	Description	Dependencies	Value
Server	All regional offices have a Windows Server 2003 Active Directory domain controller, which participates in A. Datum's single domain. The most significant factor in this asset's value is that it maintains a copy of the domain user database. This server also acts as a central file and print server.	Router, Switch, VPN	2 (Very serious)
Printer	Used for daily printing tasks.	Server, switch	4 (Not serious)
Router and Internet connection	Connects the local area network to the Internet. Used by sales staff to send and receive e-mails, and used by the VPN to connect to headquarters.		3 (Moderately serious)

Table 2-7 **Boston Asset Inventory**

Asset	Description	Dependencies	Value
Firewall	Acts as a VPN endpoint and filters traffic from the Internet.	Router	3 (Moderately serious)
Switch	A simple, inexpensive, unmanaged switch that connects computers on the local network.		4 (Not serious)
Wireless access point	Provides unencrypted 802.11g access to the local area network. A compromise could reveal network traffic.	Switch	2 (Very serious)
VPN	Connects the remote office network to the corporate headquarters. Compromise could grant access to internal corporate network.	Firewall	1 (Catastrophic)
Wired and wireless clients	Laptop computers that connect to the network via a docking station and wired Ethernet. Contain copies of confidential documents that the sales staff uses while traveling.	Switch, wireless access point, router, firewall, server, printer	2 (Moderately serious)

1. Today you must assess threats, vulnerabilities, and risks, and then create a Security Action Plan. For each asset listed in Table 2-7, perform step 3 (Assess Threats) of the assessment phase; list the possible threats to each asset and the associated vulnerability level.

2. For each threat and vulnerability you identified, qualitatively assess the risk by grouping it into one of the three categories, low risk, medium risk, or high risk.

3. Create a Security Action Plan by assigning a response and identifying a countermeasure that could reduce each risk cost effectively.

CHAPTER 3
REDUCING THE RISK OF SOFTWARE VULNERABILITIES

Upon completion of this chapter, you will be able to:

- Assess the risks of software vulnerabilities.

- Assemble a patching team and identify your software update requirements.

- List the different technologies available for distributing Microsoft security updates on your network.

- Implement a process for discovering, evaluating, deploying, and auditing Microsoft security updates.

- Design a Software Update Services (SUS) infrastructure.

- Deploy new computers with security updates.

- Audit the delivery of security updates by using the Microsoft Baseline Security Analyzer (MBSA).

Viruses and worms such as Klez, Nimda, and SQL Slammer exploit known patchable security vulnerabilities in software to attack computers, and then use those compromised computing resources to launch new attacks. After a computer is infected, the virus or worm often opens new security vulnerabilities that enable an attacker to explore your internal network, shut down network resources, and gather confidential files. Considering how widespread worms and viruses are, it is clear that they present a significant security risk to every organization.

The best way to control the risk of viruses and worms, as well as other attackers who would exploit updated software vulnerabilities, is patch management. Patch management is a process that gives you control over the deployment and maintenance of software updates on your network. An effective patch management process could have prevented a majority of the security compromises that have occurred on Microsoft Windows networks in the past few years. Although patch management can seem time-consuming and costly, it is far more efficient to proactively update computers than it is to repair them after a known vulnerability is exploited.

PROTECTING AGAINST SOFTWARE VULNERABILITIES

As you learned in Chapter 2, "Analyzing Risk," threats and vulnerabilities appear in many different forms, and present different levels of risk to different organizations. There is one type of vulnerability that is common to all organizations that have a network: software vulnerabilities.

Only malicious threat agents present a risk of compromising software vulnerabilities. Sophisticated attackers often begin an attack by identifying any widely known software vulnerabilities on the target network. In essence, a sophisticated attacker will audit your network for vulnerabilities using exactly the tools security administrators use to ensure that their network is up to date. If a sophisticated attacker identifies a widely known vulnerability and a tool exists to exploit it, the attacker is one step closer to reaching the targeted asset.

If the threat agent does not identify any widely known vulnerabilities, the attacker is forced to resort to more risky, time-consuming attack methods. The threat agent might resort to social engineering, password guessing, or other easily detectable attack methods. As an alternative, the threat agent might attempt to identify a software vulnerability that is not widely known, and for which an update does not yet exist, and then create an exploit for that vulnerability. Identifying new software vulnerabilities requires very strong programming and reverse-engineering skills, however, and only the most sophisticated of attackers will be capable of that.

Although protecting against software vulnerabilities alone does not eliminate the risk of being compromised, it does reduce the risk by making it more difficult for an attacker. In many cases, attackers will target a different asset that is not as well protected. For this reason, it is very important to use countermeasures to protect yourself from software vulnerabilities.

The most important software vulnerability countermeasure is applying security updates as quickly as possible after they are released. Software vendors release security updates to software after the software vendor, or an outside security organziation, discovers and announces a vulnerability. The typical security update is easy to install and changes no aspect of the software except to remove the newly discovered vulnerability. Most of this chapter discusses implementing a security update process to protect against well-known software vulnerabilities.

> **NOTE   Worthwhile Countermeasures**   Security updates are the most important software vulnerability countermeasure. However, as you might recall from Chapter 2, not all countermeasures are cost effective. Sometimes, the risk of an update causing an unexpected incompatibility is greater than the risk posed by the vulnerability the update is intended to fix. You must carefully consider both the benefits and the risks of every patch your software vendors release.

Although security updates should be your primary defense for security vulnerabilities, remember that the principle of defense-in-depth states that high-risk vulnerabilities deserve multiple layers of protection. Because software vulnerabilities are so commonly exploited, it is worthwhile for most organizations to use multiple layers of protection for software vulnerabilities. Besides security updates, there are several useful countermeasures:

- **Network firewalls**   For a threat to attack a software vulnerability, the threat agent must be able to communicate with it. Although some software vulnerabilities require the threat agent to have physical access to a computer, the vast majority of software vulnerability compromises occur across a network. Network firewalls, by default, block unrequested packets from reaching a private network. This eliminates the possibility that a software vulnerability in a network service can be exploited by a threat on an external network. However, network firewalls do not protect against threats on the internal network, and cannot protect against viruses or Trojan horses delivered by e-mail, a Web browser, or another mechanism that is allowed through the firewall.

- **Host-based firewalls**   Similar to network firewalls, host-based firewalls block unrequested incoming communications. This protects a single computer from software vulnerabilities in unnecessary network services. However, it cannot protect software vulnerabilities in services that are being actively used. For example, a host-based firewall running on a Web server cannot protect against a vulnerability in the Web server software because the firewall must allow incoming connections to the Web server—even if they are from a threat. As with network firewalls, host-based firewalls cannot protect against e-mail or browser-based attacks.

> **MORE INFO   More about Firewalls**   For more information about firewalls, refer to Chapter 10, "Protecting Intranet Communications."

■ **Antivirus software**   Antivirus software technically doesn't protect a software vulnerability from compromise, but it does reduce the risk of a compromised computer spreading a worm or virus that exploits a vulnerability. Antivirus software detects malicious software and prevents it from being installed, including most common software vulnerability exploits: worms, viruses, Trojan horses, and remote-control software that might be installed by a sophisticated threat agent. Therefore, antivirus software is a key component of software vulnerability risk management, but it cannot be the only countermeasure.

■ **The principle of least privilege**   Many software vulnerabilities allow a threat to gain elevated privileges. Specifically, the threat gains the same privileges that the compromised process has. Therefore, if a service running as a system account is compromised, the threat might be able to perform any action that the system account can perform. In a similar way, if a service running as a standard user account is compromised, the threat will be limited by standard user account permissions, and the damage caused by the compromise will be limited. Therefore, to use the principle of least privilege to reduce the risk of software vulnerabilities, run services using limited user accounts rather than System accounts, and have users log on with standard user accounts rather than administrator accounts.

> **NOTE**   **Refresher: Principle of Least Privilege**   The principle of least privilege states that users and services should have the minimum level of permissions required to do their jobs.

■ **Reducing the attack surface**   Many historical software vulnerabilities were in optional operating system components, such as a Web server, file server, or database server. Microsoft Windows XP and Microsoft Windows Server 2003 follow the secure-by-default development principle, and have a limited attack surface without additional configuration. However, you can dramatically improve the overall security of previous versions of Windows by disabling unnecessary services. In addition, audit all computers regularly to verify that unnecessary services have not been installed. Software vulnerabilities in a disabled service cannot be exploited.

■ **Hardening security configurations**   Any steps you take to harden the security configuration of software will reduce the risk of software vulnerabilities. Microsoft has published guides for hardening all Microsoft operating systems and many other services and applications.

Following these guidelines can increase application compatibility problems and user frustration, but they have historically protected users from many software vulnerability exploits.

> **MORE INFO** **Hardening Operating Systems** Hardening is the process of adjusting configuration settings to reduce the risk of vulnerabilities in an operating system's default configuration. For more information about hardening Microsoft software, read Chapter 7, "Hardening Servers," and Chapter 8, "Hardening Client Computers," and visit *http://www.microsoft.com/technet/security*.

- **Configuration diversity** Often, you can avoid software vulnerability exploits simply by using a non-default configuration. For example, if you had changed the Internet Information Server (IIS) port number from 80 to 81, you would not have been vulnerable to every single widespread IIS exploit. However, because configuration diversity is a form of security-by-obscurity, this would not eliminate the vulnerability. Whereas you would be protected from most worms, you would still be vulnerable to any attacker who discovered you were using port 81 and had the knowledge to exploit a nonstandard port number. Whenever possible, use nonstandard port numbers, account names, and other identifiers to reduce the risk of being compromised because of a software vulnerability. Never rely only on security-by-obscurity, but use it to reduce risk as part of a defense-in-depth strategy.

- **Software diversity** When using software to protect a network, such as with antivirus software or firewalls, use multiple layers of protection from different vendors. For example, you could reduce the risk of a software vulnerability in your perimeter firewall by using two firewalls: one based on Windows, such as Microsoft Internet Security and Acceleration (ISA) Server, and one hardware firewall. If an attacker discovers a vulnerability in Windows that can be used to bypass your firewall, the attacker would still need to circumvent the hardware firewall. Requiring an attacker to bypass multiple layers of security exponentially reduces your risk.

- **Uncommon software** Most software vulnerability exploits target common software because the number of potential targets is much higher. Therefore, you can reduce the risk of being exploited by using less-common software. For example, the risk of software vulnerabilities in Microsoft Outlook Express is very high because the software is widely distributed. Indeed, Outlook Express has had many different, well-known vulnerabilities over its history. Less-popular e-mail clients have had fewer well-known vulnerabilities because fewer potential attackers have sought out software vulnerabilities. Less-popular software probably has more unknown vulnerabilities, but unless those vulnerabilities are discovered, they cannot be compromised. As mentioned previously, although security-by-obscurity should never be relied on solely, it can be used to reduce risk as part of a defense-in-depth strategy.

Using these security techniques will reduce the risk of well-known software vulnerabilities for which an update has been released that you have not been able to install. More important, these security techniques will reduce the risk posed by newly discovered software vulnerabilities for which an update does not exist. Software vendors create security updates when they discover or are told about a newly discovered vulnerability. However, if a sophisticated, malicious threat agent discovers a vulnerability, the threat agent is not likely to tell anyone else about the vulnerability. Instead, that person will use the vulnerability to compromise their own targets. Remember, sophisticated attackers targeting your critical assets are likely to cause much more damage than widespread worms or viruses.

THE PROCESS OF UPDATING NETWORK SOFTWARE

You must plan to update every network component that uses software. This naturally includes client and server operating systems and applications, but it also includes routers, firewalls, wireless access points, and switches. To keep your systems up to date, follow this process:

1. Assemble a patching team.

2. Inventory all software in your organization.

3. Contact each software vendor and determine its process of notifying customers of software updates. Some vendors will directly notify you of updates via e-mail, while others require you to check a Web site regularly.

4. Assign individuals to identify software updates on a regular basis. For example, someone on your team should be responsible for checking every software vendor's Web site for new updates on at least a weekly basis.

5. Create a patching process for evaluating, retrieving, testing, installing, auditing, and removing updates. Although most of the process will be the same for all vendors, you might have to customize parts of the process to accommodate different uptime and testing requirements for

servers, clients, and network equipment. As an example, this chapter will thoroughly document the patching process to use for Microsoft operating system updates.

The sections that follow discuss the first two steps of this process in more detail.

The Patching Team

Identifying individuals with the right mix of technical and project management skills for deploying updates is one of the first decisions that you, and your management, will make. Even before staffing can begin, however, you need to identify the team roles, or areas of expertise, required for patch management. Microsoft suggests using the Microsoft Solutions Framework (MSF) team model, which is based on six interdependent, multidisciplinary roles: product management, program management, development, testing, user experience, and release management. This model applies equally well to both Microsoft and non-Microsoft software.

- **Product management**   Product management is responsible for identifying the organization's business needs and the needs of the end users, and for making sure those needs are supported by the patching process.

- **Program management**   The program management team's goal is to deliver updates within project constraints. Program management is responsible for managing the patching schedule and budget, and for reporting status, managing project-related risk factors (such as staff illnesses), and managing the design of the patching process.

- **Development**   The development team builds the patching infrastructure according to specification. The team's responsibilities include specifying the features of the patching infrastructure, estimating the time and effort required to deploy the patching infrastructure, and preparing the infrastructure for deployment.

- **Testing**   The testing team ensures that updates are released into the production environment only after all quality issues have been identified and resolved. The team's responsibilities include developing the testing strategy, designing and building the patching lab, developing the test plan, and conducting tests.

- **User experience**   The user experience team ensures that the patching process meets the users' needs. The team gathers, analyzes, and prioritizes user requirements and complaints.

- **Release management**   The release management team is responsible for deploying the updates. In large environments, the release management team also designs and manages a pilot deployment of an update to ensure that the update is sufficiently stable for deployment into the production environment.

The MSF team roles are flexible; they can be adapted to your organization's own processes and management philosophy. In a small organization or a limited deployment, one individual might play multiple roles. In larger organizations, a team might be required to perform all the tasks assigned to each role.

> **MORE INFO   Microsoft Solutions Framework**   For more information about the MSF team model, see the MSF Team Model white paper at http://www.microsoft.com/technet/itsolutions/tandp/innsol/msfrl/MSFTM31.asp.

Inventorying Software

After you create a patching team, you must inventory the software on your network. Specifically, you need to know what operating systems and applications you have installed to identify updates that need to be deployed. You also need to understand the security requirements for each computer system, including which computers store highly confidential information, which are connected to the public Internet, and which will connect to exterior networks.

For each computer in your environment, gather the following information:

- **Operating system**   Document the operating system version and patch level. Remember, most routers, firewalls, and switches have operating systems. Also document which optional components, such as IIS, are installed.

- **Applications**   Document every application installed on the computer, including versions and updates.

- **Network connectivity**   Document which networks the computer connects to, including whether the computer is connected to the public Internet, whether it connects to other networks across a virtual private network (VPN) or dial-up connection, and whether it is a mobile computer that might connect to networks at other locations.

- **Existing countermeasures**   Firewalls and virus checkers might protect a computer against a patched vulnerability, making the update less critical. For firewalls, document which ports are open. For antivirus software, document the update process and frequency of updates.

- **Site**   If your organization has multiple sites, you can choose to deploy updates to computers from a server located at each site to optimize bandwidth usage. Knowing which site a computer or piece of network equipment is located in allows you to efficiently deploy the updates.

- **Bandwidth**   Computers connected across low-bandwidth links have special requirements. You can choose to transfer large updates during nonbusiness hours. For dial-up users, it might be more efficient to bypass the network link and transfer updates on removable media such as CD-ROMs.

- **Administrator responsibility**   You must understand who is responsible for deploying updates to a particular device, and who will fix a problem if the device fails during the patching process. If others are responsible for individual applications or services, make note of that as well.

- **Uptime requirements**   Understand any service-level agreements or service-level guarantees that apply to a particular device, and whether scheduled downtime counts against the total uptime. This will enable you to prioritize devices when troubleshooting and testing updates.

- **Scheduling dependencies**   Applying updates requires planning systems to be offline. This can be a disruption for users, even if the device only requires a quick reboot. Understand who depends on a particular device so that you can clear downtime with them ahead of time.

Some of this information, including operating system and installed applications, can be gathered in an automated fashion. Most network management tools have this capability, including Microsoft Systems Management Server (SMS). You can also inventory Microsoft software on a computer by using Microsoft Software Inventory Analyzer (MSIA), a free download.

> **MORE INFO**   *Software Inventory Tools*   For more information about using SMS for patch management, visit *http://www.microsoft.com/ technet/itsolutions/cits/mo/swdist/pmsms/2003/pusmscg3.mspx*. For information about MSIA, visit *http://www.microsoft.com/ resources/sam/msia.mspx*. To find non-Microsoft software inventory tools, visit *http://www.microsoft.com/resources/sam/aspx/findtool.aspx*.

UNDERSTANDING MICROSOFT PATCHING

Microsoft continually works to reduce the risk of software vulnerabilities in Microsoft software. There are, however, many different types of software vulnerabilities. Some have known exploits that are propagating quickly, and it is critical that these vulnerabilities be quickly patched. Others are less critical, and the risk of them being exploited isn't high enough to justify the cost of rapidly deploying an update. To address the wide variety of vulnerabilities, Microsoft provides several different types of updates throughout the life cycle of a supported product.

This section describes the different types of updates released by Microsoft. It will also describe the Microsoft product life cycle, which affects patch management because Microsoft stops releasing security updates for products at the end of the life cycle.

What Is a Security Update?

A security update is an update that the Microsoft Security Response Center (MSRC) releases to resolve a security vulnerability. Microsoft security updates are available for customers to download and are accompanied by two documents: a security bulletin and a Microsoft Knowledge Base article.

A Microsoft security bulletin notifies administrators of critical security issues and vulnerabilities. Usually, but not always, the security bulletin is associated with a security update that can be used to patch the vulnerability. Security bulletins generally provide detailed information about whom the bulletin concerns, the impact of the vulnerability, the severity of the vulnerability, and a recommended course of action for affected customers.

Security bulletins usually include the following pieces of information.

- **Title**   The title of the security bulletin, in the format MSyy-###, where yy is the last two digits of the year and ### is the bulletin number for that year

- **Summary**   Information about who should read the bulletin, the impact of the vulnerability and the software affected, the security rating, and the MSRC's recommendation for how to respond to the bulletin

- **Technical description**   A detailed description of the vulnerability and the circumstances under which the vulnerability could be exploited

- **Mitigating factors** Technical factors that reduce the likelihood of a vulnerable system being exploited

- **Severity rating** A rating of None, Low, Moderate, Important, and Critical for each type of software that the vulnerability might affect

- **Vulnerability identifier** Links to organizations external to Microsoft that classify the security vulnerability

- **Tested versions** A list of software that Microsoft has tested for the vulnerability

- **Frequently asked questions** Answers to questions that Microsoft anticipates about the specific security bulletin

- **Update availability** Locations from which to download the update

- **Additional information** Information about installation platforms, whether a reboot is needed, whether the update can be uninstalled, and how to verify that the update was successfully installed

The severity level of a bulletin gauges the risk posed by the vulnerability that the update fixes. This severity level can be None, Low, Moderate, Important, or Critical. The MSRC judges the severity of a vulnerability on behalf of the entire Microsoft customer base. The impact a vulnerability has on your organization might be more, or less, serious.

> **NOTE** Security Bulletin Sample The following is an excerpt from an actual security bulletin released for Windows Server 2003 and other Windows operating systems on July 23, 2003. This version has been edited to save space. You can find the original bulletin at http://www.microsoft.com/technet/security/bulletin/ms03-030.mspx.
>
> Unchecked Buffer in DirectX Could Enable System Compromise (819696)
>
> Originally posted: July 23, 2003
>
> Updated: August 20, 2003
>
> Summary:
>
> **Who should read this bulletin:** Customers using Microsoft Windows
>
> **Impact of vulnerability:** Allow an attacker to execute code on a user's system
>
> **Maximum Severity Rating:** Critical
>
> **Recommendation:** Customers should apply the security update immediately
>
> **Affected Software:**
>
> DirectX 5.2 on Windows 98

DirectX 8.1 on Windows XP or Windows Server 2003

An End User version of the bulletin is available at http://www.microsoft.com/security/security_bulletins/ms03-030.asp.

Technical description:

There are two buffer overruns with identical effects in the function used by DirectShow to check parameters in a Musical Instrument Digital Interface (MIDI) file. A security vulnerability results because it could be possible for a malicious user to attempt to exploit these flaws and execute code in the security context of the logged-on user.

An attacker could seek to exploit this vulnerability by creating a specially crafted MIDI file designed to exploit this vulnerability and then host it on a Web site or on a network share, or send it by using an HTML-based e-mail. A successful attack could cause DirectShow, or an application making use of DirectShow, to fail. A successful attack could also cause an attacker's code to run on the user's computer in the security context of the user.

Mitigating factors:

By default, Microsoft Internet Explorer on Windows Server 2003 runs in Enhanced Security Configuration. This default configuration of Internet Explorer blocks the e-mail-based vector of this attack because Microsoft Outlook Express running on Windows Server 2003 by default reads e-mail in plain text. If Internet Explorer Enhanced Security Configuration were disabled, the protections put in place that prevent this vulnerability from being exploited would be removed.

Severity rating:

DirectX 9.0a	Critical
DirectX 9.0a	when installed on Windows
Server 2003	Important

Vulnerability identifier: CAN-2003-0346

Tested versions: Microsoft tested DirectX 9.0a, DirectX 8.1, DirectX 7.0.

DirectX 7.0 on Windows 2000

In addition to security bulletins, Microsoft also creates Knowledge Base articles about security vulnerabilities. However, Knowledge Base articles undergo more review than security bulletins, and they are not released until after the bulletin. Therefore, they tend to contain more information than security bulletins, and are more accurate. Knowledge Base articles generally include more detailed information about the vulnerability and step-by-step instructions for updating affected computers.

What Is a Security Rollup Package?

There have been times when Microsoft has released a significant number of security and critical updates between service packs. It is cumbersome to install a large number of updates separately, so Microsoft releases a security rollup package (SRP) to reduce the labor involved in applying updates. An SRP is a cumulative set of hotfixes, security updates, critical updates, and other updates that are packaged together for easy deployment. An update rollup generally targets a specific area of a product such as security, or a component of a product such as IIS. SRPs are always released with a Knowledge Base article that describes the rollup in detail.

SRPs receive more testing from Microsoft than individual security updates, but less testing than service packs. In addition, because SRPs consist of updates that have been previously released and are being run by many other Microsoft customers, it is more likely that any incompatibilities associated with the SRP have already been discovered. Therefore, the risk associated with deploying SRPs is overall lower than the risk of deploying security updates. However, you still need to test SRPs with critical applications before deploying them.

What Is a Service Pack?

A service pack is a cumulative set of all the hotfixes, security updates, critical updates, and other updates that have been created for a Microsoft product. A service pack also includes fixes for other problems that have been found by Microsoft since the release of the product. Service packs can also contain customer-requested design changes or features. Like security updates, service packs are available for download and are accompanied by Knowledge Base articles.

The chief difference between service packs and other types of updates is that service packs are strategic deliveries, whereas updates are tactical. That is, service packs are carefully planned and managed, and the goal is to deliver a well-tested, comprehensive set of fixes that is suitable for use on any computer. In contrast, security updates are developed on an as-needed basis to combat specific problems that require an immediate response.

> **NOTE   Microsoft Testing Levels**   *Service packs undergo extensive regression testing that Microsoft does not perform for other types of updates.*

Microsoft does not release a service pack until it meets the same quality standards as the product itself. Service packs are constantly tested as they are built, undergo weeks or months of rigorous final testing that includes testing in conjunction with hundreds or thousands of non-Microsoft products, and undergo a beta phase during which customers participate in the testing. If the testing reveals bugs, Microsoft will delay the release of the service pack.

Even though Microsoft tests service packs extensively, they frequently have known application incompatibilities. However, they are less likely to have unknown application incompatibilities. It is critical that you review the service pack release notes to determine how the service pack might affect your applications.

Sometimes, it might be in your best interest to delay deploying the service pack for several months after release. Early adopters who deploy service packs to production computers frequently discover new application incompatibilities. Early adopters must dedicate the time to resolving these incompatibilities. However, if you wait several months, most incompatibilities will be identified, workarounds will be documented, and non-Microsoft software vendors will have released updates to resolve the known incompatibilities. Microsoft security updates can be applied to systems with the current or previous service pack, so you can continue with your typical Microsoft patching process until after you have deployed the new service pack.

Microsoft Product Life Cycles

Every product has a life cycle, and, at the end of the life cycle, Microsoft stops providing updates. This doesn't mean that no new vulnerabilities will be discovered in the product, however. To keep your network protected from the latest vulnerabilities, you will need to upgrade to a more recent operating system.

Microsoft offers a minimum of five years of mainstream support from the date of a product's general availability. When mainstream support ends, businesses have the option to purchase two years of extended support. In addition, online self-help support, such as the Knowledge Base, will still be available.

Security updates will be available through the end of the extended support phase—seven years after the date of the product's general availability—at no additional cost for most products. You do not have to have an extended support contract to receive security updates during the extended support phase. This means that Microsoft will release security updates for Windows Server 2003 until at least 2010, as shown in Figure 3-1. In all likelihood, your organization will have upgraded its Windows Server 2003–based computers to a newer operating system by then. However, you must keep the product life cycle in mind, particularly the period during which security updates will be released, when planning future operating system upgrades.

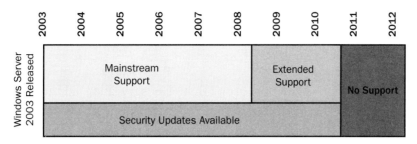

Figure 3-1   The Windows Server 2003 product life cycle

You have to keep reasonably up to date on updates to continue to receive Microsoft support because Microsoft provides support only for the current and immediately preceding service pack. This support policy allows you to receive existing hotfixes, or to request new hotfixes, for the currently shipping service pack, the immediately preceding service pack, or both during the mainstream phase.

Methods for Deploying Updates

To meet the needs of various types of organizations, Microsoft provides several different methods for applying updates. The preferred method for deploying updates is Software Update Services (SUS) and the successor to SUS, Windows Update Services (WUS). Large organizations currently using Group Policy objects (GPOs) to distribute software might prefer to use GPOs for deploying updates as well, because it allows them to deploy the update to many systems simultaneously. GPOs can be used to automatically install updates on computers, or to make them available to users through the Add/Remove Programs tool. Finally, enterprises that use SMS can use that software to deploy updates. You can even avoid installing updates manually on new systems by integrating the update directly into the Windows Server 2003 setup files.

Smaller organizations that cannot allocate computing resources to a patching infrastructure can choose to deploy updates manually by using the express or network installations. Small organizations can take advantage of automated patch deployment without adding any infrastructure servers by using the Automatic Updates client and the Windows Update server.

Table 3-1 lists the advantages and disadvantages of each of the update distribution methods described here and the network size for which the method is effective.

Table 3-1   **Patch Distribution Methods Compared**

Patch Distribution Method	Network Size	Advantages	Disadvantages
Automatic Updates	50 or fewer computers	Does not require that any infrastructure be deployed.	Does not allow administrators to test or approve updates. Wastes Internet bandwidth in large organizations.
SUS/WUS	Any number of computers	Allows administrators to test, approve, and schedule updates. Reduces Internet bandwidth usage. WUS is also capable of updating some Microsoft applications.	Requires an infrastructure server.
Group Policy	Any number of computers	Provides granular control over which clients receive updates. Can be used to distribute other types of software.	Requires Active Directory directory service. Other than service packs, updates must be manually added to a Windows Installer package.
Add/Remove Programs	Any number of computers	Gives end users control over which updates are applied, and when. Can be used to distribute other types of software.	Requires Active Directory, and requires end users to choose to install updates.
SMS with SUS Feature Pack	Any number of computers	Provides highly customizable, centralized control over patch deployment, with the ability to audit and inventory client systems. Can be used to distribute other types of software.	Requires infrastructure servers and additional software licenses.

The sections that follow describe each of these methods in more detail.

Automatic Updates Client   Both Windows Update and Software Update Services use the same client to download and install updates: the Automatic Updates client. The Automatic Updates client can automatically notify users of critical updates and security updates available either at Windows Update or at a specified Software Update Services server.

Available in Windows 2000 Service Pack 3, Windows XP Home Edition, Windows XP Professional, and Windows Server 2003, the Automatic Update client is a proactive "pull" service that allows for automatic detection, notification, download, and installation of important updates. The Automatic Updates client will even reboot a computer at a scheduled time to ensure that updates take effect as soon as possible.

The Automatic Updates client provides for a great deal of control over its behavior. You can configure individual computers by using the System Control Panel (Automatic Updates) utility. Networks that use Active Directory can specify the configuration of each Automatic Update client by using Group Policy settings to install the service. In non–Active Directory environments, you can configure computers by changing a set of registry values.

Systems administrators can configure Automatic Updates to automatically download updates and schedule their installation for a specified time. If the computer is turned off at that time, the updates can be installed as soon as the computer is turned on. Downloading updates won't affect a user's network performance either, because the client downloads the updates by using the Background Intelligent Transfer Service (BITS), a bandwidth-throttling technology that uses only idle bandwidth.

If complete automation is not acceptable, you can also give users control over when updates are downloaded and installed. As shown in Figure 3-2, the Automatic Updates client can be configured by using Group Policy settings to only notify the user that updates are available. The updates are not downloaded or applied until the user clicks the notification balloon and selects the desired updates.

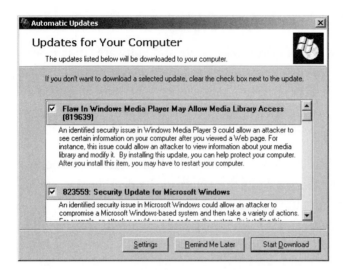

Figure 3-2   The Automatic Updates client configured to prompt the user to download

After the Automatic Updates client downloads updates, the client checks the digital signature on the updates before applying them to prevent a threat agent from sneaking in a Trojan horse. To verify that updates were installed, you can specify the address of a Web server to which the Automatic Updates client should send statistics about updates that have been downloaded, and whether the updates have been installed. These statistics appear in the IIS usage log file of the Web server.

Windows Update   Windows Update is a free Microsoft service for keeping computers running Windows up to date with the latest software updates. Windows Update is made up of three components: the Windows Update Web site, the Automatic Update client, and the Windows Update Catalog. Millions of people use the Windows Update Web site (at *http://windowsupdate.microsoft.com*) each week as a way to keep their Windows-based systems current. When a user connects to the Windows Update site, Windows Update evaluates the user's computer to check which software updates and updated device drivers should be applied to keep the system secure and reliable.

The Windows Update Web site includes a catalog of all software update installation packages for downloading by administrators. These software update installation packages can then be stored on CD, distributed, and installed through other means, such as SMS or non-Microsoft software distribution tools, or they can be used when installing new computers.

Software Update Services and Windows Update Services SUS and WUS (collectively referred to as SUS in this book) are simplified versions of Windows Update that you can host inside your corporate firewall for critical updates and security updates. SUS connects to the Windows Update site, downloads critical updates, security updates, and service packs, and adds them to a list of updates that require administrative approval. SUS will then notify administrators by e-mail that new updates are available. After an administrator has approved and prioritized these updates, as illustrated in Figure 3-3, SUS will automatically make them available to any computer running Automatic Updates. Automatic Updates (when properly configured) will then check the SUS server and automatically download and install updates as configured by the administrators.

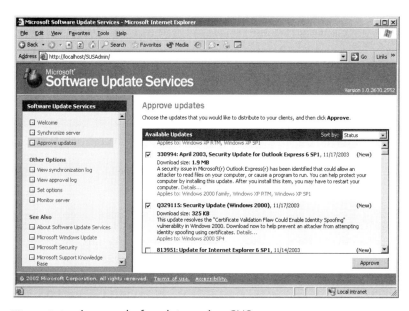

Figure 3-3   Approval of updates using SUS

SUS is designed to be used in medium-sized and large organizations. Almost every aspect of the behavior can be customized. For example, the SUS server can download updates from Microsoft automatically, manually, or on a schedule specified by an administrator. SUS servers can be tiered, as shown in Figure 3-4, with multiple parent/child SUS servers synchronizing updates between each other. This optimizes the use of your Internet connection by requiring each update to be downloaded only once for the entire organization. It also optimizes traffic on your wide area networks (WANs) by allowing clients to download updates from a local SUS server.

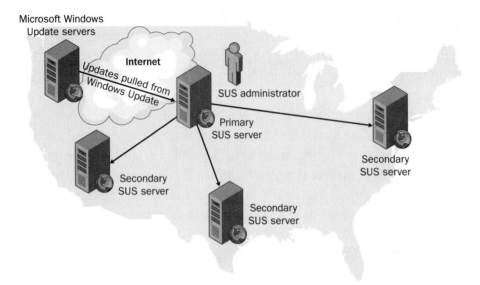

Figure 3-4   Tiered SUS architecture

You can take advantage of the ability to approve updates for internal users without storing updates locally. Administrators can configure SUS to direct the Automatic Updates client to retrieve approved downloads directly from Microsoft. This reduces the storage requirements on the SUS server, and can be more efficient for large networks spread over geographically disparate sites.

> **MORE INFO   SUS**   The section "Designing a Software Update Services Infrastructure," later in this chapter, contains more information about SUS. To download the software, visit *http://www.microsoft.com/sus*.

SUS does not provide a browser interface similar to that of Windows Updates, in which users can scan their computers and choose the updates they want to apply. Only the Automatic Updates client can access SUS.

Group Policy Objects   Any software contained in a Windows Installer package can be delivered to computers by using the Software Installation node of a GPO. Windows Installer is a Windows component that standardizes and simplifies the way you install and manage software programs such as updates. You can use Windows Installer to manage the installation, modification, repair, and removal of software programs. Windows Installer facilitates consistent deployment, which enables you to manage shared resources, customize installation processes, and solve configuration problems.

The only updates Microsoft typically releases with Windows Installer packages are service packs. But it is possible to package other updates within an .msi file if you determine that Group Policy software installation is the best way to deploy updates in your organization. Because service packs are applied across organizations to computers rather than to specific users, consider delivering the package by using a computer-level Group Policy deployment.

The key advantage to using Group Policy over SUS is the ability to uninstall updates if you run into compatibility issues or other problems. Although it is possible to uninstall updates deployed by SUS, you must run a script on each individual client computer. There is no way to uninstall updates by using the SUS management tools. In addition, although SUS is an excellent way to distribute frequently released security updates to a large number of client computers, you cannot use a single SUS server to stage a pilot deployment to a small number of computers in your organization. Instead, you would need to create a separate SUS server for the staged deployment, and configure client computers participating in the pilot to use that SUS server.

Best Practices for Deploying Updates with GPOs   To deploy a service pack or other update by using a Windows Installer file, follow these best practices:

- **Create site-specific distribution folders**   To optimize network utilization in enterprises with multiple locales, identify shared folders at each site. Then apply separate GPOs to each location by linking GPOs to location-based organizational units (OUs), by linking the GPOs to Active Directory sites, or by using security to allow only the computers in a specific location to apply that location's GPO.

- **Assign service packs only to computers**   Do not assign service packs to user GPO settings. In addition, use Windows Management Instrumentation (WMI) filtering to ensure that the update is applied only to computers with software that requires the update.

- **Create Windows Installer packages for updates**   Only service packs include Windows Installer packages. To distribute other updates by using GPOs, including non-Microsoft updates, create a custom Windows Installer package. Developers who are familiar with the files, registry entries, and other requirements that are necessary for an update to work properly can author native Windows Installer packages by using tools that are available from non-Microsoft software vendors.

■ **Assign or publish applications at a high level in the Active Directory hierarchy** Because Group Policy settings apply by default to child Active Directory containers, it is efficient to assign or publish applications by linking a GPO to a parent OU or domain. Configure restrictive permissions on the GPO for finer control over which computers receive the software.

Add/Remove Programs In some circumstances, you might want to make an update available to users without actually requiring them to apply the update. This is an ideal way to encourage other administrators, developers, and power users to update their own machines without forcing them to apply an update. Development and lab environments often require that the administrators manually apply updates to avoid conflicts with other work that the administrator or developer is using the system for. In addition, users who access the network across a dial-up link might want to choose to manually apply updates when they are not going to be using the network connection for several minutes.

If you want to advertise an update by using the Add/Remove Programs tools instead of forcibly installing the update, you can use a .zap file to allow the update to be published. Updates don't include .zap files, but they can be easily created. Installations that use .zap files require the user to be logged on as the local administrator because the update process will run under the current user's context.

> **NOTE** .Zap Files For more information about using .zap files, refer to Microsoft Knowledge Base article 231747 at http://support.microsoft.com/?kbid=231747.

Systems Management Server Although simply applying updates is not reason enough to deploy SMS, if you already use SMS, it is an excellent way to keep your network's computers up to date. SMS provides a variety of tools to help you deploy updates in your organization. With the software distribution feature of SMS, you can automatically update all of the SMS client computers in your organization with the new update. You can allow your users to run the update installation whenever they like, or you can schedule the update installation to run at a specific time. You can also schedule it to run on SMS client computers at a time when your users are not logged on.

If you are still using SMS 2.0, evaluate the SUS Feature Pack. With SMS 2.0 and the SUS Feature Pack, administrators are able to easily manage security updates throughout the enterprise. SMS has always been able to distribute any type of software, but the SUS Feature Pack adds functionality that streamlines the security patch management process. The SUS Feature Pack for SMS 2.0 is designed to quickly and effectively assess and deploy security updates for Windows, Microsoft Office, and other products scanned by the Microsoft Baseline Security Analyzer (MBSA). The Feature Pack provides the following new tools for SMS:

- **Security Update Inventory Tool**   This adds MBSA-style patching inventory capabilities to the existing hardware inventory capabilities of SMS.

- **Microsoft Office Inventory Tool for Updates**   This provides inventory capabilities for Office updates.

- **Distribute Software Updates Wizard**   This component provides a tool that reliably installs updates on end-user computers without forcing the computer to restart before the user is ready.

- **Web Reports Add-in for Software Updates**   This provides administrators with reports describing the current status of deployed updates in the enterprise.

UNDERSTANDING THE PROCESS OF PATCHING MICROSOFT SOFTWARE

Deploying updates involves more than just choosing a technology to install the updates. An effective patching process involves planning, discussion, and testing. Although you should use your organization's existing change management process (if one exists), this section will describe the fundamental components of a patch process. Figure 3-5 illustrates an effective patching process.

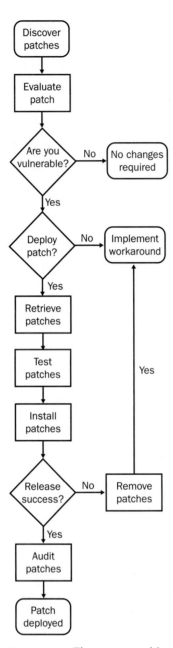

Figure 3-5   The core patching process

The sections that follow describe each of these steps in more detail.

Discovering Updates

The security patching process starts when Microsoft releases or updates a security bulletin. Reissued bulletins that have a higher severity rating should be evaluated again to determine if an already-scheduled security release should be reprioritized and accelerated. You might also initiate the security patching process when a new service pack is released.

You can be notified of Microsoft-related security issues and fixes by subscribing to the Microsoft Security Notification Services. You can register for this service from the following Web site: *http://www.microsoft.com/technet/security/bulletin/ notify.mspx*. If you subscribe to this service, you will receive automatic notification of security issues by e-mail. Note that you won't ever receive the update as an attachment from Microsoft. E-mail is easy to spoof, so Microsoft includes a digital signature that can be verified. However, it's generally easier to simply check the Microsoft Web site to ensure that the bulletin is officially listed.

In addition, use non-Microsoft sources to receive an objective opinion of vulnerabilities. The following is a list of sources of security alert information.

- Security alert lists, especially Ntbugtraq (*http://www.ntbugtraq.com*) and SecurityFocus (*http://www.securityfocus.com*)

- Security Web sites such as *http://www.sans.org* and *http://www.cert.org*

- Alerts from antivirus software vendors

Although many organizations start the patching process immediately when Microsoft releases an update, others choose to check for updates on a regular basis. For example, some organizations have a person assigned to check for updates every Thursday, and then initiate the patching process if required. You can retrieve a list of updates available for a product by visiting the Microsoft HotFix & Security Bulletin Service at *http://www.microsoft.com/technet/security/CurrentDL.aspx*. On this Web site, you can search for patches by product and service pack level.

You can also discover updates by using Automatic Updates. If the service determines that a critical update is applicable, it can notify you that the update is available, download the update and notify you that it is ready to install, or automatically download and install the updates on a schedule you define. Using Automatic Updates to discover and apply updates is great for organizations with only a handful of servers, but the approach does not scale well enough to be used by enterprises.

Evaluating Updates

After you learn of a security update, you need to evaluate the update to determine which computers at your organization, if any, should have the update applied. Read the information that accompanies the security bulletin and refer to the associated Knowledge Base article after it is released.

Next, look at the various parts of your environment to determine whether the vulnerability affects the computers on your network. You might not be using the software component that the update patches, or you might be protected from the vulnerability by other means such as a firewall. For example, if Microsoft releases a security update for Microsoft SQL Server and your company doesn't use SQL Server, you don't need to act. If Microsoft releases a security update for the Windows Messenger service, but you have blocked the vulnerable ports by using Windows Firewall, you don't necessarily need to apply the update. As an alternative, you might decide that applying the update is not the best countermeasure for a security vulnerability. Instead, you might choose to add a firewall or adjust firewall filtering rules to limit the vulnerability's exposure. Of course, for defense-in-depth, you can combine both countermeasures.

Determining whether an update should be applied is not as straightforward as you might think. Microsoft updates are a free download, but applying an update does have a cost. You will need to dedicate time to testing, packaging, and deploying the update. In larger organizations, applying a software update to a server requires that many hours be dedicated to justifying the update and scheduling the associated downtime with the groups who use the server.

Any type of update also carries the risk of something going wrong when the update is applied. In fact, any time you restart a computer, there is a small risk that the server won't start up successfully. There's also the very real risk that the update will interfere with existing applications. This risk, fortunately, can be off-set by extensively testing the update before applying it. There's a cost to deciding not to apply a security update, too: an increased risk of a security vulnerability being exploited.

Besides testing, you can offset the risk associated with an update causing problems by having a plan to roll back the update. When evaluating an update, determine whether the release can be easily uninstalled if it causes a problem that isn't identified during testing. Functionality for uninstalling updates can vary from fully automated uninstall support to manual uninstall procedures to no uninstall.

If an update cannot be uninstalled, your only option might be to restore the computer from a recent backup. Regardless of the uninstall method required for an update, ensure that there is a defined rollback plan in case the deployment doesn't match the success encountered in the test environment.

To be prepared for the worst, verify that you have recent backups of all computers that will be updated, and that you are prepared to restore those systems if the update cannot be successfully removed. It's not likely that an update will cause your systems to fail completely and require them to be restored from backup, but it is a circumstance you must be prepared to handle.

> **NOTE   Update Compatibility in the Real World**   *Updates really can break applications. Sometimes, after you restart a computer, one of your applications will simply refuse to start. In this case, you can immediately uninstall the update and have the application up and running within a few minutes. Other times, the update causes more subtle problems. For example, the update might cause your application to run slightly slower— a performance decrease small enough that nobody would notice. However, a month later, when many users are trying to access the application simultaneously, it might crash under a user load that it would have been able to handle before the update was applied. The problem was caused by the update you applied, but identifying the connection between the crash and an update you applied a month ago can be difficult, if not impossible.*

Choosing whether to apply an update is such a complicated, yet critical, decision that larger organizations should create a security committee that collectively determines which updates should be applied. The committee should consist of employees that are familiar with the patching requirements of each different type of computer on your network. For example, if you have separate organizations that manage desktop and client computers, both organizations should have a representative in the committee. If separate individuals manage each of the Web, messaging, and infrastructure servers on your network, each should have input into whether a particular update is applied. Ask members from your UNIX, database, and networking groups, and from your internal audit teams, to play an active role–their experience and expertise can be an asset in determining risk. Depending on your needs, the committee can discuss each update as it is released, or it can meet on a weekly or biweekly basis.

If the committee determines that an update needs to be deployed, you then need to determine the urgency. If there is an active attack, you must make every effort to apply the update immediately before your system is infected. If the attack is severe enough, it might even warrant removing vulnerable computers from the network until the update can be applied.

NOTE **Speeding the Patching Process** If it typically takes your organization more than a few days to deploy an update, create an accelerated process for critical updates. Use this process to speed or bypass time-consuming testing and approval processes.

For example, assume that you have an IIS computer connected to the public Internet when a security bulletin is announced. If the vulnerability enables an attacker to take complete control of a computer and an exploit is already known to be spreading outside of your network, your system could be infected at any moment. On the other hand, if a vulnerability only allows an attacker to perform a denial-of-service attack by restarting the computer, your risk is much lower. You can safely choose to delay the update until the update is tested and downtime can be scheduled. If you discover that an attacker is exploiting the vulnerability to restart your IIS computer, you could apply the update immediately without risking the loss of confidential data.

Retrieving Updates

Once you have decided to test and/or deploy an update, you must retrieve it from Microsoft. If you are using SUS as your deployment mechanism, SUS will automatically download the update. If you are deploying updates by using another mechanism, download the update from a trusted Microsoft server.

Testing Updates

After applying an update or group of updates to your test computers, test all applications and functionality. The amount of time and expense you dedicate to testing the update should be determined by the potential damage caused by a problematic patch deployment. There are two primary ways you can test an update: in a test environment and in a pilot deployment. A test environment consists of a test lab or labs and includes test plans that detail what you will test and test cases that describe how you will test each component. Organizations that have the resources to test updates in a test environment should always do so because it will reduce the number of problems caused by update incompatibility with applications. Even if your organization does not have the resources to test critical updates and security updates, always test service packs before deploying them to production computers.

The test lab can be made up of a single lab or of several labs, each of which supports testing without presenting risk to your production environment. In the test lab, members of the testing team can verify their deployment design assumptions, discover deployment problems, and improve their understanding of the changes implemented by specific updates. Such activities reduce the risk of errors occurring during deployment and allow the members of the test team to rapidly resolve problems that might occur while deploying an update or after applying an update.

Many organizations divide their testing teams into two subteams: the design team and the deployment team. The design team collects information that is vital to the deployment process, identifies immediate and long-term testing needs, and proposes a test lab design (or recommends improvements to the existing test lab). The deployment team completes the process by implementing the design team's decisions and then testing new updates on an ongoing basis.

During the beginning of the lifetime of the patching test environment, the deployment team will test the update deployment process to validate that the design is functional. Later, after your organization has identified an update to be deployed, the deployment will test the individual updates to ensure that all the updates are compatible with the applications used in your environment.

A patching test environment should have computers that represent each of the major computer roles in your organization, including desktop computers, mobile computers, and servers. If computers within each role have different operating systems, have each operating system available either on a dedicated computer or in a multiboot configuration or virtual desktop environment.

> **NOTE**   **Justifying a Lab Budget**   It can be tough to convince management to allocate budget for a lab. To help justify that cost, calculate the potential cost of an update that causes widespread problems and the likelihood of that problem occurring, and determine how long it will take to recoup the investment.

After you have a set of computers that represent each of the various types of computers in your organization, connect them to a private network. You will also need to connect test versions of your patching infrastructure computers. For example, if you plan to deploy updates by using SUS, connect a SUS server to the lab network.

Load every application that users will use onto the lab computers and develop a procedure to test the functionality of each application. For example, to test the functionality of Internet Explorer, you could visit both the Microsoft Web site and an intranet Web site. Later, when testing updates, you will repeat this test. If one of the applications fails the test, it is possible that a problem was caused by the update you are currently testing.

NOTE   Automating Testing   If you will be testing a large number of applications, identify ways to automate the testing of updates by using scripting.

The server patch testing process is not complete unless the test servers are tested under a heavy load. To facilitate this, Microsoft provides several tools for testing applications under an artificial load. For testing updates to IIS, use the Web Application Stress (WAS) tool to simulate load on the server. For testing Microsoft Exchange Server computers, use the Exchange Stress And Performance Tool. For Microsoft SQL Server computers, use the SQLIOStress Utility. Each of these tools can be downloaded from *http://www.microsoft.com/downloads*.

In addition to testing your implementation of an update, conducting a pilot provides an opportunity to test your deployment plan and the deployment processes. It helps you to determine how much time is required to install the update, and the personnel and tools needed to do so. It also provides an opportunity to train support staff and to gauge user reaction to the patching process. For example, if a particular update takes an hour for a dial-up user to download, you might have to identify an alternative method for delivering the update to the user.

NOTE   Test Service Packs Thoroughly   The more significant the update, the more important it is to use a pilot program. Service packs, in particular, require extensive testing both in and out of the lab.

Besides testing the update yourself, subscribe to mailing lists and visit newsgroups frequented by your peers. People tend to report problems with updates to these forums before an official announcement is made by Microsoft. If you do discover a problem, report it to Microsoft. Microsoft, historically, has fixed and rereleased security updates that caused serious problems. On the other hand, Microsoft support might be able to suggest an alternative method for reducing the vulnerability's risk.

Installing Updates

After you are satisfied that you have sufficiently tested an update, you can deploy it to your production environment. During the installation process, be sure to have sufficient support staff to handle problems that might arise. Have a method in place to monitor the progress of the updates, and have an engineer ready to resolve any problems that occur in the patch deployment mechanism. Notify network staff that a patch deployment is taking place, so that they are aware of the cause of the increased network utilization.

For detailed information about installing updates, refer to the sections titled, "Designing a Software Update Services Infrastructure," and "Deploying Updates to New Computers," later in this chapter.

Removing Updates

Despite following proper planning and testing procedures, problems can arise when you deploy an update to production systems. Before deploying updates, have a plan in place to roll back updates from one, many, or all of the target computers. Although you can remove updates from individual computers by using Add/Remove Programs, be prepared to remove the updates by using the same method you used to distribute the updates if possible. For example, if you deploy a service pack by using a GPO, plan to explicitly remove that service pack by using the same GPO. Every Microsoft update can also be removed from the command line, allowing you to remove multiple updates with a batch file.

> **NOTE   Removing Updates to Solve Problems**   Small organizations might be better off skipping the testing phase and simply planning to remove problematic updates. Testing is an expensive process and isn't worth the expense for every organization.

As part of every patch deployment, you will need to define a rollback plan in case the deployment doesn't succeed as it did in the test environment. The following are the main steps for the rollback and redeployment of patches.

1. Stop the current deployment. Identify any steps necessary for deactivating release mechanisms used in your environment.

2. Identify and resolve any patch deployment issues. Determine what is causing a patch deployment to fail. The order in which updates are applied, the release mechanism used, and flaws in the update itself are all possible causes for a failed deployment.

3. Uninstall updates if necessary. Updates that introduce instabilities to your production environment should be removed if possible.

4. Reactivate release mechanisms. After resolving update issues, reactivate the appropriate release mechanism to redeploy updates. Security bulletins issued by Microsoft will always indicate whether an update can be uninstalled. Because reverting computers to a previous state is not always possible, pay close attention to this detail before deploying an update that cannot be uninstalled.

When a simple uninstall process is not available for a security update, ensure that the necessary provisions are in place for reverting your critical computers back to their original state in the unlikely event that a security update deployment causes a computer to fail. These provisions might include having spare computers and data backup mechanisms in place so a failed computer can be rebuilt quickly.

Auditing Updates

After you have deployed an update, it is important to audit your work. It is ideal to have someone not responsible for deploying the update perform the actual auditing. This reduces the possibility that the person or group responsible for deploying the update would unintentionally overlook the same set of computers during both patch deployment and auditing; it would also reduce the likelihood of someone covering up oversights or mistakes.

Auditing an update that resolves a security vulnerability can be done in one of two ways. The simplest way to audit is to use a tool such as MBSA to check for the presence of the update. This can also be done by checking the version of files that have been updated by an update and verifying that the version matches the version of the file included with the update.

> **NOTE** **Real World** Although the staff responsible for deploying an update should be represented on the security committee, they cannot be solely responsible for deciding which updates are deployed, and their work should be audited by an objective individual or group.

A more complicated, but thorough, method of auditing is to scan the computers on your network for the actual security vulnerability. This requires a non-Microsoft network scanning and auditing tool, however. To adequately test that the vulnerability has been removed, the tool must be designed specifically to exploit the security vulnerability. Although no such tool exists for every security vulnerability, various companies might release scanners to check for widely exploited vulnerabilities. For example, eEye Digital Security has released a scanner to check for the vulnerability exploited by the Nimda worm. The scanner can be downloaded from *http://www.eeye.com*.

> **NOTE** **Quarantine Control for Unpatched Computers** Require updates for remote computers connecting via dial-up and virtual private network solutions because they might miss your patching and auditing. A Windows Server 2003 feature such as Microsoft Network Access Quarantine Control can be used to restrict access for computers that do not meet specific security requirements such as having up-to-date updates.

> For more information about quarantine control, refer to Chapter 11, "Protecting Extranet Communications."

For detailed information about auditing updates, refer to the section, "Auditing Software Updates," later in this chapter.

DESIGNING A SOFTWARE UPDATE SERVICES INFRASTRUCTURE

Most organizations should use SUS or its successor, WUS, to deploy updates to Microsoft software. Whereas implementing SUS is straightforward, designing an efficient SUS infrastructure is complicated. This section lists SUS server requirements and guidelines for how to configure SUS servers, use SUS to deploy service packs, design a SUS hierarchy, and configure SUS clients by using GPOs.

> **NOTE** **SUS and WUS** At the time of this writing, WUS is in beta. Therefore, this section focuses on SUS. However, planned changes to WUS are noted, and security design guidelines between the two products should be very similar.

Requirements for Deploying SUS

A SUS server configured to the minimum hardware specification can update approximately 15,000 clients. To deploy SUS, you must provide the following features and capabilities:

- A minimum of a Pentium 700 MHz CPU or equivalent.

- 512 MB RAM.

- A network adapter.

- An NTFS partition of at least 100 MB free space for SUS installation and a minimum of 6 GB storage for updates if they are to be hosted locally.

- Windows 2000 Server SP2 or later or Windows Server 2003 member servers, a Windows 2000 or Windows Server 2003 domain controller, or Small Business Server.

- IIS.

- Internet Explorer 5.5 or later.

■ At least several hundreds of megabytes of free disk space, but SUS might consume several gigabytes, depending on the options you choose when configuring SUS.

> **NOTE   Download SUS**   *You can download SUS from the downloads page of the Microsoft Web site by going to http://www.microsoft.com/ downloads and searching for SUS.*

Guidelines for Configuring a SUS Server

The SUS server itself must be protected. Although it is not likely that an attacker could cause the SUS server to issue non-Microsoft security updates (and thus could not use it to launch a worm or virus attack), the attacker could remove approval of security updates and, thus, prevent computers from being updated, block the SUS server's access to the Internet or to its parent SUS server, or otherwise prevent it from synchronizing. In addition to the normal security hardening and defensive processes that you adopt for all servers, follow the guidelines for hardening Web servers provided in Chapter 7.

The Web site SUS is installed within must use port 80 because the Automatic Updates client cannot be configured to use a different port. Because you can't configure the SUS Web site to use any port other than the default of 80/tcp, and installing SUS requires installing optional application server components that can expose the IIS server to additional vulnerabilities, avoid installing SUS on a publicly accessible Web server. You can, however, install SUS on an IIS server that hosts only internal applications without exposing significant additional vulnerabilities. If you must install SUS on a public Web server, create a separate Web site for SUS and configure the Web site to use a private Internet Protocol (IP) address.

> **NOTE   Updates Are Signed**   *Protecting the updates themselves is not critical because they are signed by Microsoft and the Automatic Updates client will refuse to install them if the file has been modified since it was originally signed.*

SUS server performance is limited by the network bandwidth. Because clients retrieving updates might saturate a server's network bandwidth, networks with more than 2,000 clients per SUS server should avoid installing SUS on a server that provides other critical network services. If you do, users will experience degraded performance when accessing network services residing on the SUS server while a large update such as a service pack is deployed. If a SUS server services fewer than 2,000 clients, or if you have more than 100 Mbps bandwidth, you can safely combine SUS with other network services.

Although SUS servers are not as critical as, say, domain controllers, you might choose to deploy them redundantly to protect against long-term outages or to provide the scalability to service thousands of client computers. The easiest way to configure redundant SUS servers is to configure two or more SUS servers identically. Then create a round-robin Domain Name System (DNS) record with the IP addresses of all SUS servers. As an alternative, you can use Network Load Balancing (NLB) to distribute incoming requests. If you choose to manually approve updates, you must approve updates on all redundant computers.

> **NOTE   What Is Round-Robin DNS?**   Round-robin DNS is a technique for distributing requests between multiple servers. Basically, you create a DNS entry with multiple IP addresses. When clients look up a DNS address, the DNS server returns alternating IP addresses. For example, you could configure the DNS address *sus.contoso.com* to return the IP addresses 192.168.10.1, 192.168.10.2, and 192.168.10.3. The first client to request *sus.contoso.com* would use the IP address 192.168.10.1, and the second would use 192.168.10.2. For an example of this, run this command at a command prompt: *nslookup www.microsoft.com.*

As with any server, it is important to back up a SUS server. Most important, back up the configuration settings and the list of approved updates. These settings are stored in a Microsoft SQL Server 2000 Desktop Engine (MSDE) or SQL Server database, which usually resides on the same physical computer. If you choose to not back up the updates, SUS will automatically retrieve the updates from Microsoft in the event of a failure after you restore the SUS server.

Guidelines for Deploying Service Packs

An exception to the performance guidelines occurs when distributing very large updates such as service packs. Because service packs can be very large (approximately 270 MB in the case of Windows XP Service Pack 2), SUS administrators need to consider the impact on internal network traffic and on the machine on which the SUS server is running.

For the vast majority of SUS implementations, server and network load will not be a concern and SUS administrators will not have to take any mitigating actions. However, monitor the performance and load on the SUS server after initially approving a service pack. Under ideal conditions for a dedicated SUS server, assuming a 100-Mbps server network card capacity with 20 percent of this capacity consumed as overhead, it will take approximately 30 seconds for a SUS client to download a 250-MB service pack update from the server.

This, theoretically, translates to about 3,000 client downloads in a 24-hour period. You can count on about 2,000 service pack downloads per server per day (rounding down the 3,000-download-per-day figure to accommodate network traffic and inefficiency). Increasing bandwidth between the SUS server and clients will proportionally increase the number of clients serviced per day. Clients that cannot be serviced by the SUS server because of capacity limitations will attempt to contact the server again after approximately 5 hours.

Designing a SUS Hierarchy

Because a single SUS server can handle at least 15,000 clients, server performance isn't an issue for even large organizations. In this scenario, performance is limited by the performance of a 100-Mbps network card. To service more clients, you will need a higher bandwidth network. On the other hand, you can deploy multiple servers in a SUS hierarchy. In general, use one SUS server for each large site and have all SUS servers synchronize with a single primary SUS server that contains the list of approved updates.

If you are using WUS, you can use GPOs to enable client-side targeting and assign client computers to multiple WUS groups. Therefore, you can use a single WUS server to deploy updates to test computers and production computers at different times.

This is not an option if you are using SUS, however. All clients that connect to a single SUS server will apply the same updates at approximately the same times. Therefore, you need to deploy multiple SUS servers to deploy different sets of updates to client computers. Common scenarios in which this is a requirement include the following:

- You need to test the process of deploying updates to Automatic Updates clients by using SUS.

- You need to use SUS to deploy updates to a pilot group of production servers.

- You have multiple IT organizations that each want to determine which patches are deployed to the computers they manage.

- Different types of computers in your organization should receive different updates.

Even though you might need to deploy multiple SUS servers, all servers within your organization should participate in a single SUS hierarchy. When multiple SUS servers participate in a hierarchy, only a single SUS server (the primary SUS server) needs to download updates from Microsoft. Other SUS servers in the hierarchy (secondary SUS servers) can retrieve the updates from the primary SUS server.

Consider a scenario in which you need to design a SUS hierarchy to deploy updates to client computers first in a test environment, and later to computers at both the headquarters and a regional office (after updates have been tested and approved). The SUS hierarchy needs to meet the following conditions:

- Administrators need to deploy updates to client computers in the test environment before approving updates for production use.

- After an update is approved, clients at the organization's headquarters should retrieve updates from the primary SUS server, and clients at the regional office should retrieve updates from that local SUS server. This will reduce the bandwidth on the network link connecting the regional office to the headquarters.

- Administrators should have to approve production updates only once for both the headquarters and the regional office.

The SUS hierarchy shown in Figure 3-6 will meet these conditions if properly configured. As the illustration shows, the parent SUS server retrieves updates directly from Microsoft. The child SUS server at the regional office retrieves both the update files and the list of approved updates from the parent SUS server across the WAN link. The child SUS server in the test environment retrieves the update files from the parent SUS server, but does not retrieve the list of approved updates. In this way, administrators can approve updates on child SUS servers in the test environment, verify that they do not negatively impact the test clients, and then approve the updates for the production clients.

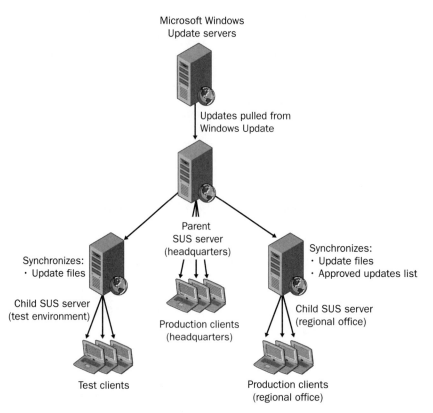

Figure 3-6   A SUS hierarchy is useful for deploying updates to different locations or at different times.

You can also have more than two levels in a hierarchy to minimize the bandwidth used on expensive WAN links, as shown in Figure 3-7. In this example, the primary SUS server in North America downloads updates directly from Microsoft. Child SUS servers on each continent retrieve updates from the primary SUS server. Regional SUS servers, in turn, retrieve updates from the SUS servers located on each continent. In this way, updates are transferred between continents only once. If each regional SUS server retrieved updates directly from the primary server, more updates would need to cross the expensive transcontinental links.

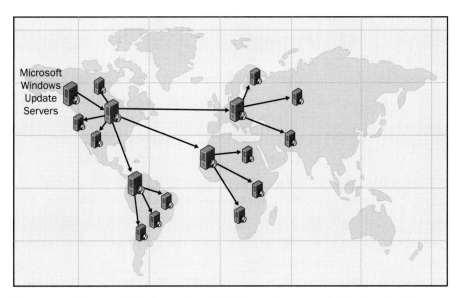

Figure 3-7   Use multiple layers in a SUS hierarchy to optimize bandwidth usage in large organizations.

Configuring SUS Clients by Using Group Policy Objects

You can improve the scalability and performance of your SUS infrastructure by carefully configuring GPOs to control the behavior of SUS clients. Table 3-2 lists the GPO settings that you can use to configure SUS clients with Windows XP and at least Service Pack 1, Windows 2000 with at least Service Pack 3, or Windows Server 2003. All settings are contained within the Computer Configuration\Administrative Templates\Windows Components\Windows Update node.

Table 3-2   **SUS GPO Settings**

GPO Setting	Description
Configure Automatic Updates	Specifies whether this computer will receive security updates and other important downloads through the Windows automatic updating service. You also use this setting to configure whether the updates are installed automatically and what time of day the installation occurs.
Specify intranet Microsoft update service location	Specifies the location of your SUS or WUS server.
Enable client-side targeting	Specifies of which group the computer is a member. This option is useful only if you are using WUS, and cannot be used with SUS.

Table 3-2 **SUS GPO Settings**

GPO Setting	Description
Reschedule Autoamtic Updates scheduled installations	Specifies the amount of time for Automatic Updates to wait, following system startup, before proceeding with a scheduled installation that was missed previously. If you don't specify this, a missed scheduled installation will occur one minute after the computer is next started.
No auto-restart for scheduled Automatic Update installations	Specifies that to complete a scheduled installation, Automatic Updates will wait for the computer to be restarted by any user who is logged on instead of causing the computer to restart automatically.
Automatic Updates detection frequency	Specifies how frequently the Automatic Updates client checks for new updates. By default, this is 22 hours.
Allow Automatic Updates immediate installation	Specifies whether Automatic Updates will immediately install updates that don't require the computer to be restarted.
Delay restart for scheduled installations	Specifies how long the Automatic Updates client waits before automatically restarting.
Re-prompt for restart with scheduled installations	Specifies how often the Automatic Updates client prompts the user to restart. Depending on other configuration settings, users might have the option of delaying a scheduled restart. However, the Automatic Updates client will automatically remind them to restart based on the frequency configured in this setting.

In addition, you can use the GPO settings described in Table 3-3 to configure clients with Windows XP Service Pack 2 or later installed.

Table 3-3 **SUS GPO Settings**

GPO Setting	Description
Do not display Install Updates And Shut Down option in Shut Down Windows dialog box	Specifies whether Windows XP with Service Pack 2 or later shows the Install Updates And Shut Down option.

Table 3-3 **SUS GPO Settings**

GPO Setting	Description
Do not adjust default option to Install Updates And Shut Down in Shut Down Windows dialog box	Specifies whether Windows XP with Service Pack 2 or later automatically changes the default shutdown option to Install Updates And Shut Down when Automatic Updates is waiting to install an update.

Configuring Group Policy Objects to Configure SUS Clients

Follow these guidelines to develop a Group Policy design for SUS clients operations.

- Use GPOs linked to OUs to set the time for clients to install downloaded security updates. Set different times in different OU policies. In this way, security update installation can be staggered. Clients poll the SUS server every 22 hours, minus up to 20 percent for randomization. Clients download and install new security updates according to the schedule you set. Randomization of this activity is also advised. Set a default time in the site GPO. OU-based GPOs will take precedence.

- Consider developing a site GPO whose main function is to identify the local SUS server using the Specify Intranet Microsoft Update Service Location policy. When a site GPO is used, clients that move between sites will download the GPO and point to the SUS server nearest them.

- Create OU-based GPOs to manage all other settings and to point clients to additional SUS servers if you have multiple SUS servers in a site. Because OU GPOs will take precedence over site GPOs, local clients will use the proper SUS server.

- Manage traveling laptops that are rarely in the office by linking a GPO to an OU to which the laptop account belongs. Because the laptops might be used across a VPN and might not have an IP address in any site, they will not be affected by the site policy. The OU-linked GPO policy, however, can provide them with the location of a SUS server from which to download updates. When they are returned to the office, if site GPOs are used, they will receive updates from a local SUS server.

- If you need an administrator to monitor the installation of updates on servers, configure server GPOs to download updates but not automatically install them. This means an administrator will need to log on to each server and manually approve security update installation. Use auditing to detect servers that are overlooked.

- Consider how systems that are turned off during their scheduled update time will get updated. By default, these systems will be updated at their next regularly scheduled update time. However, this can be changed by creating and setting the registry value RescheduleWait-Time or the Group Policy setting Reschedule Automatic Updates Scheduled Installation.

- Prepare for failure. If you have more than one SUS server, use a temporary site GPO to point clients to an alternative SUS server. The temporary GPO must have a higher priority than the GPO that normally points clients to the local SUS server. When the local SUS server is operational again, remove the temporary GPO and clients will begin using the local SUS server after the next policy refresh. For example, this policy can be used to point clients of a failed secondary SUS server to the primary SUS server.

DEPLOYING UPDATES TO NEW COMPUTERS

The setup process is a very vulnerable time for new computers. Updates can fix the vast majority of vulnerabilities for computers running Microsoft Windows, but if you install a computer using the original distribution of Windows, those vulnerabilities will be present during the setup process. Fortunately, there are steps you can take to limit the risk of having those vulnerabilities exploited. First, leave new computers disconnected from the network during the setup process, or use a firewall to block traffic from potentially dangerous networks. Second, you can integrate as many of the updates as possible into the Windows setup files, so that the updates are present even during the setup process.

Security Considerations

Computers are under attack from the moment they connect to the Internet. Worms and viruses are constantly active, probing every IP address for vulnerabilities. Although it is possible to update a computer running Windows so that it can be safely connected directly to the Internet without becoming infected by a worm or a virus, a new Windows installation does not have the benefit of updates or security hardening during the installation process. If you attempt to install Windows on a computer while it is connected to the Internet, there is a high probability that it will be attacked and, possibly, exploited. In fact, according to researchers at the Internet Storm Center, the average survival time for an unpatched Windows computer connected to the Internet in 2004 is only 16 minutes.

NOTE   *Protecting Computers During Installation*   *Not all attacks originate from the Internet. Worms and viruses might have infected computers on the local area network, and will be scanning computers inside the firewall for vulnerabilities. Therefore, you must still take measures to protect computers while installing the operating system, even if they are only connected to a private network.*

Windows Server 2003 is much more resilient to attacks that might occur during the installation process than earlier versions of Windows because it adheres to the secure-by-default ideal. However, vulnerabilities have been discovered in unpatched computers running Windows Server 2003, and these vulnerabilities might be exploited during the setup process.

In an ideal environment, you would eliminate the possibility of being attacked across the network by installing the computer without connecting it to a network. First, place all service packs and security updates that have been released for the operating system onto removable media such as a CD-ROM. Then install the operating system by using the CD-ROM, and install the necessary service packs and security updates. Harden the computer's security configuration, as described in Chapter 7 and Chapter 8 of this book. Connect the computer to the network only after the computer has been updated and hardened.

If you must perform the installation of the operating system or updates by using the network, create a separate network segment dedicated to the installation process. Connect as few computers to this network segment as possible: the file server containing the operating system installation files, and a SUS server that can be used to retrieve the latest updates. After the installation has completed, connect the newly installed computer to the production network. Figure 3-8 illustrates a typical installation network used for installing multiple computers simultaneously.

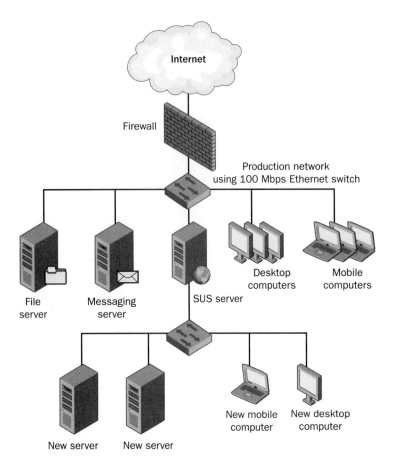

Figure 3-8   A private installation network for multiple computers

Creating a separate network segment for installing new computers has benefits other than improved security. Installing an operating system across a network is extremely bandwidth intensive and, depending on your network configuration, the bandwidth consumed while installing a computer can negatively impact the network performance of other computers on the network. In addition, you can significantly reduce the time required to install a new computer by using a higher-speed network for installations. For example, if your production network segment is 100-megabits-per-second Ethernet and you can't justify the cost of upgrading all computers to gigabit Ethernet, you might be able to justify the cost of a small gigabit Ethernet network switch and gigabit network interface cards, to be used only during the installation process.

If you are installing only one computer at a time, you do not need dedicated network hardware to create a separate installation network. Simply add an additional network interface card to your SUS server and connect the new computer directly to the SUS server by using a crossover network cable, as shown in Figure 3-9. A crossover cable is a special type of network cable used to connect two network interface cards directly to each other. This architecture dramatically reduces the risk of the new computer becoming infected during the installation process because only the SUS server could possibly infect the new computer. In addition, there is no impact on network performance because installation traffic does not traverse the production network.

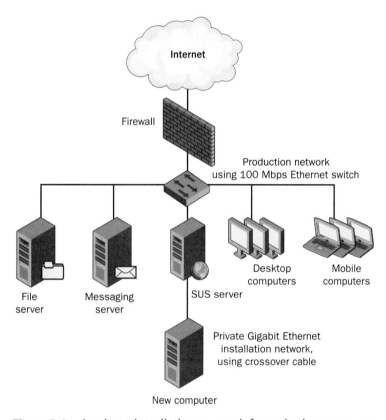

Figure 3-9 A private installation network for a single computer

If you do not maintain a SUS server, and you do not want to download updates to removable media before building a computer, you can use the Windows Update servers to update the computer. Proper network configuration can minimize the risk to which the new computer is exposed during the installation process. To allow a new computer to be installed and retrieve updates directly from Windows Update while minimizing the risk of exposing vulnerabilities, connect the computer directly to a firewall or proxy server, as shown in Figure 3-10. It is important that the new computer never have an unfiltered connection to the Internet, or even to a private network.

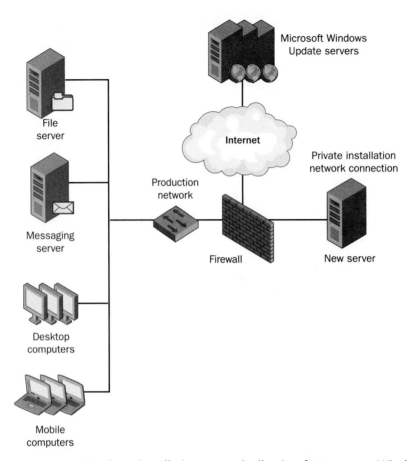

Figure 3-10   A private installation network allowing for access to Windows Update

Integrated Installation

You can apply service packs, but not necessarily other types of updates, directly to Windows 2000, Windows XP, and Windows Server 2003 installation files. The process of integrating a service pack into the original setup files for an operating system is called slipstreaming. Slipstreaming creates an integrated installation—including the latest service pack—that can be used when installing the operating system on new computers. Using this process improves the security of new computers and reduces the time required to apply updates after completing the initial installation. You can either perform the installation from a shared folder or create a CD with the integrated setup files.

Because the integrated installation replaces individual files, the space requirements for this installation type are almost identical to the space requirements for the base operating system. After you slipstream a service pack into the operating system setup files, you cannot remove the service pack.

After you create an integrated installation folder, you can install Windows directly from the shared folder. On the other hand, you can use the integrated installation to create a bootable CD-ROM. Building a new computer from an integrated installation does reduce your vulnerability to network-borne security attacks. However, it does not eliminate the risk of being attacked during the installation process. Therefore, perform the installation while the computer is disconnected from the network.

Critical updates, and other types of updates other than service packs, cannot be directly integrated into installation files. Rather, automate the installation of the critical updates and configure the Windows setup procedure to automatically launch the installation of the updates after completing setup, as described in the following section.

Scripting Non-Microsoft Updates

Although updates released by Microsoft can be integrated into the operating system installation, you might have custom, non-Microsoft updates or applications that you need to automatically install after setup has completed to further improve the security of the new computer. It is possible, fortunately, to script the installation of updates, and to run this script automatically after completing an automated installation.

> **NOTE   Integrating Updates**   This book will not discuss every step involved in creating an automated installation of Windows. However, you should understand how to integrate the application of both Microsoft and non-Microsoft updates into a new installation.

One way to apply non-Microsoft updates is to call each of the updates that need to be applied directly from the answer file. Answer files are files that provide information—without prompting the user—that all recent versions of Windows setup use to configure the system. Answer files contain a section titled [GuiRunOnce] that can include a list of commands to be run after the setup process has completed. The following is a valid section of an answer file that installs updates located in the \\server\updates shared folder:

```
[GuiRunOnce]
"\\server\updates\update1.exe /Z /M"
"\\server\updates\update2.exe /Z /M"
"\\server\updates\update3.exe /Z /M"
```

> **IMPORTANT**   **Installing Updates with an Answer File**   You can use the answer file to install updates automatically after completing the operating system installation, but you shouldn't. Rather, integrate them into the setup as described in the previous section. This ensures that the updates are applied during the setup process itself.

The applications listed in the [GuiRunOnce] section are executed in sequence, one after another. As the name indicates, the applications listed will run only once. If any of the updates called cause the computer to restart, the updates listed after that update will never be applied. Therefore, it is critical to use both the /M parameter, which causes the update to run in unattended mode, and the /Z parameter, which prevents the computer from restarting. If you use this technique to automate the application of updates, you must remember to add new updates to the answer file as they are released.

A more efficient way to install updates from the answer file is to place a batch file on a shared folder and call the updates from that batch file. If you use this technique, you can use the same answer file indefinitely. You still have to update the batch file when new updates are released, but new computers can continue to use the same answer file without modification. The following is an example of a batch file that would install three Windows Server 2003 security updates:

```
"\\server\updates\update1.exe /Z /M"
"\\server\updates\update2.exe /Z /M"
"\\server\updates\update3.exe /Z /M"
```

If you were to save this batch file as \\server\updates\post-install-updates.bat, you could automatically install those updates by using the following [GuiRunOnce] section in your answer file:

```
[GuiRunOnce]
"\\server\updates\post-install-updates.bat"
```

AUDITING SOFTWARE UPDATES

Auditing is one of security's core concepts. Without auditing, security degrades over time. Updating is certainly no exception to this; even if you configure an airtight updating infrastructure, at some point a computer on your network will go unpatched. This can happen when a mobile computer is disconnected from the network for an extended period, when a user changes a computer's configuration settings, and when the installation process of an update is interrupted. To audit the delivery of Microsoft updates, you can use either the graphical or command-line versions of MBSA or WMI scripts. The sections that follow discuss each of these tools.

Using the Microsoft Baseline Security Analyzer

MBSA is a powerful tool that you can use to assess the patch levels on your network. If and when a computer fails to install an update, MBSA can detect it. If there are rogue computers on your network that are not participating in your patching infrastructure, MBSA can find them. You can even schedule MBSA to scan your network for unpatched computers at night so you can review the reports in the morning without waiting for the scan to occur.

Requirements for MBSA Scanning

MBSA can scan the local computer and other computers on the network. During the scanning process, MBSA uses NetBIOS over Transmission Control Protocol/Internet Protocol (TCP/IP) and Common Internet File System (CIFS) protocols to connect to computers, which require TCP ports 139 and 445. If there is a firewall blocking these ports between you and the target computers, or if the computers have Internet Connection Firewall enabled and these ports have not been opened, you will not be able to scan the computers.

At the beginning of the scan, MBSA must retrieve an Extensible Markup Language (XML) file that provides information about updates and security vulnerabilities. By default, this file is retrieved from the Microsoft Web site at *http://go.microsoft.com/fwlink/?LinkId=16932*, which requires the computer running MBSA to have access to the Internet. If you use SUS to approve specific updates, MBSA will retrieve the ApprovedItems.txt file located at the root of the SUS server's default Web site. Specifying this option will configure MBSA so that it does not mark updates that you deliberately chose not to deploy.

MBSA v1.2.1 scans the following products for security misconfigurations:

- Microsoft Windows NT 4.0
- Windows 2000
- Windows XP
- Windows Server 2003
- IIS 4.0
- IIS 5.0
- IIS 6.0
- Internet Explorer 5.01+
- SQL Server 7.0

- SQL Server 2000

- Office 2000

- Office XP

- Office 2003

In addition to these products, MBSA v1.2.1 can scan the following products for missing updates:

- Exchange Server 5.5 and Exchange 2000 Server (including Exchange Admin Tools)

- Exchange Server 2003

- Microsoft Data Access Components (MDAC) 2.5

- MDAC 2.6

- MDAC 2.7

- MDAC 2.8

- Microsoft Virtual Machine

- MSXML 2.5

- MSXML 2.6

- MSXML 3.0

- MSXML 4.0

- Microsoft BizTalk Server 2000

- BizTalk 2002

- BizTalk 2004

- Commerce Server 2000 and 2002

- Content Management Server (CMS) 2001

- CMS 2002

- Host Integration Server (HIS) 2000

- HIS 2004

- SNA Server 4.0

Scanned computers must be running the Remote Registry and the Server services. If you've disabled these to reduce the computer's attack surface, or their network communications are blocked by a firewall, MBSA will fail. You must either scan computers locally (for example, by using Mbsacli, which is discussed later in this chapter), or identify a different technique for auditing patch levels.

Using the MBSA Graphical Console

After installing MBSA, you can use the graphical console to scan all computers on your network or domain for which you have administrator access. As shown in Figure 3-11, missing updates are marked by a red X, and out-of-date updates are marked with a yellow X. A green checkmark denotes a scan that was completed successfully with no missing updates found. Scan reports are stored on the computer from which you ran MBSA in the %Userprofile%\SecurityScans folder. An individual security report is created for each computer that is scanned.

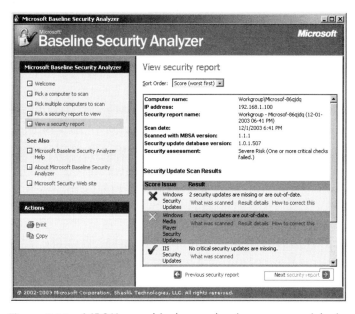

Figure 3-11   MBSA's graphical console gives you a quick view of missing updates.

There might be cases in which MBSA reports that an update is not installed, even after you complete an update or take the steps documented in a security bulletin. There are two reasons for these false reports, both of which should simply be noted and ignored for future scans:

■ Files scanned were updated by an installation that is unrelated to a security bulletin. For example, a file shared by different versions of the same program might be updated by the newer version. MBSA is unaware of the new version and, because it does not encounter what is expected, it reports that the update is missing.

■ Some security bulletins are addressed not by a file update but by a configuration change that cannot be verified. These types of flags will appear as Note or Warning messages, marked with blue asterisks or yellow Xs, respectively.

Using Mbsacli

Scanning a large network should be done on a regular basis to find computers that have not been properly updated. However, scanning a large network is a time-consuming process. Although the MBSA console is the most efficient way to interactively scan a network, the Mbsacli command-line tool provides a way to script an analysis. By using scripts, you can schedule scanning to occur automatically, without your intervention. In this way, you can have Mbsacli generate a report that you can refer to on demand.

> **NOTE Scheduling Mbsacli** It's convenient to schedule Mbsacli scans after business hours so you don't consume network resources during working hours; however, if you do this, you won't scan computers that users take home with them. It's a good idea to schedule scans at various times during the day.

Another good reason to schedule scans by using Mbsacli is to scan from multiple points on your network. For example, if your organization has five remote offices, it is more efficient to scan each remote office by using a computer located in that office. This improves performance, reduces the bandwidth used on your WAN, and allows you to scan computers even if a perimeter firewall blocks the ports that Mbsacli uses to scan.

As with the MBSA graphical console, you need administrative access to use Mbsacli to scan a computer. If you are scanning a remote computer and need to verify your administrative access and network connectivity from a command prompt, you can use the command **Net use \\computername\c$**. Establishing a connection to the hidden administrative C$ share uses the same network protocols that Mbsacli will use. After a connection is established, MBSA will use the existing connection and credentials. Therefore, if you need to connect to a remote computer using different credentials, first establish a connection with the Net Use command. The following example scans the remote computer with the IP address 192.168.1.204 using the user name admin1 and the password je#o23$sti:

```
net use \\192.168.1.204\c$ /user:admin1 je#o23$sti
mbsacli /i 192.168.1.204
net use \\192.168.1.204\c$ /delete
```

The real power of MBSA is its ability to post the results of scanning to a text file. You can import this information into a spreadsheet or database and generate reports that provide an audit of the patching program. For each computer, the file will contain a listing of its missing security updates. This information can be used to ensure that all computers are downloading and installing security updates, or determine that there are problems that must be investigated. For a full list of appropriate syntax, visit *http://www.microsoft.com/mbsa*. The following example command lines show how the Mbsacli command works:

- To scan computers based on their NetBIOS name:

  ```
  Mbsacli /hf -h computer1, computer2, computer3, computer4
  ```

- To scan computers using their IP address:

  ```
  Mbsacli /hf -I xxx.xxx.xxx.xxx, xxx.xxx.xxx.xxx
  ```

- To specify the name of a file (mycomputerip.txt) that contains IP addresses of computers to scan:

  ```
  Mbsacli /hf -fip mycomputerip.txt
  ```

- To specify a file (notthese.txt) that contains a list of Knowledge Base articles that represent security updates you do not want to scan for:

  ```
  Mbsacli /hf notthese.txt
  ```

- To specify a domain to scan:

  ```
  Mbsacli /hf -d tailspintoys
  ```

- To specify the name of a file (myscan.txt) to put output in:

  ```
  Mbsacli /hf -o tab -f myscan.txt
  ```

- To specify a password to be used for the scan: (Note that NTLM is used; the password is not sent in clear text over the network.)

  ```
  Mbsacli /hf -I xxx.xxx.xxx.xxx -u administrator -p password
  ```

- To specify the SUS server to use to identify approved security updates:

  ```
  Mbsacli /hf -sus "http://susserver"
  ```

- To specify a scan of tailspintoys.com and place the results in the myscan.txt file:

  ```
  Mbsacli /hf -d tailspintoys.com -o tab f myscan.txt
  ```

Mbsacli does not output information about vulnerabilities directly to the console. Rather, it only displays the computers scanned and the overall assessment. The details of the scan are stored in an XML report that is saved in your %Userprofile%\SecurityScans\ folder. By default, the file name for each report is set to domain – computername (date).

You can view the reports by using the graphical MBSA console, however. Simply start MBSA and then click View Existing Security Reports. MBSA will show the Pick A Security Report To View page, listing all of the available reports. You can also view them from the command line by using the /ld parameter and specifying the report file name.

Using WMI Scripts

How can you really tell whether all approved security updates have been installed? MBSA reports security updates that need to be installed but does not provide a list of security updates that have been installed. You could assume that by simply subtracting this list of "need to be applied security updates" from the list of approved security updates, you will create a list of security updates that have been applied. In most cases, this assumption is correct. However, spot check this equation to verify that your assumption is correct.

To verify that your list of security updates that have been applied is complete, enumerate installed security updates by using the WMI Service. Enumerate and compare the list of security updates applied to the list of approved security updates for the computer. If security updates are missing, determine why. If security updates are missing, the list should match the list generated by MBSA. If it does not, try to figure out why.

> **MORE INFO**   **Download WMI Scripts**   Sample WMI scripts are available from the TechNet Script Center at *http://www.microsoft.com/technet/scriptcenter*.

For more information about WMI filtering, refer to Chapter 7.

SUMMARY

- Although patching is one of the most effective ways to limit the risk of security vulnerabilities, it should be used in conjunction with other security techniques. In specific terms, use firewalls, antivirus software, the principle of least privilege, reducing the attack surface, hardening security configurations, configuration diversity, software diversity, and uncommon software.

- To create a security patching process, start by assembling a patching team. Then, inventory all software in your organization and contact each software vendor and determine their process of notifying customers of software updates. Assign individuals to identify software updates on a regular basis. Finally, create a patching process for evaluating, retrieving, testing, installing, auditing, and removing updates.

- Microsoft releases several different types of updates. Security Updates are released with minimal testing to enable customers to quickly resolve vulnerabilities. Security rollup packages contain multiple security updates and are released to simplify the patching process. Service packs contain many updates and can contain new features. Although service packs are tested thoroughly by Microsoft, the large volume of changes contained in a service pack means that you will need to thoroughly test the update before deploying it.

- A typical Microsoft patching process contains seven steps: discovering updates, evaluating updates, retrieving updates, testing updates, installing updates, removing updates, and auditing updates.

- To design a Software Update Services infrastructure, identify servers that meet the minimum requirements on your internal network. Configure the server properly, design a SUS hierarchy if necessary, and use GPOs to configure Automatic Updates clients to connect to the SUS server.

- You must design an infrastructure for deploying updates to new computers. Without proper care, new computers will become infected by worms and viruses within minutes after connecting to a network.

- To audit update installation, use the MBSA graphical and command-line tools. MBSA can scan an entire network of computers and produce reports listing missing updates.

REVIEW QUESTIONS

1. You need to automatically distribute updates to two different groups of computers: a pilot group, which will receive the updates first, and a production group, which will receive the updates only after they have been successfully deployed to the pilot group for a week. What is the minimum number of SUS servers you would require to support this configuration? How many WUS servers would you need? To minimize costs, would you recommend WUS or SUS?

2. Which of the following services must be running on a remote server that you wish to scan with MBSA? (Choose all that apply.)

   a. File and Print Service

   b. Workstation Service

   c. Server Service

   d. Remote Desktop Service

   e. Remote Registry Service

3. You want to create a SUS hierarchy such that the SUS clients on the intranet receive only updates that have been tested and approved by the IT group in your company. How would you configure the SUS servers? (Choose all that apply.)

   a. Configure the parent SUS server to manually synchronize with the Microsoft update servers.

   b. Configure the child SUS server to automatically synchronize the parent SUS server according to a schedule.

   c. Configure the parent SUS server to automatically synchronize with the Microsoft update servers.

   d. Configure the parent SUS server to synchronize a list of approved items from the Microsoft update servers.

   e. Configure the child SUS server to synchronize a list of approved items from the parent SUS server.

   f. Configure the child SUS server to manually synchronize from the parent SUS server.

4. You have a single SUS server that provides updates for approximately 700 computers in an Active Directory environment. You use GPOs to configure Automatic Updates on clients to retrieve updates from a SUS

server. Whenever a significant update appears and is approved, the SUS server has trouble fulfilling requests from the Web clients. You do not have the budget to purchase more hardware and must make do with current resources. Briefly describe what you would do to help ensure that the computer is not overloaded when an update arrives.

5. Which of the following types of updates are cumulative?

    a. Updates

    b. Security updates

    c. Critical updates

    d. Hotfixes

    e. Security rollup packages

    f. Feature packs

    g. Service packs

6. Which of the following types of updates can reduce the number of vulnerabilities on a computer? (Choose all that apply.)

    a. Feature packs

    b. Security updates

    c. Critical updates

    d. Hotfixes

    e. Security rollup packages

    f. Service packs

7. Which of the following types of updates have not been fully tested for compatibility by Microsoft? (Choose all that apply.)

    a. Feature packs

    b. Security updates

    c. Critical updates

    d. Hotfixes

    e. Security rollup packages

    f. Service packs

8. You are a newly hired security designer. As one of your first tasks, you speak to the executive team to determine high-level patching requirements. One of the requirements you identify is that updates must be thoroughly tested before deployment. Which of the following deploy-

ment methods could you use to distribute updates while meeting this requirement? (Choose all that apply.)

    a. Windows Update

    b. SUS

    c. Group Policy

    d. Add/Remove Programs

    e. SMS

9. Which of the following deployment methods can be used to automatically deploy all security updates that Microsoft releases to client computers, without administrator intervention? (Choose all that apply.)

    a. Windows Update

    b. SUS

    c. Group Policy

    d. Add/Remove Programs

    e. SMS

10. Which requires more testing, a service pack or a security update?

CASE SCENARIOS

Scenario 3-1: Choosing Which Updates to Deploy

You are a systems administrator for Litware, Inc., a small software consulting company specializing in assisting the publishing industry. You receive an e-mail from a friend who works as an administrator for another company. The e-mail describes four new vulnerabilities that might affect the computers on your network. Your friend describes the vulnerabilities as follows:

■ **Buffer Overrun in the HTML Converter Could Allow Code Execution (KB823559)**   There is a flaw in the way the Hypertext Markup Language (HTML) converter for Microsoft Windows handles a conversion request during a cut-and-paste operation. A vulnerability exists because a specially crafted request to the HTML converter could cause the converter to fail in such a way that it could run code in the context of the currently logged-on user. Because Internet Explorer uses this functionality, an attacker could craft a specially formed Web page or HTML e-mail that would cause the HTML converter to run arbitrary code on a user's computer. When a user visits an attacker's Web site, the attacker could exploit the vulnerability without any other user action.

- **A Buffer Overrun in RPCSS Could Allow an Attacker to Run Malicious Programs (KB824146)**   There are three identified vulnerabilities in the part of the Windows RPC service (RPCSS) that deals with remote procedure call (RPC) messages for Distributed Component Object Model (DCOM) activation. Two of the vulnerabilities could allow an attacker to run malicious programs; one of the vulnerabilities might result in a denial of service. The flaws result from incorrect handling of malformed messages. These vulnerabilities affect the DCOM interface in RPCSS. This interface handles DCOM object activation requests that are sent by client computers to the server. An attacker who successfully exploits these vulnerabilities might be able to run code with Local System rights on an affected computer, or cause RPCSS to stop working. The attacker could then take any action on the computer, including installing programs, viewing, changing, or deleting data, or creating new accounts with full rights.

- **Buffer Overrun in Windows Help and Support Center Could Lead to System Compromise (KB825119)**   A security vulnerability exists in the Help and Support Center function that ships with Windows XP and Windows Server 2003. The affected code is also included in all other supported Windows operating systems, although no known attack vector has been identified at this time because the vulnerable protocol is not supported on those platforms. The vulnerability results because a file associated with the Help and Support Center contains an unchecked buffer. An attacker could exploit the vulnerability by constructing a URL that, when clicked by a user, could run code of the attacker's choice in the Local Computer security context. The URL could be hosted on a Web page or sent directly to the user in e-mail. In the Web-based scenario, if a user clicked the URL hosted on the Web site, an attacker could have the ability to read or launch files already present on the local machine.

- **Update for Windows Media Player Script Command Behavior (KB828026)**   This update contains a change to the behavior of the ability of Microsoft Windows Media Player to launch URLs in the local computer zone from other zones. When a content owner creates an audio or a video stream, that content owner can add script commands (such as URL script commands and custom script commands) that are embedded in the stream. When the stream is played back, the script commands can trigger events in an embedded player program, or they can start a Web browser and then connect to a particular Web page.

Logic was added so that when Windows Media Player does run URL script commands, the script cannot take the user from a less-trusted security zone to a more-trusted security zone.

Your small network consists of a firewall, a router, a printer, several desktop and mobile clients running Windows XP, several desktop clients running Windows 98, a computer running Windows 2000 Server, and a computer running Windows Server 2003, as shown in Figure 3-12.

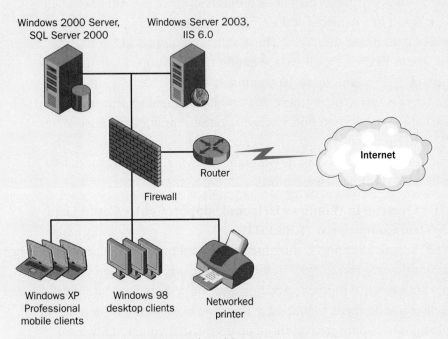

Figure 3-12   Litware, Inc., network architecture

Evaluate each of the four updates to determine their priority, and identify the computers that should receive the updates. Also, consider ways to protect the computers without applying updates.

1. How should you validate the updates your friend described to be sure that they really were released by Microsoft?

2. Which of the computers should receive the update titled Buffer Overrun in the HTML Converter Could Allow Code Execution (KB823559)? (Choose all that apply.)

   a. The computer running Windows 2000 Server

   b. The computer running Windows Server 2003

   c. The computers running Windows XP Professional

   d. The computers running Windows 98

   e. The networked printer

    f. The hardware firewall

    g. The hardware router

3. Besides applying the update, how can you protect your network from the vulnerability resolved by the update titled Buffer Overrun in the HTML Converter Could Allow Code Execution (KB823559)?

4. Which of the computers should receive the update titled A Buffer Overrun in RPCSS Could Allow an Attacker to Run Malicious Programs (KB824146)? (Choose all that apply.)

    a. The computer running Windows 2000 Server

    b. The computer running Windows Server 2003

    c. The computers running Windows XP Professional

    d. The computers running Windows 98

    e. The networked printer

    f. The hardware firewall

    g. The hardware router

5. Which of the computers should receive the update titled Buffer Overrun in Windows Help and Support Center Could Lead to System Compromise (KB825119)? (Choose all that apply.)

    a. The computer running Windows 2000 Server

    b. The computer running Windows Server 2003

    c. The computers running Windows XP Professional

    d. The computers running Windows 98

    e. The networked printer

    f. The hardware firewall

    g. The hardware router

6. Which of the computers should receive the update titled Update for Windows Media Player Script Command Behavior (KB828026)? (Choose all that apply.)

    a. The computer running Windows 2000 Server

    b. The computer running Windows Server 2003

    c. The computers running Windows XP Professional

    d. The computers running Windows 98

    e. The networked printer

    f. The hardware firewall

    g. The hardware router

7. How should you handle updates for the printer, firewall, and router?

Scenario 3-2: Designing a Security Update Infrastructure Hierarchy

You are a security designer for Contoso Pharmaceuticals. As a member of the network security steering committee, you have been asked to design a security update infrastructure for Contoso that leverages the capabilities of MBSA and SUS. If the pilot project is successful, the company will ask you to lead the security risk management process to overhaul the entire organization's security practices.

The head office in Austin currently has about 500 employees. The regional offices in Boston and Seattle have about 250 employees each. The regional offices are connected to Austin by private, 256k Frame Relay connections. All offices connect to the Internet through the Austin office's T1 connection, as shown in Figure 3-13. Users often complain about the performance of the network connections both between offices and to the Internet, but Contoso has a long-term contract with the telecommunications provider and does not have the budget to break the contract and upgrade the connections.

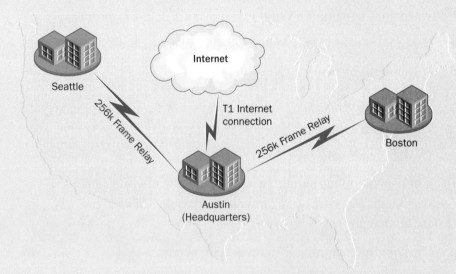

Figure 3-13 The Contoso Pharmaceuticals WAN architecture

Contoso has a single Active Directory domain. Each office has its own domain controller, and is configured as a separate site to make authentication more efficient. The Active Directory has a separate OU for each department in the organization, including separate OUs for client and server computers.

Each office has separate subnets for clients and servers and at least one IT person. The Austin network comprises a number of 100 Mbps Ethernet subnets for client computers that are connected to a gigabit Ethernet backbone switch. A number of critical servers, including an Exchange Server and two Windows Server 2003 domain controllers, are connected directly to the backbone switch.

The Austin network's connection to the Internet occurs through two layers of ISA Server 2004 firewalls to create a back-to-back screened subnet configuration (also known as a perimeter network and a demilitarized zone, or DMZ). All outbound and inbound access through the firewalls is strictly controlled. Only servers that must accept inbound connections from the public Internet are placed in the screened subnet, including the Contoso Web server, SMTP server for incoming e-mail, and DNS server. This local area network architecture is illustrated in Figure 3-14.

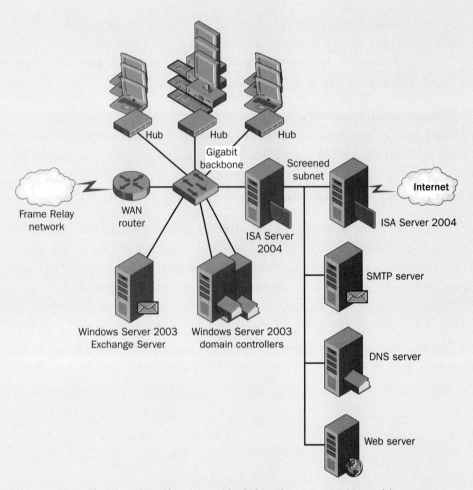

Figure 3-14   The Contoso Pharmaceuticals headquarters' LAN architecture

You gathered the following requirements from the IT manager for the update infrastructure:

- All updates must be tested and approved in an isolated test lab before being deployed to clients and servers.

- Approved updates must be deployed with the least amount of administrative effort.

- Using MBSA, weekly reports need to be automatically created that show the patch level of all computers against the list of approved updates.

In addition to providing these requirements, the network security steering committee has prepared a list of questions to assist in the design of the pilot implementation. You are to use these questions to form the basis for your proposed design, which you will take back to the committee for evaluation.

1. How many SUS servers will you need, where will you place them, and how will updates be replicated through the infrastructure?

2. Given an adequate budget to deploy dedicated computers for parent SUS servers, how could you configure them to ensure fault tolerance?

3. In your estimation, how important is it that the SUS infrastructure is fault tolerant?

4. What schedule should the SUS use to retrieve updates from Windows Update?

5. How would you use MBSA to generate weekly reports of the current patch status against the list of approved updates on the SUS servers?

Scenario 3-3: Designing Group Policy Objects for Software Update Services

You have reported back to the network security steering committee with the design for a SUS infrastructure hierarchy that you developed in Scenario 3-2. The committee is pleased with the design and wants to proceed with a GPO design to manage the SUS client configuration. Where it makes sense, you are allowed to alter the current OU design to accommodate the most efficient and administratively simple deployment of GPOs to configure SUS client settings. However, the subnet and site design will remain constant, at least for the time being.

The requirements for the SUS client settings are as follows:

- All client computers must automatically download and install approved updates at 3:00 a.m. every Sunday.

- Administrators must manually install updates on servers to allow them to immediately troubleshoot any problems caused by updates.

- Network administrators must perform installation of all updates on member servers and domain controllers manually.

- Minimize bandwidth used on the WAN.

- Use settings to block or override group policies sparingly to avoid creating a complicated troubleshooting environment.

- Minimize the number of group policies.

In addition to providing these requirements, the network security steering committee has prepared a list of questions to assist in the design of the pilot implementation. You are to use these questions to form the basis for your proposed design, which you will take back to the committee for evaluation.

1. Group policies can be applied at the OU, site, and domain levels. Also, policies can be applied directly on the local computer. In what order are group policies applied?

2. Is it possible to block a Group Policy from a higher level from being applied at a lower level? If so, what setting is used?

3. Can you force a GPO to be inherited at a lower level? If so, what setting do you use?

4. You want to ensure that the SUS clients use the SUS server located in the same office. Where could you link the GPO for the SUS clients?

5. Would you need separate group policies for client computers and servers? If so, how would the group policies differ?

6. If you were to link group policies for client computers at the site level, how could you prevent the policy from being applied to servers?

7. Briefly describe your GPO design. Keep in mind the requirement to minimize the number of group policies and the requirement to avoid the use of the block and no-override settings on the group policies themselves.

CHAPTER 4

DESIGNING A MANAGEMENT INFRASTRUCTURE

Upon completion of this chapter, you will be able to:

■ List the different tools you can use to remotely manage computers running Microsoft Windows, the advantages and disadvantages of each tool, and how to design a management infrastructure using the tools that meet your organization's security requirements.

■ Reduce the risk of a service-specific attack against the remote management tools included with Network Load Balancing, SharePoint Team Services, and Microsoft Internet Information Services (IIS).

■ Create a network architecture to enable remote management of servers and network devices while minimizing the risk of abuse.

■ Design an authentication scheme that limits the risk of an attacker impersonating an administrator.

■ Use the principle of least privilege to delegate administrative privileges without granting administrative staff excessive rights.

Systems and network administrators must be able to manage the clients, servers, and network devices on a network to keep critical services online. This creates a security risk, though, because an attacker can attempt to use your management tools against you to compromise your network. Designing a management infrastructure that enables legitimate administrators to do their jobs while limiting the risk of a security compromise is one of a security designer's most important tasks. This chapter describes the strengths and weaknesses of common computer management tools, provides guidelines for reducing the risk of an attacker compromising the management tools built into several popular network services, and discusses network architectures that can greatly reduce the risk of exploitation of your management infrastructure. In addition, you will learn best practices for authenticating administrators and allocating administrative privileges.

USING NETWORK MANAGEMENT TOOLS

The tools you use to manage computers on your network deserve special consideration because they could be the same tools an attacker uses to compromise your network. The sections that follow provide best practices for reducing the risk of Microsoft Management Console (MMC) snap-ins, Remote Desktop, Remote Assistance, Terminal Services, **Telnet**, Secure Shell (SSH), Simple Network Management Protocol (SNMP), and Emergency Management Services (EMS). Table 4-1 compares the advantages and disadvantages of each of these computer management tools.

Table 4-1 **Advantages and Disadvantages of Network Management Tools**

Tool	Advantages	Disadvantages
MMC snap-ins	Easy to use Support virtually unlimited number of simultaneous users Can be restricted with Group Policy	No automatic encryption
Remote Desktop, Remote Assistance, and Terminal Service	Easy to use Can be automatically encrypted Provides access to any administrative tool	Support limited number of simultaneous connections
Telnet	Clients and servers included in every common operating system Requires very little bandwidth	No encryption available Can be used only with command-line tools
SSH	Encrypts network communications Authenticates client and server Free client and server available for most common operating systems	Client and server not included with Windows operating systems Can be used only with command-line tools

Table 4-1   **Advantages and Disadvantages of Network Management Tools**

Tool	Advantages	Disadvantages
SNMP	Supported by almost every network device and network management software	Unsecure authentication and authorization capabilities
		Primarily used to monitor, not manage, network devices
Emergency Management Services	Useful when network access is unavailable	Can be used only with command-line tools
	Can be used on servers instead of a keyboard, mouse, video adapter, and monitor	Requires special support by the computer hardware
		Requires the addition of terminal concentrators to use over the network

Each of these tools uses different network protocols to communicate and, therefore, requires different configurations to allow or block the protocol. Table 4-2 lists the default port numbers used by these tools.

Table 4-2   **Default Port Numbers Used by Network Management Tools**

Tool	Port Numbers
MMC snap-ins	UDP 135
	TCP 135
	TCP 139
	TCP 445
	Potentially others. Whereas Microsoft snap-ins typically use this list of ports, non-Microsoft snap-ins can use any communications protocol
Remote Desktop, Remote Assistance, and Terminal Service	TCP 3389
Telnet	TCP 23
SSH	TCP 22
SNMP	UDP 161
	UDP 162
Emergency Management Services	Not applicable

Microsoft Management Console

Most administration of computers running Windows uses MMC snap-ins such as Computer Management, Disk Management, and Event Viewer. You can use these tools to administer either the computer you are currently logged on to or remote computers to which you have sufficient permissions. Using MMC snap-ins to manage remote computers is very convenient, and can make systems administration much more efficient. However, these tools introduce a security risk when used across a network. In addition, they can give administrators more capabilities than the administrators need, increasing the opportunity for abuse. The sections that follow discuss how to reduce the risk of using MMC snap-ins.

Guidelines for Improving the Privacy of Snap-In Communications
MMC snap-ins, unfortunately, don't have a standard network protocol for managing remote computers. Therefore, you can't automatically assume that network communications are encrypted to an acceptable strength, or even encrypted at all, when using a snap-in to manage a remote computer. Use the following questions to evaluate the security level of a snap-in:

■ **What protocols and port numbers does the snap-in use to communicate?**   Most snap-ins leverage existing technologies such as Distributed Component Object Model (DCOM), Server Message Block (SMB) and Common Internet File System (CIFS, an updated version of SMB) to communicate with remote computers. DCOM uses remote procedure calls (RPCs), which use TCP and UDP port 135. To use the snap-in through a firewall or other packet-filtering device, you need to tunnel traffic either inside a virtual private network (VPN) or within IPSec, or you need to open port 135. If you must open ports to use a snap-in, allow only traffic from administration systems, and you must be willing to accept the increased risk of potential RPC software vulnerabilities.

> **NOTE   The Risks of RPC**   RPC is a particularly risky protocol to allow through a firewall because many different applications use it. Therefore, if you open up RPC for one particular snap-in, any snap-in can make use of it. Malicious software such as port scanners and RPC exploits can also make use of it, unfortunately. In the past, there have been many vulnerabilities found in RPC, so it is likely that more will be found in the future.

■ **Are communications encrypted?**   With most snap-ins included with Windows, the answer is "No" for communications other than authentication. Microsoft snap-ins almost exclusively use SMB/CIFS and DCOM for communications between the client and server, which have no built-in encryption. Therefore, an attacker with a protocol analyzer such as Microsoft Network Monitor can capture and analyze the data you see presented in the snap-in. Figure 4-1 shows a frame from a Network Monitor capture generated while an administrator used the Shared Folders snap-in to view the properties of the \\192.168.1.110\NETLOGON shared folder on a remote computer. As you can see, the capture shows the name of the share. An attacker could use this information to launch a brute-force attack against the share and potentially identify valid user credentials.

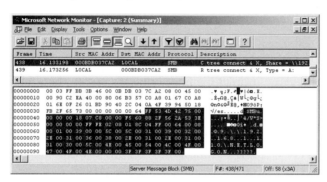

Figure 4-1   MMC communications are usually not encrypted.

If communications aren't encrypted, or if you aren't sure, use IPSec to encrypt communications between the client and server. You might be able to use Network Monitor to determine if communications are unencrypted. To analyze snap-in communications with Network Monitor, launch it on a server and start a capture. Then, launch the snap-in on your administration system, connect to the server, and perform typical administration tasks. You can then stop and analyze the capture. If communications are not encrypted, you might be able to view clear text in the data portion of the captured packets. If you can't read the packet data, it doesn't necessarily mean it's encrypted; it could simply be encoded. Although encoded data isn't readable, a skilled attacker could easily decode the information.

For more information about IPSec, refer to Chapter 10, "Protecting Intranet Communications."

■ **How are authentication credentials passed?**   Most snap-ins use NTLM and Kerberos authentication, one of which you almost certainly already use on your network. Therefore, using it for remote management is probably not introducing any additional risk. However, non-Microsoft snap-ins vary in their authentication methods. If you are using a snap-in provided by a vendor other than Microsoft, ask that vendor how it handles authentication to ensure that it meets your security requirements.

Restricting Snap-Ins

Large organizations with multiple systems administrators often choose to delegate specific tasks to administrators. For example, one group of administrators might be responsible for reviewing the event logs, another group might be responsible for managing Group Policy, while a third group handles tasks related to the Active Directory directory service schema. Although you can, and should, restrict each group's permission to the resources by following the principle of least privilege, you can further reduce the risk of administrators overstepping their bounds by limiting their access to snap-ins.

The easiest way to control access to snap-ins is to create a Group Policy object (GPO). You can modify the following settings in the object's \User Configuration\Administrative Templates\Windows Components\Microsoft Management Console node:

- **Restrict the user from entering author mode**   Enabling this setting prevents users from creating or modifying custom MMC consoles. This limits the user to the MMC consoles that you provide for that user. If you do not enable this setting, the user could add new snap-ins to a console and use the snap-ins to perform administrative tasks for which they have sufficient permissions but that you nevertheless don't want them to perform.

- **Restrict users to the explicitly permitted list of snap-ins**   Enabling this setting works in conjunction with the Restricted/Permitted Snap-Ins node to prevent users from adding unapproved snap-ins. By using these two settings together, you can be sure that a user can access only the snap-ins you specify.

- **Restricted/Permitted snap-ins**   This node contains a list of snap-ins that you can enable or disable for users. Therefore, if you want a user to be able to review event logs but not be able to manage local user accounts, first enable the Restrict Users To The Explicitly Permitted List Of Snap-Ins setting. Then, in the Restricted/Permitted Snap-Ins node, enable Event Viewer and disable Local Users And Groups.

Do not rely only on restricting snap-ins, because malicious users can find other tools to perform administrative tasks. For example, if you prevent a user from adding the Local Users and Groups snap-in, they can still use the NET USER command to manage local user accounts. However, restricting snap-ins does provide an additional layer of defense and makes it more difficult for a potential attacker to exploit a weakness in your security design.

Remote Desktop, Remote Assistance, and Terminal Services

The primary alternative to using snap-ins across the network is to use Remote Desktop for Administration. Remote Desktop is a component for Microsoft Windows 2000 Server (where it is called Terminal Services), Windows XP Professional, and Windows Server 2003 computers. Remote Desktop for Administration, like Remote Assistance, is based on, and uses, the same network protocols as Terminal Services. These tools, collectively, are an extremely useful and popular way to administer remote computers across a network. Remote Desktop brings the remote computer's desktop to a window on your computer, enabling you to perform almost any task you could perform if you were physically sitting in front of the computer with a keyboard and mouse.

> **NOTE**   **Terminal Services-Based Software**   The information in this section applies equally to Remote Desktop, Remote Assistance, and Terminal Services. This chapter refers to them collectively as "Remote Desktop."

Instead of opening a snap-in on your local computer and configuring the snap-in to connect to a remote server, you would use Remote Desktop to connect to the remote server and run the snap-in on the server itself. This is a perfect way to perform remote administration in small organizations with few systems administrators; there would be little chance that more than two administrators would need to manage a single computer at the same time. Using Remote Desktop also might allow you to block RPC, SMB, and CIFS communications required by many snap-ins, which reduces the risk posed by software vulnerabilities. You still might have to allow these protocols on your network because many other applications use them.

However, Remote Desktop allows only three clients to be simultaneously connected (two clients if you don't count the console session). In larger organizations, four or five people often need to perform different tasks on a server simultaneously—especially application servers that host applications for many different organizations. In these situations, running the snap-in on your local computer and using the snap-in to connect to the server works better because there is no practical limit on the number of users who can connect simultaneously.

Unlike other remote management solutions (such as Telnet and SNMP), Remote Desktop was designed with security in mind. Remote Desktop Protocol (RDP), the network protocol used by Remote Desktop, Remote Assistance, and Terminal Services, automatically uses 128-bit encryption (if the client supports it), following the Microsoft development team's secure-by-default principle. In addition, the service is disabled by default, and you have to manually grant users permission to use Remote Desktop.

Guidelines for Improving Remote Desktop Security

If you don't specifically need Remote Desktop for a network management application, avoid enabling it to reduce the likelihood that it would be exploited in an attack. If you do need it, you can do several things to reduce the risks of using Remote Desktop:

- **Carefully restrict users who have rights to use Remote Desktop**   In Windows XP Professional and Windows Server 2003, users must be members of the Remote Desktop Users group to log on to a computer using Remote Desktop. Restrict membership to this group and audit group membership regularly. Members of the local Administrators group can also access the computer remotely whether or not they are members of the Remote Desktop Users group. To ensure that only authorized administrators can access the computer remotely, reduce the membership of each computer's local Administrators group. In addition, remove the Domain Admins group from the local Administrators group on computers running Remote Desktop and replace it with a custom-made group for systems administrators responsible for managing that computer.

  > **MORE INFO**   **Managing Privileged Group Memberships**   For more information on managing privileged group memberships, refer to the section titled "The Process of Reducing Privileged Group Membership" later in this chapter.

- **Restrict the desktop environment**   Apply the principle of least privilege and restrict the desktop environment to control what users connected via Remote Desktop can do. In particular, prevent administrators from running user applications such as Outlook Express or Internet Explorer to reduce the likelihood of infection by malicious software while logged on with administrative privileges. For more information on hardening desktop environments, refer to Chapter 8, "Hardening Client Computers."

- **Change the port number used by Remote Desktop**   As discussed in Chapter 3, "Reducing the Risk of Software Vulnerabilities," changing a service's port number stops almost all attacks from worms and less-sophisticated attackers. The port number Remote Desktop, Remote

Assistance, and Terminal Services use to listen for incoming connections is defined by the registry value HKEY_LOCAL_MACHINE\System\ CurrentControlSet\Control\TerminalServer\WinStations\RDP-Tcp \PortNumber. By default, it is set to 3389. You will also have to change the port number in the Remote Desktop Connection tool on the client by adding a colon and a port number to the computer's name. Figure 4-2 shows the Remote Desktop Connection tool configured to connect to a server named Contoso on the nonstandard port 3390.

Figure 4-2 Change the Remote Desktop port number to reduce the risk of software vulnerabilities.

> **NOTE Changing the Port Number of Remote Desktop Web Connection** You cannot change the port number used by the Remote Desktop Web Connection client nor the Remote Desktop Connection Client for the Apple Macintosh. If you use either of these clients, you must always use port 3389.

■ **Protect Remote Desktop with IPSec** Whereas Remote Desktop can include encryption, it can still benefit from IPSec. IPSec is capable of authenticating both the client and the server, which dramatically reduces the threat of man-in-the-middle attacks in which an attacker impersonates the server.

■ **Configure a management network and block Remote Desktop on all other networks** As discussed in the section titled "Designing a Management Network Architecture," later in this chapter, you can improve the security of any management protocol by limiting its use to a dedicated management network. Block Remote Desktop using host-based firewalls, network firewalls, and IPSec on other network interfaces.

> **NOTE IPSec for Network Management** IPSec is a framework of open standards for helping to ensure private, authenticated communications over Internet Protocol (IP) networks by using cryptographic security services. IPSec supports network-level data integrity, data confidentiality, data origin authentication, and replay protection. Because IPSec is integrated at the Network layer (layer 3 of the OSI

model), it provides security for almost all protocols in the TCP/IP suite, and because IPSec is applied transparently to applications, there is no need to configure separate security for each application that uses TCP/IP.

IPSec can be used to provide packet filtering, to encrypt and authenticate traffic between two hosts, and to create a VPN. When designing a server management infrastructure, you can use IPSec to do the following tasks:

- Reduce the risk of attackers using man-in-the-middle tactics to gather administrative credentials by requiring servers to authenticate themselves with a certificate.

- Reduce the risk of an attacker capturing unencrypted traffic by encrypting all management traffic.

- Reduce the risk of an attacker exploiting a vulnerability in a network service by requiring computers that initiate a client connection to have a valid client certificate.

- Limit connections to management services to clients with approved IP addresses.

IPSec is natively available and can be used to protect network communications for Windows 2000, Windows XP Professional, and Windows Server 2003. In addition, a legacy client is available for Microsoft Windows NT 4.0, Windows 98, and Windows Millennium Edition (Windows Me). You can download the legacy client from http://www.microsoft.com/windows2000/server/evaluation/news/bulletins/l2tpclient.asp. For more information about IPSec, refer to Chapter 10.

Using Group Policy to Configure Remote Desktop

You can use Group Policy to configure several Remote Desktop security-related configuration items to reduce the risk of abuse of Remote Desktop. You can set the following security-related settings from the Computer Configuration\Administrative Templates\Windows Components\Terminal Services\Encryption and Security node of a GPO:

- **Always prompt client for password upon connection**   Users initiating Remote Desktop connections can choose to save their credentials in a file, which enables them to connect to a remote computer without typing their password. This makes administration easier but presents a security risk because any attacker who gains control of the client computer can then authenticate to any previously configured Remote Desktop server. Enable this setting to require users to provide a password even if they have previously saved a valid password.

- **Set client connection encryption level**   Specifies whether to enforce an encryption level for all data sent between the client and the remote computer during a Terminal Services session. If the status is set to Enabled, encryption for all connections to the server is set to the level you specify: High Level, Low Level, or Client Compatible. Specify High Level whenever possible, because it encrypts Remote Desktop communications by using strong 128-bit encryption. Low Level uses 56-bit encryption for communications from the client to the server (such as a user typing a password), but no encryption for communications from the server to the client (such as information about the current position of a window). If you have clients that do not support encryption, you will have to use the Client Compatible setting, which uses the maximum level supported by the client, but will use no encryption if the client is unable to encrypt communications. If the law requires you to comply with Federal Information Processing Standards (FIPS) encryption requirements, do not define this Group Policy setting. Instead, enable the following policy: Computer Configuration\Windows Settings\Security Settings\Local Policies\Security Options\System Cryptography: Use FIPS Compliant Algorithms For Encryption, Hashing, And Signing.

■ **Secure Server (Require Security)**   This setting, located within the RPC Security Policy sub-node, specifies whether a Remote Desktop server requires encrypted communication with all clients or allows encrypted communication. You can use this setting to strengthen security by allowing only authenticated and encrypted requests. If the status is set to Enabled, the server accepts requests from clients that support encrypted requests, and does not allow unencrypted communication with untrusted clients. If the status is set to Disabled, the server always requests security, but will allow unencrypted communication for clients that do not respond to the request.

For optimum security, enable all settings and set the encryption level to high. If you run into problems, change the settings for the Remote Desktop servers experiencing the problems.

Telnet

Telnet is one of the oldest technologies used to manage computers across a network. The Telnet client, as shown in Figure 4-3, is just like a command prompt except that the commands you type are run on a remote computer. To connect to a remote computer using Telnet, the client must have a Telnet client application installed, and the server must have a Telnet server installed and running. All versions of Windows include a command-line Telnet client called Telnet.exe. The

Telnet service is disabled by default on Windows Server 2003 computers and is set to start manually on Windows 2000 Server computers.

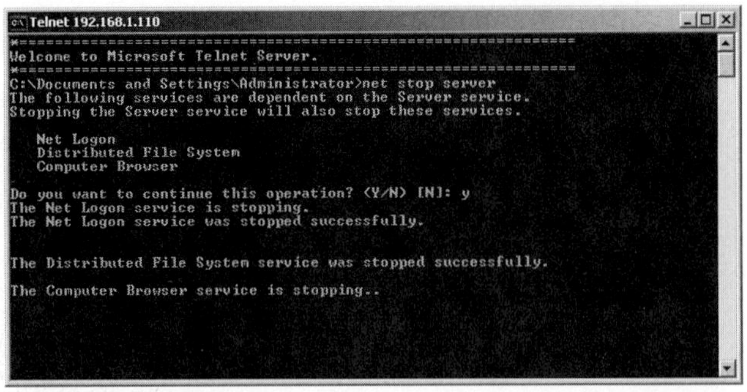

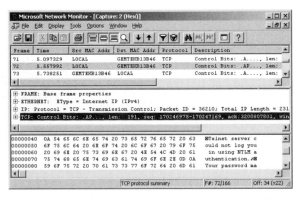

Figure 4-3   Telnet is one of the oldest network management tools.

> **MORE INFO**   **Telnet**   For detailed information on Telnet, read RFC 854. You can download RFCs from *http://www.ietf.org/rfc.html.*

Telnet is very useful, but it's rarely used on modern networks because of its inherent security problems. Telnet's underlying network protocol transmits everything in clear text. If an attacker captures traffic on your network, they can see everything you type, and everything displayed in your Telnet session. Figure 4-4 shows the use of Network Monitor to analyze captured Telnet traffic. As you can see from the captured packet, the server sent the client an unencrypted message: "Telnet server could not log you in using NTLM authentication."

Figure 4-4   Telnet traffic is easy to capture and analyze.

The risk of traffic being captured is reduced somewhat because the Microsoft Telnet client and server will attempt to authenticate the user by using NTLM. NTLM uses a difficult-to-crack hashing algorithm to protect your credentials when they are transmitted across a network. However, other Telnet clients might not support NTLM authentication, and will instead transmit your credentials in clear text. Also, if you need to authenticate with a different account than your currently logged-on user account, NTLM authentication will fail and you will need to type in a different username and password. These credentials will be transmitted in clear text, exposing them to any threat agent with a protocol analyzer, such as Network Monitor, and access to the network.

You cannot enable encryption in Telnet; however, you can encrypt network connections using IPSec. If you require IPSec to establish an encrypted Telnet connection to a server, all Telnet traffic will be encrypted during transmission.

SSH

SSH provides exactly the same management functionality as Telnet, except that it adds the following security features:

- Encryption of all network communications
- Client authentication
- Server authentication

These benefits make SSH the obvious choice for remote command-line management. In fact, SSH is the standard way of remotely managing most UNIX computers and network equipment. Windows operating systems, unfortunately, do not currently include an SSH server or client. You can install non-Microsoft SSH servers and clients, however. The most popular free server and client are part of the Cygwin environment.

> **MORE INFO** **Cygwin** For more information about Cygwin, visit *http://www.cygwin.com*.

SNMP

Simple Network Management Protocol (SNMP) is the communications protocol used by most network management software to collect data from servers, clients, and network equipment. SNMP is a relatively unsecure protocol. However, almost every server operating system and network device available supports SNMP, which makes the protocol useful for network management applications. As illustrated by Figure 4-5, network management software that makes use of SNMP can query almost any device on a network.

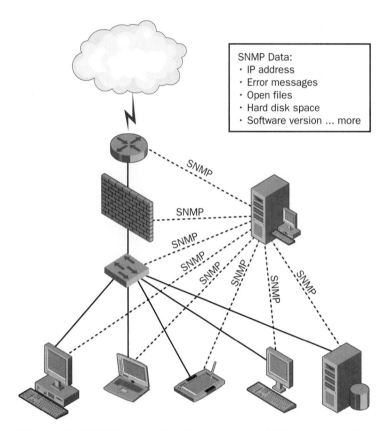

SNMP Data:
· IP address
· Error messages
· Open files
· Hard disk space
· Software version ... more

Figure 4-5   SNMP is capable of managing a wide variety of devices.

MORE INFO   SNMP   *For detailed information on SNMP, read RFCs 1213, 1902, and 1157. You can download these RFCs from http:// www.ietf.org/rfc.html.*

Using SNMP, network management software can request hundreds of types of data from managed computers and other networked devices (also known as **SNMP agents**). The following are commonly requested types of information:

- Network protocol identification and statistics
- Dynamic identification of devices attached to the network (a process referred to as discovery)
- Hardware and software configuration data
- Device performance and usage statistics
- Device error and event messages
- Program and application usage statistics

SNMP is inherently unsecure because all data is transmitted in clear text, but it does provide a rudimentary form of authentication and authorization security through the use of **SNMP community names** and **SNMP traps**, as described in the following sections.

SNMP Community Names

An SNMP community name is a simple credential that acts as both a username and a simple password for SNMP agents and servers to use to identify themselves. Community names can be used to authenticate SNMP messages and thus provide a very basic security scheme for the SNMP service. You can configure SNMP agents with multiple community names, and the SNMP agent will not accept requests from a management system that provides a different community name.

Because SNMP community names are used like passwords, use traditional password protection techniques, including requiring password complexity, long passwords (up to 32 characters), changing the community name on servers and agents on a regular basis, and changing the community name when someone with knowledge of the community name leaves your organization. Even if you follow these guidelines, the SNMP community name will be very vulnerable to attack. Every SNMP agent must be configured with the community name, which means that a user with access to any managed computer's registry can potentially determine the community name and use it to query any managed device.

> **NOTE** Community Names, Domain Names, and Workgroup Names
> There is no relationship between community names and domain names or workgroup names.

You can control the permissions an SNMP agent grants to an SNMP management server based on the community name it presents. You can grant the following types of permissions to a community:

- **None (and Notify)** The SNMP agent does not process the request. When the agent receives an SNMP message from a management system in this community, it discards the request and generates an authentication trap.

- **Read Only** The agent does not process requests from this community to update settings. It processes requests to retrieve information (including the SNMP commands GET, GET-NEXT, and GET-BULK). The agent discards update requests (known as SET requests) from manager systems in this community and generates an authentication trap.

- **Read Create (and Read Write)** The SNMP agent processes or creates all requests from this community. It processes requests to both retrieve information and update settings.

Figure 4-6 shows the Windows Server 2003 interface for configuring community names and permissions. To access this dialog box, open the Services snap-in, double-click SNMP Service, and then click the Security tab.

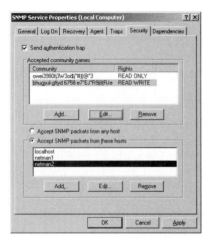

Figure 4-6   You can restrict permissions based on community names.

Community names are transmitted as clear text. As a result, any attacker who can capture network traffic can determine your community name. As with the Telnet protocol, encrypt SNMP communications by requiring IPSec encryption. For more information about IPSec, refer to Chapter 10.

SNMP Authentication Traps

SNMP authentication traps are SNMP messages sent from an SNMP agent to a server after an agent receives a request with an invalid community name. A message from such a management system is sent to a pre-configured SNMP management server known as the trap destination. Figure 4-7 shows the Windows Server 2003 user interface for configuring traps. Trap messages can also be generated for events such as host system startup, shutdown, or password violation.

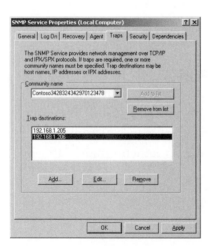

Figure 4-7   Use SNMP traps to notify servers of potential attacks.

NOTE   Configuring Authentication Traps   In addition to specifying the trap destinations and community name, you must select the Send Authentication Trap check box on the Security tab of the SNMP Service Properties dialog box.

Guidelines for Improving SNMP Security

SNMP is an optional component for all recent Windows operating systems. If you do not specifically need it for a network management application, avoid installing it to reduce the likelihood that it would be exploited in an attack. If you do need it, you can do several things to reduce the risks of using SNMP:

- **Use complex community names**   Many systems are configured by default to respond to the community name "public." Because it is a well-known vulnerability, many threats will attempt to exploit it. Assign a complex community name and change it on a regular basis.

- **Use the principle of least privilege**   Restrict the permissions assigned to community names to the most restrictive level acceptable.

- **Restrict hosts that can submit SNMP queries**   Configure each SNMP agent with the list of SNMP management nodes you use. In addition, use only a limited number of computers for SNMP management. Administrators do not need to be able to issue SNMP queries from any computer.

- **Change the port number used by SNMP**   As discussed in Chapter 3, changing a service's port number stops almost all attacks from worms and less-sophisticated attackers. SNMP uses the default UDP port 161 for general SNMP messages and UDP port 162 for SNMP trap messages. You can change the settings by modifying the local Services file on the agent. The Services file is located in \%System-Root%\System32\Drivers\Etc. Configure the management system also to listen and send on the new ports.

- **Protect SNMP with IPSec**   If you want to use IPSec to protect SNMP messages, you must configure all SNMP-enabled systems to use IPSec, or the communications will fail.

- **Configure a management network and block SNMP on all other networks**   As discussed earlier in this chapter, you can improve the security of any management protocol by limiting its use to a dedicated management network.

Emergency Management Services

Emergency Management Services (EMS) is a new feature in Windows Server 2003 that provides management control (often via command-line access) of a server when the server is not accessible across the network or by using a keyboard. Windows Server 2003 can start and operate without most video card support and, depending on the hardware, without legacy keyboard controllers. If properly equipped, you can use the EMS management port to replace the standard input and output devices. Depending on how the server hardware implements the **service processor**, you might connect to EMS via the serial port or a dedicated network adapter.

EMS is useful in several situations:

- When a software or hardware problem prevents the server from starting normally

- For locally controlling servers in a datacenter that lack a keyboard, mouse, video controller, or monitor

- For remotely managing a server without enabling network management services such as Remote Desktop

- For remotely managing servers using an out-of-band connection in conjunction with a terminal concentrator or modem

Once you establish an EMS connection, you can do many useful management tasks:

- View Stop errors (also known as blue screens)

- Start or reset the server

- Change basic input/output system (BIOS) settings

- View power-on self test (POST) information

- Install Windows by using Remote Installation Services (RIS)

- Use Windows Management Instrumentation (WMI), Terminal Services Remote Desktop for Administration, Telnet, Windows Script Hosts, and other tools

- Manage the operating system when it is not available via the network

If you plan to use EMS only to troubleshoot servers that lack a keyboard, mouse, monitor, or video adapter and you are willing to perform all troubleshooting while standing directly beside the server, you may not need to take any security measures. In this scenario, you should perform most management tasks across your network by using MMC snap-ins or Remote Desktop for Administration. If a server is unreachable across a network, you can bring a laptop computer into the datacenter with the failing server and connect your laptop directly to the EMS management port. The EMS management port does present a security vulnerability in this scenario. However, you can rely on the same physical countermeasures that you use to protect the server itself from access by unauthorized users. An attacker must be able to connect physically to the server's EMS management port to exploit EMS.

Accessing EMS across a Network

If you must be able to access an EMS serial port across a network, you need to use a device known as a **terminal concentrator**. A terminal concentrator connects to the EMS management port of one or more computers. The terminal concentrator also connects to a network to accept Telnet or SSH connections from administrators. The terminal concentrator may also be able to connect directly to a modem to allow for dial-in access to EMS. The Telnet, SSH, or modem connections are then bridged to the EMS management port of one of the servers. Figure 4-8 illustrates this configuration.

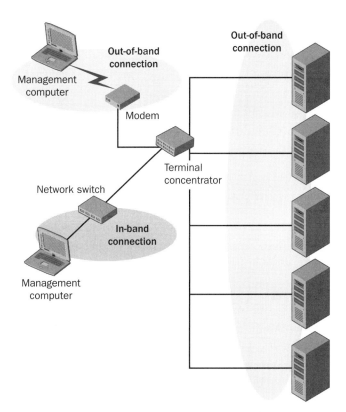

Figure 4-8   Use a terminal concentrator to connect to EMS across a network.

In this architecture, the terminal concentrator serves to bridge **in-band** and **out-of-band connections**. The in-band connection is the network connection from the management system to the terminal concentrator. It's called an in-band connection because it's using the same network used for traditional computer management. The out-of-band connections link the terminal concentrator to the EMS management ports by serial connections, and link the management computer through a modem to the terminal concentrator or service processor. These connections are considered out-of-band because they do not use the standard network connection for communications. As a result, they can be used when the computer's network card has failed or the computer is not available for another reason.

If you connect to a terminal concentrator across the network, you are using a partially out-of-band connection. If the network is inaccessible, you will not be able to connect to EMS. By allowing modem connections to the terminal concentrator, you provide an entirely out-of-band connection that is accessible even if the network is completely offline. Allowing either modem or network connections to a terminal server adds points of entry to your network that a threat could exploit, so you must weigh the costs and benefits of out-of-band connections. To mitigate the risk of these attacks, use terminal concentrators that support encrypted SSH sessions and multifactor authentication with smart cards.

If the server's service processor provides a network interface instead of a serial interface, you should connect the network interface to a network segment that is separate from your primary network. To protect EMS from abuse, this management network should not be accessible from users' computers and certainly should not be routable from the Internet. For more information, refer to the section titled "Designing a Management Network Architecture," later in this chapter.

Out-of-band connections are extremely useful for diagnosing and troubleshooting problems involving your standard network infrastructure. For example, if you are called to troubleshoot a problem and you discover that a server is inaccessible across the network, the problem could be caused by a failure in the server, the server's network adapter, or the network infrastructure. You cannot further troubleshoot the problem across an entirely in-band connection. If you had an out-of-band connection to EMS, you could further troubleshoot the problem. Without EMS, you would have to physically visit the server to perform further troubleshooting. If the server is at a remote location, using EMS with an out-of-band connection could save you hours of downtime.

Using EMS During Security Events

Having out-of-band management capabilities is useful during security events. Security scenarios in which you can use EMS out-of-band connections to troubleshoot are:

- **Identifying the target of a denial-of-service (DoS) attack when a network is inaccessible**   Connect to EMS by using an out-of-band connection, and then ping components of your network infrastructure from the inside out. The first unavailable component is almost certainly the target of the DoS attack.

- **Investigating a server compromise with the server offline**   When you discover a server has been compromised, immediately take the server off the network to prevent the attacker from destroying data to remove evidence. However, once you remove it from the network, conventional management methods will be unavailable. By using EMS with an out-of-band connection, you will still be able to use command-line tools to manage the server with the network disconnected.

- **Reconfiguring a server to minimize a DoS attack**   DoS attacks that target a server often make the server impossible to manage across the network. In these circumstances, you could connect to the server by using an out-of-band EMS connection and changing the IP address of the server, or by stopping the service being attacked to alleviate the impact of the DoS attack and allow you to manage the server across a network.

Guidelines for Designing Security for EMS

Follow these guidelines to improve the security of EMS:

- **Provide physical security**   An attacker must connect a cable physically to the EMS management port before attacking EMS. If an attacker does connect to the EMS management port, there might be no other countermeasures to protect your server. Passwords and logon requirements do not safeguard EMS, though some servers include service processors that include security features.

- **Consider terminal concentrators a significant risk and focus your countermeasures on protecting them**   The specific countermeasures you can use will vary depending on the terminal concentrator. However, you can always use standard countermeasures such as changing the port numbers on which it listens for incoming network connections and requiring multifactor authentication to the terminal concentrator.

■ **Choose service processors that provide security features**   Service processors are implemented by server hardware vendors, and therefore the security feature sets are not standardized. Some service processors include password protection, smart card authentication, and network encryption capabilities.

MANAGING SPECIFIC SERVICES

Many network services provide management tools specific to that service and, therefore, require special attention when designing a management infrastructure. The sections that follow provide guidelines for managing several popular servers that require additional attention from security designers because those servers provide custom management mechanisms: Network Load Balancing (NLB), IIS, and Microsoft SharePoint Team Services. Other services on your network may require similar considerations.

> **MORE INFO**   **Hardening Server Roles**   For information about hardening the servers themselves (as opposed to just protecting the management mechanisms), refer to Chapter 7, "Hardening Servers."

Management of Network Load Balancing

NLB and clusters exist to ensure availability in the event of a failure and scalability to handle large numbers of incoming requests. Critical systems such as firewalls, Web servers, and databases typically are connected in this manner. Attacks against these clustered systems via DoS attacks or system compromises can pose a major threat to network stability and security.

To reduce the risk of managing NLB, perform the following tasks:

■ **Leave remote access to Wlbs.exe disabled on all cluster hosts**   Using Wlbs.exe, the NLB control program, remotely is not recommended because of the risks it creates. Unless wlbs.exe is protected by a firewall that blocks UDP ports 1717 and 2504, the possibility exists of fraudulent remote control messages reaching the hosts. Even on a protected network, local console use of Wlbs.exe is preferred.

■ **Instead of using wlbs.exe, use the Network Load Balancing Manager (NLM) administration tool**   Use this tool because it uses an encrypted method of communication to access NLB hosts.

■ **Use a VPN connection to administer servers remotely**   Connecting to servers across an untrusted network for administrative purposes presents additional risk. You can mitigate that risk by using a virtual private network (VPN).

- **Do not use the cluster service account to administer the cluster** Do not allow the cluster service account to be a member of the Domain Admins group. The service account should be a domain account (and it must be the same account on all cluster members). When assigned, it is added automatically to the local Administrators group on each cluster member and is given required additional privileges. These include the ability to act as part of the operating system, to back up files and directories, increase quotas, increase scheduling priority, load and unload device drivers, lock pages in memory, log on as a service, and restore files and directories. When domain accounts are used for NLB management, Kerberos will be used for authentication. This is a more secure protocol.

- **Restrict access to the quorum disk** The quorum disk is a shared disk that cluster members use to exchange data after a failover. Allow access only to the quorum disk from the cluster service account and members of the local Administrator group. Access to the quorum disk by others is not necessary.

- **Restrict access to the cluster log** Grant access to the cluster log to the cluster administrators and the cluster service account only. This log has information about the cluster and should not be publicly available. Knowledge of the cluster might provide an attacker the means to attack it successfully.

Administration of SharePoint Team Services

You can use SharePoint Team Services for the collaborative efforts of groups within an organization. Exposing the content of one group's communications to others, allowing public access to communications, or allowing unauthorized participation can expose critical privileged information. If Web sites are unprotected, unauthorized individuals might delete them.

If you do not use SharePoint, disable the SharePoint Administration Web site entirely. If you need to use SharePoint, consider the following techniques to reduce the risk of administering these services:

- Use Secure Sockets Layer (SSL) to protect names and passwords used for remote administration of SharePoint Team Services.

■ Restrict NTFS file permissions to fpadmdll.dll and fpadmcgi.exe, which are files used for administration.

■ Use a nonstandard TCP port number for administration. In Windows, by default, a nonstandard port is created for you, but this can be changed. If the extensions are used on UNIX, you must create the administration port. On Windows, do not use IIS to change the port because this can break the shortcut to the HTML admin pages from the Start menu. Instead, use the setadminport program as follows:

```
owsadm.exe -o -setadminport -p <port>
```

Remote Web Administration of IIS

If possible, you should disable the Remote Web Administration feature of IIS and use other techniques, such as Remote Desktop, to manage the servers. If your organization needs this feature installed, follow these guidelines to minimize the risk:

■ Change the default port used for access to the administrative Web site.

■ Require IPSec for connections to the port number used by the Web site.

■ In organizations where different people have responsibility for site content and site configuration, create accounts with only the permissions required for each role. This will limit the damage that an attacker could do if he or she compromises one of the accounts.

■ Verify that authentication requests are encrypted by either requiring SSL or requiring Integrated Authentication.

■ Configure the administrative Web site to allow access from IP addresses only on your internal network.

DESIGNING A MANAGEMENT NETWORK ARCHITECTURE

One of the best ways to improve the security of servers and network equipment is to create a separate local area network (LAN) for managing the devices. To understand this concept, first consider a conventional network architecture, as shown in Figure 4-9.

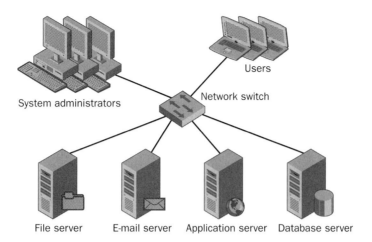

Figure 4-9   A conventional network used for both user and management communications

As you can see in Figure 4-9, both users and administrators access servers by using the same network interface. Therefore, the server network interfaces must allow protocols used by both users (such as HTTP) and administrators (such as Remote Desktop Protocol). A disgruntled user could easily launch the Remote Desktop Client, connect to a server, and attempt to authenticate. Of course, the user would need administrative credentials to log on—but that is only a single layer of protection, which means the architecture is one human error away from a compromise. The sections that follow discuss more secure management network architectures and provide guidelines for enabling remote management.

Designing a Separate Management Network

Compare the conventional architecture to a network architecture with a dedicated management network, as shown in Figure 4-10. On this network, most client computers have a single network interface card that connects to the user network. All servers have two network cards, one for the user network, and one for the management network. Computers used by systems administrators must be connected to the management network and, optionally, can be connected to the user network.

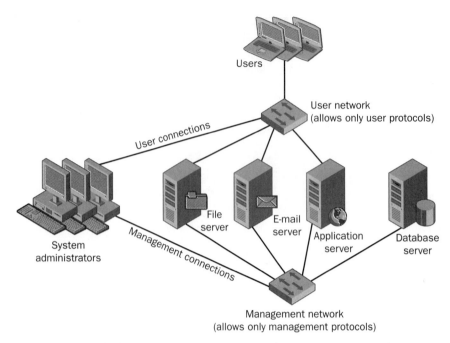

Figure 4-10   A dedicated management network separates user and management communications.

The architecture shown in Figure 4-10 has a distinct advantage over using a single network: you can block management protocols from the user network. With this architecture, for a user to connect to a server by using the Remote Desktop Client, the user would need to gain administrator credentials *and* gain physical access to the management network. That's defense-in-depth because there are two layers of defense. If an administrator makes a mistake and uses a weak password, it's not as easy for a disgruntled employee to gain access.

An additional benefit of connecting servers to multiple networks is that server-to-server communication can happen across the management network. For example, in Figures 4-9 and 4-10, the application server must send database queries to the database server. If there is only a single network, those queries must occur across the user network. This means that the database server must be configured to accept connections on the network interface connected to the user network. As a result, a disgruntled employee could attack the database server directly, and exploit any vulnerabilities in the database. However, if server-to-server communications and management tasks are performed across a separate network, the database server can be completely disconnected from the user network, as shown in Figure 4-10. This makes it much more difficult for a disgruntled employee to attack the database server directly.

NOTE *Crossover Cables* *For even better performance and security, you could connect the application and database servers directly with a crossover cable using a third network interface. Then, you could allow database connections only across this private interface.*

Besides allowing you to block management protocols on the user network, this architecture dramatically improves your ability to audit administrator actions and detect threats. It is extremely difficult to monitor network communications on user networks because there is such a huge volume of traffic. The management network is used only for privileged management tasks, however. Therefore, the total number of security events is much lower, and it is much easier for you to spot an attack.

Designing a Separate Management Network with a Gateway

A third, more popular network architecture connects all servers to a management network, but to only a single client—a gateway. Administrators connect to the gateway, and then establish connections to the servers across the management network. The gateway server can be hardened to meet extremely high security requirements, such as requiring multifactor authentication. All actions on the gateway server can be audited. This architecture is illustrated in Figure 4.11.

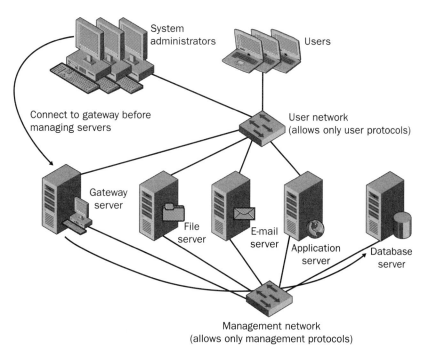

Figure 4-11   A gateway server reduces the risk of compromise of the management network.

Using a gateway provides an advantage over connecting multiple client computers to the management network because it is easier to harden and monitor a single gateway computer than it is to harden and monitor multiple administrative computers. With the architecture shown in Figure 4-11, an attacker can gain access to the management network by compromising any administrator's computer. When a gateway server is used, the attacker has only one option: attack the gateway itself. The disadvantage of this architecture is that it makes systems administration slower because administrators have to connect to a gateway before performing an administrative task.

If you manage your servers by using command-line tools such as SSH and Telnet, you can simply connect to the gateway server, and then connect to the IP address of the server you wish to manage. If you use graphical tools such as MMC snap-ins or Remote Desktop, use a Windows Server 2003 Terminal Server for the gateway server. Administrators will establish a terminal server desktop session on the gateway server, and then launch an MMC or the Remote Desktop Connection tool to connect remotely to the management interfaces of servers.

As with most choices that improve security, management networks also add cost. To determine whether a management network is worthwhile for you, you have to weigh these costs against the reduced risk of a server compromise:

- Additional network interfaces for every server and client connected to the management network

- Up-front and ongoing maintenance costs of network switches required for the management network

- Additional time required to tune server security configurations on a per-network interface basis

- If using a gateway, the cost of the gateway server

Add these costs up, and you will be spending several hundred dollars per server to support the management network. Use the Security Risk Management process to determine if this is the best way to spend your budget.

Guidelines for Using Remote Access for Systems Administration

It is unfortunate that most systems administrators occasionally (at the very least) need to work after hours. Often, work on servers must be performed after working hours to reduce the impact on users, and servers that fail after hours must be fixed immediately. To allow systems administrators to perform these tasks from remote locations, such as their home, most organizations provide remote network access for administrators.

The most common ways to provide remote administrative access is by using a VPN or a dial-up connection. If you have a separate management network with a gateway server, administrators can connect directly to the gateway server, as shown in Figure 4-12. If you do not have a separate management network, administrators could connect to your internal network. In environments with few critical servers, administrators could connect directly to the server that needs to be managed.

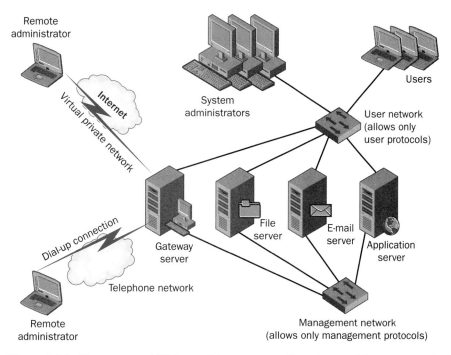

Figure 4-12 You can use VPNs or dial-up connections to provide remote administrative access.

Enabling administrators to perform administrative tasks remotely introduces significant security vulnerabilities because remote administrative access is convenient to both administrators and threats. Any remote-access mechanism you use has the potential to be abused by an attacker. However, the benefits can be significant:

- Because administrators can connect to the network remotely, they can troubleshoot after-hours problems from home rather than commuting to the datacenter. This allows administrators to respond faster, reducing downtime.

- If an administrator can troubleshoot the problem faster, they will spend less time working after hours. This can lead to greater job satisfaction and reduced overtime expenses for the IT department.

- You may need fewer administrators working at a datacenter on after-hours shifts to troubleshoot problems because administrators could solve problems remotely. Paying fewer after-hours administrators reduces IT expenses.

- Administrators can manage computers when they are unable to commute to the office. For example, they may be unable to reach the office because of severe weather. This is critical to many businesses' continuance plans.

- You might require fewer administrators at remote locations. If your organization has offices that are spread around the world, remote access can enable a single administrator to manage computers in all locations. The administrator would still need to work with local staff for tasks that require physical presence, such as replacing a failed hardware component. However, this is more efficient and less costly than hiring full-time administrators for each location.

> **MORE INFO** **Configuring Remote Access**   For detailed information about configuring remote access, including best practices for countermeasures, refer to Chapter 11, "Protecting Extranet Communications."

GUIDELINES FOR AUTHENTICATING ADMINISTRATORS

As you learned in Chapter 2, "Analyzing Risk," risk is a combination of the likelihoods of both a compromised vulnerability and the damage that the threat could do in the event of a successful compromise. If a threat successfully impersonates an administrator, the potential damage is more significant than if the threat successfully impersonates a standard user with lesser privileges. Therefore, the risk of administrator impersonation is greater than the risk of standard-user impersonation, and administrative credentials might deserve more protection in your organization, depending on how you value the risk during the security risk management process. For these reasons, consider requiring multifactor authentication for administrative tasks, even if you allow users to authenticate with a standard username and password.

Although most users will only need to authenticate to servers, administrators may need to manage servers, routers, network switches, dial-up servers, and other types of network equipment. Whereas Active Directory makes it extremely easy to configure centralized authentication for servers, you will need to design additional components to enable centralized authentication for administrators managing network equipment that does not participate in a domain. The most common technique is to use a Remote Authentication Dial-In User Service (RADIUS) server.

The sections that follow discuss multifactor authentication and RADIUS services in more detail.

Using Multifactor Authentication

Passwords can be guessed, and smart cards can be stolen. One form of authentication alone may not meet your organization's security requirements. Multifactor authentication combines two or more authentication methods and significantly reduces the likelihood that a malicious attacker will be able to impersonate a user during the authentication process.

The most common example of multifactor authentication is combining a smart card and a password. The password typically is required to retrieve a key stored on the smart card. Before you can authenticate to such a system, you must provide a password (something you know) and a smart card (something you have). Windows Server 2003 supports multifactor authentication using smart cards, and can support a variety of other authentication mechanisms using third-party hardware and software.

Smart cards can be required for all users in an organization. However, because of the additional cost, smart cards are often assigned only for administrators. To require a smart card for interactive logon for a specific user, launch the Active Directory Users And Computers console. Double-click the user account to view the properties, and then click the Account tab. In the Account Options list, select Smart Card Is Required For Interactive Logon, as shown in Figure 4-13.

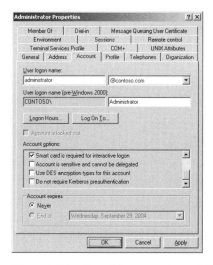

Figure 4-13   Requiring smart cards for authentication is built into the Active Directory.

Requiring smart cards for authentication can cause problems with existing applications. However, if an application includes the "Certified for Windows Server 2003" logo, the application has been tested to ensure that it meets Microsoft security standards for Windows Server 2003. From a security perspective, an application that is identified as Certified for Windows Server 2003 meets the following criteria:

- **Supports smart-card logons**   The application should work correctly with smart-card authentication and allow smart-card authentication to a terminal service.

- **Follows security best practices for credential management**   The application ensures that users will get appropriate prompting for credentials and storing credentials; it also means that the application can use Kerberos, NTLM, and Secure Sockets Layer (SSL) protocols. A user can also log on using a UPN format.

- **Runs in a highly secure configuration**   Applications can perform all primary functions in a highly secure configuration. In a highly secure configuration, applications cannot use the unsafe communication protocol NTLM, strong authentication and account policies are set, and group membership is restricted. A highly secure configuration is a system with a clean installation of Windows and with the predefined security template Hisecws.inf applied.

- **Provides encrypted network connections**   Applications using network connections must not depend on protocols known to have vulnerabilities.

Using RADIUS for Authentication

RADIUS is an Internet Engineering Task Force (IETF) standardized service used primarily to authenticate dial-up users. Windows Server 2003 includes a RADIUS service and proxy named Internet Authentication Service (IAS). The traditional use for IAS on Windows-based networks is to allow an Internet service provider (ISP) to authenticate an organization's users based on the Active Directory domain credentials stored on the organization's private network. Because most network devices support RADIUS authentication, administrators can also use IAS to authenticate to network devices using their standard username and password.

IAS Overview

IAS is a mechanism for authenticating users, not unlike Kerberos. IAS is also capable of providing user authorization and accounting for connection times, however. IAS acts as a RADIUS server and proxy that provides compatibility with a wide variety of non-Microsoft hardware and software, including wireless routers, authenticating switches, remote-access dial-up servers, and VPN connections.

Authentication services like IAS require special security considerations. When you configure IAS for a RADIUS client, you configure the IP address of the client. If an incoming RADIUS Access-Request message does not originate from at least one of the IP addresses of configured clients, IAS automatically discards the message, providing protection for an IAS server. However, do not rely solely on source IP addresses for authentication because they can be spoofed.

Shared secrets (a form of password) are used to verify most RADIUS messages sent by a RADIUS-enabled device that is configured with the same shared secret. Shared secrets also verify that the RADIUS message has not been modified in transit. Finally, the shared secret encrypts some RADIUS attributes, such as User-Password and Tunnel-Password. To provide verification for messages, you can enable use of the RADIUS Message Authenticator attribute, as shown in Figure 4-14.

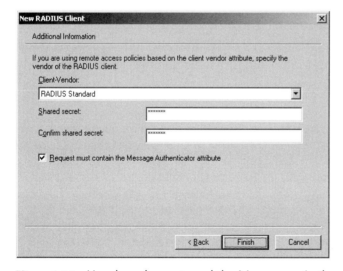

Figure 4-14 Use shared secrets and the Messenger Authenticator attribute to improve the security of RADIUS communications.

> **NOTE** **Using Shared Secrets**   If you specify RADIUS clients by using an IP address range, all RADIUS clients within the address range must use the same shared secret.

IAS Logging Considerations

IAS is capable of logging authentication requests and accounting requests. This information is vital for tracking when users attempt to connect, and for identifying successful and unsuccessful attacks. By using RADIUS to authenticate administrators connecting to network devices, you gain the ability to easily audit login attempts.

When IAS logging is enabled, log files are located by default in the %Systemroot%\System32\LogFiles folder. Configure these permissions to reduce the risk of an attacker modifying the log files. As with IIS, IAS logging can also be sent to a database server.

> **NOTE   Packet Filtering for IAS**   If a firewall is positioned between the IAS server and a client or another IAS server, ports must be opened in the firewall. Authentication traffic uses UDP ports 1645 and 1812. Accounting traffic uses UDP ports 1813 and 1646.

ALLOCATING ADMINISTRATIVE RIGHTS

The principle of least privilege is an important guideline for many aspects of network security. Least privilege is particularly critical for privileged user accounts used by systems administrators, however. The more administrators there are in an organization, the more important it is to restrict their permissions to the minimum required by the user to do their job. The sections that follow discuss how to reduce privileged group membership and provide guidelines for hardening Group Policy administration.

> **NOTE   Logging On As a User to Your Desktop, As an Administrator to Your Servers**   Most administrators know that they are not supposed to log on as an administrator to perform day-to-day tasks such as reading e-mail or browsing the Web. Instead, they should log on as a standard user and use the Run As capability of Windows XP and Windows Server 2003 to launch applications that require elevated privileges. This guideline does not apply when logging on to server computers, however. If you're logging on to a server, you should *only* be performing administrative tasks. Therefore, log on with administrative privileges, complete your task, and log off.

The Process of Reducing Privileged Group Membership

Privileged groups, such as the local Administrators group or the Domain Admins, Enterprise Admins, and Schema Admins domain groups, are user groups that have more access and authority than ordinary users. Privileged groups can be built-in groups assigned privileges by default, or they might have elevated privileges assigned them via Group Policy, delegation of authority, or direct manipulation of resource access control lists (ACLs).

The first thing to do when managing privileged groups is reduce their membership. To reduce privileged group membership:

1. Make a list of privileged local and domain groups.

2. Rank groups by the amount and range of privilege and access they have.

3. Starting with the most highly privileged groups, identify the owner of the group. In other words, who tells you who should be in the group? (You might have to work with the owners of the group to help them understand when they should and should not be granting memberships.) Then, validate the process of identifying group membership by answering the following questions:

    ❑ What is the group's procedure for determining membership?

    ❑ Does the group owner carefully consider whether the proposed member really requires access to the resources the group can use?

    ❑ Are members of the group properly trained in security best practices?

    ❑ How does the group owner verify that there is no lesser privileged group that would meet the user's needs?

4. Contact each group owner and verify that each member is authorized to be in the group. Discuss the user's job responsibilities and verify that the user is a member of the group that most closely meets the user's requirements without granting excessive permissions.

5. Verify that membership in the group does not break your security policies. In specific terms, if your security policies require separation of duties to prevent a single user from performing certain privileged tasks alone, verify that group memberships enforce that policy.

6. Verify that the owner of the group understands the importance of notifying you to remove a user from the group if that user leaves the organization or if his or her job responsibilities change.

7. Determine who can add members to the group or modify the group's permissions. Verify that administrators who can manage group memberships have proper security training. In addition, verify that auditing

is in place to record changes to group memberships and the use of administrative privileges.

Harden Group Policy Administration

Group Policy is an integral part of security administration on Windows-based networks. The ability to implement or block Group Policy is a security privilege that should be granted with extreme caution. To harden Group Policy administration:

- Restrict membership in the Group Policy Creator Owners group to a limited subset of administrators. Membership in this group enables full administration of Group Policy in the domain.

- When using the Delegation of Control Wizard, instead of providing administrators with Full Control over their organizational unit (OU), limit them to specific administrative practices. With respect to Group Policy, guidelines for common task choices are as follows:

  - Manage Group Policy links. Do not give delegated administrators the ability to remove or add GPO links to their OU.

  - Generate a Resultant Set of Policy (Planning). Provide this ability if administrators are to be involved in planning new GPOs or if Logging mode cannot be used on all computers that administrators might manage.

  - Generate a Resultant Set of Policy (Logging). Provide this ability if administrators should troubleshoot GPO applications.

    NOTE Software Restrictions   You can apply software restriction policies to privileged accounts to limit them to running just the management tools required to do their job. This reduces the risk of a privileged user either directly or indirectly running malicious software by using an e-mail client or Web browser on a server. For more information about software restriction policies, refer to Chapter 8.

SUMMARY

■ Most MMC snap-ins use RPC, SMB, and CIFS. Minimize the risk of exposing these protocols to attack by limiting traffic to a management network and requiring IPSec.

■ Managing computers by using Remote Desktop exposes fewer vulnerabilities than using MMC snap-ins, but the limited number of simultaneous administrative connections is challenging in enterprise environments with dozens of systems administrators.

■ You can use Telnet, SSH, and EMS to manage computers remotely from a command line. Telnet has no security, SSH is encrypted and authenticated, and EMS provides command-line management across a serial port. When combined with a modem or a terminal concentrator, you can use EMS for out-of-band access.

■ SNMP is a common, but unsecure, protocol for monitoring computers and network devices across a network.

■ Examine every network service to determine whether management tools expose any vulnerabilities that require additional countermeasures.

■ To reduce the risk of attacks against management services on servers and network devices, create separate LANs for user and management traffic. On the user network, block all management communications. Protect the management network by connecting only servers that need management and a gateway server. Protect the gateway server with requirements for multifactor authentication and security auditing.

■ Use multifactor authentication to protect administrator user accounts. To save administrators from maintaining separate credentials for servers and network devices, configure network devices to use RADIUS to send authentication requests to an IAS server.

■ Use the principle of least privilege when assigning administrative rights. Systems administrators should have only the minimum permissions required to perform their specific jobs. Placing too many users in powerful groups, such as Domain Admins, increases risks dramatically.

REVIEW QUESTIONS

1. Which level of encryption is required for MMC snap-ins when communicating with remote computers?

    a. No encryption

    b. 56-bit encryption

    c. 64-bit encryption

    d. 128-bit encryption

2. Which of the following management tools encrypts command-line management of remote computers?

    a. Telnet

    b. SSH

    c. SNMP

    d. EMS

    e. Remote Desktop

3. Which of the following management tools is used for out-of-band command-line management of servers?

    a. Telnet

    b. SSH

    c. SNMP

    d. EMS

    e. Remote Desktop

4. Which of the following management tools can you use to manage computers running Windows XP Professional?

    a. Telnet

    b. SSH

    c. EMS

    d. Remote Desktop

5. You are designing a separate LAN for the management of servers. On which ports should you allow incoming communications on the server

host-based firewalls to enable SNMP and Remote Desktop? (Choose all that apply.)

    a. TCP 135

    b. UDP 135

    c. TCP 3389

    d. UDP 161

    e. UDP 162

    f. TCP 22

    g. TCP 23

6. Which of the following are advantages of using out-of-band management tools? (Choose all that apply.)

    a. Less expensive than in-band management

    b. Can be used when the network is inaccessible

    c. Can be used when the power has failed

    d. Can be used to locally manage computers without a keyboard and mouse

    e. Requires smart-card authentication

7. Which technology can you use to enable administrators to manage network devices, using the same credentials they use to authenticate to an Active Directory domain controller?

    a. IPSec

    b. RADIUS

    c. SNMP

    d. SSH

8. Which of the following are advantages of creating a separate management network? (Choose all that apply.)

    a. Easier to maintain than using a single network

    b. More granular control over access to network management services

    c. Less expensive network hardware

    d. Uses Remote Desktop

9. To reduce the risk of software vulnerabilities, you change the Remote Desktop port number from 3389 to 3390 for all computers on your network. Which of the following clients will be unable to connect by using Remote Desktop? (Choose all that apply.)

   a. Remote Desktop Connection on computers running Windows XP Professional

   b. Remote Desktop Web Connection on computers running Windows XP Professional

   c. Remote Desktop Connection on computers running Windows 98

   d. Remote Desktop Connection Client for the Macintosh

CASE SCENARIOS

Case Scenario 4-1: Designing a Management Infrastructure with an Unlimited Budget

You are a security consultant hired by The Phone Company to design a management infrastructure for their new LAN. On your first day at the assignment, the IT manager, Shaun Beasley, describes your assignment:

"Did you read the paper today? I've known about it for months, but they finally made the official announcement. The FCC is requiring that our parent company split us into an independent company in order to comply with antitrust laws and enable our parent company to complete the big merger.

"This is great news, but it's a lot of work. We have to separate completely from the parent company's infrastructure. That means we need new buildings, new networks, new servers, new everything. The parent company has set aside a very healthy budget for us. It's an IT manager's dream—starting from scratch with plenty of cash. We're calling it Project Greenfield.

"Your task is to design a secure management infrastructure for our future Windows-based network. We have other people figuring out how many servers we're going to have and what services we're using, so just provide as much flexibility as possible in your design. Security is a priority—that's why I hired you."

Take some time to think about how you would design a management infrastructure, and answer the following questions from the IT manager:

1. What network architecture do you recommend using?

  a. A single network architecture for user and management communications

  b. Separate LANs for users and administrators, with administration systems connected directly to the management network

  c. Separate LANs for users and administrators, with a gateway server providing access to the management network

2. What tools should we use to monitor servers and network devices remotely? (Choose all that apply.)

  a. MMC snap-ins across the network

  b. Remote Desktop

  c. Telnet

  d. SSH

  e. SNMP

  f. EMS

3. What tools should we use to manage servers remotely? (Choose all that apply.)

  a. MMC snap-ins across the network

  b. Remote Desktop

  c. Telnet

  d. SSH

  e. SNMP

  f. EMS

4. Which ports will you allow in Internet Connection Firewall on the Windows Server 2003 network adapters connected to the management network?

  a. TCP 22, TCP 23, TCP 3389

  b. TCP 80, UDP 135, TCP 135, TCP 139, TCP 445, TCP 3389

  c. TCP 23, UDP 135, TCP 135, TCP 137, UDP 138, TCP 139, UDP 161, UDP 162, TCP 445

  d. UDP 135, TCP 135, TCP 139, UDP 161, UDP 162, TCP 445, TCP 3389

Case Scenario 4-2: Designing a Management Infrastructure with No Budget

You are a consultant hired by Alpine Ski House to improve the efficiency of its network management. After having your coffee, you step into your boss's office to discuss his goals.

"We have only one systems administrator. He's a great guy, but I think his resistance to change is slowing him down. He's been managing computers running Windows for about a decade now, and I don't think he's changed his practices a bit. If one of our Windows Server 2003 servers breaks, he walks all the way downstairs to the server room to investigate it. If it's a tough problem, he might spend hours in the server room. Meanwhile, if anyone else has a different problem and we try to call him on the phone, he's not at his desk to help us. Isn't there some way he can manage those servers from his desk? Oh, one more thing. I spent our capital budget for the year. We're out of cash. So, I'm hoping whatever you do is free. It has to be."

Take some time to think about how you would design a management infrastructure and answer the following questions from your boss:

1. Which tools would you recommend the systems administrator use to manage the servers from his desk? (Choose all that apply.)

    a. MMC snap-ins across the network

    b. Remote Desktop

    c. Telnet

    d. SSH

    e. SNMP

    f. EMS

2. What additional security risks does the remote management introduce?

3. How can you reduce the risk of users abusing the remote management capabilities of the servers?

CHAPTER 5
DESIGNING ACTIVE DIRECTORY SECURITY

Upon completion of this chapter, you will be able to:

- List the different authentication protocols used in Active Directory environments, and describe the different security levels provided by each protocol.

- Select password security requirements to minimize the risk of password-cracking attacks.

- Use multifactor authentication to minimize the risk of attackers gaining user credentials without the user's knowledge.

- Use trusts in forest designs to enable sharing of resources across security boundaries while limiting security risks.

- Weigh the risks of enabling anonymous authentication to support earlier versions of Microsoft Windows.

- Assess and minimize the risks of interoperating with computers running non-Windows-based systems in Active Directory environments.

Enterprises rely on Active Directory directory service to act as a gateway to their confidential information. Because Active Directory is responsible for authenticating users, computers, and services, a vulnerability in your Active Directory design can allow an attacker to gain access to your organization's most valuable resources. Although every authentication mechanism is vulnerable to some types of attacks, such as password dictionary attacks and attacks from authorized administrators, as a security designer you have the power to mitigate those risks significantly.

This chapter assumes you understand the fundamentals of Active Directory, including its purpose, how to configure it, and the basics of Active Directory design. The focus of this chapter will be assessing Active Directory vulnerabilities and the threats that can exploit those vulnerabilities. You will learn how to use Active Directory design to limit your exposure to security risks while maintaining support for computers running the early versions of Windows and UNIX that are present on most Windows networks.

CHOOSING ACTIVE DIRECTORY AUTHENTICATION METHODS

Active Directory supports many different operating systems running on member computers. To support this wide variety of operating systems, Active Directory supports several different authentication protocols: LAN Manager (LM), NTLMv1, NTLMv2, and **Kerberos**.

The LM, NTLMv1, and NTLMv2 authentication protocols use a challenge-response mechanism to authenticate users and computers running Windows Millennium Edition (Windows Me) and earlier operating systems, or computers running Windows 2000 or later that are not part of a domain. A user is prompted (the challenge) to provide some private piece of information unique to the user (the response). Whereas these three protocols are very similar because NTLMv1 and NTLMv2 are based on the original LM authentication protocol, their features did change with each new version. In order from least secure to most secure:

- **LM**   Developed jointly by IBM and Microsoft for use in OS2 and Microsoft Windows for Workgroups, Windows 95, Windows 98, and Windows Me. It is the least secure form of challenge-response authentication because it is susceptible to eavesdropping attacks. In addition, servers that authenticate users with LM authentication must store credentials in an **LM hash**, which is easily cracked.

- **NTLM version 1**   A more secure form of challenge-response authentication than LM. It connects to servers running Microsoft Windows NT 4.0 with Service Pack 3 or earlier. NTLMv1 uses 56-bit encryption to secure the protocol. Servers that authenticate users with any version of NTLM authentication must store credentials in an **NT Hash**. An NT Hash provides similar function to an LM hash, but is much more resistant to attack.

■ **NTLM version 2**   The most secure form of challenge-response authentication available on Windows networks; however, it is still less secure than using Kerberos. This version includes an encrypted channel to protect the authentication process. It is used for connecting to servers running Windows 2000, Windows XP, Microsoft Windows Server 2003, and Windows NT 4.0 with Service Pack 4 or later. NTLMv2 uses 128-bit encryption to protect the protocol from eavesdropping.

Kerberos is the default Active Directory authentication protocol for Windows Server 2003, Windows 2000, and Windows XP Professional. Kerberos is designed to be more secure and scalable than NTLM across large, diverse networks. Kerberos provides the following additional benefits to those provided by LM, NTLMv1, and NTLMv2:

■ **Efficiency**   When a server needs to authenticate a client, the server can validate the client's credentials without contacting a domain controller.

■ **Mutual authentication**   In addition to authenticating the client to the server, Kerberos enables the server to be authenticated to the client.

■ **Delegated authentication**   Allows services to impersonate clients when accessing resources on their behalf. This is particularly useful for architectures in which a front-end server (such as a Web server) must pass user credentials to a back-end server (such as a database server). For more information on delegated authentication, refer to Chapter 7, "Hardening Servers."

■ **Simplified trust management**   Kerberos can use **transitive trusts** between domains in the same **forest** and domains connected with a **forest trust**.

■ **Interoperability**   Kerberos is based on the Internet Engineering Task Force (IETF) standard (described in RFC 1510) to improve compatibility. Although interoperability is not guaranteed, most common non-Microsoft Kerberos software vendors do offer compatibility with the Active Directory Kerberos implementation.

For communication between systems in a heterogeneous network with both Windows and non-Windows clients to occur, all operating systems must support a common authentication algorithm. If you have non-Windows operating systems that haven't been updated for several years, it is possible that the operating system is not capable of supporting modern Windows authentication methods such as NTLMv2 and Kerberos. However, most popular non-Windows operating systems (especially Linux with the SAMBA package) are capable of supporting all standard authentication protocols on Windows networks. Table 5-1 lists common Windows and non-Windows operating systems and the current status of compatible authentication protocols.

Table 5-1   **Authentication Protocol Support**

Operating System	LM	NTLMv1	NTLMv2	Kerberos	Certificates
Windows 95/ Windows 98 out of the box	Yes	No	No	No	No
Windows 95/Windows 98 with Active Directory client	Yes	Yes	Yes	No	No
Windows NT 4.0 Service Pack 4	Yes	Yes	Yes	No	Yes
Windows 2000	Yes	Yes	Yes	Yes	Yes
Windows XP	Yes	Yes	Yes	Yes	Yes
Windows Server 2003	Yes	Yes	Yes	Yes	Yes
Linux with Samba Services	Optional	Optional	Optional	Yes	Yes
AS 400	No	No	No	Yes	Yes
Mainframe	No	No	No	Yes	Yes

NOTE   Authentication vs. Authorization: A Refresher   Whether you are withdrawing money from a bank, entering a restricted building, or boarding an airplane, gaining access to a restricted resource requires both authentication and authorization. The two processes are closely related and often confused. To understand the difference between authentication and authorization, consider an example in the physical world that most people are familiar with: boarding an airplane. Before you can board a plane, you must present both your identification and your ticket. Your identification, typically a driver's license or a passport, enables the airport staff to determine who you are. Validating your identity is the *authentication* part of the boarding process. The airport staff also checks your ticket to make sure that the flight you are boarding is the correct one. Verifying that you are allowed to board the plane is the *authorization* process.

Although Active Directory has authorization capabilities to restrict users from accessing specific objects in the Active Directory, its primary role is authentication. Authorization on Windows networks is typically handled by access control lists (ACLs) residing on the network resources themselves.

Windows networks have many other authentication methods, including mechanisms for authenticating IPSec hosts, virtual private network (VPN) clients, and Web servers and clients. Later chapters discuss these authentication methods. This chapter focuses on Active Directory authentication methods.

The sections that follow discuss LM, NTLM, and Kerberos authentication in more detail.

Assessing the Vulnerability of LM Authentication

You will need to use LM authentication to provide compatibility with earlier operating systems, including Windows 95, Windows 98, and Windows NT 4.0 Service Pack 3 or earlier. There are also earlier applications that might rely on this authentication mechanism. For example, earlier versions of third-party browsers support only LM authentication.

LM authentication is the weakest available authentication protocol and the easiest for a threat agent to compromise. Whenever possible, do not use LM authentication in an Active Directory environment. As the following section describes, LM authentication requires the Active Directory domain controllers to store LM hashes of passwords, and LM hashes are very vulnerable to attack.

You can eliminate the need for LM authentication by upgrading all operating systems and applications to support NTLMv1, NTLMv2, or Kerberos. In theory, this is a simple and obvious solution. In practice, most large organizations have computers and applications that cannot be upgraded without great expense. As you learned in Chapter 2, "Analyzing Risk," it's only worth it to upgrade earlier computer systems that require LM authentication support if the cost of the vulnerability introduced by LM authentication is greater than the cost of the upgrade. In many organizations, the cost of the upgrade is too high to justify, and you will have to focus on mitigating LM authentication vulnerabilities, rather than eliminating them.

The sections that follow discuss the LM authentication process (shared by LM, NTLMv1, and NTLMv2), the vulnerabilities of the LM hash store required by LM authentication, and how to mitigate those vulnerabilities by disabling LM passwords.

LM Authentication Process

As mentioned earlier, Windows networks support three methods of challenge-response authentication: LM, NTLMv1, and NTLMv2. The authentication process for all the methods is the same, but they differ in the level of encryption.

The following steps demonstrate the flow of events that occur when a client authenticates to a domain controller using any of the NTLM protocols:

1. The client and server negotiate an authentication protocol.

2. The client sends the user name and domain name to the domain controller in clear text.

> **NOTE**   **Discovering User Names**   Because user names and domain names are sent in clear text, anyone who can capture packets on your network can identify valid user names. This makes password-cracking attacks much easier. If you have account lockout enabled, the attacker could perform a denial-of-service attack by intentionally locking out user accounts knowing only the user name. This chapter discusses account lockouts in more detail in the section titled "Account Lockout Policy," later in this chapter.

3. The domain controller generates a 16-byte random character string called a **nonce** and sends the nonce to the client.

> **NOTE**   **The Need for a Nonce**   The purpose of the nonce might not be immediately obvious. After all, an attacker could capture the nonce as it is sent across the network. The nonce is key to protecting the authentication process because it keeps the LM hash or NT Hash secret and prevents replay attacks. If the nonce weren't used and the hashed password were sent across the network without further encryption, an attacker could authenticate to a server by simply resubmitting the captured hash—without ever knowing the original password that the hash is based on. By using a nonce, the attacker needs to crack the encryption created in step 4 to identify the hash before impersonating the user.

4. The client encrypts the nonce with the LM hash or NT Hash of the user password and sends it back to the domain controller.

5. The domain controller retrieves the valid hash of the user password from the security account database and encrypts the nonce with the hash. If the newly encrypted value matches what the client provided, the client is authenticated.

You don't need to memorize the LM authentication process to design Windows networks. However, understanding the process reveals several noteworthy vulnerabilities, and understanding those vulnerabilities will influence your network designs. In the first step, the client and server *negotiate* an authentication protocol. This enables the server to support multiple authentication mechanisms, which provides greater interoperability. It also introduces the possibility that a less-secure authentication protocol (such as LM rather than NTLM) will be used.

In the second step, the user name and domain name are transmitted to the domain controller in clear text. An attacker with the ability to capture traffic on your network, a client computer, or the authenticating server can therefore gather user names. Although user names alone do not enable an attacker to authenticate, they are a prerequisite for dictionary-based password attacks.

Storing LM Passwords

A major reason to use NTLMv1 or NTLMv2 instead of the original LM authentication protocol is that when a user creates a password and stores it for use with LM, LM converts it to an LM hash. The LM hash contains user names and hashes of the corresponding user password. When a client attempts to authenticate a user with LM authentication, LM transmits an encrypted version of the hash of the password, rather than the password itself, across the network. The server will be able to authenticate the user only if the server has the LM hash stored.

Using an LM hash is far more secure than storing the password in clear text. However, the LM hash has several weaknesses that make it more vulnerable to attack than the NT Hash used for NTLMv1 and NTLMv2. The LM hash is stored in all uppercase, is limited to 14 characters, and is divided into two discrete components before hashing. If a knowledgeable, malicious attacker does obtain access to LM hashes for a large number of users, it is likely that the attacker would be able to identify at least one user's password. Table 5-2 shows examples of passwords and the corresponding LM hashes that would be stored.

Table 5-2   **LM Passwords**

Password	LM hash
tiger	C6E4266FEBEBD6A8AAD3B435B51404EE
12345	AEBD4DE384C7EC43AAD3B435B51404EE
SECTION	D5F34F69EB965B8E3AAD3B435B51404EE
SYNERGY	CE910CFA90B123F9AAD3B435B51404EE
Player24	DD4B68A4219ED226FF17365FAF1FFE89

Examine Table 5-2 and notice that all passwords with fewer than 8 characters share the last 16 characters. During the process of computing the hash, LM divides the original password into two sets of 7 characters. If the password is 7 characters or fewer, the second set of 7 characters is null. This results in the last 16 characters being a well-known value that indicates to the attacker that the original password is fewer than 8 characters. Knowing that the password is short significantly reduces the amount of work an attacker needs to perform to identify the original password. This method of storing passwords makes the LM hash vulnerable to attacks that can reveal the unencrypted password.

Disabling LM Passwords

LM hash is an easy target for an attacker and, therefore, presents a significant risk. According to the SANS (SysAdmin, Audit, Network, Security) Institute, an organization that studies network security topics, "Since LM uses a much weaker encryption scheme than more current Microsoft approaches (NTLM and NTLMv2), LM passwords can be broken in a very short period of time. Even passwords that otherwise would be considered 'strong' can be cracked by brute-force in under a week on current hardware."

> **MORE INFO   Exploring Cracking Tools**   If you're still unconvinced about the vulnerabilities of LM authentication, do an Internet search for "LOphtcrack."

As mentioned earlier, if you currently have Windows NT 4.0 clients that require LM authentication, upgrade them to Service Pack 4 or later to enable the use of NTLMv2. NTLMv1 presents a significant security vulnerability. Some networks, unfortunately, cannot install Service Pack 4 because of application incompatibilities. If your organization faces this challenge, you must focus on mitigating the risk, rather than eliminating it. If you have client computers that are running Windows 95 or Windows 98, install the directory services client. You can install the directory services client from the Windows Server 2003 operating system CD or download the directory services client from *http://www.microsoft.com.*

If you can upgrade all clients to support at least NTLMv1, you can disable the LM hash to remove the vulnerabilities presented by LM authentication. However, if you have clients running Windows 3.1, the original release of Windows 95, or Windows NT 4.0 without Service Pack 4 or later, it is imperative that you do not disable the LM hash. For detailed information about disabling the LM hash, refer to Microsoft Knowledge Base article 299656 at *http://support.microsoft.com/ ?kbid=299656.*

If you can't completely disable LM hash because the upgrades are cost prohibitive, consider creating a separate domain for the computers that require LM authentication so that you can disable the storage of LM hashes in your primary domains. If you must enable LM hash in a domain, you can reduce the risk by disabling the use of the LM hash on an account-by-account basis. This is particularly useful for protecting accounts with administrative privileges.

To disable the LM hash for a single account, use passwords that are 15 characters or longer. Another option is to use specific ALT characters in passwords. Insert ALT characters into a password by holding down the ALT key, typing the ALT code using the number pad, and then releasing the ALT key.

> **NOTE ALT Character Ranges that Disable LM Hashes** Only specific ALT character ranges will disable the LM Hash. You don't need to memorize these, but be aware that not all ALT keys will work. The ALT character ranges that will disable the LM hash are 128–159, 306–307, 312, 319–320, 329–331, 383, 385–406, 408–409, 411–414, 418–424, 426, 428–429, 433–437, 439–447, 449–450, 452–460, 477, 480– 483, 494–495, 497–608, 610–631, 633–696, 699, 701–707, 709, 711, 716, 718–729, 731, 733–767, 773–775, 777, 779–781, 783–806, 808– 816, 819–893, 895–912, 914, 918–919, 921–927, 929–930, 933, 935– 936, 938–944, 947, 950–955, 957–959, 961–962, 965, and 967–1023.

Kerberos

Kerberos is the standard authentication method for Windows 2000 and later clients in Active Directory environments. Kerberos improves on the security provided by the various generations of LM authentication. In addition, it provides greater scalability for large networks.

Because Kerberos is an open standard, it is easier for non-Microsoft clients to interoperate with Active Directory domain controllers. However, although Kerberos itself is an open standard, and the Active Directory implementation of Kerberos complies with those standards, Active Directory adds functionality that can prevent it from transparently interoperating with non-Microsoft Kerberos implementations. It is fortunate that Active Directory is very popular, and that popularity has led most common non-Microsoft operating systems to offer some level of support for Kerberos authentication in Active Directory environments. Unless you have to support older client operating systems that do not support the technology, you should be able to configure all clients on your network to use Kerberos.

The sections that follow discuss the important role of the Kerberos Key Distribution Center (KDC) in Active Directory domains, the Kerberos authentication process, default domain policies for Kerberos tickets, and the role clock synchronization plays in Kerberos authentication.

What Is the Kerberos Key Distribution Center?

The Kerberos KDC is an Active Directory domain controller service that maintains a database of account information for all users and other security principals in the domain. When a security principal joins a domain, the security principal and the KDC establish a shared secret cryptographic key that they can use in future communications to identify themselves with very little risk of impersonation. This key is known as the **long-term key**. The long-term key is derived from a user's logon password.

Although Kerberos Key Distribution Center is the name of the KDC service that runs on domain controllers, other non-Microsoft implementations of the KDC exist for use in environments without Active Directory. However, all references to the KDC in this chapter refer specifically to the Active Directory implementation of the KDC.

The Kerberos Authentication Process

The Kerberos protocol gets its name from the three-headed dog in Greek mythology. The three components of Kerberos are

- The client requesting services or authentication.

- The server hosting the services requested by the client.

- A computer that is trusted by both the client and server: the KDC. On Windows networks, this is usually the Kerberos Key Distribution Center service on an Active Directory domain controller.

Kerberos authentication is based on specially formatted data packets known as *tickets*. In Kerberos, these tickets pass through the network instead of passwords. Transmitting tickets instead of passwords or password hashes makes the authentication process more resistant to attackers who can intercept the network traffic.

In a Kerberos environment, the authentication process begins at logon. This is different from the LM authentication process, which occurs when a user attempts to access a protected resource. The following steps describe the Kerberos authentication process:

1. When a user enters a user name and password, the client computer sends the user name in clear text to the KDC.

2. The KDC looks up the user's long-term key (KA), which is based on the user's password. The KDC then creates two items: a session key (SA) to share with the user and a Ticket-Granting Ticket (TGT). The TGT includes a second copy of the SA, the user name, and an expiration time among other details. The KDC encrypts this ticket by using its own master key (KKDC), which only the KDC knows.

> **NOTE**   *Secret Key Cryptography vs. Public Key Cryptography*
> *Kerberos implements secret key cryptography, which is different from public key cryptography in that it does not use a public and private key pair.*

3. The client computer receives the information from the KDC and runs the user's password through a one-way hashing function, which converts the password into the user's KA. The client computer now has a session key and a TGT so that it can encrypt communications with the KDC. The client is now authenticated to the domain and is ready to access other resources in the domain by using the Kerberos protocol.

> **NOTE Where Session Keys Are Stored**   When a client receives the session key and TGT from the server, it stores that information in volatile memory and not on the hard disk. Storing the information in the volatile memory and not on the hard disk makes the information more secure, because the information would be lost if the server were physically removed.

When a Kerberos client needs to access resources on a server that is a member of the same domain, it uses the following process to identify itself to the resource:

1. First, it contacts the KDC. The client presents its TGT and a timestamp encrypted with the session key that is already shared with the KDC. The KDC decrypts the TGT using its KKDC. The TGT contains the user name and a copy of the SA. The KDC uses the SA to decrypt the timestamp. The KDC can confirm that this request actually comes from the user because only the user could have access to the SA.

2. Next, the KDC creates a pair of tickets, one for the client and one for the server on which the client needs to access resources. Each ticket contains the name of the user requesting the service, the recipient of the request, a timestamp that declares when the ticket was created, and a time duration that says how long the tickets are valid. Both tickets also contain a new key (KAB) that will be shared between the client and the server so they can securely communicate.

3. The KDC takes the server's ticket and encrypts it using the server master key (KB). Then the KDC nests the server's ticket inside the client's ticket, which also contains the KAB. The KDC encrypts the whole thing using the session key that it shares with the user from the logon process. The KDC then sends all the information to the user.

4. When the user receives the ticket, the user decrypts it using the SA. This exposes the KAB to the client and also exposes the server's ticket. The user cannot read the server's ticket. The user will encrypt the timestamp by using the KAB and send the timestamp and the server's ticket to the server on which the client wants to access resources. When it receives these two items, the server first decrypts its own ticket by using its KB. This permits access to the KAB, which can then decrypt the timestamp from the client.

Now both the client and the server have the KAB, a shared secret (like a password) that has not been revealed on the network. The server can be sure that the client has truthfully identified itself because the client used the KAB to encrypt the timestamp. If it is necessary for the server to respond to the user, the server will use the KAB. The client will know that the server has truthfully identified itself because the server had to use its KB to get the KAB. Next, the resource will attempt to authorize the user.

Default Domain Policies for Kerberos Tickets

You can use Group Policy settings to fine-tune many aspects of the Kerberos authentication process. Table 5-3 describes the default domain policy options available for Kerberos tickets. These policy settings are located in the Kerberos Policy node in Account Policies.

Table 5-3   **Security Policy Settings for Kerberos Ticket Policy**

Security policy setting	Description
Enforce user logon restrictions	Determines whether the KDC validates every request for a session ticket by examining the user rights policy on the target computer. This option also serves as a means of ensuring that the requesting account is still valid and had not been disabled since the Kerberos ticket was issued. This option could potentially slow down network logons.
Maximum lifetime for service ticket	Determines the amount of time a service ticket is available before it expires. This setting should be set the same as the user ticket setting, unless your users run jobs that are longer than their user tickets would allow.
Maximum lifetime for user ticket	Determines the amount of time a user ticket is available before it expires. This setting should be set according to the average amount of time a user logs on to a computer at your organization.

Table 5-3   **Security Policy Settings for Kerberos Ticket Policy**

Security policy setting	Description
Maximum lifetime for user ticket renewal	Determines the number of days for which a user's TGT can be renewed. The default is seven days. Shortening this interval will increase security but put more load on the KDC.
Maximum tolerance for computer clock synchronization	Determines the maximum time difference (in minutes) between the time on the clock of the user's computer and the time on the domain controller. Raising this value from the default of five minutes increases your vulnerability to replay attacks, in which encrypted credentials captured from the network can be resubmitted by a malicious attacker. Lowering this value will increase the number of authentication failures caused by unsynchronized clocks. The following section describes this setting in more detail.

Setting Clock Synchronization Tolerance and Kerberos Ticket Lifetimes to Prevent Replay Attacks

Unlike LM authentication, Kerberos uses timestamps as part of the encryption. This means that both clients and servers must have their time synchronized for Kerberos authentication to be successful. This does not require you, as a security designer, to do anything for Windows clients because Active Directory clients are automatically configured to synchronize their time with a domain controller by using the Windows Time service. Non-Windows clients might have to be configured manually to synchronize time with a domain controller. For all clients, you need to ensure that clients can use the NTP (Network Time Protocol) or SNTP (Simple Network Time Protocol) to communicate with domain controllers. NTP and SNTP use UDP port 123 by default.

Kerberos clients can use the ticket issued by the KDC to authenticate to network services without sending another request to the KDC. This introduces a potential vulnerability: an attacker who cracks the encryption protecting a Kerberos ticket can authenticate to network resources until that ticket expires. Although you do not need to change the defaults, you have the option of specifying shorter or longer lifetimes for Kerberos tickets.

If you decide to change the default, establish reasonable lifetimes that are short enough to prevent attackers from cracking the cryptography that protects the ticket's stored credentials. As a rule of thumb, do not set the maximum ticket lifetime to more than twice the default. Reasonable ticket lifetimes must also be long enough to ensure that requests for new tickets do not overload the KDC and network. Avoid setting the minimum ticket lifetime to less than half the default.

You can use the Maximum Tolerance For Clock Synchronization Group Policy to define how closely the client and KDC times must match. By default, it is set to 5 minutes. In most cases, this provides an acceptable level of security. You can increase protection against replay attacks by shortening the maximum tolerance for clock synchronization. Tighter synchronization requirements, however, might result in increased authentication traffic.

Shortening the maximum tolerance reduces replay attacks because the Kerberos v5 authentication protocol uses authenticators based on time to establish user identities. A shorter tolerance makes a replay attack more difficult.

> **MORE INFO   Time Synchronization**   For more information about time synchronization in Windows Server 2003, see the Distributed Services Guide of the Windows Server 2003 Resource Kit (or see the Distributed Services Guide on the Web at *http://www.microsoft.com/reskit*).

DESIGNING PASSWORD SECURITY REQUIREMENTS

An attacker can identify a weak password in a matter of hours or days, even when the attacker has access only to an encrypted version of the password. Encryption cannot protect against passwords that are easily guessed because weak passwords are vulnerable to *dictionary attacks*. Dictionary attacks encrypt a list of common passwords and compare each possibility to the captured ciphertext. If the password appears in the password dictionary, the attacker will identify the password quickly. You can defend against this vulnerability by implementing a strong password policy.

> **NOTE   Exploring Password Dictionaries**   The best way to understand how effective dictionary attacks are is to grab a password-cracking tool from the Internet. I cannot point you to a specific one, but they are not hard to find.

What Is a Strong Password?

A strong password is one that can be remembered by the user but that is also complex enough to be difficult to guess. For example, *&_I5y#<.h might appear to be a good password, but the user might be forced to write it down to remember it, creating a significant security vulnerability. There are techniques, fortunately, for creating strong passwords that the human brain can remember.

One way to make it easier to remember a long password is to use a **passphrase**. For example, you could take a password that is easy to remember (and easy to guess), such as Birthday, and add an easy-to-remember prefix to it to make it more secure: I.Can't.Forget.My.Wife's.Birthday:0705. You now have a password that is 38 characters long, uses uppercase, lowercase, symbols, and numbers, is easy to remember, and that, because of the length, is harder than the *&_I5y#<.h password to crack.

> **NOTE   The Risks of Passphrases**   There's a risk to using pass-phrases: they haven't stood the test of time. Although passphrases are a very old idea, they haven't been commonly used in enterprise environments. If passphrases do become commonly used, password dictionaries will begin to incorporate commonly used passphrases such as HappyBirthdayToMe, HastaLaVistaBaby, and FranklyMyDear. Once this happens, passphrases might be as easily guessed as passwords. To offset this risk, make your passphrases complex by adding numbers and symbols.

In the previous example, multiple English words were added to the beginning of the password to make it complex. You can also add phone numbers, addresses, URLs, lock combinations, or anything else you can remember to make a password complex.

> **NOTE   The Benefits of Complex Passwords**   Besides being harder to crack, long and complex passwords are harder to shoulder surf (that is, watching someone type his or her password).

Strong Password Policy

To help implement a strong password policy, Windows Server 2003 provides a feature known as Password Complexity. Password Complexity is enforced by default in the Windows Server 2003 Active Directory environments, but disabled on stand-alone computers running Windows Server 2003. The Password Complexity feature requires that passwords have the following characteristics:

■ Do not contain all or part of the user's account name

- Be at least six characters in length

- Contain characters from three of the following four categories:

    ❑ Uppercase characters (A through Z)

    ❑ Lowercase characters (a through z)

    ❑ Base 10 digits (0 through 9)

    ❑ Nonalphabetic characters (for example, !, $, #, %)

> **NOTE   Windows Server 2003 Minimum Password Length**   By default, Windows Server 2003 requires that passwords be seven characters long, exceeding the requirement imposed by the Password Complexity feature.

Table 5-4 describes the security policy settings that you can use to implement a strong password policy. These policy settings are located in the Password Policy node in Account Policies.

Table 5-4 **Security Policy Settings for Strong Passwords**

Security policy setting	Description
Maximum Password Age	Determines how long passwords can be used before users are required to change them. The default value of 42 days is generally appropriate. This value, ideally, should be lower than the time it takes a commercial password-cracking program to compromise the passwords in your organization. Lowering this value decreases the likelihood that a password will be cracked while it is still valid, but might increase the number of support calls relating to forgotten passwords.
Enforce Password History	Stores the passwords that users have used previously and prevents reuse of those passwords. The default setting is also the maximum: 24 passwords remembered.
Minimum Password Age	Determines how long a user must keep a password before changing it. The default setting of one day will prevent a user from immediately changing a password to a previous one.

Table 5-4   **Security Policy Settings for Strong Passwords**

Security policy setting	Description
Minimum Password Length	Determines the minimum length of a password. The minimum recommended setting is the default of 7 characters.
Passwords Must Meet Complexity Requirements	Causes Windows Server 2003 to verify that new passwords meet complexity requirements. This setting is enabled by default.

Microsoft Operations and Technology Group (OTG), the group responsible for Microsoft's own internal password requirements, uses slightly more complex password requirements:

- Be at least 15 alphanumeric characters long on accounts with administrator privileges on the domain and at least seven alphanumeric characters long on all other accounts.

- Contain both upper- and lowercase characters, for example, a–z, A–Z.

- Have digits and punctuation characters as well as letters, for example, 0–9, !@#$%^&*()_+|~-=\`{}[]:";'<>?,./. One or more of these punctuation characters must be within the second to sixth positions.

- Contain no slang, dialect, or jargon words in any language.

  - ❑ Not be based on personal information, names of family, etc.

  - ❑ Not contain words that have the Os changed to zeros and/or I's to pipes.

  - ❑ Be significantly different from prior passwords. For example, users must not use cyclical passwords because they contain the same basic content as previous passwords, but with only a part of the content changed.

In addition, Microsoft OTG requires users to use smart cards for multifactor authentication. Microsoft's authentication requirements are costly, but they fit its security requirements because the risk posed by compromised user credentials is huge. Most organizations do not face the same level of risk as Microsoft and will not require such costly authentication requirements.

> **NOTE**   *Developing Custom Password Complexity Requirements*   *You can use the Microsoft Platform Software Development Kit (SDK) to develop custom password complexity requirements for your organization.*

When implementing and enforcing a password policy, consider the users' inability to remember passwords that change too often and are too complex or too long. When passwords are too complex or too long, users will use other methods to remember their passwords, such as writing them down.

> **NOTE The Benefits of Writing Down Passwords** There is not necessarily anything wrong with a user writing down a password to remember it, as long as the written copy is not easily accessible to potential attackers. Users actually feel more comfortable if they can write down their passwords, and are more likely to create more-complex passwords.

Assessing the Risk of Password-Cracking Threats

Every directory service is vulnerable, including Active Directory. It is obvious that you can reduce this vulnerability by such measures as disabling the storage of LM hashes. However, so long as a domain controller accepts authentication requests, you can never eliminate the threat of dictionary authentication attacks.

To launch a dictionary authentication attack, a threat starts with a list of common passwords known as a **password dictionary**. A password dictionary is simply a text file with thousands of passwords that users have historically created. These passwords include common words, such as "password," names such as "Tony," and even seemingly complex passwords, such as "yabba-dabba-doo." You can find general, comprehensive password dictionaries, and shorter language- and occupation-specific password dictionaries. The following is an excerpt from an actual password dictionary, found on the Internet by searching for the phrase "download password dictionary":

```
letter lettera letteral letterale letterali letterals letterari letteraria lettera
rio letteratura letterature letterbag letterbanket letterbased letterbeg letterbod
y letterbomb letterbombs letterbox letterboxed letterboxer letterboxers letterboxe
s letterboxing letterbyletter lettercard lettercol lettercolumn
```

Many administrators of Windows Server 2003 Active Directory domains would not feel threatened by the quoted password dictionary because none of the passwords would meet the default password-complexity requirements. However, a threat with scripting skills could easily generate complex passwords based on this dictionary by replacing lowercase letters with uppercase letters or similar numbers and symbols, just as many users do when tasked with creating a complex password. For example, a script could generate the following complex passwords based on the simple "lettercard" password:

- L3ttercard

- L3tterc@rd

- le77erc@Rd

- 13773rcArd

Complex passwords are still a good idea because the script would need to try many different combinations of letters and symbols for each simple password. However, the fact that most users do not generate truly random passwords means that dictionary-based attacks will continue to be a realistic vulnerability. To reduce your vulnerability further, audit authentication failures, regularly review your audit logs, and require regular password changes. As an alternative, you can implement an account lockout policy (described in the section titled "Account Lockout Policy," later in this chapter).

Assessing the Risk of Password-Resetting Attacks

If an attacker can gain physical access to a computer, he or she might be able to completely bypass the process of password guessing and simply reset a user's password to gain access to the operating system. Tools exist to reset passwords, and they have a dual nature, as follows:

- Administrators can reset lost passwords to regain access to a computer.

- Attackers can reset an unknown password to gain access to an operating system.

These tools work by bypassing the operating system security. The administrator or attacker boots the computer from a CD containing the password reset tool, and the tool directly modifies the Windows account database file to reset a user's password. The attacker can then authenticate as that user and access any files that have not been EFS-encrypted. A screenshot of one such tool is shown in Figure 5-1.

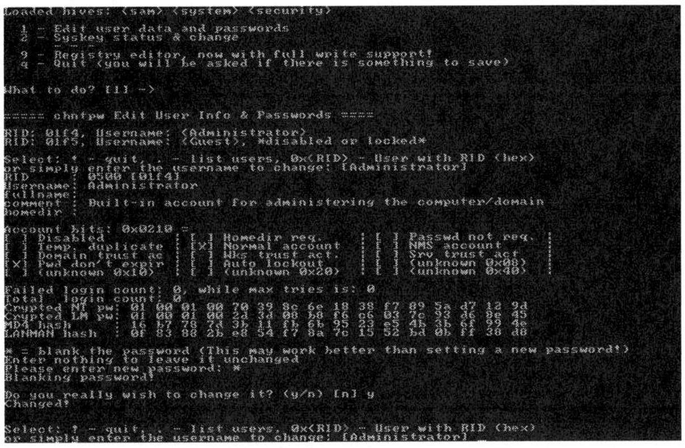

Figure 5-1   Password reset tools bypass operating system security.

Password reset tools are not typically capable of resetting Active Directory passwords. Instead, they attack the local user database on computers, granting an attacker administrative control over only the local computer. However, an attacker with administrative control on a single computer can use those privileges to acquire domain credentials by installing keyboard-monitoring software that records the user's user name and password as they type them.

To reduce the risk of password reset tools, follow these guidelines:

- Provide physical security for your servers.

- Require multifactor authentication for local logons to both servers and workstations.

- Use EFS to protect confidential user files.

Account Lockout Policy

Account lockout policies exist to limit your vulnerability to password-guessing attacks. When an account lockout policy is defined, a user account is automatically locked out after a specified number of incorrect password attempts. Windows Server 2003 does not enable account lockouts by default, and for a good reason: enabling account lockouts exposes you to a denial-of-service vulnerability. A malicious attacker with access to user names can guess incorrect passwords, causing those accounts to become locked out and denying legitimate users access to network resources.

Therefore, account lockout policies should be enabled only in environments in which the threat from guessed passwords is greater than the threat of a denial-of-service attack. Account lockout policies are set and enforced at the domain level. When enabled, these policies should be set to allow for user error, but to prevent attacks on user accounts.

> **NOTE   A Better Way to Identify Password-Cracking Attempts**
> The drawbacks to account lockout policies outweigh the benefits to most environments, and, if you have an intrusion detection system (IDS), account lockout policies are entirely redundant. An IDS will detect that an attacker is repeatedly guessing passwords and notify a system administrator. The system administrator can then track down the malicious attacker and stop the attack before the attacker successfully guesses the password.

Table 5-5 describes the various account lockout settings that you can use to secure your network. These policy settings are all located in the Account Lockout Policy node in Account Policies, except for Enforce User Logon Restrictions, which is located in the Kerberos Policy node in Account Policies.

Table 5-5   Password and Account Lockout Settings

Security policy setting	Description
Account Lockout Threshold	Determines how many logon attempts can be made before the account is locked out. This setting does not apply to attempts to log on at the console of a locked workstation or to attempts to unlock a screensaver, because locked workstations cannot be forced to run password-cracking programs.
Account Lockout Duration	Determines how many minutes a locked-out account will remain disabled before being automatically enabled. Setting this to 0 will require an administrator to unlock the account manually.
Reset Account Lockout Counter After	Determines the number of minutes that must elapse after a failed logon attempt before the counter is reset to 0 bad logon attempts.

Table 5-5   **Password and Account Lockout Settings**

Security policy setting	Description
Enforce User Logon Restrictions	When this option is enabled, the KDC validates every request for a session ticket by examining the user rights policy on the target computer. The user requesting the session ticket must be assigned the Log On Locally Policy (if the requested service is running on the same computer) or the Access This Computer From The Network Policy (if the requested service is on a remote computer) to receive a session ticket. This option also serves as a means to ensure that the requesting account is still valid. Verification is optional because the extra step takes time and might slow network access to services, but if account rights have changed or user accounts have been disabled between the time when the initial ticket was issued and the time when a service ticket was requested, these changes do not take effect. By default, the policy is enabled in the Default Domain Group Policy object (GPO). If the policy is disabled, this check is not performed. For greater security in an environment in which user accounts change frequently, enable this setting. For faster performance, particularly in a more stable user account environment, disable this setting.

Interoperability Problems with Long Passwords

Some applications have problems handling long passwords. In particular, applications that are older than a few years might not be designed to deal with passwords longer than 14 characters because when they were written, most passwords were fewer than 8 characters.

For example, if a user attempts to store a password that is longer than 14 characters for automatic logon to a computer running Windows 2000 Terminal Services, their logon will fail because Client Connection Manager can store only 14-character passwords. In a similar way, the Run.exe tool included in Windows NT 3.51 can accept passwords of up to only 14 characters in length. If you have custom applications that prompt for user credentials, they might also have similar problems with complex passwords.

NOTE **Testing with Long Passwords**   Talk to your development quality assurance team, and have it test existing and new custom applications with long passwords.

The Limitations of Technical Controls

Whenever possible, use technical controls to enforce password policy. However, understand that technical controls have limitations, as follows:

- Other risks might compromise the benefits provided by password-complexity requirements.

- Users must be forced to create passwords using characters, numbers, and symbols. This will prevent casual password guessing. However, untrained users might do the following:

  - Write down passwords in easily discovered places. This is especially true where passwords must change frequently and be complex and long. Research has shown that seven is the maximum number of letters or numbers that most people can easily remember.

  - Share passwords with co-workers. Often, employees share their passwords to provide access to temporary employees who do not have accounts or to users who lack the necessary privileges to access a resource.

  - Change only one character in their new password. The operating system sees this as a new password and the history requirement will not prevent this type of password reuse. To an attacker who knows an old password, the obvious strategy when refused its use is to change one character and try again. Attackers know the typical user will change the last character because this change is more easily remembered.

- Resetting passwords introduces vulnerabilities. Users forget their password and must have it reset. The typical resource for password changes is the Help Desk. A strong Help Desk policy, training, and enforcement practice must be used to ensure that this privilege is not abused and that the risk of social-engineering attacks is mitigated. In particular, you must have a way to authenticate the user, such as physically examining his or her identification. In addition, ensure that users immediately change their passwords. The person who reset the password knows the new password. You can force this reset by setting the account property User Must Change Password At Next Logon. If this is not set, the user might not remember to change the password. The individual who resets the password might realize this and use the opportunity to take advantage of that knowledge.

■ You can have only one effective password policy per domain. When you use a domain account to authenticate with the domain, the password is governed by only one password policy regardless of the location of the object in Active Directory or the presence of other password policies.

> **NOTE   Planning Domain Password Policies**   *A domain can have only one password policy for objects that authenticate with the domain. Separate password policies can be configured in GPOs linked to organizational units (OUs). However, that policy will affect only the local account database of the computers that reside in the domain OUs.*

DESIGNING MULTIFACTOR AUTHENTICATION

To authenticate a user on a network with some reasonable certainty that the user is who he or she claims to be, the user needs to provide two pieces of information: identification and proof of identity. In most networks, users identify themselves with a user name or an e-mail address. The way users prove their identity varies, however.

The tradition has been that a password proves a user's identity. A password is a form of a shared secret. The user knows his or her password, and the server authenticating the user either has the password stored or has some information that can be used to validate the password.

Passwords prove your identity because they are *something you know*. Other ways to prove your identity are with *something you have* or *something you are*. Many modern computer systems authenticate users by reading a secret key from a smart card—something you have. Other computer systems are satisfied that you are who you claim to be only when you prove it with something you are. Biometrics can do this by scanning a unique part of your body such as your fingerprint, your retina, or your facial features.

Passwords can be guessed and smart cards can be stolen. One form of authentication alone might not meet your organization's security requirements. Multifactor authentication combines two or more authentication methods and significantly reduces the likelihood that an attacker will be able to impersonate a user during the authentication process. The most common example of multifactor authentication is combining a smart card with a password or a personal identification number (PIN). The password typically is required to retrieve a key stored on the smart card. Before you can authenticate to such a system, you must provide a password (something you know) and a smart card (something you have).

Multifactor Authentication Benefits

Multifactor authentication can meet several important security requirements. Before considering the use of multifactor authentication, go through the Security Risk Management Process to identify potential vulnerabilities. Then, consider multifactor authentication as a countermeasure to specific vulnerabilities. Thinking about the benefits of multifactor authentication without assessing the risk of the vulnerabilities it mitigates can lead you to spend your security budget ineffectively.

With that caveat, requiring multifactor authentication can mitigate the two most common vulnerabilities in authentication systems:

- **Users sharing passwords**   Users often share their credentials to help coworkers who are having authentication or authorization problems. This is a problem for security administrators because audit logs can no longer identify the specific user who performed an action. Smart cards make sharing credentials much more difficult, because each user must physically have the smart card in his or her possession to use it.

> **NOTE**   Using Training to Minimize Risks   If you don't have multifactor authentication, you can mitigate the risk of users sharing passwords by training users about the risks. They should understand that if they share their password or smart card, they take responsibility for everything the person they loan it to does. In addition, your information technology (IT) group should have

efficient processes in place to ensure that all users, including temporary employees, receive unique passwords or smart cards as soon as they begin work. Most employees resort to sharing a password to enable other employees' productivity while the unauthorized employees are waiting for the IT group to issue official credentials.

■ **Attackers stealing passwords**   Whether by dictionary password cracking or by "shoulder surfing," a threat who gains access to a user's user name and password can authenticate as that user on most networks. A threat who steals a password on a network that requires smart card authentication would need to also steal the user's smart card—a step that is significantly more risky for the threat. Even if the threat does steal a smart card and knows how to use it, the stolen smart card is much more likely to be noticed by the user than a stolen password, increasing the likelihood that the user will call the help desk and have the account disabled before the threat can abuse the stolen credentials.

Smart-Card Costs

To decide whether smart card authentication is appropriate for your organizations, evaluate the potential benefits against the following considerations:

■ **Equipment costs**   Deploying smart cards entails initial equipment costs for the purchase of smart cards and smart-card readers, as well as administrative costs for preparing and distributing smart cards.

■ **Infrastructure costs**   A public key infrastructure (PKI) is required for smart-card authentication because the smart cards carry public key certificates to identify each unique card.

> **MORE INFO**   For more information about PKI, refer to Chapter 9, "Designing a Public Key Infrastructure."

- **Training costs**   Users must be trained to set the PIN on their smart cards, to use their smart cards properly with their computer hardware, and to care for their smart cards to avoid damaging them.

- **Administration costs**   If a user forgets a password, a quick phone call can reset it. Smart cards are more difficult and costly to replace, especially for users who travel or work in remote offices. In addition, users can have more problems with smart cards than with passwords, increasing the number of calls to the support desk.

- **User impact**   Users are accustomed to remembering a user name and password, but they're probably not used to carrying a smart card and using it each time they need to authenticate. Users will complain about the inconvenience. In addition, users on dial-up connections might experience noticeably slower logon times. If a user loses or damages a smart card, they will be unable to connect to your network until the smart card is replaced or the smart-card requirement is removed from their user account.

- **Development costs**   Applications that authenticate users, such as Web applications, must be extended to support smart cards. It might not be possible to update some applications on your network, meaning they will need to either be replaced or continue to use traditional password-based authentication. If an application includes the Certified for Windows Server 2003 logo, the application has been tested to ensure that it supports smart-card logons.

Because of the potential costs and administrative burden, many organizations choose to deploy smart cards only to certain groups of users, such as administrators or users who have access to extremely sensitive data.

DESIGNING ACTIVE DIRECTORY FORESTS

Designing an Active Directory is a huge responsibility because the way you design the Active Directory can expose you to significant vulnerabilities. For a security designer, the forest architecture, in particular, deserves a great deal of attention because forests are the only true **security boundary** in Active Directory environments (because domain administrators can elevate their privileges in trusted domains).

The process of designing a **forest** architecture is divided into five steps:

1. Assess the need for isolation.

2. Identify the forest model.

3. Identify the domain model.

4. Select the forest root domain.

5. Harden trust security.

The sections that follow give a brief overview of Active Directory components to refresh your memory and then detail each of these five steps.

Active Directory Overview

You are probably already familiar with the role Active Directory fulfills for authenticating users on a domain. Briefly, Active Directory stores and organizes a list of users that have some level of access to network resources. Network resources that participate in an Active Directory domain rely on the Active Directory domain controllers to authenticate a user's credentials before the network resource determines whether the user is authorized to access the resource. Active Directory enables administrators to organize these users in a variety of ways to delegate administrative responsibilities, simplify administration, and improve security.

Active Directory allows administrators to organize elements of a network (such as users, computers, devices, and so on) into a hierarchical containment structure. The top-level container is the forest. Within forests are domains, and within domains are organizational units.

Understanding the Role of Forests

A forest is a collection of one or more Active Directory domains that share a common structure, global catalog, directory schema, and directory configuration, as well as automatic two-way transitive trust relationships. When domains are added to a forest, they inherit the root domain name, schema, and other characteristics from the forest root domain. Figure 5-2 shows an example of a forest.

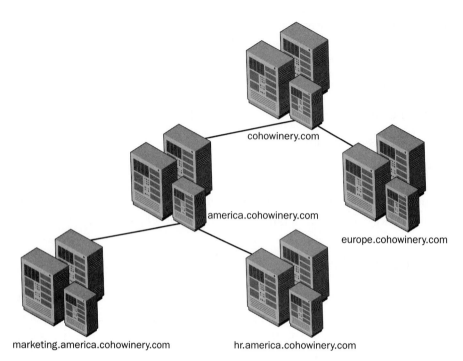

cohowinery.com

america.cohowinery.com

europe.cohowinery.com

marketing.america.cohowinery.com   hr.america.cohowinery.com

Figure 5-2   A forest is a collection of Active Directory domains.

Each forest is a single instance of the directory and defines a **security boundary**. A security boundary is a logical division that separates users outside the boundary from resources inside the boundary. Unless an administrator inside the security boundary explicitly allows it, users outside the boundary have absolutely no access.

That a forest is a security boundary is significant, and will be a key consideration when designing Active Directory architectures. This fact means that no administrators from outside the forest can control access to information inside the forest unless first given permission to do so by the administrators within the forest— even if a trust exists.

Understanding the Role of Domains

A **domain** is a partition in an Active Directory forest. In contrast to a forest, a domain is not a security boundary because within a forest it is not possible for administrators from one domain to prevent a malicious administrator from another domain from accessing data in their domain. This is a key point to understand: domain boundaries do not provide absolute protection from administrators in other domains.

Partitioning data into a domain enables you to control the replication of Active Directory data, allowing you to scale the directory globally over a network that has limited available bandwidth. In addition, creating separate domains enables you to specify different account settings for users in a domain. Creating separate domains does not prevent malicious administrators in trusted domains from accessing your resources, however.

Many smaller organizations are able to manage their network resources by using a single Active Directory domain. In the single-domain model, all user and computer accounts are contained within a single domain. Users must have an account in that domain to access network resources. Although the simplicity of a single domain makes it ideal, many circumstances require multiple domains that must interact with each other.

Windows Server 2003 requires that enterprises create multiple domains to apply different security policies to users or resources. Some aspects of an enterprise's security policy, such as minimum password length, can be defined only once for an entire Active Directory domain. Therefore, if an organization within the enterprise requires higher security than the rest of the enterprise, that organization might require its own domain.

Many enterprises use multiple domains for historical reasons. It was common practice to separate users from resources or to create separate Windows NT 4.0 domains for each geographic location. Although those are not valid reasons to create separate Windows 2000 Server or Windows Server 2003 domains, enterprises might choose to maintain an existing, if outdated, domain model.

Understanding the Role of OUs

OUs are used to form a hierarchy of containers within a domain. Organizational units are used to group objects for administrative purposes such as the application of Group Policies or delegation of authority. Control over an OU and the objects within it is determined by the ACLs on the OU and on the objects in the OU.

One of the most useful aspects of an OU is to simplify delegation of authority. By means of delegation, owners can transfer full or limited authority over objects to other users or groups. Delegation is important because it helps to distribute the management of large numbers of objects across a number of people trusted to perform management tasks.

Assess the Need for Isolation

To create a forest design for your organization, you must identify the business requirements that your directory structure needs to accommodate. The most important requirement to identify is the level of isolation IT groups need.

For example, do the IT people in different regions work together to manage resources, or do they insist that different IT groups have no access to their domain? Will they be satisfied with their own domain in a larger forest, which would give them control over their security policies? Do they need separate forests to form a proper security boundary to protect themselves from potential attacks from other domain administrators or the forest administrators? If they prefer separated forests, are they willing to fund the additional infrastructure computers that will be required to create separate forests?

Gather Requirements

To assess the need for isolation fully, discuss the following types of requirements with regional IT managers:

- **Organizational structure requirements**   Parts of an organization might participate in a shared infrastructure to save costs, but require the ability to operate independently from the rest of the organization. For example, a research group within a large organization might need to maintain control over all their own research data.

- **Operational requirements** One part of an organization might place unique constraints on the directory service configuration, availability, or security, or use applications that place unique constraints on the directory. Examples are found in the following:

  - ❏ Military organizations

  - ❏ Hosting scenarios

  - ❏ Organizations that maintain a directory that is available both internally and externally (publicly accessible by users on the Internet)

- **Legal requirements** Some organizations have legal requirements to operate in a specific way, such as by restricting access to certain information as specified in a business contract. Failure to meet these requirements can result in loss of the contract and possibly legal action. These requirements commonly apply to the following types of organizations:

  - ❏ Financial institutions that need to maintain private client financial records

  - ❏ Defense contractors that are working on classified military projects

  - ❏ Government organizations that maintain top-secret data

  - ❏ Organizations that are required to maintain separate infrastructure to conform to antitrust laws

In the short term, it's always less expensive to build a unified Active Directory design. It's simpler to manage and deploy, and fewer Active Directory domain controllers are required. However, unified Active Directory designs have security vulnerabilities, and the risk associated with those vulnerabilities might be high for your organization. To mitigate these risks, create isolated forests. Depending on your security needs, the security risks of a unified Active Directory design might outweigh the costs of building multiple, isolated forests.

Assess the Risk Posed by Administrators

All large organizations have systems administrators responsible for managing computers. These systems administrators have a job to do, and their job tasks often require them to be able to access confidential files, change permissions on protected objects, and increase a user's rights on the network.

The power granted to systems administrators, combined with their detailed knowledge of networking technologies, makes them a significant security risk. Some systems administrators might abuse their privileges for vengeance or financial gain. Others might have their account credentials compromised, enabling an outside attacker to abuse their privileges. Active Directory is no exception to this—someone must be able to manage the Active Directory, and that same individual has the power to compromise it.

At the level of an Active Directory forest, this powerful individual is known as the forest owner. Forest owners have been granted rights to administer the forest, such as being a member of the Enterprise Admins group. At the domain level, they are known as service administrators. Service administrators have been granted rights to administer a domain, such as being a member of the Domain Admins group. In theory, both roles have full access to all the data in the forest. Service administrators have the ability to do the following:

- Modify object ACLs. This enables the service administrator to read, modify, or delete objects regardless of the ACLs that are set on those objects.

- Modify the system software on a domain controller to bypass normal security checks. This enables the service administrator to view or manipulate any object in the domain, regardless of the ACL on the object.

- Use the Restricted Groups security policy to grant any user or group administrative access to any computer joined to the domain. Service administrators can thus obtain control of any computer joined to the domain, regardless of the intentions of the computer owner.

- Reset passwords or change group memberships for users.

■ Gain access to other domains in the forest by modifying the system software on a domain controller. Service administrators can affect the operation of any domain in the forest, view or manipulate forest configuration data, view or manipulate data stored in any domain, or view or manipulate data stored on any computer joined to the forest.

Because service administrators have these capabilities, organizations that participate in a forest must accept the risk that administrators will abuse the power. During the Security Risk Management Process, weigh the risk of an administrator becoming an attacker. The larger the forest, the more administrators there are likely to be, and the greater the risk involved for everyone in the forest.

If you determine this risk to be significant, you can alter your forest design to contain the potential damage from a single compromise. By dividing an organization into multiple forests, you create security boundaries. If you divide administrative responsibilities between forests, a single compromised account or disgruntled administrator can affect a single forest only. The risk still exists, but it is reduced because the scope of the damage is smaller.

You might not be able to prevent an administrator from abusing privileges, but you can detect it, limit the damage, and recover from it. In specific terms, consider using security auditing to track the actions of administrators. To reduce the risk of administrators covering their tracks by clearing the log files, develop a system that constantly moves the Security event logs to a system that your administrators do not control. Simply making administrators aware that you have implemented auditing capabilities might be sufficient to deter attacks.

Some organizations might determine that the collaborative and cost-saving benefits of participating in a shared infrastructure outweigh the risks that service administrators deliberately misuse or are coerced into misusing their authority. These organizations can share a forest and use OUs to delegate authority. However, other organizations might not accept this risk because the consequences of a compromise in security are too severe. Those organizations require separate forests. Be aware that using multiple forests carries its own costs, because you must consider the following additional complexities when designing the forests:

■ **Establishing forest trusts**   You need to design and establish trusts between the forests to allow users to access resources in remote forests.

- **Enabling DNS name resolution**   When Domain Name System (DNS) is integrated into Active Directory, you might need to enable DNS name resolution between forests to provide domain controller and resource location functionality.

- **Synchronizing sites and subnets**   To optimize performance when accessing resources in trusting forests, you need to configure identical sites and subnets in all forests. This will ensure that clients contact the closest domain controller or distributed file system (DFS) share when accessing resources in trusted forests.

- **Synchronizing printer locations**   To enable users to find the closest printer when printers are located in a trusting domain, you will need to synchronize printer information between forests using a tool such as Microsoft Identity Integration Server 2003.

- **Integrating multiple Exchange servers**   You must use synchronization, such as that provided by the Microsoft Exchange Interorg Replication Utility, to synchronize address lists and calendar information when Exchange servers are in different forests.

> **MORE INFO**   **Designing Multiple Forest Architectures**   For more information about designing multiple forests, read the white paper titled "Multiple Forest Considerations in Windows 2000 and Windows Server 2003," at *http://www.microsoft.com/technet/prodtechnol/windowsserver2003/ technologies/directory/activedirectory/mtfstwp.mspx*.

Identify the Forest Model

To determine the number of forests you must deploy, you need to carefully identify the isolation requirements for each group in your organization and map those requirements to the appropriate forest design models.

If you are coming from a Windows NT 4.0 environment, the decision process for creating your Active Directory logical structure design is different from the decision process for deploying Windows NT 4.0 domains. It is not always appropriate for you to attempt to model your existing Windows NT 4.0 infrastructure when creating your Active Directory forest design.

Determining the number of forests to deploy involves balancing costs against benefits. A single-forest model is the most cost-effective option and requires the least amount of administrative overhead. In addition, a single forest is the easiest configuration to manage and allows for maximum collaboration within the environment because all objects in a single forest are listed in a single global catalog. Therefore, no cross-forest synchronization is required.

Although a group in the organization might prefer to be isolated, the isolation might not be in the best interests of your organization as a whole. Your design decisions must be driven by the priorities of executive management. If first-level managers or employees who are not managers push you to make forest design decisions that will cost your organization a great deal of money, verify the justification with higher-level management.

You can apply one of the following four forest design models (or a combination of one or more) in your Active Directory environment:

- Single-forest model
- Organizational forest model
- Resource forest model
- Restricted-access forest model

The sections that follow describe each of these four models.

Single-Forest Model

In the single-forest model, several autonomous groups each own a domain within a forest. Because each group owns its own domain, it can make some kinds of design decisions (such as password length requirements) without needing to come to a consensus with other groups.

Because a domain is not a security boundary, groups are not protected from attacks launched by administrators of other domains. In a single-forest model, a malicious service administrator in one domain can access any other domain within the forest. Before choosing the single-forest model, make sure that all domain owners are aware of this risk and are willing to accept it.

Organizational Forest Model

In the organizational forest model, user accounts and resources are contained in the forest and managed independently. The organizational forest can be used to selectively provide both unification and isolation where you need it. Simply group the organizations that need to share resources without being isolated into a single forest. Create separate domains within the forest as needed. Organizations that need total isolation belong in a separate forest.

If users in an organizational forest need to access resources in other forests, or vice versa, trust can be established between one organizational forest and the other forests, as shown in Figure 5-3. This makes it possible for administrators to grant access to resources in the other forest, providing selective sharing.

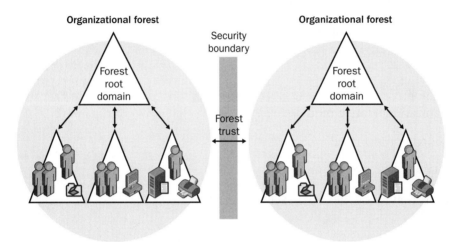

Figure 5-3   The organizational forest model provides isolation for organizations that require confidentiality.

Resource Forest Model

In the resource forest model, a separate forest is used to manage resources. Resource forests do not contain user accounts other than those required for service administration and those required to provide alternate access to the resources in that forest if the user accounts in the organizational forest become unavailable. Forest trusts are established so that users from other forests can access the resources contained in the resource forest, as shown in Figure 5-4.

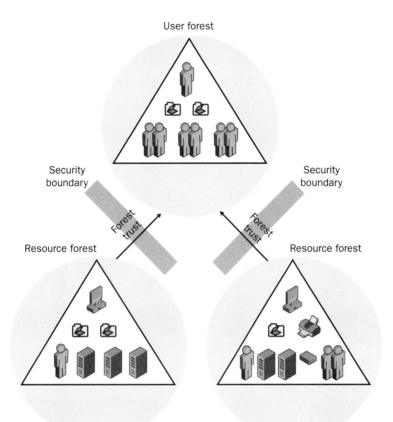

Figure 5-4 The resource forest model separates user accounts from resources.

Resource forests provide isolation that can protect areas of the network that need to maintain a state of high availability. For example, if your company includes computers that run manufacturing equipment that needs to continue to operate when there are problems on the rest of the network, you can create a separate resource forest for the manufacturing group. This does not provide any guarantee that the resource forest will not fail. However, the resource forest is less likely to be affected by problems in other forests.

Determine whether the cost of a resource forest is justified by using the Security Risk Management Process, as described in Chapter 2. First, estimate the likelihood of a failure in a single forest architecture affecting critical resources, and then estimate the cost of that failure. Then, estimate the likelihood of a forest failure when using the resource forest model; it should be slightly lower. Compare the annualized loss expectancy for each model to determine the savings. In most environments, the savings that result from the very slightly improved theoretical uptime won't be great enough to justify the cost of maintaining a separate resource forest, and you will be better off using a single-forest model.

Restricted-Access Forest Model

In the restricted-access forest model, a separate forest is created to contain user accounts and data that must be isolated from the rest of the organization. Restricted-access forests are usually used to isolate data for highly confidential projects that should be accessed only by a limited number of users. Figure 5-5 shows a restricted-access forest model.

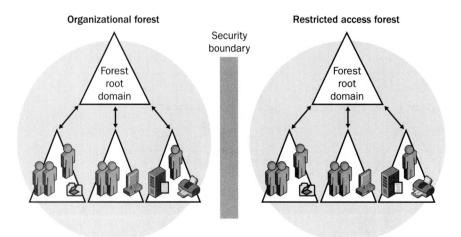

Figure 5-5   The restricted-access forest model completely separates resources involved in highly confidential projects.

Users from other forests cannot be granted access to the restricted data because no trust exists. In this model, users have an account in an organizational forest for access to general organizational resources and a separate user account in the restricted-access forest for access to the classified data. These users must have two separate workstations, one connected to the organizational forest and the other connected to the restricted-access forest. This protects against the possibility that a service administrator from one forest can gain access to a workstation in the restricted forest.

In extreme cases, the restricted-access forest might be maintained on a separate physical network. Organizations that work on classified government projects sometimes maintain restricted access forests on separate networks in order to meet government security requirements.

Identify the Domain Model

Once you have identified your forest model, determine how domains will be organized within each forest. If you are migrating from an existing Windows NT 4.0 environment with separate domains for different organizations, you can't use the same domain model and achieve the same level of isolation. Domains within an Active Directory forest do not have the same administrative and security boundaries that exist in a Windows NT 4.0 environment. Rather than basing your new design on the previous Windows NT 4.0 domain model, start from scratch by gathering requirements from each organization.

As an example of how multiple domains can be used within a forest, Figure 5-6 shows a single-forest model with a forest root domain and three other domains. These domains might exist to create a logical separation of resources, to enable different divisions to have different domain-wide security policies, or to maintain a legacy domain design.

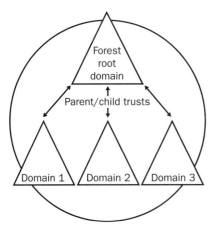

Figure 5-6   A single-forest model provides no solid security boundaries, but meets the needs of many organizations.

Unless you specifically need multiple domains within your forest, always use a single domain. Single domains simplify management and reduce infrastructure costs. The sections that follow describe why you would want to create multiple domains rather than having just a single domain in your forest, and the risks that domain owners must accept when participating in a forest with other domains.

Reasons to Create Multiple Domains

Domains in a forest cannot be used for security boundaries, but this doesn't mean that you should never design a forest with multiple domains. Creating separate domains does give the domain owners options that they would not have if you created a single domain. Table 5-6 lists the types of service management that can be controlled at the domain level.

Table 5-6   **Types of Service Management Controlled at the Domain Level**

Type of service management	Associated tasks
Management of domain controller operations	■ Creating and removing domain controllers ■ Monitoring the functioning of domain controllers ■ Managing services that are running on domain controllers ■ Backing up and restoring the directory
Configuration of domain-wide settings	■ Creating domain and domain user account policies, such as password, Kerberos, and account lockout policies ■ Creating and applying domain-wide Group Policies
Delegation of data-level administration	■ Creating OUs and delegating administration ■ Repairing problems in the OU structure that OU owners do not have sufficient access rights to fix
Management of external trusts	■ Establishing trust relationships with domains outside the forest

Other types of service management, such as schema or replication topology management, are the responsibility of the forest owner.

Accepting the Risks of Participating in a Forest

In a single-forest model, domain owners are responsible for domain-level service management tasks. Domain owners have authority over the entire domain, as well as some level of access to all other domains in the forest. The domain owner can escalate his or her user account privileges to perform domain management functions in any domain in the forest, so if this domain owner becomes malicious, or his or her credentials are compromised, the forest becomes vulnerable to attack.

For this reason, domain owners in a forest must trust each other. If one domain owner doesn't enforce a high level of security for his or her domain, every domain in the forest is exposed to their security vulnerabilities. If this risk is not acceptable to all domain owners, then create multiple forests. In addition, if these conditions change in the future, you might need to migrate the domains into a multiple-forest deployment.

Select the Forest Root Domain

The first domain that you deploy in an Active Directory forest is called the forest root domain. This domain remains the forest root domain for the life cycle of the Active Directory deployment.

The forest root domain contains the Enterprise Admins and Schema Admins groups. These service administrator groups manage forest-level operations such as the addition and removal of domains and the implementation of changes to the schema.

Selecting the forest root domain involves determining whether one of the Active Directory domains in your domain design can function as the forest root domain, or whether you need to deploy a dedicated forest root domain.

If you are applying a single-domain model, then the single domain functions as the forest root domain. If you are applying a multiple-domain model, you can choose to deploy a dedicated forest root domain or select a regional domain to function as the forest root domain. The sections that follow discuss each of these approaches.

Dedicated Forest Root Domain

A **dedicated forest root domain** is a domain created specifically to function as the forest root. It does not contain any user accounts other than the service administrator accounts for the forest root domain, and it does not represent any region in your domain structure. All other domains in the forest are children of the dedicated forest root domain.

Using a dedicated forest root provides the following advantages:

- **Operational separation of forest service administrators from domain service administrators**   In a single-domain environment, members of the Domain Admins or built-in Administrators groups can use standard tools and procedures to make themselves members of the Enterprise Admins and Schema Admins groups. In a forest that uses a dedicated forest root domain, members of the Domain Admins or built-in Administrators groups in the regional domains cannot make themselves members of the forest-level service administrator groups by using standard tools and procedures.

> **CAUTION**   The Risks of Using Domains as Security Boundaries
> Because a domain is not a security boundary, it is possible for a malicious service administrator, such as a member of the Domain Admins group, to use nonstandard tools and procedures to gain full access to any domain in the forest or to any computer in the forest. For example, service administrators in a non-root domain can make themselves members of the Enterprise Admins or Schema Admins group.

- **Protection from operational changes in other domains**   A dedicated forest root domain does not represent a particular region in your domain structure. For this reason, it is not affected by reorganizations or other changes that result in the renaming or restructuring of domains.

- **A neutral root so that no region appears to be subordinate to another region**   Some organizations might prefer to avoid the appearance that one country/region is subordinate to another country/region in the namespace. When you use a dedicated forest root domain, all regional domains can be peers in the domain hierarchy.

In a multiple regional domain environment in which a dedicated forest root is used, the replication of the forest root domain has minimal impact on the network infrastructure. This is because the forest root hosts only the service administrator accounts. The majority of the user accounts in the forest and other domain-specific data are stored in the regional domains.

The only significant disadvantages to using a dedicated forest root domain are that it creates additional management overhead to support the additional domain and requires additional infrastructure servers to act as domain controllers.

Regional Domain as a Forest Root Domain
If you choose not to deploy a dedicated forest root domain, you must select a regional domain to function as the forest root domain. This domain is the parent domain of all the other regional domains and will be the first domain you deploy. The forest root domain contains user accounts and is managed in the same way that the other regional domains are managed. The primary difference is that it also includes the Enterprise Admins and Schema Admins groups.

The advantage to selecting a regional domain to function as the forest root domain is that it does not create the additional management overhead that maintaining an additional domain creates, and doesn't require any additional domain controllers.

Select an appropriate regional domain to be the forest root, such as the domain that represents your headquarters or the region that has the fastest network connections. If it is difficult for your organization to select a regional domain to be the forest root domain, you can choose to use a dedicated forest root model instead.

In a Windows Server 2003 environment, global availability of the forest root is not as important as it is in Windows 2000 because forest-wide application partitions automatically replicate the forest-wide locator record zone to all domain controllers that are running DNS. Any domain controller can be used to write updates to the forest-wide locator records zone. In a Windows 2000 environment, DNS does not use a forest-wide application partition; therefore, it is recommended that a dedicated forest root be used to make the zone containing the writable copy of the forest-wide locator records highly available.

Harden Trust Security

A **trust** is a relationship established between domains or forests that enables users and other security principals from one domain to be authenticated by domain controllers in another domain. Enterprises that have multiple domains often need to allow users in one domain to access resources in another domain. Active Directory provides security across multiple domains and forests by using domain and forest trusts. Trusts are a critical part of a networking infrastructure, and one of the concepts that seems to be misunderstood quite frequently.

Configuring a trust enables a domain to authenticate users and other security principals that exist in a remote domain. A trust does not authorize users to access resources in the remote domain, however. Network resources authorize trusted users just as they would authorize a user in the local domain: through security descriptors on the resources that need to be accessed.

For example, if John has an account in domain A and attempts to print to a printer in domain B immediately after the trust has been created, he will be denied access. However, because the trust is in place, an administrator will be able to grant John's account access to print to the printer. Without the trust in place, the administrator would not be able to select John's user account when authorizing users to print.

You can also create trusts between forests. Use these trusts when two organizations need to share resources, but require a security boundary that exposes each organization to minimal risk of attack from the trusted organization. For example, if two organizations are in the process of a merger and they each have their own Active Directory forests, a forest trust would simplify sharing of resources.

In another common forest trust scenario, a service provider with an Active Directory forest containing user accounts needs permissions to manage resources within a customer's forest. A forest trust is ideal for this situation because it enables some level of access without requiring the customer to trust the service provider with full access to their forest.

Table 5-7 describes the types of trusts supported in Windows Server 2003.

Table 5-7 **Windows Server 2003 Trusts**

Trust type	Description
Parent/child trust	In Windows Server 2003, this is a default trust between all domains in the forest. This two-way transitive trust allows security principals to be authenticated in any domain in the forest. These trusts are created by default and cannot be removed.
Tree/root trust	In Windows Server 2003, this is a default trust between all domain trees in the forest. This two-way transitive trust allows security principals to be authenticated in any domain in the forest. These trusts are created by default and cannot be removed.
External	This trust type is created manually between domains that are not part of the forest. These trusts can be **one-way** or two-way and are not transitive.
Realm	This trust type is created manually between a non-Windows-brand operating system domain (referred to as a *Kerberos realm*) and a Windows Server 2003 domain. These trusts can be one-way or two-way and can be transitive or **non-transitive**.
Forest	This trust type is created manually between forests that use the Windows Server 2003 domain functional level. These trusts can be one-way or two-way and can be transitive or non-transitive.
Shortcut	This trust type is created manually within a Windows Server 2003 forest to reduce logon times between domains in a forest. This one-way or two-way trust is particularly useful when traversing tree-root trusts because the trust path to a destination domain is potentially reduced.

Trust Authentication Protocols

Because trusts allow you to facilitate access to resources in a multidomain environment, it is important that you use the most secure authentication protocol whenever possible when creating trusts between domains and realms. You also need to understand the various authentication types associated with each trust type. For example, if you have secured your authentication in your organization to accept only Kerberos authentication, an external trust to a Windows NT 4.0 domain will fail because a Windows NT 4.0 domain cannot use Kerberos.

Table 5-8 lists the various authentication protocols that can be used with specific trust types.

Table 5-8 **Authentication Protocols Used with Trusts**

Trust type	Authentication protocol
Parent/child trusts	Kerberos, NTLM
Tree/root trusts	Kerberos, NTLM
External	NTLM
Realm	Kerberos
Forest	Kerberos, NTLM
Shortcut	Kerberos, NTLM

Strive to use Kerberos authentication for trusts whenever possible because it provides better security than NTLM. However, Kerberos trusts work only between Windows Server 2003 forests. You cannot create transitive Kerberos trusts between Windows Server 2003 forests and Windows 2000 forests or Windows NT 4.0 domains because Windows 2000 is not able to find Kerberos Key Distribution Centers (KDCs) in other domains. To establish trusts between Windows Server 2003 and Windows 2000 forests or Windows NT 4.0 domains, create one-way or two-way external trusts between forests.

Using SID Filtering to Reduce the Risk of Trusts

As you might know, Windows grants or denies users access to resources by using ACLs. ACLs use security identifiers (SIDs) to identify users and their group membership uniquely. Every SID is made up of two parts: a domain SID that is shared by all users for that domain, and a relative ID (RID) that is unique to the user within the domain.

When a user's credentials are verified during authentication, a process known as the local security authority subsystem (lsass.exe) retrieves the user's SID, in addition to SIDs for all the groups to which the user belongs. For example, when a user Amy, who belongs to the Managers group, is authenticated, the local security authority subsystem retrieves Amy's user SID and the SID for the Managers group. When Amy requests access to a resource, her SIDs are checked by the local security authority subsystem against the ACL to determine if she is allowed to perform the action.

Users with the proper privileges, such as domain administrators, can manipulate the SIDs that are associated with specific accounts. **SID spoofing** occurs when a domain administrator from a trusted domain attaches a well-known security principal to the SID of a normal user account from the trusted domain. In the SID spoofing process, an attacker who has gained administrative privileges in a trusted domain captures packets from the trusted domain to find the SID of a security principal that has full access to resources in the trusted domain. Using a variety of programs, an administrator can attach the sniffed SID to the SID History attribute of a user. By doing this, administrators from trusted domains can escalate their privileges in the trusted domain to access resources that they are not authorized to access.

Security identifier filtering is a process that prevents users from outside the forest from using their SIDs to access resources within the forest. When a user from one forest attempts to access resources across another forest's boundaries, SID filtering removes the SID from their access credentials. This is the primary way to mitigate the risk of SID spoofing.

> **NOTE Understanding SIDs**   The SID of a security principal identifies not only the security principal, but also the domain where its account resides. In Windows NT 4.0, a user has only one user account SID, but in Windows 2000 and later, a user might have additional SIDs located in his or her SID History. This means that a user's access token could possibly contain SIDs from multiple domains. This possibility is by design, and it allows the user to continue to access resources in his former domain. If SID filtering is used, it might break this process.

When an external or forest trust is created, SID filtering is turned on by default. This enables you as a security designer to consider forests a security boundary. Although it will expose you to SID spoofing vulnerabilities, SID filtering can be turned off by using the Netdom.exe tool, included with the Windows Support Tools on the Windows Server 2003 operating system CD-ROM.

Guidelines for Restricting Trusts

Follow these additional guidelines for restricting trust relationships:

- **Use the most limited trust possible**   Always use the most limited trust that meets your needs. Forest trusts provide features that other trust types cannot support, such as Kerberos authentication, user principal name (UPN) logon, and security policy support. If a forest trust feature or forest-wide authentication is needed, you must use a forest trust. Before establishing a trust between two Windows Server 2003 forests, determine if all domains will need to authenticate users from all other domains. For example, if the trust were required only to allow users from only one domain in a forest to authenticate to a single domain in a remote forest, a forest trust would be excessive. When authentication is required between only a limited number of domains, establish one-way or two-way external trusts, rather than forest trusts, between the domains that require authentication.

- **Disable the domain info record**   The domain info record within the trust properties specifies the domains that are part of the forest trust relationship. If you disable access to the domain info record, you effectively prevent any access to the domain across the trust.

- **Use a TopLevelExclusion record to limit trust**   You can exclude a section of a domain namespace from the trust by setting a TopLevelExclusion record on the Name Suffixes To Exclude From Routing tab.

- **Restrict authentication**   You can restrict authentication across a Windows Server 2003 external trust and forest trust. To restrict authentication means to require explicit permission for authentication to be granted at the server or domain level. Until this permission is granted, no user from the trusted domain will be able to access the resources on the trusting domain. During the trust creation process, you have the opportunity to select the authentication requirements. You can either select that authentication be restricted or not, and if the trust is being created as a two-way trust, each one-way trust can be independently configured for the authentication level. Figure 5-7 shows the configuration selection during the trust creation process.

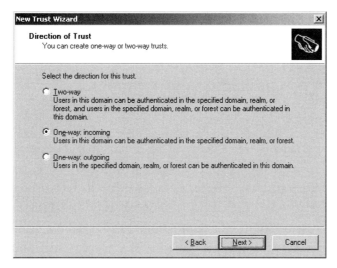

Figure 5-7   Restricting authentication during trust creation

- **Grant permission to authenticate**   After the trust is created, if **selective authentication** was chosen, you grant permission to authenticate each group of users before they can access any resources. Two types of permission can be granted:

  - ❏ To set authentication per domain in a forest trust, access the Security properties page of each domain controller in the Domain Controller OU in Active Directory Users and Computers.

  - ❏ To set authentication per server in a Windows Server 2003 external trust, use Active Directory Users And Computers to access the Security properties page of each server on which you want to grant access.

On either of the Security properties pages, add the groups that should be allowed to access the servers or the domain controllers. Then grant the Allowed To Authenticate permission.

NOTE **Understanding Selective Authentication**   When selective authentication is in effect and a user requests access across a trust boundary, an "Other Organization" SID is added to the user's credentials. This triggers a check on the resource server or domain controller to check the user's right to authenticate. A user who is not making a request across the trust boundary has the "This Organization" SID added to their account after they authenticate. These two SIDs are mutually exclusive. Only one of them can be within a user's credentials.

ENABLING ANONYMOUS AUTHENTICATION TO SUPPORT EARLIER VERSIONS OF WINDOWS

Anonymous authentication allows users and network clients to be authenticated (but not necessarily authorized to access network resources) without providing any credentials. Unlike earlier Windows operating systems, in Windows Server 2003, anonymous users are not considered to be members of the Everyone group and, therefore, will not be authorized to use any network resources. However, anonymous access is necessary to provide compatibility with systems prior to Windows 2000 in some scenarios. Situations in which this access might be necessary include the following:

- Remote Access Server (RAS) servers on Windows NT 4.0 use anonymous access to determine dial-in permissions.

- Windows NT 4.0 might use anonymous access to enumerate shares or gather information from domain controllers.

- Anonymous access might be used to enumerate shares and users in a one-way, cross-forest trust.

- Earlier operating systems might use anonymous access to change passwords in Active Directory.

- An administrator in the trusting domain of a one-way, cross-forest trust relationship needs to list users and shares in the trusted domain of another forest.

If you are running earlier versions of Windows in your Windows Server 2003 domain, you will need to determine which resources need anonymous access. You can then enable anonymous access by performing one of the following tasks:

- Add the Anonymous Logon security principal to the ACL that needs access. This is the preferred method for enabling anonymous access to resources because it is the most granular.

- Enable the Network Access: Share That Can Be Accessed Anonymously security policy setting. This security policy setting contains a list of shares that can be accessed, and is useful for enabling anonymous access to a specific share on multiple computers.

- Enable the Network Access: Let Everyone Permissions Apply To Anonymous Users security policy setting. This setting causes unauthenticated users to be considered members of the Everyone group, which might authorize users to access network resources without being authenticated as valid users. This setting should be enabled only when necessary because it creates a significant, exploitable vulnerability.

- Add the accounts to the Pre-Windows 2000 Compatible Access group. By default, this group has read access to user and group objects in Active Directory. For example, you can add users who need to change their passwords from operating systems released prior to Windows 2000 to this built-in group.

> **CAUTION** **Minimize the Scope of Risky Settings** Apply the Anonymous Logon, Network Access: Share That Can Be Accessed Anonymously, Network Access: Let Everyone Permissions Apply To Anonymous Users settings only to the OU or server that needs them. Enabling these settings at the domain level will decrease network security.

INTEROPERATING WITH UNIX

Some organizations have clients running UNIX or other operating systems. To allow for the secure exchange of information with non-Windows clients, you can configure the clients to authenticate to Windows Server 2003 domain controllers to obtain the required credentials. In a similar way, Windows clients can be configured to authenticate to other KDCs.

To enable interoperability with UNIX or other clients, you must do the following:

- Establish a Realm trust, a particular type of external trust with a UNIX realm. This enables an authentication that is completed in one realm or domain to be trusted by another realm or domain.

- Create account mappings so that other clients have mapped accounts in Active Directory. This enables other clients to access resources that are secured in a Windows environment.

The sections that follow discuss each of these two approaches.

Establishing Trusts with Kerberos Realms

To enable authentication between Windows domains and UNIX realms or other clients, you must establish a one-way or two-way trust between the two so that tickets generated in one are recognized and accepted by resources in the other. For example, a one-way trust relationship in which a Kerberos realm trusts a Windows Server 2003 domain allows Windows Server 2003 users to log on to the Kerberos realm; in other words, the UNIX server accepts or trusts the authentication performed by the Windows Server 2003 KDC. Another trust can be created so that users logged on to the Kerberos realm can access resources in the Windows Server 2003 domain.

Configuring Accounts for Kerberos Clients Running Other Operating Systems

After you have established trusts between a UNIX or other realm and a Windows domain, you might have to perform additional configurations to enable sharing of resources. The sections that follow describe several important considerations.

Configuring Linux User Accounts

You must configure clients to authenticate to the appropriate KDC. For example, you might configure a Linux desktop to authenticate to a Windows Server 2003–based KDC at logon. Most Kerberos clients allow for the specification of a KDC for authentication as part of the logon to the local computer. Windows Server 2003 provides the Kerberos KDC services as part of the domain controller, so the clients log on to the domain controller itself. The domain controller locates the KDC by means of service location records in the DNS. This frees the administrator from having to maintain explicit Kerberos configuration data for each client.

Exposing Services in Remote Kerberos Realms

Windows Server 2003 supports the authentication of other Kerberos services in a Windows Server 2003 domain. If you require services to access resources across the domain or realm, you must create service accounts in Active Directory to represent those services. For example, you can make a UNIX-based Telnet service accessible to Kerberos clients in a Windows domain by creating a service account in Active Directory for that service. In this case, the Telnet service is part of the Windows domain rather than the other Kerberos realm, as is the case with trust relationships established between Windows and other Kerberos realms.

Creating Account Mappings for Users in Remote Kerberos Realms

When a Windows Server 2003 domain trusts a Kerberos realm, the principals in the Kerberos realm do not contain the group associations that are used for access control in the Windows Server 2003 environment. You can use account mapping in the Windows Server 2003 domain to provide authorization information for Kerberos principals from trusted realms. You can map accounts either one to one, by mapping each account in a realm to a corresponding account in the Windows Server 2003 domain, or you can use one-to-many mapping, by which multiple individual accounts in a realm are mapped to one account in the Windows Server 2003 domain.

MORE INFO **Account Mapping**   For more information about account mapping, see the Distributed Services Guide of the Windows Server 2003 Resource Kit (or see the Distributed Services Guide on the Web at http://www.microsoft.com/reskit).

To ensure seamless interoperability, you must keep the accounts in the Kerberos realm and the Windows Server 2003 domain synchronized. You can use Microsoft Metadirectory Services (MMS) to synchronize accounts.

MORE INFO **About MMS**   For more information about MMS, visit http://www.microsoft.com/windows2000/technologies/directory/MMS.

SUMMARY

- Active Directory has four authentication methods: LM, NTLMv1, NTLMv2, and Kerberos. Kerberos is the most secure, but not every client on your network may support it. LM authentication exposes your entire Active Directory domain to significant vulnerabilities, and should be disabled whenever possible.

- Any directory service is vulnerable to password-cracking attacks. To mitigate your vulnerability, enforce the use of long, complex passwords. The more privileges a user has, the more critical it is that their password be complex.

- If the vulnerabilities inherent in password-based authentication are unacceptable to you and you can justify a costly countermeasure, multifactor authentication using smart cards or biometrics will greatly reduce your risk.

- Designing Active Directory forests is a complex process involving weighing many different costs and benefits. To summarize, create a new forest only when an absolute security boundary is required. Create domains where organizations have varying security requirements. Use trusts to share resources between domains and forests.

- If you have early versions of Windows on your network, you might have to enable anonymous authentication for specific services and applications to function.

- Active Directory domains can interoperate with non-Windows Kerberos realms and non-Windows clients. However, they require additional configuration, such as creating accounts in Active Directory to map to accounts in the remote Kerberos realm.

REVIEW QUESTIONS

1. Which of the following is an advantage of NTLMv2 over LM authentication?

    a. Authentications happen noticeably faster.

    b. Domain controllers can support more simultaneous users.

    c. The encryption is more time consuming to crack.

    d. User names are not transmitted in clear text.

2. Which of the following are advantages of Kerberos authentication over NTLMv2 authentication? (Choose all that apply.)

    a. Tickets, rather than encrypted passwords, are transmitted across the network.

    b. Both servers and clients can be authenticated.

    c. Kerberos is an open standard.

    d. User names are not transmitted in clear text.

3. Which of the following are strong passwords?

    a. tyia

    b. imsitrjs5itr

    c. passwordpassword

    d. l%@3tty7&

4. Which of the following passwords will not be stored in an LM Hash?

    a. tyia

    b. imsitrjs5itr

    c. passwordpassword

    d. l%@3tty7&

5. Which of the following are valid reasons to enable LM authentication? (Choose all that apply.)

    a. Users will access network resources using computers running Windows 95.

    b. Users will access network resources using computers running Windows 98.

    c. Users will access network resources using computers running Windows NT.

    d. Users will access network resources using computers running Windows Me.

    e. Users will access network resources using computers running Windows 2000.

    f. Users will access network resources using computers running Windows XP.

6. Enabling account lockout accomplishes which of the following goals?

    a. Makes it impossible to steal a user's password

    b. Reduces the likelihood that a malicious attacker will successfully use brute-force techniques to discover a user's password

    c. Eliminates the need for strong passwords

    d. Reduces Help desk costs

7. Which type of trust should you create to enable users from a UNIX-based Kerberos realm to access resources in a Windows Server 2003 domain?

    a. Parent/child trust

    b. Tree/root trust

    c. External

    d. Realm

    e. Forest

    f. Shortcut

8. Which type of trust is automatically created when a new domain joins an existing forest?

    a. Parent/child trust

    b. Tree/root trust

    c. External

    d. Realm

    e. Forest

    f. Shortcut

9. Creating a two-way trust between DomainA and DomainB will have which of the following effects? (Choose all that apply.)

    a. Enable all users in DomainA to access all shared folders in DomainB.

    b. Enable members of the Domain Admins group in DomainA to access all shared folders in DomainB.

    c. Enable administrators of DomainA to grant access to shared folders to users in DomainB.

    d. Enable administrators of DomainA to view a list of users and groups in DomainB.

10. In a Windows Server 2003 forest, which types of trusts automatically have SID filtering enabled? (Choose all that apply.)

    a. Parent/child trust

    b. Tree/root trust

    c. External

    d. Realm

    e. Forest

    f. Shortcut

CASE SCENARIOS

Case Scenario 5-1: Migrate from Windows NT 4.0 Domains

You are a security designer for Fabrikam, Inc. Fabrikam is a 20,000-employee company whose principal activity is to manufacture, distribute, and market nonalcoholic beverages. You were hired about a year ago, and were given responsibility for the security of the existing Windows NT 4.0–based domains. The current multiple master domain architecture is shown in Figure 5-8.

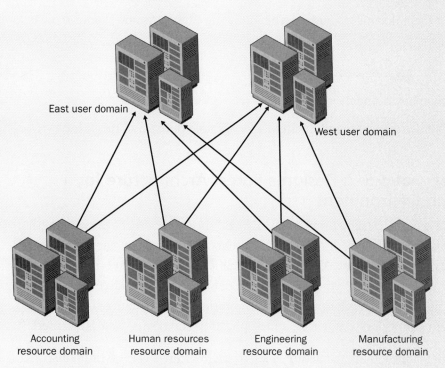

Figure 5-8 Fabrikam's existing domain architecture

You've spent much of your first year as an employee of Fabrikam lobbying to find the budget to upgrade the infrastructure to Windows Server 2003. Finally, when faced with the fact that Microsoft will no longer release security updates for Windows NT 4.0, management has granted you a budget to create a brand-new Active Directory domain architecture. As always, your budget is limited to the bare minimum you can spend while meeting management's security requirements.

Fabrikam's requirements for the domain haven't changed much since the original Windows NT 4.0 domain architecture was created. They still need to be able to scale to about 30,000 employees because they're planning for additional growth. They need to authenticate users on both the East and West coast offices.

Although Fabrikam has IT staff on both the East and West coasts, management has no desire to isolate the East and West coasts from each other. Your predecessor, who designed the original Windows NT 4.0 domains, created only separate master domains for the East and West coast for scalability purposes. Separate resource domains were created both to improve scalability and to logically divide the large number of network resources.

Based on this information, answer the following questions about your new architecture.

1. How many forests will you have?

2. How many domains will you have?

3. What security vulnerabilities exist for a single domain of this size?

Case Scenario 5-2: Design a Forest Architecture for a Hosting Environment

You are a security designer for Contoso, Ltd., a hosting services provider with about 500 employees. Your company's primary business is managing other businesses' computer systems. Many of your smaller customers have a single computer acting as a Web server at one of your datacenters. Your larger customers have hundreds of computers serving in traditional infrastructure capacities such as domain controllers, databases, and application servers in your datacenters.

Although Contoso's infrastructure is based on Windows NT 4.0 domains, Windows 2000 Active Directory domains, and Windows Server 2003 Active Directory domains, your customers have a wide variety of computers to support. You still manage Windows NT 3.51 computers that your customers refuse to upgrade, and every version of Windows through Windows Server 2003 is represented. Some of your customers use Solaris- and Linux-based computers.

Today, Contoso has three primary domains with no trusts between them, as follows:

■ A Windows Server 2003 internal domain used by all employees to access internal resources.

■ A Windows NT 4.0 customer domain that contains accounts for Contoso staff responsible for managing customers' computers. Most of your smaller customers' computers running Windows NT 4.0 are members of this domain, and the customers have user accounts in each computer's local user database.

■ A Windows 2000 Active Directory domain that contains duplicate accounts for Contoso staff responsible for managing customer computers. Most of your smaller customers' computers running Windows 2000 and Windows Server 2003 are members of this domain, and the customers have user accounts in each computer's local user database.

This domain architecture annoys the Contoso hosting staff because they have to have three separate user accounts. It annoys some of your customers, too, because they have to have separate accounts in the local user database of each computer, and you host multiple computers for many of your customers. Despite these annoyances, the model did a reasonably good job of protecting Contoso from attack by a customer, and protecting customers from attacks by each other.

However, some of your large customers are threatening to cancel their services because they want to have their own domains to enable them to log on to all of their computers with a single logon. In addition, they're upset because other customers can see their computers when browsing domain resources, and they'd rather protect their privacy from other customers. Management has asked you to redesign Contoso's domain and forest architectures using Windows Server 2003 Active Directory to meet the administrative requirements of Contoso and the security requirements of your customers.

Based on this information, create a diagram showing your new Active Directory design. Be sure to meet the following requirements, which your Product Management group gave you:

- Contoso administrators can use a single user account to access any customer computer after the migration to the new design is complete. It's okay if they need to use a separate account to access internal resources.

- Contoso staff that are not responsible for managing customer computers, including Contoso's internal IT department, must be completely isolated from customer computers to protect the security of your customers.

- Customers should not be able to authenticate to other customer computers under any circumstances.

- Customers who want their own domain, and are willing to purchase computers to act as domain controllers, must have the option while meeting all of the previous requirements. They must be able to have rights to administer the computers in the domain for times they need to perform administrative tasks without contacting Contoso.

- Customers who do not want their own domain must also have that option.

Based on your design, answer the following questions.

1. How many Windows Server 2003 Active Directory forests does Contoso need to create?

2. Will you create a forest trust between Contoso forests?

3. How many Windows Server 2003 Active Directory domains does Contoso need to create?

4. For customers that require their own domains, will you add their domain to a Contoso forest, or will you require them to create their own forest?

5. What type of trust will you create between the Contoso domain and customer domains?

CHAPTER 6
PROTECTING DATA

Upon completion of this chapter, you will be able to:

■ Describe the purpose of authorization and how Microsoft Windows uses discretionary access control lists (DACLs) and security access control lists (SACLs).

■ List the different types of groups available in Active Directory directory service environments, how they can be used to effectively manage assigning permissions to resources, and how to name groups to avoid confusion.

■ Explain the different approaches to assigning permissions to network resources.

■ Delegate rights to manage an Active Directory domain while minimizing the security risks.

■ List the different types of permissions that can be assigned to files, Active Directory objects, the registry, services, printers, and shares.

■ Harden permissions on servers and clients while allowing users to do their jobs.

■ Configure auditing for critical network resources and interpret the event logs.

■ Use Encrypting File System (EFS) to protect critical folders and files while minimizing the risk of data loss.

For many organizations, the most critical, irreplaceable resource is data. The most basic technique for protecting data is authorization, which enables you to choose which users can access data.

Windows networks use permissions to determine which users are authorized to access data or other network resources. It's easy to configure permissions for a single resource, but in an enterprise, managing permissions for thousands of resources is a daunting, error-prone task. Unfortunately, the cost of human error can be tremendous: it can expose critical network resources to attack.

As a security designer, you must understand how to control authorization on the thousands of network resources that exist in an enterprise, including files, registries, and Active Directory domains. Enterprises have thousands of users, too, so learn how to organize these users into groups, and how to provide groups with access to network resources most effectively. Effectively assigning permissions reduces the risk of a compromise but doesn't eliminate it. To be prepared for the inevitable attacks, you must configure auditing and know how to manage those audit logs.

UNDERSTANDING AUTHORIZATION

Authorization is the process of determining whether an authenticated user is allowed to perform a requested action. For example, each time you open a file, Windows checks whether your user account or your group memberships, and then grants you the right to open that file. If you do not explicitly have the right to open the file, you are denied access. Similarly, each time you print, Windows verifies that you have Print permissions to that printer. In fact, Windows verifies your authorization to access just about every object you can imagine, including files and folders, shared folders, printers, services, Active Directory directory service objects, Terminal Services connections, Windows Management Interface objects, and registry keys and values.

Security designers use authorization to mitigate the risk of a legitimate user abusing unnecessary rights to an object. For example, if all users have permission to delete important files, there is a good chance that someone will unintentionally or possibly intentionally delete those files and/or deny other users access to the file. You can reduce the risk posed by these threats by using the principle of least privilege. In brief, grant users only the minimum access they need to each object on your network.

Understanding how authorization works for each of these different types of objects is complicated because each type requires unique permissions. For example, you need to control whether users can read files or write to files, but for services, your concern is whether a given user can start or stop the service. Fortunately, Windows simplifies authorization management by using a standard model for all types of objects. This model uses access control lists, **inherited permissions**, and both standard and special permissions. Even the user interface for specifying permissions for each object type is similar.

To refresh your memory about the fundamentals of authorization on Windows networks, the sections that follow discuss the various types of access control lists (ACLs), and how Windows calculates a user's permissions.

What Is an Access Control List?

All recent members of the Microsoft Windows family (including Windows NT, Windows 2000, Windows XP, and Windows Server 2003) keep track of the privileges users have to resources by using a **discretionary access control list** (DACL). DACLs, or simply ACLs, identify the users and groups that are assigned or denied access permissions on an object. If an ACL does not explicitly identify a user, or any groups that a user is a member of, the user is implicitly denied access to that object. Figure 6-1 illustrates the relationship between authentication, authorization, and access control lists.

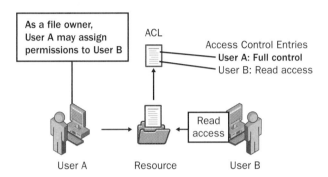

Figure 6-1   The ACL determines whether an authenticated user has access to a resource.

ACLs contain **access control entries** (ACEs) that determine user access to the object. An ACE is an entry in an object's ACL that grants permissions to a user or group. Figure 6-2 shows how Windows uses the ACEs within an ACL to determine if a user should be granted access to a resource.

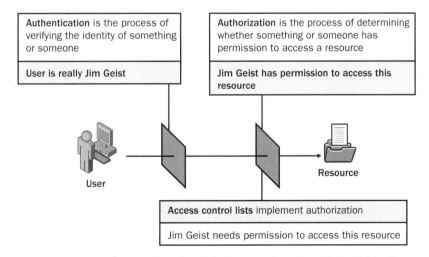

Figure 6-2   An ACL consists of multiple ACEs that identify individual users and groups.

Although a description of ACLs and ACEs is complex, they are very easy to manage. Figure 6-3 shows the Microsoft Windows Server 2003 graphical user interface dialog box for managing permissions to a folder named Secret. The GG Boston Research security group is highlighted so that the dialog box displays the permissions assigned to that group: Read & Execute, List Folder Contents, and Read. Collectively, these permissions allow members of the GG Boston Research security group to read the contents of the folder.

> **NOTE   The Deny Permission**   All of the users and groups listed in the dialog box have an ACE defined for the folder, but that does not necessarily mean they have any access to the folder. If the Deny permission is assigned, that user or group will not be able to access the object because permission has been explicitly denied—even if they have also been granted access through another group membership.

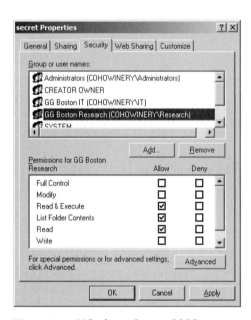

Figure 6-3   Windows Server 2003 represents ACLs by listing the permissions assigned to users and groups.

Other types of resources (such as the registry or printers) use different tools for managing permissions. However, the interface is usually very similar to the interface used to manage file and folder permissions. This book assumes you are familiar with using the interface, and will focus on providing the information security designers need to choose which permissions users receive.

What Is a Security Access Control List?

A **security access control list** (SACL) is a usage event logging mechanism that determines how object access is audited. Unlike a DACL, an SACL cannot restrict access to a file or folder. However, an SACL can cause an event to be recorded in the Security event log when a user accesses a file or folder. This auditing can be used to troubleshoot access problems or to identify intrusions.

A systems administrator or a security designer is likely to use SACLs to identify permissions that a user needs to allow an application to run correctly. A developer uses SACLs to track resources that her application cannot access, so that she can customize the application to allow it to run, without problems, under a less privileged account. To a security auditor, an SACL is a critical tool for intrusion detection.

> **NOTE SACLs vs. DACLS** It is important to understand the difference between SACLs and DACLs because the difference between the two is also a common question in technical interviews. Fortunately, it's simple: DACLs restrict access, whereas SACLs audit access. Realistically, though, most people refer to DACLs as simply "ACLs." For that reason, this book will use the term ACL to refer to DACLs.

UNDERSTANDING WINDOWS GROUP FUNDAMENTALS

To design group architectures effectively, you must understand the types of groups available in an Active Directory environment, and the function of those groups. The sections that follow describe the types of groups that you can create in a Windows Server 2003 Active Directory environment, the behavior of global, domain local, and universal groups, and the strategies to use when implementing groups.

Types of Active Directory Groups

You use groups to organize user accounts, computer accounts, and other group accounts into manageable units. Although the local user databases on member servers and stand-alone servers support only security groups, there are two types of groups in Active Directory: distribution groups and security groups.

Multiple users use distribution groups primarily for sending e-mail. You can use distribution groups with Active Directory–aware applications and e-mail applications, such as Microsoft Exchange Server and Microsoft Outlook, to send messages to users that are contained in the distribution group. Distribution groups are not security-enabled, and cannot be listed in ACLs. In other words, if you have created a distribution group for the human resources department, you cannot use the group to grant the members of that group access to a printer. You can, however, send the group an e-mail message telling them that they will have access to their new printer as soon as you create a security group.

Security groups can be used to grant (or deny) access to network resources because security groups can be listed in ACLs. For example, granting the Research security group Read access to a shared folder will enable the members of that group to access the files. Security groups can also be used for e-mail distribution. Therefore, you could use the Research security group to grant access to a shared folder, and then send an e-mail message to the group letting them know that they now have access to their files.

You can use *nesting* to place one or more groups into another group. For example, if you need two separate groups named Accounts Payable and Accounts Receivable for users in the Accounting group, you could nest them into another group called All Accounting. You can then use the All Accounting group when assigning permissions for resources that all members of the accounting department should access. When you use nested groups, a group inherits the permissions of the group of which it is a member, which simplifies the process of assigning permissions to several groups at one time.

NOTE *Group Nesting Limitations in Mixed-Mode Domains* In a mixed-mode domain, you cannot nest groups that have the same group scope. For example, if your domain were at the Windows 2000 Mixed-Mode domain functional level, you would not be able to nest global groups inside of other global groups. You can nest global groups only when the domain functional level is set to Windows 2000 native or higher. Group scope is described in the next section.

Group Scopes

Each group in an Active Directory system has a scope attribute that determines which security principals can be members of the group and where you can use that group in a multi-domain or multi-forest environment. Windows Server 2003 Active Directory supports the following group scopes:

- **Local groups** Local groups reside on member servers and client computers. Use a local group to grant access to local resources on the computer where they reside.

  > **NOTE** *Groups in a Workgroup Environment* *Local groups are the only group type available in a non-domain environment.*

- **Global groups** Global groups reside in Active Directory at the domain level. Use a global group to organize users who share the same job tasks and need similar network access requirements, such as all accountants in an organization's accounting department. Global groups can be members of other global groups, universal groups, and domain local groups.

- **Domain local groups** Domain local groups reside in Active Directory at the domain level. Use a domain local group when you want to assign access permissions to resources that are located in the same domain in which you create the domain local group. You can add all global groups that need to share the same resources to the appropriate domain local group.

- **Universal groups** Universal groups reside in Active Directory at the forest level. Use universal groups when you want to nest global groups so that you can assign permissions to related resources in multiple domains. Universal groups can be members of other universal groups, global groups, and domain local groups. The Windows Server 2003 domain functional level must be at Windows 2000 native mode or higher to use universal security groups.

If you are using the Windows 2000 mixed-domain functional level, you can use universal groups for only distribution lists. To use universal security groups, you must upgrade or remove all Microsoft Windows NT 4.0 domain controllers and raise the domain functional level to Windows 2000 native or higher. This also gives you the ability to nest groups, which is critical for creating a complex group strategy, and for converting groups between different types.

Built-In Groups

Windows Server 2003 provides many built-in groups. Built-in groups are automatically created when you create an Active Directory domain. You can use built-in groups to manage access to shared resources and to delegate specific domain-wide administrative roles. For example, you could put the user account of a junior administrator into the Account Operators group to allow the junior administrator to create user accounts and groups. This is more secure than adding the junior administrator to the Domain Admins group.

Built-in groups are automatically assigned a set of user rights that determine what each group and their members can do within the scope of a domain or forest. User rights authorize members of a group to perform specific actions, such as logging on to a local system or backing up files and folders. For example, a member of the Backup Operators group has the right to perform backup operations for all domain controllers in the domain.

Built-in groups make it easy to assign users a specific, predefined set of rights. However, these rights aren't very specific, and probably don't exactly match the needs of any single organization. For example, the Account Operators group has the ability to manage user accounts, which is useful for members of a typical enterprise help desk. However, they also have the ability to shut down domain controllers, which is excessive for a typical help desk role. Assigning help desk members this excessive right introduces a vulnerability to your network: a help desk operator could shut down a domain controller maliciously or accidentally. Even if the user would never intentionally misuse the elevated privileges of the Power Users group, a virus or Trojan horse might take advantage of the additional privileges without the awareness of the user.

If you have determined that the risk of an internal administrator becoming a threat is very low, using built-in groups is an easy way to delegate domain-wide administrative capabilities, especially with smaller networks that have only a few administrators. However, in larger networks, it will be worth your time to disregard the built-in groups and create your own groups that exactly match the privileges required by each different role within your organization. If you create custom groups, you can still make use of built-in groups to assign privileges. For example, if you are creating a security group called Monitoring for members of a team responsible for monitoring your domain's servers, you can make that group a member of the Performance Log Users group. Then, you can assign them additional privileges as needed.

To create an effective security strategy for a network, it is important that you understand the default rights associated with each built-in group. This section describes each built-in group and the rights and capabilities associated with each.

Account Operators

Members of the Account Operators group can create, modify, and delete accounts for users, groups, and computers located in the Users or Computers containers and organizational units (OUs) in the domain, except the Domain Controllers OU. Members of this group do not have permission to modify the Administrators or the Domain Admins groups, nor do they have permission to modify the accounts for members of those groups. Members of this group can log on locally to domain controllers in the domain and shut them down. Because this group has significant power in the domain, add users with caution.

Besides the rights to create some types of Active Directory objects, members of this group have the following default user rights:

- Allow logon locally
- Shut down the system

> **CAUTION**   Do not change the default user right assignments on a production computer unless you really know what you are doing. If you do find that you need to restore the default user right assignments, use the setup security.inf security template provided with Windows Server 2003.

Administrators

Members of the Administrators group have full control of the server and can assign user rights and access control permissions to users as necessary. Add users with caution. When joined to a domain, the Domain Admins group is automatically added to this group. The default Administrator user account becomes a member of the Administrators group. Members of this group have almost every user right available on a system.

Backup Operators

Members can back up and restore all files on domain controllers in the domain, regardless of their own individual permissions on those files. Backup Operators can also log on to domain controllers and shut them down. This group has no default members. Because this group has significant power on domain controllers, add users with caution. Members of this group have the following default user rights:

- Back up files and directories
- Allow logon locally

- Restore files and directories

- Shut down the system

Incoming Forest Trust Builders

This group appears in the forest root domain only. Members of this group can create one-way, incoming forest trusts to the forest root domain. For example, members of this group residing in Forest A can create a one-way, incoming forest trust from Forest B. This one-way, incoming forest trust allows users in Forest A to access resources located in Forest B. Members of this group are granted the Create Inbound Forest Trust permission on the forest root domain. This group has no default members and no default user rights.

Network Configuration Operators

This group is the staff responsible for managing the network configuration of servers and workstations in a domain. Members of this group can make changes to Transmission Control Protocol/Internet Protocol (TCP/IP) settings, renew, and release TCP/IP addresses on domain controllers in the domain. This group has no default members and no default user rights.

Performance Log Users

Members of this group can manage performance counters, logs, and alerts on domain controllers in the domain, locally and from remote clients, without being a member of the Administrators group. Members of this group have no default user rights.

Performance Monitor Users

Members of this group can monitor performance counters on domain controllers in the domain, locally and from remote clients, without being a member of the Administrators or Performance Log Users groups. This group has no default members and no default user rights.

Pre–Windows 2000 Compatible Access

Members of this group have read access on all users and groups in the domain. This group is provided for backward compatibility with computers running Windows NT 4.0 and earlier. By default, the special identity Authenticated Users is a member of this group. Members of this group have the following default user rights:

- Access this computer from the network

- Bypass traverse checking

Print Operators

Members of this group can manage, create, share, and delete printers connected to domain controllers in the domain. They can also manage Active Directory printer objects in the domain. Because members of this group can load and unload device drivers on all domain controllers in the domain, add users with caution. A member of the Print Operators group with malicious intent could take control of a domain controller. This group has no default members. Members of this group have the following default user rights:

- Allow logon locally
- Shut down the system

Remote Desktop Users

Members of this group can remotely log on to domain controllers in the domain. This group has no default members and no default user rights.

Replicator

This group supports directory replication functions, and the File Replication service uses this group on domain controllers in the domain. This group has no default members and no default user rights. Because the operating system owns this group,, adding users to this group can cause problems with the File Replication service.

Server Operators

On domain controllers, members of this group can log on interactively, create and delete shared resources, start and stop some services, back up and restore files, format the hard disk, and shut down the computer. This group has no default members. Members of this group have the following default user rights:

- Back up files and directories
- Change the system time
- Force shutdown from a remote system
- Allow logon locally
- Restore files and directories
- Shut down the system

Terminal Server License Servers

Members of this group have access to Terminal Server License Servers on the system. This group has no default members and no default user rights.

Users

Members of this group can perform most common tasks, such as running applications, using local and network printers, and locking the server. By default, the Domain Users group, the Authenticated Users group, and the Interactive group are members of this group. All user accounts in the domain are members of this group. Members of this group have no default user rights.

Windows Authorization Access Group

This group exists to simplify granting accounts permission to query a user's group information. Members of this group have access to the computed token-GroupsGlobalAndUniversal attribute on User objects. Add members to this group only when specifically required by an application. By default, only the Enterprise Domain Controllers group is a member of this group.

> **MORE INFO** For more information about built-in groups, see *http://www.microsoft.com/technet/prodtechnol/windowsserver2003/proddocs/entserver/sag_ADgroups_9builtin_intro.asp.*

Special Groups and Accounts

Servers running Windows Server 2003 include several special identities in addition to the groups in the Users and Built-in containers. These identities are generally referred to as *special groups*. Special groups, also called *special identities*, are designed to provide access to resources without administrative or user interaction.

> **NOTE**   **Recognizing Special Groups**   You can recognize most special groups because their names are in all capital letters. There are a few exceptions to this, however, such as the Authenticated Users special group.

Users become members of special groups by simply interacting with the operating system. For example, when users log on locally to a computer, they become members of the Interactive group. You can grant user rights and permissions to these special groups, but you cannot modify or view their memberships. In addition, group scopes do not apply to special groups.

It is important to understand the purpose of special groups because you can use them for security administration; they allow you to create more granular access policies and control access to resources. To understand how special groups help provide secure access, consider blocking access for dial-up users to a folder containing confidential documents. As shown in Figure 6-4, denying access to a folder is as simple as adding the Dialup special group to the folder's ACL.

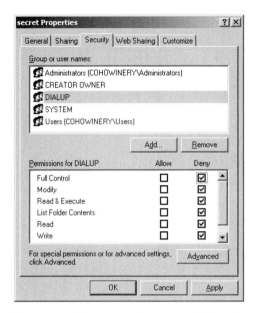

Figure 6-4   You can assign permissions to special groups that apply to users based on how they connect to the network.

The following list describes the special groups included in Windows Server 2003 that can be used to control access to resources in an organization.

> **NOTE**   **Rarely Used Special Groups**   Digest Authentication, Schannel Authentication, NTLM Authentication, Proxy, Remote Interactive Logon, and Restricted are special groups and accounts that appear when browsing accounts. However, you will probably never need to use them during a security design.

- **Anonymous Logon**   The Anonymous Logon special group represents users and services that access a computer and its resources through the network without using an account name, password, or domain name. On computers running Windows NT and earlier, the Anonymous Logon special group is a member of the Everyone group by default. On computers running a member of the Windows Server 2003 family, the Anonymous Logon special group is not a member of the Everyone group by default. If you want to create a file share for an anonymous user, grant permissions to the Anonymous Logon special group.

- **Authenticated Users**   The Authenticated Users special group represents all authenticated users and computers. Authenticated Users does not include Guest even if the Guest account has a password. Membership in the Authenticated Users special group is mutually exclusive to membership in the Anonymous Logon special group.

- **Batch**   The Batch special group includes all users and services that access a computer and its resources through the network by using a batch queue facility, such as task scheduler jobs.

- **Creator Group**   The Creator Group special group includes the user account for the user who created the resource. The Creator Group special group is a placeholder in an inheritable ACE. When the ACE is inherited, the system replaces this security identifier (SID) with the SID for the primary group of the object's current owner.

- **Creator Owner**   The Creator Owner special group includes the user account for the user who created or took ownership of a resource. If a member of the Administrators group creates a resource, the Administrators group is the owner of the resource. The Creator Owner special group is a placeholder in an inheritable ACE. When the ACE is inherited, the system replaces this SID with the SID for the object's current owner.

- **Dialup**   The Dialup special group includes all users who log on to the system through a dial-up connection.

- **Everyone**   The Everyone special group represents all current network users, including guests and users from other domains. Whenever a user logs on to the network, the user is automatically added to the Everyone special group. The Anonymous Logon special group is no longer contained in the Everyone special group as in earlier versions of Windows Server.

- **Interactive** The Interactive special group represents all users currently logged on to a particular computer and accessing a given resource located on that computer, as opposed to users who access the resource over the network. Whenever a user accesses a resource on the computer to which they are currently logged on, the user is automatically added to the Interactive special group.

- **Local Service** The Local Service account is a special built-in account that is similar to an authenticated user account. The Local Service account has the same level of access to resources and objects as members of the Users group. This limited access helps safeguard your system if individual services or processes are compromised. Services that run as the Local Service account access network resources as a null session with no credentials.

- **Network** The Network special group represents users currently accessing a given resource over the network, as opposed to users who access the resource by logging on locally at the computer on which the resource is located. Whenever a user accesses a given resource over the network, the user is added automatically to the Network special group.

- **Network Service** The Network Service account is a special built-in account that is similar to an authenticated user account. The Network Service account has the same level of access to resources and objects as members of the Users group. This limited access helps safeguard your system if individual services or processes are compromised. Services that run as the Network Service account access network resources using the credentials of the computer account.

- **Other Organization** This special group contains users who authenticated from another domain. Adding this special group to an ACL causes a check to ensure that a user from another forest or domain that is trusted has permission to authenticate to a particular service in the trusted domain.

- **Self** The Self special group is a placeholder group in an ACE on a user, group, or computer object in Active Directory. When you grant permissions to Principal Self, you grant them to the security principal represented by the object. During an access check, the operating system replaces the SID for Principal Self with the SID for the security principal represented by the object.

- **Service**   The Service special group is a group that includes all security principals that have logged on as a service. The operating system controls membership.

- **System**   The System special group is used by the operating system and by services that run under Windows. It has privileges that are similar to those of the Administrators group. The System account is an internal account, does not show up in User Manager, cannot be added to any groups, and cannot have user rights assigned to it. The System account does show up when assigning file permissions, however.

- **Terminal Server Users**   The Terminal Server Users special group includes all users who have logged on to a Terminal Services server that is in Terminal Services version 4.0 application compatibility mode.

- **This Organization**   When there are trusted domains for forests, the authentication server adds the This Organization special group to the authentication data of a user to identify the user's organization, provided the Other Organization SID is not already present.

DESIGNING A GROUP STRATEGY

As mentioned earlier, you would never have time to assign each individual user the permissions they need to every object on a network. Rather, put users into groups and assign permissions to the groups. In large enterprises, you could still end up with hundreds of different groups, however. To avoid problems with users not having the permissions they need or, worse, having excessive permissions, you need to develop a group strategy that enables you to assign permissions to employees that closely match the minimum permissions they need to do their job, without being so complicated that administrators get confused and assign permissions to the wrong groups.

In the sections that follow, you learn how to design authorization strategy, choose group naming conventions, define which users are trusted to create groups, nest groups within each other, and use Group Policy settings to control group memberships on Active Directory member computers.

Designing an Authorization Strategy

Your first group strategy design decision is to identify an authorization strategy, which will define how you assign permissions to users and groups. The sections that follow describe three different commonly used authorization strategies. Although it's important to understand them all, in most enterprise environments you will choose the Account Group/Resource Group authorization method.

User/ACL Authorization Method

When using the User/ACL method of controlling access to resources, you add the user account that needs access directly to the ACL of the resource. For example, a user, John, creates a file share and adds Sarah as an authorized user, giving her read-only permission to the share.

The User/ACL method might be acceptable for small organizations with fewer than 10 users. Generally, smaller organizations require fewer groups to manage access to resources, which reduces the complexity of the process of assigning permissions. Using the User/ACL method in large organizations has the following limitations:

- Users within the same job function might have inconsistent access to resources. Usually, users who share the same job role need uniform access to resources. For example, one engineer might have access to a laser printer, a plotter, a backup device, and many file shares. Another engineer in the same department might need access to the same resources, but might have access to only a subset of those resources. Therefore, when there is not uniform access, the network administrator will have to modify the rights for every individual who needs more access.

- Administrator overhead increases because administrators will need to control access to resources on a user-by-user basis.

- This method does not scale well for larger organizations.

- Troubleshooting and tracking which users have access to which resources can be time-consuming and result in higher administrative overhead.

- Access control lists will grow very large, which will cause performance degradation.

> **NOTE The User/ACL Method** Even small organizations will regret using the User/ACL method the first time an employee is replaced, however, because they will need to examine all resource ACLs to find the previous employee and assign his or her equivalent permissions to the new employee.

Account Group/ACL Authorization Method

When using the Account Group/ACL method, you place the user accounts into a global group. Instead of adding the user accounts to the ACL, you add the global group to the ACL. You then assign the group a set of access permissions. The Account Group/ACL method provides the following benefits over the User/ACL method:

- Grouping users into groups makes management easier.

- By placing users performing the same role in a common group, you provide them with the same set of permissions.

- You can add global groups to the access control lists of trusted domains.

For example, an administrator can put all accounting user accounts into a global group called GG All Accountants and then put that global group on an ACL and assign permissions. The Account Group/ACL method also has some limitations. These include the following:

- As more account groups are added to the resource, the resource administrator will experience some of the same challenges posed by the User/ACL method.

- Determining which groups need which permissions can be complicated.

- It is not as straightforward for non-administrators to assign access as it is when using the User/ACL method.

Account Group/Resource Group Authorization Method

The Account Group/Resource Group method of controlling access to resources is similar to the Account–Global Group–Domain Local Group–Permission (AGDLP) method. When using this method, you add users with similar access requirements into account groups, and then add account groups as members to a resource group that has specific resource access permissions. This strategy provides the most flexibility while reducing the complexity of assigning access permissions to the network. Large organizations most commonly use this method for controlling access to resources.

When creating a resource group to control access to a resource, you can create a local group at the resource or create a domain local group on a domain controller. By creating a domain local group instead of a local group to control access, an administrator can configure groups for access from the Active Directory Users And Computers console. A local group would require the administrator to connect directly to the resource to administer it.

To understand how the Account Group/Resource Group authorization method can be used in an organization, consider the following example. Nwtraders.msft needs to provide its users access to a printer named ColorLaser. However, the requirements of various users differ. Some users need only to be able to print with the printer, whereas others need to be able to print and manage the printer. In such a scenario, instead of adding each user or group into the ACL for the printer, you can create resource groups for the two sets of users and then provide the resource groups with appropriate permissions.

The Account Group/Resource Group authorization method is highly scalable and provides the following benefits:

- Instead of modifying permissions for an individual group, you can add the account group into a resource group configured with the appropriate permissions.

- You can place account groups on ACLs in trusted domains.

- You can provide groups with access to resources by simply placing account groups into resource groups.

The Account Group/Resource Group authorization method is not practical or necessary for small organizations that have fewer groups. With fewer groups, it is more practical to use the Account Group/ACL or even the User/ACL authorization method.

Defining Which Users Can Create Groups

In large organizations, the task of creating and managing groups can be time-consuming for IT personnel. In such cases, you can delegate the task of creating and maintaining groups to other users in the organization, such as directors, managers, or members of the human resources team. By delegating security group maintenance to the appropriate individuals, you can help to ensure that requests for changes in membership are evaluated by individuals who:

- Can judge the appropriateness of the request

- Have the authority to make the change

- Are motivated to keep group membership and access permissions correct and up to date

However, delegating the right of managing groups to other users could also lead to security breaches because the delegated group administrators might incorrectly configure access to resources. Therefore, it is important that you carefully determine who can create and maintain groups in your organization.

When delegating users to administer and maintain groups, keep the following considerations in mind:

- Select users who are familiar with the department in which the resource is located and who have an understanding of the access needs of that department. In general, an administrative assistant in a department has a good understanding of the access needs and requirements for those users and is a good choice for administering groups.

- After you select the appropriate users, assign them permission to create and maintain groups. Delegating permissions to these departmental administrators can be done at the OU level, or by giving them the appropriate permissions on the resources they will need to configure.

> **CAUTION** **Restricting Group Memberships**   After you have created and delegated permissions to the departmental administrators, ensure that only the users you have selected are members of this group. Accidentally adding users to this group can result in loss of data or other security compromises. To prevent these risks, you can use restricted groups at the OU level.

When to Retire Groups

As organizations grow and evolve, security groups can become obsolete. Obsolete security groups provide users with permissions they might no longer need, which can lead to security vulnerability. Although account groups for very small teams might not change frequently, large account groups experience almost continuous turnover in membership. If an account group's membership has not changed at all for some time, the group might be obsolete. Therefore, it is important that you constantly monitor which groups your organization no longer needs.

In addition, develop and enforce processes to remove groups that are no longer in use. For example, you might create an account group called GG Picnic Planners for a new morale project in your organization. To facilitate the project, you provide the group access to the color laser printer to print handouts. When the project is over, if you do not retire the group, the users will still have access to the color laser printer. To provide protection against human error, make two people responsible for ensuring that the group is removed: the project manager running the project (who will know when the project is officially over), and a member of the IT department (who should be given the expected completion date, and can check with the project manager to be sure).

Creating Restricted Groups Policy

Groups make it easier to assign permissions, but it would still be very time-consuming to manually add a new IT group that you created in Active Directory as a member of the Administrators local group on every computer in an enterprise. Fortunately, you can use Group Policy settings to control local group memberships on computers that are members of your domain.

Active Directory includes a security policy setting called Restricted Groups that allows you to control group membership. By using the Restricted Groups policy, you can specify the membership of a group anywhere in your Active Directory domain. For example, you can create a Restricted Groups policy to limit the access on an OU that contains computers containing sensitive data. The Restricted Groups policy would remove domain users from the local users group and thereby limit the number of users who can log on to the computer. Group members not specified in the policy are removed when the Group Policy setting is applied or refreshed to the computer or OU. The Restricted Groups policy settings include two properties: Members and Member Of. The Members property defines who belongs and who does not belong to the restricted group. The Member Of property specifies the other groups to which the restricted group can belong.

When a Restricted Groups policy is enforced, any current member of a restricted group that is not on the Members list is removed. Members who can be removed include Administrators. Any user on the Members list who is not currently a member of the restricted group is added. In addition, each restricted group is a member of only those groups specified in the Member Of column.

Figure 6-5 shows Restricted Groups being used to add the IT security group from the *cohowinery.com* domain to the local Administrators group on all domain member computers.

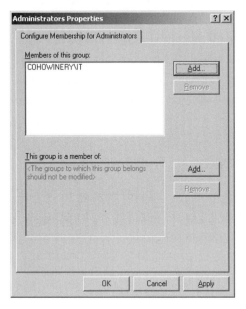

Figure 6-5   Use Restricted Groups to control group membership on domain members.

You can apply a Restricted Groups policy in the following ways:

- Define the policy in a security template and manually apply that template to computers.

- Define the setting directly on a Group Policy object (GPO). Defining the setting in this way will ensure that the operating system continually enforces the restricted groups.

▶ **How to create a Restricted Groups policy**

1. Open a new Microsoft Management Console (MMC) on a computer running Windows 2000 Server or Windows Server 2003 and add the Group Policy Object Editor snap-in. When prompted, select the GPO you want to use to enforce restricted groups, such as the Default Domain Policy.

2. In the console tree, expand Computer Configuration and Security Settings.

3. Right-click Restricted Groups, and then click Add Group.

4. In the Group field, type the name of the group to which you want to restrict membership, and then click OK.

5. In the Properties dialog box, click Add beside the This Group Is A Member Of field.

6. Under Group Membership, type the name of the group you want to add to this group, and then click OK.

7. Click OK again.

Group Naming Conventions

Designing naming standards might not seem like an important job, but a non-intuitive group naming convention can potentially lead to a security compromise. For example, if you named three global groups Group1, Group2, and Group3, a resource owner might not know which group contains the users who need access to the resource, and could grant access to the incorrect group, thereby granting users excessive permissions. The less intuitive the naming convention, the more likely users are to accidentally receive unnecessary permissions.

Table 6-1 lists the components of an intuitive naming convention.

Table 6-1 **Components of a Naming Convention**

Components	Example
Group type	GG for global group, UN for universal group, DLG for domain local group
Location of the group	Sea for Seattle
Purpose of the group	Admins for administrators

Your group naming convention can be based on geographic location, domain membership, or a resource. The main goal is to make the group name intuitive so that resource owners know the type and purpose of the group; then they can grant appropriate access to users. Windows and Active Directory do not provide any means of enforcing a group naming convention. Enforce a group naming convention in your organization by educating users who create groups, and by monitoring group names. In addition, someone in your organization should have the responsibility of auditing group names on a weekly or monthly basis and correcting any groups that have been misnamed.

> **NOTE Creating Group Names**   When creating a name, ensure that the important details are in the first 20 characters of the name. This placement will allow you to view the important details in most dialog boxes without resizing the window.

To design a naming convention, you must understand how your organization will assign resources. For example, the organization might have resources divided by regions. If an organization has marketing departments in Boston, Austin, and San Diego, and each of these marketing departments uses separate resources, include location in the group naming convention because you will be required to make separate groups for each team in each location. Following are examples of possible group names:

- GG BOS Marketing

- GG SAN Marketing

- GG AUS Marketing

However, if the marketing teams from all locations work closely together and do not maintain separate resources, you do not need to include location in the group name. For example, the group name GG Marketing would be sufficiently granular. If there are resources that only users in a particular location should access, regardless of the department they work in, you can create groups for each location, such as GG Austin, GG Boston, and GG San Diego.

> **NOTE Designing Group Names for Sorting**   Keeping the most general information toward the left of the name string and more specific information toward the right makes sorting more logical.

If you decide to use resource groups, you must determine how to name the groups uniquely and logically so that it is obvious to which resources those groups should be assigned. For example, in a small office with a single laser jet printer and a single bubble jet printer, the following names would be acceptable for resource groups:

- DL LJ Print Only

- DL LJ Managers

- DL LJ Administrators

- DL BJ Print Only

- DL BJ Managers

- DL BJ Administrators

However, in an enterprise with hundreds of printers, that naming convention would be confusing. Larger organizations need to include a description of the location in the group name. For example, if an enterprise uses a building code and office code to describe locations, the following names would be acceptable for resources groups:

- DL 25-2003C LJ Print Only

- DL 25-2003C LJ Managers

- DL 25-2003C LJ Administrators

DELEGATING ADMINISTRATIVE PRIVILEGES

In Chapter 5, "Designing Active Directory Security," you learned that it's typically better for an organization to share a single Active Directory domain unless it requires security boundaries. This is true—but when many organizations participate in a domain, you must avoid granting too many administrators rights to manage the entire domain. To allow a group of systems administrators to manage only a particular part of a domain, you can delegate only the administrative privileges they need to do their job. By increasing administrative efficiency and decentralizing administration, delegation reduces administrative costs and improves manageability of IT infrastructures. This, in turn, improves an organization's overall security level.

A good delegation model has the following attributes:

- Provides coverage for all aspects of Active Directory management

- Meets your isolation requirements

- Efficiently distributes administrative responsibilities

- Delegates administrative responsibilities in a security-conscious manner

> **MORE INFO**   *Delegating Active Directory Administration*
> *For more information, read "Best Practices for Delegating Active Directory Administration" at http://www.microsoft.com/downloads/ details.aspx?FamilyID=631747a3-79e1-48fa-9730-dae7c0a1d6d3. In addition, "Best Practices for Delegating Active Directory Administration: Appendices" provides a very useful mapping of common administrative tasks to the user rights required. You can find the appendices at http:// www.microsoft.com/downloads/details.aspx?FamilyID=29dbae88-a216- 45f9-9739-cb1fb22a0642.*

The most efficient way to assign permissions to objects in Active Directory is to open the Active Directory Users And Computers console, right-click the object, and then click Delegate Control. You can also assign permissions to objects by using ADSI Edit.

Each right you delegate has some potential for abuse. There are too many rights to list each of the possible vulnerabilities in this book. For detailed information about the vulnerabilities and potential threats to each right, refer to the document titled, "Threats and Countermeasures: Security Settings in Windows Server 2003 and Windows XP" at *http://www.microsoft.com/downloads/ details.aspx?FamilyId=1B6ACF93-147A-4481-9346-F93A4081EEA8.*

UNDERSTANDING PERMISSION TYPES

Most of the guidelines in this book apply equally well to any type of permission, whether they will apply to Active Directory objects, files and folders, the registry, or services. However, each of these resources has slightly different permissions that you must understand. The sections that follow discuss the resource-specific permissions of each of the major object types on Windows networks.

> **NOTE** **Standard and Special Permissions** Use both standard and special permissions to configure access control lists for the file system, registry, printers, services, and Active Directory. Special permissions are very granular and enable minute control over a user's access to an object. Standard permissions exist to make special permissions easier to manage. When you select a standard permission, Windows selects a set of special permissions assigned to that standard permission.
>
> The permissions available when you view the Security tab of a file or folder's properties dialog box are standard permissions. These include the Full Control, Modify, Read & Execute, Read, and Write standard permissions. If you grant Read & Execute standard permission, Windows automatically grants the List Folder/Read Data, Read Attributes, Read Extended Attributes, and Read Permissions special permissions. Similarly, if you deny the Read & Execute standard permission, the same special permissions are denied. You could choose to select those special permissions manually, but selecting the standard permission is more efficient.

File System Permission Types

File and folder permissions enable users to restrict access to content stored on NTFS volumes. You can grant access to open, edit, or delete files and folders. Files and folders also have the concept of *ownership*: the user who creates a file or folder is the owner of that object and, by default, has the ability to specify the level of access that other users have.

The following are the standard permissions that can be applied to files and folders:

- **Full Control**   Users can perform any action on the file or folder, including creating and deleting it, and modifying its permissions.

- **Modify**   Users can read, edit, and delete files and folders.

- **Read & Execute**   Users can view files and run applications.

- **List Folder Contents**   Users can browse a folder.

- **Read**   Users can view a file or the contents of a folder. If an executable file has Read but not Read & Execute permission, the user will not be able to start the executable.

- **Write**   Users can create files in a directory but not necessarily read them. This permission is useful for creating a folder in which multiple users can deliver files but not access each other's files or even see what other files exist.

- **Special Permissions**   There are more than a dozen special permissions that can be assigned to a user or group. This permission shows as selected if the set of selected special permissions does not match a standard permission.

When any of these standard permissions are selected, Windows Server 2003 automatically selects one or more of the following special permissions:

- **Traverse Folder/Execute File**   Traverse Folder, which applies only to folders, allows moving through folders to reach other files or folders, even when the user has no permissions for the traversed folders. Traverse Folder takes effect only when the group or user is not granted the Bypass Traverse Checking user right, which the Everyone group has by default. Execute File, which applies only to files, allows running program files. Setting the Traverse Folder permission on a folder does not automatically set the Execute File permission on all files within that folder.

> **NOTE The Effect of Special Permissions**   Some special permissions, such as Traverse Folder/Execute File and List Folder/Read Data, have a different effect depending on the object type to which the permission is applied.

- **List Folder/Read Data**   List Folder, which applies only to folders, allows viewing filenames and subfolder names within the folder. Read Data, which applies only to files, allows viewing the contents of a file.

- **Read Attributes**   Allows viewing the attributes of a file or folder, such as read-only and hidden.

- **Read Extended Attributes**   Allows viewing the extended attributes of a file or folder. Programs define extended attributes and can vary by program.

- **Create Files/Write Data**   Create Files, which applies only to folders, allows creating files within the folder. Write Data, which applies only to files, allows or denies making changes to the file and overwriting existing content.

- **Create Folders/Append Data**   Create Folders, which applies only to folders, allows or denies creating folders within the folder. Append Data, which applies only to files, allows or denies making changes to the end of the file but not changing, deleting, or overwriting existing data.

- **Write Attributes**   Allows changing the attributes of a file or folder, such as read-only or hidden.

- **Write Extended Attributes**   Allows changing the extended attributes of a file or folder.

- **Delete Subfolders And Files**   Allows deleting subfolders and files, even when the Delete permission is not granted on the subfolder or file.

- **Delete**   Allows deleting the file or folder. If you don't have Delete permission on a file or folder, you can still delete it if you are granted the Delete Subfolders And Files permission on the parent folder.

- **Read Permissions**   Allows reading permissions of the file or folder, such as Full Control, Read, and Write.

- **Change Permissions**   Allows changing permissions of the file or folder, such as Full Control, Read, and Write.

- **Take Ownership**   Allows taking ownership of the file or folder. The owner of a file or folder can always change permissions on it, regardless of any existing permissions that protect the file or folder.

> **NOTE**   **The Relationship Between Standard and Special Permissions** Neither standard nor special permissions map directly to ACEs. However, for the sake of the exam, it's sufficient to understand that standard permissions are used to simplify management of special permissions. You do not need to memorize all the special permissions.

When you are editing file and folder permissions and you specify the Full Control standard permission, every possible special permission is added to the ACE for the user or group. When you specify the Modify standard permission, every special permission is assigned except the Change Permissions and Take Ownership special permissions. Selecting the Read & Execute standard permission adds ACEs for Traverse Folder/Execute File, List Folder/Read Data, Read Attributes, Read Extended Attributes, and Read Permissions special permissions. The standard Read permission is identical to Read & Execute, except that it lacks the Traverse Folder/Execute File special permission. Finally, the friendly Write standard permission grants Create Files/Write Data, Create Folders/Append Data, Write Attributes, and Write Extended Attributes special permissions.

> **NOTE**   **The Real Usefulness of Special Permissions (or Lack Thereof)** In the real world, you rarely have to deal with special permissions. In fact, avoid it whenever possible because managing special permissions is more difficult than managing standard permissions. Standard permissions are granular enough to meet all but the tightest security requirements.

Active Directory Permission Types

It's important to understand access control on Active Directory objects. However, avoid changing the permissions whenever it is not required by your applications or your environment's security requirements. If you do need to modify the permissions, do so carefully. A user who intentionally or accidentally changes Active Directory objects, or the permissions assigned to those objects, can quickly affect many users and applications on the network.

Specifying too many **explicit permissions** on Active Directory objects can cause performance problems, particularly in environments with multiple domain controllers. Active Directory objects, and the ACEs associated with the assigned permissions, must be replicated between domain controllers. Therefore, the more permissions you assign, the longer replication will take, and the more significant an impact replication will have on your network.

> **NOTE** **Active Directory Default Security Settings** Active Directory applies default security settings designed to provide an out-of-the-box security configuration. These security settings grant specific pre-configured permissions to specific security groups created by default.

The following are the standard permissions that can be applied to Active Directory objects:

- **Full Control** Users can perform any action on the Active Directory object, including creating and deleting new child objects and modifying permissions.

- **Read** Users can view all object properties, the object permissions, and the object's contents (if any).

- **Write** Users can edit object properties.

- **Create All Child Objects** If the object is a container, such as an OU, users can create any type of child object in the container. You can use special permissions to limit the types of objects that a user can create. For example, special permissions allow a user to create users, but not to create groups or computers.

- **Delete All Child Objects**   If the object is a container, such as an OU, users can delete any type of child object in the container. You can use special permissions to limit the types of objects that a user can delete. For example, special permissions allow a user to delete users, but not to delete groups or computers.

- **Special Permissions**   There are more than twenty special permissions that can be assigned to a user or group. This permission shows as selected if the set of selected special permissions does not match a standard permission.

In addition, different types of objects have object-specific standard permissions. For example, a computer or user object has the Allowed To Authenticate, Change Password, and Reset Password standard permissions (among others). Security group objects also have the Add/Remove Self As Member, Send To, Read Phone And Mail Options, and Write Phone And Mail Options standard permissions.

As with other types of resources, selecting standard permissions selects one or more special permissions. Active Directory has hundreds of different permissions, and the permissions available vary depending on the type of object. For example, the available permissions for the Computers container differ from those for a computer object located in that container. The following are examples of special permissions that control the ability to perform low-level Active Directory operations.

- **Create *Child* Objects**   The right to create various types of children within the object. Different permissions exist for different types of child objects, including containers, computers, and user objects, as well as dozens of other object types. Unless you specifically need to control the types of objects a user creates, specify the Create All Child Objects standard permission.

- **Delete *Child* Objects**   The right to delete various types of children within the object. As with the Create *Child* Objects permission, use the Delete All Child Objects standard permission whenever possible.

- **Delete**   The right to delete the object.

- **Delete Subtree**   The right to delete all children of the object, regardless of the permissions on the children.

- **Read Permissions**   The right to read data from the security descriptor of the object, not including the data in the SACL.

- **Modify Permissions**   The right to modify the ACL in the object security descriptor.

- **Modify Owner**   The right to assume ownership of the object.

- **Read Property**   The right to read properties of the object.

- **Write Property**   The right to write properties on the object.

- **List Contents**   The right to list children of the object.

- **Access System Security**   The right to get or set the SACL in the object security descriptor.

For information about hardening domain controllers, refer to Chapter 7, "Hardening Servers."

Under most circumstances, control Active Directory permissions using the Delegation of Control Wizard, discussed later in this chapter. To control Active Directory permissions on a granular level, use the ADSI Edit tool. To use ADSI Edit, install the Windows Support Tools (included on the operating system CD-ROM), open a blank Microsoft Management Console (MMC), and add the ADSI Edit snap-in. As shown in Figure 6-6, it provides a user interface for modifying Active Directory permissions that is very similar to the interface that Windows Explorer provides for modifying file permissions.

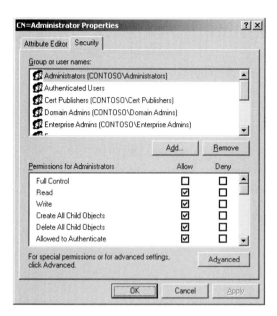

Figure 6-6 Use ADSI Edit, a Windows Support tool, to examine and modify permissions on Active Directory objects.

Registry Permission Types

Like most operating system objects, default registry permissions have changed with each new version of Windows. The default permissions in Windows Server 2003 are very restrictive, and protect the operating system from registry-based attacks from most non-administrative user accounts. The default registry permissions in Windows 2000 and earlier versions of Windows were significantly vulnerable to registry attacks. Use auditing to determine the registry permissions that users need, and limit their privileges to all other parts of the registry.

The registry stores the bulk of configuration information for both the operating system and applications. Being able to control registry permissions is important. In some cases, restrict permissions to prevent users from modifying registry keys that could present a security vulnerability or cause other problems on their computers. In other cases, you might grant users additional permissions to parts of the registry to allow them to run applications that they could not otherwise run. You can assign permissions to the values and keys in the registry by using the registry editor. To edit permissions within the registry editor, right-click the registry key, and then select Permissions.

The following are the standard permissions applied to registry keys and values:

- **Full Control**   Users can perform any action on the registry key or value, including creating and deleting new values and subkeys.

- **Read**   Users can view values and subkeys, but cannot create, delete, or edit them.

- **Special Permissions**   There are more than ten special permissions that can be assigned to a user or group. This permission shows as selected if the set of selected special permissions does not match a standard permission.

Service Permission Types

Service permissions are among the least frequently used permissions, but they can be useful in some environments. If your organization has separate groups that manage various services on a computer, you can grant the members of those groups the ability to control only the permissions they manage. For example, you could grant the team responsible for managing your Web site access to restart the World Wide Web Publishing Service without allowing them to stop the Terminal Services service.

You might expect to modify service permissions by using the Services console. There is no user interface for modifying permissions in the Services console, however, so you have to use the System Services node in a security template. I discuss security templates in more detail in Chapter 3, "Reducing the Risk of Software Vulnerabilities."

The following are the standard permissions that can be applied to services:

- **Full Control**   Users can perform any action on the service, including starting and stopping the service, modifying the service's permissions, and specifying whether a service starts automatically.

- **Read**   Users can view the status, permissions, and dependencies of a service.

- **Start, Stop, And Pause**   As you would expect, users can start, stop, and pause the service.

- **Write**   Users cannot directly start or stop a service; however, they can specify whether the service is disabled, set to start manually, or starts automatically when the server reboots.

- **Delete**   Users can delete the service.

- **Special Permissions**   There are more than ten special permissions that can be assigned to a user or group. This permission shows as selected if the set of selected special permissions does not match a standard permission.

Printer Permission Types

Controlling access to printers is useful for specifying users who can manage the printers and the print queue. You can assign permissions to printers by using Printers And Faxes, viewing the printer's properties, and clicking the Security tab. The following are the standard permissions that can be applied to printers:

- **Print**   The user can connect to a printer and send documents to the printer. By default, the Print permission is assigned to all members of the Everyone group.

- **Manage Printers**   The user can perform the tasks associated with the Print permission and has complete administrative control of the printer. The user can pause and restart the printer, change spooler settings, share a printer, adjust printer permissions, and change printer properties.

- **Manage Documents**   The user can pause, resume, restart, cancel, and rearrange the order of documents submitted by all other users. The user cannot, however, send documents to the printer or control the status of the printer. By default, the Manage Documents permission is assigned to members of the Creator Owner special group to allow users to manage their own print jobs. When a user is assigned the Manage Documents permission, the user cannot access existing documents currently waiting to print. The permission will apply only to documents sent to the printer after the user has permission

- **Special Permissions**   There are only six special permissions for printers. Besides the standard permissions, there are permissions for Read Permissions, Change Permissions, and Take Ownership.

By default, members of the Administrators and Power Users groups have full access to printers, which means that the users are assigned the Print, Manage Documents, and Manage Printers permissions.

Share Permission Types

Use Windows Explorer to specify permissions for shared folders. To do so, right-click the shared folder, select Sharing And Security, and then click the Permissions button. The following are the standard permissions that can be applied to shared folders:

- **Full Control**   Users can read, write, and change permissions on files and folders within the share if allowed to do so by file and folder permissions.

- **Change**   Users can read and write to files and folders within the share if allowed to do so by file and folder permissions.

- **Read**   Users can read files and folders within the share if allowed to do so by file and folder permissions.

Share permissions are simpler than other types of permissions, and there is no need for special share permissions. Consider share permissions an additional layer of security beyond file and folder permissions. In most cases, rely on file and folder permissions to secure the file system, regardless of whether it is accessed locally or across a network. Share permissions are used primarily on servers with FAT32 volumes, since FAT32 volumes lack the file system security of NTFS.

DESIGNING PERMISSIONS

There are two main philosophies for designing permissions: remove all default permissions and grant only those that users need, and use the default permissions but remove those that users don't need. In theory, removing all default permissions provides a more secure environment. In practice, your time is usually better spent modifying the default permissions. The sections that follow discuss each of these two approaches in detail and provide best practices for designing permission structures.

Remove All Permissions and Add Only Required Ones

The most secure method for designing any kind of permissions is to remove all of the default permissions, determine the exact permissions a user requires, and grant the users only those permissions. This technique requires that users do not even have the default permissions assigned to the Domain Users group, which might be excessive for an environment extremely concerned with users abusing their privileges. This technique can also be applied to administrators responsible for managing only particular aspects of a resource, such as an administrator who is responsible for a Web server application, but should not be able to manage other aspects of a server. To determine the permissions an application or task requires, refer to the section titled, "The Process of Hardening Permissions" later in this chapter.

Designing permissions by removing all default permissions ensures that you follow the principle of least privilege. Unfortunately, this technique is extremely costly to pursue. First, it can take weeks of work in a lab environment testing user applications and administrative tasks to determine exactly what permissions a user or administrator requires. Once you identify the permissions, you have to find a way to delegate those permissions to the user. In itself, the process of initially identifying permissions isn't the biggest drawback to this approach, however.

The biggest drawback to this approach is the overwhelming cost of maintaining the restrictive permissions. In practice, you will discover that users run into problems because an application assumes that it has permissions you have not granted the user. Even if an application works during your initial testing, it's possible for the user to find application functionality that you didn't adequately test. Deploying application updates might change the permission requirements, meaning each update you deploy will require extensive testing and modification to your permissions structure. If you do choose to use this approach, you must use extremely thorough testing procedures.

Consider an example: You are deploying standardized desktop clients to 200 users in the customer service department. You want their permissions on the desktop to be as restrictive as possible. Even the Users group provides more permissions than you would like to allow. Therefore, you create a new local group for the users and grant it no access to any resources on the network or the local computer. You test each function of the application thoroughly to ensure that users can perform every task you expect them to.

A month later, you hire an employee who requires the Windows XP Magnifier accessibility tool. However, the privileges you assigned do not allow this tool to function. The employee will either need to wait while you identify the additional permissions needed and change your permission structure (causing your organization to lose productivity), or you will need to add the employee's user account to a group with excessive privileges (creating a security risk).

This challenge is significant because application developers do not currently plan for security designers to analyze the permissions required by an application. Most tools that developers create for systems administration–type tasks assume the user is a member of the local Administrators group. Most productivity tools (such as word processors) assume the user is a member of the local Users group or, possibly, the local Administrators group. Trying to force these applications to run with fewer permissions is a significant challenge, and few application developers are willing to dedicate the time required to change their development practices to work better in a more restrictive environment.

Because of the trade-offs, use this technique only when you have determined that the risk of users abusing standard privileges exceeds the very high cost of constantly adjusting user permissions.

Reduce Default Permissions as Required

Although not as secure as removing all default permissions and adding only those a user needs, this approach is much easier to implement and maintain. With this approach, you place users and administrators in standard, built-in user groups such as the local Users and Administrators groups. Then, you reduce their permissions to prevent them from accessing system and network resources that you have identified as vulnerabilities.

For example, consider an enterprise datacenter with 100 servers managed by ten different administrators. You need the administrators to be able to do their jobs and to manage the servers. However, during the security risk management process, you determined that an administrator acquiring and abusing another administrator's privileges would pose a significant risk because it would bypass your auditing system. Therefore, you identify resources that an administrator would use in such an attack (such as the RunOnce registry key) and restrict his or her permissions to those resources. Then, you add additional auditing to identify administrators attempting to modify those keys.

This approach is significantly easier to maintain than the previous approach because most applications and tools will run without changing the permission structure. However, just as most application developers create their applications to run in the context of a standard user or administrator account, most attack tools also abuse these standard privileges. Therefore, monitor attack tools and techniques closely, and modify your permissions to reduce specific vulnerabilities that you identify. This can be time-consuming, but overall is significantly easier than adding permissions that users lack. Additionally, software vendors typically release updates to simplify fixing well-known vulnerabilities.

Best Practices for Designing Permissions

When designing permissions, keep the following best practices in mind.

- **Use security templates and GPOs to specify permissions**   Rather than set individual permissions, use security templates whenever possible. Security templates make it easier to audit configurations and to apply settings to multiple objects.

  Use Group Policy to specify local user database group memberships, system service settings, registry permissions, and file system permissions for computers in your domain. As shown in Figure 6-7, Group Policy settings can specify very granular permissions.

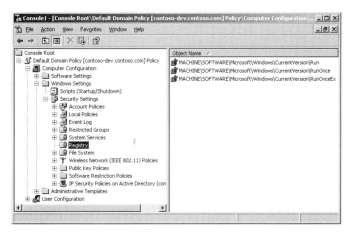

Figure 6-7   Use Group Policy settings and security templates to distribute permission settings to multiple computers.

■ **Assign permissions to an object as high on the tree as possible and then apply inheritance to propagate the security settings through the tree**   You can apply access control settings to all children or the sub-tree of a parent object quickly and effectively. By doing this, you gain the greatest breadth of effect with the least effort. The permission settings you establish should be adequate for the majority of users, groups, and computers.

■ **Minimize the number of access control entries that apply to child objects**   Use the fewest number of ACEs possible to meet your security requirements. This improves performance, reduces complexity, and reduces the opportunity for error. For example, allow "Read All Properties" or "Write All Properties" rather than individual properties.

> **NOTE   Minimizing Risk by Assigning Individual Permissions**   There are times when assigning individual permissions is appropriate. For example, if a help desk operator needs Write access to two properties of a User object, use one ACE for each property to reduce the risk of abuse, rather than granting permission to the entire user object.

■ **Avoid changing default permissions whenever possible**   Most applications are designed to function correctly with the default permissions. Use default permissions whenever possible to improve application compatibility.

■ **Avoid Deny permissions except when necessary**   Never deny the Everyone group access to an object. Use Deny permissions to exclude a subset of a group that has Allowed permissions. Use Deny to exclude one special permission when you have already granted full control to a user or group.

■ **In Active Directory, assign the same set of permissions to multiple objects**   ACLs in the Windows Server 2003 family feature single instancing: If multiple objects have identical ACLs, Active Directory will store only one instance of the ACL. Therefore, using the same sets of permissions improves efficiency.

■ **In Active Directory, avoid use of domain local groups for controlling Read access to global catalog data**   Using domain local groups to control Read permissions on global catalog objects can result in unpredictable searches because a domain controller from a different domain in the same forest might be queried.

The Process of Hardening Permissions

On Windows networks, you can use the following process to harden the permissions of almost any resource type, including file systems, the registry, Active Directory, and other Microsoft applications and services.

1. Use MBSA to Identify Significant Vulnerabilities

MBSA is an extremely useful tool for identifying a wide variety of software vulnerabilities, including problems related to weak permission settings. Use MBSA on the test systems that you use to design your organization's standard permission settings. As shown in Figure 6-8, MBSA can detect file system permissions that lead to vulnerabilities.

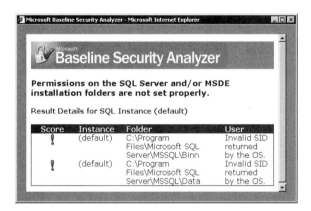

Figure 6-8   Use MBSA to scan for file permission vulnerabilities.

For more information about MBSA, refer to Chapter 3.

2. Review Security Guides

Microsoft has published hardening guides for all recent versions of Windows and many services. These security guides provide extremely detailed coverage of permissions and other security settings that can lead to or mitigate vulnerabilities. As of the time of this writing, the following security guides are available:

- Windows 2000 Security Hardening Guide

- Windows XP Security Guide

- Windows Server 2003 Security Guide

- Exchange 2000 Security Guide

- Exchange Server 2003 Security Hardening Guide

- Microsoft Internet Security and Acceleration (ISA) Server 2004 Security Hardening Guide

- Microsoft Operations Manager 2005 Security Guide

In addition, the Microsoft Web site contains security guidance for most Microsoft client and server business applications. As Microsoft releases new software, they will also release updated security guides.

This book cannot provide guidance regarding specific permissions that you would need to set to protect computers because the guidance varies based on the environment and deserves several books unto itself. Therefore, this book focuses on design concepts that will remain true for many generations of operating systems and applications. Refer to detailed security guides provided by vendors and third parties for more detailed technical information about specific products.

3. Identify Missing Permissions

Whether you choose to grant or deny access to all resources by default, users are bound to have problems with running applications or performing their normal job tasks because they lack an important permission. Often, help desk administrators resolve this type of problem quickly, by either making the user a member of a privileged group (such as Administrators or Domain Admins) or granting the user full privileges to all network resources that the application might possibly require. Unfortunately, both of these approaches result in granting the user excessive permissions; however, auditing can identify exactly the permissions the user needs. Then, you can decide whether to adjust permissions on the network resources, grant the user additional rights, or add the user to an additional group to resolve the problem.

Windows 2000, Windows XP, and Windows Server 2003 each include auditing capabilities that add an event to the Security event log each time a user with insufficient permissions accesses a resource. Identifying the source of authorization problems using auditing is complex, but auditing identifies exactly the missing permissions a user requires to perform a task or run an application. The flow chart in Figure 6-9 shows the authorization troubleshooting process that occurs when you use auditing.

> **NOTE Auditing for Intrusion Detection**   Most people think of auditing as solely an intrusion detection mechanism. In reality, its usefulness for intrusion detection is limited because it tends to generate far too many events to parse successfully. However, it is immensely useful when troubleshooting authorization problems.

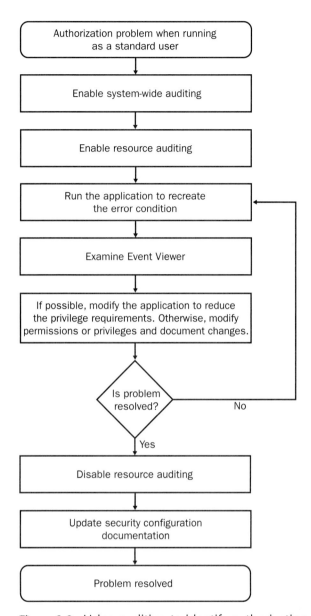

Figure 6-9   Using auditing to identify authorization problems

Most of the troubleshooting process is self-explanatory, but enabling system auditing, enabling resource auditing, and analyzing events by using Event Viewer deserve further explanation.

▶ How to enable system auditing

The first step in identifying resources with insufficient privileges is to enable auditing on a system-wide basis, as follows:

1. Log on to your computer using an administrator account.

2. Click Start, and then click Administrative Tools. If this is a domain members or a stand-alone computer, click Local Security Policy. If this is a domain controller, click Domain Controller Security Policy.

3. Expand Local Policies, and then click Audit Policy.

4. If you are troubleshooting access to Active Directory objects, double-click Audit Directory Service Access. If you are troubleshooting access to any other type of object, double-click Audit Object Access.

5. Make note of the current setting. You will return this setting to its original state after you complete the troubleshooting process.

6. Select Define These Policy Settings, and then select Failure, as shown in Figure 6-10. Click OK.

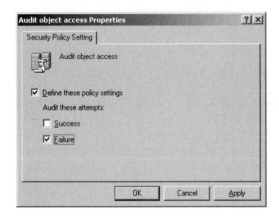

Figure 6-10   Enable system auditing before resource auditing.

► How to enable resource auditing

After enabling failure auditing for the Audit Object Access or Audit Directory Services Access policies, you must enable auditing for the individual resources that are being accessed. The exact process varies depending on the type of object you want to audit. The following process applies to enabling auditing for folders or files, the most common source of authorization problems. The process for auditing other types of objects is very similar, although you will use a different tool for each object.

1. Click Start, point to All Programs, point to Accessories, and then click Windows Explorer.

2. Navigate to the file or folder you want to audit. If you are not sure which object is being accessed, you can enable auditing for entire disks.

3. Right-click the file or folder, and then click Properties.

4. On the Security tab, click the Advanced button.

5. In the Advanced Security Settings dialog box, click the Auditing tab. Make note of the current settings, and then click Add.

6. In the Select User Or Group dialog box, type the name of the user account you are using to debug the application, and then click OK. The Auditing Entry dialog box appears.

7. Select the Failed check box for the Full Control entry, as shown in Figure 6-11. All Failed check boxes are selected automatically.

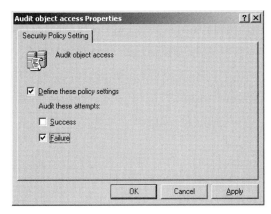

Figure 6-11 Enable resource failure auditing to detect unsuccessful attempts to access protected resources.

8. Click OK twice. Windows will apply the auditing setting to the folder, subfolder, and files automatically. If you are applying settings to a large number of files, such as the entire C drive, this can take a moment.

9. Click OK to close the Properties dialog box and return to Windows Explorer.

Now that failure auditing is enabled for those resources, every time the specified user is denied access to the resource, Windows will add an event to the Security event log. If you are using auditing for troubleshooting, be sure to disable auditing after the problem is resolved. Auditing a large number of objects adds many events to the event log and can affect performance severely.

▶ **How to analyze events in Event Viewer**

After you enable auditing and re-create the problem condition, Windows adds events to the Security event log that describe which resource could not be accessed and the type of operation that was attempted. To view failure audit events by using Event Viewer, perform the following steps:

1. Log on to the computer using an administrator account.

2. Click Start, click Administrative Tools, and then click Event Viewer.

3. In the left pane, click Security. The Security event log displays.

4. On the View menu, click Filter. The Security Properties dialog box appears.

5. Clear the Information, Warning, Error, and Success Audit check boxes. Only the Failure Audit check box should remain selected. Click OK.

6. Event Viewer will now display only failure audits in the right pane. Double-click the most recent failure audit to examine the contents of the event. The Event Properties dialog box appears, as shown in Figure 6-12.

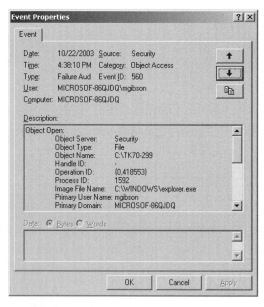

Figure 6-12 Event Viewer is the most common tool for manually analyzing events.

7. Examine the Description box. This box shows the type of object, the object name, the process ID, and image filename of the application used to access the object, and the type of operation that was performed on the object. For example, the following are the contents of the Description box for a user, mgibson, who was denied access to the C:\Private folder when she attempted to access the folder using Windows Explorer.

```
Object Open:
 Object Server:Security
 Object Type:File
 Object Name:C:\Private
 Handle ID:-
 Operation ID:{0,419122}
 Process ID:1592
 Image File Name:C:\WINDOWS\explorer.exe
 Primary User Name:mgibson
 Primary Domain:MICROSOF-86QJDQ
 Primary Logon ID:(0x0,0x60641)
 Client User Name:-
 Client Domain:-
 Client Logon ID:-
 Accesses:SYNCHRONIZE
ReadData (or ListDirectory)
Privileges:-
 Restricted Sid Count:0
 Access Mask:0x100001
```

Notice that the *Accesses* line lists *Synchronize* and *ReadData*. This indicates that the application was attempting to gain read access to the C:\Private directory. To resolve this problem, you would either modify the way the user performs the task so that it no longer requires the right to read the directory, or you would document the fact that the user requires the permission and follow your organization's change management process to grant the additional access. There are two ways to grant the additional access:

❑ Modify the folder's ACL to grant the user (or a group to which the user belongs) Read access to that folder.

❑ Add the user to a group that already has Read access to the folder.

8. Browse through other failure audit events to determine other resources to which the user might require access.

After identifying the resources the user requires access to and assigning new permissions, repeat the troubleshooting process by re-creating the problem. Often, you will have to run through the process three or four times to identify all the permissions required by the user.

Benefits of Delegation

By enabling efficient, security-conscious delegation and distribution of administrative responsibilities among various administrative groups that addresses the specific requirements imposed by participating business units, delegation of administration provides the means to manage an Active Directory environment successfully. Delegation of administration provides the following benefits:

- Allows distribution of administrative responsibility among multiple administrative groups, each with a defined scope of authority and a defined set of responsibilities

- Enables decentralization of administrative authority

- Allows the security-conscious distribution of administrative responsibility

In addition, delegation of administration allows organizations to efficiently manage their IT infrastructures and enforce their security precautions by enabling organizations to:

- Distribute administrative responsibilities based on least privilege, which ensures that the individual or group of individuals to whom the task has been delegated can perform only the tasks that are delegated, and cannot perform tasks that have not been explicitly delegated or authorized.

- Increase administrative efficiency by easily and conveniently assigning the responsibilities for managing Active Directory content and the directory service itself.

- Reduce administrative costs by facilitating shared administrative responsibility. For example, administrative responsibility for providing account support to all accounts in the organization can be easily achieved within a matter of minutes.

An Example of Delegation of Administration

A brief example of delegation at work will help you better understand the value and the benefits of delegation that organizations can use to enhance security, decrease the total cost of ownership (TCO), and make Active Directory and IT resource management more tractable and efficient.

Contoso Pharmaceuticals, a fictitious company, has recently deployed Active Directory. Contoso Pharmaceuticals is a large organization that has its headquarters in Chicago, Illinois, and has operations in five other locations in North America and Europe. The Active Directory infrastructure consists of a single forest, three domains, and six sites. The company has about 16,000 users, 20,000 end-user workstations, and about 3000 servers spread across five physical locations. Contoso has four business units in each of the five physical locations. These business units include:

- Research and Development

- Production

- Business Management

- IT

With Active Directory delegation, Contoso could delegate responsibility in the following areas:

- **Workstation management**   Contoso could delegate all aspects of workstation management to local administrative groups, one for each physical location, seamlessly and easily.

- **Account management**   Contoso could delegate all aspects of account management to the Account Admins of each business unit, regardless of the physical location of the managed users, while centrally retaining help desk operations.

- **Security-sensitive operations**   Contoso could grant security personnel sufficient authority to carry out security-sensitive operations on every user account in the company, such as allowing security personnel to disable or lock out any user account in the entire company without contacting the IT group.

- **Resource management**   Contoso could delegate all aspects of resource management to the appropriate resource owners, enabling the resource owners to manage and retain control over their resources. For example, this might include:

  ❑ A human resources portal on the intranet, hosted on a small cluster of three high-performance servers running Microsoft Internet Information Services (IIS). Contoso could delegate full control over the servers to the administrators of this application and grant them the ability to authorize access to their portal.

  ❑ Multiple in-house applications hosted on a set of high-performance servers, with the administration of the servers entrusted to one set of administrators in the data center and the administration of each application entrusted to a separate set of administrators. Using delegation, Contoso could easily delegate to the administrative group responsible for managing the servers the ability to manage the servers while delegating to the administrative group responsible for managing each application the ability to manage their applications.

- **Self-service user accounts**   Contoso could enable self-service on user accounts so that users could change and finely control specific information themselves. With delegation, Contoso could allow their users to modify their phone numbers and personal information while retaining control over the ability to modify such sensitive data as the password-not-required flags on user objects. Contoso could also grant other stakeholders, such as human resources managers, the ability to modify a user's manager and office location information.

- **Active Directory–enabled applications**   Contoso could delegate all aspects of Microsoft Exchange mailbox administration to its Exchange administrators, which increases productivity while achieving separation of duties. In addition, Contoso has an in-house application that stores data in Active Directory. Contoso administrators could delegate complete control over the application's data to the application's administrators, including the ability to control access to data by using account and resource groups.

- **Service management**   Contoso could distribute Active Directory service management among specific administrative groups based on the principle of least privilege. This increased accountability could provide a clear separation of responsibility and decrease the number of highly trusted administrators that Contoso needed to hire and maintain.

As demonstrated by the Contoso example, organizations can realize multiple benefits from the delegation capabilities of Active Directory. These benefits include distributing administrative responsibilities based on least privilege, increasing administrative efficiency by easily and conveniently assigning the responsibilities for managing directory content and the directory service itself, and reducing administrative costs by facilitating shared administrative responsibility.

Typical Roles for Delegation

The great thing about the granular permissions provided for different types of objects on Windows networks is that they give you a great deal of flexibility for delegating administrative rights. You can use this flexibility to create delegated administrative roles that provide just the permissions required for various employees to do their job, with no excessive permissions. You do not have to structure your organization around predefined roles such as Backup Operators or Server Operators. In fact, your organization's upper management typically specifies organizational structure. As a security designer, it's not your job to determine what responsibilities different groups will have. It is your job, however, to design a group structure to simplify management of user rights, and to map job responsibilities to user rights and permissions.

Although you should take advantage of the flexibility to create very customized delegated roles, most organizations have roles similar to these:

- **Regional administrators**   This role is useful in organizations that distribute responsibility to regional IT organizations. This role typically has unlimited rights to all resources within their region, and can further delegate rights to local staff as needed.

- **Application administrators**   Many organizations have different IT groups to manage different critical applications. For example, they might have two or three people dedicated to maintaining the company's internal payroll application. These administrators probably need permissions to restart the servers involved in the application they administer, as well as to stop and start services, and add or remove users from the servers' local user databases. They don't need permissions to modify the Active Directory or to manage other computers, however.

- **Database administrators**   The database administrator role is similar to the application administrator role, except database administrators typically need permissions only to the database portion of an application. This means that a database administrator wouldn't necessarily be able to access an application's front-end servers.

- **Help desk operators**   Help desk operators typically need some permissions to both end-user computers and portions of the Active Directory. Depending on the specific responsibilities, they might also need access to server resources. The following is a list of common help desk operator tasks:

    - ❑ Create user accounts
    - ❑ Delete user accounts
    - ❑ Move user accounts
    - ❑ Reset a user's password

❑ Unlock user accounts

❑ Modify non–security-sensitive information, such as phone numbers

❑ Modify security-sensitive information

■ **Infrastructure administrators**   Infrastructure administrators manage Active Directory, Domain Name System (DNS), Windows Internet Naming Service (WINS), virtual private network (VPN) servers, firewalls, proxy servers, and the network infrastructure. They don't necessarily need any permissions to desktop computers or servers that aren't related to the infrastructure itself.

■ **Developers**   Developers need more permissions than standard desktop users because they need to be able to debug applications running on their computers. If the developers use Microsoft Visual Studio, the installation creates a local group named VS Developers specifically to grant the necessary rights to the desktop environment. In addition, developers creating Web applications might need elevated permissions on the Web server to debug Web applications remotely.

■ **Managers**   Most management tasks require no more permissions than standard users. However, some organizations push the responsibility for delegating rights and auditing the actions of their teams to managers. If you decide that managers are the most capable of performing these tasks, assign additional privileges to that role.

■ **Security administrators**   Security-conscious organizations have different groups responsible for performing day-to-day management of computers and for managing the security configuration and audit logs. If your organization requires a separate group for security administrators, grant this group rights to perform auditing, to export log files, and to shut down systems (in the event of a compromise). Restrict standard administrators from performing actions that might interfere with security administrators' work such as clearing the event log.

Guidelines for Delegating Administration

Use the following recommendations to guide your delegation design:

- Create a separate security group for each administrative role your organization needs.

- If users tend to perform multiple roles, such as managing infrastructure servers and auditing desktop security, create separate roles for each task. This will make re-assigning permissions easier if responsibilities change in the future.

- Whenever possible, delegate permissions only on OUs. OUs specifically facilitate delegation of administration. Delegating permissions on OUs enables easy and reliable revocation.

- Unless required, do not specify permissions on individual objects within an OU.

- Consider granting access to modify Group Policy settings to be a significant vulnerability. Users who can create or modify Group Policy settings can maliciously elevate their privileges by configuring a logon script that runs the next time one of the higher-privileged administrators logs on. The logon script could add their user account to the Domain Admins group.

- Avoid granting Full Control permissions over an object or OU. Granting someone Full Control allows that person to take ownership of an object and modify the permissions on it. If someone has Full Control on a container, he or she can take ownership of, and have Full Control over, all objects in that container. As far as possible, instead of allowing Full Control, give only the permissions needed by the user.

- Carefully consider who should own the root object for each domain partition. The owners of these directory partition root objects have the ability to change the security settings of all other objects in the partition through inheritable ACEs, which is a significant vulnerability. The Schema Admins group owns the schema directory partition, Enterprise Admins group owns the configuration directory partition, and the Builtin\Administrators group owns the domain directory partition.

■ On domain controllers that are running Windows Server 2003, set quotas that limit the number of objects that a user can own in a domain or application directory partition. This type of quota reduces the risk of a denial-of-service attack caused by creating unlimited numbers of objects in a directory partition. For more information about Active Directory quotas, refer to *http://www.microsoft.com/resources/documentation/WindowsServ/2003/standard/proddocs/en-us/sag_ADintro_9.asp*.

Inheritance and Organizational Units

OUs are special-purpose containers in that they are intended to contain domain objects such as user accounts, computer accounts, and groups. In addition, OUs can contain other OUs within them. In this manner, domain objects are stored within a hierarchy of OUs that serve the role of containers for domain objects. Unlike other Active Directory containers, such as computers and users, GPOs can be applied directly to OUs. GPOs applied to OUs are inherited automatically by all child objects. The precedence of GPOs is determined by the order in which the Group Policy has been applied.

Use OUs to form a hierarchy of special-purpose containers within a domain. These OUs can be used to store computer accounts, user accounts, and resources based on specific Group Policy requirements.

OUs also play a major role in delegation of administration. Delegation of administration involves granting an administrative group sufficient permissions to allow the group to perform specific administrative tasks. Usually, administrative authority is delegated to manage a set of users. Although it is possible to grant an administrative group permissions on the specific user accounts that belong to a set of users, individually modifying the ACL of every single user account in a set is usually unmanageable and impractical. To simplify the application of the permissions required to delegate authority and control access, the inheritance feature of Active Directory enables the application of inheritable permissions on objects.

Instead of having to specify permissions in the ACL of every managed object explicitly, administrators can simply specify the same permission on an OU or any object that contains one or more objects, and mark the specified permissions as inheritable. Because domain information is typically stored in OUs, inheritable permissions usually are applied on OU objects, and inheritance takes care of propagating all inheritable permissions down to all objects in the sub-tree rooted at the OU on which these inheritable permissions were applied.

> **NOTE** **Applying Inheritable Permissions to the Computers and Users Containers**   Inheritable permissions can be applied to the Computers and Users containers even though they are not OUs because the concept of inheritance of permissions applies to other containers as well as to OUs. Inheritance works the same in every directory partition, whether the Configuration partition, the Schema partition, or a domain partition.

Thus, after you design your Active Directory forest and domain architectures, you must create an OU structure to store domain objects, including user and computer accounts and groups. When designing an OU structure, take into account both Group Policy application requirements and requirements for delegation of administration.

AUDITING

As Chapter 2, "Analyzing Risk," discussed, you can't realistically expect to prevent all compromises. For many risks, the best you can hope to do is detect that a compromise has occurred, identify the vulnerability the threat agent targeted, and identify the threat itself. You can do this with auditing.

Auditing, a feature built into Windows NT, Windows 2000, Windows XP, and Windows Server 2003, adds an event to the Security event log when a user attempts to perform a task for which auditing has been enabled. For example, auditing can add an event when a user attempts to open an important file, or each time a user attempts to log on. Most security designers use auditing to determine what an attacker has done to a system after a compromise has been detected. Auditing can also detect both attacks currently in progress and unsuccessful attacks that occurred earlier.

There are two types of audit events: success and failure. Success audits occur when a user attempts to access a resource and is granted access. Failure audits occur when a user attempts to access a resource, but is denied access because of insufficient permissions. Failure audits can be very useful for identifying attempted attacks.

The sections that follow describe best practices for how to use auditing as an intrusion detection tool, various tools that you can use to examine log files, and the meaning of important events created when auditing is enabled.

Default Auditing Settings

By default, Windows 2000, Windows XP, and earlier versions of Windows do not have auditing enabled. However, computers running Windows Server 2003 do have the most useful types of auditing enabled by default, In Active Directory environments, the Default Domain Controller policy enables several types of auditing on domain controllers. However, the Default Domain policy does not enable any auditing. Unless the Local Security Policy of member computers enables auditing, most computers on your network will not be audited unless you change the Default Domain Controller policy.

The easiest way to configure auditing for computers in an Active Directory environment is to use the Group Policy settings located within Computer Configuration\Windows Settings\Security Settings\Local Policies\Audit Policy\. Table 6-2 lists the different types of events and whether they are enabled by default on computers running Windows Server 2003. As you can see, domain controllers by default have several additional types of auditing enabled.

Table 6-2 **Windows Server 2003 Default Auditing Policies**

Policy	Default Settings	Domain Controller Default Settings
Audit Account Logon Events	Success	Success
Audit Account Management	No auditing	Success
Audit Directory Service Access	Undefined	Success
Audit Logon Events	Success	Success
Audit Object Access	No auditing	No auditing
Audit Policy Change	No auditing	Success
Audit Privilege Use	No auditing	No auditing
Audit Process Tracking	No auditing	No auditing
Audit System Events	No auditing	Success

You might not need to make any adjustments to the default auditing settings of computers running Windows Server 2003, but be sure to examine the settings on earlier versions of Windows to ensure that they meet your requirements for tracking user actions. By default, earlier versions of Windows did not enable any auditing. In particular, analyze Active Directory resource auditing on Windows 2000 Server domain controllers and Windows Server 2003 domain controllers that were upgraded from Windows 2000 Server. Windows Server 2003 domain controllers not upgraded from Windows 2000 have extensive auditing enabled on Active Directory objects to detect potential attacks.

> **MORE INFO**   For more information about auditing Active Directory objects, read the paper titled, "Best Practice Guide for Securing Active Directory Installations and Day-to-Day Operations" at http://www.microsoft.com/technet/prodtechnol/windows2000serv/technologies/activedirectory/maintain/bpguide/default.mspx.

When deciding how much to audit, bear in mind that the more you audit, the more events you generate and, therefore, the more difficult it can be to spot critical events. If you are doing extensive auditing, strongly consider using additional tools, such as Microsoft Operations Manager (MOM), to help you filter events that are of greater importance.

Archiving Logs to Meet Security Requirements

Log files of any type present a challenge because they contain important information that you might need to refer to in the future, but they also grow constantly and can fill up your disk space. Audit logs are no exception. To make managing audit logs easier, Windows can automatically delete old events after a certain number of days or after the log file grows to a specified size. This prevents the audit logs from filling up your computer's disk capacity, but it also prevents you from referring to deleted log files.

You already know that you can't prevent all compromises. Unfortunately, you also can't detect all compromises. Often, successful compromises go completely unnoticed. Sometimes, however, you will find out that an attacker compromised your networks months, or even years, after the compromise occurred. In fact, the most dangerous threats make no noticeable changes to your computer so that they can continue to abuse your network indefinitely.

You want to be able to review audit logs to determine when an attacker compromised your system, even if it occurred months or years in the past. To store audit logs for an extended period without filling up disk space, you need a plan to archive log files. Generally, this plan should include the ability to store log files in a centralized location to prevent an attacker who compromises a computer from clearing the local log files and covering his or her tracks.

Sophisticated attackers often try to cover their tracks by deleting audit logs. One technique attackers use to remove audit logs is to generate so many events that the events created during the compromise are automatically deleted to save space. You can prevent this from happening by enabling the Shut Down System Immediately If Unable To Log Security Audits policy setting. However, if you do this, you give the attacker the ability to perform a denial-of-service attack.

In fact, anyone who can generate security events could use this setting to shut the computer down, without necessarily having any privileges to it. Most likely, the log files fill by accident; perhaps an application begins to generate excessive log entries, or maybe your log archive application fails without you noticing. If the computer does shut down because the audit logs are full, an administrator will need to start the computer and log on to clear the logs. This requirement can cause the computer to be offline for an extended time. Preventing events from being erased usually isn't worth the risk of the extended downtime, so leave this setting disabled in most environments.

Most organizations should copy log files to a central location and archive them for two years. To implement this, you can use tools such as DumpEL.exe or Microsoft Operations Manager (MOM), discussed later in this section. If you schedule a batch file to regularly copy and archive log files, the log files on each computer need to be only large enough to store events that occur between scheduled archiving sessions, plus sufficient capacity to allow for failure of the archiving mechanism and malicious attempts to fill the event log. Given the constantly increasing size of hard disks, you might decide that you can allocate 500 MB to each of the Security event logs and automatically delete older events. Then, you could schedule log file archiving of new events on a nightly basis, which would ensure that all events are archived in all but the most extreme circumstances.

Using Auditing for Intrusion Detection

In theory, you can use auditing as an intrusion detection mechanism. Because auditing adds events when users or applications access resources or perform specific system tasks, you can audit events that would occur during the course of an attack. For example, an attacker using a dictionary-based password-cracking tool would generate hundreds or thousands of repeated failure audits for a user attempting to log on. However, these same events would also be generated by a user who mistypes his or her password (albeit, in smaller numbers). Table 6-3 lists the various events that you can audit to detect specific types of attacks, as well as to detect nonthreatening sources for the same events.

Table 6-3 **Auditing to Detect Specific Threats**

Potential Threat	Events to Audit	Other Event Sources
Dictionary attacks	Failure audit for logon	Users mistyping a password Services that have been configured with an incorrect password
Impersonating an authorized user	Success audit for logon	Legitimate successful authentication
Misuse of privileges by an internal attacker	Success audit for: Privilege use User and group management Security change policies System restart System shutdown Other system events	Legitimate administration tasks
Improperly accessing sensitive files	Success and failure audit for file access by suspect users or groups	Legitimate file access
Improperly accessing printers	Success and failure audit for printer access by suspect users or groups.	Legitimate printer access
Virus outbreak	Success and failure auditing for Process Tracking	Normal, legitimate application usage

If you use auditing extensively, you will quickly discover that normal, legitimate, day-to-day tasks generate thousands of events. Finding events generated by an attacker in a list that long is almost impossible. In fact, it's very impractical, and would take too much administrative time. Most environments don't use Windows auditing to proactively detect attacks. Instead, they use the auditing after they have detected an attack by other means to determine how the attacker compromised the computer and what actions the attacker took.

Microsoft does not currently produce an **intrusion detection system** (IDS). Therefore, to properly detect intrusion, you will need an IDS from someone other than Microsoft. IDS software uses algorithms to detect a possible attack from the thousands of legitimate events, and then alerts administrative staff so that they can analyze it further and respond if necessary. For example, an IDS could parse the Security event log and alert an administrator to a possible password-guessing attack if a single source generated more than ten failed authentication attempts. The administrator could then either block traffic from that computer, trace the source IP address of the computer in an attempt to identify the threat agent that initiated the attack, or contact law enforcement officials for assistance.

Some non-Microsoft IDS systems go far beyond simple log file analysis. Many systems gather and analyze network traffic, and use this information to detect attacks that might not trigger a computer running Windows to add a Security event to the event log. IDS software can detect an attack by either looking for traffic that matches predefined signatures (signature recognition), or by simply learning what normal traffic is on your network and creating an alarm when something unusual is detected (anomaly detection).

Another type of IDS system is a **honeypot**. Honeypots impersonate an entire network and wait for an attacker to launch an attack. Because there is no legitimate reason to send traffic to a honeypot, you can be certain that any traffic it receives is malicious. In all likelihood, an attacker who unknowingly targets a honeypot is also targeting your legitimate network resources. You can create your own honeypot by installing Windows on one or more computers and configuring the computer for extensive auditing. Alternatively, you can purchase software from non-Microsoft vendors that simulate one or more networked computers.

Tools for Analyzing Events

You are probably already familiar with the Event Viewer console (Eventvwr.msc), the primary tool used to analyze event logs. Event Viewer is useful for manually reviewing logs; however, it is not powerful enough to be used for regular Security event log reviews. Besides Event Viewer, Microsoft offers three tools: Event-CombMT, a powerful graphical event-filtering tool; DumpEL, a command-line event-filtering tool; and Microsoft Operations Manager (MOM), a more expansive server management tool. The sections that follow describe each of these tools.

EventCombMT.exe

Figure 6-13 shows EventCombMT configured to filter out failed logon attempts with Event ID 681 on the server CONTOSO-SERVER.

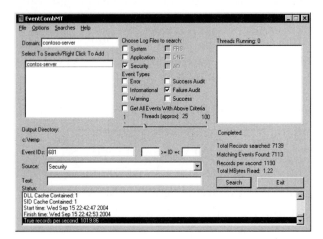

Figure 6-13   Use EventCombMT to manually search for specific events in an event log.

After running EventCombMT on a production Web server with that configuration, it produced a text file containing over 7000 failed logon attempts that occurred during a period of about two years, similar to what you would find on any popular Web server. Figure 6-14 shows a portion of this text file. In addition, as you would commonly find, the vast majority of the authentication failures were not malicious. In fact, because authentication failures happen accidentally with such high frequency, it would still be hard to identify an attacker among the typos.

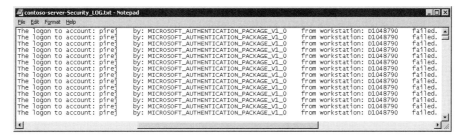

Figure 6-14 EventCombMT outputs important events to a text file for easy analysis.

You can download EventCombMT as part of the Account Lockout and Management Tools download at Microsoft.com.

Dumpel.exe

Dumpel.exe performs a similar function to EventCombMT, but works from the command-line without a graphical user interface. This makes it useful for scripting and scheduling. For example, you can use Dumpel as part of a batch file or script to extract all failed authentications from the Security event log and mail them to your e-mail address. Naturally, you can also perform additional script-based processing on the text file.

To create a text file named Output.txt containing all failed authentication attempts, you would run the following command:

```
dumpel -f output.txt -e 681 -m Security -l Security
```

> **MORE INFO** For more information about Dumpel and to download it, visit *http://www.microsoft.com/windows2000/techinfo/reskit/tools/existing/dumpel-o.asp*.

> **NOTE** Analyzing Events with Perl If you are familiar with Perl, you can use the EventLog.pl and EventQuery.pl scripts to parse and analyze log files. For more information about Perl, visit *http://www.ActiveState.com*. To download the EventLog.pl and EventQuery.pl tools, visit *http://www.microsoft.com*.

Microsoft Operations Manager

Microsoft Operations Manager (MOM) 2000 offers a comprehensive set of tools that allow enterprises to analyze thoroughly the built-in event reporting and performance monitoring of Windows 2000 and its applications. MOM 2000 can collect, store, and report events and performance data to a single location through the use of Intelligent Agents at remote computers, allowing an administrator to centrally review the collected information.

The core MOM 2000 management pack collects events that appear in the System, Application, and Security event logs, and aggregates the results into a central event repository. These events are stored in a Microsoft SQL Server database, which means you can access them quickly and from multiple applications. Administrators can use the Operations Manager Administrator Console, Web Console, or Operations Manager Reporting to view, print, or publish the data. Each view includes predefined views for analyzing the archived data, and allows definitions for customized views and reports.

Interpreting Audit Log Events

The biggest challenge of auditing is not determining what should be audited, but interpreting the events that result from the auditing. The sections that follow describe each category of auditing in more detail and provide a summary of important events that can be generated when you enable that type of auditing.

Audit Logon Events

This security setting determines whether to audit each instance of a user logging on to or logging off from a computer. Account Logon Events are generated on domain controllers for domain account activity and on local computers for local account activity. If both account logon and logon audit policy categories are enabled, logons that use a domain account generate a logon or logoff event on the workstation or server, and they generate an account logon event on the domain controller. In addition, interactive logons to a member server or workstation that use a domain account to generate a logon event on the domain controller as the logon scripts and policies are retrieved when a user logs on.

By auditing success events in the logon event category, you have a record of when each user logs on to or logs off from a computer. Although the vast majority of success audits will be legitimate users connecting, this information is still valuable because it provides a time when a user, even someone inside your organization, began an attack. Events are generated both when a user logs on to a computer locally and when he or she connects to a remote computer across a network. If an unauthorized person steals a user's password and logs on to a computer, this type of auditing enables you to determine when the breach of security occurred.

If you decide to audit failure events in the logon event category, you will see multiple failure audits in the event of a dictionary-based password-guessing attack. In all likelihood, you will see thousands of failure audits. The following types of security incidents can be diagnosed using logon event entries:

- **Local logon attempt failures** Any of the following Event IDs indicates failed logon attempts: 529, 530, 531, 532, 533, 534, and 537. You will see events 529 and 534 if an attacker tries and fails to guess a user name and password combination for a local account. However, these events can also occur when a user forgets his or her password, or starts browsing the network through My Network Places. In a large-scale environment, it can be difficult to interpret these events effectively. As a rule, investigate these patterns if they occur repeatedly or coincide with other unusual factors. For example, a number of 529 events followed by a 528 event in the middle of the night could indicate a successful password attack. More likely, someone was working late and was too tired to type their password correctly.

- **Account misuse** Events 530, 531, 532, and 533 can all represent misuse of a user account. The events indicate that the user entered the account/password combination correctly, but other restrictions are preventing a successful logon. Wherever possible, investigate these events to determine whether misuse occurred, or if the current restriction needs modification. For example, you might need to extend the logon hours of certain accounts.

- **Account lockouts** Event 539 indicates that an account was locked out. This can indicate that a password attack has failed. Look for earlier 529 events (failed logins due to password or user name error) by the same user account to try to discern the pattern of logon attempts.

- **Terminal Services attacks** Terminal Services sessions can be left in a connected state that allows processes to continue running after the session is ended. Event ID 683 indicates when a user does not log out from the Terminal Services session, and Event ID 682 indicates when a connection to a previously disconnected session has occurred.

Audit Account Logon Events

Audit events in the Account Logon Event category to see when users attempt to log on to or log off from the domain. When a user logs on to a domain, the logon is processed at a domain controller. If you audit Account Logon Events at domain controllers, you will see this logon attempt recorded at the domain controller that validates the account. It is not necessary to audit events in the Account Logon Event category on member servers because those logons show up in the Logon Event category.

Because the Account Logon event can be recorded in any valid domain controller in the domain, consolidate the Security event log across domain controllers to analyze all Account Logon events in the domain. As with Logon Events, Account Logon Events include both computer and user logon events.

For each of these events, the event log shows detailed information about each authentication attempt. The following types of security incidents can be diagnosed using logon event entries.

- **Domain logon attempt failures**   Event IDs 675, 677, and 681 indicate failed attempts to log on to the domain. The event contains the user name the user provided during the authentication. The event log also provides the workstation name (also known as the computer name). However, the client provides this information. In the event of an attack, the client will probably provide a fake user name. The error code indicates the specific problem:

    - **3221225572**   User logon with misspelled or bad user account
    - **3221225578**   User logon with misspelled or bad password
    - **3221225583**   User logon outside authorized hours
    - **3221225584**   User logon from unauthorized workstation
    - **3221225585**   User logon with expired password
    - **3221225586**   User logon to account disabled by administrator

- ❑ **3221225875**   User logon with expired account

- ❑ **3221226020**   User logon with Change Password At Next Logon selected

- ❑ **3221226036**   User logon with account locked

Figure 6-15 shows this type of event as viewed within Event Viewer.

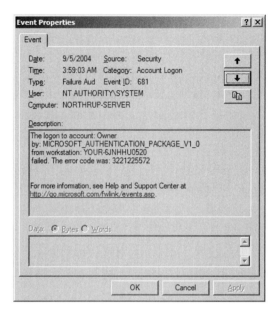

Figure 6-15   Failure audits for logon attempts show the user name and computer name—but you can't trust the computer name.

- ■ **Time synchronization issues**   If a client computer's time differs from the authenticating domain controller's by more than five minutes (by default), the domain controller adds Event ID 675 to the Security event log. This might not indicate a security event, but you probably should inform a system administrator of the problem so that he or she can configure time synchronization on that computer.

- ■ **Terminal Services attacks**   Terminal Services sessions can be left in a connected state that allows processes to continue running after the terminal server session is ended. Event ID 683 indicates when a user does not log out from the Terminal Services session, and Event ID 682 indicates when a connection to a previously disconnected session has occurred. To prevent disconnections, or to terminate these disconnected sessions, define the time interval to end a disconnected session in the Terminal Services Configuration console, in the properties of the RDP-TCP protocol.

Audit Account Management

Account Management auditing is used to determine when users or groups are created, changed, or deleted. This audit can be used to determine when a user or computer account was created, and who performed the task. In addition, it will identify when accounts are renamed, disabled, or enabled, and when passwords are reset. Audit success events in this event category to verify changes made to account properties and group properties. Although the vast majority of these changes will occur because of normal day-to-day systems administration tasks, they are also the types of changes that an attacker would make if he or she had administrative privileges.

If you decide to audit failure events in the Account Management event category, you can see if unauthorized users or attackers are trying to change account properties or group properties. The following Account Management events can be diagnosed using Security event log entries:

- **Creation of a user account**   Event IDs 624 and 626 identify when user accounts are created and enabled. If account creation is limited to specific individuals in the organization, you can use these events to identify whether unauthorized personnel have created user accounts.

- **User account password changed**   The modification of a password by someone other than the user can indicate that another user has taken over an account. Look for Event IDs 627 and 628 to indicate that a password change is attempted and successful. Review the details to determine whether a different account performed the change, and whether the account is a member of the help desk or other service team that resets user account passwords.

- **User account status changed**   An attacker might attempt to cover his or her tracks by disabling or deleting the account used during an attack. After you discover a compromise, investigate all occurrences of Event IDs 629 and 630 to ensure that these are authorized transactions. Look for occurrences of Event ID 626 followed by Event ID 629 a short time later. This can indicate that a disabled account was enabled, used, and then disabled again.

- **Modification of Security Groups**   Review membership changes to Domain Admins, Administrators, any of the operator groups, or to custom global, universal, or domain local groups that are delegated administrative functions. For global group membership modifications, look for Event IDs 632 and 633. For domain local group membership modifications, look for Event IDs 636 and 637.

- **Account Lockout**   When an account is locked out, two events will be logged at the primary domain controller (PDC) emulator operations master. A 644 event indicates that the account name was locked out, and then a 642 event is recorded, indicating that the user account is changed to indicate that the account is now locked out. This event is logged at the PDC emulator only.

Audit Directory Services Access

This security setting determines whether to audit the event of a user accessing an Active Directory object that has its own SACL specified. You can use Directory Services Access auditing to track administrative changes to Active Directory objects. By default, this value is set to success auditing in the Default Domain Controller GPO of a Windows Server 2003 domain that was not upgraded from a Windows 2000 Server domain. Windows 2000 domains do not have this auditing enabled by default, but seriously consider enabling it and enabling auditing on key Active Directory objects. This type of auditing is particularly important in environments that use delegation extensively.

Audit Object Access

This security setting determines whether to audit the event of a user accessing an object such as a file, folder, registry key, or printer that has its own SACL specified. If you want events to appear in the Security event log, you must first enable Auditing for Object Access and then define the SACL for each object you wish to audit.

Object access auditing occurs *before* the object is accessed. Write audits are generated before a file is written to, and read audits are generated before a file is read. This introduces a slight delay in actually accessing the object. Therefore, enable auditing only for objects that you really need to monitor, and only for those users whom you are interested in monitoring. Although you could enable auditing for an entire file system, the performance degradation would be tremendous and the number of events that the operating system generated would be unmanageable.

If you are looking for specific Object Access events, you primarily need to filter everything except Event ID 560 events. You need to search the event details to find the specific events you are looking for. Table 6-4 shows how you might perform some actions.

Table 6-4 Finding Auditing Events Related to Specific Tasks

Auditing Action	How It Is Achieved
Determine which user accessed a specific file, folder or object	In the Event 560 details, search for the full path of the file or folder you wish to review.
Determine actions by a specific user	Define a filter that identifies the user name in a 560 event.
Determine actions performed at a specific computer	Define a filter that identifies the specific computer account where the task was performed in a 560 event.

Audit Policy Change

Enable Audit Policy Change event auditing to audit every incident of a change to user rights assignment policies, audit policies, or trust policies. If you decide to audit failure events in the Policy Change event category, you can see if unauthorized users or attackers are trying to change policy settings, including security policy settings. However, sophisticated attackers who have gained privileges to modify policy will also attempt to alter the audit policy itself, so that any changes they make are not audited.

The two most important events to look for here are Event IDs 608 and 609. Many attacks begin by attempting to acquire elevated privileges. The following list shows how to identify which right was being acquired:

- **Act as part of the operating system**   Look for Event IDs 608 and 609 with user right seTcbPrivilege in the event details.

- **Add workstations to the domain**   Look for the events with user right SeMachineAccountPrivilege in the event details.

- **Back up files and directories**   Look for the events with user right SeBackupPrivilege in the event details. An attacker could abuse this right to access files to which he or she does not have assigned permission.

- **Bypass traverse checking**   Look for events with user right SeChangeNotifyPrivilege in the event details. This user right allows users to traverse a directory tree even if the user has no other permissions to access that directory.

- **Change the system time** Look for events with user right SeSystemtimePrivilege in the event details. This user right allows a security principal to change the system time, potentially masking when an event takes place.

- **Create permanent shared objects** Look for events with user right SeCreatePermanentPrivilege in the event details. The holder of this user right can create file and print shares.

- **Debug Programs** Look for events with user right SeDebugPrivilege in the event details. A holder of this user right can attach to any process. This right is, by default, assigned only to administrators.

- **Force shutdown from a remote system** Look for events with user right SeRemoteShutdownPrivilege in the event details.

- **Increase scheduling priority** Look for events with user right SeIncreaseBasePriorityPrivilege in the event details. A user with this right can modify process priorities.

- **Load and unload device drivers** Look for events with user right SeLoadDriverPrivilege in the event details. A user with this right could load a Trojan horse version of a device driver.

- **Manage auditing and Security event log** Look for events with user right SeSecurityPrivilege in the event details. A user with this right can view and clear the Security event log.

- **Replace a process-level token** Look for events with user right SeAssignPrimaryTokenPrivilege in the event details. A user with this right can change the default token associated with a started subprocess.

- **Restore files and directories** Look for events with user right SeRestorePrivilege in the event details.

- **Shut down the system** Look for events with user right SeShutdownPrivilege in the event details. A user with this right could shut down the system to initialize the installation of a new device driver.

- **Take ownership of files or other objects** Look for events with user right SeTakeOwnershipPrivilege in the event details. A user with this right can access any object or file on an NTFS file system disk by taking ownership of the object or file.

These audit events show only that a user was assigned a right, not that he or she used the right.

Audit Privilege Use

This security setting determines whether to audit each instance of a user exercising a user right. Here are examples of some of the event log entries that can exist when specific user rights are used:

- **Act as part of the operating system**   Look for Event ID 577 or 578 with the SeTcbPrivilege access privilege indicated. The event details identify the user account that used the right. This event can indicate a user's attempt to elevate security privileges by acting as part of the operating system. For example, the GetAdmin attack, in which a user attempts to add his or her account to the Administrators group, uses this privilege. The only entries for this event should be for the System account and any service accounts assigned this user right.

- **Change the system time**   Look for Event ID 577 or 578 with the SeSystemtimePrivilege access privilege indicated. The event details identify the user account that used the right. This event can indicate a user's attempt to change the system time to hide the true time that an event takes place.

- **Force shutdown from a remote system**   Look for Event IDs 577 and 578 with user right SeRemoteShutdownPrivilege access privilege indicated. The specific SID the user right is assigned to and the user name of the security principal that assigned the right are included in the event details.

- **Load and unload device drivers**   Look for Event ID 577 or 578 with the SeLoadDriverPrivilege access privilege indicated. The event details identify the user account that made use of this right. This event can indicate a user's attempt to load an unauthorized or Trojan horse (a type of malicious code) version of a device driver.

- **Manage auditing and Security event log**   Look for Event ID 577 or 578 with the SeSecurityPrivilege access privilege indicated. The event details identify the user account that used this right. This event will occur both when the event log is cleared and when events for Privilege Use are written to the Security event log.

- **Shut down the system** Look for Event ID 577 with the SeShutdownPrivilege access privilege indicated. The event details identify the user account that used this right. This event will occur when an attempt to shut down the computer takes place.

- **Take ownership of files or other objects** Look for Event ID 577 or 578 with the SeTakeOwnershipPrivilege access privilege indicated. The event details identify the user account that used the right. This event can indicate that an attacker is attempting to bypass current security settings by taking ownership of an object.

Audit Process Tracking

This security setting determines whether to audit detailed tracking information for events such as program activation, process exit, handle duplication, and indirect Object Access. Audit Process Tracking can be useful for security auditing under very specific circumstances, such as testing a known worm or virus on an isolated system. However, it requires a very detailed understanding of operating system internals. For that reason, this book will not list the event IDs used for tracking processes.

Audit System Events

This security setting determines whether to audit when a user restarts or shuts down the computer or when an event occurs that affects either the system security or the Security event log. If you audit system events, audit when the Security event log also is cleared. This is very important because attackers will often attempt to clear their tracks after making changes in an environment.

The most important system events from a security perspective are event IDs 512, 513, and 517. The first two IDs are important because they tell you that the computer was restarting. Although most computer restarts are not part of an attack, an attacker might intentionally restart a computer to which he or she has physical access to bypass the operating system security. Alternatively, if the attacker is stealing hardware such as memory from the computer, he or she would have to restart the computer.

Windows operating systems released prior to Windows Server 2003 and Windows XP with Service Pack 2 also have network vulnerabilities during startup. Therefore, an attacker might initiate a restart or wait for a computer to restart to attack it from across the network.

If the restart was unexpected, Windows adds Event ID 6008. This probably means there was a power failure or a device driver failure. However, it can be indicative of a denial-of-service attack that caused the computer to shut down.

An attacker might try to modify the Security event logs, disable auditing during an attack, or clear the Security event log to prevent detection. If you notice large blocks of time with no entries in the Security event log, look for Event IDs 612 and 517 to determine which user modified the audit policy. Compare all occurrences of Event ID 517 to a physical log indicating every time the Security event log was cleared. An unauthorized clearing of the Security event log can be an attempt to hide events that existed in the previous Security event log. The name of the user that cleared the log is included in the event details.

Reviewing Application Event Logs

In addition to reviewing the event logs for security events, review the logs created by applications. The application logs might include valuable information regarding potential attacks that can supplement the information found in the Security event logs. To make it easier to correlate events, make sure application servers synchronize system time with other computers on your network. Depending on your environment, you might need to look at log files for IIS, ISA Server, Internet Authentication Service (IAS), and non-Microsoft applications.

USING EFS TO PROTECT FILES

The **Encrypting File System (EFS)** is a transparent file encryption service provided by the Windows 2000, Windows XP Professional (not Windows XP Home Edition), and Windows Server 2003 family for files on NTFS volumes. EFS provides what file permissions cannot: protection when the operating system is bypassed. If an attacker steals a hard disk with confidential files, file permissions are meaningless because the operating system isn't running. EFS encryption remains, however, and can be accessed only when the operating system is running and the user has a valid key.

EFS is especially useful for securing sensitive data on portable computers, such as those commonly used by consultants or sales people who frequently conduct business away from the offices of an organization. It can also be useful on computers shared by several users, such as in banks or medical facilities. Both kinds of systems are susceptible to attack by techniques that circumvent the restrictions of ACLs. In a shared system, an attacker can gain access by starting a different operating system. An attacker can also steal a computer, remove a hard disk, place the hard disk in another system, and gain access to the files stored on the disk. Files encrypted by EFS, however, appear as unintelligible characters when the attacker does not have the decryption key.

Figure 6-16 shows EBCD (Emergency Boot CD), a typical tool used to compromise files on an NTFS volume that are protected with file permissions. EBCD is a free download from the Internet and facilitates creation of a bootable CD-ROM with tools for accessing a computer's file system and even resetting user passwords. As Figure 6-16 demonstrates, an attacker with physical access to a computer can bypass NTFS file permissions and access files directly.

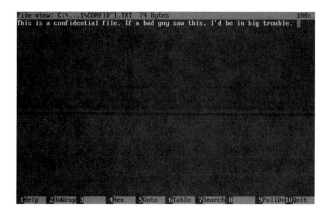

Figure 6-16 An attacker can gain access to unencrypted files in a few minutes with a bootable recovery CD-ROM.

This is not possible when the file is encrypted, however. Figure 6-17 shows how EBCD responds when trying to open an encrypted file. Without access to the private key necessary to decrypt the file, the contents are indecipherable.

Figure 6-17   Encrypted files cannot be read by a file recovery tool.

The default configuration of EFS allows users to start encrypting files with no administrative effort. In fact, as shown by Figure 6-18, enabling encryption for a folder requires only selecting a check box from the folder's Properties dialog box. EFS automatically generates a public-key pair and file encryption certificate for file encryption for a user the first time a user encrypts a file. Because EFS works transparently, you don't have to decrypt a file manually to open it and use it. EFS automatically detects an encrypted file and locates a user's file encryption key from the system's key store.

Figure 6-18   Encrypting a folder is as simple as selecting a check box.

File encryption and decryption is supported per file or for an entire folder. Folder encryption is transparently enforced. All files (and folders) created in a folder marked for encryption are automatically encrypted. Each file has a unique file encryption key, making it safe to rename. If you rename a file from an encrypted folder to an unencrypted folder on the same volume, the file remains encrypted. However, if you copy an unencrypted file into an encrypted folder, the file state will change. In this case, the file becomes encrypted. Command-line tools and administrative interfaces are provided for advanced users and recovery agents.

> **NOTE** *Choosing Files to Encrypt* *System files and any files in the %Systemroot% folder or its subfolders cannot be encrypted (not that there's any reason to encrypt them). No files or directories in a roaming user profile can be encrypted. A file cannot be both compressed and encrypted. Being compressed does not prevent encryption, but when the file is encrypted, it is uncompressed. You can, however, encrypt compressed file types such as .ZIP files. You can encrypt the %Temp% directory, but this can cause some applications to malfunction and, therefore, is not currently recommended.*

How EFS Works

EFS uses both public-key (asymmetric) and private-key (symmetric) encryption to protect files. When EFS encrypts a file, it creates fast symmetric keys designed for bulk encryption. The file is encrypted one block at a time, using a different encryption key for each. These file encryption keys are themselves encrypted and then stored in the file header. When you attempt to decrypt a file, EFS uses your certificate and asymmetric private key to unlock the encrypted fields within the file header. It then uses the decrypted symmetric key to decrypt the rest of the file. Chapter 9, "Designing a Public Key Infrastructure," provides a detailed explanation of how public-key encryption works.

EFS Costs

EFS can be an important countermeasure to mitigate the risk of threats with physical access to your computer. When assessing the countermeasure value of EFS as part of the Security Risk Management Process, do not assume that its cost is zero just because it's included for free with the operating system. EFS has significant costs. It makes recovering from disk-related problems more difficult because you cannot simply copy files from a failing hard disk to a new hard disk.

In addition, you cannot use file recovery tools (such as Recovery Console) to access encrypted files. The cost of losing a key is substantial because it means you lose access to your encrypted files—probably the most important files on your network. Furthermore, EFS carries a performance cost. The operating system must both read the file from the disk and decrypt it, which adds processing overhead.

EFS does reduce the risk of an attacker with physical access to a hard disk accessing your private files. It does not eliminate the risk, however. Encrypted files are still vulnerable to an attacker who can access the user's private key. Typically, the private key is stored on the computer itself, and Windows will automatically use it after authenticating the user. Therefore, an attacker who gains access to the user's credentials also gains access to the encryption key. In Active Directory environments, a recovery key agent can also access the files. Therefore, recovery key agents are another vulnerability.

Finally, because an attacker cannot gain access to protected files without the user's private key, a determined attacker could escalate the threat. The attacker might threaten the user personally to acquire the files or private key, rather than simply taking the hard disk. Given these costs and limitations, implement EFS only for folders that are at significant risk of a physical attack.

Managing EFS Keys

If a user encrypts a file and then loses the private key, he or she can't access the encrypted files. In fact, this user would face the same challenges that an attacker would have. Losing access to critical files is a significant risk. To mitigate this, EFS supports data recovery agents (DRAs). DRAs have the ability to recover encrypted files without the user's private key.

EFS establishes a DRA by default on Windows 2000 systems. The DRA is optional on Windows XP Professional and Windows Server 2003 to provide organizations with greater flexibility in implementing data recovery strategies. Managing these keys is a challenge in enterprises with thousands of computers. Rely on a Public Key Infrastructure (PKI) such as Certificate Services to issue keys for EFS and manage recovery agents. For more information about PKI and certificate services, refer to Chapter 9.

The DRA deserves protection. Always keep it in a different location from the physical computer to make it more difficult for an attacker with access to the hard disk to also acquire the DRA. The DRA should be reasonably accessible to authorized staff, however. If you ship the DRA to another country to protect it, it might take you several days to recover critical encrypted files. For more information about DRAs, refer to Chapter 9.

Using Syskey to Protect the EFS Encryption Key

By default, EFS stores the user certificates and private keys in the user's profile. The private keys are encrypted with a master key that is unlocked when the user logs on to a system. This, itself, presents a vulnerability.

You can mitigate this vulnerability by using a tool called Syskey to move the system startup password to a floppy disk. The Security Accounts Manager (SAM) database, including the keys used to protect the EFS private key, is protected by encryption that is unlocked with the system startup password. When Syskey is used to move the startup key to a floppy disk, you cannot start the computer or access the system startup key without the floppy disk, providing an extra level of protection for encrypted files.

> **NOTE Encrypting the SAM** Windows 2000, Windows XP, and Windows Server 2003 encrypt the system startup key by default. The Microsoft Windows NT 4.0 SAM database was not encrypted by default. You can encrypt the Windows NT 4.0 SAM database by using the Syskey utility.

▶ To configure Windows system key protection

1. Click Start and then click Run. Type **syskey**, and then press ENTER.

2. In the Securing the Windows Account Database dialog box, note that the Encryption Enabled option is selected and is the only option available. When this option is selected, Windows will always encrypt the SAM database.

3. Click Update.

4. Click Password Startup if you want to require a password to start Windows. Use a complex password that contains a combination of uppercase and lowercase letters, numbers, and symbols. The startup password must be at least 12 characters long and can be up to 128 characters long. You cannot remotely restart a computer that requires a password. Therefore, do not select this option for remotely managed servers, or servers that automatically restart after applying Automatic Updates.

5. Click System Generated Password if you do not want to require a startup password. Select either of the following options.

❑ Click Store Startup Key On Floppy Disk, as shown in Figure 6-19, to store the system startup password on a floppy disk. This provides the highest level of protection for the SAM database, but requires that someone insert the floppy disk to start the operating system.

❑ Click Store Startup Key Locally to store the encryption key on the hard disk of the local computer. This is the default option.

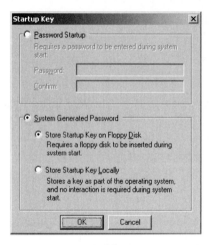

Figure 6-19   Provide extra protection for the EFS key by moving the system startup disk to a floppy.

6. Click OK twice to complete the procedure.

Always create a backup floppy disk if you use the Store Startup Key On Floppy Disk option. You can restart the system remotely if someone is available to insert the floppy disk into the computer when it restarts.

EFS Best Practices

Keep the following best practices in mind when deciding how to use EFS in your organization.

Ensure That Files Intended for Encryption Are Created—and Remain—Encrypted

- Encrypt folders before creating sensitive files in them for maximum security. This encrypts the files when they are created, preventing the data from ever being written to the disk as plaintext.

- Encrypt the My Documents folder if you save most of your documents to the My Documents folder. This ensures that your personal documents are encrypted by default. For Roaming User Profiles, this should be done only when the My Documents folder is redirected to a network location.

- Encrypt folders rather than individual files so that, if a program creates temporary files during editing, these are encrypted as well.

Manage Private Keys to Ensure File Security

- The designated recovery agent should export the data recovery certificate and private key to disk, secure them in a safe place, and delete the data recovery private key from the system. In this way, the only person who can recover data for the system is the person who has physical access to the data recovery private key.

- Keep the number of designated recovery agents to a minimum. This exposes fewer keys to cryptographic attack and provides a higher level of assurance that encrypted data is decrypted inappropriately.

- Use Microsoft Certificate Services to manage EFS and DRA certificates and private keys.

Push Responsibility to End Users

- Train users to enable encryption for private files on their own computers.

- Describe scenarios in which encryption is the only defense against confidential files being compromised. Specifically, demonstrate how easy it is to steal a laptop, and provide examples of people you know who have had their laptop stolen.

- Describe the consequences of compromised confidential files. Confidential files, if they find their way into the hands of your competitors, could destroy your business.

- Create separate folders in the default My Documents folder named Encrypted and Unencrypted. Users can then easily choose whether a file requires encryption or not.

SUMMARY

- Authorization is the process of analyzing the ACLs assigned to a resource and determining whether the user, with consideration for group memberships, has permission to access the resource.

- Active Directory environments have four group types: local, global, domain local, and universal. There are many built-in groups; use those groups to assign permissions whenever possible.

- There are three different authorization methods: User/ACL, Account Group/ACL, and Account Group/Resource Group. Most enterprises should use the account group/ resource group method to reduce the labor associated with assigning permissions and to reduce the risk of assigning excessive permissions because of a human error.

- Enterprises require many administrators to manage their networks. How you choose to delegate permissions can result in a very high level of security. Careless delegation can expose you to significant security risks from internal administrators. Careful delegation can improve your network security by distributing responsibility for security to the individuals who are most able to make security decisions.

- Although objects on Windows networks offer extremely consistent permission models, each type of object has a set of permission types that is unique to the object type.

- There are two approaches to assigning permissions: remove all default permissions and assign only those permissions users require, or use the default permissions but restrict them to protect critical resources. Most environments should start with the default permissions and fine-tune them. However, environments that identify extremely high-cost risks might find it beneficial to spend the time analyzing user needs to create a more restrictive permission strategy.

- Auditing is an important part of security because it enables you to detect successful and unsuccessful attacks. Your network's default security settings might not have sufficient auditing configured. Therefore, determine your auditing requirements and use Group Policy settings to ensure that auditing configuration is distributed to every computer on your network.

■ File permissions are an effective way to protect files when the operating system is running. However, file permissions are meaningless if the attacker has physical access to the computer. Use EFS to encrypt files so that they can be accessed only when the operating system is running. Take care to protect the encryption keys, though. If an attacker acquires the keys, they can decrypt the files. If you lose a key, you also lose access to the file you were trying to protect.

REVIEW QUESTIONS

1. Which of the following is a standard permission for a file or folder?

    a. Read Attributes

    b. Delete

    c. Read & Execute

    d. Take Ownership

2. Which of the following special groups could you assign to an ACL to allow access from unauthenticated users?

    a. Everyone

    b. Anonymous Logon

    c. Authenticated Users

    d. Interactive

3. Which of the following group types could be nested within a universal group?

    a. Local group

    b. Domain local group

    c. Global group

    d. Distribution group

4. You have created a forest trust between your organization's forest and a partner organization's forest. Which of the following group types should you create to enable administrators in the remote forest to assign privileges to a group of users in your forest?

    a. Local group

    b. Domain local group

    c. Global group

    d. Universal group

5. Which of the following group names was created with an effective group naming strategy?

    a. HR

    b. GG BOS HR

    c. Cohowinery Global Group Boston Human Resources

    d. Resources Human

6. Is the User/ACL or the Account Group/ACL method more effective in large enterprises?

7. Which of the following is an intrusion detection system most likely to accomplish?

    a. Prevent an attacker from compromising a system

    b. Detect an attack in progress

    c. Gather evidence required to prosecute the attacker

    d. Identify the vulnerability the attacker exploited after the compromise is successful

8. What is an SACL?

9. Which of the following are costs associated with EFS? (Choose all that apply.)

   a. You must deploy a PKI.

   b. Attackers with physical access to the computer can still access encrypted files.

   c. Performance is reduced.

   d. There is an increased risk of losing access to files.

10. Which type of auditing should you enable to detect dictionary-based password-cracking attacks against domain user accounts?

    a. Success logon events

    b. Failure logon events

    c. Success account logon events

    d. Failure account logon events

11. How can Syskey improve the security of EFS?

12. What is the best way for an enterprise to allow help desk operators to reset the passwords of Active Directory user accounts in one particular department, while minimizing the risk of those users abusing their privileges?

CASE SCENARIOS

Case Scenario 6-1: Designing a Group Strategy for a Pharmaceutical Company

You are consulting for a pharmaceutical company named Fabrikam, Inc., that specializes in the development of drugs that fight heart disease. Fabrikam employs a staff of over 600 scientists and researchers, many of whom have worked for other companies in the pharmaceutical industry. Fabrikam's headquarters are located in Ithaca, New York. Fabrikam has remote offices in Boston, Massachusetts, and Palo Alto, California.

Fabrikam is in the planning phase of a new Active Directory deployment and has asked you to design their group strategy. The consultant responsible for the Active Directory design informs you that Fabrikam's business groups are not limited to a single office. In other words, members of the accounts payable team in both Ithaca and Palo Alto will be granted access to the same resources. However, each location has resources, such as printers, that only users at a specific location should be allowed to access.

1. Which of the following group names is most fitting to an appropriate naming strategy?

    a. Accounts Payable

    b. Boston AP

    c. GG Accounts Payable

    d. GG Ithaca Accounts Payable

    e. GG Ithaca New York Accounts Payable

2. How will you recommend that Fabrikam enforce the group naming conventions?

3. Will you recommend the User/ACL, Account Group/ACL, or Account Group/Resource Group authorization method?

Case Scenario 6-2: Designing a Permissions Strategy for a Financial Company

You are a security consultant hired by Contoso, Inc., to evaluate their existing permissions structure and, if necessary, redesign it. Your boss, Maria Hammond, calls you into her office to discuss the current state of their network and your assignment.

"Hi. I've heard good things about you. We need your help. Our network has grown up slowly over the past 10 years as Contoso's financial services have expanded. When Contoso was started, the founders set up their own computers. For better or worse, they were financial geniuses, not network gurus. They slowly developed a network over the first several years, relying heavily on favors from technically savvy friends and relatives. I started a couple of years later and added a Windows NT 4.0 domain. That domain is still running, although I added a Windows 2000 domain controller and am now running it as an Active Directory in Windows 2000 mixed mode.

"Here's the problem: I don't know much about security. Actually, that's not the problem. The problem is, I don't know much about security, and we now have some very highly confidential files on our network, and there are people out there who could turn a nice profit if they gained access to those files and misused the information.

"Right now, we have a Windows NT 4.0 domain controller and a Windows 2000 domain controller. We also have two Windows Server 2003 computers. One is a file server, and the other is a Web server with a SQL Server database. We got our ISP to give us a big block of IPs, so all the computers have their own public IP addresses. Cool, huh?

"Anyway, I can sum up the current security settings on our network with one word: defaults. I'm good about patching, though. I have everything on Automatic Updates. That's probably the only reason we haven't been compromised yet. I'm a little concerned, though, because some of the temps we hire seem a little shady—and a little too skilled with computers."

Based on this brief description, Maria asks you the following questions:

1. "What are the chances we will be hacked?"

    a. "Not high at all. You're fine as long as you're patched."

    b. "Moderately high. You might get compromised in the next year, but it's not too late to protect yourselves."

    c. "Very high. Odds are good that you'll be compromised in the next year."

    d. "*Will* be? You've probably already been compromised and you don't know it."

2. "How do we start the process of improving the security?"

3. "Off the top of your head, which of the computers do you want to secure first?"

4. "In the future, how can I find out if someone attacks me? How would you set that up?"

5. "When we hire temps, I make user accounts for them in the Domain Admins group. I delete them after they leave. Is that okay? Which user group should they be in instead?"

CHAPTER 7
HARDENING SERVERS

Upon completion of this chapter, you will be able to:

- Describe how client and server security settings can be designed using security templates and GPOs.

- Apply security settings to servers in an enterprise.

- Audit a computer's configuration to determine if security settings match those in a security template.

- Apply server hardening techniques that apply equally well to any server role.

- Design security for the following types of server roles:

  - Domain controllers
  - DNS servers
  - DHCP servers
  - File servers
  - Web servers
  - IAS servers
  - Exchange Server computers
  - SQL Server computers

To be effective, security settings must be fine-tuned to the role that each computer serves on a network. Database servers, such as SQL Server computers, must be configured to allow authorized user accounts to issue database queries. Messaging servers, such as computers running Exchange Server, must be configured to authenticate messaging users, and must have security configured to allow messages to be exchanged with other systems.

Each network service added to a computer system inherently exposes another potential vulnerability. For example, although adding the Dynamic Host Configuration Protocol (DHCP) server role does not necessarily expose you to a specific, known vulnerability, configuring that role does cause the server to listen for an additional type of request from clients. Without the DHCP server role installed, the server would simply ignore those types of requests. At some point in the future, if a vulnerability is discovered that can exploit DHCP servers, the computer would be at risk.

Although each additional role increases a computer's attack surface, and thereby introduces an additional security risk, you as a security designer can do a great deal to mitigate that risk. Some of those mitigating steps, such as enabling restrictive **packet filtering**, are implemented by using tools provided by the operating system. Other steps can be taken by using the tools provided with the server role, such as requiring encryption for all database queries.

DESIGNING SECURITY TEMPLATES

Without a strategy for configuring and maintaining security settings on all computers on your network, the security of the systems will degrade over time. Even if you are willing to configure the security of every computer manually, you cannot count on the reliability of that security. Administrators who troubleshoot problems, install new applications, or apply updates will inadvertently leave important configuration settings in a different, and possibly less secure, state.

> **MORE INFO**   Security Templates Apply to Both Servers and Clients
> The information about security templates in this chapter applies equally well to both servers and clients. However, Chapter 8, "Hardening Client Computers," provides detailed information about hardening client platforms.

Administrators use security templates to configure security settings on computers running Microsoft Windows. By itself, a security template is a convenient way to configure the security of a single system. When combined with GPOs or scripting, security templates make it possible to maintain the security of networks with hundreds or thousands of computers running Windows.

> **NOTE**   Degrading Security Configurations   When you harden the security of a system, you are bound to break some applications that were designed to work on a system with a standard security configuration. This isn't unusual; it just means that an administrator needs to identify the security settings required by the application and set them in a manner that allows the application to function without compromising the security of the system. Unfortunately, unless you implement auditing, it's possible that administrators will adjust security settings in a manner that exposes a vulnerability. This can lead to a compromise.

This scenario can be avoided by using security templates and GPOs. When properly configured, administrators would need to request permission from a Domain Admin to change the centralized Group Policy to allow the new permissions. This gives the Domain Admin the opportunity to suggest something more secure.

What Is a Security Template?

Security templates are text files that describe a set of security configuration settings. You can make your own security templates from scratch. However, it is usually easier, and more thorough, to start with one of the default security templates included with Windows Server 2003 or Microsoft Windows 2000 Server (depending on the version of Windows running your domain controllers). Windows Server operating systems include several predefined security templates that you can copy and modify to meet the security requirements for your organization and apply to computers in your network. By default, these predefined security templates are stored in the %Systemroot%\Security\Templates\folder.

> **IMPORTANT**   *Create New Templates Instead of Modifying Existing Templates*   *Do not modify the predefined security templates. These files are well known, and an administrator might attempt to use your modified file without being aware of the changes you have made. Instead, copy the predefined security templates to create a new security template that you can modify as needed.*

The names of the security templates are somewhat descriptive. If the name ends with *ws*, the template is intended for workstations (otherwise known as client computers) and member servers. If the name ends with *dc*, the template is intended for domain controllers. If the name starts with *Compat*, the template increases backward compatibility by reducing security. If it starts with *Secure*, it improves security while limiting compatibility problems. If it starts with *Hisec*, it significantly improves security, but can definitely cause compatibility problems that demand extensive testing before deployment.

The following list describes each of these predefined security templates.

■ **Setup Security.inf and DC Security.inf**   These templates represent the default security settings of a new install of the Windows Server 2003 family. Setup Security.inf is different depending on whether the operating system was installed as part of an upgrade or as a fresh install. When a server is promoted to a domain controller, it creates the DC Security.inf template. Use this template to re-apply a server's default security settings, but be aware that this might overwrite security configurations performed by applications.

- **Compatws.inf**   If you have problems with users running applications when logged on as a member of the Users group, this client computer template makes the default permissions for the Users group less restrictive so that older applications are more likely to run correctly. This reduces the security of the desktop environment compared to having users log on as a member of the Users group, but it offers better security than making users a member of the Administrators group to bypass the security restrictions. Among other changes, this template will remove all members in the Power Users group on Windows Server 2003 member servers.

- **Securews.inf and Securedc.inf**   These templates increase security for areas of the operating system that are not covered by permissions, including Account Policy, Auditing, and selected security-relevant registry keys. This template will remove all members in the Power Users group on computers running Windows XP.

- **Hisecws.inf and Hisecdc.inf**   These templates are provided for networks in which all computers are running Windows 2000 or newer operating systems. In this configuration, all network communications must be digitally signed and encrypted at a level that Windows operating systems released prior to Windows 2000, Windows XP, and the Windows Server 2003 family did not provide. Thus, a highly secure computer running a Windows 2003 Server–family operating system can communicate only with another computer running one of those operating systems.

- **Rootsec.inf**   This template resets the default permission entries of the system root folder and propagates the permissions to all subfolders and files. All files and subfolders, except those files or subfolders that have had explicit permissions set, inherit the permission entries of the root folder. This template is new to Windows Server 2003.

- **Iesacls.inf**   This template is provided to enable auditing of registry settings that control Microsoft Internet Explorer security. Applying this template does not improve Internet Explorer security; rather, this security template is a starting point for creating a template for Internet Explorer–related security.

MORE INFO *The Best Reference for Security Configuration Details*
The Windows Server 2003 Security Guide includes many other useful security templates. To find it, visit http://www.microsoft.com and search for "Windows Server 2003 Security Guide."

It might be tempting simply to apply the high-security, predefined security templates. After all, more security is better, right? Unfortunately, it is not that simple. Remember, security requires compromise, and you usually give something up for increased security. The Secure*.inf and Hisec*.inf templates do increase security, but they will cause problems in some environments. Analyze the changes as part of the Security Risk Management Process to determine if the benefits outweigh the costs. If the benefits are significant enough, perform extensive testing with each of your organization's applications before deploying the template.

Security Template Planning

The predefined security templates are designed to provide baseline security levels, but not to provide security for specific computer roles such as file servers, Web servers, or Exchange Server computers. Therefore, choose a security template to use as your baseline and apply it to all servers in your organization that have similar security requirements. If different computers require different levels of security, you might be required to create a separate baseline template for each security level. Create role-specific security templates and apply those templates to servers with specific roles.

The exception to this is domain controllers. Domain controllers have their own organizational unit (OU) in the Active Directory, so leave them in this OU. In addition, they have their own security templates. Rather than applying the same baseline security template you apply to other servers and then applying a domain-controller-role security template, simply copy one of the predefined security templates (DC Security.inf, SecureDC.inf, or HiSecDC.inf) and modify it to meet your needs.

When deciding how to design your security templates, think in terms of computer roles rather than of individual computers. It's simple to apply multiple security templates to a single computer, but much more complicated to separate the security settings required by each of the individual roles a computer might serve. For example, if you have a domain controller that also acts as a file server, create separate security templates for the domain controller role and the file server role. In the future, if you add a dedicated domain controller or file server, you can apply only the security template that is required.

In large organizations, it is likely that different divisions within the organization will have different security requirements. This is most evident in government organizations, where material classified at different levels has distinctly different security requirements. In this case, first determine which roles are required, and then determine the security levels required by each role. If one organization has a file server that stores only public content, and another organization has a file server that stores highly confidential files, create two file-server security templates.

Security Template Settings

In Chapter 6, "Protecting Data," you learned how you use security policies to control authorization. The structure of security policies is identical to that of security templates, so you are already familiar with many of the settings available within a security template. For example, you can use a security template to configure the permissions associated with files, folders, registry entries, and services. Security templates can have more security options than any single computer's Local Computer Policy, however, because security templates include options for both stand-alone computers and computers that are participating in a domain.

Understanding the types of security settings that can and cannot be configured using security templates is critical for designing security templates successfully. The following sections describe the various types of settings that can be defined in a security template.

> **NOTE** **Getting to Know Security Templates** There are far too many security options in a security template to describe them all in detail. The best way to become familiar with the options available is to browse through them, open each policy, and view the choices available.

Account Policies

Account policies affect how user accounts can interact with the computer or domain. Account policies can be defined only once within a domain. The Account Policies node contains three nodes:

- **Password Policy** Determines settings for passwords, such as whether a password history is maintained, the minimum and maximum password ages, and password complexity and length requirements.

> **NOTE** **How to Use Minimum Password Age** Set the minimum password age only if you have also defined a maximum password age and password history requirement. The minimum password age prevents users from changing their password back to the original pass-

word after being required to change it because it reached the maximum password age.

- **Account Lockout Policy**   Determines the circumstances and length of time that an account will be locked out of the system.

- **Kerberos Policy**   Determines Kerberos-related settings, such as ticket lifetimes and enforcement. Kerberos policies do not exist in Local Computer Policy.

There can be only one account policy per domain for domain accounts. This account policy must be defined in the Default Domain Policy Group Policy object (GPO), and the domain controllers that make up the domain enforce it. A domain controller always obtains the account policy from the Default Domain Policy even if there is a different account policy applied to the OU that contains the domain controller. For this reason, if a group within your domain requires a different account policy, you must create a separate domain for them. For more information about domain architectures, refer to Chapter 5, "Designing Active Directory Security."

By default, workstations and servers joined to a domain (such as member computers) will receive the same account policy for their local accounts. However, local account policies can be different from the domain account policy, such as when you define a local security policy specifically for the local accounts.

Local Policies

The Local Policies node in a security template contains policies that control auditing, user rights, and miscellaneous security options for a computer. The Local Policies node contains three nodes:

- **Audit Policy**   The auditing policies that you choose for the event categories define your auditing policy.

  For information on using auditing, refer to Chapter 6.

- **User Rights Assignment**   These policies define dozens of options that specify which users can perform various actions on a computer. You can use the policies contained in this node to control who can and cannot log on to a computer, back up files on a computer, and restart a system (among other actions). Generally, it is better to add users who need additional rights to built-in groups, such as Power Users, or to custom security groups that you design to meet your organization's specific needs.

■ **Security Options**   The Security Options node contains policies that didn't fit well into the other policy groups. These options include whether a computer will shut itself down when the Security event log is full, whether unsigned drivers can be installed, and whether CTRL+ALT+DEL is required to log on.

Event Logs

The Event Log node in a security template contains policies that define how the computer's event logs behave. These policies define the maximum size for the three main log files: the Application event log, the Security event log, and the System event log. You can also use these policies to control which users are authorized to access each of the three primary event logs. Of particular importance for environments that require retaining a history of actions performed on a computer, you can define policies that control how log files are retained.

For information on designing event log retention, refer to Chapter 6.

Group Memberships

Unlike the Account Policies, Local Policies, and Event Logs nodes, the Restricted Groups node does not contain a list of policies. Instead, you can use this node to specify security groups by name and limit the memberships of those groups. For each group you specify, you can define two properties: Members and Members Of. The Members list defines who belongs and who does not belong to the restricted group. The Members Of list specifies to which other groups the restricted group belongs.

When Windows enforces a Restricted Groups Policy, any current member of a restricted group that is not on the Members list is removed. Any user on the Members list who is not currently a member of the restricted group is added.

Services

This node of a security template defines the startup type and authorization for system services on a computer. For example, if you want users to be able to start the Messenger service as needed, you can define a policy setting to set the Messenger service startup type to manual, and then configure the Messenger service authorization so that only Domain Users have permissions to start, stop, and pause the service.

Registry Permissions

This node of a security template defines the authorization for registry keys and values. Although the default registry authorization settings for Windows Server 2003 are sufficient for most environments, earlier versions of Windows may not be restrictive enough for your environment. In addition, applications that create their own registry keys and values might not adequately restrict the permissions associated with that information, but you can use security templates to restrict those permissions further.

File and Folder Permissions

The File System node of a security template allows you to use the security template to specify file and folder permissions on computers on which the template is applied.

> **MORE INFO** **Restricted Groups**   For more information on using Restricted Groups and assigning permissions for services, the registry, and files and folders, refer to Chapter 6.

Security Configuration for Earlier Versions of Windows

Most administrators will use Group Policy to deploy security templates through a network. Windows Server 2003, Windows 2000 Server, Windows 2000 Professional, and Windows XP Professional all fully support Group Policy, making it simple to apply a security template. However, many enterprise networks will include other Windows operating systems, including Windows Millennium Edition (Windows Me), Windows 98, and Windows NT 4.0. You must consider the potential security vulnerabilities of earlier versions of Windows when deploying security configurations to systems on your network. After all, earlier versions of Windows are more likely to have security vulnerabilities than later versions.

Windows NT 4.0, Windows 95, Windows 98, and Windows Me clients use System Policy rather than Group Policy. System Policy is a policy based on registry settings specified by using the System Policy Editor (Poledit.exe). You can find the System Policy Editor on a Windows NT 4.0 CD.

> **NOTE** **Drawbacks to Using Both System Policy and Group Policy**
> You can use System Policy and Group Policy together, but it makes life much more difficult for you. You'll experience more problems deploying security settings because you'll have to configure settings using two separate tools. In addition, administrators at your organization will spend more time troubleshooting the settings because they will have to learn how to isolate problems using both tools. If you can justify the cost, upgrade Windows NT 4.0 domains to Windows 2000 or Windows Server 2003 domains, and upgrade older computers to an operating system that supports Group Policy.

Although Group Policy mostly replaces the System Policy Editor, it is still useful to create .pol files that can define security-related registry settings on computers that do not support Group Policy. These .pol files contain a list of registry values and can be automatically deployed to a computer on startup or when a user logs on. The .pol file you create varies depending on the operating system you are targeting:

- **Windows 95 or Windows 98**   System Policy Editor must run locally on computers that run Windows 98 or Windows 95 to create Config.pol files that are compatible with the local operating system.

- **Windows NT 4.0 Workstation and Windows NT 4.0 Server**   Run System Policy Editor on a Windows NT 4.0 computer, as shown in Figure 7-1, to create a file named Ntconfig.pol.

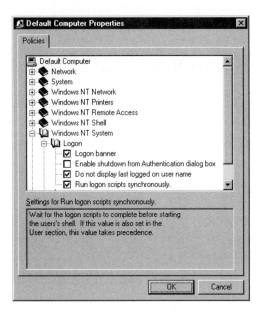

Figure 7-1   Use System Policy Editor on Windows NT 4.0 to create a file named Ntconfig.pol.

After creating a system policy, copy the resultant .pol file to the Netlogon share (%Systemroot%\Sysvol*DomainName*\Scripts) of any domain controller. Client computers running Windows XP and Windows 2000 ignore System Policy settings in the Netlogon share of a Windows Server 2003 domain controller. Rather, they will apply Group Policy settings. These clients will apply System Policy if they're joined to a Windows NT 4.0 domain controller, however.

> **NOTE   Windows Clients Not Intended for the Enterprise**   Neither System Policy nor Group Policy apply to Windows XP Home Edition, Windows NT 3.51, Windows 3.1, and MS-DOS operating systems. There's no straightforward way to manage these clients in an enterprise network, so you have little alternative to migrating these clients to newer platforms. If you can't upgrade them, you will have to develop manual procedures for deploying and auditing the security configurations.

Defining Baseline Security Templates

Your baseline server security template should include settings that you can broadly apply to all servers in your organization. Certainly, there will be exceptions to the settings you define in the baseline security template. In fact, all servers will probably be an exception because they will have a role-specific security template applied. However, by defining a separate baseline security template, you can define security settings that should apply across all servers.

The baseline security template should define your organization's most secure settings. You can then use the role-specific security templates to weaken security settings as needed to allow different server roles to function. For example, if you plan to have backups scheduled to run nightly on every server in your organization, configure your baseline security template to start the Task Scheduler service automatically. However, if only a portion of your servers will be running the World Wide Web Publishing Service, your baseline security template should disable that service. You can use your Web server security template to override that particular security setting and set that service to start automatically.

Consider the following configuration settings when defining your baseline security template:

- Services that should be set to Automatic or Disabled
- Group memberships
- File and registry permissions
- Password and account lockout policy for the server's local user database
- Auditing
- Maximum event log size and other event log settings
- User rights assignments and other security options

In addition, there are many security settings that you cannot define in a security template that need to be considered. Specifically, the following settings can be defined with Group Policy settings but not with a security template:

- Configuration of Automatic Updates
- Which Windows components and applications are installed
- IPSec policies
- Software restrictions

- Wireless network policies

- EFS settings

- Certificate Authority settings

In addition, some settings cannot be defined with either Group Policy or security templates. Therefore, you must develop custom mechanisms, such as scripts or batch files, for configuring and auditing the following types of settings:

- Configuration of Internet Connection Firewall, including which ports are open and closed by default. Configure Windows Firewall by using Group Policy settings.

- How logs are archived to external storage.

- Configuration of applications installed on all servers, such as monitoring agents or antivirus software.

As you can see, you cannot define a large portion of the settings you need to consider when designing a baseline security configuration with security templates. Despite this limitation, security templates are a useful tool for maintaining consistent security settings on the servers in your organization.

APPLYING SECURITY CONFIGURATION

Deploying your security templates can be a more complex, time-consuming process than creating the templates. Depending on the network environment, you can choose from several different methods of deploying security templates, including the following:

- Manually importing the templates into Local Group Policy on individual computers

- Importing the templates automatically by using scripting

- Importing the templates into GPOs linked to Active Directory directory service

In addition, you have a great deal of flexibility in configuring which templates to apply to which computers. Designing an infrastructure to efficiently deploy and maintain security configurations is a key aspect of designing security for Windows networks.

The sections that follow discuss how to deploy security templates in both Active Directory environments and to servers that are not members of a domain.

Deploying Security Templates with Active Directory

Most environments with security requirements complex enough to require the use of security templates will also deploy Active Directory to simplify the management of the computers. One of the challenges of designing security for Windows networks is applying the correct settings to different computers on your network. Group Policy is the preferred method, because security templates can be imported easily into Group Policy.

The sections that follow discuss how to use Group Policy to apply security templates to different computers. In particular, you learn the different ways you can control which computers receive security settings by using inheritance, security group memberships, and Windows Management Instrumentation (WMI) filtering.

Using Group Policy

Use Group Policy to configure security settings on member computers running Windows XP, Windows 2000, and Windows Server 2003 in your domain. All systems have a Local Group Policy that, in the absence of a higher-priority Group Policy setting, defines configuration settings. In a domain, Group Policy simplifies management of large numbers of computers by allowing administrators to define software configurations, install new software, deploy updates, and many other tasks for both servers and user computers. An administrator can use Group Policy to set policies that apply across a site, a range of OUs, or an entire domain. These network Group Policy settings take priority over the Local Group Policy when present.

> **NOTE   Platforms that Support Group Policy**   Support for Group Policy is available on computers running Windows 2000 Server, Windows 2000 Professional, Windows XP Professional, and Windows Server 2003. Earlier operating systems do not support Group Policy.

A GPO is a collection of Group Policy settings. GPOs are essentially the documents created by the Group Policy Object Editor. GPOs are stored at the domain level, and they affect users and computers that are contained in sites, domains, and OUs. Briefly, one or more security templates can be imported into a GPO. Then, that GPO should be linked to OUs created for different types of servers, as shown in Figure 7-2. When you deploy the GPO to client systems, those systems will automatically apply the settings contained within the imported security templates.

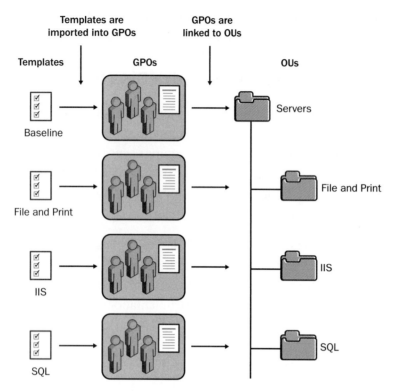

Figure 7-2   Import security templates into GPOs, and then link those GPOs to role-specific OUs.

NOTE   Updating Security Templates   If you make an update to a security template, be sure to reimport it into the GPO.

MORE INFO   This book provides a brief overview of Group Policy that you need to understand to deploy security templates. A complete discussion of Group Policy is outside the scope of this book. For more information, refer to "Introduction to Group Policy in Windows Server 2003" at http://www.microsoft.com/windowsserver2003/techinfo/overview/gpintro.mspx.

It might take several hours after you import a security template into a GPO for the settings to be applied to domain members. You can use the Gpudate.exe tool to apply the template immediately to an individual system, or you can wait until the updated GPO is automatically applied. By default, the security settings refresh every 90 minutes on a workstation or server and every five minutes on a domain controller. You see this event if any changes have occurred during these intervals. In addition, the settings refresh every 16 hours, regardless of whether new changes have taken place.

If multiple GPOs are linked to a single domain, site, or OU, verify that the order in which the policies are applied is correct. The higher policy in the list has higher precedence and will overwrite conflicting settings from other policies. As shown in Figure 7-3, you can use the Up and Down buttons on the Group Policy tab of the domain, site, or OU properties to set the precedence.

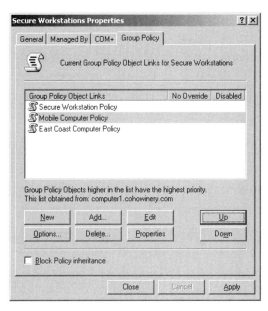

Figure 7-3   Modify Group Policy precedence to define the order in which policies are applied.

Standard Group Policy Inheritance

In general, Group Policy is passed down from parent to child containers within a domain. Group Policy is not inherited from parent to child domains. For example, *accounting.cohowinery.com* does not inherit Group Policy from *cohowinery.com*. However, if you assign a specific Group Policy setting to a high-level parent container, that Group Policy setting applies to all containers beneath the parent container, including the user and computer objects in each container.

Group Policy inheritance follows these rules:

- If a policy setting is defined for a parent OU and the same policy setting is not defined for a child OU, the child inherits the parent's enabled or disabled policy setting.

- If you explicitly specify a Group Policy setting for a child container, the child container's Group Policy setting overrides the parent container's setting.

- When multiple GPOs apply, and they do not have a parent/child relationship, the policies are processed in this order: local, site, domain, OU.

- If a policy setting that is applied to a parent OU and a policy setting that is applied to a child OU are compatible, both policy settings will be applied.

- If a policy setting that is configured for a parent OU is incompatible with the same policy setting that is configured for a child OU (because the setting is enabled in one case and disabled in the other), the child does not inherit the policy setting from the parent. The policy setting in the child is applied.

You can block policy inheritance at the domain or organizational-unit level by opening the properties dialog box for the domain or OU and selecting the Block Policy inheritance check box. You can enforce policy inheritance by setting the No Override option on a GPO link. When you select the No Override check box, you force all child policy containers to inherit the parent's policy, even if that policy conflicts with the child's policy and even if Block Inheritance has been set for the child. You can set No Override on a GPO link by opening the properties dialog box for the site, domain, or OU and making sure that the No Override check box is selected.

> **NOTE   Preventing Settings from Being Overridden**   Set No Override for policies that must be applied to computers in child OUs for which you have delegated other administrative responsibilities.

Group Policy Inheritance with Security Groups

You cannot link GPOs directly to a security group. However, you can use security group membership to allow or disallow members of the group to apply a GPO. In this way, you can control which users receive a GPO by placing them into specific groups.

By default, all Authenticated Users are authorized to apply a GPO. Therefore, to allow only specific groups to apply a GPO, you must first remove the default permissions for Authenticated Users, and then grant permissions for the specific groups to apply the GPO. You can use Active Directory Users and Computers, Active Directory Sites and Services, Group Policy Object Editor, or the Group Policy Management Console to edit GPO properties. After you have opened the properties dialog box for a GPO, enable only a specified group to apply a GPO by following these steps to edit the permissions:

1. Click the Authenticated Users group. In the Permissions box, select the Deny Apply Group Policy check box.

2. Click the Add button to add the security group to the Group Or User Names list.

3. Click the new security group. In the Permissions box for the selected security group, select the Allow Apply Group Policy check box, as shown in Figure 7-4, to explicitly allow the selected security group to apply the GPO.

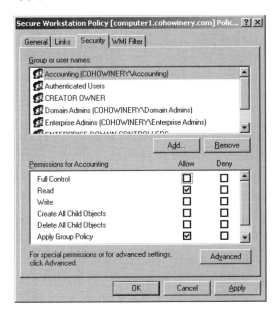

Figure 7-4   Denying a security group access to a GPO

WMI Filtering

When you need to restrict the application of GPOs based on a property of the user or computer, rather than on security group memberships, you can use WMI filters. The WMI filter is evaluated on the destination computer (running either Windows XP or Windows Server 2003) during Group Policy processing. You can use WMI filters to decide whether to apply a GPO based on any of the following aspects of a computer:

■ **Services**   Use WMI filters to apply a GPO to a computer that is running a specific service. This is an excellent way to ensure that computers apply security settings appropriate for that specific role. For example, you could apply Web server–specific security settings to computers running the World Wide Web Publishing service, or you could apply database server–specific security settings to computers running the MSSQLSERVER service.

NOTE **Determining Server Roles**   Determining whether a service is installed is not the ideal way to distribute security configurations because some servers have unnecessary services installed. For example, if your organization requires IPSec for all internal connections, but you create a security template for your external Web servers that overrides that requirement, you wouldn't necessarily want that security template to be applied to a domain controller on which an administrator accidentally installed Internet Information Server (IIS). It's less likely that a server will be moved from one OU to another, however, so it's better to rely on Active Directory organization to determine security configurations.

- **Registry**   Apply security settings based on whether specific registry keys exist. This is an excellent way to determine if a computer has a particular application or patch installed. For example, if a vulnerable application is installed, you can use WMI filtering to check for the presence of a registry key that the application creates during setup and apply security settings that protect that vulnerability better. If an application requires less restrictive security settings to run, you could even reduce the security level to improve compatibility. By using WMI filtering, you can allow the application to run on the computers on which it is installed, without reducing the security level of all computers within the domain or OU to which you attach the GPO.

- **Operating system version**   In many circumstances, you need to design different security configurations for different versions of Windows. WMI filtering is the best way to apply GPOs only to specific platforms. Use this property of WMI filtering to provide more or less restrictive security settings for those operating systems that require them.

- **Hardware inventory and configuration**   During the Security Risk Management Process, you may identify hardware components that expose you to particularly risky vulnerabilities. With WMI filtering, you can apply security settings only to those computers.

- **Other properties**   You can also make WMI filtering decisions based on properties of the Windows event log, service associations, and network response times (using Ping).

WMI Filtering Drawbacks WMI filtering might be the only way you can apply security settings to specific computer roles without manually applying the settings to each computer's local security policy. Although it is very useful, WMI filtering has significant drawbacks:

- Each GPO can have only one WMI filter. If applications have different inventory requirements, you need multiple WMI filters and therefore multiple GPOs. Increasing the number of GPOs impacts startup and logon times and increases management overhead.

- WMI filters can take significant time to evaluate, so they can slow down logon and startup time. The amount of time depends on the construction of the query.

Given these drawbacks, use WMI filtering only when more conventional methods of distributing security settings (such as organizing computers into different OUs according to their roles) are not sufficient.

How WMI Filtering Works A WMI filter consists of one or more WMI Query Language (WQL) queries. The WMI filter applies to every setting in the GPO, so administrators must create separate GPOs if they have different filtering requirements for different settings. The WMI filters are evaluated on the destination computer after the list of potential GPOs is determined and filtered based on security group membership. Windows XP and Windows Server 2003 will apply the GPO only if the WMI filter evaluates to TRUE. Windows 2000 does not support WMI filtering, so computers running Windows 2000 ignore the WMI filter and will always apply the GPO.

Because computers running Windows 2000 ignore WMI filters, a filtered GPO will always be applied on them. However, you can work around this by using two GPOs and giving the one with Windows 2000 settings higher precedence. Then, use a WMI filter for that Windows 2000 GPO, and apply it only if the operating system is Windows 2000 rather than Windows XP Professional. The computer running Windows 2000 will receive the Windows 2000 GPO and will override the settings in the Windows XP Professional GPO. The client running Windows XP Professional will receive all the settings in the Windows XP Professional GPO. Figure 7-5 shows the Manage WMI Filters window with a filter designed to apply the GPO only to computers running Windows XP Professional.

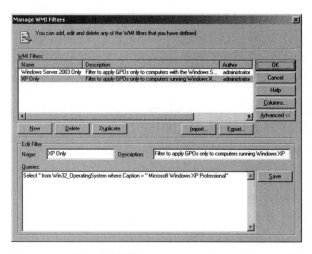

Figure 7-5   Use WMI filters to control security templates based on operating system or other computer properties.

Because this book focuses on design rather than on implementation, this book will not cover the details of creating WMI filter queries. As a security designer, understand that computers running Windows 2000 and earlier do not support WMI filtering, and will always apply a GPO with WMI filtering. Know also that you can use WMI filters to apply a GPO to computers based on operating system, hardware, and other factors that the computer applying the GPO is able to evaluate. If you need to apply security settings to a set of computers, but attaching a GPO to an OU would apply the settings to too many computers, you might be able to use WMI filtering to further control the computers that apply the GPO.

> **MORE INFO**   For more information about creating WMI filters with WQL, refer to Querying with WQL at *http://msdn.microsoft.com/library/en-us/ wmisdk/wmi/querying_with_wql.asp*.

Deploying Security Templates without Active Directory

Using Active Directory makes managing a large network of computers running Windows much easier, which makes the environment more secure by reducing the possibility for human error. However, not all networks use Active Directory. Even in Active Directory environments, there are often computers that do not participate in the Active Directory. Fortunately, you can still deploy security templates by using tools that do not rely on Active Directory, including the Group Policy Object Editor, the Security Configuration And Analysis snap-in, and Secedit.

■ Group Policy Object Editor and Security Configuration And Analysis are both graphical tools, and are therefore more useful when manually applying a security template. Use the Secedit command-line tool to automate the application of security templates in non–Active Directory environments by applying security templates as part of a batch file. Depending on whether the security template should be applied on a per-computer or per-user basis, you can configure Secedit to be automatically called when the computer starts (by using Task Scheduler or the HKEY_LOCAL_MACHINE\SOFTWARE\Microsoft\Windows\CurrentVersion\Run registry key) or when a user logs in (by using the Startup group).

AUDITING SECURITY CONFIGURATION

Whereas security templates do simplify creating GPOs, the real advantage comes from the ability to audit servers and clients easily to determine if the effective security settings match those defined by the security template you created. This enables you to verify that security settings are being distributed throughout your organization.

The Security Configuration And Analysis snap-in gives you an immediate, detailed list of security settings on a computer that do not meet your security requirements. Recommendations are presented alongside current system settings, and icons or remarks are used to highlight any areas where the current settings do not match the proposed level of security. Security Configuration And Analysis uses a database to perform analysis and configuration functions. Using a database gives you the ability to compare the current security settings against custom databases created by importing one or more security templates. After the analysis is complete, examine the results by expanding the nodes contained within the Security Configuration And Analysis node, as shown in Figure 7-6.

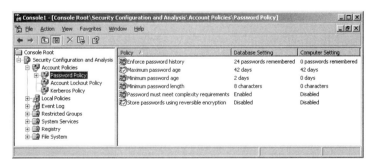

Figure 7-6 Use Security Configuration and Analysis to verify that security templates are applied.

GENERAL BEST PRACTICES FOR HARDENING SERVERS

Although each type of server role has guidelines specific to that role to consider, the following best practices apply equally well to any server role:

- Read the role-specific security guides at Microsoft.com. Although this book provides high-level guidelines for designing security for server roles, it cannot provide the detail of role-specific security guides. Among other guides for hardening specific roles, Microsoft provides the following:

  - ❏ Exchange Server 2000 Security Guide

  - ❏ Exchange Server 2003 Security Hardening Guide

  - ❏ Microsoft Internet Security and Acceleration (ISA) Server 2004 Security Hardening Guide

  - ❏ Microsoft Operations Manager 2005 Security Guide

  - ❏ Windows Server 2003 Security Guide, which includes chapters covering domain controllers, infrastructure servers, file servers, IIS, Internet Authentication Service (IAS), certificate services, and **firewalls**

- On Windows Server 2003, use the Configure Your Server Wizard to add roles. Configure Your Server Wizard is designed to minimize the security risk of adding additional roles by installing only the necessary software and configuring it with Secure By Default settings.

- Disable unnecessary services. By default, computers running Windows Server 2003 have most unnecessary services disabled or set to start manually. Earlier versions of Windows will have many unnecessary services running. In particular, consider disabling the following services: Alerter, Computer Browser, License Logging Service, Messenger, Print Spooler, and Removable Storage.

- Have a process for updating all software components on the server, including the operating system, optional Windows components, additional Microsoft server software, and non-Microsoft services and applications.

  For more information about patching, refer to Chapter 3, "Reducing the Risk of Software Vulnerabilities."

- When installing new servers, apply all updates before connecting the computer to a network. The new server is likely to have well-known vulnerabilities that can be exploited during the installation process before the software is updated.

■ Enable encryption whenever possible. For internal services that do not have encryption built in, enable IPSec to protect the privacy of communications and to authenticate the server and client.

■ When possible, change the default port numbers used by services on both the clients and servers. All common viruses, worms, and other attack tools attempt to connect to services on their well-known port number. By changing the default, you dramatically decrease the risk of attack from these types of threats.

■ Use packet filtering to block any incoming communications you do not plan for the server to receive. Use IPSec, host-based firewalls, and network firewalls as needed. Research the port numbers used by the server applications running on each server and open only those port numbers.

■ When communications to a particular service will be limited to connections from one specific computer or computers on a limited number of subnets, use packet filtering to drop connections from invalid IP addresses. For more information about IPSec and packet filtering, refer to Chapter 10, Protecting Intranet Communications."

■ Place servers accessed from the Internet in **perimeter networks** (also known as screened subnets or demilitarized zones). Perimeter networks have two layers of firewalls: one firewall to protect the servers from attacks on the Internet, and another firewall to protect the internal network from attacks originating from your own servers in the event they are compromised.

■ Use physical security to restrict physical access to servers. In security, there is a saying, "If an attacker touches your computer, it's not your computer anymore."

■ In addition to physical security, restrict access to removable media to make it more difficult for an attacker to copy confidential files or to restart the server using a CD-ROM with a non-Windows operating system installed. To accomplish this, you need to either use security settings built into the computer's BIOS or remove floppy and CD-ROM drives completely.

■ Ensure backup of configuration information and data specific to the server's role. For example, you must ensure backup of the data within a SQL Server database separately from your standard backup practices because SQL Server databases must be dumped to a file before they can be backed up.

- Audit backup and restore events. An attacker might have initiated events that occur at unusual times.

- Rename the default Administrator and Guest accounts in the local user databases of computers. Keep track of the name of the Administrator account. You might need it for troubleshooting.

- If the application or service maintains its own user database separate from the local user database or Active Directory, consider requiring complex passwords for that user database. Depending on the application, this might not be feasible because the application might not provide the functionality to enforce complex password requirements.

- Design a way to monitor the unique functionality provided by each server role. For example, monitor a Domain Name System (DNS) server by submitting DNS queries and validating the response. Monitor a file server by retrieving a file across the network. This monitoring can alert you to a server that has failed or is experiencing a denial-of-service attack.

HARDENING SERVER ROLES

This chapter has discussed concepts that apply equally well to any type of server. Each server role requires some customized hardening, however. The sections that follow provide hardening guidelines for domain controllers, DNS servers, DHCP servers, file servers, Web servers, IAS servers, Exchange Server computers, and SQL Server computers.

Hardening Domain Controllers

Domain controllers are responsible for authenticating users on your network. In addition, they contain detailed information about your organization's network resources. If an attacker compromises a domain controller, the attacker can use the information contained in Active Directory to map out network resources, and might be able to use the information to access those resources. If that attacker gains administrative privileges, he or she can create additional user accounts, which would make it very difficult to remove the attacker's privileges from your network.

> **IMPORTANT**   **Storing Application Directory Data**   Do not use a domain controller to store application data. If you have a Web application and you need to store user account information about external users, use Active Directory Application Mode (ADAM) instead. ADAM is more flexible than Active Directory, it's a free download, and, most important from a security perspective, user accounts created in an ADAM database do not receive any rights to your network. For more information about ADAM, visit *http://www.microsoft.com/adam*.

The sections that follow describe domain controller threats, provide information about the Active Directory database, describe Active Directory event logging considerations, list domain controller services that you cannot disable, explains how to reduce the risk of viruses and threats attacking by using the backup service account, and lists the port numbers you need to allow domain controller communications across a firewall.

Assessing Threats to Domain Controllers

For two main reasons, domain controllers will be one of the first targets of any type of threat who wishes to gain elevated privileges on your network:

1. If a domain controller is compromised, the threat can grant permissions to any member computer.

2. Domain controllers are easy to find because there must be a DNS record to identify them. The following shows an attacker finding the IP address of the domain controller for the *contoso.com* domain:

```
C:\>nslookup

Default Server:  localhost

Address:  127.0.0.1


> set type=all

> _ldap._tcp.dc._msdcs.contoso.com

Server:  localhost

Address:  127.0.0.1


_ldap._tcp.dc._msdcs.contoso.com         SRV service location:

        priority      = 0

        weight        = 100

        port          = 389

        svr hostname  = contoso-dev.contoso.com

contoso-dev.contoso.com internet address = 192.168.1.107
```

As you can see from this Nslookup output, the *contoso.com* domain controller has the IP address 192.168.1.107. An attacker could then target the domain controller directly. For these two reasons, any threat with access to your internal network and knowledge of Active Directory domains will very likely target your domain controllers.

> **NOTE   Making It More Difficult for Attackers to Find Your Domain Controllers**   *Being able to look up the IP address of a domain controller is a good reason to maintain separate DNS servers for internal and external namespaces. Some domains allow anyone on the Internet to perform a query to find his or her domain controller. This is likely to invite avoidable attacks from the Internet.*

Protecting the Active Directory Database

Safeguarding the Active Directory database and log files is crucial to maintaining directory integrity and reliability. Moving the ntds.dit, edb.log, and temp.edb files from their default locations will help to conceal them from an attacker if a domain controller is compromised. Furthermore, moving the files off the system volume to a separate physical disk will also improve domain controller performance.

If an attacker does gain access to a domain controller, it is likely that the attacker will attempt to discover user credentials by using password-cracking software. The System Key utility (Syskey) provides an extra line of defense against offline password-cracking software by using strong encryption techniques to secure account password information. By default, Syskey is enabled on all computers running Windows Server 2003 in Mode 1 (obfuscated key). There are many reasons to recommend using Syskey in Mode 2 (console password) or Mode 3 (floppy storage of Syskey password) for any domain controller exposed to physical security threats.

Although Syskey does make the user database more difficult to crack, an administrator must be physically at the computer to type the console password or insert the floppy disk. This prevents you from restarting the computer remotely, and will cause the computer to remain offline if it restarts—such as after a Stop error (also known as a blue screen). For more information about Syskey, refer to Chapter 6.

Logging Considerations

When you add the Domain Controller role to a computer, Windows adds several event logs:

- Directory Service
- DNS Server
- File Replication Service

As described in Chapter 6, you need to make special accommodations to archive these logs.

Services Required by Domain Controllers

As with all servers, follow the general best practice and disable unnecessary services. In addition to the standard services discussed in the general best practices, you can disable the Distributed Link Tracking Server service, which is installed when the domain controller role is added. This is particularly important on domain controllers because of the high risk of a compromise. The following services must be running on domain controllers, however.

- **File Replication Service**   Enables files to be automatically copied and maintained simultaneously on multiple computers. This service replicates SYSVOL between all domain controllers.

- **Inter-Site Messaging**   Required by SMTP replication in Active Directory, DFS, and Netlogon.

- **Kerberos Key Distribution Center**   Provides the ability for users to log on using the Kerberos V5 authentication protocol.

- **Netlogon**   Maintains protected channels between the domain controller, other domain controllers, member servers, and workstations in the same domain and in trusting domains.

- **Remote Procedure Call (RPC) Locator**   Enables RPC clients to locate RPC servers and manage the RPC name service database.

- **Windows Management Instrumentation**   Provides management information about the domain controller through the WMI interface.

- **Windows Time**   Synchronizes time between computers on the network, which is critical for Kerberos authentication.

Protecting Domain Controllers with Virus Scanners

Domain controllers, just like every client and server, should be protected by a virus scanner. Domain controllers will have problems, however, because the virus scanner may lock important files during the scanning process. To prevent problems, exclude the following folder, files, and file types from virus scans on domain controllers (default locations are shown):

- %SystemRoot%\NTDS\Edb.chk

- %SystemRoot%\NTDS\Edb*.log

- %SystemRoot%\NTDS\Edb*.pat

- %SystemRoot%\NTDS\ntds.dit

- %SystemRoot%\NTDS\ntds.pat

- %SystemRoot%\NTDS\Res.log

- %SystemRoot%\NTDS\Res2.log

- %SystemRoot%\NTDS\Temp.edb

- %SystemRoot%\ntfrs\jet\ntfrs.jdb

- %SystemRoot%\ntfrs\jet\log*.log

- %SystemRoot%\ntfrs\Jet\sys\edb.chk

- %SystemRoot%\SYSVOL*

> **NOTE** *Save Your Brain for the Important Information* *Don't memorize this list. Just remember to run antivirus software on domain controllers, and that it requires some special configuration.*

Protecting Domain Controllers during Backups

The service account you use to back up domain controllers must have a high level of privilege on your domain controllers. To reduce the risk of a threat abusing these privileges, use different backup agent service accounts for backing up domain controllers and other servers.

When a domain controller is promoted, a special built-in group, Backup Operators, is created in Active Directory. To back up a domain controller, the backup agent must run in the security context of an account with Backup Operator privileges and, thus, a very high level of privilege to the Active Directory. If the same backup agent service account is used for backups on both domain controllers and other application servers, the application servers could potentially be compromised to gain access to this highly privileged account.

As a general recommendation, membership in groups with service administrator privileges should be highly restricted. Do not make users that are responsible for backing up data on member servers only a member of the Backup Operators group in Active Directory. Instead, create a new security group for them and use Restricted Groups to add the new security group to the local Backup Operators group in each member server's local user database. Figure 7-7 shows how to design user accounts for backup services in an Active Directory environment.

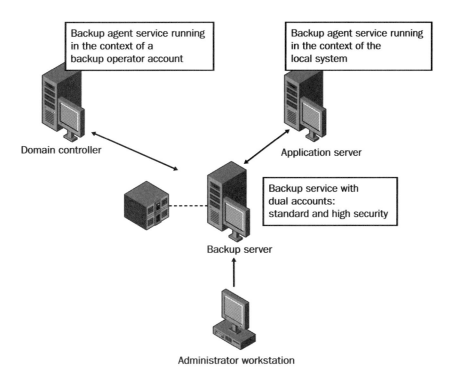

Figure 7-7   Use separate accounts to back up domain controllers and member servers.

Protecting Domain Controllers with Firewalls

Use a firewall to limit the opportunity an attacker has to connect to your domain controllers. Use packet filtering to block all unnecessary traffic to and from your domain controllers. Domain controllers use several different protocols for communicating with clients and peers. Whenever possible, limit the communication so that only the necessary ports are opened between a domain controller and another computer. Table 7-1 shows common domain controller communications and the port numbers used.

> **NOTE   Don't Memorize Port Numbers**   This table, and similar tables in this chapter, are provided as reference. Don't memorize this information, because it's easy enough to look up when you need it.

Table 7-1   **Ports Used by Active Directory**

Active Directory Communication	Traffic Required
A user network logon across a firewall	Microsoft-DS traffic (445/tcp, 445/udp)
	Kerberos authentication protocol (88/tcp, 88/udp)
	Lightweight Directory Access Protocol (LDAP) ping (389/udp)
	DNS (53/tcp, 53/udp)

Table 7-1 **Ports Used by Active Directory**

Active Directory Communication	Traffic Required
A computer logon to a domain controller	Microsoft-DS traffic (445/tcp, 445/udp) Kerberos authentication protocol (88/tcp, 88/udp) LDAP ping (389/udp) DNS (53/tcp, 53/udp)
Establishing a trust between domain controllers in different domains	Microsoft-DS traffic (445/tcp, 445/udp) LDAP (389/tcp or 686/tcp if using SSL) LDAP ping (389/udp) Kerberos authentication protocol (88/tcp, 88/udp) DNS (53/tcp, 53/udp)
Trust validation between two domain controllers	Microsoft-DS traffic (445/tcp, 445/udp) LDAP (389/tcp or 686/tcp if using SSL) LDAP ping (389/udp) Kerberos (88/tcp, 88/udp) DNS (53/tcp, 53/udp) Net Logon

Hardening DNS Servers

DNS is the TCP/IP name resolution service the Internet uses. The DNS service enables client computers on your network to register and resolve user-friendly DNS names. It also allows network services to resolve IP addresses to host names, a common, but unreliable, method of filtering requests. Most network applications rely on DNS and, as a result, a successful attack against DNS can have serious consequences.

Assessing Threats to DNS Servers

Safeguarding DNS servers is essential to any environment with Active Directory because clients use DNS to find their Active Directory servers. When a DNS server is attacked, one possible goal of the attacker is to control the DNS information being returned in response to DNS client queries. In this way, clients can be misdirected to computers controlled by the attacker. Cache poisoning is an example of this type of attack. To use cache poisoning in an attack, an attacker inserts false information into the cache of a DNS server. This results in a legitimate DNS server returning incorrect results, thereby redirecting clients to unauthorized computers. The unauthorized computers can then perform a man-in-the-middle attack.

Protect the DNS cache by selecting the Secure Cache Against Pollution check box on the Advanced tab of the DNS server's Properties dialog box, as shown in Figure 7-8. This is selected by default on Windows Server 2003 computers, but is not selected in earlier versions of Windows.

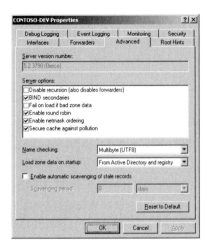

Figure 7-8   On Windows 2000 and earlier DNS servers, select Secure Cache Against Pollution.

The Windows Server 2003 DNS client service supports Dynamic DNS updates, which allow client systems to add DNS records directly into the database. Dynamic DNS (DDNS) servers can receive malicious or unauthorized updates from an attacker using a client that supports the DDNS protocol if the server is configured to accept unsecured updates. At a minimum, an attacker can add bogus entries to the DNS database; at worst, the attacker can overwrite or delete legitimate entries in the DNS database. Using secure DDNS updates guarantees that registration requests are processed only if they are sent from valid clients in an Active Directory forest. This greatly limits (but does not eliminate) the opportunity for an attacker to compromise the integrity of a DNS server.

DNS servers provide a mechanism called a *zone transfer* to replicate information about a DNS zone between servers. A DNS server that is not configured to limit who can request zone transfers will transfer the entire DNS zone to anyone who requests it. Unfortunately, this can make the entire domain's DNS dataset available, including which hosts are serving as domain controllers, Web servers, and databases.

NOTE   Protecting DNS Clients   DNS clients deserve protection, too. If an attacker can change the client's configured DNS server address or modify the client's HOSTS file, they can redirect traffic to a malicious server, just as they could if they compromised your DNS server. For more information about hardening clients, refer to Chapter 8.

Logging Considerations

The DNS service generates logging information that is useful for determining whether an attack occurred and how it was carried out. DNS logging is enabled by default, and can be modified from the Event Logging tab of the DNS server properties dialog box. To view the DNS server logs, open the DNS console, expand Event Viewer, and then click DNS Events. DNS events will appear in the right-hand pane. Alternatively, you can view DNS events by using the standard Event Viewer console.

Protecting DNS Servers with Firewalls

A great deal of damage can be done to an organization if a DNS server is compromised. To mitigate this risk, limit access to your DNS server to only those clients that should be making DNS requests. Use packet filtering to block all traffic from DNS clients, except for packets transmitted by means of UDP or TCP port 53. If you plan to receive DNS requests from the Internet, you will have to allow requests on UDP and TCP port 53 from all addresses. However, use packet filtering to block all other traffic destined for your DNS servers from the Internet.

Best Practices for Hardening DNS Servers

Besides the general best practices that apply to all servers, consider the following when designing DNS servers into your network architectures:

- Whenever possible, use Active Directory–integrated zones. Replication between zones is easier to manage and much more secure.

- If a DNS zone is not stored in Active Directory, improve the security of the DNS zone file by modifying permissions on the DNS zone file or on the folder in which the zone files are stored. The zone file or folder permissions should be configured to allow Full Control only to the System group. By default, zone files are stored in the %Systemroot%\ System32\Dns folder. Secure the DNS registry keys also. Find the DNS registry keys in the registry under HKEY_LOCAL_MACHINE\ System\CurrentControlSet\Services\DNS.

- On DNS servers that do not respond to DNS clients directly and are not configured with forwarders, disable recursion. A DNS server requires recursion only if it responds to recursive queries from DNS clients or is configured with a forwarder. The DNS server will use iterative queries to communicate with other DNS servers.

- If your DNS server will not be resolving Internet names for clients, configure the root hints to point only to the DNS servers hosting your root domain. By default, the root hints contain a list of Internet DNS servers to enable any public domain names to be resolved.

- Use IPSec to protect zone transfers between DNS servers within your organization.

- Use separate servers and zones for DNS servers that resolve names for addresses within your organization and for those that resolve names for your public IP addresses. If your external DNS server is compromised, the attacker will not be able to redirect internal clients.

- If possible, allow only secure dynamic DNS updates.

- Use forwarders instead of secondary zones. Forwarders provide most of the performance benefit of a secondary zone by responding to and caching DNS queries for clients on the local network. However, forwarders are less of a security risk because secondary zone data is not stored in Active Directory; it is stored in a text-based zone file, which makes the data more vulnerable to attack. Using forwarders is another way to distribute the load on the DNS servers; however, forwarders do not require zone files to be stored on every server.

Hardening DHCP Servers

Dynamic Host Configuration Protocol (DHCP) is an IP standard designed to reduce the complexity of administering address configurations. DHCP servers enable an administrator to assign TCP/IP configurations to client computers automatically on startup. When a client computer moves between subnets, its old IP address is freed for reuse. The client reconfigures its TCP/IP settings automatically when the computer restarts in its new location.

> **NOTE Filtering DHCP Messages** Packet filtering isn't much of a concern with DHCP servers because DHCP requests are broadcast messages and don't cross a router unless specifically configured to do so.

Authorizing DHCP Servers

Although the role of a DHCP infrastructure server might seem mundane, a DHCP server can be used maliciously to compromise the security of DHCP client computers. DHCP clients trust the DHCP server that assigns an IP address to provide them with information about the default gateway and DNS servers. An attacker could place a DHCP server on a network segment and replace the default gateway and DNS server information with the IP addresses of computers owned by the attacker. These computers could then intercept all traffic from the client, allowing the traffic to be analyzed for confidential information, and enabling man-in-the-middle attacks.

Physical and network security is the only way to ensure that an attacker does not place a rogue DHCP server on your network. However, Windows Server 2003 can limit the risk of a user unintentionally starting a Windows-based DHCP server on your network, which could result in DHCP clients getting incorrect address information and inability to access network resources. Active Directory contains a list of IP addresses available for the computers that you authorize to operate as DHCP servers on your network, and supports detection of unauthorized DHCP servers and prevention of their activity on your network.

> **NOTE** **Authorization with Earlier Versions of Windows** Microsoft Windows NT 4.0 and earlier Windows operating systems do not check for DHCP server authorization.

A DHCP server running Windows Server 2003 uses the following process to determine whether Active Directory is available. If it finds an Active Directory domain, the server validates its own authorization by using one of the following procedures, depending on whether it is a member server or a stand-alone server.

For member servers (a server joined to a domain that is part of an enterprise), the DHCP server queries Active Directory for the list of authorized DHCP server IP addresses. If the server finds its IP address in the authorized list, it initializes and starts providing DHCP service to clients. If it does not find itself in the authorized list, it does not initialize and stops providing DHCP services. When installed in a multiple forest environment, DHCP servers seek authorization from within their forest only. After authorization, DHCP servers in a multiple forest environment lease IP addresses to all reachable clients. Therefore, if clients from another forest are reached using routers with DHCP/BOOTP forwarding enabled, the DHCP server leases IP addresses to them. If Active Directory is not available, the DHCP server continues to operate in its last known state.

For stand-alone servers (a server not joined to any domain or part of an existing enterprise), when the DHCP service starts, it sends a DHCP information message (DHCPINFORM). This message includes several vendor-specific option types that are known and supported by other DHCP servers running Windows Server 2003. When received by other DHCP servers, these option types enable the query and retrieval of information about the root domain. When queried, the other DHCP servers reply with DHCP acknowledgement messages (DHCPACK). If the stand-alone server receives no reply, it initializes and starts providing DHCP services to clients. If the stand-alone server receives a reply from a DHCP server authorized in Active Directory, the stand-alone server does not initialize and does not provide DHCP services to clients.

Authorized servers repeat the detection process at a default interval of 60 minutes. Unauthorized servers repeat the detection process at a default interval of 10 minutes. Efforts to detect unauthorized servers are noted as "Restarting rogue detection" entries in the audit log.

Dynamic DNS Updates

DHCP and DNS are closely related, because you can configure the DHCP server to perform updates on behalf of its DHCP clients to any DNS servers that support dynamic updates. This is an important concept to understand for security reasons because network services such as IIS might use DNS when authorizing requests. In addition, network services that create usage or auditing log files might store DNS information about clients. Therefore, having DNS information for every computer on the network increases your network security by enabling you to trace IP communications back to the correct computer more easily.

The DHCP server can be used to register and update the pointer (PTR) and host (A) resource records on behalf of its DHCP-enabled clients. The PTR record resolves the client's IP address to its host name, and the A record resolves the fully qualified domain name (FQDN) to the IP address. Although end users rely on A records to find services on the network, PTR records are more useful for security-related tasks such as filtering incoming requests based on the client's domain name.

By default, Windows Server 2003 registers and updates client information with the authoritative DNS server of the zone in which the DHCP server is located according to the DHCP client request. In this mode, the DHCP client can request the manner in which the DHCP server performs updates of its host (A) and pointer (PTR) resource records. If possible, the DHCP server accommodates the client request for handling updates to its name and IP address information in DNS. This is the default setting, but it can lead to DHCP clients not having DNS records updated because the client is trusted to register its own DNS records. To select this setting, view the properties of the DHCP server or a DHCP scope. Click the DNS tab and select the Dynamically Update DNS A and PTR Records Only If Requested By The DHCP Clients check box.

To configure the DHCP server to always update the DNS records for a client, view the properties of the DHCP server or a DHCP scope, click the DNS tab and select the Always Dynamically Update DNS A and PTR Records check box. In this mode, the DHCP server always performs updates of the client's FQDN, leased IP address information, and both its A and PTR resource records, regardless of whether the client has requested to perform its own updates. If you prefer to trust the clients to update their own DNS records, you can clear the Enable DNS Dynamic Updates According to the Settings Below check box.

Although all recent versions of Windows are capable of registering their own DNS records, including Windows 2000, Windows XP, and Windows Server 2003, earlier versions of Windows such as Windows 98 do not have this capability. Configure the DHCP server to register DNS records on behalf of these clients by selecting the Dynamically Update DNS A And PTR Records For DHCP Clients That Do Not Request Updates check box, as shown in Figure 7-9.

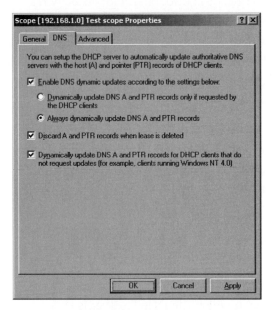

Figure 7-9   DHCP can update DNS for clients who are not capable.

NOTE   **The Security Usefulness of Reverse DNS Lookups**   Although being able to look up the PTR record registered to a particular IP address can be useful when tracking down the source of a request, it's hardly a reliable tool when attempting to identify an attacker. An attacker either would use an IP address without registering with the DHCP server or would spoof another user's IP.

Known DHCP Server Security Risks

The DHCP protocol itself, an open Internet standard, has several known security vulnerabilities. First, DHCP is an unauthenticated protocol. When a user connects to the network, the user is not required to provide credentials to obtain a lease. Therefore, an unauthenticated user can obtain a lease for any DHCP client whenever a DHCP server is available to provide a lease. Any option values that the DHCP server provides with the lease, such as Windows Internet Naming Service (WINS) server or DNS server IP addresses, are available to the unauthenticated user. If the DHCP client is identified as a member of a user class or vendor class, the options that are associated with the class are also available.

Malicious users with physical access to the DHCP-enabled network can instigate denial-of-service attacks on DHCP servers by requesting many leases from the server, thereby depleting the number of leases that are available to other DHCP clients. In addition, such a denial-of-service attack can also impact the DNS server when the DHCP server is configured to perform DNS dynamic updates.

> **NOTE** *802.1X Authentication and DHCP* When clients running Windows XP use 802.1X-enabled LAN switches or wireless access points to access a network, authentication occurs before the DHCP server assigns a lease, thereby providing greater security for DHCP.

To mitigate these risks, ensure that unauthorized persons do not have physical or wireless access to your network, and enable audit logging for every DHCP server on your network as described in the next section. Configure DHCP servers in pairs, splitting DHCP server scopes between servers so that 80 percent of the addresses are distributed by one DHCP server and 20 percent by another to ensure that clients can continue receiving IP address configurations in the event of a server failure.

Logging Considerations

Enable audit logging for every DHCP server on your network. Regularly check audit log files and monitor them when the DHCP server receives an unusually high number of lease requests from clients. Audit log files provide the information you need to track the source of any attacks made against the DHCP server. The default location of audit log files is %Systemroot%\System32\Dhcp. You can also check the system event log for explanatory information about the DHCP server service.

By default, the DHCP service logs only startup and shutdown events in the Event Viewer. Enable a more detailed log on the DHCP server by following these steps:

1. Start the DHCP console, right-click the DHCP server, and then click Properties.

2. Click the General tab, and then select Enable DHCP Audit Logging.

Use the DHCP audit logs to monitor DNS dynamic updates by the DHCP server. The Event ID 30 represents a dynamic update to a DNS server. Event ID 31 means that the dynamic update failed, and Event ID 32 means the update was successful.

The IP address of the DHCP client is included in the DHCP audit log, providing the ability to track the source of the denial-of-service attack.

DHCP clients are often difficult to locate in log entries because the only information stored in most event logs are computer names, not IP addresses. The DHCP audit logs can provide one more tool for locating the sources of internal attacks or inadvertent activities. However, the information in these logs is not by any means foolproof because both host names and media access control (MAC) addresses can be forged or spoofed. (*Spoofing* is making a transmission appear to come from a user other than the user who performed the action.) Nevertheless, the benefits of collecting this information by far exceed the costs incurred by enabling logging on a DHCP server. Having more than just an IP address and a machine name can be of great assistance in determining how a particular IP address was used on a network.

By default, Server Operators and Authenticated Users have read permissions to these log files. To preserve the integrity of the information logged by a DHCP server most effectively, limit access to these logs to only server administrators. Remove the Server Operators and Authenticated Users groups from the access control list (ACL) of the %Systemroot%\System32\Dhcp folder.

Hardening File Servers

File servers are likely targets because most organizations use them to store highly confidential documents. In addition, because they are commonly accessed and typically are visible in My Network Places, threats without significant technical experience are likely to find them and at least attempt to access confidential files. In addition to the general best practices for hardening servers, carefully restrict file and share permissions as described in Chapter 6. Use auditing to generate security events when highly confidential files are accessed.

Table 7-2 shows the ports used by file servers that must be opened at any firewalls protecting the file server to enable communications.

Table 7-2 **Ports Used by File Servers**

File Server Communication	Traffic Required
Communications with Windows clients or non-Windows clients supporting Windows file sharing	Common Internet File System (CIFS) (445/tcp) NetBIOS over TCP/IP (NBT)/Server Message Blocks (SMB) (137/udp, 138/udp, 139/tcp)

Table 7-2 **Ports Used by File Servers**

File Server Communication	Traffic Required
Communications with NFS clients when Windows Services for UNIX is installed	Portmapper (111/tcp, 111/udp) Status (1039/tcp, 1039/udp) Nlockmgr (1047/tcp, 1047/udp) Mountd (1048/tcp, 1048/udp) NFS Server (2049/tcp, 2049/udp)
Communications with Apple clients when File Server for Macintosh is installed	File Server for Macintosh (548/tcp)

Hardening Web Servers

Web servers are the servers most likely to be attacked in your organization. The likelihood for Web servers to be attacked stems from the large number of Web servers connected to the Internet. Because so many Web servers are publicly accessible, threat agents have dedicated a tremendous amount of time to developing tools to exploit known Web server vulnerabilities.

Hardening Web servers deserves so much of your attention that Chapter 12, "Designing Security for Web Servers," is dedicated entirely to this topic.

Hardening IAS Servers

IAS is a mechanism for authenticating users, not unlike Kerberos. IAS is also capable of providing user authorization and accounting for connection times, however. IAS acts as a Remote Authentication Dial-In User Service (RADIUS) server and proxy that provides compatibility with a wide variety of non-Microsoft hardware and software, including wireless routers, authenticating switches, remote-access dial-up servers, and virtual private network (VPN) connections.

Often, IAS is used to allow an Internet service provider (ISP) to authenticate dial-in users against an organization's Active Directory database. This enables users to dial in to an ISP by using their Active Directory user names and passwords, even if the ISP does not maintain the Active Directory service. RADIUS, like the Internet protocols that Windows Server 2003 supports, is an Internet Engineering Task Force (IETF) standard.

RADIUS Message Authenticators

When you configure IAS for a RADIUS client, you configure the IP address of the client. If an incoming RADIUS Access-Request message does not originate from at least one of the IP addresses of configured clients, IAS automatically discards the message, providing protection for an IAS server. However, as discussed earlier, source IP addresses can be spoofed and are therefore unreliable.

Shared secrets are used to verify that RADIUS messages, with the exception of Access-Request messages, are sent by a RADIUS-enabled device that is configured with the same shared secret. Shared secrets also verify that the RADIUS message has not been modified in transit (known as *message integrity*). Finally, the shared secret is used to encrypt some RADIUS attributes such as User-Password and Tunnel-Password. To provide verification for messages, you can enable the RADIUS Message Authenticator attribute, as shown in Figure 7-10.

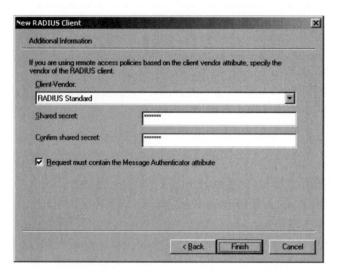

Figure 7-10 Use shared secrets and the Messenger Authenticator attribute to encrypt private RADIUS communications.

> **NOTE Configuring RADIUS Shared Secrets** If you specify RADIUS clients by using an IP address range, all RADIUS clients within the address range must use the same shared secret.

Account Lockout

You can use the remote-access account lockout feature to specify how many times a remote-access authentication can fail against a valid user account before the user is denied access. Remote-access account lockout is especially important for remote-access VPN connections over the Internet. An attacker on the Internet can attempt to access an organization intranet by sending credentials (valid user name, guessed password) during the VPN connection authentication process. During a dictionary attack, the attacker sends hundreds or thousands of credentials by using a list of passwords based on common words or phrases.

To enable remote-access account lockout, set the MaxDenials value in the HKEY_LOCAL_MACHINE\SYSTEM\CurrentControlSet\Services\ RemoteAccess\ Parameters\AccountLockout registry key to 1 or greater. MaxDenials is the maximum number of failed attempts that can occur before the account is locked out. By default, MaxDenials is set to 0, which means that remote-access account lockout is disabled.

To modify the amount of time that passes before the failed-attempts counter resets, set the ResetTime (mins) entry in the HKEY_LOCAL_MACHINE\ SYSTEM\ CurrentControlSet\Services\RemoteAccess\Parameters\AccountLockout registry key to the required number of minutes. By default, ResetTime (mins) is set to 0xb40, or 2,880 minutes (48 hours).

To reset a user account manually that has been locked out before the failed attempts counter is automatically reset, delete the HKEY_LOCAL_MACHINE\ SYSTEM\CurrentControlSet\Services\RemoteAccess\Parameters\ AccountLockout\ *domain:user* registry key that corresponds to the user's account name.

Quarantine Control

A remote-access user provides credentials to demonstrate that he or she is a valid user, which offers some proof that the user is not an attacker. Authenticating a user does not determine whether that user's computer contains malicious software, such as a Trojan horse, a worm, or a virus. Fortunately, IAS provides quarantine control to help provide a way to determine whether a remote-access user's computer is safe, which can prevent a user from unknowingly spreading worms and viruses into an otherwise secure network.

Network Access Quarantine Control, a new feature in Windows Server 2003, delays normal remote access to a private network until an administrator-provided script has examined and validated the configuration of the remote-access computer. When a remote-access computer initiates a connection to a remote-access server, the user is authenticated and the remote-access computer is assigned an IP address. However, the connection is placed in quarantine mode, in which network access is limited. The administrator-provided script is run on the remote-access computer. When the script notifies the remote-access server that it has successfully run, and the remote-access computer complies with current network policies, quarantine mode is removed and the remote-access computer is granted normal remote access.

The quarantine restrictions placed on individual remote-access connections consist of a set of quarantine packet filters that restrict the traffic that can be sent to and from a quarantined remote-access client, and a quarantine session timer that restricts the amount of time the client can remain connected in quarantine mode before being disconnected. Tools for configuring and implementing quarantine control are included with the Windows Server 2003 Resource Kit, available from *http://www.microsoft.com/windowsserver2003/techinfo/reskit/resourcekit.mspx.*

Logging Considerations

IAS is capable of logging authentication requests and accounting requests. This information is vital for tracking when users attempt to connect, and for identifying successful and unsuccessful attacks. When IAS logging is enabled, log files are located by default in the %Systemroot%\System32\LogFiles folder. The access control list in the LogFiles folder provides the best security for the IAS log files. The access control list is a list of users and groups that can access the folder. In addition, each user or group is assigned specific permissions that determine what actions the user or group can take with the folder. As with IIS, IAS logging can be sent to a database server.

Protecting IAS with Firewalls

If a firewall is positioned between the IAS server and a client or another IAS server, ports must be opened in the firewall. Authentication traffic uses UDP ports 1645 and 1812. Accounting traffic uses UDP ports 1813 and 1646. The notification and listener components of quarantine control use port 7250 by default. Therefore, allow network traffic on port 7250 through the firewall to enable the client computers to communicate with the remote-access server listener.

Hardening Exchange Server Computers

Many enterprises build their messaging infrastructure on Exchange Server. Exchange Server provides a scalable, reliable, Active Directory–integrated messaging platform. Exchange Server 2003 usually enables users to gain access to critical business communications whenever and wherever they need to, and it is designed to deliver greater security, availability, and reliability than that delivered by other messaging platforms, and even by earlier versions of Exchange Server.

> **MORE INFO**   For detailed information on hardening Exchange Server, including security templates, read the Microsoft Exchange Server 2003 Security Hardening Guide at *http://www.microsoft.com/technet/ prodtechnol/exchange/2003/library/exsecure.mspx*. In addition, read the book *Secure Messaging with Microsoft Exchange Server 2003* (Microsoft Press, 2004), by Paul Robichaux.

Encrypting Mail Traffic

Exchange uses the Transport Layer Security (TLS) protocol, which is based on and interoperable with SSL, to encrypt network communications. IIS uses SSL and earlier versions of Exchange, including Exchange Server 5.5. Turning on TLS protects messages traveling between mail servers using SMTP, but doesn't protect traffic traveling from clients to the server. To encrypt communications between Web browsers and Outlook Web Access (OWA), enable the use of SSL on the

Web server. Post Office Protocol version 3 (POP3) or Internet Message Access Protocol version 4 (IMAP4) users should use a client that supports the use of SSL with POP3 and IMAP4, such as Microsoft Outlook Express. Alternatively, you can use IPSec to encrypt all traffic between clients and servers. IPSec encryption is transparent to both Exchange and the client application. For more information about IPSec, refer to Chapter 10, "Protecting Intranet Communications."

Logging Considerations

Exchange is capable of logging almost every activity that occurs within the messaging server, including detailed information about messages sent to and from the server, by using the Message Tracking Center. Although these logging options are essential for troubleshooting messaging problems, they are not likely to be used for security purposes (unless your server is being misused to transfer spam, which does happen).

The built-in auditing capabilities of Exchange Server are extremely useful for tracking use and misuse, however. Auditing in Exchange Server is implemented by means of the same mechanisms Windows Server 2003 uses, and auditing events will appear in the Security event log. After enabling auditing, you can review auditing events in the Security event log by using the Event Viewer console.

Protecting Exchange Server with Firewalls

Use a firewall to stop unnecessary traffic from reaching your computers running Exchange Server. Computers running Exchange Server can use several different protocols for communicating with clients and other mail servers. Whenever possible, limit the communication so that only the necessary ports are opened between a computer running Exchange Server and another computer. Table 7-3 shows common Exchange Server communications and the port numbers used.

Table 7-3 **Ports Used by Exchange Server**

Network Communication	Traffic Required
Communications with domain controllers	LDAP standard protocol (389/tcp, 636/tcp if using SSL) Site Replication Service LDAP communications (379/tcp) Global Catalog LDAP communications (3268/tcp, 3269/tcp if using SSL)
Outgoing DNS queries to a DNS server	DNS (53/tcp and 53/udp)

Table 7-3   **Ports Used by Exchange Server**

Network Communication	Traffic Required
Message transfer between servers	SMTP traffic (25/tcp, 465/tcp if using TLS)
	SMTP Link State Algorithm (691/tcp)
Client downloading e-mail using POP3	POP3 (110/tcp, 995/tcp if using SSL)
Client downloading e-mail using IMAP4	IMAP4 (143/tcp, 993/tcp if using SSL)
Client using newsreader	NNTP (119/tcp, 563/tcp if using SSL)
Web browsers downloading e-mail from OWA	HTTP protocol (80/tcp, 443/tcp if using SSL)
Clients using instant messaging	RVP (80/tcp and ports above 1024/tcp)
Clients using chat protocol	IRC/IRCX (6667/tcp, 994/tcp if using SSL)

Assessing Threats to Mail Servers

Besides the standard threats faced by any networked server, mail servers face two additional significant threats: spam and viruses. The sections that follow discuss each of these threats.

Relaying Spam

One of the most common threats to mail servers is spammers. Spammers distribute messages, typically filled with advertisements, to thousands of users who would rather not receive the message. Spam is one of the Internet's most significant nuisances. As a result, the systems engineers who manage e-mail servers have gone to great lengths to stop spam messages from reaching the mailboxes on the servers they manage. They have been mostly successful.

One of the ways systems engineers block spam is by refusing messages from mail servers that are known to send outgoing spam. To increase the likelihood that the unwanted messages reach their recipients, spammers will attempt to use other people's servers to relay outgoing spam. Many servers on the Internet are **open relays**, which are mail servers that accept messages from anyone and attempt to forward the message on to its final destination. Spammers use scripts to find open relays: the script searches for computers accepting inbound SMTP messages on TCP port 25, and attempts to send a message through the SMTP server to its own mailbox. If the message is delivered, the server is an open relay. Once a spammer has identified an open relay, he or she might send thousands of messages through it.

Exchange Server computers and the SMTP server included with IIS, by default, are not open relays. This means that if someone from the Internet attempts to send a message through the server to an external address without properly authenticating, the mail server will refuse to deliver the message. It's very common for administrators to unknowingly configure a mail server to be an open relay while troubleshooting delivery problems, however. If this open relay is on the Internet, it's only a matter of a few days before a spammer finds the server and begins to abuse it.

A related threat is third-party organizations that search the Internet for open relays with the purpose of blacklisting them. These organizations want to reduce spam by creating a list of known open relays, and distributing this list so that mail server administrators can block messages from the server. If they identify your server as an open relay, a large number of mail servers will begin to reject messages from your organization, interfering with important outgoing communications.

To reduce the likelihood of spammers abusing your mail server, discuss the threat of spammers with messaging administrators and ensure that they understand the potential for abuse. In addition, implement defense-in-depth by blocking incoming connections on TCP port 25 from the Internet (if possible), requiring authentication for SMTP connections, and regularly auditing your own mail servers.

To audit your own mail server to determine if it is an open relay, connect a computer to the Internet. Open the mail client of your choice and configure the SMTP server IP address with the public IP address of your mail server. Then, attempt to send an e-mail to a mailbox on a different mail server outside of your organization.

▶ To Audit a Mail Server for Being an Open Relay

1. Determine the IP address of the public SMTP server. If you do not know it, you can look it up by using the Nslookup command to find the domain's MX (Mail eXchange) records. The following example demonstrates how to look up Microsoft's public mail servers:

```
C:\>nslookup
Default Server:  dns.contoso.com
Address:  10.172.3.10

> set type=mx
> microsoft.com
Server:  dns.contoso.com
Address:  10.172.3.10

Non-authoritative answer:
microsoft.com   MX preference = 10, mail exchanger = mailc.microsoft.com
```

```
microsoft.com     MX preference = 10, mail exchanger = maila.microsoft.com
microsoft.com     MX preference = 10, mail exchanger = mailb.microsoft.com


microsoft.com     nameserver = ns1.msft.net
microsoft.com     nameserver = ns2.msft.net
microsoft.com     nameserver = ns3.msft.net
microsoft.com     nameserver = ns4.msft.net
microsoft.com     nameserver = ns5.msft.net
mailc.microsoft.com        internet address = 131.107.3.126
mailc.microsoft.com        internet address = 131.107.3.121
maila.microsoft.com        internet address = 131.107.3.125
maila.microsoft.com        internet address = 131.107.3.124
mailb.microsoft.com        internet address = 131.107.3.122
mailb.microsoft.com        internet address = 131.107.3.123
ns1.msft.net     internet address = 207.46.245.230
ns2.msft.net     internet address = 64.4.25.30
ns3.msft.net     internet address = 213.199.144.151
ns4.msft.net     internet address = 207.46.72.123
ns5.msft.net     internet address = 207.46.138.20
```

2. In your e-mail client, change the Outgoing Mail Server text box to the mail server's IP address. Make sure the e-mail address is set to a mailbox outside of the organization that you can receive messages on. Figure 7-11 shows this configuration in Microsoft Office Outlook 2003.

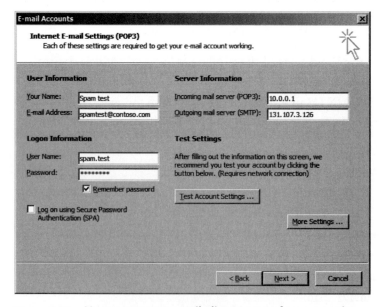

Figure 7-11   You can use any mail client to test for open relays.

3. Compose a new message and send it. If the server is not configured as an open relay, you will probably receive an immediate error message. If it is configured as an open relay, you will receive the message in your mailbox.

If you determine that the server is an open relay, immediately reconfigure it by blocking incoming connections on TCP port 25 from the Internet (if possible), and requiring authentication for SMTP connections.

Receiving Spam

Besides relaying spam, spam presents a threat because almost certainly it will be addressed to your users' mailboxes. Spam wastes mail-server capacity and end-user productivity. In addition, as the number of unwanted messages increases, so does the risk that a user will overlook an important message.

The most effective countermeasures to combat this threat are to implement server- and client-side anti-spam solutions. In large environments, it may be most cost effective to implement only a server-side solution. In small environments, client-side solutions tend to be less expensive. Use the Security Risk Management Process to identify the cost of receiving spam and weigh that cost against the cost of implementing either or both types of anti-spam solutions.

There are many non-Microsoft anti-spam solutions. One solution provided by Microsoft without cost to Exchange Server 2003 users is the Exchange Intelligent Message Filter. Of course, there are costs to implementing it: the time required by your staff to learn how to use it and to design the filters. There's also a good chance that some legitimate, and possibly important, messages will be filtered. These costs exist in varying degrees for any anti-spam solution, however.

> **MORE INFO**   **Anti-Spam Software**   For more information about the Exchange Intelligent Message Filter, visit *http://go.microsoft.com/fwlink/?LinkId=28649*. For a list of Microsoft partners providing anti-spam software for Exchange Server computers, visit *http://go.microsoft.com/fwlink/?LinkId=28649*.

Receiving Viruses

Besides spammers, the most common threat to mail servers is transferring a virus. These viruses are rarely a threat to the mail server itself. Instead, attackers use mail servers as a conduit to transfer a virus from an infected computer to uninfected computers. These viruses typically send outgoing messages from an infected computer and attach an executable file or script (sometimes hidden in an archive such as a ZIP file). The recipient of the message might run the attachment and become infected with the virus, which then replicates itself by sending additional messages.

Block these messages at your mail server. The most effective way is to install antivirus software for your mail server. Microsoft provides a list of antivirus partners on its Web site at *http://www.microsoft.com/exchange/partners/antivirus.asp*.

You can also block e-mail viruses from spreading at the client. By default, recent versions of Outlook block potentially dangerous attachments, as shown in Figure 7-12. Running client-side antivirus software further reduces this risk. For more information about client-side non-Microsoft antivirus software, visit *http://www.microsoft.com/security/antivirus*.

Figure 7-12   Outlook blocks messages that contain potentially dangerous attachments.

Best Practices for Hardening Exchange Servers

Besides the general best practices that apply to all servers, consider the following when designing Exchange Server computers into your network architectures:

- Adding members to the Pre–Windows 2000 Compatible Access group always weakens security because members of this group have read access to user and group objects in Active Directory. For the exam, understand the implication for Exchange Server: members of the Pre–Windows 2000 Compatible Access group can view a member list for mail-enabled groups that otherwise would be hidden.

- Exchange Server enables users to access their e-mail from a Web browser by connecting to an Outlook Web Access (OWA) server. OWA uses IIS; therefore, you must understand IIS to know how to configure security for OWA. After installing Exchange Server, you manage it by using the System Manager in the Microsoft Exchange Server program group.

■ Use Microsoft Baseline Security Analyzer (MBSA) to identify known vulnerabilities and missing security updates on your Exchange Server computers.

■ Use strong passwords. Whereas this best practice is true of any computer, it is particularly true of computers such as e-mail servers that are exposed on the Internet, because they are the most likely to be attacked. For more information about strong passwords, refer to Chapter 5, "Designing Active Directory Security."

Hardening SQL Server Computers

Microsoft SQL Server is a popular database that acts as a back-end data store for many business applications. After installing SQL Server, you manage it by using the Enterprise Manager in the Microsoft SQL Server program group.

The sections that follow discuss SQL authentication, authorization, the risk of SQL injection attacks, SQL logging considerations, ports you must open in your firewall to allow SQL communications, and best practices for hardening SQL Server computers.

SQL Authentication

SQL Server supports two modes of authentication for clients connecting to the SQL Server computer: Windows Authentication Mode and Mixed Mode. Windows Authentication Mode is the default authentication mode in SQL Server 2000. In Windows Authentication Mode, SQL Server 2000 relies solely on the Windows authentication of the user. Windows users or groups are then granted access to the SQL Server database resources.

Whenever possible, require Windows Authentication Mode for connections to SQL Server. This simplifies administration, provides single sign-on for users, and enables you to use Windows security enforcement mechanisms such as stronger authentication protocols and mandatory password complexity and expiration. In addition, credentials delegation (the ability to bridge credentials across multiple servers) is available only in Windows Authentication Mode. On the client side, Windows Authentication Mode eliminates the need to store passwords, which is a major vulnerability in applications that use standard SQL Server logons.

In Mixed Mode, either Windows Authentication or SQL Server Authentication can authenticate users. Users authenticated by SQL Server have their user name and password pairs maintained within SQL Server. If the client accessing the SQL Server database is unable to use a standard Windows logon, SQL Server requires a user name and password pair, and compares this pair against those stored in its system tables.

You can specify this choice by using the SQL Server Properties dialog box in the SQL Enterprise Manager, as shown in Figure 7-13.

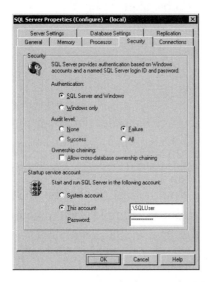

Figure 7-13   Use Windows-only SQL Server authentication whenever possible.

When using Mixed Mode, be aware of an account named *sa*. The sa account in SQL Server is similar to the Administrator account in Windows; it is both highly privileged and built-in. Because it is built into SQL Server, it is the target of many SQL Server attacks. To decrease the risk of being exploited by such an attack, assign a strong password to the sa account.

SQL Authorization

SQL Server provides three authorization mechanisms: object permissions, statement permissions, and implicit permissions. Object permissions in SQL Server provide granular control over authorization to databases, tables, and even rows and columns of data contained within tables. You control access to these objects by granting, denying, or revoking the ability to run particular statements or stored procedures. For example, you can grant a user the right to SELECT information from a table, but deny the right to INSERT, UPDATE, or DELETE information in the table.

> **NOTE   SQL Commands**   SELECT, INSERT, UPDATE, and DELETE are Structured Query Language (SQL) commands.

Statement permissions control administrative actions such as creating a database or adding objects to a database. Only members of the System Administrators role and database owners can assign statement permissions. By default, normal logons aren't granted statement permissions, and you must specifically grant these permissions to logons of users that aren't administrators. For example, if a user needs to be able to create views in a database, you would assign permission to execute CREATE VIEW.

Only members of predefined system roles or database/database-object owners can assign implied permissions. Implied permissions for a role can't be changed or applied to other accounts (unless these accounts are made members of the role). For example, members of the System Administrators server role can perform any activity in SQL Server. They can extend databases and kill processes. You can't revoke or assign these rights to other accounts individually.

Owners of databases and database objects also have implied permissions. These permissions allow them to perform all activities with either the databases or the objects they own, or with both. For example, a user who owns a table can view, add, change, and delete data. That user can also alter the table's definition and control the table's permissions.

SQL Injection Attacks

SQL injection attacks insert database commands into user input to modify commands sent from an application to a back-end database. Applications that employ user input in SQL queries can be vulnerable to SQL injection attacks.

Consider the following simplified C# source code, intended to determine whether an order number (stored in the variable *Id* and provided by the user) has shipped:

```
sql.Open();

sqlString="SELECT HasShipped FROM orders WHERE ID='" + Id + "'";

SqlCommand cmd = new SqlCommand(sqlString,sql);

if ((int)cmd.ExecuteScalar() != 0) {

    Status = "Yes";

} else {

    Status = "No";

}
```

Legitimate users will submit an order ID such as **1234**. The second line of code would add this to the existing sqlString command to generate the following SQL query:

```
SELECT HasShipped FROM orders WHERE ID='1234'
```

Then, the remaining code would set the Status variable to *"Yes"* if the *HasShipped* value in the row with that ID number were true. However, a malicious attacker could submit a value such as, **1234' drop table customers** − . The preceding C# code would then construct the following SQL query.

```
SELECT HasShipped FROM orders WHERE ID='1234' drop table customers --
```

> **NOTE SQL Variances** The exact structure of SQL commands varies between database servers. Some database servers, for example, require each command to be separated by a semicolon. SQL Server does not have this requirement, however.

Assuming a table named *customers* existed, and the user had the right to drop the table, the table would be lost. Dropping a table is one of the least-damaging types of SQL injection attacks. Depending on the application and the database configuration, such maliciously malformed queries can also be used to retrieve data from the database and run operating system commands. An attacker could potentially retrieve a list of passwords or credit card numbers stored in the database, install a Trojan horse to gather credentials from administrators, or create a new administrator account.

As a security designer, you can't prevent this type of attack with firewalls because SQL Server computers have to be able to receive queries. In fact, the burden of preventing this type of attack lies in the hands of the developers. As a security designer, it is your responsibility to ensure that the developers use security best practices. In addition, you must ensure that applications connecting to databases are auditing for SQL injection attacks. As a third line of defense, use Windows authentication and apply the principle of least privilege to restrict authorization to objects in the SQL database.

> **MORE INFO** It's vital that developers receive security training. Two good books for developers on the topic are *Writing Secure Code, Second Edition* (Microsoft Press, 2002) by David LeBlanc and Michael Howard, and *MCAD/MCSD Self-Paced Training Kit: Implementing Security for Applications with Microsoft Visual Basic .NET and Microsoft Visual C# .NET* (Microsoft Press, 2004) by Tony Northrup.

Logging Considerations

SQL Server includes its own authentication mechanism. To provide auditing of logon attempts for SQL Server logons, configure SQL Server to add events to the Application event log. This setting can be found on the Security tab of the server Properties dialog box. You can choose from four different auditing levels:

- **None** No authentication logging is performed.

- **Failure** Events are added to the Application event log when a user attempts to authenticate but fails.

- **Success** Events are added when a user is successfully authenticated.

- **All** Events are added with each authentication attempt, successful or unsuccessful.

Even if you enable authentication auditing to the Application log, you won't find details in the logs about certain user activities, such as which tables users access, which queries users run, and which stored procedures users invoke. To log details about these kinds of activities, use the Profiler tool, which can be started from within the SQL Server program group. Use Profiler to create a trace of almost every activity that happens within a SQL Server database, including the exact queries submitted by users, as shown in Figure 7-14. If you believe you are being actively attacked, recording the queries submitted to SQL Server can provide you with a great deal of information about the attacker.

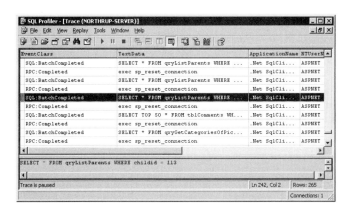

Figure 7-14   Use SQL Profiler during an attack to gather the exact queries used by the attacker.

Protecting SQL Server with Firewalls

SQL Server databases should never be connected to the Internet without at least a packet-filtering firewall in place. Connecting a SQL Server database to even an internal network is risky because other internal systems might become infected with a worm that could infect a system that accepts incoming database connections. To allow database clients to submit queries to the database server, allow packets with a TCP port of 1433 to be passed. However, because of the risk of worms that attempt to connect to this port, use a firewall to drop packets that are not from authorized database clients.

Using Delegated Authentication

Delegated authentication occurs when a network service accepts a request from a user and assumes that user's identity to initiate a new connection to a second network service. Delegated authentication occurs by default when anonymous access is disabled for IIS. A typical architecture in which delegated authentication is used is shown in Figure 7-15.

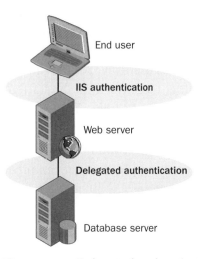

Figure 7-15   Delegated authentication enables a Web server to pass credentials to a back-end SQL database.

Using delegated authentication increases the security of back-end network services such as SQL Server. Without delegated authentication, a back-end database must grant the Web server service user account access to all data that any user would potentially need to access. In essence, without delegated authentication, the database must rely entirely on the Web server to authenticate and authorize users.

With delegated authentication, the Web server presents the end user's credentials when accessing data from the back-end database. The database can then determine whether the user should be able to access the requested piece of information. In the case of a human resources database, the database administrators could configure the database to allow employees to view only the names and locations of users. However, employees working in the human resources department could be granted access to view and update specific rows and columns in the database that should not be accessible to all users.

To delegate this right, assign the Enable Computer And User Accounts To Be Trusted For Delegation user right to the selected individuals. By default, Administrators have this right. Users who are assigned the right to enable delegated authentication can then edit the properties of computer accounts in the Active Directory Users And Computers console, select the Delegation tab, and click one of the two Trust This Computer For Delegation options. This setting should be specified for computer and service accounts that provide users information that is stored on back-end servers and must be accessed securely.

> **NOTE** **Risks of Trusting for Delegation** Misuse of this user right, or of the Trusted For Delegation setting, could make the network vulnerable to sophisticated attacks such as Trojan horse programs that impersonate incoming clients and use their credentials to gain access to network resources. As a result, set the Account Cannot Be Delegated option on accounts that are particularly sensitive.

By enabling delegated authentication, you can prevent an attacker who gains control of a server from accessing data stored on other servers that require user credentials to access. By requiring that all data be accessed by means of credentials that are delegated to the server for use on the client's behalf, you ensure that the server cannot be compromised and then used to gain access to sensitive information on other servers. However, if a server itself has access to information stored on other servers, an attacker who gains control of this server would be able to access the information stored on the other servers.

> **NOTE** **EFS and Delegation** If you enable Encrypting File System (EFS) on a file server, that server must be trusted for delegation to obtain certificates on behalf of a user to encrypt and decrypt files.

When you enable delegated authentication for a computer account by selecting the Trust This Computer For Delegation To Any Service option, delegation is automatically enabled for all services on that computer. Constrained delegation allows administrators to specify particular services from which a computer that is trusted for delegation can request resources. By using constrained delegation, you can prevent attackers who compromise a server from accessing resources that are not intended to be accessed by that server. Specify constrained delegation by selecting the Trust This Computer For Delegation To Specified Services Only option, specifying the available authentication protocols, and then selecting the services, as shown in Figure 7-16.

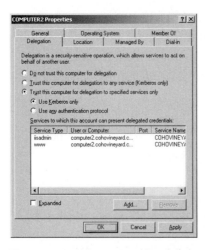

Figure 7-16   Use constrained delegation to limit the risk of delegated authentication.

Best Practices for Hardening SQL Servers

Besides the general best practices that apply to all servers, consider the following when designing SQL Server computers into your network architectures:

- Use MBSA to identify known vulnerabilities and missing security updates on your SQL Server computers.

- Applications often store confidential information in a SQL Server database and, as a result, knowing how to harden the security of a SQL Server computer is important both in the real world and for this exam. However, this exam will not require detailed knowledge of SQL Server. There are other certification exams dedicated to SQL Server. Become familiar with the role SQL Server and other databases fulfill on the network, understand the potential vulnerabilities associated with this role, and know about the tools used to configure security for SQL Server.

- Disable every SQL communication protocol except TCP/IP, and then force encryption for that protocol, as shown in Figure 7-17. This will limit the potential attack surface.

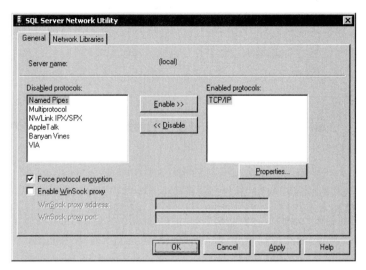

Figure 7-17   Use the built-in encryption in SQL Server to protect communications.

■ Change the port numbers SQL Server computers and clients use to something other than the default. This will prevent the vast majority of worms and viruses from infecting your server, even if they bypass your other layers of defense.

SUMMARY

- Create a baseline security template that you can apply to all servers in your organization, and then create security templates for individual computer roles in your organization.

- Apply security templates and other security settings to computers in an Active Directory by using GPOs.

- Use the Security Configuration and Analysis snap-in to verify that security settings are applied to the target computers in your organization.

- Although different server roles require security settings specific to a particular role, many guidelines apply to any type of server. In particular, reduce the attack surface by disabling unnecessary services, blocking unwanted traffic, and uninstalling unnecessary Windows components.

- Active Directory domain controllers are common targets because a threat that compromises a domain controller can gain access to any member computer. Therefore, dedicate more time to hardening domain controllers than to hardening other computers. In particular, protect the Active Directory user database and use separate accounts for backing up domain controllers.

- DNS servers contain the IP addresses of computers on your internal network. This information enables attackers to map your network, which enables them to identify and target the most critical servers. For this reason, take measures to protect internal records from being queried, including configuring separate DNS servers for internal and external networks. In addition, be very careful to limit the risk of a threat updating or adding records, because a sophisticated attacker could add records to direct private traffic to a malicious server.

- DHCP servers distribute network configurations to servers and clients on many networks. They are likely threat targets because an attacker who can configure the network configuration of computers can redirect requests to malicious servers. To reduce the threat of malicious DHCP servers, Windows DHCP servers in Active Directory environments must be authorized.

- File servers store many of your organization's confidential documents. To protect them, use access control lists to restrict authorization to confidential files. In addition, audit access to your most critical documents.

- IAS servers provide authentication for remote access to your network. As a result, they are likely targets of attack. You can reduce the risk of remote-access attack by using a password to enable encryption and authentication of communications to the IAS server. You can also use quarantine control to restrict access to authenticated remote-access users until you verify that the computer they are using meets your network's security requirements.

- Mail servers—and Exchange Server computers in particular—can greatly benefit from hardening. You can reduce the risk of attacks from spammers and viruses by creating custom filters with Exchange Intelligent Message Filter. Alternatively, it may be more cost effective to purchase third-party anti-spam and antivirus software.

- SQL Server computers store confidential application data and should rarely be connected to external networks. In fact, allow only communications from front-end servers with static IP addresses. In addition, require encryption for those communications. Besides improving communication security, you can dramatically reduce the risk of a SQL Server computer being compromised by applying the principle of least privilege to table and query permissions.

REVIEW QUESTIONS

1. Which predefined security template can be used to improve the ability of members of the Users group to run applications without being logged on as administrators?

    a. Setup Security.inf

    b. Compatws.inf

    c. Securews.inf

    d. Hisecws.inf

2. Which predefined security template can be used to return a system to its original security settings?

    a. Setup Security.inf

    b. Compatws.inf

    c. Securews.inf

    d. Hisecws.inf

3. Which is the correct tool to use to deploy a security template to dozens of stand-alone computers most efficiently?

   a. Group Policy Object Editor snap-in

   b. Security Configuration And Analysis snap-in

   c. Security Templates snap-in

   d. Local Security Policy console

   e. Secedit command-line tool

4. Which of the following types of servers should have traffic allowed on UDP port 53?

   a. DHCP servers

   b. DNS servers

   c. Domain controllers

   d. Web servers

   e. RADIUS servers

   f. Database servers

   g. Messaging servers

5. You manage an Active Directory network, but some servers are not members of the domain. What are the risks of having some computers in a domain and others that do not participate in the domain?

6. Your organization has an auditing process based on aggregating and monitoring Event Viewer logs, but each type of event log being monitored must be specially configured. Which of the following types of servers creates a dedicated event log that can be viewed by using Event Viewer? (Choose all that apply.)

   a. DHCP servers

   b. DNS servers

   c. Domain controllers

   d. Web servers

   e. RADIUS servers

   f. Database servers

   g. Messaging servers

7. Security templates alone are insufficient for distributing security configuration settings. What other techniques will you use to establish standardized security settings for servers in your organization?

8. Which of the following types of servers support communications encryption without using IPSec? (Choose all that apply.)

    a. SQL Server computers

    b. Exchange Server computers

    c. File servers

    d. DNS servers

    e. DHCP servers

9. Which of the following types of servers should you spend the most time hardening?

    a. SQL Server computers

    b. Web servers

    c. IAS servers

    d. DNS servers

    e. DHCP servers

CASE SCENARIOS

Case Scenario 7-1: Maintaining Security in an Active Directory Environment with Legacy Computers

Your manager has asked you to stabilize the security configurations of the 10 servers and 150 portable and desktop computers in your Active Directory domain environment. In the past, computers have been compromised because users modified the security configurations of their computers, introducing vulnerabilities that you hadn't planned for. Your manager wants the solution you create to ensure that users cannot reduce the security of their computers.

Most servers perform multiple tasks. In total, your 10 servers perform the following roles:

- Six file servers

- Three domain controllers

- Three mail servers

- Two external Web servers

- Two internal Web servers

- Two proxy servers

- Four database servers

Although you have been pushing management to fund upgrades for all portable and desktop systems, you still have many older operating systems in use. Of the 150 portable and desktop computers, you have

- 120 computers running Windows XP Professional

- 10 computers running Windows NT Workstation 4.0

- 5 computers running Windows XP Home Edition

- 7 computers running Windows 2000 Professional

- 4 computers running Windows Me

- 4 computers running Windows 95

All computers should use a standardized security configuration that you and your team designed. This security configuration includes standardized user rights, wireless network policy, file, folder, and registry permissions, and renamed Administrator and guest accounts in each computer's local user database.

1. How many different security templates will you create, and what will each one be used for?

2. Which of the portable and desktop computers will not be able to use Group Policy? (Choose all that apply.)

   a. The computers running Windows XP Professional

   b. The computers running Windows NT Workstation 4.0

   c. The computers running Windows XP Home Edition

   d. The computers running Windows 2000 Professional

   e. The computers running Windows Me

   f. The computers running Windows 95

3. Which of the following is the right choice for deploying security templates in your environment to those computers that support Group Policy?

    a. Importing the security templates into Local Group Policy

    b. Importing the security templates by using Secedit

    c. Importing the security templates by using the Security Configuration And Analysis tool

    d. Importing the security templates by using GPOs linked to Active Directory

4. How will you apply security settings to those systems that do not support Group Policy?

5. How will you configure wireless network policy using security templates?

Case Scenario 7-2: Deploying Public Mail and DNS Servers

The Chief Security Officer (CSO) of your organization has asked you to create a network design for the two new servers that you will be deploying: an Exchange Server 2003 computer and a Windows Server 2003–based DNS server. Currently, your ISP provides these services, but the Chief Information Officer (CIO) wants to reduce costs by bringing these services in-house. Both computers must be accessible to users on both the Internet and the internal network, so you have decided to place them in your organization's perimeter network. The Exchange Server computer needs to be able to receive e-mail from other mail servers on the Internet, but employees do not need to be able to check their mail from the Internet. Instead, they will connect to an existing VPN server and check their e-mail through the internal network.

Your CSO stresses that security is extremely important. The employees of your organization frequently send confidential information through e-mail, and if your computer running Exchange Server were compromised, the losses could be huge. Your DNS server holds records for every system on your internal network and, if compromised, it would provide an attacker with a roadmap for future attacks against your intranet. Worst yet, a perceptive attacker could modify your DNS records to get internal computers to communicate confidential information to computers controlled by the attacker.

1. Which of the following ports will you have to configure the firewall to forward to the perimeter network? (Choose all that apply.)

    a. 53/udp

    b. 53/tcp

    c. 25/udp

    d. 25/tcp

    e. 110/udp

    f. 110/tcp

    g. 1433/udp

    h. 1433/tcp

2. How many security templates would you use to configure and analyze the security settings on this network?

3. Besides configuring the initial security settings on the Exchange and DNS servers, what security-related tasks should be performed on an ongoing basis?

4. What types of attacks are likely to be directed at the DNS server?

5. How can you reduce the risk of an attacker identifying IP addresses of computers on your private network by querying the public IP address of your DNS server?

6. What types of attacks are likely to be directed at the Exchange Server computer, and how can you prevent them?

CHAPTER 8
HARDENING CLIENT COMPUTERS

Upon completion of this chapter, you will be able to:

■ Assess the features and limitations of different versions of Microsoft Windows client operating systems.

■ Plan client computer security to meet your security needs, including:

   ❏ Using software-restriction policies to limit the applications that can run on client computers.

   ❏ Understanding the various mechanisms for restricting software and explaining the advantages of each.

   ❏ Designing security configurations for desktop computer systems.

   ❏ Reducing the risk of mobile computers being compromised while connected to unprotected networks and limiting the loss of confidential information if a mobile computer is stolen.

■ Explain how you must design security differently for client computer roles including desktops, laptops, and kiosks.

■ Explain the benefits of Code Access Security (CAS) and use CAS to reduce the risks of running applications based on the Microsoft .NET Framework.

Many threats will attempt to compromise your critical resources through your client computers. If a threat compromises one of your client computers, it can abuse the user's privileges to access network resources. It can use the client computer to attack your network from inside your firewall, bypassing at least one of your layers of security. If the threat is searching for confidential files, it might even find copies of the files on the client computers themselves.

Many security designers put little effort into hardening client computers because they trust their network's perimeter firewalls to protect client computers on the internal network. This design is outdated, however. Today, more and more client computers are mobile, and they are vulnerable to attack while attached to a user's home network, hotel Internet connection, or a Wi-Fi hotspot. After one computer is compromised, threat agents such as viruses can spread to other computers on your internal network.

To protect against these threats, you must harden every client computer in your network. This may seem like a daunting task because you probably have many times more client computers than servers. However, security templates, Group Policy objects (GPOs), and non-Microsoft software reduce the time required to deploy and maintain hardened client configurations in enterprise environments.

The challenge of hardening client computers is weighing the costs and benefits of security. It's quite simple to harden desktop environments to allow only users to run a handful of approved applications; however, the productivity of power users will suffer. Employee efficiency might drop because of the lack of flexibility. As a security designer, your challenge is to use the Security Risk Management Process to determine which client-side countermeasures reduce risk enough to justify their cost, and which are too much trouble to implement. In all likelihood, you need to create different policies for client computer roles such as desktop computers, mobile computers, and kiosks.

This chapter teaches you the different techniques to harden client computers and gives you the information you need to choose the hardening techniques that meet your organization's security requirements.

ASSESSING CLIENT OPERATING SYSTEM FEATURES

The latest version of Windows will usually be the most secure. Unfortunately, most enterprises still have many computers running earlier versions of Windows. As a security designer, understand the weaknesses of those earlier versions of Windows so that you can weigh the risks against the cost of upgrading.

Where you can't justify the cost of an upgrade, find ways to configure the client computers to meet your organization's security requirements. Because early versions of Windows lack important security features, you might need to identify non-Microsoft software to supplement the security configuration of these computers. Alternatively, you might determine that the least expensive option is upgrading the computers to Windows XP. Table 8-1 compares the security features of recent Windows client operating systems.

Table 8-1 **Comparison of Windows Client Security Features**

Feature	Description	Win 95, Win 98, and Win Me	Win NT 4.0	Win 2000 Pro	Win XP Pro	SP 2 for Win XP Pro
Internet Connection Firewall	Windows XP offers a firewall client that can help protect small businesses from common Internet attacks.	Not supported	Not supported	Not supported	Fully supported	Not supported; upgraded to Windows Firewall
Windows Firewall	Service Pack 2 for Windows XP includes an improved firewall client that is more resistant to attacks, easier to configure, and enabled by default.	Not supported	Not supported	Not supported	Not supported	Fully supported
Encrypting File System (EFS) with multiuser support	EFS encrypts each file with a randomly generated key. The encryption and decryption processes are transparent to the user. Only Windows XP Professional supports the ability to have multiple users accessing an encrypted document and encrypting offline folders.	Not supported	Not supported	Partly supported; no support for use with multiple users or offline access	Fully supported	Fully supported
Security Center	Security Center provides a central location for users to change security settings and install security updates; it's primarily intended for home users.	Not supported	Not supported	Not supported	Not supported	Fully supported
IP Security (IPSec)	IPSec helps protect data transmitted across a network, as described in Chapter 10, "Protecting Intranet Communications."	Partly supported	Partly supported; requires free download	Fully supported	Fully supported	Fully supported
Kerberos support	Kerberos provides high-strength authentication in Active Directory directory service domains.	Not supported	Not supported	Fully supported	Fully supported	Fully supported

Table 8-1   **Comparison of Windows Client Security Features**

Feature	Description	Win 95, Win 98, and Win Me	Win NT 4.0	Win 2000 Pro	Win XP Pro	SP 2 for Win XP Pro
Smart Card support	Windows XP Professional integrates smart-card capabilities into the operating system, including support for smart-card logon to terminal server sessions hosted on computers running Microsoft Windows Server 2003.	Partly supported; subset of features	Not supported	Partly supported; subset of features	Fully supported	Fully supported
Data execution prevention	Data execution prevention reduces vulnerability to worms and viruses by enabling applications to mark blocks of memory containing data, rather than by application instructions, with a special code that prevents the processor from running potentially malicious software.	Not supported	Not supported	Not supported	Not supported	Fully supported
Microsoft Internet Explorer security improvements	Internet Explorer reduces the risk of Web sites running malicious software or accessing private data on user computers.	Not supported	Not supported	Not supported	Not supported	Fully supported
Attachment manager	The attachment manager helps users determine whether files are safe to open/execute when attached to messages in Outlook Express and Windows Messenger, or opened via Internet Explorer.	Not supported	Not supported	Not supported	Not supported	Fully supported
Alerter service, Messenger service, DCOM, and RPC security enhancements	Windows XP offers improved resistance to attacks that exploit vulnerabilities in the Alerter and Messenger services by disabling them by default and provides granular control over Distributed Component Object Model (DCOM) and Remote Procedure Call (RPC) privileges.	Not supported	Not supported	Not supported	Not supported	Fully supported

Table 8-1   **Comparison of Windows Client Security Features**

Feature	Description	Win 95, Win 98, and Win Me	Win NT 4.0	Win 2000 Pro	Win XP Pro	SP 2 for Win XP Pro
Group Policy	Group Policy is your most important tool for deploying and maintaining security settings. Without it, security settings on client computers degrade over time.	Not supported	Not supported	Partly supported; subset of features	Partly supported; subset of features	Fully supported
Automatic Updates	Patching is critical for security. Most Windows client operating systems support Automatic Updates, but computers running Windows NT 4.0 do not.	Partly supported; subset of features in Windows Me	Not supported	Fully supported	Fully supported	Fully supported

PLANNING MANAGED CLIENT COMPUTERS

When planning the requirements for managed client computers, start by identifying the baseline privilege level appropriate for users to have on their computers. The baseline user privilege level is specified by granting users membership to one of these groups: Users, Power Users, and Administrators. Membership in the Users group gives the most protection from a number of external threats, such as viruses, and it limits the damage users can cause accidentally or intentionally to their computers. However, Users permissions have the most incompatibility problems with earlier applications. Take particular care before you give users privileged access to computers that they share with other employees.

Next, identify the types of systems with which users need to operate. Interoperability with earlier systems, such as Microsoft Windows NT 4.0–based servers and UNIX file servers, necessitates that some of the security you might use in a pure Windows Server 2003 environment must be relaxed. For example, you might have to add users to the Pre–Windows 2000 Compatible Access group, which grants the users privileges to view users and groups in the domain. You might also have to enable the storage of LM hashes, which can make the password database more vulnerable to password-cracking attacks.

Finally, consider the level of support users provide for their own computers. Users who use portable computers and provide their own support might require administrative rights on their computers. Other high-performance users, such as developers, might also need administrative rights.

Testing Client Security Settings

Before deploying your management solutions to a wide base, fully test your design in a lab environment. At a minimum, your test environment should consist of a domain controller and one computer representative of each client computer type in your organization (which might include a desktop computer, mobile computer, and highly restricted kiosk computer). If you are testing software installation through Group Policy, include one or more servers set up as software distribution points. By setting up a test-to-production environment deployment process, you can ensure that you provide a reliable and consistent configuration management solution.

Document the testing network in addition to all steps required to set it up. If you are adding new hardware, such as a new server, to your organization's network, use this same hardware in your test deployment if possible. To minimize variables and to ensure that testing does not interfere with your organization's network services, keep the testing network on its own isolated local area network (LAN).

After completing tests in a controlled environment, select a group of users to pilot your configuration. Keep the users to a manageable number: fewer than fifty in an enterprise, and even fewer in smaller organizations. A pilot deployment can expose unexpected problems on a small scale so that you can resolve them before deploying on a large scale. Verify that the deployed technology is operating as expected.

> **MORE INFO**   In addition to the topics discussed here, regular patching is a requirement for all client computers. For more information about patching, refer to Chapter 3, "Reducing the Risk of Software Vulnerabilities."

Designing Client Security Templates

You can use security templates to simplify the management and auditing of client security configuration settings in your organization, as described in Chapter 7, "Hardening Servers." In addition to the client security templates included with

Windows XP (and Windows Server 2003), the Windows XP Security Guide v2, published by Microsoft, includes several more up-to-date templates. The document provides templates in two categories: enterprise and high-security. For each category, the document provides separate templates for desktop and laptop computers so that laptop users have additional privileges such as restoring files while traveling away from IT support.

Use the enterprise templates from the Windows XP Security Guide in most cases, because the high-security settings are for organizations willing to sacrifice administrative costs for security only. For example, the enterprise templates set the minimum password length to 8 characters, but the high-security templates set the minimum password length at 12 characters. For most organizations, 12 characters is too long and will increase the number of help calls and password resets required; 12-character passwords won't dramatically reduce the risk of password-cracking attacks for most organizations, either.

> **MORE INFO** *You can download the Windows XP Security Guide at http://www.microsoft.com/technet/security/prodtech/winclnt/secwinxp/.*

Designing a Client Computer Organizational Unit Model

Each time Microsoft releases a new client operating system, it includes significant security enhancements. Windows 2000 Professional is much more secure at the outset than Windows Millennium Edition (Windows Me), and Windows XP Professional is significantly more secure than any earlier client operating system. Because of these differences, you need to design security configurations for each platform separately and create separate GPOs for different versions of Windows client operating systems.

As you learned in Chapter 7, it is possible to use Windows Management Instrumentation (WMI) filtering to apply different GPOs to computers based on their operating systems. However, WMI filtering is complicated, and using WMI filtering to apply GPOs to computers running Windows 2000 requires some trickery. Rather than using WMI filtering, group computers into different organizational units (OUs) based on their current operating systems.

Subdivide those operating system OUs further for each client computer role. The design you choose should reflect the way you design client platforms. Typically, this means creating separate OUs for different client computer roles in your organization. Typical roles and OUs include

- Laptops

- Desktops

- Kiosks

Figure 8-1 illustrates this type of OU model.

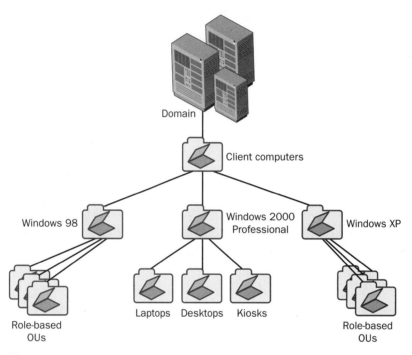

Figure 8-1   Design an OU structure for client computers that simplifies assigning GPOs.

Depending on your organization's security requirements, you might not base the roles you choose for your client platforms on how users use the computer. Rather, you might base them on the users' tasks or business units. For example, you might have a different client platform for users in your development, accounting, and executive groups because each group probably has access to a different set of applications. In addition, developers need a different operating system configuration to perform debugging tasks. Figure 8-2 illustrates this type of OU model.

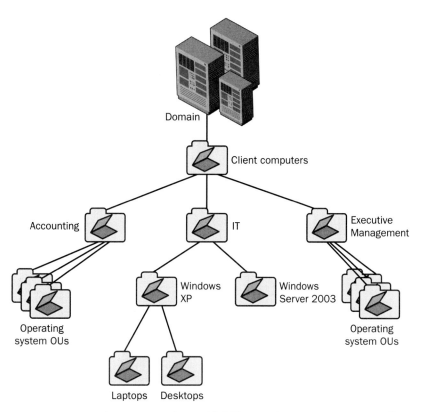

Figure 8-2 Use departmental OUs if different departments have different security needs.

If users in all departments have similar security requirements, create OUs based on the computer roles. If users in different departments have different security requirements, create departmental OUs. If necessary, create OUs for each computer role used by each department.

Although there is no practical limit to the number of OUs you can create, avoid an overly complex client-computer OU structure by using group memberships to control which computers receive a GPO within a single OU. For example, rather than subdividing your custom Laptops and Desktops OUs to assign a special GPO to development computers, you could add development computers to a security group called Development Computers. Then, you could assign permissions on the GPO so that only members of the Development Computers group can apply the policy.

For more information about using security groups to restrict access to GPOs, refer to Chapter 7.

Restricting GPO permissions is a useful technique for testing changes to GPOs with small pilot groups. Although you could create an OU for the pilot group and then move the computers into that OU, there is a good chance you would make a mistake when returning the computers to their original OU after the pilot was complete. In addition, any changes made to GPOs assigned to the production OUs would not be applied to the pilot computers. Instead, create a security group for computers in the pilot group, restrict access to the test GPO so that only members of the pilot group can apply it, and then link the test GPO to a high-level OU that includes all client computers, as illustrated in Figure 8-3.

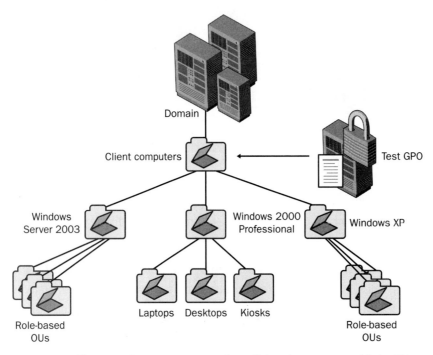

Figure 8-3   Use security groups to apply policies that span multiple OUs.

Adding Non-Microsoft Client Security

Even environments with minimal security requirements will need to add non-Microsoft software to their client computers. In particular, you must address several needs currently lacking in some or all Windows clients:

- **Antivirus protection**   Viruses are the most frequent threat on Windows networks, and antivirus software must be running on every client computer, regardless of your security requirements. Even if you have no budget to allocate, find a free antivirus solution. Most enterprises need a sophisticated antivirus solution that gives administrators centralized control over the antivirus configuration and that automatically updates antivirus signatures.

> **MORE INFO** For a listing of Microsoft antivirus partners, visit *http://www.microsoft.com/security/partners/antivirus.asp*.

- **Network backups** Backing up the data on client computers is critical for security and disaster recovery, but challenging. Enterprises typically purchase non-Microsoft network backup software. Then they install backup agents on all client computers and configure critical data (such as My Documents and the system state) to do backup across the network every night to a central backup server. The backup server typically stores the data on multiple hard disks for quick restorations, and it copies data to removable backup tapes that can be shipped off site to protect the data in the event of a fire or other catastrophe. For more information about backups, refer to Chapter 13, "Creating a Disaster Recovery Plan."

- **Host-based firewalls** Host-based firewalls protect a single computer from many network attacks by examining all network traffic sent to the computer and dropping unrequested communications. Host-based firewalls have an advantage over perimeter firewalls because they protect the computer from attacks originating from the internal network, and they protect the computer when it connects to external networks such as an employee's home network or a wireless hotspot. Windows XP was the first Microsoft client operating system to include a true host-based firewall: Internet Connection Firewall (ICF). Windows XP Service Pack 2 upgraded ICF to Windows Firewall. If you use Windows XP on your network, be sure to use Group Policy to enable the host-based firewalls. If you use earlier versions of Windows that cannot be upgraded to Windows XP, you must use non-Microsoft software. For more information about firewalls, refer to Chapter 10.

Designing Software-Restriction Policies

Software-restriction policies are a feature in Windows XP and Windows Server 2003 that can regulate unknown or untrusted software. Businesses that do not use software-restriction policies put the burden of identifying safe and unsafe software on the users. Users who access the Internet must constantly make decisions about running unknown software. Malicious users intentionally disguise viruses and Trojan horses to trick users into running them. It is difficult for users to make safe choices about what software they should run.

With software-restriction policies, you can protect your network from untrusted software by identifying and specifying the software permitted to run. You can define a default security level of Unrestricted or Disallowed for a GPO to regulate what software is allowed to run by default. In most cases, if you choose to implement a restrictive desktop environment, you will disallow all software by default. You can then make exceptions to this default security level by creating software-restriction policy rules for specific software.

Software-restriction policies define the default security level and all the software rules that apply to a GPO. Apply software-restriction policies across a domain, to local computers, or to individual users. Software-restriction policies provide a number of ways to identify software, and they provide a policy-based infrastructure to enforce decisions about whether the identified software can run. With software-restriction policies, when users run software programs, they must adhere to the guidelines that administrators set up.

With software-restriction policies, you can control the ability of software to run on your system. For example, if you are concerned about users receiving viruses through e-mail, you can apply a policy setting that does not allow certain file types to run in the e-mail attachment directory of your e-mail program. You can even restrict policies based on users, allowing only certain users on a computer to run an application.

You can use four types of rules to create a software-restriction policy:

- Hash rules
- Certificate rules
- Path rules
- Internet zone rules

The sections that follow describe each of these types of policies.

Hash Rules

When you create a hash rule for a software program, software-restriction policies calculate a unique hash of the executable file, as illustrated by Figure 8-4. When a user tries to start an application, Windows generates a hash of the application and compares it to existing hash rules for software-restriction policies. The hash of a software program is always the same, regardless of where the program is located on the computer. However, if a user alters a software program in any way, its hash also changes and it no longer matches the hash in the hash rule for software-restriction policies.

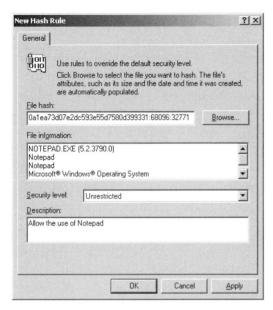

Figure 8-4 Hash rules cause Windows to verify that a file has not been modified before a user can run it.

Hash rules will not allow a user to run a modified file, including those updated by a patch or maliciously modified by a virus. Therefore, use hash rules only when users are allowed to run only a particular version of an application's executable file *and* when you have an existing process for testing patches before deployment. You must add a new rule every time you update an application; therefore, hash rules require very high maintenance.

Certificate Rules

Use certificate rules to allow users to run applications developed within your company. However, to take advantage of certificate rules, you must ensure that your developers sign their applications and executables with a certificate issued by a Public Key Infrastructure (PKI). You need a copy of that certificate when you create the certificate rule. You can also use certificate rules to allow applications from external developers, provided that they provide you with a copy of their certificate and public key (you don't need their private key). For more information about PKIs and certificates, refer to Chapter 9, "Designing a Public Key Infrastructure."

Certificate rules require lower maintenance than hash rules because developers can update an application and the certificate rule software restriction will still allow the updated application to run if it is signed with the same certificate. Therefore, you need to update certificate rules only when you generate a new certificate, which needs to happen only if the certificate is compromised.

To reduce the risk of a developer with access to your allowed certificate adding malicious code to an internal application, ensure that your internal development teams use **code review** procedures and **delayed signing**. Code review procedures require that a manager who has access to your organization's certificate review and approve all code written by a developer.

After that manager approves the code, the manager can then sign the code using delayed signing. Delayed signing is a two-part application-signing process that separates the public and private keys in a developer's certificate, enabling your internal development team to centralize application signing and restrict the distribution of the private keys used to generate application signatures. The fewer people who have access to a private key, the lower the risk of abuse of the key. In this scenario, only the manager has access to the certificate's private key. Therefore, injecting malicious code requires the cooperation of the manager, greatly reducing the risk.

Path Rules

A path rule identifies software by its file path. For example, if you have a computer that has a default security level of Disallowed, you can still grant unrestricted access to a specific folder for each user. You can create a path rule by using the file path and setting the security level of the path rule to Unrestricted. Some common paths for this type of rule are %Userprofile%, %Windir%, %Appdata%, and %Temp%. You can also create registry path rules that use the registry key of the software as the path. Because the path specifies these rules, if a software program is moved, the path rule no longer applies.

Use path rules any time you have a structured desktop environment that disallows users to install their own applications. If you create path rules so that only executables in approved folders can be run, a user cannot run an executable directly from a Web site, which is an excellent countermeasure against the risk of allowing users to browse the Web. In addition, users would not be able to run executable e-mail attachments unless you created a path rule that allowed executables in the e-mail client's temporary directory.

Internet Zone Rules

An Internet zone rule can identify software from a zone specified through Microsoft Internet Explorer. Internet zone rules are useful for preventing users from running applications downloaded from the Internet but still allowing programs stored on the local computer or other trusted computers to run. The zones you can choose from are Internet, Local Intranet, Restricted Sites, Trusted Sites, and My Computer.

The My Computer zone includes any applications installed on the local computer. The Local Intranet zone is for computers located within your organization's internal network, but it does not include any sites by default. The Trusted Sites zone, by default, includes only Web sites used to download updates from Microsoft and to submit error messages to Microsoft. By default, the Restricted Sites zone is empty. The Internet zone includes any computers not located in any of the other zones.

To specify which computers on the network are included in the Local Intranet, Restricted Sites, and Trusted Sites zones for a single computer, start Internet Explorer and, on the Tools menu, click Internet Options, and then click the Security tab as shown in Figure 8-5. You can then select Local Intranet, Restricted Sites, or Trusted Sites and click Sites to add additional locations that will be included in that zone.

Figure 8-5   Internet zone rules enable you to restrict software run directly from the network.

You also can configure zones by using a GPO. Zone settings are located in the User Configuration\Windows Settings\Internet Explorer Maintenance\Security\Security Zones and Content Ratings Policy.

The default settings on clients are sufficient for most organizations. However, if you are creating a restrictive desktop environment and all applications are run directly from local computers, use Internet zone rules to prevent computers from running any application across the network.

Restricting the Desktop Environment

Whereas security templates are useful for configuring client as well as server computers, there are many desktop settings within GPOs that can't be defined in the security template but that can be used to help secure a desktop computer. In particular, examine each Group Policy setting contained in the User Configuration\Administrative Templates node, as shown in Figure 8-6. These settings allow you to carefully configure the desktop and remove items that might be unnecessary or undesired, such as the Run option on the Start menu.

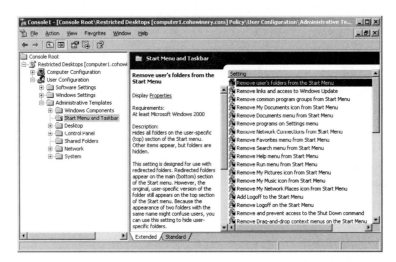

Figure 8-6   Control the desktop environment by using Administrative Templates GPO settings.

The sections that follow describe the settings to consider restricting in your desktop environment. You can't go through the entire Security Risk Management Process to weigh the costs and benefits of each setting as a separate countermeasure, so you'll have to rely primarily on common sense. However, have at least one other person review your choices, and then test those choices thoroughly before deploying the configuration to your users, computers, or both.

For each setting, consider what types of attackers might try to abuse the setting being restricted, and how effective the setting is at blocking the attack. Also consider how much inconvenience having the setting restricted causes to users doing their jobs.

This book can't describe every setting in detail because there are literally thousands of settings. Instead, this book focuses on the settings that are most critical to a security designer. The following sections discuss important security-related Group Policy settings, divided in the same way as they are within a GPO.

Restricting Windows Components

This node, located within the Administrative Templates node of both Computer Configuration and User Configuration, contains settings for configuring important (but primarily optional) components of Windows client operating systems. Spend time examining the settings in the Windows Explorer node, which enable you to fine-tune the client user interface to make it more difficult for users to perform potentially malicious tasks such as burning a CD (which an attacker could use to transport confidential files) and browsing the network (which an attacker could use to identify network resources). Components include the following:

- **Application Compatibility**   Although not very relevant to security, these settings enable you to disable support for 16-bit applications. All recent Windows applications are 32-bit or 64-bit.

- **Internet Explorer**   These policies give you a great deal of control over Internet Explorer's capabilities on client computers in your domain. The most useful settings relate directly to those you would see in Internet Explorer's security options, giving you control over the access granted to Web sites located in various zones (such as the Internet zone and the Trusted Sites zone). Tweak these settings to enable users to browse the Web safely. Most organizations will find the default settings provided with Windows XP Service Pack 2 to be too restrictive, blocking features of Web sites that are very important to your users. To determine how to configure Internet Explorer settings, create a list of commonly accessed, complex Web sites. Then, start with the default settings and test the Web site's functionality. Address compatibility issues by either adjusting the properties of the Web site's zone or moving the Web site to a different zone for the computers in your organization.

- **Internet Information Services**   Web servers, particularly Internet Information Services (IIS)-based Web servers, are frequent targets. As a result, it's vital that you prevent IIS from being installed on computers that do not require it. Unfortunately, all recent Windows client operating systems include a version of IIS. Enable the Prevent IIS Installation setting for computers that do not act as servers and will not be used by developers. Because of the high risk of having IIS installed, it is better to globally prevent it and then make exceptions as needed. In addition, use System Services policies to prevent the various IIS services from starting in the event IIS is installed.

- **NetMeeting**   NetMeeting is a conferencing tool included with several Windows operating systems, but not typically installed by default. If you use NetMeeting, these policies enable you to configure NetMeeting on client computers. You can enable the Set Call Security Options policy to require encryption for both incoming and outgoing calls. If you don't use NetMeeting, use Software Restrictions to prevent it from running and a host-based firewall to block network communications. Because it listens for incoming connections, it is a potential target for threats attacking across the network.

- **Task Scheduler**   You can prevent users from scheduling their own tasks or running tasks that you have scheduled. Leave this enabled for power users who might want to schedule administrative tasks such as defragmenting their disk drives or backing up important files. These benefits typically outweigh the minimal security risks.

- **Terminal Services**   In the Terminal Services\Encryption And Security node, you can require encryption for Remote Desktop connections and require that users type their passwords each time they connect. For most organizations, there is no drawback to requiring encryption. However, test every different Remote Desktop client that you plan to use to verify that it supports encryption—some clients, such as those for Linux computers, might not support encryption. To prevent an attacker who gains physical control over a client computer from using the same credentials to log on interactively to other computers on your network, require that users retype their passwords each time they connect.

- **Windows Digital Rights Management**   This node has a single policy: Prevent Windows Media Digital Rights Management (DRM) Internet Access. This policy applies to copy-protected Windows Media files that your users might have purchased on the Internet, such as songs or videos. To play back the audio or video files, Windows Media Player needs to send a request to an Internet server and validate the license. The security risk is minimal, so leave it disabled under most circumstances. However, it does have the potential to expose which copy-protected files your users are watching. This policy will not affect Windows Rights Management Services (RMS) that you might be running internally.

- **Windows Explorer**   This node within the User Configuration branch of a GPO provides control over the Windows Explorer (also known as My Computer) interface. You can also control the common open file dialog—the dialog box that applications prompt you with to open a file. Consider enabling each of the options in this node if you need to restrict your users' access to content on their computers. In particular, you can hide drives, remove tabs from file and folder properties dialogs, remove CD-burning features, and prevent users from using aspects of My Network Places to browse the network. Each of these settings can both mitigate the risk of an attack and frustrate users, so disable Windows Explorer features with care.

- **Windows Installer**   Windows Installer handles the installation, updating, and removal of software on client computers. Domain administrators can use Active Directory software distribution to install software contained in Windows Installer packages on all computers in a network. Windows Installer also provides update and removal features. The Windows Installer Group Policy settings give you control over these features, such as granting users control over installs, or prohibiting patching. Review each of these settings if you do not want users to install new software in your environment, or if you use Windows Installer packages to distribute software in your network. Note that restricting these settings is not sufficient for preventing users from installing or running unapproved applications because it affects only applications that use Windows Installer. Other applications, such as Trojan horses or attack tools, will be affected only by software restrictions.

- **Microsoft Management Console**   Administrators use MMC snap-ins to perform most management tasks on client computers. Many snap-ins are very powerful tools, particularly in the hands of a skilled attacker. They can also be dangerous in the hands of an ambitious user who wants to perform management tasks on his or her computer but does not have the necessary skills. This node enables you to create a list of permitted and restricted snap-ins to use to restrict users' access to snap-ins on a case-by-case basis. You can also enable the Restrict The User From Entering Author Mode setting to prevent users from saving custom consoles, thus restricting them to consoles you create for their specific tasks. This is very useful when delegating administrative tasks.

- **Windows Media Player**   Windows Media Player queries databases on the Internet to retrieve information about CDs, music files, and Internet radio stations. Although this information probably won't reveal anything useful to an attacker, you can enable the settings in this node to prevent those communications.

- **Windows Messenger**   The only security-related setting in the Windows Messenger node is a policy named Do Not Allow Windows Messenger To Be Run. You can enable this if you don't want users to use Windows Messenger. Windows Messenger does carry some security risks because it allows files to be transferred and thus can be used to transfer malicious software or confidential documents. However, instant communications can improve employee productivity. In general, the benefits of Windows Messenger outweigh the costs. If you choose to use instant communications, consider mitigating the security risks by implementing additional software to monitor and control this mode of communication. Naturally, you must make employees aware that they are being monitored.

- **Windows Update**   You can use these settings to restrict users from entering author mode and restrict the snap-ins they have access to, as shown in Figure 8-7. Removing access to snap-ins will prevent most attackers from attempting to perform administrative tasks; however, sophisticated attackers might still be able to call the underlying management functions by directly accessing the Windows application programming interfaces (APIs).

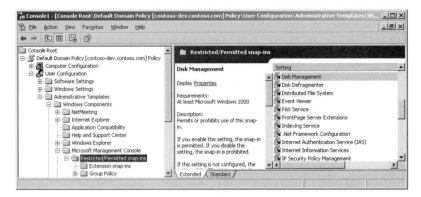

Figure 8-7   Restrict access to MMC snap-ins to make it more difficult for users to perform malicious administrative tasks.

Restricting the Start Menu

If, during the Security Risk Management Process, you determine that restricting the desktop environment is a cost-effective countermeasure, spend some time exploring each of the settings in the User Configuration\Administrative Templates\Start Menu And Taskbar node of a GPO. The policies in this node give you almost complete control over the menu items that appear on the Start menu of a client computer including the ability to do the following:

- Remove the Run menu item, making it more difficult to run arbitrary processes

- Disable the My Recent Documents menu, making it more difficult for an attacker to find important documents

- Remove My Network Places, reducing an attacker's ability to browse for critical network resources

Figure 8-8 shows the standard Start menu when Windows XP is newly installed. As you can see, there are many opportunities for an attacker. The attacker could click Run and launch any arbitrary process. The attacker could open Help And Support Center, which in the past has had several known vulnerabilities. If an attacker used another user's computer (for example, by sitting at the person's desk when he or she stepped away), the attacker could use the My Recent Documents menu to identify quickly the files the user had most recently been working on. The attacker could use the Control Panel to change system settings, or even to create his or her own user account.

Figure 8-8   The Windows Start menu prior to customization provides several opportunities for an attack.

If any of the previously described attacks pose too much of a risk for your organization, you can significantly restrict the options in the Start menu, as shown in Figure 8-9. Most of the previously described attacks are no longer effective. Of course, the attacker has options other than the Start menu. The attacker could press CTRL+ALT+DEL to launch Task Manager, click the File menu, and then click New Task to run an arbitrary task rather than using the Run command on the Start menu. The attacker could also navigate the All Programs menu (which can also be removed) to identify an application with a known weakness. You need to set different policies to restrict those activities.

Figure 8-9   The Windows Start menu can be severely restricted to limit an attacker's opportunities.

As with most countermeasures, restricting the Start menu does not eliminate risk, but it does reduce it. When combined with other desktop restrictions and customized program menus, you can make it much more difficult for an attacker to perform malicious actions on a computer.

Restricting the Desktop

When discussing Group Policy restrictions, the term *desktop* literally means the client computer's desktop, which might include icons for My Computer, My Network Places, and several applications. In this context, desktop does not refer to the complete *desktop environment*. Other Group Policy settings provide control over the Control Panel and Start menu.

The Desktop Group Policy settings (located only within User Configuration) enable you to remove icons from a user's desktop, including the My Computer, My Documents, Recycle Bin, and My Network Places. You can even enable a setting named Hide And Disable All Items On The Desktop. In general, restrict the desktop icons only for those resources to which you choose not to grant your users access. For example, if you don't want your users accessing My Network Places, remove it from both the desktop and the Start menu. Some users are accustomed to using the desktop to access resources such as My Documents, so avoid removing icons unnecessarily because it will confuse users.

Restricting Control Panel

Use the Control Panel Group Policy settings (available with User Configuration) to remove tools your users do not need. If users should not configure the Control Panel at all, enable the Prohibit Access To The Control Panel setting, which prevents the user from opening Control Panel using any mechanism—even running Control.exe from a command prompt. In addition, remove the Control Panel icon from the start menu.

Users might need access to some aspects of Control Panel, but not to others. In this circumstance, use the Hide Specified Control Panel Applets and Show Only Specified Control Panel Applets to restrict access to the unneeded components. In addition, you can configure which features users can access in Add Or Remove Programs, Display settings (as shown in Figure 8-10), Printer settings, and Regional And Language Options.

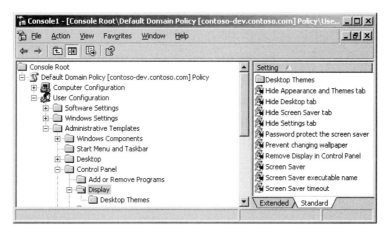

Figure 8-10 Use the Display Group Policy settings to grant control over some aspects of display settings, but not over others.

Restricting Shared Folders

The Shared Folders Group Policy node provides two self-explanatory settings: Allow DFS Roots To Be Published and Allow Shared Folders To Be Published. If you don't plan to use the peer-to-peer networking functions of your client computers running Windows, disable both of these settings to reduce the likelihood of users sharing confidential files with excessive permissions, which can lead to an attacker gaining access to the files.

Restricting the Network

The Network node in Administrative Templates in both Computer Configuration and User Configuration gives you control over several key aspects of client computers' network configurations. Most network settings apply to the entire computer and, as a result, exist within Computer Configuration. The only per-user settings in the User Configuration are related to offline files and network connections.

By default, the Network node in GPOs on a Windows Server 2003 domain contain the DNS Client, Offline Files, Network Connections, QoS Packet Scheduler, and Simple Network Management Protocol (SNMP) sub-nodes. Of these default policies, the following are the most interesting to security designers:

- **Offline Files: Encrypt The Offline Files Cache**   Encrypting offline files is critical. Without encryption, it is very easy for an attacker who steals a notebook computer to gain access to confidential files located in shared folders on your internal network because the notebook can contain unencrypted copies of those files.

- **SNMP: Communities, Traps For Public Community, and Permitted Managers**   If you use SNMP for monitoring client computers on your network and run the SNMP service, use the SNMP node to control community names, permitted managers, and the hosts to which to send SNMP traps. If you don't have the SNMP service running on your computers, use the System Services policy to ensure that the service is disabled. For more information about SNMP, refer to Chapter 4, "Designing a Management Infrastructure."

However, Microsoft added many additional policies when it released Service Pack 2 for Windows XP. In particular, the Network node now contains settings for Microsoft Peer-to-Peer Networking Services, Windows Firewall (within Network Connections), and the Background Intelligent Transfer Service (BITS). If you are not using Peer-to-Peer Networking Services, enable the Turn Off Microsoft Peer-To-Peer Networking Services setting.

If you use Automatic Updates and you are concerned downloading updates will affect your network usage, you can limit the per-client bandwidth used by BITS and restrict it to specific times of day by enabling and configuring the Maximum Network Bandwidth That BITS Uses setting, as shown in Figure 8-11. You probably don't need to adjust this, however, because BITS is designed not to affect the performance of most networks.

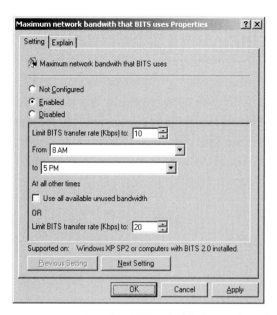

Figure 8-11   Restrict BITS only if clients downloading patches through Automatic Updates impacts critical network services.

The most important Windows XP Service Pack 2 security settings in the Network node are in the Network Connections\Windows Firewall node. As shown in Figure 8-12, you can create separate standard and domain profiles for Windows Firewall. Windows Firewall will apply the domain profile to network interfaces when the client computer is connected to a domain. It will apply the standard profile when the computer is not connected to a domain, such as when a user has connected to a home network or a wireless hotspot at an airport or café.

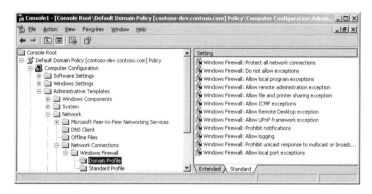

Figure 8-12   Create separate profiles for standard and domain network connections.

Take advantage of these multiple profiles to configure the standard profile as more restrictive than your domain profile. For example, if you use Internet Control Message Protocol (ICMP) to ping client computers on your domain, you must configure an exception in the domain profile for ICMP. However, you can use Windows Firewall to block ICMP traffic when the computer is not connected to the domain, greatly reducing the risk of an attacker outside your network exploiting an ICMP vulnerability. Figure 8-13 shows the Allow ICMP Exceptions setting being configured to enable pings when connected to a domain. To disable ping requests when away from the domain, you would disable this policy within the Standard Profile node.

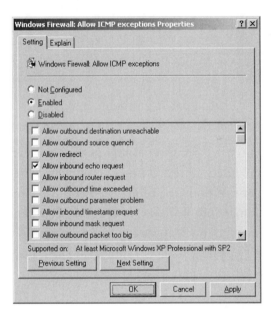

Figure 8-13   You can enable pings when connected to the domain, but block them when a client computer is away from your network.

Restricting System Settings

The System node contains many sub-nodes that enable you to configure user profiles, scripts, logon settings, disk quotas, net logon, Group Policy, Remote Assistance, System Restore, error reporting, Windows File Protection, RPCs, Distributed COM, Power Management, Internet communications, and the Windows Time Service.

In Computer Configuration, pay attention to the Scripts sub-node; if you use scripts for security-related tasks, consider enabling the Run Logon Scripts Synchronously policy. In the Remote Assistance sub-node, configure the policies to restrict Remote Assistance so that only authorized desktop support personnel can use it. Environments with very strict security requirements should configure the policies in the Error Reporting node to upload error reports to a server on your private network. This prevents error reporting from uploading potentially confidential information to the Microsoft error-reporting server.

Service Pack 2 for Windows XP added Internet Communication Management settings, which enable you to stop Windows XP clients from contacting computers on the Internet for tasks such as Windows Error Reporting, updating root certificates, and dynamic Help And Support Center content. If you are extremely concerned about your organization's privacy, disable these settings. However, the information sent over the Internet by these services contains little, if any, private information (although crash dumps sent to the error-reporting service have the potential to contain private information). In addition, there have been no known compromises stemming from information sent to Microsoft across the Internet.

In User Configuration, you can set the Ctrl+Alt+Del Options settings to define whether users can change their passwords, lock their computer, log off, or open Task Manager. These settings might be useful if you are configuring extremely restrictive desktop environments. Otherwise, power users will appreciate the ability to use Task Manager to change process priorities and kill processes that they can't stop by using normal methods. The sole Power Management setting enables you to require the user to enter a password when resuming a portable computer from standby or hibernation.

Restricting Printers

This node contains policies that control printers connected to your client computers. Your primary concern with printers is whether client computers should be allowed to share them on the network, and whether printers are published to Active Directory.

PROTECTING COMMON CLIENT ROLES

Different computer roles require different security considerations. The sections that follow discuss how to design security for desktop computers, laptops, and kiosks.

> **NOTE   What Is a Kiosk?**   A *kiosk* is a stand-alone computer that users can typically access unsupervised. They are often located in public places to enable people to access the Internet or limited intranet applications, such as an employee directory.

Security for Desktop Computers

When a computer manufacturer delivers a new computer, the operating system typically is configured to provide the greatest flexibility to the average user. Many organizations then install additional software such as Microsoft Office on top of the operating system. This provides power users with the tools they need to do their jobs.

However, many types of employees do not require much flexibility and will actually be more productive if the software on their computers is restricted. For example, a user in the accounts payable department might need access only to an e-mail client, accounting software, and a Web browser. For such users, restricting the applications they can run can make them more productive (for example, by removing Solitaire). In addition, it can reduce the risk of malicious software, such as viruses and Trojan horses, infecting the computer.

In a typical restricted desktop computer role, the desktop and Start menu are significantly simplified. Users cannot make extensive customizations other than a limited number of application-specific settings. Administrators typically allocate applications to users based on their job roles, and users cannot add or remove applications. This type of desktop configuration is appropriate in a marketing or finance department, for example. In these areas, users require only a specific and limited set (typically three to five) of productivity and in-house applications to do their jobs.

If your environment requires secure desktops, create a security template that contains the standard desktop security settings. Base this new security template on the Hisecws.inf predefined security template, which contains the majority of the settings you would need to specify. Besides the settings already defined in the Hisecws.inf template, consider enabling both the Accounts: Rename Administrator Account and Accounts: Rename Guest Account policies. Your organization's security policy might also require that you warn users as they log on by enabling the Interactive Logon: Message Text For Users Attempting To Log On and Inter-active Logon: Message Title For Users Attempting To Log On policies. Consult your legal department for the exact messages used to warn users. The message will vary depending on your local laws and whether your organization is private, military, or part of the government. For more information on security templates, refer to Chapter 7.

Security for Mobile Computers

Mobile computers require that you attend to several additional security consider-ations beyond those of desktop computers. Mobile users might use their comput-ers while traveling, which could require them to perform administrative tasks that a member of the IT group would normally perform. For example, a mobile user might need to print a document using a different printer than the one installed in the office and would need to install the correct printer driver. To allow this, disable the Devices: Prevent Users From Installing Printer Drivers security option. If you anticipate that users who work away from the office will need to install or reinstall applications while working remotely, you might want to enable the Always Install With Elevated Privileges setting in the Administrative Tem-plates\Windows Components\Windows Installer node.

Mobile users might connect to foreign networks, such as a wireless hotspot at a coffee shop. These foreign networks won't have the benefit of your organization's network security, so mobile users have an elevated risk of being attacked across the network. To mitigate this risk, enable Windows Firewall or another host-based firewall on all network interfaces for mobile computers.

It is more likely that a mobile computer will be stolen than will a desktop com-puter, which makes EFS extremely important on mobile computers. To reduce the likelihood that an act of theft will compromise your business's secrets, any confidential documents should be encrypted with EFS. Although EFS cannot be enabled for specific folders using security templates, you can create a logon script that enables EFS for folders that might contain confidential data. For more infor-mation about EFS, refer to Chapter 6, "Protecting Data."

Mobile users might require additional flexibility to configure their systems; for example, they might need to configure virtual private network (VPN) connec-tions. In such cases, modify the appropriate settings under the User Configura-tion\Administrative Templates\Network\Network Connections node of the applicable GPO.

Security for Kiosks

A kiosk is a public workstation that runs only one application, runs unattended, and uses a single user account that automatically logs on. A kiosk should be highly secure, should be simple to operate, and should not allow users to make changes to the default settings. The Start menu, and even the desktop, should be unavailable. Users should not be able to customize the computer, install applications, save any data, or access the file system directly.

> **NOTE   Hacking Kiosks**   Have you ever picked up the quarterly hacker's magazine *2600*? It's always an interesting read, and it can be educational for those of us working on the lawful side of the information-security industry. If you read a couple of issues of it, you are bound to find detailed descriptions of how to hack into some kind of kiosk computer. It seems as though there's always a way to make a kiosk computer do something it's not intended to do. One common trick is to press CTRL+C during startup when a script is running—this can interrupt the script and give the user a command prompt.

Kiosks usually run dedicated applications. The dedicated application could be a custom application, a Web application accessed by means of Internet Explorer, or another application, such as Microsoft PowerPoint. The default application should not be Windows Explorer or any other shell-like application because of the flexibility, and potential for misuse, that Windows Explorer provides. Be sure the command prompt is disabled and Windows Explorer is inaccessible. Applications used for kiosk scenarios must be carefully checked to ensure that they do not contain "backdoors" that allow users to circumvent system policies.

When creating a security template for a kiosk computer, start by creating a copy of the Hisecws.inf template. Assuming that you plan to make the primary kiosk user account a member of the local Users group on the computer, modify the security template so that the Users group is not granted the Shut Down The System user right, which might be granted by default.

Within the Audit Policy node of the template, enable restrictive password and account-lockout policy settings for the local accounts. If a user does manage to get to a logon prompt, the account-lockout settings will prevent the user from successfully guessing a password. Enable extensive security logging and system auditing. This can be useful for proving that a user did attempt to misuse the system, and for identifying how the attacker compromised the computer.

Within the Security Options node of the security template, enable both the Accounts: Rename Administrator Account and the Accounts: Rename Guest Account policies. Use file and folder permissions to prohibit changes to files or folders outside of the user's profile folder. In particular, apply more-restrictive access controls in the root directory. Restrict registry permissions to limit access to the computer registry hive, which prohibits the user from making changes.

After importing the kiosk security template into the kiosk GPO, specify several GPO settings that are not configurable by means of security templates. Specifically, expand User Configuration\Administrative Templates and examine each node contained within. Enable every setting, starting with Remove in the Start Menu And Taskbar node. Also, carefully review and configure the settings contained within the Desktop, Network, System, and Control Panel nodes of the GPO.

DESIGNING SECURITY FOR .NET FRAMEWORK APPLICATIONS

Everyone knows you should not log on to your computer as an Administrator. The reason isn't because you don't trust yourself not to delete your hard drive—it's because you don't trust the *applications* you run. When you run a standard Windows application, that application gets all the privileges your user account has. If you accidentally run a virus or a Trojan horse, the application can do anything your user account has permissions to do. So, you are forced to restrict application permissions by logging on with minimal privileges.

That doesn't make much sense, does it? You should be able to control the permissions that individual applications have. If a friend sends you a new text editor, you should be able to restrict it to opening a window and prompting you to open and save files—and nothing else. It shouldn't be able to send e-mails, upload files to a Web site, or create files without asking you.

Code access security (CAS) gives you the ability to restrict on a very granular level what .NET Framework applications can do. As illustrated by Figure 8-14, CAS can block applications from accessing resources to which the user running the application has access.

Figure 8-14   CAS restricts an application's access.

CAS is a relatively new concept to Windows desktop computers, and the vast majority of applications you will run on Windows client computers, such as Microsoft Office, do not use the .NET Framework and thus do not support CAS. More and more applications are built on the .NET Framework (such as Microsoft SharePoint Services), however, and all .NET Framework applications support CAS.

As a security designer, understand how you can use CAS to restrict the permissions granted to applications built on the .NET Framework. The sections that follow discuss the .NET Framework, CAS, and configuring them to improve the security of your client computers.

What Is the .NET Framework?

The *.NET Framework* is a relatively new set of tools and interfaces developers can use to create applications. Every version of Windows includes many such tools and interfaces; however, the .NET Framework provides new capabilities. In particular, the .NET Framework offers significantly improved security. The .NET Framework is so different from other Windows application interfaces that applications must be rewritten to use it.

The .NET Framework was first included with Windows Server 2003. You can download and install the .NET Framework on earlier versions of Windows, however. Versions of Windows that support the .NET Framework are the following:

■ Windows NT 4.0 with Service Pack 6a

■ Windows 98

■ Windows Me

■ Windows 2000

■ Windows XP

To download and install the .NET Framework on a computer, visit Windows Update, perform a custom install, and then click Select Optional Software Updates. If the computer does not already have the latest version of the .NET Framework installed, you have the option to install or update it.

What Is CAS?

Code access security (CAS) is a security system that allows administrators and developers to control application authorization similar to the way they have always been able to authorize users. With CAS, you can allow one application to read and write to the registry, while restricting access for a different application. You can control authorization for most of the same resources you've always been able to restrict using the operating system's **role-based security (RBS)**, including the following:

- The file system

- The registry

- Printers

- The event logs

You can also restrict resources that you can't control by using RBS. For example, you can control whether a particular application can send Web requests to the Internet, or whether an application can make DNS requests. These are the types of requests that malicious applications are likely to make to abuse a user's privacy, so it makes sense that CAS allows you to restrict those permissions.

Unfortunately, CAS can be applied only to **managed applications** that use the .NET Framework runtime. **Unmanaged applications** run without any CAS restrictions and are limited only by the operating system's RBS. If CAS is used to restrict the permissions of managed applications, the applications are considered **partially trusted applications**. Partially trusted applications must undergo CAS permission checks each time they access a protected resource. Some applications are exempt from CAS checks and are considered **fully trusted applications**. Fully trusted applications, like unmanaged applications, can access any system resource that the user has permissions to access.

> **NOTE** **The Performance Impact of the .NET Framework** Applications designed for the .NET Framework do suffer a slight performance penalty when compared with applications designed to run using native Windows application interfaces. The additional security checks imposed by CAS and the additional layer of isolation that the .NET Framework provides cause this performance penalty.

The Elements of Code Access Security

Every security system needs a way to identify users and determine what a user can and can't do, and CAS is no exception. However, because CAS identifies and assigns permissions to applications rather than to people, it can't use the user names, passwords, and access control lists (ACLs) that you're accustomed to.

Instead, CAS identifies applications using *evidence*. Each piece of evidence is a way an application can be identified, such as the location where the application is stored, a hash of the application's executable file, or the application's signature. An application's evidence determines to which code group it belongs. Code groups, in turn, grant an application a permission set. The sections that follow describe each of these components in more detail.

What Is Evidence?

Evidence is the information that the runtime gathers about an application to determine to which code groups the application belongs. Common forms of evidence include the folder or Web site the application is running from and digital signatures.

> **NOTE   Misnomer: Evidence**   The term "identification" would be more accurate than evidence. Evidence sounds like a set of clues you would use to track down someone who didn't want to be identified. CAS uses evidence just like a person's passport, password, and PIN—information that proves identity and describes an individual as deserving a certain level of trust.

Table 8-2 shows the common types of evidence that a host can present to the runtime.

Table 8-2   **Evidence Types**

Evidence	Description
Application directory	The directory in which the application resides. This type of evidence is similar to the path-rule software restriction.
Hash	The cryptographic hash of the application, which uniquely identifies a specific version of an application. Any modifications to the application's executable file will make the hash invalid. This type of evidence works exactly like a hash-rule software restriction.
Publisher	The application's publisher's digital signature, which uniquely identifies the software developer. This type of evidence works exactly like a certificate-rule software restriction.

Table 8-2 **Evidence Types**

Evidence	Description
Site	The site from which the application was downloaded, such as *http://www.microsoft.com*.
Strong name	The cryptographic strong name of the application, which uniquely identifies the application's namespace.
URL	The URL from which the application was downloaded, such as *http://www.microsoft.com/application.exe*.
Zone	The zone in which the application is running, such as the Internet Zone or the Local Intranet Zone. This type of evidence works exactly like an Internet zone–rule software restriction.

What Is a Permission?

A *permission* is a CAS **access control entry (ACE)**. For example, the File Dialog permission determines whether an application can prompt the user with the Open dialog box, the Save dialog box, both, or neither. Figure 8-15 shows the File Dialog permission being configured.

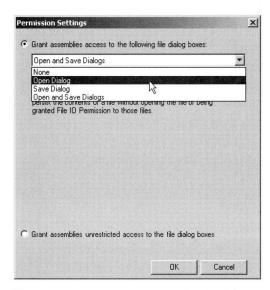

Figure 8-15 Permissions specify whether an application can or can't perform specific actions.

By default, 19 permissions are available for configuration in the .NET Framework Configuration tool. Table 8-3 describes each of these permissions.

Table 8-3 **Default Permissions**

Permission	Description
Directory Services	Grants an application access to Active Directory. You can specify paths, and whether Browse or Write access is available.
DNS	Enables or restricts an application's access to submit DNS requests.
Environment Variables	Grants applications access to environment variables such as *Path*, *Username*, and *Number_Of_Processors*. You can grant an application access to all environment variables, or specify those that the application should be able to access. To view all environment variables, open a command prompt and run the command Set.
Event Log	Provides an application access to event logs. You can grant unlimited access or you can limit access to browsing or auditing.
File Dialog	Controls whether an application can prompt the user with the Open dialog box, the Save dialog box, or both.
File IO	Restricts access to files and folders. You can grant an application unrestricted access, or you can specify a list of paths and whether each path should grant Read, Write, Append, or Path Discovery access.
Isolated Storage File	Grants applications access to isolated storage. You can configure the level of isolation and the size of the disk quota.
Message Queue	Allows an application to access message queues, which can be restricted by path and access type.
OLE DB	Lists the Object Linking and Embedding Database (OLE DB) provider that an application can access, and controls whether blank passwords are allowed.
Performance Counter	Controls whether an application can read or write performance counters.
Printing	Limits an application's ability to print.
Reflection	Controls whether an application can discover member and type information in other applications.
Registry	Restricts access to registry keys. You can grant an application unrestricted access, or you can specify a list of keys and whether each key should grant Read, Write, or Delete access.

Table 8-3 **Default Permissions**

Permission	Description
Security	Provides granular control over the application's access to various CAS features. All applications must at least have the Enable Application Execution setting to run. This permission also controls whether applications can call unmanaged code, assert permissions, and control threads, among other settings.
Service Controller	Specifies which services, if any, an application can browse or control.
Socket Access	Controls whether an application can initiate TCP/IP connections. You can control the destination, port number, and protocol.
SQL Client	Controls whether an application can access SQL Server computers and whether blank passwords are allowed.
User Interface	Determines whether an application can create new windows or access the clipboard.
Web Access	Determines whether the application can access Web sites, and which Web sites can be accessed.

What Is a Permission Set?

A *permission set* is a CAS ACL. For example, the Internet default permission set contains the following permissions:

- File Dialog
- Isolated Storage File
- Security
- User Interface
- Printing

The Local Intranet zone contains the following additional permissions based on the theory that code running on your local network deserves more trust than code running from the Internet:

- Environment Variables
- File Dialog
- Isolated Storage File

- Reflection

- Security

- User Interface

- DNS

- Printing

- Event Log

The .NET Framework includes seven default permission sets, as described in Table 8-4.

Table 8-4 **Default Permission Sets**

Permission Set	Description
Full Trust	Exempts an application from CAS permission checks.
Skip Verification	Enables an application to bypass permission checks, which can improve performance, but sacrifices security.
Execution	Enables an application to run and grants no other permissions.
Nothing	Grants no permissions to an application. The application will not even be allowed to run.
Local Intranet	Grants a generous set of permissions to applications, including the ability to print and access the event log. Notably, it does not allow the application to access the file system except through the Open and Save dialog boxes.
Internet	Grants a restricted set of permissions to an application. In general, you can run an application with this permission set with very little risk. Even malicious applications should not be able to cause any serious damage when run with this permission set.
Everything	Grants applications all permissions. This is different from FullTrust, which skips all CAS security checks. Applications with the Everything permission set will still be subject to CAS checks.

What Are Code Groups?

Code groups are authorization devices that associate applications with permission sets. Code groups provide a service to CAS similar to that provided by user security to RBS. For example, if you wanted to grant a set of users access to a folder, you would create a user group, add the users to the group, and then assign file permissions to the group. Code groups work similarly, except that you don't have to manually add individual applications to a group. Instead, group membership is determined by the evidence that you specify as the code group's membership condition.

For example, any code running from the Internet should be a member of the Internet_Zone code group. As you can see from Figure 8-16, the Internet_Zone code group's default membership condition is that the host presents Zone evidence, and that piece of Zone evidence identifies the application as being in the Internet zone.

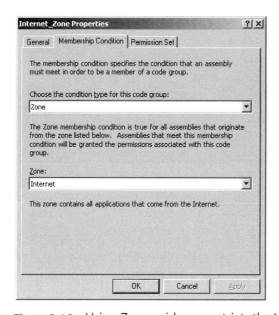

Figure 8-16 Using Zone evidence restricts the Internet_Zone code group membership.

Whereas user groups control authorization based on distributed ACLs associated with each resource, code groups use centralized permission sets. For example,

Figure 8-17 shows that the Internet_Zone code group assigns the Internet permission set. For convenience, the dialog box lists the permission set's individual permissions. However, you cannot specify individual permissions for a code group. A code group must be associated with a permission set.

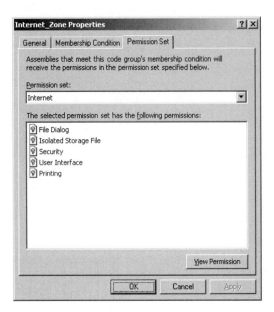

Figure 8-17   The Internet_Zone code group assigns the Internet permission set.

It might seem limiting that you can specify only a single type of evidence and a single permission set for a code group. However, just as a user account can be a member of multiple user groups, an application can be a member of multiple code groups. The application will receive all the permissions assigned to each of the code groups (known as the *union* of the permission sets). In addition, you can nest code groups within each other and assign permissions only if the application meets all the evidence requirements of both the parent and child code groups. Nesting code groups allows you to assign permissions based on an application having more than one type of evidence. Figure 8-18 shows the Microsoft_Strong_Name code group nested within the My_Computer_Zone code group, which in turn is nested within the All_Code group.

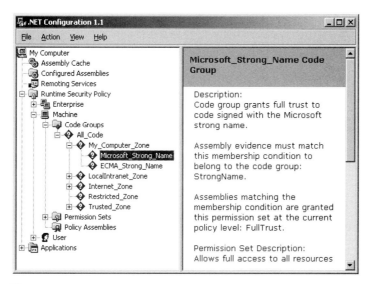

Figure 8-18 You can nest code groups to require multiple types of evidence.

What Is Security Policy?

A *security policy* is a logical grouping of code groups and permission sets. In addition, a security policy can contain custom applications that define other types of policies. Security policies provide you with the flexibility to configure CAS settings at multiple levels. By default, there are three configurable policy levels: Enterprise, Machine, and User.

> **NOTE** **The Fourth Policy Level** There's actually a fourth policy level: the Application Domain. Only developers need to worry about application domains, though.

The Enterprise level is the highest security policy level, describing security policy for an entire enterprise. Use Active Directory to configure Enterprise security policy. Machine policy, the second security policy level, applies to all code run on a particular computer. User policy is the third level, and it defines permissions on a per-user basis. The runtime evaluates the Enterprise, Machine, and User levels separately, and it grants an application the minimum set of permissions granted by any of the levels (known as the *intersection* of the permission sets). By default, the Enterprise and User security policies grant all code full trust, which causes the Machine security policy to restrict CAS permissions alone.

How CAS Works with Operating System Security

CAS is completely independent of operating system security. In fact, you must use entirely different tools to administer CAS. Although you can control a user's or a group's file permissions using Microsoft Windows Explorer, you have to use the .NET Framework Configuration tool to grant or restrict an application's file permissions.

CAS works on top of existing operating system security. When determining whether an application can take a particular action, both CAS and the operating system security are evaluated. The most restrictive set of permissions is applied. For example, if CAS grants an application access to write to the C:\Windows\ folder, but the user running the application does not have that permission, the application will not be able to write to the folder. Figure 8-19 shows how CAS relates to operating system security.

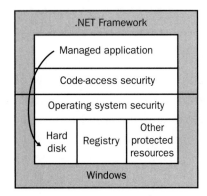

Figure 8-19   CAS complements, but does not replace, role-based security.

NOTE   RBS Limits CAS   No application can have more permissions than the user running the application, regardless of how the application uses CAS.

Figure 8-20 shows the decision-making process used to determine whether an application can access a file.

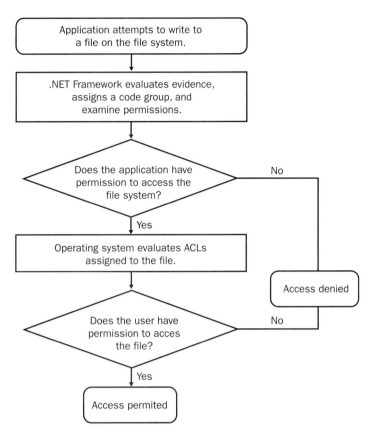

Figure 8-20 Before an application can access a file, both the runtime and the operating system must approve the request.

Guidelines for Configuring CAS

Using managed applications has the potential to reduce the risk of security vulnerabilities greatly. When designing CAS for your client computers, keep the following guidelines in mind.

- Use the principle of least privilege to configure CAS. In other words, grant applications only the minimum privileges they require to do the tasks you expect them to do.

- Test every function of a managed application with your CAS settings to verify that the rights are not too restrictive.

■ Encourage your internal development groups to switch to creating managed applications by using the .NET Framework. In addition, encourage them to migrate unmanaged applications to the .NET Framework so that you can use CAS to improve the security of your client computers. If they need justification, explain that CAS reduces the likelihood of a security vulnerability in their code from being exploited—potentially saving them from making a very costly security mistake.

■ Encourage your external software vendors to migrate their applications to the .NET Framework.

■ When evaluating new software for client computers, ask vendors whether their applications use the .NET Framework and how they support CAS.

SUMMARY

- Microsoft has added security features to each new version of Windows. You might be able to add some security features to previous versions of Windows with free downloads available from Microsoft. Adding other security features, such as a host-based firewall, requires the use of non-Microsoft software.

- Use security templates and GPOs to implement client security configurations. In addition, you need non-Microsoft software to perform network backups, check for viruses, and add host-based firewall features to versions of Windows released prior to Windows XP. Use software-restriction policies to prevent users from running unapproved software and restrict the desktop environment to prevent them from using aspects of Windows.

- Desktop computers, laptop computers, and kiosks each have different security design considerations. Desktop computers are the simplest to secure because they remain connected to your internal network. Laptops are more complex because they will connect to both your internal network and other untrusted networks. Kiosks must have an extremely restricted desktop environment to reduce the risk of an attacker abusing the computer.

- CAS can control .NET Framework applications. CAS enables you to restrict a specific application's access to computer and network resources, which is extremely effective for reducing the risk of a developer adding malicious code to an application. In addition, CAS reduces the risk of a threat agent exploiting a vulnerability in a .NET Framework application.

REVIEW QUESTIONS

1. You create a default software restriction to block all executable files. Which type of rule would you create to allow internal applications developed by your IT department to run?

   a. Hash rules

   b. Certificate rules

   c. Path rules

   d. Internet zone rules

2. You thoroughly test for security vulnerabilities all applications that users run. You're wary of vulnerabilities that might be introduced to an application during an update, so you don't want users to be able to run

an application if the file has been modified or updated. Which type of rule should you create to allow a specific testing application to run?

   a. Hash rules

   b. Certificate rules

   c. Path rules

   d. Internet zone rules

3. During the Security Risk Management Process, you determine that the risk of users running malicious e-mail attachments is unacceptable. You would like to use software restrictions as a countermeasure. Which type of rule should you create to block e-mail attachments from being run?

   a. Hash rules

   b. Certificate rules

   c. Path rules

   d. Internet zone rules

4. Which of the following rules would you *not* enforce on a computer that will be used as a kiosk?

   a. Remove the Run menu item from the Start menu.

   b. Deny the Everyone group the right to log on locally.

   c. Require a user to log on automatically.

   d. Deny the interactive user the right to change his or her own password.

5. Your network has several different Windows client operating systems. Which versions require a host-based firewall from a non-Microsoft software developer? (Choose all that apply.)

   a. Windows NT 4.0 with Service Pack 4

   b. Windows Me

   c. Windows 2000 Professional with Service Pack 4

   d. Windows XP Professional with Service Pack 1

   e. Windows XP Professional with Service Pack 2

6. What type of evidence would you use to apply a permission to assemblies created by your internal development group?

   a. Hash

   b. Publisher

     c. Strong name

     d. URL

7. Your internal development group asks you to attend a meeting during which the group will plan a new application that will grant users access to a confidential database. What guidance can you provide to improve the security of the finished application?

8. What are some of the risks facing mobile computers that don't affect desktop computers? What can you do to mitigate these risks?

CASE SCENARIOS

Case Scenario 8-1: Designing Enterprise Client Computer Security

You are a security designer at Woodgrove Bank, a national bank with about 250 branches. Woodgrove Bank has a significant history that includes many different types of computers. As a result, there are many different operating systems in use at Woodgrove Bank, including Windows NT 4.0 Workstation, Windows 2000 Professional, and Windows XP Professional. The staff uses most of the computers, but many branches have a computer configured as a kiosk to allow customers to access *http://www.woodgrovebank.com/* to check their account balances. Your patch-management process is working well, so all client computers are up to date on patches.

At a high level, you can divide the staff at Woodgrove Bank into three categories:

- **Customer support**   Employees who deal directly with customers to perform tasks such as making withdrawals, deposits, and opening new accounts. These employees need access to only a handful of internal applications. Because their client computers are used to access account information, the risk of them using a Web browser or reading e-mail is too great to be acceptable.

- **Management**   Employees who manage customer support personnel. They must communicate with management in other branches, which requires them to use an e-mail client to access Woodgrove Bank's e-mail system. In addition, they need access to the Web for research. Management has both desktop and laptop computers.

- **Internal support**   This category includes you and the rest of the IT team. You don't need any access to customer information. However, you do need to access e-mail, the Internet, and other internal resources. Internal support uses both desktop and laptop computers.

Based on this information, answer the questions that follow:

1. How will you design your client computer OUs? Create a diagram.

2. For which groups do you recommend creating a restrictive desktop environment? (Choose all that apply.)

    a. Kiosks

    b. Customer support

    c. Management

    d. Internal support

3. What non-Microsoft software do you need to set aside part of your budget for?

Case Scenario 8-2: Evaluating the Security Benefits of the .NET Framework

You are a security designer at Blue Yonder Airlines. The CEO of your company read an article that quoted a security analyst who stated that the .NET Framework can prevent viruses from spreading. You run into the CEO in the hallway and he says, "Hey, I just read this article in the paper. What's this about the .NET Framework? It's got some kind of new security that can stop programs from doing bad things, eh? Maybe you can install it on my computer so that I don't have to worry about viruses spreading, or about other dangerous software sending my private files off to the Internet somewhere." He then asks you a series of questions.

1. Can .NET Framework CAS prevent viruses from spreading? Why or why not?

2. Will installing the .NET Framework on my computer improve the security? If not, what will it accomplish?

3. Could a .NET Framework–based virus running in the Internet zone, with the default CAS permissions, effectively replicate itself across our network? Why or why not?

4. Could a malicious .NET Framework–based application running in the Intranet zone, with the default CAS permissions, delete files on your hard drive? Why or why not?

CHAPTER 9
DESIGNING A PUBLIC KEY INFRASTRUCTURE

Upon completion of this chapter, you will be able to:

- Compare private and public key cryptography, and describe the components of a Public Key Infrastructure (PKI).

- Evaluate your organization's need for a PKI and determine your certificate requirements.

- Choose the type of certification authority (CA) that best meets your needs, and harden it to protect it from attacks.

- Scale your PKI by designing a CA hierarchy and trust model.

- Define procedures for issuing, renewing, revoking, and archiving certificates.

Public key cryptography is a tremendously powerful security tool, providing authentication and high levels of privacy and data integrity that would otherwise be impractical or impossible. Public key cryptography is the basis for the most useful types of encryption, digital signatures, and authentication technologies. For public key cryptography to be useful in an enterprise, deploy a **public key infrastructure (PKI)**. Microsoft Windows Server 2003 and Windows 2000 Server implement PKI functionality in Certificate Services. As a security designer, you need to be able to design and deploy a PKI infrastructure to suit the needs of organizations ranging from small businesses to enterprises.

Deploying the infrastructure is only the beginning, however. You also need to make the enrollment and distribution of certificates to end users a straightforward task while meeting your organization's security requirements. Depending on your needs, you can require users to show identification physically to receive a **certificate**, or you can deploy certificates automatically with no user interaction whatsoever. After deploying your PKI, threats to your certificate servers will present a significant risk. To mitigate this risk, you must be able to design security to protect the Certificate Services servers themselves.

This chapter starts with an overview of PKI fundamentals to refresh your memory and then walks you through the four steps of designing a PKI:

1. Planning a PKI deployment

2. Designing certification authorities (CAs)

3. Creating trust models

4. Defining procedures for issuing, renewing, revoking, and archiving certificates

UNDERSTANDING PUBLIC KEY INFRASTRUCTURE

A PKI is a set of policies, standards, and software for managing certificates and public key pairs. A PKI consists of a set of digital certificates, CAs, and tools used to authenticate users and computers and to verify transactions. To place the PKI implementation provided by Windows Server 2003 in the proper context, this section provides a general overview of public key cryptography and encryption, and then describes the components that make up a PKI: certificates and certification authorities.

> **MORE INFO** PKI Standards   The data formats and network communications used by a PKI are (mostly) standardized. For detailed information about PKI standards, refer to RFC 2459 at http://www.faqs.org/rfcs/rfc2459.html.

Fundamentals of Cryptography and Encryption

Cryptography is essential for protecting information sent across shared networks such as intranets, extranets, and the Internet. From a technical point of view, cryptography is the science of protecting data by mathematically transforming it into an unreadable format, otherwise known as *encryption*. To a business, cryptography is a means to reduce the likelihood of a costly security compromise by providing authentication, confidentiality, and data integrity.

Network encryption comes in two main varieties: **private key encryption** and **public key encryption**. The sections that follow describe each of these types of encryption.

What Is Private Key Encryption?

Private key encryption, also known as **symmetric key encryption** or shared key encryption, requires both the sender and the recipient of an encrypted message to have a **shared secret**. A shared secret is, fundamentally, a password used to encrypt and decrypt the message. Figure 9-1 shows symmetric key encryption and decryption.

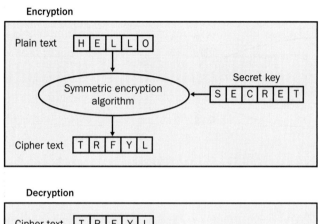

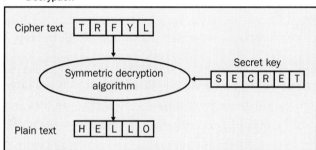

Figure 9-1   Symmetric encryption uses the same key for encryption and decryption.

For example, if Sam wants to send an encrypted electronic message to Toby, Sam first walks over to Toby and whispers a password in his ear. Then, when Toby receives the electronic message, Toby decrypts it with the password. So long as nobody else knows the password, Sam can be reasonably sure that the contents of the message are private, even if a threat sees the message while it's being transferred. The challenge here is that Sam and Toby have to exchange a password and keep it secret—and if this were easy to do, they would not be worried about encryption in the first place.

Private key encryption is easy to understand, but it is difficult to implement on a large scale. After all, to allow encrypted communication between 1,000 employees at a company would require the exchange of about 1 million passwords because any two users who wanted to communicate would need to exchange a unique password.

Figure 9-2 shows how users must transfer both the encrypted message and the key by using different communication mechanisms to prevent an attacker—who can capture communications across one of the two networks—from decrypting the message. Users often transfer keys by physically carrying them to the recipient, by voice across the phone network, or by sending them through the mail system. After establishing the shared secret, the two peers can use it to encrypt and decrypt any number of messages.

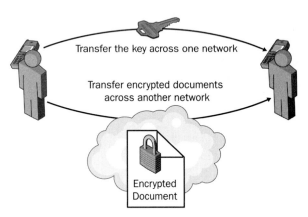

Figure 9-2   Symmetric key encryption requires separately exchanging both the key and the encrypted document.

Symmetric algorithms are extremely fast and are well suited for encrypting large quantities of data. Even though symmetric encryption is very secure, an attacker can identify the plaintext given the **cipher text** and enough time. To identify the plaintext, the attacker needs to use only a brute-force attack to generate symmetric keys sequentially until the attacker has tried every single possibility. The time required to try all keys is typically hundreds of years, if not longer, because the attacker would need to try at least 2^{56} key possibilities to crack a 56-bit symmetric encryption algorithm. More secure symmetric algorithms use longer keys that would take exponentially longer to crack.

What Is Public Key Encryption?

The need to establish a shared secret key rules out private key encryption for encrypting spontaneous network communications. For example, private key encryption is not used initially between a Web client and Web server because users on the Internet typically are not willing to wait several days while the Web site physically mails them a secret key. Instead, Web sessions are established initially by using public key encryption, also known as **asymmetric key encryption**.

Public key encryption uses one key to encrypt a message and a second, related, key to decrypt the message. These two keys form a key pair. One of these keys is kept private, and the other key can be shared publicly (hence the name "public key encryption"). Figure 9-3 shows a simple public key encryption arrangement in which only one side of the communications provides a public key.

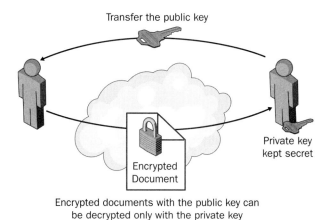

Transfer the public key

Private key
kept secret

Encrypted
Document

Encrypted documents with the public key can
be decrypted only with the private key

Figure 9-3   Public key cryptography uses separate keys for encryption and decryption.

For example, if Sam wants to send an encrypted message to Toby, Toby must generate a public key pair. Then, Toby sends his public key to Sam. Sam then uses Toby's *public* key to encrypt the message. When Toby receives the message, Toby uses his *private* key to decrypt it. Only Toby's private key can decrypt a message encrypted with his public key, so Sam can be sure that nobody else was able to view the contents of the message.

Public key encryption algorithms are not as fast as private key algorithms, but are much more difficult to break. Public key algorithms are not well suited to encrypting large amounts of data because of the performance overhead. One common use of public key algorithms is to encrypt and transfer a symmetric key and initialization vector (a random value used to improve security). The private key encryption algorithm is then used for all messages being sent back and forth. This is the technique used by Hypertext Transfer Protocol Secure (HTTPS) and Secure Sockets Layer (SSL) to encrypt Web communications—public key encryption is used only during session establishment. Figure 9-4 shows this common combination of public and private key encryption.

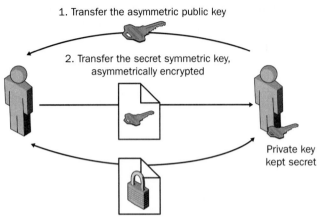

1. Transfer the asymmetric public key

2. Transfer the secret symmetric key, asymmetrically encrypted

Private key kept secret

3. Communicate using symmetric encryption

Figure 9-4   Combine public and private key algorithms to optimize security and performance.

There is another interesting way to use public key encryption: digital signatures. If Sam wants to prove to Toby that Sam, and not somebody else, sent the message, Sam can use his own private key to encrypt the message. After Toby receives it, Toby needs to use Sam's public key to decrypt the message. If it decrypts properly, Toby can be certain that Sam's private key was used to encrypt it and that the message had not changed since Sam sent it. This provides **non-repudiation**. Non-repudiation is a security concept that ensures that a specific user (and not an imposter) actually performed an action, such as sending an e-mail.

Of course, public key encryption takes a great deal of processing power, so Sam would probably choose to encrypt a short hash of the message instead of the entire message, and append the hash onto the end of the message. That would be sufficient to prove that Sam sent the message and that it was not modified in transit.

> **NOTE   The Point of PKI**   *Public key encryption would not be much easier than private key encryption if everyone had to manually exchange public keys. That's why we use a PKI—to make the process of managing and exchanging public keys simpler.*

What Is a Certificate?

A **public key certificate**, referred to in this chapter as simply a certificate, is a tool for using public key encryption for authentication and encryption. Certificates are issued and signed by a **certification authority (CA)**, and any user or application that examines the certificate can safely assume that the CA did indeed issue the certificate. If you trust the CA to do a good job of authenticating users before handing out certificates, and you believe that the CA protects the privacy of its certificates and keys, you can trust that a certificate holder is who he or she claims to be.

Certificates can be issued for a variety of functions, including Web user authentication, Web server authentication, secure e-mail, encryption of network communications, and code signing. CAs even use certificates to identify themselves, create other certificates, and establish a certification hierarchy between themselves and other CAs. If an organization uses the Windows Server 2003 enterprise CA, clients can use certificates to log on to the domain.

Certificates contain some or all of the following information, depending on the purpose of the certificate:

- The user's principal name.

- The user's e-mail address.

- The computer's host name.

- The dates between which the certificate is valid.

- The certificate's serial number, which is guaranteed by the CA to be unique.

- The name of the CA that issued the certificate and the key used to sign the certificate.

- A description of the policy that the CA followed to authenticate the subject originally.

- A list of ways the certificate can be used.

- The location of the **certificate revocation list (CRL)**, a document maintained and published by a CA that lists revoked certificates. A CRL is signed with the private key of the CA to ensure its integrity.

> **NOTE   Reminder: CRLs and Delta CRLs**   *CRLs contain every certificate that has ever been revoked. As a result, they can grow very large in enterprise environments. To reduce the bandwidth consumed by clients regularly retrieving new versions of the CRL, CAs publish delta CRLs. Delta CRLs contain only newly revoked certificates and, as a result, are much smaller than the full CRL.*

Figure 9-5 shows how Microsoft Internet Explorer represents an SSL certificate.

Figure 9-5   Certificates store many different pieces of information about the recipient.

What Is a Certification Authority?

A CA is a server trusted to issue certificates to an individual, a computer, or a service. A CA accepts a certificate request, verifies the requester's information according to the policies of the CA and the type of certificate being requested, generates a certificate, and then uses its private key to digitally sign the certificate. A CA can be a public third party, such as VeriSign, or it can be internal to an organization. For example, you might choose to use Windows Server 2003 Certificate Services to generate certificates for users and computers in your Active Directory directory service domain. Each CA can have distinct proof-of-identity requirements for certificate requesters, such as a domain account, an employee badge, a driver's license, a notarized request, or a physical address.

Registration is the process by which subjects make themselves known to a CA. Registration can be accomplished automatically during the certificate enrollment process, or it can be accomplished by a trusted entity such as a smart-card enrollment station. *Certificate enrollment* is the procedure that a user follows to request a certificate from a CA. The certificate request provides identity information to the CA, and the information the user provides becomes part of the issued certificate.

What Are Certificate Templates?

Certificate templates are the sets of rules and settings that define the format and content of a certificate based on the certificate's intended use. Certificate templates also provide the client with instructions on how to create and submit a valid certificate request. In addition, certificate templates define which security principals are allowed to read, enroll, or autoenroll for certificates based on that template. Certificate templates are configured on a CA and are applied against the incoming certificate requests.

Windows Server 2003 supports two types of certificate templates: version 1 and version 2. Version 1 templates provide backward compatibility for servers running Microsoft Windows 2000–family operating systems. Version 1 templates have a major limitation, however: the information they contain is hard-coded in the certificate. You cannot modify certificate template properties such as certificate lifetime and key size. Version 2 certificate templates address some of these limitations.

When the first enterprise CA is installed in a forest, version 1 templates are created by default. Unlike version 2 templates, these cannot be modified or removed, but they can be duplicated. When you duplicate a version 1 template, you create a version 2 template. Version 1 templates provide a certificate solution as soon as the CA is installed because they support many general needs for subject certification. For example, there are certificates that allow EFS encryption recovery, client authentication, smart-card logon, and server authentication.

PLANNING A PKI DEPLOYMENT

Before you configure your first CA, identify the need for the PKI and determine how certificates issued by the PKI will be used. The sections that follow discuss these concepts.

Identify the Need for a PKI

Before you deploy a PKI, you must use the Security Risk Management Process to determine that your organization can benefit from it. The benefit needs to be significant because deploying and maintaining a PKI is a costly endeavor. Although you don't necessarily need to purchase any software if you have any existing Windows network, planning, distributing, managing, and revoking certificates requires significant administration time for the lifetime of the PKI. In fact, many organizations will not be able to justify the cost of a PKI.

Organizations typically use PKIs to support the following security applications.

- **Digital signatures** Much as a person's signature on a document can be used as proof that the person reviewed the document, you can use digital signatures to verify that an individual created or reviewed an electronic document. Digital signatures work by creating a hash of a file and then encrypting that hash with the user's private key. Anyone with access to the user's public key can generate a new hash of the file, unencrypt the hash included with the digital signature, and then verify that the hashes match. Decrypting by using the user's public key verifies that only the user's private key could have been used to encrypt the hash. Assuming the user has kept his or her private key secure, you can be very sure that nobody else generated the digital signature.

- **Encrypted and signed e-mail**   Most Internet e-mail completely lacks security. If your organization does not use certificates to protect e-mail, you could send a message to your boss to quit your job—but spoof a coworker's e-mail address. This does not require the skills of a sophisticated attacker; just change the e-mail address in your e-mail client software. A PKI can make spoofing e-mails dramatically more challenging by issuing certificates to users to automatically sign messages digitally. Although you could still spoof your coworker's e-mail address, without his private key you couldn't create his digital signature. In addition, you can use certificates to protect the privacy of e-mail by encrypting each message with a user's public key before sending it. This would prevent e-mail server administrators from reading your messages.

- **Software code signing**   Trojan horses and viruses often modify or replace applications that users need to do their jobs. Unfortunately, there is no way to detect this with most applications. However, you can use software code signing and a PKI to enable your internal developers to sign their applications. You can even implement software code signing with delayed signing to reduce the risk of your internal developers inserting malicious code into your applications. For more information on delayed signing, refer to Chapter 8, "Hardening Client Computers."

- **Web authentication**   You can use a PKI to issue certificates to both clients and servers for the purpose of authentication. Server certificates, known as SSL certificates, enable the session to be encrypted and, by adding server authentication, greatly reduce the risk of an attacker impersonating the Web server. If you issue certificates to users, they can use the certificate to authenticate rather than using a traditional username and password.

- **IPSec**   A PKI is not *technically* a requirement for IPSec, but in practice, you need a PKI to deploy IPSec in an enterprise. IPSec provides client and server authentication and communications encryption, regardless of the application or communication protocol. For more information about IPSec, refer to Chapter 10, "Protecting Intranet Communications."

■ **Smart-card logon**   Most organizations use traditional usernames and passwords for authentication. As you know, passwords can be stolen, lost, or cracked. Smart cards enhance the security of your organization by allowing you to store extremely strong credentials in an easy-to-use form. Smart cards store a certificate issued by a PKI and use the private key to authenticate the user. Requiring a physical smart card for authentication virtually eliminates the potential for spoofing the identities of your users across a network. In addition, you can also use smart-card applications in conjunction with virtual private networks (VPNs) and certificate mapping. For many organizations, the potential to use smart cards for logon is one of the most compelling reasons for implementing a public key infrastructure.

> **NOTE**   **Reminder: Certificate Mapping**   Certificate mapping associates user certificates with Active Directory users. With certificate mapping, a user who is authenticated by using a user certificate can access resources based on permissions granted to their Active Directory user account.

■ **Encrypting File System (EFS) user and recovery certificates**   EFS doesn't require a PKI because it generates its own key pairs by default. However, this strategy has a significant weakness: if the user loses his or her private key, he or she can't access encrypted files. If you issue EFS keys using a PKI, you can archive a copy of the private key on your server. The key recovery agent (KRA) can then use this copy of the private key to restore access to the user's files if the user loses his or her copy of the private key.

■ **802.1x authentication**   Wireless network authentication is very challenging in an enterprise. Although you can encrypt wireless network communications without a PKI, you have to distribute keys to users manually. If you use a PKI with 802.1x authentication, you can distribute certificates to users and they can use the certificate to authenticate to your wireless access point. Then, if you need to remove a specific user's access to the wireless network, you just revoke a specific key. Without a PKI, you would need to change your encryption key, which would require changing the wireless configuration of every computer on your network.

Determining Certificate Requirements

After you have identified the need for a PKI, identify the users, computers, and services that will use certificates. For example, you may decide that only members of your information technology (IT) organization need to use the PKI to fulfill your organization's requirement that users with administrative rights authenticate by using a smart card and multifactor authentication.

> **NOTE For Simplicity's Sake** You can issue certificates to users, computers, and services. For simplicity, this chapter will simply refer to all three types of recipients as users.

For each of the groups that you have identified, determine:

- **The types of certificates to be issued** This is based on the security application requirements of your organization because different types of certificates are issued for signing e-mail, authenticating to Web servers, and connecting with IPSec.

- **The number of users that need certificates** This number can include as few as one or as many users, computers, or applications as are in an entire organization.

- **The number of certificates required for each user** In some cases, you can issue one certificate to each user and meet all your requirements. At other times, you might need to issue separate certificates for each application a user requires.

- **The physical location of the users** You might need to adjust your PKI design or your certificate procedures to accommodate remote offices or users who travel frequently. Requirements can differ based on local laws also. For example, some countries consider specific types of encryption illegal. You would need to adjust your PKI design to accommodate offices in such countries to ensure that you complied with local laws.

DESIGNING CERTIFICATE AUTHORITIES

Once you determine that you need a PKI and how you're going to use it, you have to decide how it should be designed. You have several key decisions to make:

- Should you build a PKI internally or use an external service provider?

- If you build your PKI internally, can you use an Active Directory–integrated enterprise CA, or do you need to deploy stand-alone CAs? Do you need both?

- How many CAs do you need to meet your capacity and performance requirements?

- How will you protect your CAs?

The sections that follow give you the information you need to answer each of these questions.

Choosing an Internal or External CA

Depending on the functionality you require, the capabilities of your IT infrastructure and IT administrators, and the costs your organization can support, you might choose to base your certification authority infrastructure on internal CAs, third-party CAs, or a combination of internal and third-party CAs. The sections that follow describe the advantages and disadvantages of each.

Internal CAs

If your organization conducts most of its business with partner organizations and wants to maintain control of how certificates are issued, internal CAs are the best choice. Internal CAs do the following:

- Allow an organization to maintain direct control over its security policies

- Allow an organization to align its **certificate policy** with its overall security policy

- Can be integrated with the Active Directory infrastructure of the organization

- Can be expanded to include additional functionality and users at relatively little extra cost

The disadvantages associated with using internal CAs include the following:

- The organization must manage its own certificates, which requires training of administration staff and ongoing administration time.

- The deployment schedule for internal CAs might be longer than that for CAs available from third-party service providers.

- The organization must accept liability for problems with the PKI.

> **NOTE**   **Specifying the Common Name for the CA**   If you choose to deploy internal CAs, do not use the fully qualified domain name (FQDN) for the common name of the CA. The CA's common name is part of every certificate it issues. If you don't use an FQDN, it's more difficult for an attacker who obtains a copy of a certificate (for example, by stealing a laptop computer) to identify the organization and abuse any rights granted to the holder of the certificate.

External CAs

If your organization conducts most of its business with external customers and clients, and wants to outsource certificate issuing and management processes, you might choose to use external CAs.

External CAs do the following:

- Provide certificates that give customers and partners outside confirmation of your identity as a certificate holder

- Have more technical expertise managing a PKI than you can easily develop because their full-time focus is managing the PKI

- Have greater knowledge of the legal and business issues associated with certificate use

- Enable you to use certificates immediately while you take your time to develop an internal PKI

The disadvantages associated with use of external CAs include the following:

- A potentially higher per-certificate cost. Costs vary, however, and some external CAs can be less costly than managing an internal CA.

- Less flexibility in configuring and managing certificates.

- Lack of Active Directory integration features such as autoenrollment.

- Limited integration with the internal directories, applications, and infrastructure of the organization.

Whereas clients will automatically trust internal enterprise CAs, you might need to configure clients to trust external CAs if they are not one of the CAs automatically trusted by Windows clients. You can add certificates for external CAs that you trust to issue certificates to your organization to the Computer Configuration\Windows Settings\Security Settings\Public Key Policies\Trusted Root Certification Authorities Group Policy node, as shown in Figure 9-6. These root CAs then become trusted root CAs for the computers within the scope of the Group Policy. For example, if you want to use a third-party CA as a root CA in a certification hierarchy, you must add the certificate for the third-party CA to the Trusted Root Certification Authorities Group Policy.

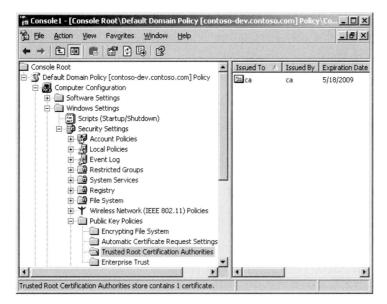

Figure 9-6   Add external CA certificates to Group Policy to make them a trusted root CA.

Enterprise and Stand-Alone Root CAs

If you decide to deploy an internal CA, you can create two types of root CAs: enterprise and stand-alone. The most significant difference is that enterprise CAs use and require Active Directory while stand-alone CAs do not. In addition, enterprise CAs are capable only of issuing certificates to computers and users in the Active Directory forest.

> **NOTE**   **Reminder: Root and Subordinate CAs**   Root CAs are self-signed CAs, meaning they issue their own certificate, and then use that certificate to sign client certificates. Clients must trust the CA in order to trust the certificates issued by the CA. Root CAs issue certificates to subordinate CAs, which can then issue other certificates to clients. Subordinate CAs can then issue certificates to other subordinate CAs. In this way, root and subordinate CAs form a hierarchy very similar to domains in an Active Directory forest.

Although you have to have an Active Directory environment, enterprise CAs offer some important advantages. Most important, you can use autoenrollment and certificate templates with an enterprise CA to reduce the labor associated with managing certificates dramatically. Users performing certificate enrollment with a stand-alone CA must use Web enrollment.

Stand-alone CAs can be used in an Active Directory environment, but they do not require Active Directory. If you use stand-alone CAs, all information about the requested certificate type must be included in the certificate request. By default, all certificate requests submitted to stand-alone CAs are held in a pending queue until a CA administrator approves them. You can configure stand-alone CAs to issue certificates automatically upon request, but this is less secure and usually is not recommended because the requests are not authenticated.

However, unless you are using auto-issuance, using stand-alone CAs to issue large volumes of certificates usually comes at a high administrative cost because an administrator must manually review and then approve or deny each certificate request. For this reason, stand-alone CAs are best used with public key security applications on extranets and the Internet, when users do not have Windows 2000 or Windows Server 2003 accounts, and when the volume of certificates to be issued and managed is relatively low. You must use stand-alone CAs to issue certificates when you are using a third-party directory service or when Active Directory is not available.

Table 9-1 summarizes the criteria used to determine if a CA should be a stand-alone or enterprise CA.

Table 9-1 **Stand-Alone and Enterprise CA Criteria**

Stand-Alone CA Criteria	Enterprise CA Criteria
■ It is an offline root or offline intermediate CA (discussed later in this chapter).	■ A large number of certificates must be enrolled and approved automatically.
■ Support of templates that you can customize is not required.	■ Availability and redundancy is mandatory.
■ A strong security and approval model is required.	■ Clients need the benefits of Active Directory integration.
■ Fewer certificates are enrolled and the manual work that you must do to issue certificates is acceptable.	■ Features such as autoenrollment or modifiable V2 templates are required.
■ Clients are heterogeneous and cannot benefit from Active Directory.	■ Key archival and recovery is required to store backups of encryption keys.
■ It is combined with a third-party Registration Authority solution in a multi-forest or heterogeneous environment.	
■ It issues certificates to routers.	

Table 9-2 compares the features of stand-alone and enterprise CAs based on Windows Server 2003.

Table 9-2 **Stand-Alone and Enterprise CAs Compared**

Stand-Alone CA Features	Enterprise CA Features
CA configuration can be published into Active Directory.	CA configuration is always published into Active Directory.
CRL and CA certificates must be manually published into Active Directory.	CRL, Delta CRL, CA certificate, and cross certificates are automatically published to the forest where the CA configuration was registered. Certificates are automatically published into a directory service if this is specified on a per-template level. Certificate publishing may be defined as an attribute on the template in Active Directory.
By default, certificate enrollment is available only by using Web enrollment support.	By default, certificate enrollment is possible by using Web enrollment or the Certificates Microsoft Management Console (MMC).
Hypertext Transfer Protocol (HTTP) or HTTPS facilitates certificate request processing.	Remote Procedure Call (RPC)/Distributed Component Object Model (DCOM) or HTTP and HTTPS protocols facilitate certificate request processing.
The certificate is based on V1 templates with custom object identifier (also known as OID).	Also issues certificates that can be modified and duplicated, based on V2 templates.
The enrollment method (automatic or pending) is valid for all templates. You cannot apply a configuration to individual templates.	You can individually set the enrollment method on each template.
Certificates are manually approved.	Certificates are manually approved or they are approved through Active Directory authentication and access control.
Certificates are not published to a directory location, but to the client or the CA.	Depending on the type of certificate, it is automatically enrolled into the requester's certificate store and published to Active Directory, based on template definition.

Table 9-2   **Stand-Alone and Enterprise CAs Compared**

Stand-Alone CA Features	Enterprise CA Features
Stand-alone CAs do not support certificate publishing and object management based on Active Directory.	Enterprise CAs support certificate publishing and object management based on Active Directory.
Stand-alone CAs can be installed on a domain controller, member server, or stand-alone server (workgroup member).	Enterprise CAs can be installed on a domain controller or member server. (The CA is registered as a forest resource.) It must not be installed on a stand-alone server (workgroup member).

Naturally, you can use both stand-alone and enterprise CAs in your organization if one type of CA cannot meet all of your requirements. Throughout this chapter, differences between enterprise and stand-alone CAs will be pointed out.

Planning CA Capacity

The load placed on a CA is minimal compared to the capabilities of modern computing hardware. Therefore, you only need to deploy multiple CAs to meet redundancy, network performance, or risk management requirements, but not scalability requirements. For example, a stand-alone Windows 2000 CA supports more than 7 million certificates per physical CA without any degradation of performance; Windows Server 2003 CA supports more than 35 million certificates. An individual departmental certification authority running on a server with a dual processor and 512 megabytes (MB) of RAM can issue more than 2 million certificates per day—enough to meet the needs of even the largest enterprises. Even with an unusually large CA key, a single stand-alone CA with the appropriate hardware is capable of issuing more than 750,000 user certificates per day.

Using multiple CAs in a hierarchy reduces the risk that your organization might be forced to revoke and reissue all certificates if a single CA is compromised. However, using a greater number of CAs also increases your administrative overhead. Depending on the number of certificates you manage, the cost of the additional administrative overhead might outweigh the risk of a single CA's private key being compromised.

For many organizations, network performance is the primary limitation to CA performance because of high latency connections between clients and a remote CA. Whereas CA requests require minimal bandwidth and are unlikely to saturate even a low-bandwidth link, high-latency links such as satellite connections will cause autoenrollment requests to be delayed. If slow autoenrollment requests become a significant issue, consider placing a CA at a remote office.

> **NOTE   Real World: Bandwidth Concerns**   You probably do not need to place a CA at a remote office to reduce bandwidth usage—the bandwidth consumed by CA requests is typically minimal. Nonetheless, it is important to understand because technical interviewers often ask about ways to reduce bandwidth on wide-area network (WAN) links.

Some hardware components affect PKI capacity and performance more than others do. When you are selecting the server hardware for your CAs, consider the following:

■ **Number of CPUs**   CPU power is the most critical resource for a certification authority. The greater the number of CPUs, the better the responsiveness and scalability of the CA. Although CA performance is processor-limited, you probably do not need to invest in expensive multiprocessor systems for a dedicated CA. If hardware costs are a concern, deploy a CA with low-end, single-processor server hardware and monitor the performance closely. The performance will probably be acceptable. If you determine that the processor is averaging higher than 60 percent use during peak hours, and performance is affecting end users, you can then choose to upgrade your hardware.

> **NOTE   Weighing the Value of Longer Key Lengths**   In most cases, the default key length provides an acceptable balance between security and CA performance. Generating larger keys can place a high load on computer processors and might increase the amount of time needed for signing operations to excessive levels. Because key length only helps reduce the already extremely low risk of a certificate being cracked by brute force, the benefits of using longer-than-default keys is minimal. You are more likely to have a security compromise because a certificate was lost or stolen than because it was cracked.

■ **Disk performance**   In general, a high-performance disk subsystem allows for a faster rate of certificate enrollment. However, key length influences disk performance. With a shorter CA key length, the CPU has fewer calculations to perform and, therefore, it can complete a large number of operations. With longer CA keys, the CPU needs more time to issue a certificate, resulting in a smaller number of disk input/output (I/O) operations per time interval. You can also improve performance by using a redundant array of independent disks (RAID).

However, invest in expensive server hardware only after you have determined that disk I/O is going to negatively impact your end users.

- **Amount of memory**   The amount of memory you use does not have a significant impact on CA performance, but must meet operating system requirements.

- **Hard disk capacity**   Plan for your hard disk requirements to grow over time. In general, every certificate you issue requires 17 kilobytes (KB) in the database, 15 KB in the log file, and 4 KB if the private key is archived. Certificate key length does not affect the size of an individual database record. Therefore, the size of the CA database increases linearly as more records are added.

If availability or distributed functionality of Certificate Services is a priority, you must deploy multiple CAs. You also need multiple CAs if you want separate CAs to issue certificates for different purposes. To determine the number of CAs required, answer the following questions.

- **Do you require more than one CA?**   If you are supporting only a single application and location, and if greater than 99.9 percent availability of the CA is not critical, you might be able to use a single CA. Otherwise, you probably require at least one root and multiple subordinate CAs.

- **If so, how many root CAs do you require?**   Generally, experts recommend that you have only one root CA as a single point of trust. This is because significant cost and effort is required to protect a root CA from compromise. With multiple root CAs, root maintenance becomes much more difficult. However, organizations with a decentralized security administration model, such as corporations with multiple, largely independent business units and no strong central administrative body, might require more than one root CA.

In addition, you have to determine how many intermediate and issuing CAs you need, which depends on the following factors:

- **Usage**   Certificates can be issued for a number of purposes (for example, secure e-mail, network authentication, and so on). Each of these uses might involve different issuing policies. Using separate CAs provides a basis for administering each policy separately.

- **Organizational or geographic divisions**   You must have different policies for issuing certificates, depending on the role of an entity or its physical location in the organization. You can create separate subordinate CAs to administer these policies.

- **Distribution of the certificate load**   You can deploy multiple issuing CAs to distribute the certificate load to meet site, network, and server requirements. For example, if network links between sites are slow or discontinuous, you might need to place issuing CAs at each site to meet Certificate Services performance and usability requirements.

- **The need for flexible configuration**   You can tailor the CA environment (key strength, physical protection, protection against network attacks, and so on) to provide a balance between security and usability. For example, you can renew keys and certificates more frequently for the intermediate and issuing CAs that are at high risk for compromise, without requiring a change to established root trust relationships. In addition, when you use more than one subordinate CA, you can turn off a subsection of the CA hierarchy without affecting established root trust relationships or the rest of the hierarchy.

- **The need for redundant services**   If one enterprise CA fails, redundancy makes it possible for another issuing CA to provide users with uninterrupted service.

Strive to have only as many CAs as you need to function efficiently. Deploying more CAs than you need creates an unnecessary management burden and introduces additional areas of security vulnerability.

Protecting CAs

The cost of a compromised CA is significant. If an attacker can gain access to your CA, either physically or by means of the network, the threat might be able to retrieve the private key of the CA and then impersonate the CA to issue certificates, which might grant the attacker access to valuable network resources. If the attacker can retrieve archived private keys, the attacker can encrypt documents, impersonate users, and gain access to other protected resources on the network. To limit this risk, harden your CA configuration, consider using offline CAs, evaluate hardware cryptographic service providers (CSPs), and configure auditing on your CAS. I discuss each of these strategies in the following sections.

Hardening CAs

CAs should be hardened to meet your organization's security requirements, just like any other server. Several security considerations are unique to CAs, however.

First, CAs are likely to be targeted by an attacker to retrieve either the CA's private key or archived copies of private keys that have been issued to users. To reduce the risk of an attacker with physical access to the computer copying private keys, use Group Policy settings to restrict access to floppy disks, Compact Disc-Recordables (CD-Rs), flash drives, and other removable media.

As with any server, use physical security to limit a threat agent's access to the computer. In particular, take measures to reduce the risk of an attacker booting the CA into a non-Windows operating system by inserting a bootable CD-ROM. This would enable the threat to bypass operating system security and potentially copy files that, with sufficient computing power, could reveal private keys to the attacker.

As you do with any computer, disable any unnecessary services. In particular, ensure that the Computer Browser service is disabled. You will need to specifically allow the Certificate Services service to run, however.

If your CA server does not have redundant disks, try to place the certificate database directory and the database logs on separate physical disks. By placing them on separate disks, you can recover from the failure of a single disk much easier. If the disk containing the database fails, you will be able to recover the database from a backup and bring it up to date by using the certificate database logs. By default, the certificate database is stored in the %SystemRoot%\System32\CertSrv folder and the logs are stored in the %SystemRoot%\System32\CertLog folder. Standard users need to have Read And Execute NTFS permissions to the CertSrv folder, but only administrators and the SYSTEM should have any permissions on the CertLog folder.

In addition to the CA hardening guidelines contained in this section, take care to harden the security of Microsoft Internet Information Services (IIS) if you add the Application Server role to provide Web-based enrollment or to publish CRLs by using HTTP. If you determine that the risk of a Web server being compromised is high and the value of your CA is high, run IIS on a different computer than your root CA to reduce the risk of a vulnerability in IIS leading to a compromise of your root CA. For more information on hardening Web servers, refer to Chapter 7, "Hardening Servers."

Using Offline CAs

The compromise of even one CA key invalidates the security protection that it and any CAs below it in the hierarchy provide. For this reason, it is important to avoid connecting root CAs to the network.

To ensure the reliability of your CA infrastructure, specify that any non-issuing root and intermediate CAs must be offline. This minimizes the risk of the CA private keys becoming compromised. You can isolate your server in several different ways (listed in order of increasing protection).

- By shutting down the CA service

- By physically removing the computer from the network

- By shutting down the computer

Install Certificate Services on a computer running Windows 2000 or Windows Server 2003 that is not a member of a domain and configure it as a stand-alone CA. Installing an offline CA on a server that is a member of a domain can cause problems when you bring the CA back online after a long offline period. This is because the computer account password changes every 30 days. Installing an offline CA as an enterprise CA will cause Active Directory to have problems replicating when you disconnect the server from the network.

When a CA is supposed to be an offline CA, you can still publish its certificate and CRL in Active Directory. You must bring an offline CA online at regular intervals (at least as frequently as your CRL publication schedule) and generate a new CRL. You must also bring the CA online to process new certificate requests and revoke existing certificates for subordinate CAs.

Using Hardware CSPs

You can use a hardware CSP to reduce the damage if a CA is compromised. Hardware CSPs store keys in tamper-resistant hardware cryptographic devices that are more secure than keys stored on local computer hard disks. Therefore, keys stored in hardware cryptographic devices can have key lifetimes that are longer than keys stored by software CSPs on hard disks. Another advantage to using hardware CSPs is that the key material is kept outside the memory of the computer and within the hardware device. This makes it impossible to access the key of the CA by means of a memory dump.

Hardware CSPs may also provide hardware cryptographic operations such as random number generation, encryption key generation, digital signatures, and key archive and recovery. Although these are all services that Windows Server operating systems also provide, the hardware CSP may provide different algorithms that suit your needs better. In addition, if you are experiencing processor performance limitations on your CA, offloading processing to the hardware CSP will improve performance or scalability.

If you choose to use hardware cryptographic service providers for CA private key storage, you must ensure that the hardware device is secured physically or at least that the operator cards or tokens are backed up. You might, for example, keep it in a highly secured area in the computer room of your company or locked in a safe.

If you determine that a hardware CSP is too costly, consider using smart cards for key storage. When you store cryptographic keys on a smart card, no one in your organization can issue or revoke certificates without the appropriate smart card together with the correct personal identification number (PIN).

Auditing CAs

As with most components of Windows Server 2003, you can and should audit Certificate Services events that might be useful in identifying attacks. You can choose from the following self-explanatory events:

- Back up and restore the CA database
- Change the CA configuration
- Change the CA security settings
- Issue and manage certificate requests
- Revoke certificates and publish CRLs
- Store and retrieve archived keys
- Start and stop Certificate Services

If you use certificates for any type of authentication or authorization in your organization, it's critical that you enable both success and failure auditing. Certificate Services typically do not generate so much auditing data that they become difficult to manage. However, if you suspect that your Certificate Services have been compromised, the auditing information will be vital to determining the scope of the compromise.

In addition to auditing CA events, enable auditing on the HKEY_LOCAL_MACHINE\SYSTEM\CurrentControlSet\Services\Certsvc\Configuration registry key. In particular, enable all types of Failure auditing for Everyone, Full Control. This adds an event to the Security event log if someone without proper permission attempts to access this key, which is very likely to be part of an attack.

In addition, consider auditing successful changes for the Everyone group for the Set Value, Create Subkey, Create Link, Delete, Change Permissions, and Take Ownership actions.

Audit access to the CertSrv and CertLog folders as well. Audit all failed attempts by the Everyone group to access the CertLog folder, and audit all successful attempts by the Everyone group to modify the CertSrv folder. This auditing is likely to generate events during attacks against Certificate Services by authenticated users.

DESIGNING A CA TRUST MODEL

CAs can be hierarchical, just as Active Directory forests can be designed in a hierarchy. Just as two trusting domains or forests trust each other to authenticate users, CAs in a hierarchy must trust each other. There are three basic types of CA trust hierarchies:

- **Rooted trust model**   In a rooted trust model, a CA is either a root or a subordinate, and you can use offline root CAs for the highest level of security.

- **Network (or cross-certification) trust model**   In a network trust model, every CA is both a root and a subordinate.

- **Hybrid trust model**   Hybrid trust models combine elements of both the rooted and network trust models.

The sections that follow discuss both the rooted and network trust models, and then provide information on limiting the risks of trusts. The hybrid trust model is simply a combination of the other two trust models and is not covered in more detail.

Rooted Trust Model

The rooted trust model is the model you will probably use within your organization. In a rooted trust model, two or more CAs are organized in a structure with a single root CA and one or more subordinate CAs. The root CA provides a certificate to the subordinate CAs, which in turn can generate certificates for additional subordinate CAs or end users. In Active Directory, trusts are automatically created between domains in a hierarchy. In a CA hierarchy, **trust chaining** enables certificates issued by subordinate CAs to be trusted by clients who trust the root CA.

Within an organization's certification hierarchy, some subordinate CAs might be intermediate CAs. In other words, they do not issue certificates to end users or computers; they issue certificates to other subordinate CAs below them in the certification hierarchy. Intermediate CAs are not required. However, using an intermediate CA allows you to take your root CA offline, which greatly increases the security of the root CA. After all, if the root CA is unplugged, it is invulnerable to network attacks.

Subordinate CAs that do issue certificates to end users are known as *issuing CAs*. Of course, root and intermediate CAs are also capable of issuing certificates to end users. Figure 9-7 shows the relationships between root, intermediate, and issuing CAs and the users and computers who use certificates. If you create a new CA hierarchy, your existing CA hierarchy needs to trust only the root CA of the new PKI to trust all the subordinate CAs in the new hierarchy.

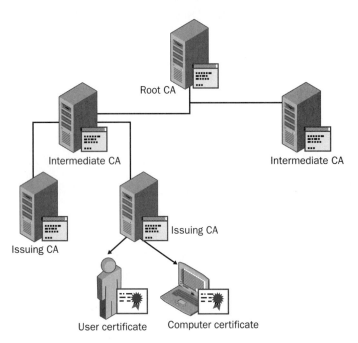

Figure 9-7   In a CA hierarchy, root CAs issue certificates to intermediate CAs, and issuing CAs issue certificates to end users.

Rooted trust hierarchies are more scalable and easier to administer than network trust hierarchies because you have control over the entire hierarchy. Because you can potentially revoke the root CA certificate and invalidate every certificate ever issued, you have complete control over the risks associated with a PKI.

Because CAs in a rooted trust hierarchy can be online or offline, rooted trust hierarchies allow great flexibility in the ways you can deploy and manage a PKI. You can protect the private key of a CA by taking the CA offline. Because offline CAs are typically the root and/or policy CAs that issue certificates only to other CAs, taking the CA offline does not affect other parts of the hierarchy.

If you choose a rooted trust model, you also need to design the CA architecture. Designing a CA architecture is very similar to creating an Active Directory domain architecture. Use a single CA whenever possible (just as a single Active Directory domain is ideal). If different groups within your organization perform their own IT management, they will probably also want to control how certificates are issued, renewed, and revoked. To give them that control, create subordinate CAs.

Ultimately, your CA architecture should mirror the structure of your organization. If you have a single IT group that manages all your computers, you need only a single CA. If different locations perform their own IT management, you have a geographical CA hierarchy with subordinate CAs at each location. If different groups perform their own IT management, you have an organizational CA hierarchy with subordinate CAs for each organization. For more information about Active Directory architectures, refer to Chapter 5, "Designing Active Directory Security."

Network Trust Model

If your organization has multiple, distributed IT departments, you might not be able to establish a single, trusted root. Similarly, if you need to trust certificates issued by partners, customers, or vendors outside of our own organization, but you don't want to give them control over issuing and revoking certificates in your organization, you will not be able to rely on a rooted trust model. In these situations, you can implement a network trust model in which all CAs are self-signed and trust relationships between CAs are based on **cross-certificates**. Cross-certificates are special certificates that establish complete or qualified one-way trusts between otherwise unrelated CAs.

The network trust model is very similar in function to the rooted trust model. In essence, trusting a cross-certificate from another CA makes your CA a subordinate CA. You can establish two one-way trusts in the network trust model, however, causing two separate rooted hierarchies to trust certificates issued by the trusted CA. In addition, although you can stop trusting a cross-certificate, you cannot revoke a trusting CA's certificates, because you did not issue the CA's certificates.

Figure 9-8 shows an example of a network trust model.

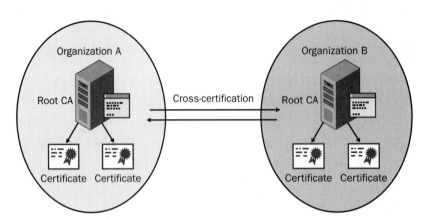

Figure 9-8   The network trust model enables your PKI to trust certificates issued by other organizations.

The trusts in Figure 9-8 are bidirectional, which means that the CA for Organization A issued a cross-certificate of trust to the CA for Organization B and that Organization B issued a cross-certificate of trust to Organization A. You can also remove a trust for a CA by revoking its cross-certificate.

Cross-certificates usually need to be installed on all clients of the PKI in a network trust model. Otherwise, clients won't trust certificates issued by the trusted CA. You could theoretically add the cross-certificate to every client computer; however, this would be extremely time-consuming to deploy and difficult to maintain. Typically, you will deploy cross-certificates to clients by using Group Policy objects (GPOs) in an Active Directory environment.

As an alternative to installing cross-certificates on all PKI clients, you can generate a cross-certification authority certificate. Cross-certification authority certificates essentially give a remote organization's CA the capabilities of a subordinate CA. For more information about cross-certification authority certificates, read the white paper "Planning and Implementing Cross-Certification and Qualified Subordination Using Windows Server 2003" by Brian Komar and David Cross at *http://www.microsoft.com/technet/prodtechnol/windowsserver2003/technologies/ security/ws03qswp.mspx.*

Cross-certification does not need to be bidirectional, and typically is not. For example, your Web browser trusts certificates from dozens of different root CAs by default, including VeriSign, Microsoft, and Equifax. Therefore, you trust certificates published by these CAs. However, these CAs do not trust you to publish certificates. This is known as **unilateral cross-certification**, in which one CA cross-certifies another CA but not the reverse.

Cross-certification doesn't need to happen between two root CAs; cross-certification can happen between two subordinate CAs or between a root and a subordinate CA, as shown in Figure 9-9. For example, imagine that you have an internal rooted CA hierarchy with separate subordinate CAs for each regional office. The team in Boston needs to be able to exchange encrypted e-mails with a partner company. In this case, you could have the Boston CA trust the partner's company with the cross-certificate, rather than configuring your root CA to trust the cross-certificate. This limits the risk of the cross-certification being abused because other CAs in your organization are not exposed to any additional risk.

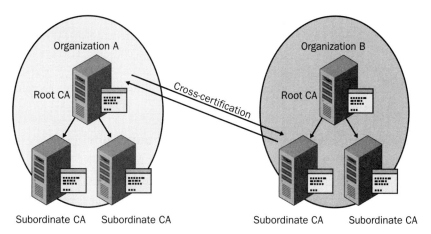

Figure 9-9 Cross-certification can occur between root and subordinate CAs.

Limiting Unplanned Trusts

When you extend your CA trust infrastructure beyond the boundaries of the PKI of your organization, you can inadvertently create unplanned trust relationships.

Unplanned trusts that can occur include the following:

- Allowing certificates to be used for unintended applications.

- Allowing external certificates to be used for longer than intended.

- Enabling trust with the extended business partners of a business partnership.

For example, if company A trusts company B by means of an unconstrained cross-certificate, and company B trusts company C, then company A unintentionally trusts company C. Equally serious problems can occur when company A and company B cross-certify, and company A does not realize that company B does not have the same level of control over the manner in which its certificates are issued and used.

In both Windows 2000 and Windows Server 2003 environments, you can use **certificate trust lists (CTLs)** to limit unplanned trusts. A CTL is a predefined list of certificates that is signed by a trusted entity. The CTL includes either hashes of certificates or a list of the actual certificate names. In most cases, the CTL is a list of hashed certificate contexts. The CTL allows you to limit the purposes for which certificates issued by an external CA can be used, and the validity period of those certificates.

You might use a CTL to allow users to trust certificates issued by a commercial CA and restrict the permitted uses for those certificates. You might also use CTLs to control trust on an extranet for certificates issued by CAs managed by your business partners. After a CTL is defined, it must be applied to client computers by a GPO.

In addition, Windows Server 2003 certificate trust lists allow you to impose the following types of restrictions:

- **Create trust certificates from specific CAs without requiring broader trust for the root CA**   For example, you can use CTLs on an extranet to trust certificates issued by certain commercial CAs. If you map certificates issued to an account stored in Active Directory, you can grant appropriate permission to users who need access to restricted extranet resources. This is possible because they have certificates issued by the trusted commercial CAs.

- **Restrict the permitted use of certificates issued by trusted CAs**   For example, you can use a certificate trust list on an extranet to restrict the permitted use of certificates to applications such as secure mail.

- **Control the period of time in which third-party certificates and CAs are valid**   For example, the CA of a business partner can have a lifetime of five years and issue certificates with lifetimes of one year. However, you can create a CTL with a lifetime of six months to limit the time that certificates issued by the CA of the business partner are trusted on your extranet.

To further limit the creation of unplanned trust relationships in Windows Server 2003 environments, you can use CA constraints, also known as **qualified subordination**. You can use qualified subordination to exert a great deal of control over what subordinate CAs are allowed to do. For example, you can configure a subordinate CA so that it issues certificates for only a specific namespace such as partners.cohowinery.com. You can also restrict a subordinate CA to issuing specific types of certificates. This would allow you to create a subordinate CA that issued only smart-card certificates.

Qualified subordination in Windows Server 2003 can be based on the following constraints and policies:

- **Basic constraints**   Enable you to limit the path length for a certificate chain. For example, if you don't configure basic constraints and you trust a root CA, you will automatically trust certificates issued by any subordinate CAs. If you define a path length of zero, you will trust certificates issued only by the root CA itself, and not by subordinate CAs. Figure 9-10 shows a second example, with a path length of 2. In this example, you would trust CorpCA, RegionCA, AsiaCA, and User1. You would not, however, trust Japan CA, because the path length for that CA would be equal to 3.

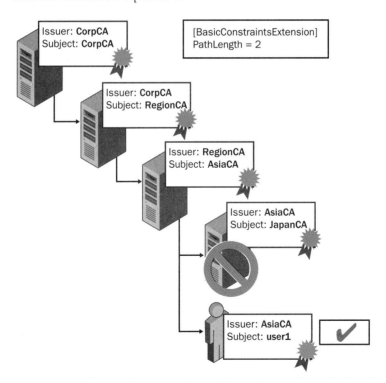

Figure 9-10   Use basic constraints to limit the number of subordinate CAs you trust.

■ **Name constraints**   Enable you to control which namespaces each trusted CA manages. For example, you could use name constraints to ensure your partner's CA infrastructure cannot issue trusted certificates containing names in your organization's namespace. You can define permitted or excluded name lists for the following types of names: relative distinguished names, DNS domain names, Universal Resource Identifiers (URIs), e-mail addresses, user principal names (UPNs), and IP addresses.

■ **Issuance policy**   Enables you to identify the extent to which your organization trusts the identity presented in a certificate issued by another organization's CA hierarchy. For example, an issuance policy might describe that you trust certificates issued only during a face-to-face meeting with a network administrator, such as the issuance of a smart-card certificate.

■ **Application policy**   Enables you to restrict the ways in which a certificate can be used. For example, you could allow server and client authentication certificates, but reject code signing and document signing certificates.

> **MORE INFO**   Qualified subordination is a complex, detailed topic, and is not covered in more detail in this book. For more information, refer to "Planning and Implementing Cross-Certification and Qualified Subordination Using Windows Server 2003," available at http://www.microsoft.com/technet/prodtechnol/windowsserver2003/technologies/security/ws03qswp.mspx.

DEFINING CERTIFICATE PROCEDURES

If a threat can acquire a certificate, it might be able to use it maliciously. Technology can't protect you from human error, so define a set of procedures for performing PKI-related tasks such as issuing certificates, renewing certificates, and revoking certificates. Document these procedures well; users with privileges to perform PKI management tasks need to follow the procedures closely to avoid a security compromise. The sections that follow provide you with the information you need to develop each of these PKI procedures.

Issuing Certificates

Issuing certificates, otherwise known as **certificate enrollment**, is the process of requesting and installing certificates for a user, computer, or service. You, as a security designer, define the policies and processes of your CA. Before issuing certificates, determine how users will obtain their certificates, and how they will prove their identity.

There are two primary approaches to enrollment: manual and automatic. The type of CA, the client operating system, and whether the client and CA can communicate across a network will dictate your choice of enrollment method. The following circumstances require you to use manual enrollment:

- **Client computers run operating systems earlier than Windows 2000**   You must manually enroll these clients for certificates because the client operating systems do not support Group Policy and, therefore, cannot take advantage of autoenrollment.

- **Clients are not members of an Active Directory domain**   Autoenrollment is applied to clients by using GPOs. If the client is not participating in the Active Directory domain, it cannot apply domain Group Policy settings and, therefore, cannot use autoenrollment.

- **You are using a stand-alone CA**   A stand-alone CA does not have the ability to issue a certificate automatically.

- **The client or CA is not connected to the network**   Autoenrollment requires the client to communicate directly to the enterprise CA. In these circumstances, users must manually submit all certificate requests.

> **NOTE**   **Enrolling User Certificates**   *The most secure way to enroll user certificates initially is to do a face-to-face authentication at the registration authority, and then have the registration authority store user certificates on smart cards. This provides a very high level of security because a threat agent would need to physically appear before your staff and provide false credentials, such as a fake employee badge. This would be very risky for the threat agent because the risk of being caught is very high. Unfortunately, manually requesting and issuing certificates also has a high cost of deployment. In addition, it takes several weeks or months to meet with every employee in an enterprise.*

The sections that follow discuss manual and automatic enrollment.

Manual Enrollment

If all or part of the enrollment process is manual, you must decide between having users request certificates using the Web Enrollment Support pages, the Certificate Request Wizard, or the Certreq.exe command-line utility. Web-based enrollment is by far the easiest and most intuitive method for end users to enroll for certificates. If users have the ability to use the Certificates snap-in, they have the option of using the console to submit certificate requests directly to the CA. This method will require end users to load and configure a MMC snap-in—hardly a user-friendly process. The final method for certificate enrollment is to use the Certreq.exe command directly from the command line. Certreq.exe is used primarily for scripting certificate tasks that cannot be accomplished by using Group Policy settings. Although it is used to request certificates, it is not intended to be used by end users.

To enroll for certificates manually by using a Web-based interface, ensure that the CA has IIS installed. The Web Enrollment application is installed when Certificate Services is installed. It allows users to perform various tasks that are related to requesting certificates from both stand-alone and enterprise CAs. The Web Enrollment Web site is located at *http://ServerName/certsrv*.

> **NOTE** **Enable SSL to Provide Encryption for Web Enrollment**   By default, SSL is not enabled on the Web-based interface. For increased security, enable SSL on the certsrv virtual directory using a certificate trusted by all clients, such as a certificate issued by a public CA. This will provide server authentication and reduce the risk of someone impersonating your CA.

You can also enroll for certificates by using the Certificate Request Wizard in the Certificates snap-in to request certificates from a computer running Windows Server 2003 configured as an enterprise CA. The Certificates snap-in displays the active certificates and other PKI client properties, such as trusted root CAs and existing certificate trust lists. As the administrator of a computer, you can manage certificates issued to users, computers, and services. As a user without administrative privileges, you can manage certificates only for your user account.

Unless an organization uses firewalls between one part of the organization and another, you can use the Certificates snap-in or the Web interface interchangeably. If a firewall exists between the CA and the requesting client, you must request certificates by means of the Web Enrollment Support pages or ensure that TCP port 135 and a dynamic port above 1024 is open for communications.

Whether you choose to use the Web Enrollment Support pages or the Certificate Request And Renewal Wizard, prepare documentation that describes how users can request a user certificate, what users can expect after they request the certificate (for example, automatic enrollment or a delay pending administrator approval), and how they can use the certificates after they receive them.

Automatic Enrollment

For the ultimate in automation, use GPOs to configure clients for autoenrollment. Autoenrollment enables organizations to deploy certificates to both users and computers automatically. The autoenrollment feature allows you to manage all aspects of the certificate lifecycle centrally, including certificate enrollment, certificate renewal, and the modification and supersession of certificates.

Autoenrollment of user certificates provides a quick and simple way to issue certificates to users. It also enables faster deployment of PKI applications, such as smart-card logon or EFS, within an Active Directory environment by eliminating the need for interaction with the end user. Autoenrollment is typically a requirement for large environments because you must be able to justify the cost of a PKI as a cost-effective countermeasure during the Security Risk Management Process. Manually enrolling certificates has a very high cost, while autoenrollment minimizes the cost of a PKI deployment and reduces the total cost of ownership for a PKI implementation.

There is an important restriction placed on automatic enrollment, however. Although computers running Windows 2000 can participate in autoenrollment for computer certificates deployed by means of the Automatic Certificate Request Settings Group Policy setting, autoenrollment of user certificates is not possible for clients running Windows 2000.

> **NOTE   Autoenrollment Delay**   When Windows XP and Windows Server 2003 perform autoenrollment, there is a short delay between when a user logs on and autoenrollment starts. This delay allows services to start and the user to finish logging on.

In contrast, Windows XP and Windows Server 2003 support autoenrollment for both user and computer certificates by means of Autoenrollment Settings policies and version 2 certificate templates. This solution reduces the number of certificates issued by combining certificate purposes into fewer certificates. It also reduces administration and end-user interaction by using autoenrollment. Remember that autoenrollment settings in Group Policy require the use of version 2 certificate templates.

In a Windows Server 2003 PKI, there are two methods of enabling autoenrollment of certificates: Automatic Certificate Request Settings and Autoenrollment Settings:

- **Automatic Certificate Request Settings**   A Group Policy setting that enables the deployment of version 1 certificates to computers running Windows 2000, Windows XP, and Windows Server 2003. This type of autoenrollment is used only to deploy computer certificates, and it occurs each time the computer starts or Group Policy is refreshed. It is used most commonly to deploy certificates to be used for encrypted IPSec connections.

- **Autoenrollment Settings**   Based on a combination of Group Policy settings and version 2 certificate templates. This combination allows the client computer running Windows XP Professional or Windows Server 2003 to enroll user or computer certificates automatically when the user logs on.

> **NOTE**   *The Scope of the Automatic Certificate Request Settings Group Policy*   Remember that the Automatic Certificate Request Settings Group Policy setting does not apply to users. It applies only to computers. Because Windows 2000 cannot use Autoenrollment Settings, Windows 2000 can autoenroll in computer certificates only.

Some types of certificates require user interaction to be enrolled. For example, smart-card certificates require the user to insert the smart card before the certificate can be generated. In these cases, you can still use autoenrollment by configuring the version 2 certificate template to prompt the user during enrollment. When users are autoenrolled, a pop-up window (like those used in update notifications) will prompt the user that interaction is required.

Renewing Certificates

All certificates have a limited lifetime.

Although this lifetime is probably several years in the future, plan now to renew the certificates when they expire. Users might not need to be involved in the certificate renewal process. However, document whether certificates are automatically renewed, which administrators are authorized to manually renew certificates, and the process that they will use.

In general, the process will be similar to the process you used to issue the certificate initially. If you performed a face-to-face authentication for each user and issued them a smart card, they should bring their smart card to the registration authority to have the certificate renewed. If they manually requested the certificate by using a Web interface, they should use the same interface to request renewal. Similarly, autoenrolled computer certificates can be automatically renewed.

> **NOTE Reminding Users to Renew Certificates** Users won't think about certificates expiring. Therefore, if you need users to submit renewal requests manually, you'll need to send out reminder notices to have them renew certificates before they expire.

How often you go through the certificate renewal process will be determined by the lifetimes of the certificates you issue to your CAs and to your end users. The sections that follow discuss important aspects of how to select certificate lifetimes.

End-User Certificate Lifetimes

Certificates cannot be used forever; that would give an attacker too much time to crack the corresponding private key. Certificates have a predefined life cycle and expire at the end of this life cycle. You, as the security designer, maintain control over the certificate life cycle. You can define how long certificates will last when initially issued, extend the lifetime of a certificate by renewing it, or end the usefulness of a certificate before the expiration date by revoking it.

A number of factors influence the length you will choose for a certificate lifetime, such as the type of certificate, the security requirements of your organization, the standard practices in your industry, and government regulations. In general, longer keys support longer certificate lifetimes and key lifetimes because they take an attacker longer to crack. Longer lifetimes reduce administrative labor, which reduces costs.

> **NOTE Risks to Private Keys** Most compromised private keys aren't cracked, regardless of their lifetime. Rather, an attacker steals them. All that encryption is useless if you don't protect your private keys.

When establishing certificate and key lifetimes, consider how vulnerable your keys are to compromise and what the potential consequences of compromise are. The following factors influence the lifetimes that you choose for certificates and keys:

- **The length of private keys for certificates**   Because longer keys are more difficult to break, they justify longer safe key lifetimes.

- **The security of the CAs and their private keys**   In general, the more secure the CA and its private key, the longer the safe certificate lifetime. CAs that are operated offline and stored in locked vaults or data centers are the most secure.

- **The strength of the technology used for cryptographic operations**   In general, stronger cryptographic technology supports longer key lifetimes. You can extend key lifetimes if you enhance private key storage by using smart cards and other hardware cryptographic service providers.

- **The vulnerability of the CA certification chain**   In general, the more vulnerable your CA hierarchy is to attack, the longer the CA private keys and the shorter the key lifetimes required.

- **The users of your certificates**   Organizations typically trust their own employees more than they trust employees of other organizations. If you issue certificates to external users, you might want to shorten the lifetimes of those certificates to reduce the time window during which a compromised private key can be abused.

An expiration date is defined for each certificate when it is issued. An enterprise CA issues certificates with lifetimes that are based on the certificate template for the requested certificate type.

CA Certificate Lifetimes

Every certificate issued by a CA has a validity period that ends with the certificate's expiration date. Because a CA is, really, just another entity that has been issued a certificate—either issued by itself (in the case of a root CA) or issued by a parent (in the case of a subordinate CA)—every CA has a built-in expiration date. The expiration date of a CA's certificate is more important than that of other certificates, however.

Although a CA's certificate can be renewed just as easily as any other certificate, a CA cannot issue a certificate with an expiration date valid beyond the expiration date of its own certificate. Therefore, when a CA's certificate reaches the end of its validity period, all certificates it has issued also expire. Because of this, if you purposely do not renew a CA, you can be assured that all the certificates that the now-expired CA has issued can no longer be used. In other words, there will be no "orphaned" certificates that are still within their validity period but that have been issued by a CA that is no longer valid.

Because a CA that is approaching the end of its own validity period issues certificates valid for shorter and shorter periods of time, have a plan in place to renew the CA well before it expires to avoid issuing certificates of a very short validity period. For example, in the case of Windows Server 2003, the root CA's certificate defaults to a validity period of five years. Renew it every four years, however, to prevent the root CA from publishing new certificates with lifetimes shorter than a year.

You can reduce the time required to administer a PKI by increasing the validity period of the root CA. As with any certificate, choose a validity period shorter than the time required for an attacker to break the root CA key's cryptography. Given the current state of computer technology, one estimate is that a 4096-bit private key would take about 15 to 20 years to crack. Although a determined attacker could eventually crack a private key by using the corresponding certificate, the result would be useless if the certificate had expired by the time the attack completed.

Revoking Certificates

In some situations, you might need to invalidate a certificate before it has reached the end of its lifetime. Creating policies for certificate revocation involves the following tasks:

- Defining the conditions that warrant the revocation of a certificate, such as when employees leave your organization or abuse their user rights

- Selecting a certificate-revocation-list location

- Selecting the type or types of CRLs you intend to use

- Establishing schedules for the publication of CRLs and determining the cached CRL validity period.

The sections that follow describe each of these tasks in more detail.

> **NOTE** **The Problem with CRLs** So, if you can revoke certificates, why do certificates have an expiration date? Why not just have the CA revoke the certificate after a certain date? The reason is that certificate revocation isn't useful in many circumstances.
>
> Consider a Web site that has an SSL certificate issued by a public CA: https://www.woodgrovebank.com/. Woodgrove Bank uses the SSL certificate for two reasons: to enable communications encryption and to authenticate the server. A disgruntled administrator at the School of

Fine Arts manages to steal Woodgrove Bank's SSL certificate, and he uses it to set up a malicious Web site. Then, the disgruntled administrator changes the School of Fine Arts' internal DNS servers to redirect traffic to the malicious server. Because the disgruntled administrator has Woodgrove Bank's actual SSL certificate, users at the School of Fine Arts who attempt to visit the Web site do not receive an error message that the Web site's certificate is invalid. They would have no reason to believe they were entering their financial information into a malicious server because SSL would be protecting the transaction.

If Woodgrove Bank discovered that the certificate had been compromised, they would immediately contact the public CA who issued the SSL certificate, and the CA would immediately revoke the certificate by adding it to their CRL. However, this wouldn't stop the disgruntled administrator; users could continue to visit the malicious Web server until their browsers retrieved the updated CRL. This is key: *Until the client retrieves an updated CRL, it will still consider a revoked certificate to be valid.* How often the CRL is checked is defined by the CRL's validity period, discussed later in this chapter.

Defining Conditions for Certificate Revocation

Not all PKIs need support by the publication of CRLs. For example, if your certificates provide only a low or medium level of security and are unlikely to be misused, or if they have short lifetimes, there might not be a need to create and distribute lists of revoked certificates. If, on the other hand, your certificates have a high value and a lifetime that is long enough to cause potential misuse, create and distribute certificate revocation lists on a regular basis.

Before you create certificate revocation schedules, define all the circumstances that justify the revocation of certificates in your organization. For example, you might choose to revoke certificates for any of the following reasons:

- An unauthorized user has gained access to the private key of the certificate.

- An unauthorized user has gained access to the CA. In this case, all the certificates that the CA has published must be revoked and reissued.

> **NOTE Revoking Root Certificates**   A root certificate cannot be revoked by means of a CRL because a root CA is self-signed.

- Certificate criteria have changed; for example, an employee has moved to a different department.

- The certificate has been superseded. For example, you might decide to use a different encryption protocol or a longer key.

- The CA that issued the certificate is no longer operating.

- The status of the certificate is on hold. When a certificate has been revoked, it cannot be renewed. However, if the status of a certificate is questionable, you can revoke it and then rescind the revocation if necessary, or revoke it again for another reason.

- A user's private key is compromised (a smart card is lost, for example).

- A computer is replaced or permanently removed from service, or the private key of the computer is compromised.

Selecting CRL Publication Locations

If you need to download a file from a server, you might access the file in several different ways. If you're logged onto the computer locally, you would use Windows Explorer to navigate to the folder containing the file. If you were on a different computer on the same network, you might map a drive to the server and download the file from a shared folder. If the server were behind a firewall and running IIS, you could open a Web browser to retrieve the file.

Having multiple ways to retrieve a file from a server is important, especially when the server will be accessed by a variety of different clients. Certificate Services enables clients to retrieve CRLs by using a wide variety of different protocols: shared folders, HTTP, File Transfer Protocol (FTP), and Lightweight Directory Access Protocol (LDAP).

By default, CRLs are published in three different locations. For clients accessing the CRL from a shared folder, they are located in the *Server*\CertEnroll\ share, which is created automatically when Certificate Services is installed. Clients who need to retrieve the CRL by using LDAP can access it from CN=*CAName*,CN=*CAComputerName*,CN=CDP,CN=Public Key Services, CN=Services,CN=Configuration,DC= *ForestRootNameDN*. Web clients can retrieve the CRLs from *http://Server/certenroll*.

There's little risk in enabling all three methods for CRL distribution. Ensure, however, that all clients can access the CRL. In general, publish CRLs to Active Directory if they are for internal clients and all computers are members of your domain and to a Web server if you issue certificates to external clients or you have non-Windows clients. If you issue certificates to both internal and external clients, you can configure both or direct all clients to retrieve the CRL from your Web server.

If you need clients to be able to retrieve a CRL even if the server hosting the publication location is offline, configure redundancy. If you publish CRLs to Active Directory, the CRLs are replicated between domain controllers automatically.

Therefore, you would need to worry only about configuring multiple domain controllers. If you publish CRLs to a Web server, configure multiple Web servers.

Figure 9-11 shows this decision-making process.

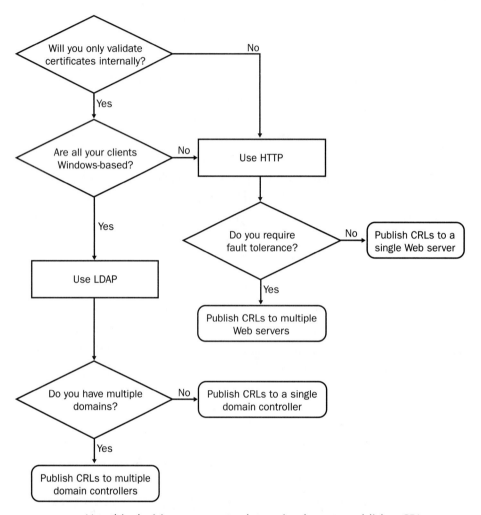

Figure 9-11   Use this decision process to determine how to publish a CRL.

Because the CRL path is included in every certificate, you must define the CRL location and its access path before deploying certificates. If an application performs revocation checking and a valid CRL is not available on the local computer, it rejects the certificate.

You can modify the CRL distribution point by using the Certification Authority MMC snap-in, as shown in Figure 9-12. In this way, you can change the location where the CRL is published to meet the needs of users in your organization. Move the CRL distribution point from the CA configuration folder to a Web server to change the location of the CRL, and move each new CRL to the new distribution point, or else the chain will break when the previous CRL expires.

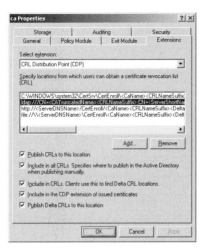

Figure 9-12   You can publish a CRL to multiple locations.

If you publish CRLs to Active Directory, consider the replication schedule. It may take longer than expected for every directory server to receive the latest version of the CRL, depending on the size and replication schedule of the Active Directory environment. In addition, make sure the CRL validity period is longer than the replication convergence time for the Active Directory forest.

Using Delta CRLs

Windows Server 2003 includes two types of CRLs: base CRLs and delta CRLs. **Base CRLs** include a complete list of revoked certificates and, therefore, they can grow quickly in organizations that issue a large number of certificates. **Delta CRLs** contain only the certificates revoked after the last base or delta CRL was published; therefore, the data in a delta CRL is accurate throughout its lifetime. Because delta CRLs are smaller than base CRLs, they require less bandwidth to replicate across the network and they can be published more frequently, which improves the security of your PKI.

Delta CRLs have drawbacks, though. The most significant is that only Windows XP and newer clients support delta CRLs. Other clients, such as computers running Windows 2000 Professional, can read only base CRLs. Therefore, if you have older clients and you want the same level of security for all clients, you still need to update base CRLs frequently. Windows XP clients can still take advantage of the delta CRLs, but the overall benefit is reduced.

In addition, avoid using delta CRLs if you use an offline CA. Because you have to bring the CA online manually, and then publish the CRL, creating delta CRLs is not worth the administration time. Instead, manually generate and publish base CRLs when you bring an offline CA online.

Consider the following factors to determine if you should use delta CRLs in addition to base CRLs:

- **Compatibility**   Only Windows XP and newer clients can recognize delta CRLs. Publish base CRLs for other types of clients. Unless all clients are running Windows XP or newer operating systems, use only base CRLs.

- **Volume**   If you revoke a large number of certificates, your delta CRLs can approach base CRLs in size. Therefore, it is not useful to use delta CRLs when large numbers of certificates are revoked between base CRL publication dates.

- **Bandwidth**   In most organizations, CRLs consume an extremely small percentage of the network's bandwidth. If you are not currently constrained by bandwidth, you won't realize any benefit from the use of delta CRLs; use only base CRLs.

- **Online status**   If you use an offline CA, use only base CRLs. Publishing CRLs from an offline CA is too time-consuming to worry about publishing separate base and delta CRLs.

Establishing a CRL Publication Schedule and Validity Period

Determine how often your CAs will publish CRLs. Basically, the more frequently you publish CRLs, the more quickly clients will consider the revoked certificates invalid. Publishing new CRLs consumes some bandwidth; however, the amount of bandwidth used is minimal.

By default, enterprise CAs publish CRLs weekly to Active Directory, and stand-alone and enterprise CAs publish CRLs weekly to a directory on the CA server. If you're willing to allow a revoked certificate to be considered valid for up to a week, these settings are sufficient. If you consider a stolen certificate to be a significant risk, you should probably increase the frequency to as high as daily.

If you use delta CRLs, you might choose to publish base CRLs every week and delta CRLs daily. These are the default settings, as Figure 9-13 demonstrates. This configuration speeds the process of effectively revoking certificates, while keeping the bandwidth used by transferring CRLs to a minimum. If you choose not to use delta CRLs, increase the frequency with which base CRLs are published.

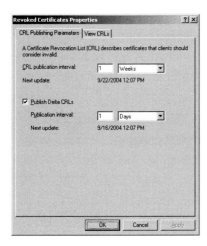

Figure 9-13   By default, base CRLs are published weekly, and delta CRLs are published daily.

Unfortunately, a CRL is effective only if clients retrieve it. Clients do not automatically retrieve new CRLs because they keep them cached and retrieve a new CRL only when the *validity period* of the cached CRL has expired. The CRL publication schedule and the validity period, therefore, determine the frequency with which clients retrieve a CRL. Worry only about configuring the publication schedule. The CA automatically sets the validity period to a time slightly longer than the publication schedule. By default, certificates have a validity period of eight days and the CRL publication interval is seven days.

To prevent certificate misuse, certificates are considered invalid if the cached CRL has expired and the client cannot download a new CRL. Therefore, it's critical that the CRL is valid for the amount of time it takes for you to recover a failed CA. For example, a one-hour CRL validity period isn't long enough for you to restore a failed CA. After the cached CRL expired on clients, the clients might consider *all* certificates invalid—which might cause many applications on your network to come crashing to a halt.

For most organizations, the cost associated with the bandwidth consumed by clients retrieving the CRL every two days will be minimal. Nonetheless, compare the cost of the additional bandwidth with the reduced risk as determined by the Security Risk Management Process.

> **NOTE   Revoking Certificates When Issuing a New CA Key**   If you issue new keys to a CA, you need to publish two CRLs: one CRL for certificates issued with the old key pair, and one CRL for certificates issued with the new key pair.

These guidelines relate only to CAs that issue certificates to end users. Root and intermediate CAs that issue certificates to other CAs should have a longer CRL validity period than issuing CAs because revocation of a CA certificate should be a very rare operation. Set the CA CRL publication schedule in the range of 90 to 180 days.

Planning for Data Recovery and Key Recovery

One of the most costly aspects of maintaining a PKI is the loss of private keys and certificates due to corrupted files or disk failure on client computers. For this reason, as part of your certificate management plan, evaluate the risks of lost private keys and the data they encrypt, and create a strategy for recovering files that have been encrypted. There are two approaches to this: **data recovery** and **key recovery**. The sections that follow describe each of these approaches, as well as how to limit the risks associated with key archival.

Data Recovery

Data recovery enables more than one private key to retrieve encrypted files. In this way, data can be decrypted (and thereby recovered) if a single private key is lost. This saves you from having to back up private keys, the approach used by key recovery. Use data recovery if you need to be able to recover data in your organization but do not need to have access to individual private keys of users.

The advantages of data recovery include the following:

- You can use it with EFS even if you do not have a CA or a PKI infrastructure.

- Manage data recovery policies centrally by means of Active Directory.

- Users do not have to manage certificates or private keys for data recovery.

The disadvantages of data recovery include the following:

- An administrative process must recover user data. Users cannot recover their own data.

- You cannot define the scope of what data the data recovery agent can or cannot recover.

- Data recovery occurs manually on a file-by-file basis.

- Only data is recovered, not the user keys. Therefore, after data recovery is completed, the user must reenroll for new certificates.

- It is assumed that, when a key is lost, the certificate is compromised. Therefore, administrators must revoke old certificates.

- Stand-alone workstations or workstations in non–Active Directory environments cannot be centrally managed.

Key Archival and Recovery

Key recovery is a process that allows a trusted agent to gain access to user private keys that have been archived on a CA. The advantages of key recovery include the following:

- Existing certificates do not have to be revoked.

- After a key recovery, users do not have to reenroll for certificates or change security settings as they would after data recovery.

- Users do not have to recover any data or e-mail due to lost private keys.

- All data encrypted by means of a public key in a certificate can be recovered after a private key has been recovered.

- Windows Server 2003 does not accept signing keys for archival and recovery.

The disadvantages of key recovery include the following:

- Administrators and users must perform user key recovery manually.

- Key recovery allows administrative access to the private keys of users.

- Key recovery does not work with hardware security tokens such as smart cards.

- Key recovery lessens non-repudiation assurance.

To enable key recovery, complete the following tasks:

1. **Configure the key recovery agent template** Before you configure a key recovery agent certificate, you must decide which users or groups can have Read and Enroll permissions on the key recovery agent certificate template. By default, only an Enterprise Administrator or a Domain Administrator can request a key recovery agent certificate. If you choose to change these defaults, configure the new Read and Enroll permissions on the template itself.

2. **Configure the CA to allow key archiving**   You must mark the keys as exportable to enable the key recovery agent to export the private keys from the local store of the workstation to a floppy disk or other medium for safe storage. It is also best to protect the key recovery agent certificate private key with a strong password requirement. You can use a smart card as a key recovery agent. The default key recovery agent certificate template requires manual approval of requests for key recovery agent certificates. It is best if a certificate manager manually approves all key recovery agent certificate requests. The certificate manager might choose to use fewer key recovery agents than the number of available key recovery agent certificates. In this way, no individual key recovery agent can decrypt all the private keys in the CA database. The CA chooses the key recovery agent certificate randomly as a means to ensure that the key recovery agent selection is not predictable.

3. **Enroll users and archive their keys**   Windows Server 2003 will automatically archive keys when the version 2 certificate template and the CA have been properly configured. Version 1 certificate templates cannot be automatically archived by this process. You can archive only keys generated by means of a Rivest-Shamir-Adleman (RSA)–based CSP. The Digital Signature Standard (DSS) and Diffie-Hellman CSPs are not supported for key archiving.

> **NOTE   Requirements for Key Recovery**   The default templates in Windows Server 2003 do not allow for key archiving. You must create new version 2 templates, which are available only in Windows Server 2003, Enterprise Edition, to support user enrollment with archiving. Therefore, only a Windows Server 2003 Enterprise Edition CA can implement Windows Server 2003 key recovery.

An important aspect of the CA's archival and recovery attributes is that the CA does not hold any information that can be used to decrypt the archived private keys. Decrypting archived private keys requires one of the KRAs' private keys, which is stored in each KRA user's profile. Only public key certificates encrypt the keys needed to gain access to the archived private keys. This ensures that an attacker who compromises the CA cannot compromise the security of the archived keys.

To implement a key archival and recovery strategy successfully in your organization, you must first ensure that you meet the following requirements:

- All certificates that require archiving are based on version 2 certificate templates and have been configured for key archival.

- The issuing CAs are running Windows Server 2003.

- All clients are using Windows XP or Windows Server 2003.

- You are using enterprise CAs and the Windows Server 2003 schema extensions apply to the forest.

> **NOTE**   **Limitations of Using a Windows 2000 Forest**   *You can run an enterprise CA running Windows Server 2003 in a Windows 2000 forest without modifying the schema; however, you will not be able to use version 2 certificate templates. When you run* `adprep.exe /forestprep` *in a Windows 2000 forest, the version 2 templates will be installed the next time you open the certificate templates administration tool.*

Assessing and Mitigating the Risks of Key Archival

The purpose of key archival is to mitigate the risk of lost private keys and lost data, but key archival itself includes some level of risk. Because an attacker with KRA privileges can abuse a recovered private key, you must sacrifice some level of non-repudiation. Certificates and digital signatures can be used for non-repudiation, but if a KRA exists, it is theoretically possible that an attacker acting as the KRA can recover a user's private key and use it to impersonate a user to generate a message. This risk shouldn't necessarily rule out the use of a KRA, but weigh the risk as part of the Security Risk Management Process.

> **NOTE**   **Choosing Keys to Archive**   *Because of the risk of an attacker abusing key recovery, you typically should only archive keys that are used for encryption and therefore required to recover data. Keys used for digital signature do not typically need to be archived, because they can be easily revoked and re-issued.*

Be conscious of the potential for key recovery to be misused. Many companies do not entrust this role to even network administrators because it would give them the ability to decrypt files created by individuals with higher security clearance, such as managers. Many companies use a dedicated user account as the data recovery agent. This account might require a smart card for logon, or it might even be disabled with the password kept in a secure location, such as a safe. Some companies even break the password in half or into thirds and entrust two or three different individuals with knowledge of only part of the password. This strategy ensures that no one individual can activate the data recovery agent.

Beyond requiring collusion, you can reduce the likelihood for abuse of the recovery process by revoking the certificate that is associated with the lost private key immediately after you recover the data. For example, if a laptop computer is stolen and the user has encrypted files on a network share, recover the private key, decrypt the files, and then revoke the certificate. Then issue the user a new certificate so that the user can re-encrypt the files. After you revoke the certificate, the key pair cannot be used for encryption or digital signing purposes. The private key can still be used to decrypt previously encrypted files, but further attempts to encrypt files by using the public key will fail during the certificate validation process.

When planning how you will transport the keys to the original owner, choose a process that does not involve copying the key or sending it across the network. E-mailing the key is a bad idea, as is copying it to a shared folder. A better approach is to *move* the key to a CD-R and physically carry the CD-R to the user. After you move the key to a CD-R, ensure that the original key file is no longer available on the disk by deleting the key permanently (not placing it in the recycle bin). Then obscure the remnants of a file by using a non-Microsoft software tool that overwrites the file's data multiple times to prevent an internal threat from restoring the private key. If you must ship the CD-R or trust another user with transporting the CD-R, encrypt the private key with a non-Microsoft file encryption tool. After copying the private key off the CD-R, destroy the CD-R in a shredder.

SUMMARY

- Private key cryptography provides high levels of security and performance. However, users have to exchange private keys prior to exchanging encrypted messages and the keys might be vulnerable during transmission. Public key cryptography is slower, but the keys are not vulnerable during transmission. Managing the keys is still challenging. PKIs simplify the distribution and management of certificates, which contain public key pairs.

- Not every organization requires a PKI. However, a PKI is the best way to implement many types of countermeasures that you might identify, including IPSec, encrypted e-mail, digital signatures, and 802.1x authentication.

- When you design a PKI, you can choose to use an external service provider or you can use Certificate Services to deploy a PKI internally. Certificate Services CAs can be configured as either stand-alone CAs, or enterprise CAs that are tightly integrated into Active Directory. Environments with a single, unified IT group can probably use a single CA because a single CA can handle an extremely large number of requests. However, you might need to deploy multiple CAs to meet organizational requirements or to provide redundancy.

- There are two main types of CA trust models: the rooted trust model and the network trust model. In addition, you might combine the two models to enable separate organizations to work with each other's certificates in a controlled way. Adding a CA trust creates a vulnerability. Fortunately, you can limit your risk from that vulnerability by using certificate trust lists (CTLs) and qualified subordination.

- Many compromises are caused not by vulnerable technologies, but by weaknesses in procedures. To reduce your risks, carefully design procedures for issuing, renewing, revoking, archiving, and recovering certificates.

REVIEW QUESTIONS

1. Which of the following scenarios would use public key encryption to keep a message sent from User A to User B private?

    a. User A encrypts a message with User B's public key.

    b. User A encrypts a message with User A's public key.

    c. User B encrypts a message with User B's private key.

    d. User B encrypts a message with User A's public key.

2. Which of the following is a feature unique to enterprise CAs?

    a. Web enrollment.

    b. Certificate autoenrollment.

    c. Certificates can be revoked.

    d. Certificates can be renewed prior to their expiration date.

3. You are a certificate manager for your company's PKI. You are review-ing enrollment methods and have determined that you will implement three methods for certificate enrollment: Web-based enrollment, MMC enrollment by using the Certificate Request Wizard, and autoenroll-ment. Under what circumstances must you use Web-based enrollment to perform certificate enrollment? (Choose all that apply.)

    a. When enrolling certificates that are issued by an enterprise CA

    b. When performing enrollment from computers running Windows 95 or Windows 98

    c. When enrolling certificates that are issued by a stand-alone CA

    d. When performing enrollment from computers running Windows 2000

    e. When enrolling for certificates that are issued by a CA on comput-ers running Windows 2000

4. How many CAs will you need to support 100,000 certificates?

    a. One

    b. Two

    c. Three

    d. Four

5. Which of the following is an advantage of using an external CA managed by a PKI service provider?

    a. Complete control over how CAs are issued

    b. No per-certificate charges

    c. Reduced liability in the event of a compromise

    d. Ability to use autoenrollment

6. Which of the following conditions would require you to use a stand-alone CA instead of an enterprise CA?

    a. You must use Certificate Services on a domain controller.

    b. No Active Directory is available.

    c. You must use autoenrollment to issue certificates.

    d. You must use cross-certificates to trust certificates issued by a partner's CA.

7. Which of the following operating systems supports autoenrollment for user certificates? (Choose all that apply.)

    a. Windows Millennium Edition (Windows Me)

    b. Windows 2000 Professional

    c. Windows XP Home Edition

    d. Windows XP Professional

    e. Windows Server 2003

8. What are some of the ways you would limit the risk of a root CA being compromised?

9. Which is more risky, creating a two-way forest trust, or creating a two-way cross-certificate trust between CAs? Discuss this question with the class.

CASE SCENARIOS

Case Scenario 9-1: Providing Protected E-mail for a Small Organization

You are a systems administrator for Coho Vineyard. Your organization is planning to conduct a research project with Coho Winery, a partnering firm. This project will involve users in both organizations' research departments. These users will exchange documents and information by means of e-mail messages. Much of this information is considered secret, so competitors must not be able to access the information. There are approximately 75 users working in the research department.

Coho Winery has expressed some concern about your ability to ensure that all users in its research department will be able to exchange secure e-mail messages with users in the Coho Vineyard research department. You must present Coho

Winery with a plan that illustrates how you will address these concerns. In particular, they want to know how you will meet the following requirements:

- Users in the Coho Winery research department must be able to send secure e-mail messages.

- Users who leave the Coho Winery research department must no longer be able to send secure e-mail messages.

- Security requirements relating to e-mail might need to change from time to time.

1. How will you ensure that users in the Coho Winery research department can send secure e-mail messages?

   a. Configure a stand-alone CA and instruct users to enroll for user certificates by using the Web enrollment tool.

   b. Configure an enterprise CA and use a certificate template to issue certificates automatically that support S/MIME to the domain users group.

   c. Configure an enterprise CA and use a certificate template to issue certificates that support EFS to the research group.

   d. Configure a stand-alone CA and instruct users to perform advanced certificate requests by using the Web enrollment tool.

2. How will you ensure that when users leave the Coho Winery research department they are no longer able to send secure e-mail messages?

   a. Configure a Group Policy setting to delete certificates from the local computer when the certificates are revoked.

   b. Create a group that has been denied the Read permission on the certificate template that the certificates were based on. Add users to this group when they leave the research department.

   c. Place a copy of your certificate revocation list on a public Web server that is accessible by users in Coho Winery.

   d. Provide Coho Winery with a copy of each certificate that belongs to a user who has left the research department. Instruct the administrator to place the certificates in the Untrusted Certificates store.

3. How will you reconfigure users in the Coho Winery research department when a new requirement for secure e-mail, such as a longer key, is introduced?

   a. Create a new template with the new parameters. Configure the new template to supersede the old template.

   b. Configure the existing template to contain the longer key length. Configure the template to reenroll all certificate holders.

   c. Create a second template with the new parameters. Deny research users the right to enroll for certificates based on the old template.

   d. Revoke all certificates. Instruct users to enroll for new certificates based on a new template with the longer key length.

Case Scenario 9-2: Planning PKI to Support IPSec

You are a network security designer for Contoso Pharmaceuticals, a publicly traded company with about 10,000 employees. Contoso has offices in Los Angeles, Dallas, Miami, New York City, and Boston, connected via high-speed virtual private networks. Each employee has his or her own computer, and all computers are based on Windows 2000 Professional or Windows XP Professional and participate in a single Active Directory domain.

Recently, during the Security Risk Management Process, you identified the use of IPSec internally as a cost-effective countermeasure to reduce the risk of a threat capturing and analyzing traffic or impersonating a client or server. The first step in deploying IPSec is to deploy a PKI internally to issue the required computer certificates to clients and servers.

You have a meeting with Craig Dewar, your Chief Information Officer (CIO), to allocate resources for the PKI deployment. Craig says:

"Do you listen to the quarterly analyst meetings? Well, if you do, you probably already know that Wall Street is hounding us to control cash flow. A couple of years ago, all they cared about was that we were EBITDA positive, which means we have to make more money than we spend on day-to-day operations. Now, we have to be *cash flow positive*, which means we have to make more money than we spend on day-to-day operations *and* that we invest. So you ask about budget, and my answer is that the budget is as little as possible. We have cash, but we can't really spend it. You want those options we gave you to be worth something, right?"

With your project's budget clarified, you head to a meeting with other engineers to decide on the PKI design. They bring up the following questions.

  1. How many CAs will we need to meet the performance and scalability requirements?

2. How important is it that the PKI be fault tolerant?

3. Given the performance and fault-tolerance requirements, how many total servers do you need for your new PKI?

4. How will you issue the required computer certificates?

5. Will you create an enterprise or a stand-alone CA?

6. Will you use delta CRLs?

CHAPTER 10
PROTECTING INTRANET COMMUNICATIONS

Upon completion of this chapter, you will be able to:

- Use network firewalls and host-based firewalls to provide Internet Protocol (IP) filtering and thereby reduce the risk of software vulnerabilities.

- Use **Internet Protocol Security (IPSec)** to reduce the risk of an attacker capturing confidential, unencrypted communications, and to make man-in-the-middle attacks almost impossible.

- Design wireless network security to reduce the risk of attackers connecting to your intranet.

The majority of your enterprise's confidential communications happen between computers on the *intranet* (the internal network). Unfortunately, most successful compromises also originate from your intranet. Your intranet communications clearly deserve protection.

The simplest countermeasure is to implement IP filtering by using network and host-based firewalls. Whereas your network security can probably benefit by using some of your budget to purchase firewall software, recent versions of Microsoft Windows include host-based firewalls that you can implement without purchasing additional software, and with little administrative time.

Firewalls protect servers from many types of attacks, but they do not protect communications from being captured by an attacker as they cross your intranet. To enable encryption for network communications, use IPSec. IPSec also enables you to authenticate both clients and servers, making man-in-the-middle attacks almost impossible for an attacker. In addition, IPSec includes IP filtering capabilities, enabling you to add another layer of firewalls.

Filtering and IPSec can greatly reduce your intranet vulnerabilities, but most enterprises have another potential weakness: wireless networks. Organizations frequently deploy wireless networks without sufficient security planning. As a result, attackers outside your building may be able to connect to your internal network, anyone within range might compromise private communications, and uninvited guests may abuse your Internet connection. You can reduce these types of risks by enabling encryption and authentication on your public and private wireless networks.

DESIGNING IP FILTERING

Firewalls examine network traffic, forward permitted traffic, and drop potentially dangerous packets. All computers deserve the protection of a firewall, whether it's the thousands of servers and desktops that compose the network of a Fortune 500 company, a traveling salesperson's laptop connecting to the wireless network of a coffee shop, or your grandmother's new PC with a dial-up connection to the Internet. Each of these environments needs different types of firewalls, however. As a security designer, you must be able to choose cost-effective firewall solutions to protect computers and networks.

Firewalls are not impregnable. No firewall, whether a host-based firewall or a several-thousand-dollar enterprise firewall array, will make your computers impervious to attack. Firewalls are merely barriers to attack. By making it difficult for attackers to get into your network, by making them invest much time, you can make your organization less attractive to them. However, it is impossible to prevent every intrusion fully; as long as you must allow legitimate traffic through your firewall, an attacker can misuse the network connection. In addition, all software has bugs, and someone might find an obscure bug in your firewall that allows that person to launch an attack. Briefly, there is no such thing as absolute security. As the Security Risk Management Process teaches, how much you invest in firewalls should be a function of how much you have to lose if an attack is successful.

This section covers the concepts and design of both network firewalls and host-based firewalls (also called personal firewalls).

Types of Firewalls

There are two main types of firewalls: network firewalls and host-based firewalls. Network firewalls, such as software-based Microsoft Internet Security and Acceleration (ISA) Server or the hardware-based Nortel Alteon Switched Firewall (ASF) or the Cisco PIX firewalls, protect the perimeter of a network by watching traffic that enters and leaves. Host-based firewalls, such as Internet Connection Firewall (ICF–included with Windows XP and Microsoft Windows Server 2003) and

Windows Firewall, protect an individual computer regardless of the network to which it's connected. You might need one or the other—but most businesses require a combination of both to meet their security requirements.

Host-Based Firewalls

Host-based firewalls are software firewalls installed on individual computers to protect communications regardless of the network to which the computer connects. Depending on the software you choose, a host-based firewall can offer features beyond those of network firewalls, such as protecting your computer from **spyware** (a component of some software programs that track your Web-browsing habits) and Trojan horses.

Although only home users have traditionally used host-based firewalls, recent trends in security exploits highlight the importance of enterprises using both types of firewalls together. Traditional firewall architectures protect only the perimeter of a network. However, once an attacker penetrates that perimeter, internal systems are completely unprotected. Hybrid worms, in particular, have penetrated enterprise networks through e-mail systems, and then have spread quickly to unprotected internal systems by exploiting vulnerabilities in network services. Figure 10-1 illustrates this process.

① E-mail passes through firewall to bypass client computer

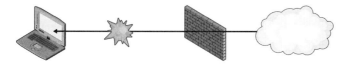

② Virus spreads to servers within internal network using other exploits

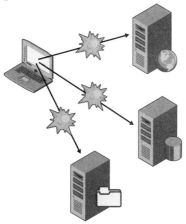

Figure 10-1   Once a virus penetrates an internal network, it might spread quickly.

Installing host-based firewalls on all systems, including those behind the corporate firewall, should now be standard practice. For users traveling with a laptop, a host-based firewall is a necessity—they need protection wherever they connect to the Internet.

Recent Windows client and server operating systems include host-based firewalls—Windows XP and Windows Server 2003 shipped with ICF. When you install Service Pack 2 on Windows XP or Service Pack 1 on Windows Server 2003, the patch upgrades ICF to the easier-to-use Windows Firewall. Earlier versions of Windows include some packet-filtering capabilities, but nothing robust enough to be considered a firewall.

> **NOTE Packet Filtering with IPSec**   Although the primary purpose of IPSec is to ensure the integrity of hosts and to encrypt traffic, IPSec also provides limited host-based firewall capabilities. This is extremely important with versions of Windows released prior to Windows XP. However, Windows XP and Windows Server 2003 include ICF and can be upgraded to Windows Firewall, both of which provide more powerful stateful packet filtering than IPSec. If you must maintain versions of Windows released before Windows XP and you do not have the budget for a non-Microsoft host-based firewall, consider using IPSec.

Because Windows Firewall inspects all incoming communications, some programs, especially e-mail programs, might behave differently when Windows Firewall is enabled. Some e-mail programs periodically poll their e-mail server for new mail, and some e-mail programs wait for notification from the e-mail server.

Outlook Express, for example, automatically checks for new e-mail when its timer tells it to do so. When new e-mail is present, Outlook Express prompts the user with a new e-mail notification. Windows Firewall will not affect the behavior of this program because the request for new e-mail notification originates from inside the firewall. The firewall makes an entry in a table noting the outbound communication. When the mail server acknowledges the new e-mail response, the firewall finds an associated entry in the table and allows the communication to pass, and then the user receives notification that a new e-mail message has arrived.

Microsoft Outlook 2000, however, is connected to a computer running Microsoft Exchange Server that uses a remote procedure call (RPC) to send new e-mail notifications to clients. Outlook 2000 does not automatically check for new e-mail when it's connected to a computer running Exchange Server. Exchange Server notifies Outlook 2000 when new e-mail arrives. Because Exchange Server (which is outside the firewall) initiates the RPC notification, Windows Firewall does not identify the connection as allowed, and it drops the RPC notification. Users can send and receive e-mail, but cannot be notified automatically of new messages.

> **IMPORTANT** **Firewalls and Antivirus Software** Host-based firewalls do not replace antivirus software. You need both.

Popular host-based firewall products include ZoneAlarm, Tiny Personal Firewall, Agnitum Outpost Firewall, Kerio Personal Firewall, and BlackICE PC Protection from Internet Security Systems. Most host-based firewall software is available in free or trial versions, so it will not cost you anything to download these packages and determine whether they meet your needs better than Windows Firewall.

Network Firewalls

Network firewalls protect an entire network by guarding the perimeter of that network. Network firewalls forward traffic to and from computers on an internal network and filter that traffic based on the criteria the administrator has set. Network firewalls come in two flavors: hardware firewalls and software firewalls. Hardware-based network firewalls are generally less expensive than software-based network firewalls (when you factor in the computer hardware and configuration effort required for software-based network firewalls), and are the right choice for home users and many small businesses.

Software-based network firewalls often have a larger feature set than hardware-based firewalls, and might fit the needs of larger organizations. Software-based firewalls can also run on the same server as other services, such as e-mail and file sharing, allowing small organizations to make better use of existing servers. Network firewalls often include additional features that are not necessary for host-based firewalls, such as caching Web requests issued by multiple computers, and generating reports on network bandwidth usage.

Types of Packet Filtering

Although the primary task of any firewall is to filter network communications, different types of firewalls do it in different ways. Almost every firewall supports the most basic of packet-filtering capabilities: stateful inspection. More-advanced firewalls also support Application Layer filtering, which looks inside the data portion of packets to filter traffic based on the content of a request. The sections that follow discuss the differences between basic packet filtering, stateful inspection, and application layer filtering.

Basic Packet Filtering

By default, most firewalls block everything that you have not specifically allowed. Routers with filtering capabilities are a simplified example of a firewall. Administrators often configure them to allow all outbound connections from the internal network but to block all incoming connections. A user on the internal network would be able to download e-mail without a problem, but an administrator would need to customize the router configuration to allow users to connect to their work computers from their homes by using Remote Desktop.

You use packet filters to instruct a firewall to drop traffic that meets certain criteria. For example, you could create a filter that would drop all ping requests. You can also configure filters with more-complex exceptions to a rule. For example, a filter might assist with troubleshooting the firewall by allowing the firewall to respond to ping requests coming from a monitoring station's IP address. By default, ISA Server does not respond to ping queries on its external interface. You would need to create a packet filter on the computer running ISA Server for it to respond to a ping request.

The following are the main Transmission Control Protocol/Internet Protocol (TCP/IP) attributes used in implementing filtering rules:

- Source IP addresses

- Destination IP addresses

- IP protocol

- Source TCP and UDP ports

- Destination TCP and UDP ports

- The interface at which the packet arrives

- The interface to which the packet is destined

If you have configured the firewall to allow all traffic by default, you can use filters to block specific traffic. If you have configured the firewall to deny all traffic, filters allow only specific traffic through. A common packet-filtering configuration is to allow inbound Domain Name System (DNS) requests from the Internet so that a DNS service can respond.

Some types of firewalls (including Windows Firewall, but not Internet Connection Firewall) can filter traffic based on source or destination IP address. Filtering based on source or destination address (known as *source filtering* or *destination filtering*) is useful because it enables you to allow or deny traffic based on the computers or networks that are sending or receiving the traffic. This allows administrators to disable instant messaging from the computer in one organization, while allowing the same protocol from a different set of computers.

Source filtering also allows you to give greater access to users on internal networks than those on external networks. It's common to use a firewall to block all requests sent to an internal e-mail server except for those requests from users on the internal network. You can also use source filtering to block all requests from a specific address, for example, to block traffic from an IP address identified as having attacked the network.

> **IMPORTANT   Blocking Internet Control Message Protocol (ICMP) Traffic**   Most people block ICMP traffic to make it more difficult to find hosts on a network and protect against ICMP-based denial-of-service (DoS) attacks. When designing IP filtering to block ICMP traffic, keep in mind that such a policy might cause services and tools that rely on ICMP to measure network response times to produce misleading results. For example, Windows 2000 and Windows XP domain members have an IP/DNS-compatible locator, which measures ICMP response times for domain controller load balancing within a site. In addition, Group Policy measures ICMP response times to determine if the connection to the domain controller is a slow link. Tools that depend on ICMP, such as Tracert, will not work when ICMP traffic is blocked.

Stateful Inspection

Stateful inspection is a firewall feature that enables the firewall to keep track of all valid connections and drop all packets that are not part of an existing session. In a typical configuration where a firewall is protecting a private network, stateful inspection enables the firewall to remember requests from clients on the private network that are sent to the Internet. When the firewall receives packets addressed from the Internet to clients on the private network, the firewall first checks if the packet is part of an existing connection. If it is, it forwards the packet to the client on the private network. If it is not, it drops the packet.

> **NOTE   Proxy Servers and NAT**   Proxy servers and firewalls that support Network Address Translation (NAT) always provide stateful inspection.

In addition to maintaining the conversation based on IP addresses and ports, firewalls also check the TCP flags, the sequence and acknowledgment numbers within the TCP header fields for TCP conversations. The flags represent the state of the conversation, whether it is the beginning of a conversation (SYN), the middle of a conversation (ACK), or the end of the conversation (FIN). If any of the flags are out of sequence, the stateful firewall blocks the connection. The sequence and acknowledgment fields provide the information to ensure that the next packet received in the conversation is the correct one. Once again, any request that does not fit the state of the conversation is blocked.

Application-Layer Filtering

Application-layer firewalls can examine packets on a deeper level than firewalls that support only basic packet filtering or stateful inspection. Application-layer firewalls can allow or deny traffic based on the content. For example, basic packet filtering could allow you to drop all Simple Mail Transfer Protocol (SMTP) traffic. An application-layer firewall could block SMTP requests that contain viruses. Similarly, whereas basic packet filtering could drop every packet except for valid Hypertext Transport Protocol (HTTP) requests, an application-layer firewall could go a step further and drop all requests except for valid HTTP requests for files with a .HTM extension. In this way, an application-layer firewall could protect a Web server from attacks that target .PL, .ASP, or .ASPX files.

> **NOTE**   **Application-Layer Firewall Capabilities**   You can tell any firewall to "Drop all Web requests" or "Allow all Web requests." You can tell an application-layer firewall to "Allow *some* Web requests."

Host-based firewalls with application-layer filtering, often used to block objectionable Web content based on keywords contained in the Web pages, are a form of application-layer firewall. You also use application-layer firewalls to inspect packets bound for an internal Web server to ensure that the request is not really an attack in disguise.

Currently, the ability to inspect a packet's contents is one of the best ways to distinguish between firewall products. ICF and Windows Firewall currently lack application-layer filtering. However, most business-oriented firewalls do include this capability.

ISA Server is an application-level proxy that is able to read data within packets for a particular application and perform an action based on a rule set. In addition, ISA Server comes with predefined application filters that inspect each packet and block, redirect, or modify the data within the packet. For instance, you can implement Web-routing rules that tell the computer running ISA Server to redirect an HTTP request to a certain internal computer running Microsoft Internet Information Server (IIS), based on the URL in the packet. Another example is the DNS intrusion detection filter. This filter blocks packets that are not valid DNS requests, or that fit common types of DNS attacks. You can invoke application filtering on ISA Server when Web Publishing or Server Publishing is configured.

Firewall Auditing

Firewalls do not prevent attacks; they simply reduce the likelihood of a break-in. When you deploy a firewall, you will still get just as many attacks as you always did—you just won't have to worry about them as much. All firewalls provide some capability for logging these attacks for later, manual review. This allows administrators to watch for attacks that are out of the ordinary. It is also useful for forensics purposes. If an attacker does manage to defeat your firewall, you can refer to the firewall's log and gather information to determine how the attacker carried out the attack. This log can be useful to law enforcement officials if they are involved in a related investigation.

Auditing and intrusion detection capabilities are two of the features that different firewall products use to distinguish themselves. With the host-based firewalls built into Windows XP and Windows Server 2003, the best you can do for auditing and intrusion detection is to review a text file filled with a list of dropped packets. Unfortunately, even on quiet, private networks, host-based firewalls will drop a great deal of non-malicious traffic. This makes distinguishing between malicious attacks and innocent traffic impractical. Figure 10-2 shows a portion of an audit log file generated by Windows Firewall running on a computer located on a private network protected by a perimeter firewall. The log file shows only innocent traffic; there are no malicious attacks shown in this file.

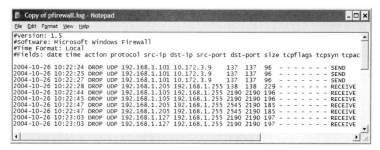

Figure 10-2   Windows Firewall logs dropped packets, but identifying actual attacks is almost impossible.

Even though it is almost impossible to monitor firewall audit logs manually to detect attacks in progress, log dropped packets and archive them as long as possible. Although you probably won't identify an attack by using these logs, if you discover a compromise, you will want to examine the log files to determine how the attacker compromised the computer. For example, Figure 10-3 shows that an attacker at the IP address 192.168.1.103 performed a port scan on TCP ports 3012 to 3022. Port scans are a common technique for identifying holes in a firewall.

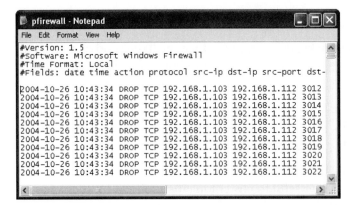

Figure 10-3   Audit logs can be useful for reactively identifying methods used prior to a compromise.

Using a Screened Subnet

One of the most practical uses for a network firewall is to create a **screened subnet**, also known as a demilitarized zone (DMZ). A screened subnet provides users on the Internet with limited access to some internal servers, while still providing protection for users and servers on the private network. Most organizations use their Internet connection to expose services to the Internet. At a minimum, SMTP services are exposed to allow inbound e-mail. You can use filtering and port forwarding to allow this traffic through a firewall, but many organizations require a DMZ to further protect the internal network. This section discusses how to secure your DMZ—the area in which you typically place your servers that expose public services to provide the best security.

A DMZ consists of public servers, private servers, and two layers of firewalls. The first layer of firewalls protects the public servers from the public network. The second layer of firewalls filters traffic between the private network and the public servers. A screened subnet provides a multilayer protection system between the Internet and the internal network of an organization.

Figure 10-4 and Figure 10-5 show screened subnet configurations common in corporate environments today. Both provide excellent protection for the internal network. Figure 10-4 shows a simple configuration in which one firewall filters traffic for both the screened subnet and the private network. In this configuration, the firewall is configured as a "three-legged firewall" because it connects to three subnets: the screened subnet, the private network, and the Internet.

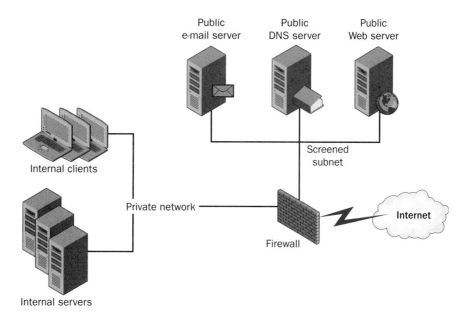

Figure 10-4   Use a three-legged firewall to create a screened subnet with a single firewall.

Figure 10-5 shows a configuration that provides defense-in-depth by using two separate layers of firewalls. Each of these layers of firewalls ideally would be based on different hardware and software, requiring an attacker to identify different vulnerabilities for each layer to penetrate the private network. In Figure 10-5, the external firewall is a hardware-based firewall, whereas the internal firewall is a software-based firewall.

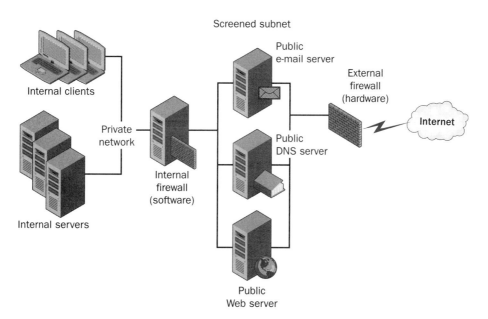

Figure 10-5   Use two layers of firewalls to provide defense-in-depth (at a higher cost).

The external firewall filters requests from the Internet, allowing only those requests directed to one of the services running in the screened subnet. The internal firewall blocks all incoming requests, and allows only requests originating from the internal network to the Internet. For example, the internal firewall would allow users on the internal network to browse the Web, but would not allow requests from users on the Internet to enter the internal network. This limits the damage possibly caused by an attacker who manages to compromise a server in the screened subnet, because the attacker cannot easily use the compromised server to launch attacks on the internal network.

Depending on your needs, you might choose to configure the internal firewall to allow some incoming requests from servers in the screened subnet. For example, if a Web server in the screened subnet provides Internet users with information about inventory available for sale on the Web site, the Web server may have to issue requests to a database server located on the internal network. The internal firewall must be configured to allow requests between the Web server and the database server, but not to allow requests from the Web server to other computers on the internal network. This configuration enables the Web server to access data stored in the database, while protecting the database from direct access from the Internet.

DESIGNING IPSEC

Firewalls can distinguish between traffic that is probably legitimate and traffic that is potentially dangerous. By filtering potentially dangerous traffic, firewalls reduce the risk of attackers that actively send malicious traffic to your computer. However, firewalls do not mitigate the risk of attackers who passively capture traffic on your network and analyze that captured traffic to identify user names and passwords or extract confidential information. To mitigate that risk, you need IPSec.

IPSec adds security features to TCP/IP, which is extraordinarily vulnerable to attack. For two hosts to communicate via TCP/IP, their communications might be passed among as many as dozens of different network devices and, in the case of the Internet, the sender of the message has no control over who owns the network equipment that carries the messages. Without the use of IPSec, there is ample opportunity for an attacker to eavesdrop on your private communications.

Unprotected TCP/IP communications are also easy to impersonate and manipulate. When a computer receives an unprotected TPC/IP message, the computer has no way of determining whether the IP address in the message is genuine or was modified in transit. This makes TCP/IP vulnerable to such attacks as the man-in-the-middle attack, which an attacker can use to compromise private data and user credentials.

IPSec is a newer protocol suite that works with TCP/IP to verify the integrity of communications, authenticate computers, and encrypt traffic. When implemented, IPSec dramatically reduces the risk of several common kinds of attacks. Windows Server 2003, in addition to other recent versions of Windows, include IPSec capabilities. However, understanding, planning, and configuring an IPSec infrastructure is a complex task. This section teaches you the fundamentals of IPSec, provides you with information for planning an IPSec deployment, and familiarizes you with the tools used to configure IPSec.

IPSec Fundamentals

IPSec in Windows Server 2003 protects networks from active and passive attacks by securing IP packets through packet filtering, cryptography, and the enforcement of trusted communication. IPSec is useful for improving the privacy and integrity of host-to-host, host-to-network, and network-to-network communications. IPSec can also be used as a host-based firewall to harden clients and servers by using packet filtering.

This section discusses the universal, fundamental aspects of IPSec. The information in this lesson definitely applies to computers running Windows Server 2003 and other Windows-based computers. However, it also accurately represents how UNIX, Linux, and other computers would implement the IPSec standards.

IPSec Overview

IPSec is a framework of open standards for helping to ensure private, secure communications over IP networks through cryptographic security services. IPSec supports network-level data integrity, data confidentiality, data origin authentication, and replay protection. Because IPSec is integrated at the Network layer (layer 3) of the Open System Interconnection (OSI) model, it provides security for almost all protocols in the TCP/IP suite and, because IPSec is applied transparently to applications, there is no need to configure separate security for each application that uses TCP/IP.

NOTE *Review: OSI Model* *The OSI model is a seven-layer model that describes the roles of the different protocols used in network communications. These layers are as follows:*

7. *Application—High-level protocols that applications interact directly with, such as HTTP, used for Web communications, and Common Internet File System (CIFS), used for file sharing.*

6. *Presentation—In theory, this layer translates data into different formats, such as adding or removing encryption. In practice, network protocols are not implemented at this layer.*

5. *Session—In theory, this layer handles long-lasting conversations between computers that may initiate several different connections. In practice, network protocols are not implemented at this layer.*

4. *Transport—Protocols that allow for persistent and reliable communications between hosts such as TCP and UDP.*

3. *Network—Routable protocols, such as IP, IPSec, and ICMP.*

2. *Data Link—Non-routable protocols used on a single network segment such as Ethernet.*

1. *Physical—Standards for cabling and electrical transmissions.*

IPSec can be used to provide packet filtering, to encrypt and authenticate traffic between two hosts, and to create a virtual private network (VPN). Using these capabilities of IPSec helps to provide protection against the following:

- Network-based denial-of-service attacks from untrusted computers

- Data corruption

- Data theft

- User-credential theft

- Administrative control of servers, other computers, and the network

Besides simply improving security, IPSec can be used to save money. With IPSec, remote offices and remote-access clients can communicate across the Internet without the risk of sending unprotected communications. This can be implemented with much lower cost than using dedicated circuits that offer privacy at the physical level.

MORE INFO *IPSec* *This chapter provides a basic overview of IPSec's functionality. If you want to know the details, and you have the spare time, read the following Requests For Comments (RFC): 3457, 3456, 3281, 3193, 2857, 2709, 2451, and approximately 22 more. You can obtain copies at http://www.ietf.org.*

Securing Host-to-Host Communications

You can use IPSec to encrypt and validate the integrity of communications between two computers. For example, IPSec can protect traffic between domain controllers in different sites, between Web servers and database servers, or between Web clients and Web servers. When an IPSec client attempts to initiate a connection to an IPSec server, the client and server negotiate IPSec integrity and encryption protocols. After the IPSec connection is established, the application's data is transported within the IPSec connection.

For example, consider the common scenario of a user downloading e-mail from a server using Post Office Protocol version 3 (POP3). If IPSec is not enabled, the e-mail client software initiates a connection directly to the e-mail server software. The user name and password are transmitted in clear text, so that anyone with a protocol analyzer such as Network Monitor can intercept the user's credentials. An attacker who has control of a router can modify the contents of the user's e-mail messages as they download, without being detected.

Now consider the same scenario with IPSec enabled. In this case, when the server receives the POP3 request from the e-mail client, it sends a message back to the client requesting an IPSec connection. The client agrees, and IPSec negotiates encryption and integrity protocols. Then IPSec on the client computer intercepts the e-mail client's network traffic, stores it within encrypted IPSec packets, and sends the data to the server using TCP/IP. IPSec on the server receives the packets, decrypts the contents, and passes the e-mail client's original communication to the e-mail server software.

In this IPSec-enabled scenario, neither the e-mail client nor the e-mail server software is aware that IPSec protected the communications. In a similar way, routers and firewalls between the client and server cannot modify the communications or extract the user's credentials. In fact, the routers and firewalls cannot even determine that the user is downloading e-mail, because the POP3 protocol is completely hidden within the IPSec packets.

IPSec can operate in two different modes: transport mode and tunnel mode. Use transport mode to protect host-to-host communications. In **transport mode**, IPSec tunnels traffic starting at the transport layer, also known as Layer 4. Therefore, IPSec in transport mode can encrypt the UDP/TCP protocol header and the original data, but the IP header itself is unprotected.

IPSec transports an application's data by adding an IPSec header and trailer to outgoing packets. Depending on the IPSec protocol used, the original contents of the outgoing packets are encrypted. Figure 10-6 shows IPSec's position in the packet when functioning in transport mode. The diagram shows IPSec using the Encapsulating Security Payload (ESP). ESP is the more common of two IPSec protocols because it provides both authentication and encryption.

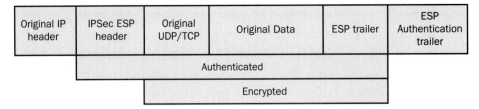

Original IP header	IPSec ESP header	Original UDP/TCP	Original Data	ESP trailer	ESP Authentication trailer
	Authenticated				
		Encrypted			

Figure 10-6   Use IPSec's transport mode to protect host-to-host communications.

In the past, IPSec traffic could not pass from a privately numbered network to a publicly numbered network through a NAT server such as a firewall or proxy server. IPSec could not deal with having the NAT server change the source and destination IP address—to IPSec, this translation was tampering with the packet, and IPSec would reject the packet. IPSec **NAT Traversal (NAT-T)** allows IPSec traffic to pass through compatible NAT servers. However, both the IPSec hosts and the NAT server must support NAT-T, and the NAT server must be configured to allow traffic on UDP port 4500. Windows Server 2003, Windows XP Professional, and Windows 2000 support NAT-T as IPSec clients. ISA Server and Windows Server 2003 support NAT-T as a firewall.

For more information about NAT-T, refer to RFC 3193.

> **NOTE   Planning for NAT-T**   Are you planning to use IPSec to authenti-
> cate or encrypt communications between a private and public network?
> Make sure your NAT server supports NAT-T. If not, factor the cost of
> upgrading into the cost of deploying IPSec.

Securing Host-to-Network Communications

IPSec is used often to authenticate and encrypt traffic sent directly between two hosts. However, IPSec can also protect traffic traveling from a single host to an entire network, as illustrated in Figure 10-7. This is used most commonly in remote-access scenarios. In the past, many organizations required users to dial in to remote-access servers connected to the organization's private network. Today, organizations can eliminate the cost of maintaining dial-in servers by using IPSec to allow remote users to connect to an organization's private network across the Internet. Most security experts agree that IPSec provides a level of security similar to that of dial-up remote access.

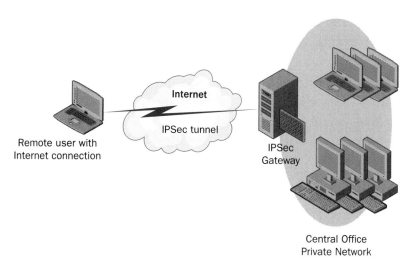

Figure 10-7   IPSec can protect communications between a host and an entire network.

As you recall, when you protect traffic sent directly between two hosts, you usually use IPSec transport mode. When you protect traffic between a host and a network, or between two networks, you must use IPSec **tunnel mode**. Although transport mode stores the UDP/TCP header and the application data between an IPSec header and trailer, tunnel mode stores the entire original packet, as shown in Figure 10-8. The IP header, including the source and destination addresses, must be stored within the IPSec packet because the traffic is destined for a computer other than the computer to which the IPSec connection was established.

NOTE   The Difference between Tunnel and Transport Modes   It is important that you understand when to use tunnel mode and when to use transport mode. Use transport mode when you communicate with one computer; use tunnel mode when you need to be able to communicate with an entire network. If an exam question asks about encapsulating or tunneling the IP header, that's a clue that it's referring to tunnel mode.

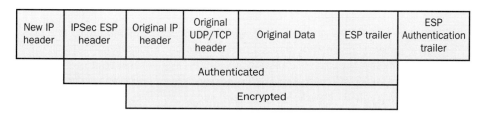

Figure 10-8   Tunnel mode IPSec stores the entire original packet, including IP headers.

Once again, consider the scenario of a remote user retrieving e-mail from a mail server on a private network. When the user's e-mail client attempts to initiate a connection to the mail server's IP address, IPSec on the client computer detects that traffic is being sent to a network that must be accessed by using IPSec tunnel mode. The client's IPSec then establishes an IPSec connection to the IPSec gateway that provides access to the internal network.

IPSec then encapsulates the entire packet generated by the e-mail client, including the source and destination IP address, the TCP header, and the application's data. IPSec adds a new IP header with the destination address of the IPSec gateway. The IPSec gateway will decrypt the packet, restoring the packet to the original condition it was in when sent by the e-mail client. The original IP header is restored too, including the original source and destination IP addresses. Finally, the IPSec gateway forwards the packet to the mail server.

As with transport mode, the e-mail client is not aware that IPSec protected the communications. Unlike with transport mode, the mail server's operating system also is unaware that IPSec was in use because the IPSec gateway removed the IPSec header and trailer before forwarding the packets to the private network.

NOTE **The Risk of Traffic Analysis** If hosts on two networks are communicating across the Internet and all clients are IPSec enabled, transport mode can be used to encrypt traffic between individual hosts, or tunnel mode can be used to encrypt all traffic sent between the two networks. Naturally, tunnel mode is more convenient because it does not require every host to have IPSec enabled—but which is more secure?

Tunnel mode is more secure than transport mode, in theory. Remember, VPNs protect against an attacker trying to capture your traffic, analyze it, and use the information gathered to do something malicious. Imagine that an attacker is capturing IPSec-encrypted packets as they travel between the private networks of two competing businesses. If tunnel mode is used, all the attacker can determine is how much traffic passes between the networks, and when it is being sent. This information might be useful because the attacker might be able to guess that a sudden increase in traffic volume is occurring because of an impending merger between the companies, and then use that information to buy some stock and make an illegal profit.

If transport mode is used, attackers can analyze the total volume of traffic being sent, just as they could with tunnel mode. However, they can also analyze the shape of traffic sent between hosts within the network. By analyzing the shape, they might be able to determine the internal IP addresses of Web and e-mail servers and build a partial map of the private network. Even though they cannot see the encrypted contents of the packets, they can examine the lengths of the packets and the communications patterns. Web traffic, for example, can be recognized even when encrypted because Web browsers send multiple, short requests to a Web server, which returns multiple, longer responses containing the files that make up a Web page. Attackers analyzing the shape of traffic can also identify e-mail servers, backup servers, and domain controllers.

Now, even if an attacker does manage to capture and analyze your traffic, would this information really be useful? Probably not, but some organizations use this possibility as a justification to avoid VPNs, so it is important to understand the risk.

Securing Network-to-Network Communications

IPSec can also be used to connect two remote networks. Before Internet connectivity was common, remote offices were connected with private links provided by communications companies. These links typically would consist of a circuit (such as a T1 in the United States or an E1 in Europe) from each of the remote offices that connected to a switched frame relay network that would carry the traffic over long distances.

Today, many organizations still use private links to connect offices. Private links offer some distinct advantages, most notably predictability and stability. Although the Internet continues to become more reliable, performance factors such as usable bandwidth, latency, and jitter fluctuate unpredictably. Private links dedicate bandwidth to a communication link and always follow the same path—guaranteeing that performance will always stay the same.

IPSec can connect two remote offices across the Internet, providing the same connectivity as a private link using an existing Internet connection. IPSec uses authentication and encryption to reduce the risk of traffic interception; a private link relies on physical security to reduce the risk of eavesdropping. For many, the security provided by IPSec and private links is similar enough that the additional cost of a private link cannot be justified.

However, IPSec does nothing to stabilize the Internet's available bandwidth or latency, or to improve its reliability. When two offices connect using IPSec across the Internet, both offices lease links to a local Internet service provider (ISP). Then administrators at both offices establish an encrypted IPSec tunnel between IPSec gateways located at each office, as shown in Figure 10-9. To the clients on both networks, the gateways act like standard routers. The clients do not need to support IPSec to make use of the tunnel.

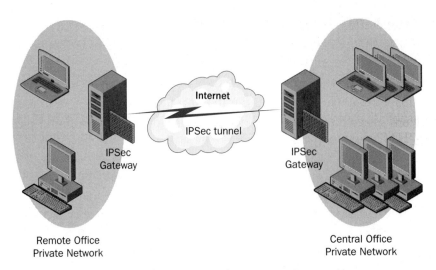

Figure 10-9   IPSec can support network-to-network tunnels.

Although both ends of the tunnel can be servers running Windows Server 2003, they do not have to be. IPSec is a set of Internet standards supported by a wide variety of operating systems and network devices. One or both of the IPSec tunnel endpoints can be non-Microsoft firewalls, network devices, Windows 2000-based servers, or UNIX/Linux servers.

Authentication Header and Encapsulating Security Payload

IPSec can use two protocols: **Authentication Header (AH)** and **Encapsulating Security Payload (ESP)**. The protocols can be used either separately or together. AH provides data origin authentication, data integrity, and anti-replay protection for the entire packet, including the IP header and the data payload carried in the packet. Naturally, AH does not provide protection for the fields in the IP header that are allowed to change in transit, such as the hop count. AH does not encrypt data, which means it does not provide privacy. Attackers can read the contents of packets if they can intercept them, but the packets cannot be modified.

ESP is used more commonly than AH because it provides data origin authentication, data integrity, anti-replay protection, and the option of privacy. Although AH and ESP can be used together, you will use ESP alone in most circumstances. Choose AH over ESP only when the data and header in the packet need to be protected from modification and authentication but not encrypted. You might do this if you have an intrusion detection system, firewall, or quality of service (QoS) router that needs to inspect the contents of the packet. Otherwise, take advantage of the privacy provided by encryption and use ESP. If IPSec traffic must traverse a NAT server, you must use ESP because ESP is the only IPSec protocol that supports NAT-T.

Planning an IPSec Infrastructure

You can enable IPSec for your entire domain with a few mouse clicks—but it would not be wise. If configured incorrectly, IPSec can cause minor problems, such as a network application that performs poorly, or major problems, such as total loss of network connectivity. Only careful planning can ensure the success of an IPSec deployment. That planning involves choosing an authentication method, deciding how to manage IPSec's integration with Active Directory directory service, and devising a testing procedure to validate application compatibility with your planned IPSec configuration.

Active Directory Considerations

To manage large numbers of computers consistently, it is best to distribute IPSec policies by using Group Policy objects. Although you can assign local IPSec policies to computers that are not members of a trusted domain, distributing IPSec policies and managing IPSec policy configuration and trust relationships is much more time-consuming for computers that are not domain members.

Another advantage of using Active Directory–based IPSec policy is that you can delegate permissions on the IP Security Policies On Active Directory container to enable specific administrators to manage IPSec throughout your organization. These administrators do not necessarily need permissions to directly manage the individual computers that receive the IPSec policy, however. This capability is vital to organizations that divide responsibility for security tasks between various groups.

To delegate permissions on the IP Security Policies container, use an Active Directory editing tool such as ADSI Edit. ADSI Edit is a Windows support tool that uses the Active Directory Service Interfaces (ADSI). Install the Windows support tools from the \Support\Tools folder on the Windows 2000 Server and Windows Server 2003 operating system CDs.

An IPSec policy administrator typically requires Write access to all IPSec policy objects. Do not attempt to assign permissions to individual IPSec policies. If many administrators in your organization want to manage Active Directory–based IPSec policy, channel all IPSec changes through existing Domain Admins. The individuals making the changes to IPSec policy can configure local IPSec policy on a computer in a lab environment, and then use IP Security Policy Management to export an IPSec policy file for the domain administrator or another delegated administrator. The Domain Admin can then import the IPSec policy file into the IP Security Policies On Active Directory container. This practice minimizes the number of administrators who can modify IPSec policy, which decreases the risk of human error negatively affecting IPSec policy.

Authentication for IPSec

Peer authentication is the process of ensuring that an IPSec peer is the computer it claims to be. By using peer authentication, IPSec can determine whether to allow communications with another computer before the communication begins. You can choose from three authentication methods: Kerberos v5, public key certificates, and preshared keys.

If you have deployed a Windows 2000 Server or Windows Server 2003 Active Directory environment and all hosts using IPSec are part of that domain (or a member of a trusted domain), use Kerberos. If you are communicating with outside organizations and your partners use a Web-based certification authority (CA), you can use public key certificates. If neither of these methods is available, you can use a preshared key.

You can mix and match authentication methods as needed. For example, you can configure your public Web server to authenticate internal clients by using Kerberos and external clients by using public key certificates. After you configure IPSec, it will compare the source IP address of the remote host against an IPSec policy rule to determine which authentication method to use.

Kerberos v5 Authentication   Kerberos v5 is the default authentication standard in Windows Server 2003 and Windows 2000 domains. Any computer in the domain or a trusted domain can use this method of authentication. Kerberos is the most natural form of IPSec authentication; configuration is straightforward and simple. However, there are a couple of important considerations.

First, earlier versions of Windows automatically allowed Kerberos traffic through IPSec filters. However, Windows Server 2003 will drop Kerberos packets if an IPSec rule determines that the traffic should be blocked. If you want to enable Kerberos authentication, create filters in the IPSec policy that explicitly allow all traffic to your domain controllers.

Second, for IPSec to use Kerberos authentication across a cross-forest trust, you must use fully qualified domain names to configure the trusts. In addition, you must configure the IPSec client policy to allow communication to any domain controller in the forest domain hierarchy so that IPSec can obtain a Kerberos ticket from a domain controller in the IPSec peer's domain.

Public Key Certificate Authentication   A Public Key Infrastructure (PKI) can be used to authenticate and encrypt communications for a wide variety of applications, including Web applications, e-mail, and IPSec. Although using public key certificates is not as convenient as using Kerberos, there are specific circumstances for which certificates are the logical choice for authentication in IPSec. In particular, use public key certificates when you need to communicate privately with external business partners or other computers that do not support the Kerberos v5 authentication protocol.

IPSec's use of certificate authentication is compatible with many different PKI architectures and IPSec places relatively few requirements on the contents of a certificate. Computers that have a common trusted root, or whose certificates can chain through a cross-certification trust relationship, typically can successfully use IPSec authentication. To use certificates for IPSec authentication, define an ordered list of acceptable root CA names in the authentication method. This list controls the certificates IPSec can select and the certificates it will select.

If IPSec authentication fails, you cannot retry the authentication using a different method. For this reason, before you apply an IPSec policy that can use certificates for authentication, ensure that all target computers have the correct root CA certificates and relevant cross-certificates, in addition to valid computer certificates. In addition, to ensure that certificate authentication works as intended, test your PKI infrastructure with various IPSec policy configurations before deployment.

In Windows 2000 Server and Windows Server 2003, you can use Certificate Services to implement the root CA. Certificate Services is integrated with Active Directory and Group Policy, and it simplifies certificate deployment by enabling certificate autoenrollment and renewal and by providing configurable certificate templates. In addition, by publishing the computer certificate as an attribute of the domain computer account, Certificate Services allows you to use IPSec to restrict access to network services.

> **MORE INFO**   Refer to Chapter 9, "Designing a Public Key Infrastructure," for information on Certificate Services.

You can also use third-party CAs, which is particularly useful when communicating with external partners. IPSec supports the use of a variety of third-party X.509 PKI systems in addition to Windows 2000 Server or Windows Server 2003 Certificate Services. Windows Server 2003 Internet Key Exchange (IKE) has basic compatibility with several certificate systems, including those offered by

Microsoft, Entrust, VeriSign, and Netscape. If you are using a third-party PKI system, the PKI system must be able to issue certificates to computers and store their certificates in the Windows Cryptographic Application Programming Interface (CryptoAPI) computer certificate store.

Preshared Key Authentication   If both IPSec peers are not in the same domain and do not have access to a CA, a preshared key can be used. For example, a stand-alone computer on a network that does not connect to the Internet might need to use a preshared key because neither Kerberos authentication through the computer's domain account nor access to a CA on the Internet is available. A preshared key is a shared secret key (in essence, a password) agreed on by administrators who want to secure the computers' communications by using IPSec. Administrators must manually configure their systems to use the same preshared key.

The preshared key authentication method uses symmetrical encryption to authenticate the hosts, which itself is very secure, but which requires that any two hosts communicating have been configured with a predefined password. Unfortunately, this key is not stored securely on the IPSec hosts. The authentication key is stored in plaintext format in the system registry and hex-encoded in Active Directory–based IPSec policy. If attackers can access your registry, they can find your preshared key, which would allow them to decrypt your traffic or impersonate one of the hosts. Use preshared key authentication only when you cannot use any stronger method.

If you must use preshared key authentication, use a local IPSec policy, a 25-character or longer random key value, and a different preshared key for each IP address pair. These practices result in different security rules for each destination, and ensure that a compromised preshared key compromises only those computers that share the key.

Testing IPSec

As a rule, perform extensive testing before making any changes to your infrastructure. This rule certainly holds true when planning to use IPSec. IPSec has the potential to interfere with all network communications and, as a result, can break any network applications your organization uses.

Begin testing IPSec in a lab environment. Configure computers with the client and server sides of your critical applications, and verify that the lab is functional and accurately simulating the production environment. Your lab environment should have computers with each of the potential IPSec client operating systems because different operating systems support different IPSec functionality.

Develop performance metrics for each of your applications, and gather baseline performance data you can use for comparison after implementing IPSec. Then implement IPSec policies on the lab computers.

Not all network equipment provides the same IPSec capabilities; use the testing phase to determine which network devices need configuration changes or upgrades. Add firewalls, proxy servers, and routers to the lab environment to simulate the potential for those devices to interfere with IPSec communications in the production environment. If you plan to use IPSec for remote access, be sure to include a remote-access client in your lab environment and have that client connect from a typical remote network. If employees will use IPSec to connect to your internal network from home, test IPSec across a variety of commonly used home routing equipment. Test non-IPSec-enabled clients with IPSec-enabled servers. There will be a transition period during which some computers will not yet have received the IPSec configuration.

After configuring IPSec clients and network equipment in the lab environment, test the application functionality. If you identify problems, document the problems and solutions so that they can be quickly resolved if they appear in the production environment. Besides verifying that applications function, verify IPSec functionality. If you allow IPSec clients to use unsecured communications if **IPSec negotiations** fail, it is possible for applications to appear to be compatible with IPSec when the computers were unable to establish an IPSec session.

After you verify that all your applications are compatible with IPSec and you document the changes required to ensure compatibility, compare the results of your performance tests against the results gathered before IPSec was enabled. If your tests are accurate, they will show a slight degradation in the time required to establish network connections and a slight increase in processor use. Note the overhead required. Monitor computers in your production environment to ensure that the performance impact is minimal.

Establishing a handful of IPSec connections is not going to bog your computer down. However, the negotiation process does use a significant amount of processing time. If you have a server that is receiving anywhere from dozens to thousands of incoming IPSec connections per second, monitor the server's processor use. If it is consistently over 30 percent during peak hours, consider adding a network interface card (NIC) that offloads the IPSec processing. This enables the NIC to handle the negotiations while the server's processor deals with more interesting tasks.

Establishing the IPSec connection is processor-intensive because it uses asymmetric public key cryptography. The data transmitted after the connection is established is encrypted using symmetric shared key cryptography and does not use a significant (by modern standards) amount of processing capacity, so off-loading processor use is going to benefit you only if the server is constantly receiving a large number of new connections.

Begin the production IPSec rollout with a pilot deployment. During the pilot phase, do not require IPSec communications on any computer. All computers should allow non-IPSec communications to support computers that are not part of the pilot. You can require IPSec communications only after all computers have received IPSec configurations. Monitor the pilot computers to verify that IPSec is functioning correctly. When users report problems, identify whether IPSec is the source of the problem and document a resolution to the problem. Gradually deploying IPSec to your production environment will reduce the problems that users experience, which saves your organization money.

Assessing the Limitations and Costs of IPSec

IPSec has costs that might be prohibitive in your environment:

- **Slower connection establishment** IPSec is not recommended for scenarios in which clients make infrequent, short-lived connections. IPSec increases the time required to establish authenticated connections initially. Depending on policy design, network round-trip time, and the load on the systems required to establish the connection, negotiating security initially using IKE typically increases connection time by one to three seconds. Make sure that you want to trade the one-to three-second increase in connection time for the added security. After an IPSec session is established, no further delays occur, typically—even if applications create multiple TCP sessions.

- **Reduced computing performance** Filtering and encryption of each packet consumes computing power. As the volume of IPSec traffic—including policies, rules, and filters—increases, the load placed on the network and on computer CPUs increases also. To reduce the performance impact of IPSec, add a NIC that offloads IPSec processing.

■ **Thwarting some networking inspection technologies** IPSec encrypts traffic to protect it from a threat analyzing it. It also protects it from legitimate analysis that a network administrator might do, unfortunately. The data contained within IPSec communications cannot be analyzed by a protocol analyzer such as Network Monitor, which limits your administrators' troubleshooting options.

■ **Reducing throughput by increasing packet size and increasing network use** IPSec protection adds overhead to IP packets, reducing effective throughput and increasing network use. Although the Internet Engineering Task Force (IETF) design and Microsoft implementation of IPSec attempt to minimize both impacts, existing networks and servers might be operating at maximum capacity even without IPSec. Before deploying IPSec, test several different IPSec policy configurations because each policy configuration is likely to result in different performance impacts on clients and servers. It might be necessary to increase the available network bandwidth or CPU power or install IPSec offload adapters to compensate for the increased overhead of IPSec.

■ **Application incompatibility with IPSec NAT-T** Windows Server 2003 supports IPSec NAT-T as described by version 2 of the IPSec NAT-T Internet drafts, but some applications might not work when IPSec protects their traffic first and then passes it through a network address translator. Test how your planned implementation of IPSec interacts with network address translators in a lab before deploying IPSec in your environment.

■ **Loss of connectivity during cluster node addition or removal** IPSec establishes and maintains a cryptographic state between computers. Many clustering and load-balancing services use the same IP address for all nodes in a cluster, which creates incompatibilities with IPSec. Windows Server 2003 IPSec has proprietary extensions that allow it to work with the Windows Server 2003 Network Load Balancing service and Windows Cluster Service. However, support for these extensions does not exist in the current Windows 2000 and Windows XP IPSec client implementations, so you might experience some loss of connectivity when you add or remove cluster nodes.

■ **Blocking connections between Active Directory domain members and domain controllers by requiring IPSec for communication**   IPSec is based on the authentication of computers on a network; therefore, before a computer can send IPSec-protected data, it must be authenticated. The Active Directory security domain provides this authentication using the Kerberos protocol. As a result, if IPSec is required from domain members to the domain controllers, authentication traffic will be blocked and IPSec communications will fail. In addition, no other authenticated connections can be made using other protocols, and no other IPSec policy settings can be applied to that domain member through Group Policy. For these reasons, using IPSec for communications between domain members and domain controllers is not supported.

DESIGNING WIRELESS NETWORKS

Since the year 2000, consumers and businesses have been adopting mobile computing and wireless networks at a breathtaking pace. The benefit to businesses is obvious: employees are more productive because they can work and stay in touch when away from their desks. In an organization that uses a VPN, an employee with a wireless mobile computer can even connect to corporate resources from the airport, the local coffee shop, or thousands of other wireless hot spots.

Wireless networks are also among the most widely compromised technologies, unfortunately. If you have a wireless network, attackers might be able to access your network without physically entering your building. This can grant them access to your internal network resources, allow them to eavesdrop on your communications, and enable them to impersonate you when attacking other computers on the Internet.

When you configure your wireless network properly, the risks of an attacker compromising it are reduced dramatically. Windows Server 2003 includes several features that allow you to improve the security of your wireless networks and realize their benefits without assuming unnecessary risk. This section describes these features and gives you hands-on experience with configuring wireless security.

Wireless Security Fundamentals

Wireless technologies expose severe security weaknesses that security designers have overlooked for years. Security designers have relied on physical security to protect the privacy of communications on private networks. In other words, the only barrier preventing an attacker from capturing another user's traffic is being unable to connect physically to the user's network. Wired networks usually rely at least partially on physical security to authorize users to access the network. If you can reach an Ethernet port, you gain access to some private resources on most companies' intranets.

Wireless networks have these weaknesses too, but they lack the inherent physical security of wired networks. In fact, people with mobile computers in the businesses' parking lots can access many corporate wireless networks. To make matters worse, attackers have significant motivation to abuse access to the networks. Accessing a wireless network might grant an attacker access to resources on an organization's internal network, or it might allow the attacker to access the Internet while hiding his or her identity, which would allow the intruder to attack hosts on remote networks while disguised with the organization's IP addresses.

The concerns over the abuse of wireless networks are far from theoretical. Intruders have a wide variety of tools available for detecting, connecting to, and abusing wireless networks. As with most aspects of security, there are technologies available that can help you to limit the vulnerabilities presented by wireless networks. In particular, you can require authentication and encryption of wireless communications. This provides assurance similar to that offered by the physical security of wired networks. The game between security experts and attackers continues, however, and an intruder can now defeat early wireless authentication and encryption technologies easily.

Wireless Network Components

Home wireless networks don't necessarily need anything other than a wireless access point. Enterprises have requirements that are more demanding, however, because of the need to manage large numbers of wireless clients and to protect the security of confidential data crossing the wireless network. Windows-based enterprise wireless networks typically have, at a minimum, the following components:

- **Active Directory**   Stores account properties and validates user credentials. Also provides Group Policy settings useful for configuring wireless clients' settings, including preferred networks and Wired Equivalent Privacy (WEP) or Wi-Fi Protected Access (WPA) settings.

- **Remote-Access Dial-In User Server (RADIUS) server**   Provides centralized authentication, authorization, and accounting. If you use Microsoft Internet Authentication Service (IAS) for your RADIUS server, you can authenticate users against Active Directory. If you use a non-Microsoft RADIUS server, ensure that it supports Extensible Authentication Protocol-Transport Layer Security (EAP-TLS) for certificate-based authentication, and Protected EAP-Microsoft Challenge Handshake Authentication Protocol version 2 (PEAP-MS-CHAP v2) for password-based authentication.

- **CA**   Issues and validates certificates required for EAP-TLS and PEAP-TLS authentication.

- **Dynamic Host Configuration Protocol (DHCP) server**   Provides IP addresses to wireless clients. Because wireless networks typically have clients frequently joining and leaving the network, you might need to decrease the DHCP lease time to avoid running out of IP addresses.

- **DNS server**   Provides name resolution for clients.

Figure 10-10 shows how these components fit together. The certificate enrollment must happen across a wired network before the wireless authentication occurs. Encryption protects the communications only as they cross the wireless network. After the access point bridges the communications to the wired network, the communications are no longer encrypted.

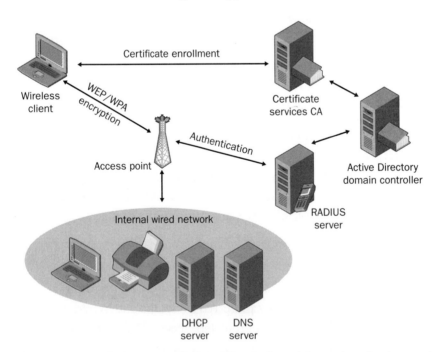

Figure 10-10   Wireless networks must be designed for authentication and encryption.

Assessing the Risks of Wireless Networks

Because wireless communications are not contained within the physical medium of a wire, wireless networks are more vulnerable than wired networks to several types of attacks, including the following:

- **Eavesdropping**   Attackers can capture traffic as it travels between a wireless computer and the wireless access point (AP). Depending on the type of antenna used and the transmitting power, an attacker might be able to eavesdrop from hundreds or thousands of feet away.

- **Spoofing**   Attackers might be able to gain access to restricted network resources by impersonating authorized wireless users.

- **Freeloading**   Attackers might use your wireless network to access the Internet. This reduces the available bandwidth to legitimate users. In addition, the attacker might use your network to launch attacks against other users on the Internet while making the attack appear to originate from your network.

- **Attacks against wireless clients**   Attackers can launch a network-based attack on a wireless computer connected to an ad hoc or untrusted wireless network.

- **Denial of service**   Attackers can jam the wireless frequencies by using a transmitter, preventing legitimate users from successfully communicating with an AP.

- **Data tampering**   Attackers can delete, replay, or modify wireless communications with a man-in-the-middle attack.

Using Encryption to Mitigate Wireless Network Risks

To reduce the vulnerability of wireless networks to these types of attacks, you can use WEP and WPA to encrypt wireless network traffic, as the following sections discuss.

WEP

WEP is a wireless security protocol that helps protect your information by using a security setting, called a *shared secret* or a *shared key*, to encrypt network traffic before transmitting it over the airwaves. This helps prevent unauthorized users from accessing the data as it is being transmitted.

WEP encryption has known vulnerabilities, however. Some smart cryptographers found several theoretical ways to discover WEP's shared secret by analyzing captured traffic. Shortly thereafter, programmers wrote and distributed free software to exploit these theoretical weaknesses. The combination of free tools for cracking WEP encryption, the ease of capturing wireless traffic, and the dense proliferation of wireless networks have led WEP to become the most frequently cracked network encryption protocol today.

> **NOTE   WEP's Weakness**   You won't need to understand the details of the WEP standard to be a security designer, but it is an interesting study on how not to make an encryption protocol. The most easily exploited weakness of WEP is that many of WEP's possible initialization vectors (IVs, which are bits of data used to generate encryption keys) are cryptographically weak and can expose individual bytes of the WEP key. WEP changes these IVs over time, and an attacker who captures millions of packets will eventually gather enough packets with weak IVs to crack the entire WEP key. Some wireless network adapters intentionally avoid using weak IVs, which makes it much more time-consuming to expose the WEP key. Ask your network adapter vendor what they've done to make WEP communications more secure. For more detailed information on WEP's weaknesses, search for the paper titled "Weaknesses in the Key Scheduling Algorithm of RC4" on the Internet.

Besides weak cryptography, another factor contributing to WEP's vulnerability is that WEP is difficult to manage because it doesn't provide any mechanism for changing the shared secret. On wireless networks with hundreds of hosts configured to use an AP, it is practically impossible to change the shared secret on all hosts regularly. As a result, the WEP shared secret tends to stay the same indefinitely. This gives attackers sufficient opportunity to crack the shared secret and all the time they need to abuse their ill-gotten network access.

If you could change the shared secret on a regular basis, however, you would be able to prevent an attacker from gathering enough data to crack the WEP key, and this would significantly improve WEP's privacy. There are techniques for changing the shared secret—dynamically and automatically—to reduce WEP's weaknesses dramatically. When WEP is used with a dynamic shared secret, it is called *dynamic WEP*. When a static shared key is used with WEP, it is called *static WEP*.

NOTE   **Cracking Tools for Wireless Networks**   Search the Internet for AirSnort and WEPCrack for information on two tools commonly used to break into WEP-protected wireless networks. These tools can derive a WEP key in anywhere from a day to a couple of weeks, depending on how much traffic is transferred across the network, the level of encryption used, and luck. They hardly provide instantaneous access to an encrypted wireless network, however.

To put it simply, if you rely only on a static shared secret, you cannot trust WEP to either protect the privacy of your network communications or to prevent uninvited (but patient) guests from accessing your wireless network. If providing compatibility with all of the wireless devices on your network forces you to use static WEP, there are a few things you can do to improve security. First, use the highest level of encryption possible: 128-bit. Short keys might be sufficient in some encryption scenarios, but WEP's 40-bit encryption is very vulnerable. Second, place APs in a perimeter network to restrict access to internal resources. If users need access to the internal network from a wireless network, they can use a VPN connection. Third, position your APs so that wireless transmissions are limited to locations that you can physically protect, such as the interior of your building. For more information about VPNs, refer to Chapter 11, "Protecting Extranet Communications."

Open and Shared Network Authentication   The initial WEP standards provided for two types of computer authentication: open system and shared secret. Shared secret authentication requires wireless clients to authenticate by using a shared secret; open system authentication allows any client to connect without providing a password.

Choosing between open system and shared secret authentication is easy, fortunately: always use open system authentication. On the surface, this seems illogical because open system authentication merely identifies the wireless client without providing any proof of identity, but shared key authentication requires knowledge of a secret key. However, shared secret authentication actually weakens security because most WEP client implementations, including Windows XP, use the same secret key for both authentication and WEP encryption. A malicious user who captures the keys used for both authentication and encryption can use cryptanalysis methods to determine the shared secret authentication key and, therefore, the WEP encryption key.

Once the WEP encryption key is determined, the malicious user has full access to the network as if WEP encryption were not enabled. Therefore, although shared key authentication is stronger than open system for authentication, it weakens WEP encryption. If you use open system authentication, any computer can easily join your network. However, without the WEP encryption key, the wireless clients cannot send or receive wireless communications, and they will not be able to abuse the wireless network.

802.1X Authentication   Although the early implementations of WEP were woefully inadequate, WEP's vulnerability was reduced significantly by using 802.1X authentication. 802.1X enables WEP to change the encryption keys regularly, which dramatically reduces the likelihood that an attacker will be able to gather enough data to identify the shared secret.

802.1X employs an IETF standard protocol called EAP to carry the authentication conversation between the client, the AP, and a RADIUS service. As part of the 802.1X secure authentication process, the EAP method generates an encryption key that is unique to each client. RADIUS forces the client to generate a new encryption key on a regular basis, which makes it more difficult for an attacker to capture enough traffic to identify a key. This allows the use of existing WEP-capable hardware while minimizing WEP's vulnerabilities.

> **MORE INFO   802.1X**   For more detailed information on 802.1X authentication, see "IEEE 802.1X Authentication for Wireless Connections" at *http://www.microsoft.com/technet/columns/cableguy/cg0402.asp.*

The process used by a client connecting to a dynamic WEP network with 802.1X authentication, as shown in Figure 10-11, is significantly more complex than the process a client uses to connect to an unsecured wireless network.

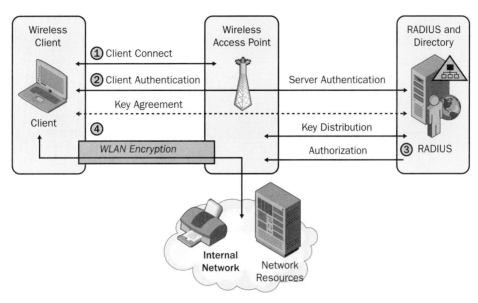

Figure 10-11   Connecting to an 802.1X authenticated wireless network

In particular, the client must perform the following steps to connect to an 802.1X authenticated wireless network:

1. When the client computer is in range of the AP, it will try to connect to the Service Set Identifier (SSID) hosted by the AP. If the client has been configured with shared network authentication, it will authenticate itself to the AP by using the network key. Because the AP is configured to allow only 802.1X authenticated connections, it issues an authentication challenge to the client. The AP then sets up a restricted channel that allows the client to communicate only with the RADIUS service.

2. The wireless client examines the RADIUS server's public key certificate to ensure that an attacker is not impersonating the RADIUS server. The client then attempts to authenticate to the RADIUS service, using 802.1X, as follows:

    ❑ If the client and RADIUS service have been configured to use PEAP authentication, the client establishes a TLS session with the RADIUS service and then transmits credentials using the configured authentication protocol.

❑ If the client and RADIUS service have been configured to use EAP-TLS authentication, the client authenticates by using public key certificates.

NOTE EAP-MD5 CHAP   There is a third authentication method called EAP-Message Digest 5 Challenge Handshake Authentication Protocol (EAP-MD5 CHAP). However, it is not suitable for authenticating wireless connections, and Windows XP Service Pack 1 removes it as an option. It is not an option in Windows Server 2003.

3. The RADIUS service checks the client credentials against the directory. If it can authenticate the client's credentials and the access policy allows the client to connect, it will grant access to the client. The RADIUS service relays the access decision to the AP. If the client is granted access, the RADIUS service transmits the dynamic shared secret to the AP. The client and AP now share common key material that they can use to encrypt and decrypt the traffic that will pass between them.

NOTE   RADIUS Implementations in Windows-Based Networks In Windows-based environments, the RADIUS service will usually be a computer running Windows Server 2003–based IAS, and the directory will be an Active Directory domain.

4. The AP then bridges the client's connection to the internal network, completing the 802.1X authentication process. If the client is configured to use DHCP, it can now request a lease.

The sections that follow describe the PEAP and EAP-TLS authentication methods and the role of the RADIUS service in more detail.

PEAP   PEAP typically is used to authenticate wireless clients by using a user name and password; EAP-TLS is used to authenticate wireless clients by using public key certificates. Although using a user name and password is not as strong as using public key certificates because passwords can be stolen or guessed, the resulting encryption is still very strong. When PEAP authentication is used with a RADIUS service that forces encryption keys to change regularly, the resulting WEP encryption is not likely to be compromised in a reasonable amount of time. PEAP's primary advantage over EAP-TLS is that it is easier to deploy because it does not require you to implement a PKI.

The PEAP authentication method has two phases. Phase 1 authenticates the RADIUS server by using the RADIUS server's public key certificate and then establishing a TLS session to the RADIUS server. Phase 2 requires a second EAP method tunneled inside the PEAP session to authenticate the client to the RADIUS service. This allows PEAP to use a variety of client authentication methods.

This is an important point: PEAP uses two separate types of authentication, one in each authentication phase. PEAP handles the first authentication without requiring administrative configuration. You must configure the second authentication protocol, however. Although wireless standards could theoretically support any authentication method, Windows Server 2003 and Windows XP support two by default: MS-CHAP v2 and certificates using EAP-TLS tunneled inside PEAP. You will usually use MS-CHAP v2 with PEAP, however, because you should use EAP-TLS for certificate-based authentication. Certificate-based authentication does not require the additional layer of encryption provided by PEAP.

> **NOTE   The Weakness of MS-CHAP**   It's good that MS-CHAP v2 authentication is protected by TLS encryption because MS-CHAP v2 is very susceptible to an offline dictionary attack. An attacker who can capture a successful MS-CHAP v2 exchange can methodically guess passwords until the correct one is determined. It would take a while, but the attacker will get the password eventually.

After the user is authenticated successfully, the authentication server supplies dynamically generated keying material to the AP. From this keying material, the AP creates new encryption keys for data protection.

> **NOTE   The Difference between PEAP and EAP-TLS**   If you have a hard time remembering the difference between PEAP and EAP-TLS, think of the P in PEAP as standing for *password*, because you usually use PEAP for password-based authentication, and you use EAP-TLS when client certificates are available.

EAP-TLS   EAP-TLS performs the same functions as PEAP by authenticating the client computer and generating keying material used for encrypting the wireless communications. However, EAP-TLS uses public key certificates to authenticate both the client and the RADIUS service. Microsoft designed EAP-TLS and based it on an authentication protocol that is nearly identical to the protocol used in the Secure Sockets Layer (SSL) protocol for securing Web transactions. Although public key certificates provide strong authentication and encryption, use EAP-TLS only if you already have a PKI in place for another application, or your organization's security requirements do not allow simple password authentication. For more information about EAP-TLS, refer to RFC 2716.

RADIUS   RADIUS is a standardized service used primarily to authenticate dial-up users. Windows Server 2003 includes a RADIUS service and proxy named IAS. The traditional use for IAS on Windows-based networks is to allow an ISP to authenticate an organization's users based on the Active Directory domain credentials stored on the organization's private network.

Because RADIUS is designed to allow network hardware to authenticate against an external user database, APs can also use RADIUS to authenticate wireless users as they join the network. Authenticating to a RADIUS service allows user authentication for wireless networks to be centralized rather than forcing administrators to store user credentials on each AP.

The RADIUS service receives a user-connection request from the AP and authenticates the client against its authentication database. A RADIUS service can also maintain a central storage database of other relevant user properties. In addition to the simple yes or no response to an authentication request, RADIUS can provide other applicable connection parameters for the user, including static IP address assignment and maximum session time.

The ability to specify a maximum session time enables the RADIUS service to force the client to re-authenticate on a regular basis. This re-authentication automatically generates a new, shared secret, which upgrades static WEP to dynamic WEP. Each time the shared secret is changed, an attacker must restart the process of cracking the encryption key. If the maximum session time is low enough, it will be practically impossible for an attacker to capture enough data to crack the shared secret key. As a result, dynamic WEP can be considered adequately secure for most environments.

Wi-Fi Protected Access

Although WEP with dynamic re-keying is secure enough to meet the needs of most organizations, WEP still has security weaknesses. WEP still uses a separate static key for broadcast packets. An attacker can analyze these broadcast packets to build a map of private IP addresses and computer names. WEP keys have to be renewed frequently, which places an additional burden on RADIUS services.

NOTE **The Not-So-Technical WEP Weakness** Dynamic WEP is very secure. Its biggest detractor might be its bad reputation. Often, executives at a company won't allow a wireless deployment because they've heard about the ability for attackers to break through WEP security. Even though standard WEP is not at all easy to exploit, and almost impossible to exploit when dynamic re-keying is used, the publicity WEP's vulnerabilities have received makes WPA even more attractive.

To address these lingering weaknesses with WEP, the Wi-Fi Alliance, a consortium of the leading wireless network equipment vendors, developed WPA. WPA can use the same authentication mechanisms and encryption algorithms as WEP. This compatibility allows support for WPA to be added to APs with a simple firmware upgrade. However, WPA virtually eliminates WEP's most exploited vulnerability by using a unique encryption key for each packet.

There are two encryption options for WPA: Temporal Key Integrity Protocol (TKIP) and Advanced Encryption System (AES). TKIP is the encryption algorithm used by WEP, and it is used in the vast majority of WPA implementations. WPA improves on WEP's implementation of TKIP, however. WPA with TKIP reuses IVs less frequently than WEP with TKIP and, as a result, significantly reduces the likelihood that an attacker will collect enough traffic to compromise the encryption. In addition, WPA with TKIP creates a unique encryption key for every frame, whereas WEP can use the same key for weeks or months. Finally, WPA with TKIP implements the message integrity code (MIC), often referred to as *Michael*, to guard against forgery attacks.

WPA can also use AES, a more secure encryption algorithm than TKIP. Although most existing wireless equipment can be upgraded to support WPA, most equipment cannot be upgraded to support AES, unfortunately. As a result, you will probably not be able to use AES unless you specifically choose equipment that supports it.

When you enable WPA, you establish a passphrase that is automatically associated with the dynamically generated security settings. This passphrase is stored with your other network settings on the base station and on each of your networked computers. Only wireless devices with the WPA passphrase can join your network and decrypt network transmissions.

WPA provides better security than WEP. However, WEP data protection, when combined with strong authentication and rapidly changing encryption keys, can meet the security requirements of most organizations. This is fortunate because many organizations are forced to continue using WEP. Not all wireless network hardware supports WPA, but WEP is universally supported. Windows 2000 and earlier versions of Windows do not have built-in support for WPA, although you might be able to download an update from the vendor of your wireless network adapter. Finally, WPA must be configured manually on Windows XP clients because WPA configuration settings cannot be defined by using Group Policy objects (GPOs) with the built-in Active Directory functionality included with Windows Server 2003. For these reasons, you might be forced to choose WEP over WPA, even though you will sacrifice some degree of security.

Other Wireless Security Techniques

Encrypting is the most important wireless network security technique. However, there are several secondary security techniques that you should be familiar with: media access control (MAC) address filtering, disabling SSID broadcasts, VPNs, detecting rogue wireless networks, and limiting wireless leakage.

MAC Address Filtering

MAC address filtering is a common technique used to make it more difficult for a casual user to connect to your wireless network. As with wired Ethernet cards, every wireless network card is assigned a unique MAC address by the manufacturer. MAC address filtering allows only a predefined set of MAC addresses.

When an AP is configured to use MAC address filtering, it will ignore any messages from wireless cards that use a MAC address not on the approved list. Although this does improve security, it has significant manageability drawbacks. First, you must manually maintain the list of MAC addresses on your AP, which would be almost impossible to do if you managed more than a dozen computers or multiple APs. Second, APs typically have limited memory, and might not be able to store your organization's complete list of MAC addresses. Third, if an attacker is knowledgeable and determined enough to circumvent your WEP or WPA encryption, the attacker will also be able to identify and spoof an approved MAC address. Finally, before a guest can access your wireless network, you need to add his or her MAC address to the approved list.

> **NOTE   Real Benefits of MAC Address Filtering**   It's important to be familiar with MAC address filtering for the exam, but, in the real world, the security gains are so minimal that it's not worth the trouble to set up.

Disabling SSID Broadcasts

APs provide the option of disabling SSID broadcasts, but do not treat this as a security feature. SSID broadcasts allow wireless clients to detect an available wireless network. In fact, Windows XP displays a notification to the user when it first receives an SSID broadcast from a wireless network. This is convenient; if you want users to be notified actively of the presence of the wireless client, enable SSID broadcasts.

Disabling SSID broadcasts will prevent the casual computer user from discovering your network, but it does nothing to prevent a skilled attacker from detecting your network. For example, a user with the free Network Stumbler tool installed can quickly identify the SSID of a wireless network that has SSID broadcasts disabled, because 802.11 association/disassociation messages always are sent unencrypted and contain the SSID that the client wants to associate to or disassociate from. You can download Network Stumbler from *http://www.stumbler.net.*

Encrypting Traffic with VPNs

Whereas a VPN is an excellent solution for securely traversing a public network such as the Internet, VPNs are not the best solution for securing wireless networks. For this kind of application, a VPN is unnecessarily complex and costly. It adds little additional security to dynamic WEP, but it significantly increases costs, reduces usability, and removes important pieces of the functionality.

VPN clients usually require the user to initiate a connection to the VPN server; therefore, the connection will never be as transparent as a wired network connection. Non-Microsoft VPN clients might also prompt for logon credentials, in addition to the standard network or domain logon, when the connection is established. If the VPN disconnects because of a poor wireless signal or because the user is roaming between APs, the user has to repeat the connection process.

Because the VPN connection is only user-initiated, an idle, logged-off computer will not be connected to the internal network. Therefore, a computer cannot be remotely managed or monitored unless a user is logged on. Certain computer GPO settings, such as startup scripts and computer-assigned software, might never be applied. Finally, mobile computers often go into standby or hibernation mode. However, resuming from standby or hibernation does not automatically reestablish the VPN connection; the user has to do this manually.

NOTE   Using IPSec   IPSec, discussed elsewhere in this chapter, is very useful for improving wireless network security.

Detecting Rogue Wireless Networks

Rogue wireless networks are APs that are connected to your network but are not officially sanctioned. These are actually very common because wireless networks are easy to set up and wireless network hardware is very inexpensive. Usually, a user sets up a rogue wireless network without any malicious intent because he or she wants to be able to access the network while in other parts of the building, such as in a meeting room.

Although the user who sets up a rogue AP might not have malicious intent, he or she does create a substantial vulnerability by making it much easier for uninvited guests to connect to your internal network. Even if he or she configures encryption, you don't have any way of controlling who that user grants access to. It's important that IT have control over who uses your organization's network, so take measures to detect and eliminate rogue wireless networks.

You can purchase tools designed to detect rogue wireless networks. An easier alternative is to use a software tool such as Network Stumbler, shown in Figure 10-12, with a laptop computer. With Network Stumbler running on a laptop, you can walk around your facilities and detect any APs. Network Stumbler displays the signal strength, which you can use to locate the AP.

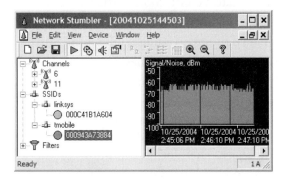

Figure 10-12   You can use Network Stumbler to find APs because it displays the signal strength of wireless networks.

Limiting Wireless Leakage

The principal vulnerability of wireless networks is that threats can access the wireless network without physically entering your facilities. You can limit this risk by making an effort to keep wireless signals limited to the interior of your buildings. To do this, place APs in central locations instead of against exterior walls. Use a tool such as Network Stumbler to walk around the perimeter of your building and identify locations where an attacker can get a strong signal.

If you determine that your wireless signal goes too far, you can reduce the power output of your AP or adjust the antennae to direct the signal away from the vulnerable location. Consider using high-gain antennas that focus wireless signals toward locations where legitimate users will access your network. Adding screens to exterior windows also reduces the risk of wireless attacks by adding significant amounts of noise to the wireless signals outside of a building.

Understanding Wireless Provisioning Services

Wireless Provisioning Services (WPS) simplify the process of connecting to a wireless hotspot by providing a standardized procedure for authenticating and authorizing a user and configuring wireless security. Without WPS, hotspots typically do not use wireless encryption (because requiring the user to type an encryption key is too difficult) and require the user to open a browser to authenticate to the AP, a process known as the Universal Access Method (UAM). With WPS, users can connect to an encrypted hotspot, authenticate, and gain network access immediately. Even the initial sign-on can be standardized because a WPS client such as Windows XP Professional with Service Pack 2 can gather the user's account and payment information using a wizard.

WPS is included with Windows XP Service Pack 2 and Windows Server 2003 Service Pack 1. WPS extends the wireless client software included with Windows XP and the IAS included with Windows Server 2003 to allow for a consistent and automated configuration process when connecting to public wireless hotspots that provide access to the Internet or private wireless networks that provide guest access to the Internet. To use WPS, you need the following components:

- **WPS-enabled wireless clients** WPS-enabled wireless clients are computers running Windows XP with Service Pack 2, Windows XP Tablet PC Edition with Service Pack 2, or Windows Server 2003 with Service Pack 1.

- **An AP that supports filtering using either virtual LANs (VLANs) or IP addresses**   With VLANs, the traffic from the wireless client can be tagged with a VLAN ID to identify whether it is authenticated, in which case the traffic is forwarded to the Internet VLAN, or not, in which case the traffic is forwarded to a provisioning resources VLAN that contains the set of servers used for configuring the wireless client. The access controller uses the VLAN ID to determine how to switch the traffic. As an alternative to VLAN support, the wireless AP must have the ability to filter traffic from individual wireless clients based on the destination IP address or tag traffic for filtering by an access controller. IP filtering allows the wireless AP to confine the traffic of unauthenticated clients to a specific set of resources on the network.

  The wireless AP is configured as a RADIUS client to the IAS server on the wireless network.

- **Access controller**   The access controller is a device that performs routing and either filtering or VLAN switching for packets coming from and going to the wireless APs. If packet filtering is being used, the access controller uses the tags placed on the frames to perform packet filtering. If VLANs are being used, the access controller uses the VLAN ID of packets coming from the wireless APs to switch the packets to a provisioning resources VLAN or the Internet VLAN. Clients connect to the provisioning resources VLAN to provide identification and payment information, and the Internet VLAN provides Internet access after they receive authorization.

- **Provisioning server**   The provisioning server must have a Web server such as IIS and XML files containing wireless client configuration settings. The Web server will be running an HTTPS-protected WPS Web application capable of processing standardized, XML-based sign-up and renewal requests. The WPS client running on the user's computer generates these requests. The Web application typically will need a database server to store information such as promotion codes.

- **Lightweight Directory Access Protocol (LDAP) directory server**   Used to store the user accounts database for active customers. When a customer performs the initial sign-up process, the Web application on the provisioning server creates a new account in the directory and adds the user account to the appropriate groups. You can use an Active Directory domain controller or another LDAP-based database that supports dynamic creation of user accounts.

■ **RADIUS server**   IAS or a non-Microsoft RADIUS server, used to authenticate and authorize users. The RADIUS server will have remote-access policies for both guest access and authenticated users. The RADIUS server must specifically support WPS, such as IAS after Windows Server 2003 Service Pack 1 is installed. In addition, the RADIUS server must have a server certificate that the client trusts. If WPS is used to authenticate clients that are not part of your domain, use a certificate issued by a third-party CA (such as VeriSign or Thawte) that is trusted by default. Otherwise, the WPS will reject the server's certificate. A certificate issued by an internal CA will suffice for test deployments of WPS.

■ **DHCP server**   Assigns IP addresses to the wireless client computers that are connecting either as guests or as authenticated clients that are accessing the Internet.

■ **Optionally, virtual AP support**   If you are migrating existing APs to WPS, virtual AP support (which enables a single AP to broadcast multiple SSIDs with different security configurations) will simplify the migration process by enabling you to offer both the legacy sign-on process and WPS side by side.

These components are shown in Figure 10-13.

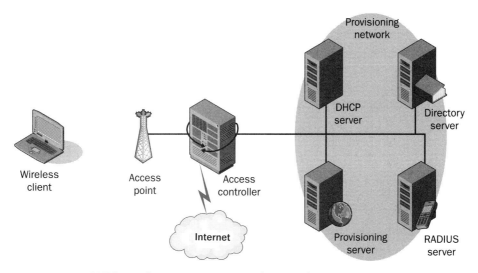

Figure 10-13 WPS requires many server and network components.

WPS uses the following steps to connect a new user:

1. The user discovers the network at a Wi-Fi hotspot.

2. The user authenticates as a guest.

3. The client is provisioned and the user establishes an account.

4. The user is authenticated with the new account credentials.

5. The user is switched to a VLAN that provides Internet access.

WPS is a security feature because it enables guests to connect easily to encrypted wireless networks. Without WPS, you typically need to provide unencrypted wireless access to your network because configuring an encryption key is too complex for guests. As a result, an attacker within range of your wireless network can capture your guests' wireless traffic and compromise their private communications.

Planning Wireless Access Policies

There are several aspects to planning wireless access policies. First, it is important to plan wireless access policies to help prevent APs from being installed in your organization with insufficient security. Draft a policy that, at a minimum, defines the following requirements for new APs:

- **Authentication requirements**   In general, require that all wireless users be authenticated, and specify whether PEAP or EAP-TLS will be used. If you plan to allow guests to access your wireless network, make provisions for creating APs providing limited access to your internal network that only guests use.

> **NOTE**   *Source IP-Based Authentication*   If you allow wireless access to guests and do not force guests to use a different IP subnet, add a policy stating that no application shall rely on the IP source address for authorization.

- **Encryption**   Some level of encryption should always be required. Unless you have wireless devices that do not support it, your policy should mandate the highest level of encryption available.

- **Physical security**   Just as with any other piece of network equipment, APs should be protected by lock and key to prevent attackers from tampering with the hardware.

- **SSID broadcast and naming conventions**   Your policy should specify whether APs are configured to broadcast the SSID and it should detail naming conventions for SSIDs.

- **Actively maintained list of APs**   You must maintain a list of all APs on your network that, at a minimum, includes the SSID, the security settings, the administrator's name, and patching requirements.

- **Auditing requirements**   Specify how usage information is gathered and how logs are archived.

Besides documenting requirements for the configuration of new APs, define how users can and cannot use wireless access. Consider restricting the times of day when wireless access is available and physically shutting down APs after business hours. To reduce the likelihood of attacks on wireless-capable computers while they are connected to untrusted wireless networks, consider forbidding users to connect to wireless networks other than your own, or restricting access to a list of approved networks.

> **MORE INFO**   **Wireless Security Policies**   The SANS (SysAdmin, Audit, Network, Security) Institute provides a template for a wireless communications policy at *http://www.sans.org/resources/policies/ Wireless_Communication_Policy.pdf*.

Another way to use policy to control the risks associated with wireless networks is to specifically state that end-user-managed APs are not allowed in your organization's computer usage policy. Notify existing employees that the computer usage agreement has been updated and that they are not allowed to connect an AP to your organization's network. If you decide not to use wireless networks in your organization, pursue this strategy in an active, rather than a passive, way. Back up this decision with a clear, published policy and ensure that all employees are aware of it and of the consequences of violating it. Consider using scanning equipment and network packet monitors to detect the use of unauthorized wireless equipment on your network.

> **NOTE**   **Take a Proactive Approach**   The single most effective way to prevent users from adding their own APs is to proactively provide wireless access and make it easy for users to connect.

Designing a Wireless Network Infrastructure

After you have identified your wireless network policies, design an authorization strategy to assign computers and users rights to access your wireless network. If you plan to use certificates for wireless authentication, design a certificate infrastructure. In addition, most environments will benefit from deploying IAS-based RADIUS servers and creating dedicated network segments for wireless networks.

Designing the Authorization Strategy

Although many organizations choose to allow all computers and users in the organization to access the wireless network, other organizations choose to restrict access. On Windows networks, you can restrict access to wireless networks by using domain security groups. Although it is possible to use the dial-up properties of domain user objects to allow and deny access to individuals, this is tedious to administer for more than a few users.

One method for implementing this is to create a three-tiered structure for assigning permissions. At the top level, create a universal group and grant this universal group access by using a remote-access policy in IAS. At the second level, create domain global groups for users and computers that will be granted wireless access. Add to these security groups users and groups that should be granted wireless access. Figure 10-14 shows an example of such a hierarchy.

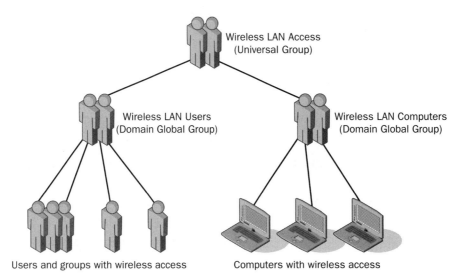

Figure 10-14   Create a group hierarchy that simplifies granting access to wireless networks.

Strive to have all wireless computers joined to the same domain as your IAS computers. You can have wireless clients that are not members of a domain, but you will have to configure the wireless network client settings manually because GPOs are not applicable. If the user does not log on to the domain, user authentication to the wireless network will require a separate user name and password prompt.

Designing the Certificate Infrastructure

Regardless of which authentication method you choose, you will need at least one computer certificate to use 802.1X authentication. This certificate must be installed on the IAS servers that will perform RADIUS services. For computer authentication with EAP-TLS, you must also install a computer certificate on the wireless client computers. A computer certificate installed on a wireless client computer is used to authenticate the wireless client computer so that the computer can obtain network connectivity to the enterprise intranet and download computer Group Policy settings prior to user logon. For user authentication with EAP-TLS after a network connection is made and the user logs on, you must use a user certificate on the wireless client computer.

Table 10-1 summarizes the certificates that need to be installed or enrolled for the two types of supported wireless authentication.

Table 10-1   **Authentication Types and Certificates**

Authentication Type	Certificates on Each Wireless Client	Certificates on Each IAS Computer
EAP-TLS	One computer certificate, one or more user certificates, and the root CA certificates for issuers of IAS server computer certificates	One computer certificate and the root CA certificates for issuers of wireless client computer and user certificates
PEAP with MS-CHAP v2	The root CA certificates for issuers of IAS server computer certificates	One computer certificate

If the certificate of the root CA that issued the IAS servers' certificates is already installed as a root CA certificate on your wireless clients, no other configuration is necessary. If your issuing CA is a Windows 2000 Server or Windows Server 2003 online root enterprise CA, the root CA certificate is automatically installed on each domain member through computer configuration GPO settings. If it is not, you must install the root CA certificates of the issuers of the computer certificates of the IAS servers on each wireless client.

In general, configure Windows Server 2003 Certificate Services to issue the IAS server certificate—even if the only reason you create the CA is to issue a single certificate for the IAS server. Alternatively, you can purchase a certificate from a public CA. Regardless of whether you deploy your own PKI or buy a certificate, the root CA certificate of the CA that issued the IAS server certificate must be installed on each wireless client.

Windows XP includes the root CA certificates of many public CAs. If you purchase your IAS server certificates from a public CA that corresponds to an included root CA certificate, no additional wireless client configuration is required. If you purchase your IAS server certificates from a public CA for which Windows XP does not include a corresponding root CA certificate, you must install the root CA certificate on each wireless client. For more information about Certificate Services, refer to Chapter 9.

If you are using a Windows Server 2003 or Windows 2000 Certificate Services enterprise CA as an issuing CA, you can install a computer certificate on the IAS server by configuring a GPO for the autoenrollment of computer certificates. If you plan to use the EAP-TLS authentication method, configure autoenrollment for computer and user certificates for computers and users that will be accessing the wireless network. Only Windows XP and Windows Server 2003 wireless clients support user certificate autoenrollment.

> **NOTE** **Duplicate the User Certificate Template** *When enrolling user certificates, consider creating a duplicate of the User certificate template specifically for wireless users.*

A client computer configured to use EAP-TLS authentication can obtain certificates for the authentication of wireless connections in three ways: autoenrollment, Web enrollment, and importing a certificate file. If you choose to import the certificates, you can either create and distribute certificates individually for each user or distribute a single certificate file to all users. A single certificate used for a group of users is known as a *group certificate*, which is the least secure certificate deployment because anyone who obtains the certificate file could use it to successfully authenticate a wireless connection.

> **NOTE** **Pocket PCs with Wireless Network Support** *Pocket PCs do not support GPOs and, as a result, you will have to manually enroll them. Pocket PCs can use only user certificates because they do not support computer certificates.*

Designing IAS Servers

IAS is a component of Windows Server 2003 that provides RADIUS services capable of authenticating users based on information contained within Active Directory. When configuring the security of a wireless network, you must configure the IAS server to use specific authentication methods and to grant access to authorized users. For more information about IAS, including how to harden IAS servers, refer to Chapter 7, "Hardening Servers."

Authenticating wireless users requires minimal processing time; a 2-GHz Pentium 4 server can authenticate about 36 users per second. Even if every access point in your organization uses a single RADIUS server, you probably do not need to configure multiple IAS or RADIUS servers to meet your scalability requirements. You might need multiple servers to meet redundancy requirements, however. The simplest way to provide redundant RADIUS servers is to configure your AP with primary and secondary RADIUS server addresses, as shown in Figure 10-15. In enterprise environments, you can configure the AP to failover to a secondary RADIUS server located in a remote office to provide redundancy without requiring each office to have multiple RADIUS servers.

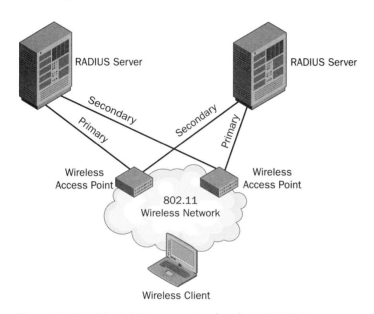

Figure 10-15   Most APs support redundant RADIUS servers.

Benefits of Segmenting Wireless Network Traffic

Wireless clients place very different demands on a LAN and infrastructure services than do wired clients, because wireless clients tend to leave and rejoin the network frequently. In addition, the risk of having a malicious computer join a wireless network is greater than having it join a wired network because the attacker would need to gain physical access to your facilities to join a wired network. For these reasons, it might be cost-effective to place wireless clients on a separate network segment. Creating a wireless network segment offers the following benefits:

- Wired network components do not have to draw from the same pool of existing IP addresses as your wireless clients.

- IP addresses for wireless clients are easier to identify, which assists in easier management and troubleshooting.

- Separate subnets give you increased control over DHCP lease times. You can provide short lease times to computers on the wireless segment, while providing long lease times for the more stable wired clients.

- You can associate each of your physical subnets (both wireless and wired) with sites within Active Directory, which enables you to assign network access policies to the specific subnets.

- If all APs are on the same subnet, you can provide seamless network-layer roaming for the wireless clients. Network-layer roaming allows a wireless client to associate with a new AP within the same subnet, in the same wireless network. When crossing subnets, applications that cannot handle a change of address, such as some e-mail applications, might fail.

Detecting Wireless Threats

Table 10-2 lists threats that you might see to your wireless network, and the symptoms that you can use to identify an attack. You can use custom scripts or Alerts (created by using the Performance console) to detect and alert you when these symptoms appear.

Table 10-2 **Wireless Network Threats**

Threat	Symptom
Authorization attempt using stolen credentials	Authentication events in the System Event log of the IAS server that indicate attempted use of revoked certificates
Brute-force authentication attacks	Repeated authentication failure events in the System Event log of the IAS server
Unsuccessful man-in-the-middle attack with a rogue AP	Increases in the Bad Authenticators or Invalid Request performance counters on an IAS server caused by requests from an invalid AP

SUMMARY

■ There are two ways to implement IP filtering: network-based and host-based firewalls. Network-based firewalls protect the perimeter of a network, but do not protect against attacks originating from your intranet, and cannot protect computers that connect to untrusted networks. Host-based firewalls protect only one computer at a time, but the protection stays with the computer wherever it goes.

■ You can use IPSec to enable encryption and authentication for network communications on your network. IPSec can protect almost any type of network communication, whether or not the applications being used natively support encryption. To use IPSec effectively in an enterprise, deploy infrastructure servers, including Active Directory domain controllers, RADIUS servers, and certification authorities.

■ Wireless networks provide your intranet users with the freedom to use the network away from their desks, but such networks introduce many significant vulnerabilities. If the network is not designed with security in mind, attackers might be able to connect to your wireless network, capture private network communications, and abuse your Internet connection. You can significantly reduce this risk by making use of wireless encryption and 802.1X authentication.

REVIEW QUESTIONS

1. Which mode would you use to protect communications between two private networks connected by the Internet?

   a. Transport mode

   b. Tunnel mode

2. Which mode would you use to protect communications between an IPSec-enabled e-mail client and an e-mail server on a private network?

   a. Transport mode

   b. Tunnel mode

3. Which of the following IPSec protocols provides encryption for network communications?

   a. AH

b. ESP

c. SA

d. IKE

e. ISAKMP

4. You are an administrator at an organization that uses Windows Server 2003 Active Directory. Which IPSec authentication method should you recommend for authenticating internal clients to an intranet Web server?

  a. Kerberos authentication

  b. Public key certificates authentication

  c. Preshared key authentication

5. You need to grant employees at an external partner company access to an application server, but you want to ensure that the communications are authenticated and encrypted. Which IPSec authentication method should you recommend?

  a. Kerberos authentication

  b. Public key certificates authentication

  c. Preshared key authentication

6. Which of the following authentication methods would you use to protect a wireless network for an organization that has an existing PKI, and in which all computers and users have been issued certificates with private keys? (Choose all that apply.)

  a. Open network authentication

  b. Shared network authentication

  c. 802.1X PEAP authentication

  d. 802.1X EAP-TLS authentication

  e. 802.1X EAP-MD5 CHAP authentication

7. Which of the following authentication methods would you use to protect a wireless network for an organization that prefers using user names and passwords for authentication? (Choose all that apply.)

    a. Open network authentication

    b. Shared network authentication

    c. 802.1X PEAP authentication

    d. 802.1X EAP-TLS authentication

    e. 802.1X EAP-MD5 CHAP authentication

8. Which of the following clients supports WPS?

    a. Windows 98

    b. Windows 2000 Professional with Service Pack 4

    c. Windows XP Professional with Service Pack 1

    d. Windows XP Professional with Service Pack 2

CASE SCENARIOS

Case Scenario 10-1: Designing IPSec to Meet Business Requirements

You are an administrator for Contoso, Ltd. Your company is in the mergers and acquisitions business, working closely with public corporations before major business deals. During the process of a merger, Contoso exchanges hundreds of confidential documents with your customer's executive and legal teams. Currently, when Contoso exchanges confidential documents with its customers, the documents must be printed and physically delivered because Contoso's Chief Information Officer (CIO) is not comfortable allowing your customers to retrieve them from the file servers on which the master copies of the documents are stored. After all, allowing electronic access to your file servers from other networks could open the file server to attack. Many people could profit from advance knowledge of a merger, and profit is a powerful motivator to a skilled attacker.

The cost of having the paperwork delivered is cutting into your company's profits, unfortunately. Even worse, waiting for the documents to be delivered overnight adds several weeks to the length of the merger process. If you can find a way to provide for secure communications with your external partners and make the

CIO comfortable with using electronic communications, you would save your company millions of dollars.

Contoso has offices in New York, Boston, and San Jose. The three offices are networked by private links that connect to a switched frame relay network. In addition, each office has an Internet connection to enable employees to do research by using Internet resources. Many of Contoso's 300 employees have to travel to customer offices on a regular basis, and dial in to Contoso's bank of modems for access to the internal network. All computers are members of a single Active Directory domain.

Based on this information, answer the questions that follow.

1. Your CIO's main concern is reducing the length of the merger process by allowing customers to retrieve documents electronically from your file servers. How would you propose that this be accomplished using the technologies discussed in this chapter?

2. How can you use IPSec to reduce the costs of the private links between the three offices?

3. How can you use IPSec to reduce the costs of maintaining the dial-up modem bank and the long-distance costs associated with remote employees dialing in?

4. How can you use IPSec to improve the security of communications on the internal network? What authentication method will you use on the internal network?

Case Scenario 10-2: Reducing the Risk of Rogue Wireless Networks

You are the lead systems administrator at a large law firm. Law firms are among the slowest to adopt new technologies and your employer is no exception. Your organization has, to date, not deployed a wireless network. After bringing up the benefits of wireless networks at a recent meeting with the senior partners, you learned that you will not be deploying a wireless network for several years, if ever.

The lack of an IT-configured wireless network has not entirely stopped its adoption, however. Yesterday, you noticed a junior attorney accessing the Web from the firm's library—without an Ethernet cable. When you asked the attorney how he connected to the network, he confessed that he plugged a consumer AP into the network port in his office.

You need to explain to the senior partners why your organization needs a wireless network security policy even if they do not want to sponsor a wireless network. Based on this information, answer the following questions:

1. Which of the following risks are posed to your organization by the presence of a rogue wireless network? (Choose all that apply.)

    a. An attacker could use a wireless network card to capture traffic between two wired network hosts.

    b. An attacker could access hosts on your internal network from the lobby of your building with a wireless-enabled mobile computer.

    c. An attacker could use your Internet connection from the lobby of your building with a wireless-enabled mobile computer.

    d. An attacker could capture an attorney's e-mail credentials as the attorney downloads his messages across the wireless link.

    e. An attacker with a wireless network card could join your Active Directory domain.

2. Which of the following would reduce the risk of a security compromise resulting from a vulnerable rogue wireless network? (Choose all that apply.)

    a. Publishing a wireless network security policy allowing employee-managed APs that have authentication and encryption enabled

    b. Publishing a wireless network security policy forbidding employee-managed APs

    c. Publishing instructions for other employees to access the current employee-managed AP

    d. Deploying an IT-managed AP using open network authentication without encryption

    e. Deploying an IT-managed AP with WEP encryption and 802.1X authentication

    f. Educating internal employees about the risks associated with wireless networks

CHAPTER 11
PROTECTING EXTRANET COMMUNICATIONS

Upon completion of this chapter, you will be able to:

- Determine whether dial-up or virtual private network (VPN) connections meet your organization's remote-access needs better.

- Describe the different remote-access communication, encryption, and authentication protocols.

- Use Connection Manager, remote-access policies (RAPs), and quarantine control to configure remote access while minimizing the security risks.

- Design demand-dial routing to connect remote networks across dial-up connections while minimizing usage costs.

- Design remote-access architectures by choosing the optimal locations for remote-access servers to meet your security and performance needs.

- Design an extranet identity management solution to grant limited access to specific applications to external partners, customers, and vendors.

Your organization's private network provides employees access to many important resources, including file servers, application servers, and intranet Web servers. These resources contain a great deal of confidential information, and you probably have taken steps to keep people outside your network from accessing them. There are many times, however, when your organization's employees will need access to these resources while outside your offices.

Microsoft Windows servers and clients support two methods of remote access: VPNs and dial-up connections. Allowing legitimate users remote access poses a risk, however, because an attacker could abuse the same connections. To minimize the risk of uninvited guests using remote access, first choose between dial-up and VPN remote access. Next, identify appropriate authentication and encryption protocols. Then, select the optimal geographic locations at which to place your remote-access servers, and, finally, choose the location in your network architecture that provides the best protection for the remote-access servers.

CHOOSING A REMOTE-ACCESS METHOD

There are two primary methods for connecting remote users to a private network: **dial-up networking** and virtual private networking. In addition, if you need to connect a remote network to your private network but do not need a site-to-site VPN like those described in Chapter 10, "Protecting Intranet Communications," you can use **demand-dial routing**. The sections that follow describe each of these approaches.

Dial-Up Networking

Dial-up networking enables a remote-access client to establish a temporary dial-up connection to a physical port on a remote-access server by using a circuit such as an analog phone line, an Integrated Services Digital Network (ISDN) connection, or an X.25 link. The most common use of dial-up networking is that of a dial-up networking client that dials the phone number of a modem attached to the remote-access server. This establishes a circuit between the two devices.

> **NOTE** **Dial-Up Connections: Still a Dedicated Circuit?** A dial-up connection was once a dedicated circuit on the Public Switched Telephone Network (PSTN). There would be, literally, a pair of copper wires—connected by a series of analog switches—that connected the dial-up client to the server. Telephone companies are constantly striving to become more efficient, and today's telephone communications are carried digitally. In fact, it is entirely possible that the only areas in which your dial-up connection will actually be a dedicated circuit are between the two modems and the telephone company. After it reaches the telephone company, your traffic might be carried in Internet Protocol (IP) packets, and it might even cross the Internet!

Virtual Private Networking

Virtual private networking is the creation of an encrypted, authenticated, point-to-point connection across a public network such as the Internet. A VPN client uses special network protocols called *tunneling protocols* to make a virtual call to a virtual port on a VPN server.

MORE INFO IPSec-based VPNs are thoroughly described in Chapter 9, "Designing a Public Key Infrastructure."

A common example of virtual private networking is that of a VPN client who makes a VPN connection to a remote-access server connected to the Internet. The remote-access server answers the virtual call, authenticates the caller, and transfers data between the VPN client and the corporate network. In contrast to dial-up networking, virtual private networking is always a logical, indirect connection between the VPN client and the VPN server over a public network such as the Internet.

The primary benefit of using VPNs is reduced cost compared with dial-up connections. Supporting dial-up connections incurs the following costs:

- **Hardware purchase and installation** Dial-up networking requires an initial investment in modems or other communication hardware, server hardware, and phone line installation.

- **Monthly phone costs** Each phone line used for remote access increases the cost of dial-up networking. If you use toll-free numbers or the callback feature to defray long-distance charges for your users, these costs still can be substantial. Most businesses can arrange a bulk rate for long distance, which is preferable to reimbursing users individually at their more expensive residential rates.

- **Ongoing support** The number of remote-access users and the complexity of your remote-access design significantly affect the ongoing support costs for dial-up networking. Support costs include network support engineers, testing equipment, training, and help desk personnel to support and manage the deployment. These costs represent the largest portion of your organization's investment.

VPN access has a significant cost advantage because providing dial-up access requires purchasing modem equipment and leasing circuits from your telecommunications provider, whereas providing VPN access uses an existing Internet connection that is probably required for other uses. Although the Internet connection might need to be upgraded to provide the additional bandwidth needed by the VPN clients, the costs will almost certainly be lower than building a dial-up infrastructure.

Compare, also, the security level provided by the two access methods. Many people immediately assume that dial-up access provides greater security than a VPN. After all, allowing people on the Internet access to your entire intranet sounds very risky. However, if you analyze the security risks point-by-point, dial-up and VPN access have similar risks:

- Attackers can methodically identify both dial-up and VPN ports. If attackers want to find your dial-up ports, they will use a *war dialer*, which is a tool that dials phone numbers until a modem answers. If attackers want to find your VPN ports, they will use an IP scanner. IP scanning can happen much faster than war dialing, and it is easier to hide your identity when scanning computers on the Internet than it is when dialing telephone numbers. Whereas both dial-up and VPN ports have similar vulnerabilities, dial-up access has a slight edge because it takes longer for attackers to identify dial-up ports.

- Once the attacker has identified the ports, he or she must authenticate to the remote-access server. Both dial-up and VPN remote-access servers use the same authentication protocols. However, attackers can send requests to a VPN server faster than they can to a dial-up server. Therefore, dial-up servers have a bit of an advantage here because the long connection time makes them less vulnerable to brute-force attacks.

- Regardless of whether a dial-up or VPN connection is used, it will be difficult for an attacker to eavesdrop on a user's traffic. Gaining access to either an Internet Service Provider (ISP) or a public telephone provider would be difficult for the attacker. It would be much simpler for the attacker to eavesdrop on traffic on either end of the remote-access connection by installing a sniffer on the remote-access client or server.

Overall, VPN servers are slightly less secure than dial-up servers, but they are significantly less expensive. In the real world, most organizations are better off using a VPN and spending the money saved on other security initiatives.

Demand-Dial Routing

If you need to connect an entire network but you do not want a persistent connection like that described in Chapter 10, you can use demand-dial routing. For example, a small, remote office connected by a dial-up link might prefer to have a VPN to the corporate headquarters only during working hours to reduce dial-up costs. For the remote office, demand-dial routing can seamlessly link that network to the network at the corporate headquarters across an analog phone line or ISDN circuit during working hours while not incurring any cost when the link isn't being used.

NOTE *Comparing Demand-Dial Routing and Remote Access*
Demand-dial routing is not the same as remote access. Whereas remote access connects a single computer to a network, demand-dial routing connects entire networks.

For more information about demand-dial routing, refer to the section titled "Designing Demand-Dial Routing," later in this chapter.

UNDERSTANDING REMOTE-ACCESS TECHNOLOGIES

After choosing your remote-access method, the next step is to configure the remote-access connection. Many aspects of configuring remote access closely resemble those used for configuring wireless access, as discussed in Chapter 10. For example, remote-access servers typically use Internet Authentication Service (IAS)–based Remote Authentication Dial-In User Service (RADIUS) servers for authentication, just as many wireless access points do. However, remote-access servers use different communication and authentication protocols, as the following sections describe.

VPN Protocols

Microsoft Windows Server 2003 supports two VPN protocols: Point-to-Point Tunneling Protocol (PPTP) and Layer Two Tunneling Protocol (L2TP). In most circumstances, either protocol will work equally well. They both provide similar levels of privacy and data integrity because they support the same authentication and encryption standards. They primarily differ in stability and compatibility. PPTP is more mature, but it is not an Internet standard. L2TP is relatively new, but a wider variety of non-Microsoft clients might support it because it is an Internet standard.

NOTE *VPN Support in Different Windows Operating Systems*   *The number of incoming connections supported is one of the factors that differentiate the various editions of Windows Server 2003. Windows Server 2003, Standard Edition, can support up to 1,000 incoming PPTP connections and 1,000 incoming L2TP VPN connections. Windows Server 2003, Enterprise Edition, and Windows Server 2003, Datacenter Edition, each support 16,384 PPTP and L2TP connections. However, Windows Server 2003, Web Edition, can accept only one VPN connection at a time, which should be used to manage the server remotely.*

PPTP and L2TP is not an either/or choice. By default, a Windows Server 2003 VPN server supports both PPTP and L2TP connections simultaneously. You can use PPTP for some remote-access VPN connections (from VPN clients that are not running Windows XP or Windows 2000 and do not have an installed computer certificate) and L2TP for other remote-access VPN connections (from VPN clients running Windows XP, Windows 2000, or Microsoft L2TP VPN Client and have an installed computer certificate). If you are using both PPTP and L2TP, you can create separate RAPs that define different connection parameters for PPTP and L2TP connections.

> **NOTE Interoperability** There are both PPTP and L2TP VPN clients available for most non-Windows clients, such as Linux and Macintosh computers.

The sections that follow describe PPTP and L2TP in more detail.

PPTP

PPTP is a VPN protocol that takes advantage of the authentication, compression, and encryption mechanisms of Point-to-Point Protocol (PPP), the most common standard used for dial-up remote access. PPTP first stores the IP datagram being transmitted inside a PPP frame. PPTP tunnels the PPP frame within a Generic Routing Encapsulation (GRE) header using IP protocol 47 and a Transmission Control Protocol (TCP) header using port 1723, as illustrated in Figure 11-1.

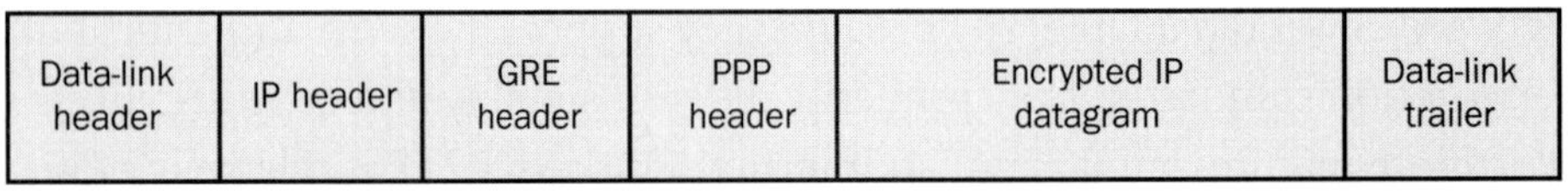

Data-link header	IP header	GRE header	PPP header	Encrypted IP datagram	Data-link trailer

Figure 11-1 PPTP tunnels data inside PPP and GRE.

PPTP relies on PPP's encryption to protect the privacy of the tunneled data. The PPP frame is encrypted with Microsoft Point-to-Point Encryption (MPPE) by using encryption keys generated from the Microsoft Challenge Handshake Authentication Protocol version 1 (MS-CHAP v1), MS-CHAP v2, or Extensible Authentication Protocol (EAP) authentication process. VPN clients must use the MS-CHAP, MS-CHAP v2, or EAP authentication protocol for the payloads of PPP frames to be encrypted. PPTP does not do the encryption itself; rather, it takes advantage of the underlying PPP encryption by encapsulating a previously encrypted PPP frame.

PPTP requires additional configuration to allow it to traverse a Network Address Translation (NAT) server or a firewall. To allow PPTP traffic through a firewall, the firewall must allow TCP port 1723 and IP protocol 47. Many NAT servers are capable of allowing a client on the internal network to connect to a PPTP server on the public network. The NAT server must specifically support PPTP, however. Although every NAT server is capable of translating standard IP traffic, the GRE protocol requires special consideration because it is not standard IP traffic, but a different network protocol entirely. The NAT server built into Routing And Remote Access is one example of a NAT server that supports PPTP.

Every version of Windows released since Microsoft Windows NT 4.0 and Windows 98 has supported PPTP, and it is still the default VPN protocol in Windows Server 2003. Earlier versions of Windows do not support either PPTP or L2TP when initially installed, but you can add support by installing additional software that can be downloaded free from Microsoft. To use a computer running Windows 95 or Windows 98 as a PPTP client, install the Windows Dial-Up Networking version 1.4 upgrade, available at *http://support.microsoft.com/kb/ 285189*. Microsoft does not support either PPTP or L2TP on Windows NT 3.5*x*, even with a software upgrade.

PPTP-based VPN connections provide data confidentiality (captured packets cannot be interpreted without the encryption key). PPTP VPN connections, however, do not provide data integrity (proof that the data was not modified in transit) or non-repudiation (proof that the data was sent by the authorized user). L2TP, described in the next section, does provide data integrity and origin authentication or non-repudiation.

L2TP

L2TP is a standardized, RFC-based tunneling protocol. Whereas PPTP uses MPPE to encrypt PPP datagrams, L2TP relies on IPSec for encryption services. The combination of L2TP and IPSec is known as *L2TP/IPSec*. To establish a VPN connection, both the VPN client and the VPN server must support both L2TP and IPSec. Because L2TP implementations always use IPSec, this chapter will simply refer to the combination as L2TP.

For many years, one of PPTP's advantages over L2TP was that PPTP could work through most NAT servers. L2TP used the source and destination IP addresses for authentication, and embedded this information inside the encrypted portion of the packet. Therefore, NAT servers were incapable of changing the source and destination IP addresses. NAT Traversal (NAT-T), a new capability of L2TP, enables you to use L2TP to connect to an L2TP server when the client is located behind a NAT server. However, the client, the server, and the NAT server must all support NAT-T. For more information on IPSec and NAT-T, refer to Chapter 10.

Encapsulation for L2TP packets consists of two layers: L2TP encapsulation and IPSec encapsulation. L2TP wraps an L2TP header and a User Datagram Protocol (UDP) header around a PPP frame containing the tunneled data, which is similar to the way PPTP performs tunneling. The resulting L2TP message is then wrapped with an IPSec Encapsulating Security Payload (ESP) header and trailer, an IPSec Authentication trailer that provides message integrity and authentication, and a final IP header, as illustrated in Figure 11-2. IPSec encrypts the message by using Data Encryption Standard (DES) or Triple DES (3DES) by using encryption keys generated from IPSec's Internet Key Exchange (IKE) negotiation process.

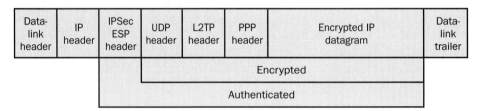

Figure 11-2   L2TP tunneling can provide both authentication and encryption.

Like most IPSec connections, L2TP generally is used with public key certificates. Unless you are using a pre-shared key for authentication (which should be used only for testing purposes), you must configure public key certificates on both the VPN server and the client. In addition, both the client and the server must trust the root CA that issued the other's certificate.

Client support for L2TP is built into the Windows Server 2003, Windows XP, and Windows 2000 remote-access client, and VPN server support for L2TP is built into Windows 2000 and Windows Server 2003. However, L2TP is not supported in out-of-the-box versions of Windows released prior to Windows 2000. To use computers running Windows 98, Windows ME, or Windows NT Workstation 4.0 as L2TP clients, install the Microsoft L2TP VPN client, which is available at *http://www.microsoft.com/windows2000/server/evaluation/news/bulletins/ l2tpclient.asp*. It can also be installed on Windows 95; however, Microsoft does not officially support the Microsoft L2TP VPN client when installed on Windows 95.

Before you can install the Microsoft L2TP VPN client on computers running Windows 95 or Windows 98, you must have Microsoft Internet Explorer 5.01 or later installed, in addition to the Dial-Up Networking version 1.4 upgrade. You can download the Dial-Up Networking upgrade from *http:// support.microsoft.com/kb/285189*.

Authentication Methods

Because dial-up, PPTP, and L2TP all use PPP for authentication, they all support the same authentication methods. There are several authentication methods available. Some you already will be familiar with because they are the same methods used for wireless networks or IPSec. Others are used primarily for authenticating remote-access users.

When choosing a remote-access authentication method, first choose between authenticating users against a RADIUS server and authenticating them against the local user database or Active Directory domain. If you choose to authenticate users against a RADIUS server, you will have configuration options similar to those used when configuring a RADIUS server to authenticate wireless users. In particular, specify the IP addresses and port numbers of one or more RADIUS servers. For information about hardening IAS servers, refer to Chapter 7, "Hardening Servers."

Regardless of whether you choose Windows or RADIUS as the authentication provider, you can choose from several authentication methods: EAP, MS-CHAP v2, MS-CHAP, CHAP, Shiva Password Authentication Protocol (SPAP), Password Authentication Protocol (PAP), pre-shared key, and unauthenticated access. Choose the most secure authentication method that all remote-access clients support. All Windows operating systems can be updated to support every standard authentication method except for EAP. Only Windows Server 2003, Windows XP, and Windows 2000 support EAP. Non-Windows operating systems might have different restrictions.

Table 11-1 shows the supported client operating systems and key features of the various authentication methods.

Table 11-1 **Authentication Methods Supported by Versions of Windows**

	EAP	MS-CHAP v2	MS-CHAP v1	CHAP	SPAP	PAP	Pre-shared Key
Supported by Windows Server 2003, Windows XP, and Windows 2000 clients		X	X	X	X	X	X

Table 11-1   **Authentication Methods Supported by Versions of Windows**

	EAP	MS-CHAP v2	MS-CHAP v1	CHAP	SPAP	PAP	Pre-shared Key
Supported on updated versions of Windows prior to Windows 2000		X (Note, however, that Windows 95 does not support MS-CHAP v2 over dial-up connections without the Dial-Up Networking upgrade installed.)	X	X	X	X	X
Supported by default on a computer running Windows Server 2003 and Routing And Remote Access	X	X	X				
Provides authentication encryption	X	X	X	X	X		X
Provides data encryption	X	X					X
Provides mutual authentication	X	X					X
Allows changing of passwords during authentication process		X	X				
Requires passwords to be stored with reversible encryption			X	X			
Vulnerable to Replay attacks					X	X	

You can use a RADIUS server to authenticate dial-up and VPN users just as you can when controlling wireless access (discussed in Chapter 10). Any standard RADIUS server will work, including IAS. If you do choose to use IAS, you can use IAS to restrict authentication, encryption, group access, and other aspects of a RAP further.

As shown in Figure 11-3, configuring Routing And Remote Access to connect to a RADIUS server involves the same information used to configure wireless users to authenticate to a RADIUS server: the primary RADIUS server's IP address, optionally an IP address for a secondary RADIUS server, and a shared secret. After completing the initial configuration, you can use the Routing And Remote Access console to add additional RADIUS servers if necessary. In addition, configure the RADIUS servers to accept the Routing And Remote Access server as a client and to use the same shared secret.

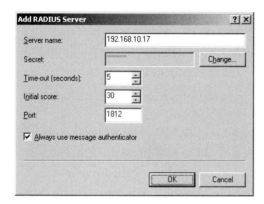

Figure 11-3 Configuring Routing And Remote Access to authenticate to a RADIUS server requires only the IP address and a shared secret.

You can use the same authentication methods whether you choose RADIUS or Windows authentication, as described in the following sections.

EAP

EAP, the protocol itself, enables an arbitrary authentication mechanism to authenticate a remote-access connection. By default, Routing And Remote Access includes support for several EAP-based authentication mechanisms: Protected EAP (PEAP), Message Digest 5 Challenge (MD5-Challenge), and Smart Card Or Other Certificate.

PEAP   PEAP is used primarily to authenticate wireless users with a user name and password. MS-CHAP v2 is the preferred method for authenticating dial-up or VPN users with user name and password credentials; therefore, never configure PEAP for use with a VPN. For more information on PEAP, refer to Chapter 10.

MD5-Challenge   MD5-Challenge is a supported EAP type that uses the same challenge handshake protocol as PPP-based CHAP, but the challenges and responses are sent as EAP messages. A typical use for MD5-Challenge is to authenticate non-Microsoft remote-access clients such as those running Mac

OSX. You can also use MD5-Challenge to test EAP interoperability. EAP with MD5-Challenge does not support encryption of connection data.

Smart Card Or Other Certificate   This authentication method, also known as EAP-Transport Layer Security (EAP-TLS), is used to enable remote-access authentication with a smart card or a public key certificate. Only Windows Server 2003, Windows XP, and Windows 2000 remote-access clients support this authentication method. The computer certificate that you assign to the L2TP client must be valid for either client authentications or IPSec. The VPN server certificate must contain the Server Authentication purpose if it is deployed as a remote-access server, or it must contain both the Server Authentication purpose and the Client Authentication purpose if it is deployed in a router-to-router VPN.

> **MORE INFO**   For more information about public key certificates, refer to Chapter 9.

Install a user certificate on all VPN clients and, if the authenticating server is a RADIUS server, install a Server Authentication computer certificate on the RADIUS server. When two or more purposes are required, they must be included in the extensions of the same certificate.

> **NOTE   EAP Support**   Remember that only Windows 2000, Windows XP, and Windows Server 2003 support EAP. Windows NT version 4.0, Windows 98, and Windows 95 do not support EAP. Remember, too, that you will always use EAP if smart cards or public key certificates are used for authentication.

MS-CHAP v1

The Windows Server 2003 family includes support for MS-CHAP v1. MS-CHAP v1 is a one-way authentication method offering both authentication encryption and data encryption. However, this encryption is relatively weak because MS-CHAP v1 bases the cryptographic key on the user's password and will use the same cryptographic key as long as the user has the same password. This gives an attacker more data with which to crack the encryption.

MS-CHAP's sole advantage is that earlier Windows clients, such as Windows 95 and Windows 98, without additional software upgrades, support it. By default, Windows Server 2003 Routing And Remote Access will accept MS-CHAP v1 authentication if the client requests it, enabling clients that haven't been upgraded to connect successfully. You can choose to disable this authentication method if all clients can use MS-CHAP v2.

MS-CHAP v2

The Windows Server 2003 family includes support for MS-CHAP v2, the preferred method for authenticating remote-access connections that do not use smart cards or public key certificates. Unlike MS-CHAP v1, MS-CHAP v2 authenticates both the client and the server. In addition, MS-CHAP v2 uses much stronger cryptography than MS-CHAP v1, including the use of a new cryptographic key for each connection and each direction of transmission.

If you do not change any of the default settings, Windows VPN remote-access clients will use MS-CHAP v2 to authenticate. Windows 95 with the Windows Dial-Up Networking Performance & Security Upgrade supports MS-CHAP v2, but only for VPN connections, not for dial-up connections. MS-CHAP (version 1 and version 2) is the only authentication protocol provided with the Windows Server 2003 family that supports password change during the authentication process. If you use a different authentication method, the user will have to connect to a domain controller through a mechanism other than a VPN to change the password.

> **NOTE   Changing Remote-User Passwords**   If you have users who always work remotely, not being able to change a password during authentication can be a real problem because they cannot simply change the password the next time they are in the office. One way to allow remote users to change their passwords is to set up a computer with Terminal Services. Have the users connect to the Terminal Server when a password change is required. When they log on, they will be prompted to change their passwords.

CHAP

CHAP is a challenge-response authentication protocol that uses the industry-standard MD5 hashing scheme to encrypt the response. Various vendors of network access servers and clients use CHAP. A computer running Windows Server 2003 and Routing And Remote Access does not allow CHAP authentication by default. However, you can enable CHAP authentication so that remote-access clients that support CHAP but do not support MS-CHAP can be authenticated.

CHAP does not support encryption of connection data. Because CHAP requires the use of reversibly encrypted passwords, avoid using it whenever possible. Enabling reversibly encrypted passwords makes it easier for an attacker to identify users' passwords if the attacker gains access to your user database. If a remote-access user uses CHAP for authentication and his or her password expires, the user cannot change the password during the remote-access authentication process. The user will need to authenticate by using MS-CHAP or connect to your internal network directly.

SPAP

SPAP is a reversible encryption mechanism used by a company named Shiva. A computer running Windows XP Professional, when connecting to a Shiva Local Area Network (LAN) Rover network device, uses SPAP, as does a Shiva client that connects to a server running Routing And Remote Access. This form of authentication is more secure than plaintext but less secure than CHAP or MS-CHAP. SPAP is not enabled by default on computers running Windows Server 2003 and Routing And Remote Access, and it should not be enabled unless specifically required.

> **NOTE   The Risks of SPAP**   When you enable SPAP as an authentication protocol, any particular user password is always sent in the same reversibly encrypted form. This makes SPAP authentication susceptible to replay attacks, in which an attacker captures the packets of the authentication process and replays the responses to gain authenticated access to your intranet. Do not use SPAP unless absolutely necessary.

PAP

PAP uses plaintext passwords and is the least secure authentication protocol. Anyone capturing the packets of the authentication process can easily read the password and use it to gain unauthorized access to your intranet. The use of PAP is highly discouraged, especially for VPN connections. It is disabled by default, and it should be used only if the remote-access client and the remote-access server cannot negotiate a more secure form of validation.

Unauthenticated Access

The Windows Server 2003 family supports unauthenticated access, which means that user credentials (a user name and password) are not required. Unauthenticated access is useful in some situations. In particular, if you are using a remote access policy (RAP) to control access by another means, such as callback or caller ID, you might decide that additional authentication is not required. Alternatively, you might encounter a scenario in which you want to allow guests to connect to a remote-access server without requiring any form of authentication.

Pre-shared Keys

Pre-shared key authentication is the only way to use L2TP without installing a computer certificate on the remote-access server. Pre-shared keys are never the preferred authentication method for enterprises because managing pre-shared keys on large numbers of computers is time-consuming. If the pre-shared key on a remote-access server is changed, a client with a manually configured pre-shared key will be unable to connect to that server until the pre-shared key on the client is changed. If the pre-shared key was distributed to the client within a Connection Manager profile, reissue that profile with the new pre-shared key and reinstall it on the client computer.

In addition, because the same pre-shared key must be distributed to all clients, the likelihood of the pre-shared key being discovered by an attacker is very high. Unless you distribute the pre-shared key within a Connection Manager profile, each user must manually type the pre-shared key. This limitation further reduces security and increases the probability of error. Pre-shared keys are unlike certificates in that the origin and history of a pre-shared key cannot be determined.

The only way to fix the vulnerability of a compromised pre-shared key is to configure a new pre-shared key on the server and either manually reconfigure the pre-shared key on all other systems or distribute the new pre-shared key in secret. During the key-change transition time, no one will have access to the server. This is equivalent to having to change the locks on the doors of your business when every employee shares the same key required for accessing the building.

Finally, the use of pre-shared keys is supported with only Windows Server 2003 and Windows XP clients. For these reasons, the use of pre-shared keys to authenticate L2TP connections is considered a relatively weak authentication method. Although pre-shared key authentication is useful for testing purposes, if you want a long-term, strong authentication method for L2TP, use public key certificates.

DESIGNING REMOTE-ACCESS SECURITY FEATURES

To help you deploy and protect your remote-access connections, Windows Server 2003 provides Connection Manager, RAPs, and quarantine control. This section describes each of these technologies, and then provides best practices for mitigating the risks of remote access.

Using Connection Manager

Connection Manager is client dial-up software that you can distribute to configure clients to connect to your remote-access servers automatically. Whereas all Windows client operating systems include dial-up software, Connection Manager includes advanced tools that make it easier for administrators to deliver preconfigured connections to network users. These tools are the Connection Manager Administration Kit (CMAK) and Connection Point Services (CPS). Rather than requiring each user to configure a dial-up or VPN connection manually on his or her client computer, you can use Connection Manager to configure the connections for them automatically.

With Connection Manager, you can automatically configure clients to connect to the closest dial-up server if you have multiple dial-in numbers, a perfect solution for environments that use a dial-up service provider, such as an ISP, that might have hundreds of numbers. If you're using a VPN, Connection Manager can automatically configure clients with the IP addresses of multiple VPN servers. You can even pre-populate the user name and password fields so that users can connect to your network with a single click. Connection Manager supports a variety of features that both simplify and enhance implementation of connection support for you and your users. Most of these features can be incorporated using the CMAK Wizard:

- **Routing table updates**   You can reconfigure user routing tables to manage your network traffic and security better.

- **Automatic proxy configuration**   You can configure user proxy settings to ensure that the user has appropriate access to internal and external resources while connected to your service.

- **Branding**   You can customize the graphics, icons, messages, Help, and phone book support in Connection Manager to provide an identity and support that are unique to your service or corporation. You can include custom logos, customer support, and phone book information to identify and represent your company.

- **Custom actions and monitored applications**   You can incorporate custom functionality, including your own programs to enhance the connection experience for your users. These programs can be run automatically at various points during the connection process, such as when users log on or disconnect. Connection Manager also supports pre-connect and pre-tunnel actions. You can set up monitored applications to disconnect automatically after the program ends.

- **Multiple-user support for each service profile**   You can provide support for users who share computers. User profiles allow two or more people to use the same computer and the same service profile. Credentials are maintained, based on the logon ID of the user, so users do not have to re-enter them for each connection.

- **Simplified distribution**   Using the CMAK wizard to automatically build your service profile (the customized software required for your users to run Connection Manager), you create a self-installing executable file that can be distributed on compact disc or downloaded by your users.

- **Custom phone books**   You can specify the phone books to provide to your users. You can download your phone book to users and provide automatic phone book updates when your users log on. To simplify maintenance, you can combine existing phone books by merging existing service profiles.

- **VPN server selection**   You can allow your users to choose a VPN server to use when connecting to your service.

- **Direct connections**   If you specify support for VPN, you can provide support for direct connections (sometimes referred to as always-on or persistent connections). Support for direct connections includes support for cable, asymmetric digital subscriber lines (ADSLs), and other types of direct connections.

- **Protocols**   You can specify whether to support VPN, which enables your users to connect to your service using PPTP, or, if running Windows 2000, Windows XP, or a member of the Windows Server 2003 family, L2TP with IPSec encryption as the tunneling protocol. These protocols enable improved security for direct and dial-up connections.

Connection Manager works with almost any Windows client operating system, including Windows 95, Windows NT 4.0, and all recent Windows operating systems. The sections that follow describe the CMAK, which is the administrative tool for configuring Connection Manager, and CPS, which manages the list of remote-access servers for the client.

CMAK

You use the CMAK to configure Connection Manager profiles. As shown in Figure 11-4, it uses a wizard interface to collect the large amount of information required to create a profile.

> **NOTE Installing CMAK**   To use CMAK, you must install the Connection Manager Administration Kit component in Add/Remove Windows Components. It is a subcomponent of Management and Monitoring Tools.

Figure 11-4   The CMAK wizard gathers information to create a Connection Manager profile.

CPS

Enterprises that manage large numbers of dial-up or VPN servers need to change the phone numbers and IP addresses of the servers frequently. You could create new Connection Manager profiles and e-mail them to all the users in your organization every time you make a change, but that would consume a great deal of administration and end-user time.

CPS provides a simpler way to distribute updated phone books. With CPS, dial-up and VPN clients can automatically retrieve updated phone books. CPS has two components:

- **Phone Book Administrator**   A tool used to create and maintain the phone book database and to publish new phone book information to the Phone Book Service.

- **Phone Book Service**   A Microsoft Internet Information Services (IIS) extension that runs on Windows NT Server 4.0 or later (with IIS). Phone Book Service automatically checks subscribers' or corporate employees' current phone books and, if necessary, downloads a phone book update.

Using Remote-Access Policies

RAPs control how or whether a connection is authorized to the network. A RAP contains a set of policy conditions that determine whether that policy applies to a given connection request. If you are using IAS as a RADIUS server, create the

RAPs by using the Internet Authentication Service console on the IAS server. Otherwise, create the RAPs by using the Routing And Remote Access console on the remote-access server.

A typical use of a dial-up or VPN RAP is to create policy conditions that specify the Active Directory security group that a client must be a member of, the time of day, or the connection type of the requesting client. A RAP is also configured to allow or deny the connection request. For example, Figure 11-5 shows a RAP that would allow connections from VPN clients who are members of the CONTOSO\Domain Users group, but only on Saturday and Sunday.

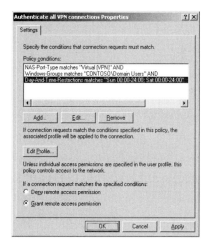

Figure 11-5   RAPs enable you to control remote-access connections based on a large number of conditions.

RAPs consist of conditions, permissions, and profile settings:

- **Conditions**   RAP conditions are one or more attributes that are com-pared with the settings of the connection attempt. If there are multiple conditions, then all of the conditions must match the settings of the connection attempt for it to match the policy. For VPN connections, you commonly use the following conditions:

    ❑ *NAS-Port-Type*–By setting the NAS-Port-Type condition to Virtual (VPN), you can specify all VPN connections.

    ❑ *Tunnel-Type*–By setting the Tunnel-Type to PPTP or L2TP, you can specify different policies for PPTP and L2TP connections.

    ❑ *Windows-Groups*–By setting the Windows-Groups to the appropriate groups, you can grant or deny access based on group membership.

■ **Permissions**   You can use the permission setting to either grant to deny remote access for the connection attempt if the remote-access permission of the user account is set to Control Access Through Remote Access Policy. Otherwise, the remote-access permission setting on the user account determines the remote-access permission.

■ **Profile Settings**   An RAP profile is a set of properties applied to a connection when it is authorized. For VPN connections, you can use the following profile settings:

❑ Dial-in constraints can be used to define how long the connection can exist or be idle before being terminated by the VPN server, among others.

❑ IP settings can define, using IP packet filters, the specific types of IP traffic that are allowed for remote-access VPN connections. With profile packet filters, you can configure the IP traffic that is allowed from remote-access clients (From client filters) or to remote-access clients (To client filters) on an exception basis: either all traffic except traffic specified by filters or no traffic except traffic specified by filters. RAP profile filtering applies to all remote-access connections that match the RAP.

❑ Authentication settings can define which authentication protocols the VPN client must use to send its credentials and the configuration of EAP types, such as EAP-TLS.

❑ Encryption settings can define the encryption strength and whether encryption is required. For encryption strengths, Windows Server 2003 supports Basic (40-bit MPPE for PPTP and 56-bit Data Encryption Standard [DES] for L2TP), Strong (56-bit MPPE for PPTP and 56-bit DES for L2TP), or Strongest (128-bit MPPE for PPTP and 3DES for L2TP).

Using conditions, permissions, and profile settings, you can control who connects to your network remotely, as well as when and how they can do it. For example, you can create a Windows group named VPNUsers whose members are the user accounts of the users creating remote-access VPN connections across the Internet. Then, you create a policy with two conditions on the policy: NAS-Port-Type is set to Virtual (VPN), and Windows-Group is set to VPNUsers. Finally, you configure the profile for the policy for a specific authentication method and encryption strength.

If there are multiple RAPs on a server, each connection request is evaluated against them according to the priority until a matching RAP either allows or denies the request. By default, two RAPs are pre-configured in Windows Server 2003. The first built-in policy is Connections To Microsoft Routing And Remote Access Server. As the name suggests, this policy is configured to match every remote-access connection to the Routing And Remote Access service. When Routing And Remote Access is reading this policy, the policy naturally matches every incoming connection. However, when an IAS server is reading the policy, a non-Microsoft vendor might provide network access; consequently, this policy will not match those connections.

The second built-in RAP is Connections To Other Access Servers. This policy is configured to match every incoming connection regardless of network access server type. However, because the first policy matches all connections to Routing And Remote Access, only connections to other remote-access servers read and match the policy when the default policy order is not changed. Unless the first policy is deleted or the default policy order is rearranged, this second policy can be read only by IAS servers.

In general, do not edit the built-in RAPs. Editing the built-in RAPs can cause confusion for administrators, which can lead to security vulnerabilities. For example, if you choose to edit the profile of the Connections To Microsoft Routing And Remote Access Server RAP to allow unencrypted communication, an administrator might assume that the policy still requires encryption without double-checking the settings. Instead of modifying the built-in RAPs, add additional RAPs that have higher priority ratings.

Using Quarantine Control

Quarantine Control is a remote-access server feature that provides phased network access for remote clients by limiting their communications to a quarantine network until the security configuration of the client computer is verified. After the client computer configuration is either brought into, or determined to be in accordance with, your organization's specific quarantine restrictions, standard VPN policy is applied to the connection, granting the user full access to internal network resources.

Quarantine control is useful because remote-access servers typically verify only the user's credentials; they do not verify that the computer itself isn't a threat. A valid user might unknowingly connect to your network using a computer infected with a worm, a virus, or other malicious software. Once they connect, the malicious software could attack computers on your internal network and might even spread like a virus. You can use quarantine control to limit the risk of this happening.

Quarantine restrictions might specify, for example, that specific antivirus software is installed and enabled while connected to your network–although Quarantine Control does not protect against sophisticated attackers because it trusts the remote-access client to report its own status. However, computer configurations for authorized users can be verified and, if necessary, corrected before they can access the network. A timer setting is also available, which you can use to specify an interval at which the connection is dropped if the client fails to meet configuration requirements.

Quarantine control uses the following process:

1. A remote-access client connects and authenticates to a remote-access server.

2. The remote-access server processes the quarantine RAP, which restricts client communications to computers in the quarantine network.

3. The client's connection manager (CM) profile starts a script to (optionally) download updates to the CM profile and verify that the client computer meets your security requirements. The script performs one of two actions:

    ❑ If the computer meets the security requirements, the script calls the *notifier component* on the client. The notifier component sends a message to the *listener component* on the server.

    ❑ If the computer does not meet the security requirements, the script notifies the user that the security check failed. You can control exactly what the script does but, typically, the script displays a Web page on a server located in a quarantine network that contains instructions for the user to update his or her computer. Alternatively, the script could automatically apply updates or install software to enable the computer to meet the requirements.

The sections that follow describe how to create the CM profile that will contain the notifier component and your client script, how to design your quarantine network, and how to configure the RAPs.

Creating the CM Profile

Quarantine Control relies on the CM profile you create for your VPN clients. The CM profile must contain:

- **A post-connect action that runs a network policy requirements script**   This is configured when the CM profile is created with CMAK.

- **A network policy requirements script**   This script performs validation checks on the remote-access client computer to verify that it conforms to network policies as part of the CM profile post-connect action. This can be a custom executable file or a simple command file (also known as a batch file). When the script has run successfully and the connecting computer has satisfied all of the network policy requirements (as verified by the script), the script runs a notifier component (an executable) with the appropriate parameters. If the script does not run successfully, it should direct the remote-access user to a quarantine resource such as an internal Web page, which describes how to install the components that are required for network policy compliance.

- **A notifier component**   This sends a message indicating a successful execution of the script to the *listener component* on the remote-access server. After the listener component receives notification, it removes the client from quarantine mode, and the remote-access server applies standard RAP to the client.

You can create your own notifier and listener components, or you can use Rqs.exe (a listener component) and Rqc.exe (a notifier component), either of which is available for download from *http://www.microsoft.com* as part of the Windows Server 2003 Resource Kit Tools. Install Rqs.exe on the remote-access server and include Rqc.exe in your CM profile along with your validation script. With these components installed, the remote-access client computer uses the CM profile to perform network policy requirement tests and to indicate its success to the remote-access computer as part of the connection setup.

Designing the Quarantine Network

Your quarantine network will contain servers that client computers must access during the security check process. The quarantine network requires special security consideration because computers on the quarantine network have not yet passed your security check and might be infected with malicious software. Therefore, take great care to harden computers connected to the quarantine network to protect them from attack during the quarantine period.

Servers that typically will be connected to the quarantine network include:

- **Remote-access server with the listening component** The remote-access server must be running a listening component. The listening component must be able to receive communications from the notifier component. If you use Rqc.exe and Rqs.exe, these communications use TCP port 7250 by default.

- **DHCP server** If you are not using your remote-access server to assign IP addresses to remote-access clients, ensure that the Dynamic Host Configuration Protocol (DHCP) server is accessible from the quarantine network. When you configure the RAP, allow communications for quarantined computers to send broadcast messages from UDP port 68 to UDP port 67.

- **DNS server** If your network policy requirements script refers to computers by hostname instead of by IP address, place a Domain Name System (DNS) server on your quarantine network. When you configure the RAP, allow communications for quarantined computers to UDP port 53 on the DNS server.

    > **NOTE You might need a WINS server, too** If some clients still rely on NetBIOS name resolution, you might need to add a Windows Internet Naming Service (WINS) server to your quarantine network.

- **File server** Your network policy requirements script might download an updated CM profile to enable you to change the client security requirements easily. To enable the file transfer, connect a file server to your quarantine network and configure the quarantine RAP to allow communications with the file server using TCP ports 139 and 445. The file server should be configured to allow anonymous access to the files that might be retrieved by quarantined clients.

- **Web server** Some client computers will not meet your security requirements. This is probably because the computer has not yet received a required update. If you simply disconnect the remote-access session, the user will be confused and probably will become frustrated. Instead, provide a friendly message describing why the user cannot connect to your internal network and listing steps the user can take to rectify the problem. The easiest way to do this is to connect a Web server to your quarantine network and have your network policy requirements script open a predefined Web page containing the friendly error message and further instructions for the user. When you configure the RAP, allow communications for quarantined computers to TCP port 80 on the Web server. The Web server should be configured to allow anonymous access to the files that might be retrieved by quarantined clients. Alternatively, the script could open a file located on a file server.

The quarantine network does not have to be a dedicated network segment. Your RAP can limit communications to specific IP addresses, so as long as each of the servers in your quarantine network has a static IP address, there is little risk in enabling quarantined computers to communicate across your internal network with the limited number of servers they need to access during the quarantine period. Figure 11-6 shows how you might configure a quarantine network.

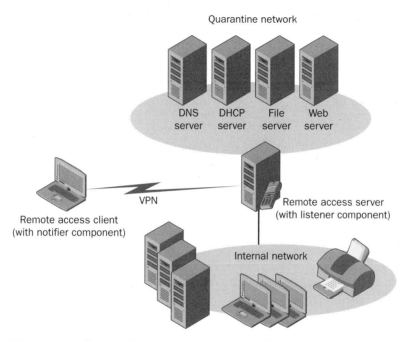

Figure 11-6   Quarantine networks must contain a remote-access server with a listener component, and they often contain a DNS server, file server, and Web server.

Configuring Remote-Access Policies for Quarantine Control

After creating listener and notifier components, configure quarantine RAPs. Create separate policies that will apply to users with full access, and those remote-access users who are restricted to quarantine. When you create the quarantine policy, configure an input filter using the MS-Quarantine-IPFilter attribute to allow network traffic on TCP port 7250 (if you use the Resource Kit tools) to the remote-access server to enable the notifier and listener components to communicate, as shown in

Figure 11-7. You can specify a different port, but be sure you reconfigure both the listener and the notifier. If your network policy requirements script communicates with other servers (for example, to perform DNS queries or retrieve the latest version of the CM profile from a file server), be sure to enable those communications as well.

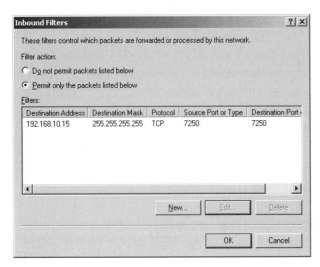

Figure 11-7   By default, the quarantine control notification and listener components use port 7250.

> **NOTE   Configuring Quarantine Input Filter**   The quarantine input filter needs to allow access only to the IP address of your remote-access server and any servers that your network policy requirements script communicates with. To allow communications with a single IP address, in the Edit IP Filter dialog box, provide the remote-access server's IP address, and use the subnet mask 255.255.255.255.

Specify a quarantine timeout period by using the MS-Quarantine-Session-Timeout attribute. Allow enough time for the script to check the client's security settings and display helpful information if the user does not meet the security requirements. If you want users to be able to install software (such as updates or antivirus software) while in quarantine, allow extra time for the user to complete those tasks. After you create the quarantine policy (as shown in Figure 11-8), ensure that it is the first policy in the list of RAPs.

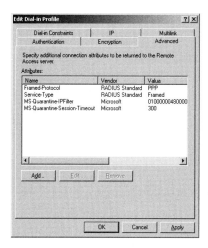

Figure 11-8   Quarantine policies use the MS-Quarantine-IPFilter and MS-Quarantine-Session-Timeout attributes.

> **MORE INFO**   **Configuring Quarantine Policy**   For detailed instructions for configuring quarantine RAPs and creating quarantine scripts, read the white paper titled "Microsoft Windows Server 2003 Network Access Quarantine Control," at *http://www.microsoft.com/windowsserver2003/ techinfo/overview/quarantine.mspx.*

Best Practices for Mitigating the Risk of Remote Access

Exposing your internal network to access from an external network always carries risk. However, you can mitigate that risk by following these best practices:

■ **Mitigate traditional authentication risks**   VPN servers typically must accept incoming connections from clients on the Internet. As a result, it is possible for an attacker to submit authentication requests and perform traditional authentication attacks such as password-guessing dictionary attacks. To limit this risk, follow these best practices:

❑ Whenever possible, use EAP-TLS with smart cards. If smart cards are too costly, deploy client certificates to VPN client computers.

❑ If you use password-based authentication, enforce strong password policies on your network to make dictionary attacks more difficult.

❑ Make sure that PAP, SPAP, and CHAP are disabled. PAP, SPAP, and CHAP are disabled by default on the profile of a RAP.

❑ Disable MS-CHAP. MS-CHAP is enabled by default on the profile of an RAP. Before you disable MS-CHAP, ensure that all of the clients of your access server are capable of using MS-CHAP v2. If your server is not running Windows Server 2003, you will need the latest service packs and dial-up networking updates to support MS-CHAP v2.

❑ If you do not disable MS-CHAP, disable LAN Manager authentication for MS-CHAP. LAN Manager authentication for MS-CHAP is enabled by default on clients running earlier versions of Windows.

■ **Avoid account lockout**   When remote-access account lockout is enabled, if a malicious user attempts a dictionary attack with the logon name of an authorized user, both the malicious user and the authorized user are locked out of the account until the account lockout threshold is reached. To limit this risk, be cautious when defining account lockout policy. If you do enable account lockouts, ensure that administrators are alerted as soon as an account is locked out so that the administrator can determine whether the lockout is caused by an attack or by user error.

■ **Use Windows 2000 Server and Windows Server 2003**   Use only servers that are running Windows 2000 Server or Windows Server 2003, if possible. Using servers running Routing And Remote Access in conjunction with servers that are running Windows NT 4.0 decreases your network security.

■ **Require the VPN server or a DHCP server to assign IP address leases to VPN clients**   Do not allow VPN clients to specify their own IP address. The method by which the VPN server assigns addresses to remote-access clients (either using addresses that the VPN server obtains from a DHCP server or using addresses from a specified range of addresses that you configure) is set when you run the Routing And Remote Access Server Setup Wizard.

■ **Always use L2TP connections for the strongest encryption**   Use smart cards for the most secure authentication, and use certificates when smart cards are not practical.

■ **Use certificates for IKE negotiations**   As discussed both elsewhere in this chapter and in Chapter 10, do not use pre-shared keys because they cause management challenges that lead to security vulnerabilities.

DESIGNING DEMAND-DIAL ROUTING

Demand-dial routing is more complex than remote-access connections involving a single computer because you must enable traffic from an entire network to be routed to the remote network. Therefore, understanding how to design demand-dial routing requires a basic understanding of routing and routing protocols. In addition, you need to understand several configuration settings that are not required for traditional remote-access or VPN connections.

Routing Across Demand-Dial Links

As you may know, routers are responsible for forwarding packets between networks. As shown in Figure 11-9, a router might have to forward packets to networks through several different neighboring routers. Therefore, each router must have a map of the entire network to understand the most efficient way to forward packets to remote networks. These maps are stored in **routing tables**. Routing tables are lists of remote networks and the neighboring routers that can forward traffic to each network.

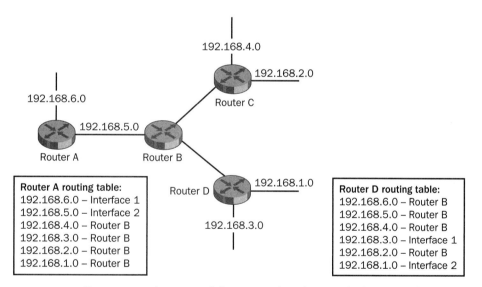

Figure 11-9   Routers need a map of the network to know which way to forward packets to distant networks.

You could manually configure each router with a map of the entire network. However, if the network changed or a router failed, you would need to reconfigure every router manually. On enterprise networks with dozens of routers, this would be extremely time-consuming. On the Internet (with thousands of routers), reconfiguring every router would be impossible.

Routers use **routing protocols** to create a map of the network automatically and to notify other routers about changes. When routing protocols are configured properly, you can add a new network and, within a few minutes, every router on your network will know about the new network and be able to forward traffic to it. Figure 11-10 illustrates this process.

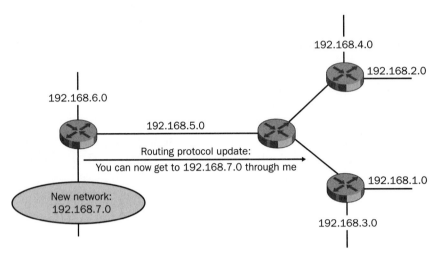

Figure 11-10   Routers use routing protocols to notify each other of new networks, failures, and changes automatically.

Site-to-site VPNs connect remote networks. As a result, routers need to be able to forward traffic to the remote network. VPN endpoints typically act like any other router, including communicating with routers and other VPN endpoints using routing protocols. Figure 11-11 shows this configuration.

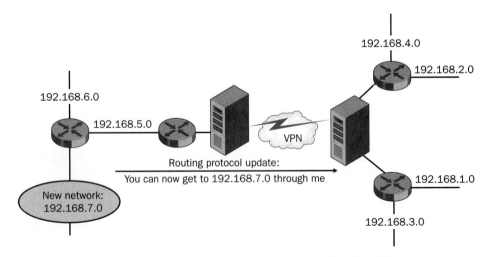

Figure 11-11   VPN endpoints send routing protocol updates just like any other router.

Routing protocols do not work well with demand-dial routing, unfortunately. Demand-dial routing automatically establishes a dial-up link when any type of traffic needs to be forwarded to a remote network, including routing protocol communications. Many routing protocols send updates on a regular basis, whether or not a network configuration has changed. For example, Routing Information Protocol (RIP) sends a message every 30 seconds. Therefore, if you use RIP with demand-dial routing, the VPN would establish the demand-dial routing connection every 30 seconds. In real terms, the demand-dial routing connection would stay up indefinitely, defeating its purpose.

To prevent this, manually configure the routing tables of demand-dial VPN endpoints with static routes. If your network configuration changes, update the routing tables manually. Figure 11-12 shows Routing And Remote Access configured with static routes. Static routes introduce a significant risk: if there is a network change or failure on either end of the demand-dial link, the network change won't be reflected until an administrator updates the routes. If an administrator is unavailable at the time of the change, static routes could lead to an extended network outage.

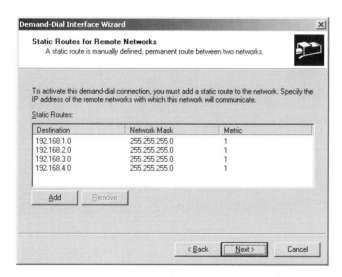

Figure 11-12   You must configure static routes for demand-dial VPN routing manually.

Configuring Demand-Dial Links

Whereas the concept of demand-dial routing is fairly simple, configuration of demand-dial routing is relatively complex compared with remote-access connections or site-to-site VPNs. This complexity is due to the following factors:

- **Differentiation between remote-access clients and calling routers**   Both routing and remote-access services coexist on the same computer running Windows Server 2003. Both remote-access clients and demand-dial routers can initiate a connection. The computer running Windows Server 2003 that answers a connection attempt must be able to distinguish a remote-access client from a demand-dial router. If the user name, which is included in the authentication credentials sent by the router that initiates the connection (the calling router), matches the name of a demand-dial interface on the Windows Server 2003 that answers the connection attempt (the answering router), the connection is a demand-dial connection. Otherwise, the incoming connection is a remote-access connection.

- **Configuration of both ends of the connection**   Configure both ends of the connection, even if only one end of the connection is initiating a demand-dial connection. Configuring only one side of the connection means that packets are successfully routed in only one direction, which is not sufficient for most networking.

- **Configuration of static routes**   Do not use dynamic routing protocols over temporary demand-dial connections. Therefore, routes for network IDs that are available across the demand-dial interface must be added, as static routes, to the routing tables of the demand-dial routers. You can add static routes manually or by using **auto-static updates**. Auto-static updates are a method of automatically adding static routes to the routing table after establishing a demand-dial connection.

- **Choosing between one-way and two-way connections**   Demand-dial connections can be one-way or two-way. With one-way initiated connections, one VPN router is always the calling router and one VPN router is always the answering router. One-way initiated connections are well suited to a permanent-connection, spoke-and-hub topology where the branch office router is the only router that initiates the connection. One-way initiated connections require the following:

❑ The answering router is configured as both a LAN and demand-dial router.

❑ A user account is added for the authentication credentials of the calling router that is accessed and validated by the answering router.

❑ A demand-dial interface is configured at the answering router with the same name as the user account that is used by the calling router. This demand-dial interface is not used to dial out; therefore, it is not configured with the host name or IP address of the calling router or with valid user credentials.

With two-way initiated connections, either VPN router can be the calling router or answering router, depending on which one is initiating the connection. Both VPN routers must be configured to both initiate and accept a site-to-site VPN connection. You can use two-way initiated connections when the site-to-site VPN connection is not active 24 hours a day and traffic from either router is used to create an on-demand connection. Two-way initiated site-to-site VPN connections require the following:

❑ Both routers are configured as LAN and demand-dial routers.

❑ User accounts are added for both routers so that the authentication credentials for the calling router are accessed and validated by the answering router.

❑ Demand-dial interfaces, with the same name as the user account that is used by the calling router, must be fully configured at both routers, including settings for the host name, IP address or phone number of the answering router, and user account credentials.

❑ Static routes are configured on both routers.

NOTE **Preventing Unnecessary Connections**   *To prevent the calling router from making unnecessary connections, you can use demand-dial filtering to control the traffic that initiates demand dialing and dial-out hours to control when the connection can be established.*

DESIGNING REMOTE-ACCESS ARCHITECTURES

The placement of remote-access servers in your network's architecture can have a profound effect on the level of risk you must accept. Determine whether VPN servers will be placed inside or outside your firewall, what geographic locations should host remote-access servers, and whether you will allow **split tunneling**, a technique for allowing VPN clients to communicate with both a private network and the Internet simultaneously. The sections that follow provide guidance for you to make these design decisions.

VPN Servers in Network Architectures

You have four choices for where to place VPN servers in your network architectures:

- Behind the firewall
- In front of the firewall
- Between two firewalls in a screened subnet
- Hosted at your ISP

The recommended location for a VPN server is behind a firewall, as shown in Figure 11-13. In this design, the firewall provides packet filtering for the VPN server. Ideally, configure the firewall to allow only PPTP (TCP port 1723 and Protocol ID 47) or L2TP (UDP port 500, UDP port 4500, Protocol ID 50) traffic through to the VPN server's IP address. The drawback to this scenario is that the firewall cannot monitor or filter traffic passing through the VPN tunnel because it is encrypted until the traffic reaches the VPN server.

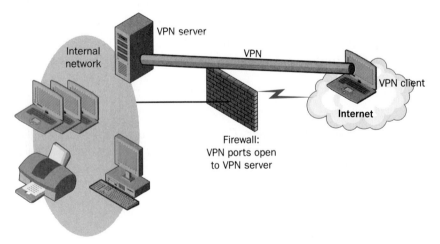

Figure 11-13   The recommended location for a VPN server is behind the firewall.

Some security designers choose to place the VPN server outside the firewall, as shown in Figure 11-14. The VPN server must decrypt the tunneled traffic from the VPN client and then send the traffic through the firewall to the internal network. This enables the firewall to filter traffic contained within the VPN connection. However, this is typically more trouble than it's worth. Because you can't always predict what types of network protocols clients need to use to connect to computers on the internal network, either open all ports from the VPN server to the internal network or spend a great deal of time troubleshooting VPN client connection problems as you determine which protocols to allow through the firewall. Because neither filtering option is ideal, this is not a recommended configuration.

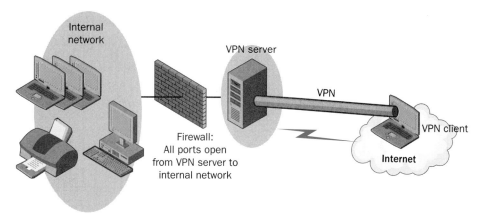

Figure 11-14   Placing the VPN outside the firewall enables you to filter tunneled traffic.

If you have a screened subnet with two layers of firewalls, you can also choose to place the VPN server in the screened subnet, as shown in Figure 11-15. In this case, enable incoming PPTP and/or L2TP to the VPN server through the external firewall. In addition, allow any network communications from the VPN server to the internal network through the internal firewall.

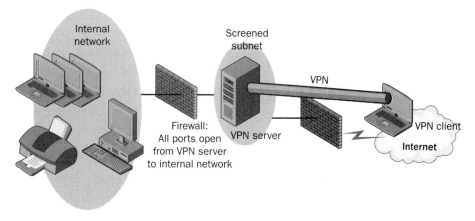

Figure 11-15   Place the VPN server in the screened subnet if you have one.

There is one final option: not hosting the VPN servers on your site at all, as shown in Figure 11-16. Many ISPs offer network-based VPNs as an additional service on top of their standard Internet access service. This puts the responsibility of protecting the VPN server on your ISP, which might be appealing to you. The service fee charged by the ISP might even be less than your ongoing management costs for maintaining the VPN.

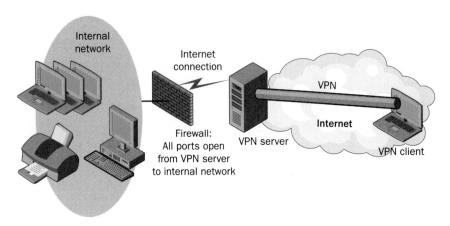

Figure 11-16   Many ISPs offer VPN services.

Geographic Placement of VPN Servers

VPN server placement is an important design choice that can influence both the security and performance of your extranet. In essence, you must decide which of your offices will host remote-access VPN servers. The more remote-access VPN servers you set up, the more choices for VPN endpoints users have. This enables users to choose VPN servers that are closer to them, which improves VPN performance. However, adding VPN servers also increases hardware and management costs, and increases your security risk by increasing the number of potential entry points to your internal network.

You might choose to enable remote access through only a single VPN server. If this meets your needs, a single VPN server is an ideal solution because it minimizes security risks and management costs. Figure 11-17 shows an extreme example of this configuration, in which a single VPN server provides access to a worldwide corporation's internal network. In this example, users anywhere on the Internet would need to connect to the VPN server located at the enterprise's North American headquarters.

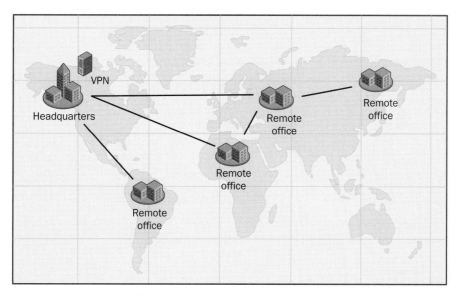

Figure 11-17 Using a single VPN server minimizes costs.

However, a single VPN server might not meet your needs if you have many offices and remote users spread around a large area. Consider Figure 11-17 again. If a user in Africa needs to connect to a file server located at the African office, the user would have to connect to the Internet and then establish a connection to the North American VPN server. The user's network traffic would then have to travel to North America across the Internet, and then back to Africa across the private network. This inefficient routing would not prevent the user from accessing the file server, but it would hurt network performance.

The primary reason that type of inefficient routing might cause poor network performance is network **latency**. Latency is the time it takes a packet to travel between two points, usually measured in milliseconds. The higher a connection's latency, the longer it takes to access the resource. High latency makes a remote network resource seem sluggish. In the case of a file server, high latency would make browsing files in a shared folder very slow.

> **NOTE Latency vs. Bandwidth**   Latency does not have a significant effect on bandwidth when transferring large files. It would not take much longer to transfer a 1-GB file across a high-latency link than it would to transfer the same file across a low-latency link.

Once again, consider Figure 11-17. If the round-trip latency—the time it takes for a packet to travel from the source to the destination and then back to the source—between Africa and North America is .5 seconds, the user's latency when accessing the file server will be about a full second; packets sent from the VPN user to the African file server must cross the Atlantic Ocean twice. When the VPN user clicked a shared folder to view its contents, it would take at least a full second—probably two—to view the contents of the folder.

This latency problem could be resolved by adding a VPN server at the African office, as shown in Figure 11-18. A user in Africa who needs to access the African file server could connect directly to the African VPN server, where latency would be negligible. Redundancy is an added benefit; if the African VPN server is offline, the user could connect to the North American VPN server, and still access internal network resources (albeit with a severe performance penalty).

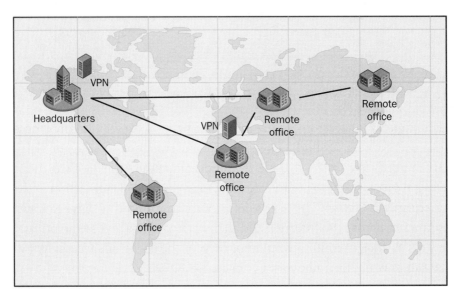

Figure 11-18   Use multiple VPN servers to improve performance and provide redundancy.

To provide optimal performance to all users, you might add VPN servers to each location. You could then add each VPN server to your phone book and instruct VPN users to choose the location closest to them.

> **NOTE**   *Choosing a VPN Server Location*   It is typically more efficient for users to choose the VPN server closest to their location, rather than choosing the VPN server closest to the network resource they are trying to access because latency over the Internet is typically higher than latency over internal networks. Therefore, when you are required to make a choice, place VPN servers close to users rather than close to network resources. Instruct users to choose the VPN server closest to their current location, and to pick a different server when traveling.

What Is Split Tunneling?

As discussed earlier in this chapter, inefficient VPN design can lead to high latency, which decreases network performance. Latency is not just a consideration when accessing resources on the internal network, however. You must also consider latency when VPN users are accessing the Internet.

If you do not enable split tunneling, VPN users must access the Internet through your internal network, as shown in Figure 11-19. This might improve the security of the connection because it routes all the users' Internet traffic through your own proxy servers and firewalls.

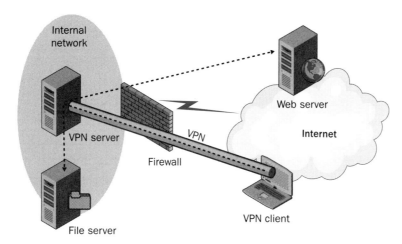

Figure 11-19   Without split tunneling, VPN users must access Internet resources through your internal network.

If you do enable split tunneling, VPN users can directly access Internet resources, and only traffic addressed to your internal network is routed through the VPN connection, as shown in Figure 11-20. This improves the performance of network connections to Internet resources, which will make common tasks such as browsing Web sites much faster. However, because Internet traffic is not routed through your internal firewalls and proxy servers, it increases the risk that the user's computer will become infected with a worm, virus, or other malicious software. If a user's computer does become infected while connected to your VPN, the malicious software can use the VPN connection to attack computers on your internal network.

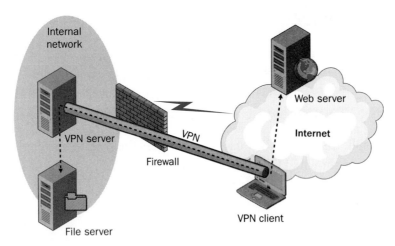

Figure 11-20   With split tunneling, VPN users can access the Internet without going through your internal network.

Split tunneling requires client computers to know which destination networks should be accessed through the VPN because all other traffic will be routed directly to the Internet. Therefore, configure routing tables on the client computer. The easiest way to do this is to use Connection Manager Administration Kit Wizard; it will prompt you to enter a list of IP subnets that clients should access through your VPN. Clients will use their default gateway (typically, their Internet connection) for all other destinations.

In summary, without split tunneling, all traffic from a VPN client is routed through the VPN connection, even if it's not destined for your internal network. With split tunneling, traffic that's not destined for your internal network can take the shortest path to the destination.

DESIGNING EXTRANET IDENTITY MANAGEMENT

Every organization works with outside customers and vendors. Often, you must allow outside organizations access to your internal applications and data to enable business processes to function efficiently. Before you can authorize them to access internal resources and data, you must have a technique for authenticating the users and managing their identity information.

You know how to manage your intranet users' identities: with Active Directory directory service. Active Directory is typically not the right solution for extranet identity management, however, because Active Directory users automatically receive some level of access to resources in your domain. This presents a significant security risk.

Active Directory Application Mode

With capabilities such as hierarchical organization, distributed architectures, and automatic replication, Active Directory seems like an ideal solution for authenticating any user type, including both intranet and extranet users. Developers love using Active Directory because Microsoft has provided very powerful development tools and application programming interfaces (APIs) for connecting to it. In fact, Active Directory is an ideal solution for managing identities of Windows users on an intranet. However, it has significant drawbacks for other uses:

- Users in Active Directory are security principals and may receive higher privileges to network resources than unauthenticated users.

- You can run only one Active Directory instance on a single computer.

- Active Directory cannot be redistributed with applications and cannot run on Microsoft Windows XP.

Because of these limitations, most enterprises should not use Active Directory for extranet identity management. However, Active Directory Application Mode (ADAM) enables you to leverage the power and flexibility of Active Directory while bypassing these limitations, making it the perfect choice for extranet application identity management. Your developers will use the same APIs to access ADAM as they would to access an Active Directory domain, so they can easily port existing applications to ADAM.

ADAM is similar to Active Directory, but you can choose to build your own schema from scratch. If you want to use aspects of a standard Active Directory schema, you can use the ADAM installation wizard, which Figure 11-21 shows, to import one of four Lightweight Directory Interchange Format (LDIF) files that contain schema for objects such as people, organizations, and users.

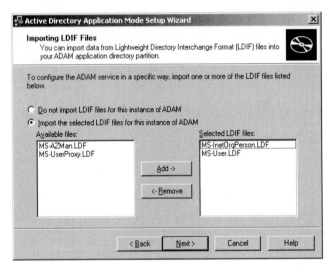

Figure 11-21   Instead of creating your own schema from scratch, you can import standard schemas into a new ADAM instance.

ADAM includes several administration tools: a version of ADSI Edit that lets you directly view and edit objects, the ADAM Schema Microsoft Management Console (MMC) snap-in for editing the schema, and a variety of command-line tools for manipulating the directory service and its data. Figure 11-22 demonstrates ADAM's version of ADSI Edit and ADAM's ability to run multiple instances on one computer. As you can see, ADSI Edit is connected to three Active Directory instances: the Active Directory domain controller on port 389, an instance of ADAM on port 50000, and a second instance of ADAM on port 51000.

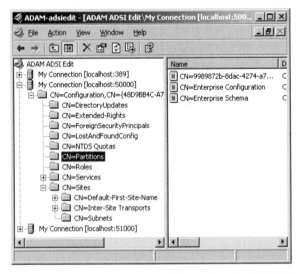

Figure 11-22   You use a special version of ADSI Edit to manage ADAM.

Active Directory to ADAM Synchronizer

Often, enterprises need to populate a directory service by copying a portion of an Active Directory domain. For these users, Microsoft provides Active Directory to ADAM Synchronizer (ADAMSync). ADAMSync is a scriptable command-line tool capable of selectively copying objects from your Active Directory domain and storing copies as instances of ADAM. Because you are working with copies, you can extend and modify the schema without touching your enterprise's Active Directory. You can even add additional users to the ADAM instance without risking any abuse of domain privileges. This solution is perfect for applications that will be accessed by both internal users with Active Directory accounts and external partners, vendors, or customers.

Authorization Manager

Both Active Directory domains and ADAM are capable of storing user credentials, but they typically do not store authorization information. If you need to restrict access to any aspect of your extranet application, you will need a way to control which users have access to which parts of your application. Developers can create custom tools to configure role-based authorization to application components, but doing so requires a significant development effort.

Rather than creating custom tools, developers should leverage Authorization Manager. Authorization Manager enables system administrators to control role-based authorization to an application from the Authorization Manager console, Azman.msc, which Figure 11-23 shows, while minimizing development effort. Authorization Manager allows developers and administrators to define operations (for instance, creating and closing trouble tickets) and tasks, which contain one or more operations. You can then grant access to groups and roles, which can be based on objects in Active Directory or can be unique to the application. Of course, developers need to write the application with Authorization Manager in mind because they must associate application components with the various operations.

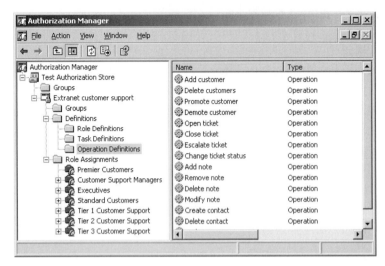

Figure 11-23   The Authorization Manager console enables developers and administrators to control authorization to a compatible application.

Guidelines for Designing Extranet Identity Management Solutions

When choosing an extranet identity management solution, be sure to balance deployment and management costs, risk management, and end-user impact. Consider each identity management solution's resistance to attack, the resources that a solution will expose if an attack is successful, your ability to detect an attempted attack, and your access to audit information that can be used as evidence in civil or criminal proceedings.

When evaluating extranet identity management technologies, use Lightweight Directory Access Protocol (LDAP)–based directories, such as ADAM, whenever possible. Using a standard protocol such as LDAP greatly increases your chances that the solution will continue to be useful if you add or update front-end applications.

> **NOTE   Designing Custom Application Authentication**   Use a single directory service for applications that have the same users. Be sure the application supports Authorization Manager so administrators can restrict which users can access which applications.

Compare non-Microsoft LDAP solutions to ADAM during your evaluation phase. Although another solution may offer important benefits to you, ADAM has some key advantages: it's a free download, it can be integrated with an Active Directory domain, and it supports the same programming interfaces as a traditional Active Directory. If you do choose ADAM, further simplify future upgrades and migrations by basing your schema on the standard LDIF files and extend them as needed.

Rather than modifying your Active Directory schema for an application, use ADAMSync to replicate relevant portions of your Active Directory's content. Create a separate user account with read-only access to the portion of the Active Directory to be replicated. Then, use Task Scheduler to schedule ADAMSync to run with the account's credentials.

> **CAUTION** **Scheduling ADAMSync** ADAMSync has a /creds parameter that you can use to specify a user name and password that ADAMSync will use to authenticate to the remote directory. However, this technique requires you to write the user's credentials in clear text, which presents a significant security vulnerability.

Figure 11-24 shows how you could give both internal customer support users and external customer users access to an extranet customer support application. ADAMSync selectively replicates primary accounts from the internal Active Directory to shadow accounts in the customer support application's LDAP directory. This grants both internal and external users access without requiring you to create user accounts for customers in your internal Active Directory domain.

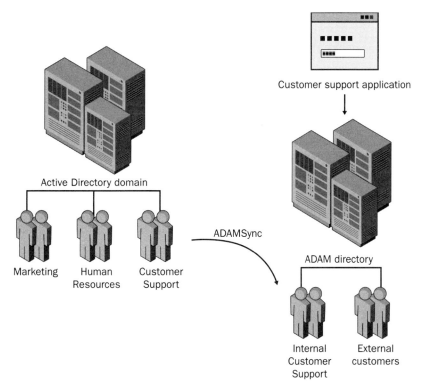

Figure 11-24 Use synchronization to copy a single user account across multiple directories.

NOTE **Identity Integration Feature Pack**   If you need to synchronize accounts between an Active Directory domain and an ADAM instance, also evaluate the Identity Integration Feature Pack for Microsoft Windows Server Active Directory. For more information, visit *http:// www.microsoft.com*.

If you need to control access to your application and you use Active Directory for identity management, recommend that your developers create an **authorization store**. An authorization store is a database that defines which users and groups can access an application's features. With an authorization store, administrators can use the Authorization Manager (Azman.msc) tool to authorize users to access the application, which means that your developers do not have to create custom authorization management tools.

If you choose to store extranet user credentials in a database, take care to improve the security by hardening the network and server before carefully analyzing the security of the database architecture. In particular, ensure that user passwords are not stored in clear text. Instead, direct developers to store keyed hashes of the user passwords. Hashing passwords with a non-keyed algorithm, such as MD5 or Secure Hash Algorithm 1 (SHA1), provides little deterrence to an attacker with a hashed-password index. However, keyed hashes, such as Hashed Message Authentication Code Secure Hash Algorithm (HMACSHA1) and Media Access Control Triple Data Encryption Standard (MACTripleDES), invalidate hashed-password indexes by introducing a secret key before generating the hash.

When evaluating authentication mechanisms, weigh the costs and benefits of user name/password authentication mechanisms, Microsoft .NET Passport, client certificates, and smart cards. For example, client certificates require you to issue a certificate to each extranet user, but the extra time required when creating a user is worthwhile if you consider password-guessing attacks to be a serious risk.

Because your partners may use different software platforms, choose standards-based extranet communication and authentication protocols whenever possible. For example, developers creating Hypertext Transfer Protocol/Simple Object Access Protocol (HTTP/SOAP) Web Services using Microsoft .NET Framework will need to choose between implementing HTTP/SOAP authentication or Web Services Security (WS-Security) authentication. HTTP/SOAP authentication is much easier to program, but it is not an open standard. WS-Security authentication is an open standard, which will enable a wider range of clients to use the Web Service.

SUMMARY

- VPNs provide remote access at low cost while meeting the security requirements of most organizations. Dial-up networking connections provide remote access without requiring clients to have an Internet connection, but the cost of maintaining dial-up equipment can be high.

- You can create VPNs by using either PPTP or L2TP, or both. In most cases, L2TP is the better choice because it offers greater compatibility and higher levels of encryption. In addition to choosing the VPN protocol, choose from several different authentication protocols.

- Connection Manager enables you to deploy complex remote-access client configuration settings easily. You can use RAPs to restrict who connects to your internal network, what resources they can access, and when they can connect. Quarantine control provides a means to verify that client computers meet your security requirements before they are granted access to your internal network.

- Demand-dial routing provides a compromise between remote-access connections and site-to-site connections by enabling you to connect remote networks using dial-up links. You can minimize the usage costs on the dial-up link by using RAPs to restrict the types of traffic that initiate the connection and the hours the connection can be used. Unlike traditional remote-access connections and site-to-site VPNs, demand-dial routing requires you to configure static routes.

- In general, place remote-access servers inside your firewall, unlike a publicly accessible Web server, which you would normally place outside your firewall. When choosing which locations to deploy VPN servers to, you must balance the cost of maintaining VPN servers with your client performance requirements. VPN connections can dramatically influence the performance of connections to Internet servers; however, you can eliminate this impact by enabling split tunneling.

- Avoid creating user accounts for external partners, vendors, and customers in Active Directory domains. Instead, use ADAM.

REVIEW QUESTIONS

1. Which of the following authentication protocols can fully updated Windows 98 VPN clients use? (Choose all that apply.)

    a. EAP

    b. MS-CHAP v2

    c. MS-CHAP v1

    d. CHAP

    e. SPAP

    f. PAP

2. Your organization's security policy requires that passwords not be stored with reversible encryption. Which of the following authentication protocols can you use? (Choose all that apply.)

    a. EAP

    b. MS-CHAP v2

    c. MS-CHAP v1

    d. CHAP

    e. SPAP

    f. PAP

3. Your organization still has clients running Windows 95. Which of the following protocols can you use to authenticate dial-up clients? (Choose all that apply.)

    a. EAP

    b. MS-CHAP v2

    c. MS-CHAP v1

    d. CHAP

    e. SPAP

    f. PAP

4. Which of the following is an advantage of using VPNs for remote access over dial-up connections?

   a. Lower costs

   b. No need for an Internet connection

   c. More resistant to password-guessing attacks

   d. More difficult for attackers to identify

5. Which of the following is an advantage of using pre-shared keys for VPN client authentication?

   a. More resistant to attack

   b. Better performance

   c. Does not require a certification authority

   d. Easier to manage

6. For which of the following reasons would you enable split tunneling?

   a. Computers running Windows 98 cannot access resources on the intranet.

   b. You are concerned about malicious software accessing your intranet through a VPN connection.

   c. Users complain about poor performance when connected to the VPN and attempting to access servers on the intranet.

   d. Users complain about poor performance when connected to the VPN and attempting to access servers on the Internet.

7. You are a security consultant. Your manager has asked you to recommend a VPN architecture to connect two remote offices. Their primary concern is that the VPN is easy to manage because they have no full-time IT support. What type of VPN architecture would you recommend?

   a. VPN servers located behind their firewalls

   b. VPN servers located in front of their firewalls

   c. VPN servers hosted by their ISP

CASE SCENARIOS

Case Scenario 11-1: Recommending a VPN Solution

You are a security designer at Fabrikam, Inc., an enterprise services company with approximately 2,000 employees. Approximately 250 of those employees are consultants who are required to travel almost constantly with mobile computers running Windows XP. They need to stay in touch with the rest of Fabrikam while they travel, so your management decided to forward Post Office Protocol 3 (POP3) requests at the NAT server that separates the public and private networks to allow consultants to retrieve their e-mail from the computer that runs Microsoft Exchange Server.

There is a problem, however. The consultants have asked to access other resources on the internal network: file servers, intranet servers, and databases. You cannot forward all of this traffic through your Windows Server 2003–based NAT server. Even if you could, you would not want to allow the communications to travel across the Internet unencrypted. In fact, your IT group has done everything it can to reduce unencrypted communications on the internal network, and it has deployed IPSec with a public key infrastructure (PKI) to provide authentication.

Your manager has asked you to provide a way to allow traveling consultants to access the resources on the internal network while minimizing the risks.

1. Which of the following solutions will you recommend? (Choose the best answer.)

    a. Deploy dial-up servers running Windows Server 2003. Configure the clients to dial directly in to the Fabrikam headquarters and authenticate to the remote-access servers by using MS-CHAP v2 authentication.

    b. Deploy dial-up servers running Windows Server 2003. Configure the clients to dial directly into the Fabrikam headquarters and authenticate to the remote-access servers by using EAP authentication with public key certificates.

    c. Configure the Windows Server 2003–based NAT server with VPN services. Configure the clients to connect directly to the VPN server and authenticate by using MS-CHAP v2 authentication.

    d. Configure the Windows Server 2003–based NAT server with VPN services. Configure the clients to connect directly to the VPN server and authenticate by using EAP authentication with public key certificates.

2. Will you recommend using a PPTP or L2TP VPN?

    a. How will you configure the network connections on the client computers?

    b. Should you recommend using a RADIUS server?

Case Scenario 11-2: Designing a VPN Architecture

You are a consultant hired by Margie's Travel. Margie's Travel is an up-and-coming travel agency with five agents in North America and four agents in Europe. In addition, Margie herself runs the worldwide headquarters in North America. There is also a dedicated regional manager in Europe. Margie and the European regional manager each have dedicated office spaces; however, all the travel agents work from their homes.

Their IT infrastructure is minimal. In Margie's Seattle-based headquarters, she has a small network with a computer running Windows Server 2003 acting as a file server, e-mail server, and intranet Web server. Each travel agent has a computer running Windows XP Professional with a small LAN connecting the computer to the Internet. Currently, agents use their computers to access a Web-based application hosted by a service provider to manage travel plans.

Margie's Travel has challenges that it hopes you can solve by using technology. First, it would like to phase out the use of the Web-based application because the service provider is charging very high monthly fees. These monthly fees are reflected on the Margie's Travel balance sheet as operating costs, which make the travel agency appear EBITDA (earnings before interest, taxes, depreciation, and amortization) negative. That's making it more difficult for Margie to identify a larger travel agency that would be willing to acquire her company.

Instead, Margie's Travel is going to invest capital into developing its own internal software, which it plans to host on two computers: the existing computer running Windows Server 2003 in North America and a new server the company plans to add at the European regional office. The company plans to place the servers in different locations because the North American and European travel standards differ, and it wants agents on each continent to be able to access their own servers without traffic needing to travel between continents. Currently, Margie's Travel is planning to connect the headquarters and the European regional office using a site-to-site IPSec-based VPN. Both locations will have firewalls.

Margie does not want the application to be available from the Internet. Therefore, before the company can make use of the application, it needs to connect all of its locations into a single network. Margie wants some assurance that an attacker won't be able to easily connect to the network, but the company doesn't have the budget for expensive security solutions. It's particularly concerned about worms, however. It plans to add more travel agents, and wants to make sure one travel agent doesn't pass worms to every other agent.

Based on this information, answer the questions that follow.

1. Would you recommend a dial-up or VPN solution? If you prefer the VPN solution, would you recommend that the company use demand-dial routing?

2. Would you recommend using PPTP or L2TP for the VPN connections?

3. What is the best way for the travel agents to configure the client-side VPN connections?

4. What client software configuration policies do you recommend to protect client computers from being infected by worms?

5. How can you ensure that travel agent computers meet the requirements set by the software configuration policies before they connect to the VPN?

6. Where will you locate the VPN servers: in North America, Europe, or both?

7. Should the VPN servers be located inside or outside the firewall?

8. Should you enable split tunneling?

CHAPTER 12
HARDENING WEB SERVERS

Upon completion of this chapter, you will be able to:

■ Harden a Microsoft Internet Information Services (IIS) Web site by configuring IIS to use encryption, configuring restrictive Web site permissions, and protecting IIS with a firewall.

■ Design IIS authentication by selecting an IIS authentication method.

■ Design authentication and authorization for ASP.NET Web applications.

■ Design a content management strategy.

■ Monitor IIS for failures and security incidents.

Microsoft Internet Information Services (IIS) is a complete Web server available in all recent versions of both client and server Microsoft Windows–based platforms. Designed for intranets, extranets, and the Internet, IIS makes it possible for organizations of all sizes to deploy powerful Web sites, applications, and Web services quickly and easily. In addition, IIS provides a high-performance platform for applications built using the Microsoft .NET Framework.

> **NOTE** **What Are Web Services?** Web services are technologies that applications use to communicate with each other across a network. For example, a client application could submit a Web services request to a weather agency connected to the Internet to retrieve the current weather conditions in an XML file. Although the Web services technologies, such as Simple Open Access Protocol (SOAP), are extremely flexible and can be implemented using many different protocols, they are usually based on Hypertext Transfer Protocol (HTTP) and implemented on Windows networks with IIS. In addition, Web services are often developed with ASP.NET, the same development environment commonly used for traditional Web applications.

In this chapter, you learn how to limit the risks of running Web servers in your organization by hardening IIS, choosing an authentication mechanism that meets your security requirements, configuring ASP.NET application security, managing Web content, and monitoring IIS.

HARDENING IIS

IIS is probably the server component most frequently targeted by attackers. Although you can and should use defense-in-depth to protect your Web servers running IIS, the most critical form of protection is hardening the IIS service. The sections that follow discuss measures you can take to improve IIS security.

Upgrading to Windows Server 2003

The most important thing you can do to improve the security of IIS is to upgrade earlier versions of Windows to Windows Server 2003. Better yet, build a new computer to run Microsoft Windows Server 2003 and transfer your Web content to the new server. Performing an in-place upgrade from Windows 2000 Server (with IIS 5.0) to Windows Server 2003 (with IIS 6.0) does increase your security, but you might still have unnecessary components installed. In fact, unless you have installed the IIS Lockdown Tool on your computer running Windows 2000 Server, Windows Server 2003 will disable IIS after completing the in-place upgrade.

> **MORE INFO** **Upgrading IIS**   To learn more about upgrading from IIS 5.0 to IIS 6.0, read the section titled "Deploying IIS 6.0" in the Windows Server 2003 Deployment Kit at http://www.microsoft.com/resources/ documentation/windowsserv/2003/all/deployguide/en-us/ iisdg_int_anhm.asp.

Windows Server 2003 was the first Windows operating system to conform to the secure-by-default security principle, and one of the most affected components was IIS. For example, to reduce the Web infrastructure attack surface, IIS 6.0, by default, is not installed on Windows Server 2003. You must explicitly select and install IIS 6.0 on all members of the Windows Server 2003 family except for Windows Server 2003, Web Edition. This means that now it does not need to be uninstalled after Windows has been installed.

In addition, IIS 6.0 is configured in a locked-down state when installed. After installation, IIS 6.0 accepts requests for only static files until configured to serve dynamic content, and all timeouts and settings are set to aggressively secure defaults. Programmatic functionality provided by Internet Server Application Programming Interface (ISAPI) extensions or Common Gateway Interfaces (CGI) must be manually enabled by an IIS 6.0 administrator. ISAPI and CGI extend the functionality of your Web pages and, for this reason, they are referred to as Web service extensions.

For example, to run Active Server Pages (ASP) with IIS 6.0, you must enable the ISAPI extension that implements ASP.dll specifically as a Web service extension. Microsoft FrontPage server extensions and Microsoft ASP.NET also have to be enabled before their functionality will work. Using the Web Service Extensions feature, Web site administrators can enable or disable IIS 6.0 functionality based on the individual needs of the organization. This functionality is enforced across the entire server. IIS 6.0 provides programmatic, command-line, and graphical interfaces for enabling Web service extensions.

By default, IIS 6.0 worker processes, which run Web service extensions, run as a Network Service account. The Network Service account is a new, built-in account with seven privileges:

- Adjust memory quotas for a process
- Generate security audits
- Log on as a service
- Replace process-level tokens
- Impersonate a client after authentication
- Allow logon locally
- Access this computer from the network

Running as a low-privileged account helps IIS 6.0 comply with the least-privilege security principles. The ability to exploit a security vulnerability can be contained effectively if the worker process has very few rights on the underlying system. Administrators can configure the application pool to run as any account (Network Service, Local System, Local Service, or a configured account) if desired. Unfortunately, earlier versions of IIS run using the Local System account, which has almost unlimited privileges.

Selecting Application Server Role Components

When using the Add/Remove Windows Components tool, you have a great deal of control over which IIS subcomponents to install. Understanding which of these components is required for your application to function is critical. Without a necessary component, parts of a Web application will simply not work. If unnecessary components are enabled, you are exposing the server to unnecessary risk. Table 12-1 describes the available Application Server subcomponents and lists whether each component is automatically installed when you add the Application Server role.

Table 12-1 **Application Server Subcomponent**

Subcomponent	Description	Default Setting
Active Server Pages	Enables ASP 3.0 applications to run. Do not enable this component unless you are running an ASP 3.0 application. You do not need to enable this component for ASP.NET applications.	Disabled
Application Server Console	Microsoft Management Console (MMC) snap-in for managing the Application Server role.	Enabled
ASP.NET	Enables ASP.NET applications to run. Do not enable this component unless you will be running an ASP.NET application.	Disabled
Background Intelligent Transfer Service (BITS) server extension	A background file transfer mechanism used by Windows Update and Automatic Update. This component is required when Windows updates or automatic updates are used to automatically apply service packs and hotfixes to an IIS server.	Disabled
Common Files	Files required by IIS. They must always be enabled on IIS servers.	Enabled
Enable Network COM+ Access	Enables COM+ communications, which some types of distributed applications use. Consult with your application developers to determine if this subcomponent is required.	Enabled
Enable Network DTC Access	Enables Distributed Transaction Coordinator (DTC) communications, which distributed applications use. Consult with your application developers to determine if this subcomponent is required.	Disabled
File Transfer Protocol (FTP) Service	Allows IIS servers to provide FTP services. This service is not required for dedicated IIS servers.	Disabled
FrontPage 2002 Server Extensions	Provides FrontPage support for administering and publishing Web sites. Disable on dedicated IIS servers when no Web sites use FrontPage extensions.	Disabled

Table 12-1 **Application Server Subcomponent**

Subcomponent	Description	Default Setting
Internet Data Connector	A tool used by some applications to publish information contained in databases. Most applications don't need this, so leave it disabled.	Disabled
Internet Information Services Manager	Administrative interface for IIS. There is little risk in enabling this, and you will probably need it for managing IIS.	Enabled
Internet Printing	Provides Web-based printer management and allows printers to be shared over HTTP. This is not required on dedicated IIS servers.	Disabled
Message Queuing	This component includes several subcomponents: Active Directory Integration, Common, Downlevel Client Support, Microsoft Message Queuing (MSMQ) HTTP Support, Routing Support, and Triggers. Disable this component unless you specifically know that your application requires it.	Disabled
NNTP Service	Distributes, queries, retrieves, and posts Usenet news articles on the Internet. This component is rarely used and should always be disabled.	Disabled
Remote Administration (HTML)	Enables you to administer IIS remotely with a browser. This component has been compromised in the past. Although all known vulnerabilities are patched, new vulnerabilities might be discovered. Always leave this disabled unless you have no other way to manage IIS.	Disabled
Remote Desktop Web Connection	Installs a small Web application and Microsoft ActiveX control to enable clients running Microsoft Internet Explorer to control the computer by using Remote Desktop. There is rarely a reason to enable this in enterprise environments, so leave this disabled.	Disabled
Server Side Includes	Some applications (primarily older applications) use files with a .shtm, .shtml, or .stm file extension. Enable Server Side Includes only if you know your application requires it.	Disabled

Table 12-1   **Application Server Subcomponent**

Subcomponent	Description	Default Setting
SMTP Service	Supports the transfer of e-mail. Leave this component disabled unless you know that a Web application sends outgoing e-mail using the local server as a Simple Mail Transfer Protocol (SMTP) server.	Disabled
WebDAV Publishing	Web Distributed Authoring and Versioning (WebDAV) is a content management technology used by some content management tools, such as recent versions of FrontPage and Microsoft Visual Studio. Enable it if you require it, but know that installing WebDAV exposes you to additional risk because it provides the ability for remote users to update content. Although attackers without credentials do not have privileges to update content by using WebDAV, vulnerabilities have been discovered (and patched) in WebDAV historically, so future vulnerabilities might be discovered.	Enabled
World Wide Web Service	Provides Web services and static and dynamic content to clients. This component is required on dedicated IIS servers.	Enabled

Using IP Address and Domain Name Restrictions

IIS can deny or allow incoming requests based on the source IP address, the network from which the request originated, or the domain name of the source IP address. Although these techniques can be used for increasing the Web site's security, they are hardly impenetrable. Source IP addresses can be spoofed, and domain name lookups are only as secure as the Domain Name System (DNS) server hosting the reverse lookup domain. Nonetheless, they can be useful as part of a layered security strategy when used in conjunction with other security mechanisms.

Figure 12-1 shows IIS configured to allow only requests from the 192.168.1.0 subnet.

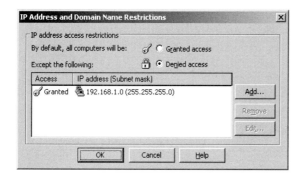

Figure 12-1   IIS can restrict access based on IP address, network ID, and domain name.

NOTE   The Risks of Source IP Filtering   Source IP filtering should not be your only authorization technique because source IP addresses can be spoofed by skilled attackers with direct access to your network. However, source IP filtering can be a useful part of a defense-in-depth approach.

If you restrict access by domain name, IIS has to perform a reverse DNS lookup for every new source IP address that sends a request. This slows down the responsiveness of the first page that each client retrieves, which will probably upset your Webmaster. In addition, if you have a busy site, all those DNS requests can really bog down your DNS server.

Using SSL Encryption

IIS supports HTTP Secure (HTTPS), an extension to HTTP that provides encryption by using a Secure Sockets Layer (SSL) certificate. If you host your own certification authority (CA), you can create your own SSL certificate. However, if your CA is not a public authority that is trusted by your visitors' Web browsers, visitors will receive a warning message (as shown in Figure 12-2) that your certificate is not from a trusted authority. To avoid this warning message, purchase an SSL certificate from a CA that is trusted by default by popular Web browsers.

Figure 12-2   Public Web servers should have certificates issued by a trusted CA to avoid this security alert.

> **MORE INFO   CAs and SSL**   For more information about CAs and details about how SSL functions, read Chapter 9, "Designing a Public Key Infrastructure."

Designing Web Site Permissions

Although file permissions are used to restrict which users can access particular files, IIS uses Web site permissions to determine what HTTP actions can occur within a Web site, such as allowing script source access or directory browsing. Unlike file permissions, Web site permissions can be defined for Web sites or directories, but they cannot apply to individual files. In addition, Web site permissions apply to all users who access the site.

Use the Internet Information Services Manager to specify Web site permissions. Valid choices are as follows:

- **Read**   Users can view the content and properties of directories or files. This permission is selected by default and must be enabled for any active Web site.

- **Write**   Users can change content and properties of directories or files. Choose this permission when you are using WebDAV or FrontPage Server Extensions to update content on your site. If you update content by using shared folders or FTP, you do not need to enable this permission.

- **Script Source Access**   Users can access source files. If Read is also enabled, users can read source code; if Write is also enabled, users can change the source code. This permission should be enabled only in development environments.

■ **Directory Browsing**   When a user requests a directory and a default file does not exist, IIS will generate a list of the directory contents that can be viewed in a browser. This setting is convenient in development environments; however, typically, it should not be enabled in production environments. If you enable this setting and forget to create a default document for every folder, users can view the contents of the folder. An attacker might be able to use this information to identify a vulnerability in your Web site.

■ **Log Visits**   A log entry is created for each visit to the Web site. This should always be enabled in production environments because the log files provide valuable security auditing information. It does not necessarily need to be enabled in development environments.

■ **Index This Resource**   Allows Indexing Service to index resources. Unless your application makes use of the Indexing Service, disable this permission.

■ **Execute Permissions**   The following options determine the level of script execution for users:

   ❏ None—Does not allow script executable files to run on the server. Choose this when you are hosting only static content, such as Hypertext Markup Language (HTML) and image files.

   ❏ Scripts Only—Allows only scripts to run on the server. Choose this setting when you are hosting ASP or ASP.NET Web applications.

   ❏ Scripts And Executables—Allows both scripts and executable files to run on the server. Do not select this setting. Historically, some Web applications have used executable files. However, allowing executable files to run is extremely risky because an attacker might be able to misuse the executable or call other executables on the computer.

   > **MORE INFO**   **File Permissions**   For general information about using NTFS file permissions, refer to Chapter 6, "Protecting Data." For detailed information about using file permissions to protect ASP.NET applications, refer to the section titled "How to Control Authorization for Folders and Files by Using File Permissions," later in this chapter.

Protecting IIS with Firewalls

Attackers commonly target Web servers and, as a result, it is common practice to place a firewall between a Web server and end users. If a simple port-filtering firewall is used, such as the Internet Connection Firewall or Windows Firewall, allow traffic using the port numbers you specify for each Web site in IIS Manager. By default, allow TCP port 80 for HTTP communications and TCP port 443 for encrypted HTTPS communications.

Application firewalls can provide greater security for IIS than that offered by simple packet-filtering firewalls. Microsoft Internet Security and Acceleration (ISA) Server and other application firewalls can examine inbound requests to your Web server, and outbound responses to Web clients, and use complex criteria to determine whether the request should be allowed or denied. For example, an application firewall could be configured to drop requests for confidential pages that originate from the Internet. IIS can be configured similarly, but specifying the rules both within IIS and at the firewall provides a double-layered security combination that remains in place even if the security settings within IIS are changed. For more information about firewalls, refer to Chapter 10, "Protecting Intranet Communications."

DESIGNING IIS AUTHENTICATION

Web applications have special requirements for authentication because, rather than using conventional authentication protocols such as Kerberos, user credentials must be passed between a Web browser and the Web server. In addition, custom authentication mechanisms are particularly common in Web applications because Web applications available on the Internet must often scale to support hundreds of thousands of users. To meet these authentication requirements, IIS supports the following types of authentication:

- **Anonymous access**   IIS accepts browser requests that do not include user credentials. Anonymous access is used by most Web sites on the Internet. If you do not allow anonymous access, every user must provide a valid set of credentials.

- **Basic authentication**   Basic authentication provides an unencrypted authentication mechanism that is supported by every common browser. User credentials are Base64 encoded, which does not provide any privacy. If an attacker captures Basic authentication traffic, the attacker can immediately determine the original password. Because of this, use Basic authentication only if communications are encrypted by HTTPS or IPSec. Basic authentication can pass through firewalls.

■ **Digest authentication**   Digest authentication allows the Web browser to submit the user's password in a Message Digest 5 (MD5) hash. If Digest authentication traffic is intercepted, an attacker would not be able to easily determine the user's password. Digest authentication provides higher security than Basic authentication and can pass through firewalls.

> **NOTE** **Digest Authentication and Reversible Encryption**
> Digest authentication functions only if the domain controller has a reversibly encrypted (clear text) copy of the requesting user's password stored in Active Directory directory service. Using reversible encryption is not recommended. As a result, Integrated Windows authentication is recommended over Digest authentication.

■ **Integrated Windows authentication**   Integrated Windows authentication provides either NT LAN Manager (NTLM) or Kerberos v5 authentication between a Web client and server. This allows the Web browser to send the user's password in the form of a hash without requiring the user's password to be stored using reversible encryption. Integrated Windows authentication is ideal for intranet use in which all users are a member of a domain, and all clients are using Internet Explorer to connect to your Web server. You cannot use Integrated Windows authentication through a firewall, however, which limits its usefulness on the Internet.

■ **Client-certificate authentication**   Client certificates use public key certificates to authenticate clients. Although this provides a very high level of security, it requires you to have a CA and to issue certificates to all Web clients. Therefore, it is used on intranets and extranets most effectively. For more information about client certificates, refer to the section titled "Authenticating Users with Client Certificates," later in this chapter.

■ **Passport authentication**   **Microsoft Passport** is a Microsoft authentication service that enables users to use a single set of credentials to authenticate to multiple Web sites on the Internet. This form of authentication requires the Web site owner to purchase additional services from Microsoft. The cost of those services, plus the development effort required to use Passport authentication, can be justified only by public Web sites that serve thousands of users and require authentication.

You can configure multiple authentication types and Web browsers will typically use the strongest supported form of authentication available. For example, as Figure 12-3 shows, you can enable anonymous, Basic, and Digest authentication. All files that have NTFS permissions granting the anonymous Web user access (IUSR_CONTOSO-DEV in this example) can be retrieved with anonymous authentication. For those files that have restrictive NTFS permissions, IIS will allow the browser to submit credentials using either Basic or Digest authentication.

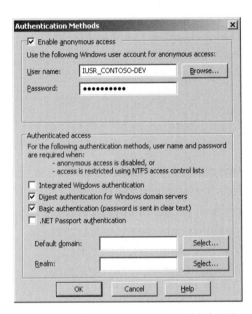

Figure 12-3   You can permit multiple IIS authentication types.

If your users have a recent version of Internet Explorer, use Integrated Windows authentication. If you can't mandate a particular browser, enable both Integrated Windows authentication and Basic authentication.

Using SSL Certificates with a Web Site

You can use SSL certificates to allow users to verify the identity of your Web site and to encrypt traffic sent between the client and the Web site. It is important to understand that an SSL certificate identifies a *Web site*, and not a *Web server*. A single Web server can host multiple Web sites. Alternatively, a single Web site can be hosted on multiple Web servers to provide redundancy and scalability.

For example, an Internet service provider (ISP) that hosts Web sites for twenty customers on a single Web server needs twenty SSL certificates to allow each site to use encryption. On the other hand, if an ISP stores a copy of a Web site on 10 different servers to allow the Web site to remain online in the event of a hardware failure, it can install the same certificate on all 10 servers.

SSL certificates use the *fully qualified domain name (FQDN)* to identify the Web site. When the client retrieves the site's SSL certificate, the client checks the FQDN of the Web site against the *subject name*, also known as the *common name*, listed in the certificate. Checking the name used to identify the site against the name listed in the certificate prevents a rogue Web site from intercepting traffic destined for a different site.

> **NOTE**   **Risks Mitigated by SSL Certificates**   SSL certificates help reduce the risk of attacks against Domain Name System (DNS). For example, an attacker could compromise your DNS server and add a DNS record for the FQDN *www.microsoft.com* so that it resolved to the IP address of a rogue Web site. When you went to visit *http://www.microsoft.com*, your requests actually would be sent to the rogue Web site. The rogue Web site could then collect any information you intended to send to *www.microsoft.com*, which might include personal information or credit card numbers.
>
> However, if you visited *https://www.microsoft.com*, the rogue Web site would have to return an SSL certificate to your Web browser. The rogue Web site could return a certificate with the common name *www.microsoft.com*, but no trusted CA would issue such a certificate. Therefore, your Web browser would warn you that the CA was untrusted. Alternatively, the rogue Web site could perform a true man-in-the-middle attack and forward your Web browser to the actual certificate of *www.microsoft.com*. However, the rogue Web site would not be able to establish an SSL session with your browser, because it would not have the private key associated with the public key in the certificate.

Although you assign SSL certificates to individual Web sites, you can configure SSL to help protect confidential data on a URL-by-URL basis. One virtual directory might require encryption of data transmissions with SSL (by specifying HTTPS in the URL), and another part of the Web site might allow unencrypted data transmission (by specifying HTTP in the URL). This flexibility in security configuration allows you to provide encryption of confidential data as required while not incurring the performance penalty inherent in encryption and decryption.

To understand better how this is used, visit your favorite e-commerce Web site. While browsing the catalog, notice that the URL specifies the *http://* protocol. Next, attempt to purchase an item. At some point during the purchase process, you will begin to use SSL, and the URL will show the *https://* protocol.

E-commerce sites typically use HTTPS only when exchanging private information because this reduces the burden of public key cryptography and encryption on their Web servers.

> **NOTE SSL Accelerators**   One way that you can reduce the processing overhead of using SSL is to use a hardware SSL accelerator. A hardware SSL accelerator is a fast, hardware-based encryption/decryption mechanism that outperforms software-based implementations. If you do not have a hardware SSL accelerator, your server will use its main processor to perform the SSL calculations required for authentication and encryption. As a result, the computer has less processing power available for serving Web pages. Accelerators offload all encryption/decryption work to the onboard CPU, similar to the way 3-D video cards take on complex graphic computations to save the main CPU for other tasks.
>
> Although hardware SSL accelerators do outperform software, you may never see the benefit. You would not know that from examining the vendor's marketing material, unfortunately. Their marketing material will show you dramatic improvements in performance, which in theory will lead to improved scalability and a better end-user experience.
>
> However, these statistics are misleading. Marketing materials often show the performance gains in terms of new SSL sessions established, but new SSL sessions are usually established only when a new user connects to the Web site. As mentioned in Chapter 9, establishing an SSL session involves using public key cryptography, which is extremely processor-intensive. However, maintaining an SSL session involves only shared key encryption, which is not nearly as processor-intensive. Therefore, highlighting the benefits of hardware SSL accelerators by showing a large number of new SSL sessions does not reflect real world benefits.
>
> Investigate hardware SSL accelerators only if your Web site is currently processor limited—in particular, if the processor time averages greater than 30 percent use during peak times. Even then, compare the cost of hardware SSL accelerators against the cost of upgrading the processor, adding an additional Web server, or optimizing your code. These other methods of adding processing capability allow all aspects of your Web site to benefit—not just SSL session establishment. When accounting for the cost of the hardware SSL accelerators, be sure to factor in the cost of managing an additional device and the risk associated with adding an additional point of failure to your Web site.

Authenticating Users with Client Certificates

Client certificates provide one of the most flexible ways to authenticate users to IIS. With client certificates, you can authenticate users in the following scenarios:

- **Internal users issued certificates by your internal CA**   If you have an internal CA, you can issue user certificates and have IIS automatically authenticate users with valid certificates. However, if all users are members of a domain, it would probably be easier to authenticate users by using Digest authentication or Integrated Windows authentication.

- **External users issued certificates by your internal CA**   If you have an internal CA and you need to authenticate users outside your organization, you can issue certificates to those users by using Web enrollment, as discussed in Chapter 9. Then, you can configure IIS to authenticate any user with a valid certificate. This saves you from having to create user accounts for each external user. To restrict access on a user-by-user basis, you can map individual certificates to Windows user accounts, and then grant those accounts access to resources.

- **External users issued certificates by a partner organization's CA**   If you are designing a Web site that will be accessed by external users at a partner organization, you can authenticate users by using certificates issued by the partner organization's CA. Figure 12-4 shows the Certificate Trust List (CTL) Wizard being used to trust a partner organization's CA, thereby enabling users with those client certificates to be authenticated. You should add each CA that will issue certificates for a particular Web site to that Web site's CTL.

Figure 12-4   Use a CTL to authenticate users with certificates issued by an external CA.

To control authorization for users with client certificates, use client certificate mapping. You can use either **one-to-one** or **many-to-one** client certificate mapping, as described in the sections that follow.

One-to-One Client Certificate Mapping

One-to-one certificate mapping relates a single exported certificate to an Active Directory user account, as shown in Figure 12-5. When Web users present the certificate, they are authenticated as if they had presented a valid user name and password for that account. IIS will impersonate that user when accessing resources, which enables you to control the certificate holder's access by granting or denying NTFS file permissions.

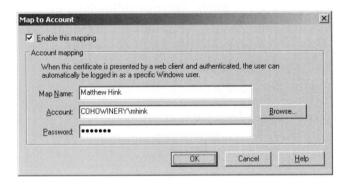

Figure 12-5   Configure one-to-one certificate mapping to further control a user's access.

If a user is issued a different certificate and attempts to authenticate with that certificate, the client certificate mapping will no longer work. You will have to re-create the mapping each time the certificate changes (which, typically, isn't that frequently).

Many-to-One Client Certificate Mapping

Many-to-one certificate mapping uses matching rules that verify whether a client certificate contains specific information about the certificate issuer (the CA) or subject (the recipient). This mapping does not identify individual client certificates; it accepts all client certificates fulfilling the specific criteria. Commonly used criteria include the following:

- Certificates issued by a specific CA
- Certificates issued by a specific CA that have a specific organizational unit (OU)
- Certificates with a specific first and last name

If a client gets another certificate containing all the same user information, the existing mapping will still work. Certificates do not need to be exported for use in many-to-one mappings.

For example, use many-to-one client certificate mappings to grant access to all users in the Accounting department by following these steps:

1. Issue client certificates to users in the Accounting department. Ensure that the organizational unit field is set to Accounting.

2. Add the CA to the Web site's CTL.

3. Create a user account in the local or domain user database.

4. Grant the user account access to the desired resources.

5. Create a many-to-one client certificate mapping that maps clients with a certificate subject organizational unit value to the user account you created in step 3. Figure 12-6 shows how you might configure this mapping.

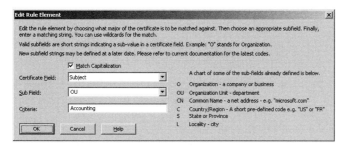

Figure 12-6   Use many-to-one certificate mapping to control access for users based on information contained within the client certificate.

You can also use wildcards in many-to-one certificate mappings. For example, if some certificates have an organizational unit set to Accounting, but others use the term Accountants, you could match either type of client certificate to the term "Account*".

Authenticating Web Users with a RADIUS Server

IIS does not directly support Remote Authentication Dial-In User Service (RADIUS) authentication, which is unfortunate because it would be useful in extranet scenarios. Besides writing your own RADIUS client software, this leaves you with three options for authenticating Web requests to a RADIUS server:

■ Use non-Microsoft software

■ Use ISA Server 2004

■ Configure a virtual private network (VPN) with RADIUS authentication and grant access to VPN clients

Using Non-Microsoft Software for RADIUS Authentication

The simplest way to authenticate IIS requests to a RADIUS server is by using non-Microsoft software. One such example is RadIIS, from TCP Data. RadIIS is an ISAPI filter that intercepts Basic Authentication requests as they are sent to the Web server and submits them to a RADIUS server for authentication. RadIIS, unfortunately, supports using only Basic Authentication requests to the Web server, which means you must use HTTPS to provide encryption for the authentication requests. In addition, RadIIS maps all requests to a single Windows user account, which does not provide accountability or the ability to configure different levels of authorization for different users and groups.

> **MORE INFO**   RadIIS   For more information about RadIIS, visit *http://www.tcpdata.com.*

If you choose to add non-Microsoft software for RADIUS authentication, add your IIS server's IP address to the list of approved clients on your RADIUS server. If you are using Internet Authentication Service (IAS) as your RADIUS server, create remote-access policies to allow your chosen client authentication method.

Using ISA Server 2004

If you are currently using ISA Server 2004 to publish your Web server, you can perform RADIUS user authentication at ISA Server. After a user has authenticated, the ISA server will pass the user's credentials to the Web server.

Using ISA Server to authenticate Web requests for a separate Web server requires you to perform the following configuration steps:

1. Connect ISA Server between your Web server and the Internet.

2. Configure a RADIUS server with Web user accounts. This RADIUS server could be on your intranet, or on a partnering organization's network.

3. Install an SSL certificate on ISA Server to enable encryption for Web communications. Although this step is optional, it is important because ISA Server must use Basic Authentication, which provides no encryption of its own.

4. Configure ISA Server to use Web Publishing to make the Web server available on the Internet.

5. Configure ISA Server to use the RADIUS server for authentication.

6. Configure the RADIUS server to allow authentication requests from the RADIUS server.

7. Configure ISA Server to require authentication for requests to the published Web site.

> **MORE INFO** **Step-by-Step Instructions** For detailed information on configuring ISA Server to use RADIUS authentication for a published Web site, refer to "Using ISA Server 2004 RADIUS Authentication in Web Publishing Rules" by Paul Baldwin at *http://www.isaserver.org/tutorials/ISA2004-RADIUS-Authentication-Web-Publishing-Rules-Part1.html*.

Figure 12-7 shows how the authentication process would occur. The steps are as follows:

1. A Web client attempts to connect to your Web server. ISA Server, configured to publish the Web server, intercepts the incoming connection and requires the user to authenticate. The user provides his or her credentials to ISA Server by using Basic authentication.

2. ISA Server forwards the user's credentials to the RADIUS server, and the RADIUS server authenticates the user.

3. ISA Server forwards the client's original request to the Web server on the internal network. The client is now considered authenticated and can continue to browse the Web site.

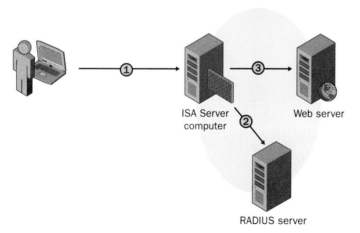

Figure 12-7 ISA Server can authenticate Web requests by using RADIUS.

Leveraging a VPN for RADIUS Authentication

Your third option for granting users access to a Web server based on credentials stored in a RADIUS server requires only Microsoft software; however, it is less than ideal because it leverages the ability of IIS to grant access based on source IP addresses. As discussed in Chapter 11, "Protecting Extranet Communications," VPNs can authenticate users with RADIUS. Therefore, you can configure a VPN server to use RADIUS authentication, and then configure IIS to allow all requests from users connecting across the VPN.

Figure 12-8 shows how you could use VPN authentication to grant a user at a partnering organization access to a Web site based on credentials stored in the partner's RADIUS server.

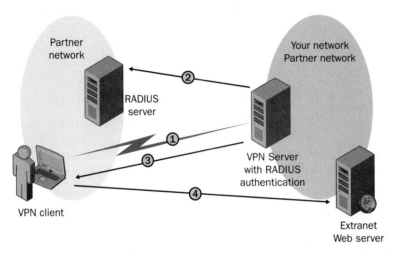

Figure 12-8   Allowing requests from VPN users can effectively simulate IIS authenticating users to a RADIUS server.

The steps are as follows:

1. A partner VPN client connects to your VPN server.

2. Your VPN server authenticates the user by sending a request to your partner's RADIUS server. This RADIUS server, in turn, might authenticate the user by sending the credentials to a domain controller.

3. After the user is authenticated, the VPN server assigns the VPN client an IP address. This IP address is in a range that you have reserved for only extranet VPN clients, such as 192.168.20.0–192.168.20.255 (although any valid network on your intranet would work).

4. The user contacts your extranet Web server, which is configured to allow requests from users with IP addresses in the extranet VPN range (such as 192.168.20.0–192.168.20.255). This Web server configuration is illustrated in Figure 12-9.

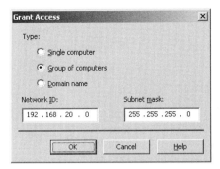

Figure 12-9   Configure IIS to allow requests from an IP address range to avoid authentication of VPN users.

If you need to authenticate users on an intranet using RADIUS, you could leverage 802.11X security to protect access to your network, and then configure IIS to allow any requests from your local network.

Although this configuration will work, you must remember that users with access to your network might be able to spoof IP addresses to bypass the IIS IP address filtering. In addition, because users are not authenticating directly to IIS, you cannot track user-specific actions. Therefore, users do not have accountability and you cannot restrict authorization to individual users and groups. For these reasons, this approach is not recommended. Instead, consider using non-Microsoft software or ISA Server 2004 to authenticate IIS requests to a RADIUS server.

DESIGNING SECURITY FOR ASP.NET WEB APPLICATIONS

Many Web server compromises have occurred because of vulnerabilities in the application itself, rather than in the computer's operating system or Web server software. As a security designer, understand how Web applications can introduce vulnerabilities and methods you can use to mitigate the risk of those vulnerabilities.

Today, many Web applications are based on ASP.NET—part of the Microsoft .NET Framework. This section discusses how to design authentication and authorization strategies for ASP.NET applications running on IIS. Although the focus of this book is on design rather than on implementation, this section provides ASP.NET configuration information along with the design information because ASP.NET security configuration is not straightforward, and most systems administrators have not had experience configuring ASP.NET applications.

> **NOTE** **For the Exam**   The 70-298 MCSE certification exam will not test your knowledge of ASP.NET configuration. However, this knowledge is very important for protecting Web applications in the real world.

Designing Web Application Authentication

As you learned earlier in this chapter, IIS provides several built-in authentication mechanisms. Systems administrators can configure one or more of these authentication mechanisms to require users to provide valid credentials before accessing any type of Web content. This enables systems administrators to restrict access to static HTML pages, images, and Web applications.

ASP.NET applications have authentication capabilities separate from IIS, however. When designing authentication for an ASP.NET application, you can choose to use IIS for authentication, ASP.NET for authentication, or both. The sections that follow describe the different ASP.NET authentication types, and then show you how to configure each type that can be configured without requiring development effort.

ASP.NET Authentication Types

ASP.NET supports four types of authentication that you can use instead of, or in conjunction with, IIS authentication:

- **Anonymous access**   ASP.NET does not require authentication and processes requests from clients who do not submit credentials.

- **Windows authentication**   ASP.NET requires users to submit credentials and verifies those credentials against the local user database or an Active Directory domain. This requires IIS to have Basic, Digest, or Integrated Windows authentication enabled.

- **Forms authentication**   ASP.NET redirects unauthenticated requests to an HTML form that prompts the user for credentials. ASP.NET can authenticate the credentials against a list of names stored in a configuration file, a database, or any custom mechanism created by the application developer. After the user has been authenticated, ASP.NET gives the client Web browser a **cookie** containing a secret key. A cookie is a piece of data that the Web browser submits in subsequent requests to identify the user. In Forms authentication, ASP.NET verifies that the cookie contains the secret key, which proves that the user has already been authenticated.

- **Passport authentication** ASP.NET can work with Passport authentication, as discussed earlier in this chapter.

> **MORE INFO** *Passport* For more detailed information about using Passport with an ASP.NET application, you can download and review the free Passport software development kit from MSDN on the Microsoft Web site at *http://msdn.microsoft.com/downloads/list/websrvpass.asp*.

You can configure any ASP.NET application to use anonymous access or Windows authentication. To use Forms or Passport authentication, however, the application must be written specifically to support these authentication mechanisms. In other words, you must have application development skills to add Forms authentication to an ASP.NET application, but you need only systems administration skills to use Windows authentication.

As stated earlier, IIS authenticates users to the Web server only, and not to the application. However, IIS does forward a user's credentials to ASP.NET, allowing your application to perform ASP.NET Windows authentication with the same credentials presented to IIS. Therefore, if you configure both IIS and ASP.NET to require Windows authentication, users will have to type their credentials only once. However, if you configure IIS to require Windows authentication and you configure ASP.NET to require Forms authentication, the user will be required to authenticate twice because credentials cannot be passed between Windows authentication and Forms authentication.

> **NOTE** *Configuring Forms and Passport Authentication* When using Forms or Passport authentication with an ASP.NET application, always configure IIS for anonymous access.

As discussed in more detail later in this chapter, ASP.NET authentication protects only ASP.NET files. To require authentication for all files in an application's virtual directory, configure Windows authentication for both the ASP.NET application and IIS when authenticating users against the local user database or an Active Directory domain. If you enable Windows authentication for ASP.NET but anonymous authentication for IIS, users can retrieve static files such as images without being authenticated.

Table 12-2 shows how you should configure IIS and ASP.NET authentication in different scenarios.

Table 12-2   How to Configure IIS and ASP.NET Authentication in Common Application Scenarios

Scenario	IIS Authentication	ASP.NET Authentication
ASP.NET application that does not require authentication	Anonymous	Anonymous
ASP.NET application that uses Windows authentication	Windows	Windows
ASP.NET application that uses Forms authentication	Anonymous	Forms
ASP.NET application that uses Passport authentication	Anonymous	Passport

What Are Web.config Files?

Each of the ASP.NET authentication methods requires configuring IIS by using the Internet Information Services Manager and creating one or more Web.config files. **Web.config files** are per-folder configuration settings for ASP.NET applications. Storing configuration settings in eXtended Markup Language (XML)–based files instead of in the registry, isolated storage, or an IIS metabase allows administrators to copy your application to a different location or to another computer and have the application run correctly. This storage method is particularly important for environments that host Web farms, where multiple Web servers run the same ASP.NET application simultaneously and incoming requests are distributed among the servers. Web farms usually have file synchronization running between the Web servers, which allows changes to a Web.config file to be replicated automatically between all computers.

Web.config files are the most granular files in the .config file hierarchy and can inherit and override the settings of higher-level configuration files. The highest .config file is the Machine.config file, which affects all .NET applications, including ASP.NET applications. The Machine.config file is located in the %Systemroot%\Microsoft.NET\Framework*Version*\CONFIG\ folder. You can create a hierarchy of Web.config files within an application, too. Place a Web.config file in the root folder of an application to apply default settings to all files and folders in that application. If a particular set of pages requires different security settings, store those files in a single subfolder and add a Web.config file to that folder.

> **NOTE** .**Config File Hierarchy**   An application's virtual folder structure
> determines the hierarchy, not its physical folder structure.

Figure 12-10 shows this hierarchy. In this example, App1 has a Web.config file.
Therefore, App1 inherits all security settings from the computer's Machine.config
file, except those overridden in the Web.config file. The Folder1 subfolder of
App1 also has a Web.config file. These settings override settings in both App1's
Web.config file and the computer's Machine.config file. However, any settings not
explicitly overridden are inherited. Folder2 does not have a Web.config file, so its
effective security settings will be the same as App1. App2 does not have a
Web.config file and will inherit all security settings from the Machine.config file.

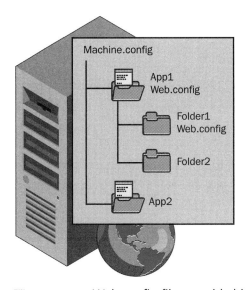

Figure 12-10   Web.config files provide hierarchical security settings.

The Machine.config file defines which settings cannot be overridden. Settings
with an *allowDefinition* property set to MachineOnly can be defined only in the
Machine.config file. Settings with an *allowDefinition* property set to Machine-
ToApplication can be defined in each application, but not overridden by placing
a Web.config file in an application's subfolders. For example, you can control
authentication on an application-by-application basis because its definition sets
the *allowDefinition* property set to MachineToApplication, as shown by this
excerpt from the default Machine.config file:

```
<section name="authentication"
     type="System.Web.Configuration.AuthenticationConfigHandler,
     System.Web,
     Version=1.0.5000.0,
     Culture=neutral,
    PublicKeyToken=b03f5f7f11d50a3a"
     allowDefinition="MachineToApplication" />
```

You cannot, however, override *authentication* with a Web.config file in an application's subfolder unless the subfolder is configured in IIS as an independent application. The *authentication* section can be specified only at the application's root folder, as configured in IIS. The *authorization* section, which doesn't explicitly define the *allowDefinition* property, can be overridden in an application's subfolders.

> **MORE INFO**   **Configuring ASP.NET Security**   This section is intended to give you an overview of the capabilities of ASP.NET security so that you can factor Web applications into security designs. It is not intended to teach you how to perform the actual configuration. For detailed information, read *.NET Framework Developer's Guide, Hierarchical Configuration Architecture* in MSDN on the Microsoft Web site at *http://msdn.microsoft.com/library/en-us/cpguide/html/cpconhierarchicalconfigurationarchitecture.asp.*

How to Configure Web Applications to Require Windows Authentication

If your application is targeted for use inside an organization and users accessing the application have existing user accounts within the local user database of the Web server or Active Directory, you will probably choose Windows authentication for your ASP.NET application. You can configure Windows authentication in two ways: within IIS and within your ASP.NET application. To provide defense-in-depth, use both techniques to require authentication.

When a Web application requires Windows authentication, the application rejects all requests that do not include a valid user name and password. The user's browser then prompts the user for a user name and password. Because the browser prompts the user for credentials, you do not have to create a page to request them. Some browsers, such as Internet Explorer, automatically provide the user's current user name and password when the server is located on the intranet. This seamlessly authenticates the user, relieving him or her from retyping the password when visiting the intranet site.

After you configure Windows authentication in IIS, all Web requests to the virtual directory will require Windows authentication—even if ASP.NET is configured for anonymous access only. Even though configuring authentication within IIS is sufficient to require users to present Windows credentials, it is good practice to edit the application's Web.config file so that it requires Windows authentication as well.

To configure an ASP.NET application for Windows authentication, edit the `<authentication>` section of the Web.config file. This section, like most sections related to ASP.NET application configuration, must be defined within the

`<system.web>` section. The `<system.web>` section, in turn, must exist within the `<configuration>` section. This example shows the `<authentication>` section of a Web.config file configured to use Windows authentication:

```
<configuration>
      <system.web>
              <authentication mode="windows" />
              <authorization>
                      <deny users="?" />
              </authentication>
      </system.web>
</configuration>
```

If you do not add the `<authentication>` section to a Web.config file, the ASP.NET application will use the setting configured in the Machine.config file. To override the Machine.config setting, add the authentication section to the application's Web.config file.

The `<authorization>` section simply requires all users to be successfully authenticated. Specifying `<deny users="?" />` within `<authorization>` denies access to unauthenticated users, whereas specifying `<allow users="*" />` within `<authorization>` bypasses authentication entirely.

How to Configure Web Applications for Only Anonymous Access

You can explicitly disable authentication for your application if you know that only anonymous users will use it. This example shows a simple Web.config file that allows only anonymous access to an ASP.NET application:

```
<configuration>
      <system.web>
              <authentication mode="None" />
      </system.web>
</configuration>
```

How to Configure Web Applications to Use ASP.NET Forms Authentication

Enabling Windows authentication causes the user's browser to open a dialog box to gather credentials, as shown in Figure 12-11. Although giving the browser the responsibility of gathering the user's user name and password enables automatic authentication in intranet sites, it requires users to be authenticated against the local user database or an Active Directory domain.

Figure 12-11   IIS authentication causes the browser to prompt the user for credentials.

Web applications developed for external sites commonly use form-based authentication (or Forms authentication) instead of Windows authentication so that user credentials can be stored in a database. Form-based authentication presents the user with an HTML-based Web page that prompts the user for credentials. Once authenticated, a cookie with information about the user is stored within the user's browser. The browser presents this cookie with all future requests to the Web site, allowing the ASP.NET application to validate requests. The Web server can optionally encrypt the cookie with a private key, enabling the Web server to detect an attacker who attempts to present a cookie that the Web server did not generate.

How to Enable Forms Authentication   To configure form-based authentication, a developer has to create an authentication page that uses an HTML form to prompt the user for credentials. Therefore, form-based authentication can be used on only those ASP.NET Web applications developed with this authentication method in mind.

You do not need to modify the Web.config file for an application that uses Forms authentication because the developer should provide it. However, you can control some aspects of how Forms authentication behaves, such as to configure the timeout period after which a user will need to log on again. A simple Web.config file requiring Forms authentication is shown here:

```
<configuration>
      <system.web>
            <authentication mode="Forms">
                  <forms loginURL="LoginForm.aspx" />
            </authentication>
            <authorization>
                  <deny users="?" />
            </authentication>
      </system.web>
</configuration>
```

In the preceding example, all users who have not yet signed in will be redirected to the LoginForm.aspx page when they attempt to access any ASP.NET file in the application. The form typically prompts the user for a user name and password and handles authentication within the application itself. In whatever way the application handles the user's input, the user's credentials are sent to the server as an unencrypted HTTP request. The best way to ensure privacy of user credentials submitted by using Forms authentication is to configure an SSL certificate within IIS and require HTTPS for the logon form.

The application can check the user name and password against a database, a list contained in the Web.config file, an XML file, or any other mechanism the developer creates. Forms authentication is tremendously flexible; however, security vulnerabilities in the ASP.NET application can expose Forms authentication to compromise.

To protect against an attacker creating a fake authentication cookie, ASP.NET can encrypt and validate the cookie. The type of encryption and validation used is controlled by the *protection* attribute of the <forms> section. If the *protection* attribute is not set, it defaults to *All*. If the *protection* attribute is set to *Encryption*, the cookie is encrypted with 3DES. This encryption ensures the privacy of the data contained in the cookie but performs no validation. If the *protection* attribute is set to *Validation*, as the following example demonstrates, the server verifies the data in the cookie at each transaction to reduce the likelihood of it being modified between the time it is sent from the browser and the time it is received by the server. If the *protection* attribute is set to *None*, neither encryption nor validation is performed. This setting reduces the overhead on the server, but it is suitable only in situations in which privacy is not a concern, such as Web site personalization.

```
<authentication mode="Forms" protection="Validation" >
  <forms loginURL="LoginForm.aspx" />
</authentication>
```

> **IMPORTANT** **The Most Secure Protection Level** For optimal security (with a slight performance cost), leave protection at the default setting of All.

Another important attribute of the <forms> section is *timeout*, which defines, in minutes, the amount of idle time allowed between requests before the user is forced to log on again. If the forms section is <forms loginUrl="YourLogin.aspx" timeout="10">, the user is forced to log on again if he does not send any requests to the ASP.NET application within 10 minutes. This number should be decreased to reduce the risk of the browser being misused while the user is away from the computer. The <forms> section has other attributes, but *LoginUrl*, *protection*, and *timeout* are the most important.

How to Configure User Accounts in the Web.Config File   To avoid creating a database to store user credentials, you can store the user credentials directly in the Web.config file. The passwords can be stored in one of three formats: as cleartext; encrypted with the MD5 one-way hash algorithm; or encrypted with the Secure Hash Algorithm 1 (SHA1) one-way hash algorithm. Using one of the two hash algorithms to mask the user credentials reduces the likelihood that a malicious user with Read access to the Web.config file will gather another user's logon information. Define the hashing method used within the <forms> section, in the <credentials> section. An example is shown here:

```
<authentication mode="Forms">
        <forms loginUrl="login.aspx" protection="Encryption" timeout="30" >
            <credentials passwordFormat="SHA1" >
                <user name="Eric" <;$RD>
password="07B7F3EE06F278DB966BE960E7CBBD103DF30CA6"/>
                <user name="Sam" <;$RD>
password="5753A498F025464D72E088A9D5D6E872592D5F91"/>
            </credentials>
        </forms>
</authentication>
```

Windows does not include a tool to generate hashed passwords. Therefore, your ASP.NET application must include a page or tool to generate these passwords if you plan to store hashed password information in the Web.config file.

Designing Web Application Authorization

ASP.NET Web applications provide multiple methods for restricting access besides NTFS file permissions. You can use Web.config files to control which users and groups can access applications, folders, and individual files. In addition, you can expand the scope of protection ASP.NET provides to files that ASP.NET does not normally process. Although most authentication and authorization techniques apply equally well to both Web applications and Web services, Web services require additional consideration because they expose the Documentation protocol, which is a potential security vulnerability.

How to Restrict Access to ASP.NET Web Applications, Files, and Folders
ASP.NET authorization is controlled with Web.config files, just as it controls authentication. This enables authorization to work with any type of authentication—even if the authorization doesn't use the local user database or Active

Directory that NTFS permissions are based on. The use of Web.config files also makes copying file permissions between multiple Web servers as easy as copying files.

In the sections that follow, you learn how to restrict access according to user and group names, to restrict access to specific files and folders using either a .config file or file permissions, and to use impersonation in an ASP.NET application.

How to Restrict Access to Users and Groups   The default Machine.config file contains the following authorization information:

```
<authorization>
        <allow users="*"/>
</authorization>
```

Unless you modified this section of the Machine.config file, or overrode the Machine.config file by adding this section to your application's Web.config file, all users permitted by your authentication configuration will be allowed to interact with all parts of every ASP.NET Web application. The `<allow users="*">` subsection of the authorization section tells ASP.NET that all users that pass the authentication requirements should be allowed access to all ASP.NET content. The * is a wildcard indicating all users, but you can also list user names or use the question mark character (?) to refer to all unauthenticated users. For example, to configure an ASP.NET application to provide access only to the users Eric and Sam, edit the Web.config file in the root of the ASP.NET application, and add the following lines within the `<system.web>` section:

```
<authorization>
      <allow users="Eric, Sam"/>
      <deny users="?"/>
</authorization>
```

The `<allow>` and `<deny>` subsections can contain *users*, *roles*, and *verbs* attributes. The *users* attribute should be set to a list of user names separated by commas; a * to indicate all authenticated or unauthenticated users; or a ? to indicate anonymous users. If Windows authentication is used, the user names should match names in the local user database or Active Directory, and might need to include a domain name (that is, "*DOMAIN\user*").

The *roles* attribute contains a comma-separated list of roles. When Windows authentication is used, roles correspond to Windows user groups. In this case, the names must exactly match group names in the local user database or Active Directory. If Forms authentication is being used, these roles are defined within the application itself and cannot be defined by the systems administrator.

The *verbs* attribute is used to restrict users and roles to specific types of HTTP requests—for example, HEAD, GET, POST, and DEBUG requests. All users should have access to the HEAD, GET, and POST verbs. Access to DEBUG can be limited to developers and administrators, if desired. Use the *verbs* attribute only when you understand how applications use each of the different requests. The following example demonstrates limiting access to different types of HTTP requests:

```
<authorization>
      <allow verbs="HEAD, GET, POST, DEBUG" roles="Developers"/>
      <allow verbs="HEAD, GET, POST" roles="Users"/>
      <deny users="?"/>
</authorization>
```

> **NOTE   The Most Common HTTP Verbs**   Browsers submit a GET request to retrieve a file. For example, the first time a user visits *http://www.microsoft.com*, the browser submits a "GET /" request to the *www.microsoft.com* Web server.
>
> If the user fills out a Web form (for example, to search the Microsoft.com Web site), the browser usually sends the response using an HTTP POST command, although forms with small amounts of input can be submitted with a GET command, too. GET and POST are the most commonly used commands; however, browsers will use the HEAD command to retrieve information about a file without actually retrieving a file. HEAD responses usually contain the date the file was modified, the length of the file, and the software the Web server is running.
>
> Tools such as FrontPage or Windows Explorer, which use Web folders to perform file management tasks, use PUT and DELETE commands. Applications use DEBUG, logically enough, for debugging, so developers need access to it but regular users do not. TRACE is rarely used, but can be useful for debugging and troubleshooting, and can provide some insight into how the remote server is handling the request. The OPTIONS command is also rarely used, but can determine what types of requests to which the Web server is capable of responding.

How to Control Authorization for Folders and Files by Using .config Files

The previous techniques are useful for controlling user access to an entire ASP.NET application. To restrict access to specific files or folders, add a `<location>` section to the `<configuration>` section of the Web.config file. The `<location>` section will contain its own `<system.web>` subsection, so do not place it within an existing `<system.web>` section.

To configure access restrictions for a specific file or folder, add the `<location>` section to your Web.config with a single section: *path*. The *path* section must be set to the relative path of a file or folder; absolute paths are not allowed. Within the

`<location>` section, include a `<system.web>` subsection and any configuration information that is unique to the specified file or folder. For example, to require Forms authentication for the file ListUsers.aspx and restrict access to the user named admin, add the following text to the `<configuration>` section of the Web.config file:

```
<location path="ListUsers.aspx">
    <system.web>
        <authentication mode="forms">
            <forms loginUrl="AdminLogin.aspx" protection="All"/>
        </authentication>
        <authorization>
            <allow users="admin"/>
            <deny users="*"/>
        </authorization>
    </system.web>
</location>
```

When using multiple `<location>` sections, files and subfolders automatically inherit all settings from their parent. Therefore, you do not need to repeat settings that are identical to the parent's configuration. When configuring authorization, inheritance has the potential to lead to security vulnerabilities. Consider the following Web.config file:

```
<configuration>
   <system.web>
       <authentication mode="Windows" />
       <authorization>
          <deny users="?" />
       </authorization>
   </system.web>

   <location path="Protected">
       <system.web>
          <authorization>
             <allow roles="CONTOSO\IT" />
          </authorization>
       </system.web>
   </location>
</configuration>
```

In this example, there are actually three layers of inheritance. The first is the Machine.config file, which specifies the default `<allow users="*"/>`. The second layer is the first `<system.web>` section in the example, which applies to the entire application. This setting, `<deny users="?"/>`, denies access to all unauthenticated users. By itself, this second layer would deny access to any user. However, combined with the Machine.config file, this layer allows access to all authenticated users and denies access to everyone else.

The third layer is the <location> section, which grants access to the CON-TOSO\IT group. However, this section also inherits the `<deny users="?"/>` and `<allow users="*"/>` settings. Therefore, the effective settings for the Protected subfolder are the same as for the parent folder: all authenticated users have access. To restrict access to *only* users in the CONTOSO\IT group, you must explicitly deny access to users who are not granted access specifically, as the following code demonstrates:

```
<location path="Protected">
   <system.web>
      <authorization>
         <allow roles="CONTOSO\IT" />
         <deny users="*" />
      </authorization>
   </system.web>
</location>
```

How to Control Authorization for Folders and Files by Using File Permissions

Even for publicly available content, it is good practice to tighten the NTFS file permissions on your Web server by removing the Everyone group's access. By default, the Everyone group has Read & Execute permissions to Web content, as shown in Figure 12-12. If you do remove the Everyone permission, you will discover that ASP.NET applications cannot execute unless both the ASPNET user account (on IIS 5.0) or the Network Service account (on IIS 6.0) and the IUSR_*MachineName* user accounts have Read permissions to the .aspx files.

Figure 12-12   The Everyone group has permission to read ASP.NET application files by default.

The IUSR_*MachineName* account needs only Read & Execute privileges to those files the browser requests directly—generally the .aspx and .asmx files. If the application was built using code-behind techniques, the .aspx files might refer to other files with extensions of .aspx.cs or .aspx.vb. If this is the case, only the ASPNET account (on IIS 5.0) or the Network Service account (on IIS 6.0) needs Read & Execute privileges to the code-behind files. Modifying permissions on a file-by-file basis can be difficult to maintain, however, because you must disable inheritable permissions for each file, and administrators must adjust the permissions for each file any time they make changes.

Table 12-3 lists the minimum permissions that an IIS IUSR_*ComputerName* Internet Guest Account and either the ASPNET account (IIS 5.0) or the Network Service account (IIS 6.0) must have. These permissions are valid only for applications in which the source code is compiled in a dynamic link library (DLL) file before the application runs, such as applications created by using Microsoft Visual Studio .NET. Individual users or groups must have additional permissions to update the files. Permissions are shown for individual file types. For all file types, if the IUSR_*ComputerName* account and the ASPNET account (IIS 5.0) or Network Service account (IIS 6.0) have these permissions, you can remove the Everyone account and the Authenticated Users account from the file's access control list (ACL).

Table 12-3   **Permissions Required for ASP.NET Applications**

File Type	Internet Guest Account Permissions	ASPNET Account (IIS 5.0) or Network Service Account (IIS 6.0) Minimum Permissions
Folders	Read (required for access to default document)	Read
.asax	No Access	Read
.ascx	No Access	Read
.ashx	No Access	Read
.asmx	Read	Read
.aspx	No Access	Read
.config	No Access	Read
.cs	No Access	No Access
.csproj	No Access	No Access
.dll	No Access	Read
.licx	No Access	No Access
.pdb	No Access	No Access
.rem	No Access	Read
.resources	No Access	No Access

Table 12-3   **Permissions Required for ASP.NET Applications**

File Type	Internet Guest Account Permissions	ASPNET Account (IIS 5.0) or Network Service Account (IIS 6.0) Minimum Permissions
.resx	No Access	No Access
.soap	No Access	Read
.vb	No Access	No Access
.vbproj	No Access	No Access
.vbdisco	No Access	No Access
.webinfo	No Access	No Access
.xsd	No Access	No Access
.xsx	No Access	No Access

How to Configure Impersonation by Using .config Files   By default, ASP.NET applications make all requests for system resources from the ASPNET account (IIS 5.0) or the Network Service account (IIS 6.0). This setting is configurable, of course, and is defined in the `<processModel>` item of the `<system.web>` section of the Machine.config file. The relevant default settings for this section are as follows:

```
<processModel
     enable="true"
     userName="machine"
     password="AutoGenerate"
/>
```

The *user Name* and *password* sections define the account ASP.NET impersonates when requesting system resources on behalf of Web users. The "machine" setting for *user Name* means that ASP.NET will use the account named ASPNET (IIS 5.0) or the Network Service account (IIS 6.0). The "AutoGenerate" setting for *password* forces ASP.NET to use a random password, which is much more secure than typing the password in the Machine.config file.

These settings are sufficient for most ASP.NET implementations. However, in many cases, you might need to configure ASP.NET to impersonate the client's authenticated user account, the anonymous user account in IIS, or a specific user account. This configuration is done by editing the impersonate section of the `<identity>` section of the Machine.config (for server-wide settings) or Web.config (for application- or directory-specific settings) files. To enable impersonation of the client's authenticated Windows account or the IUSR_*MachineName* account of IIS for anonymous access, add the following line to the `<system.web>` section of the Web.config file:

```
<identity impersonate="true" userName="" password=""/>
```

When IIS is configured for anonymous access, ASP.NET will make requests for system resources using the IUSR_*MachineName* account. When a user authenticates directly to IIS using a Windows logon, ASP.NET impersonates that user account. To enable ASP.NET to impersonate a specific user account, regardless of how IIS authentication is handled, add the following line to the `<system.web>` section of the Web.config file and replace the *DOMAIN*, *User Name*, and *Password* attributes with the account logon credentials:

```
<identity impersonate="true" userName="DOMAIN\UserName" password="Password"/>
```

How to Use Code Access Security to Limit Privileges

You can control the level of trust granted to external applications that your ASP.NET Web application might call. By default, trust is not a factor for ASP.NET applications because the Machine.config file is pre-configured to give full trust to ASP.NET applications. This snippet from the Machine.config file shows the default settings of the `<securityPolicy>` and `<trust>` sections:

```
<securityPolicy>
<trustLevel name="Full" policyFile="internal"/>
<trustLevel name="High" policyFile="web_hightrust.config"/>
<trustLevel name="Medium" policyFile="web_mediumtrust.config"/>
<trustLevel name="Low" policyFile="web_lowtrust.config"/>
<trustLevel name="Minimal" policyFile="web_minimaltrust.config"/>
</securityPolicy>

<trust level="Full" originUrl=""/>
```

The `<securityPolicy>` section defines the different levels of trust that might be specified for ASP.NET applications. Each `<trustLevel>` subsection defines a unique level of trust and has two attributes: *name* and *policyFile*. The *name* attribute gives the trust level a friendly name that will be referenced in the `<trust>` section, and the *policyFile* attribute references another configuration file (located in the same folder containing the Machine.config file) that contains the details of that level's trust settings. By default, five different levels of trust exist: Full, High, Low, None, and Minimal. The Full trust level does not have a configuration file because it receives unrestricted access.

The <trust> section defines the level of trust that ASP.NET applications run from a remote URL will receive. The default setting in the Machine.config file grants all applications Full trust. To configure an application run from *http://remoteapp/ appdir/* to run with a Low level of trust, add this line to the Web.config file:

```
<trust level="Low" originUrl="http://remoteapp/appdir/" />
```

How IIS and ASP.NET Handle File Extensions

IIS authentication, when enabled, authenticates all requests for a folder regardless of the type of file being retrieved. ASP.NET authentication works very differently, however, and can authenticate only those requests that IIS passes to .NET Framework. By default, IIS 5.0 with .NET Framework installed is configured to pass requests for files ending in the extensions .asax, .ascx, .ashx, .asmx, .aspx, .axd, .config, .cs, .csproj, .java, .jsl, .licx, .rem, .soap, .vb, .vbproj, .webinfo, .resx, .resources, .vjsproj, and .vsdisco. This means that requests for any other file will not be passed through ASP.NET and, therefore, cannot be controlled by ASP.NET authentication.

Here is a practical example. Your company uses a public Web site to sell recipes written using Adobe Acrobat. These Portable Document Format (PDF) files are located in the /Recipes virtual directory. Users should be able to download these recipes only after they pay a fee and the application assigns them a unique user name and password. You created an ASP.NET application that uses Forms authentication to verify users, and you configured the /Recipes virtual directory to require Forms authentication by setting the <authentication> section of the virtual directory's Web.config file appropriately. However, after the first user purchases a recipe, he or she e-mails the URL of the .pdf file to his friends, and other people are able to download the file directly without being authenticated.

This problem occurs because files with extensions that are not associated with the aspnet_isapi.dll file are processed directly by IIS and, therefore, cannot trigger an ASP.NET authentication event. The .pdf extension is not one of the extensions mapped to ASP.NET; therefore, IIS retrieves the file from the context of its anonymous user account and sends the file to the user. To overcome this, add .pdf to the IIS extension mappings as shown in Figure 12-13.

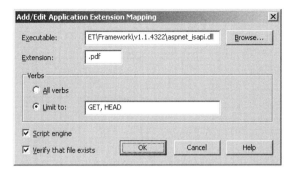

Figure 12-13   To add an extension, at a minimum, configure the Aspnet_isapi.dll executable and the file extension.

After you make this change, IIS will send all requests for files ending in .pdf to ASP.NET. ASP.NET will enforce authentication rules and redirect users requesting the file to the logon page. To ensure the security of a virtual directory authenticated with ASP.NET, map all file extensions of documents that should be protected to the aspnet_isapi.dll file.

> **NOTE   The ASP.NET Performance Overhead**   Processing static files through ASP.NET increases the overhead of each request, thereby reducing scalability. Use this technique only for file types that must have access controlled by ASP.NET.

Notice that many of the file extensions IIS is configured to pass to ASP.NET should never be called by users. Users typically call only files ending in .aspx. There is no legitimate reason for a typical user to request a file ending in .cs or .vb. However, IIS is configured to pass them to ASP.NET and ASP.NET, in turn, filters these requests. If IIS were to fulfill the request by transferring the files, the attacker would gain access to your application's source code. However, by default, ASP.NET intercepts the requested file, detects that the file extension should not be part of a legitimate request, and drops the request.

> **NOTE   Protecting ASP.NET Source Code**   If, for some reason, an ASP.NET application is installed on a Windows 2000 Server that has not been configured for ASP.NET applications, the source code might be vulnerable. Always verify that .NET Framework is installed on computers running Windows 2000 Server before copying or installing an ASP.NET application.

ASP.NET is configured by default to accept requests for some specific file extensions and to reject others. Because most applications use standard file extensions, developers rarely modify ASP.NET extension mappings in Web.config files.

Therefore, extension mappings are usually drawn from the `<httpHandlers>` sub-section of the `<system.web>` section of the Machine.config file. The following code is a sample of the `<httpHandlers>` section in the Machine.config file, which .NET Framework processes from top to bottom.

```
<add verb="*" path="*.vjsproj" type="System.Web.HttpForbiddenHandler"/>
<add verb="*" path="*.java" type="System.Web.HttpForbiddenHandler"/>
<add verb="*" path="*.jsl" type="System.Web.HttpForbiddenHandler"/>
<add verb="*" path="trace.axd" type="System.Web.Handlers.TraceHandler"/>
<add verb="*" path="*.aspx" type="System.Web.UI.PageHandlerFactory"/>
<add verb="*" path="*.ashx" type="System.Web.UI.SimpleHandlerFactory"/>
<add verb="*" path="*.asmx"
     type="System.Web.Services.Protocols.WebServiceHandlerFactory,
     System.Web.Services, Version=1.0.5000.0, Culture=neutral,
     PublicKeyToken=b03f5f7f11d50a3a" validate="false"/>
<add verb="*" path="*.rem"
     type="System.Runtime.Remoting.Channels.Http.HttpRemotingHandlerFactory,
     System.Runtime.Remoting, Version=1.0.5000.0, Culture=neutral,
     PublicKeyToken=b77a5c561934e089" validate="false"/>
<add verb="*" path="*.soap"
     type="System.Runtime.Remoting.Channels.Http.HttpRemotingHandlerFactory,
     System.Runtime.Remoting, Version=1.0.5000.0, Culture=neutral,
     PublicKeyToken=b77a5c561934e089" validate="false"/>
<add verb="*" path="*.asax" type="System.Web.HttpForbiddenHandler"/>
<add verb="*" path="*.ascx" type="System.Web.HttpForbiddenHandler"/>
<add verb="GET,HEAD" path="*.dll.config" type="System.Web.StaticFileHandler"/>
<add verb="GET,HEAD" path="*.exe.config" type="System.Web.StaticFileHandler"/>
<add verb="*" path="*.config" type="System.Web.HttpForbiddenHandler"/>
<add verb="*" path="*.cs" type="System.Web.HttpForbiddenHandler"/>
<add verb="*" path="*.csproj" type="System.Web.HttpForbiddenHandler"/>
<add verb="*" path="*.vb" type="System.Web.HttpForbiddenHandler"/>
<add verb="*" path="*.vbproj" type="System.Web.HttpForbiddenHandler"/>
<add verb="*" path="*.webinfo" type="System.Web.HttpForbiddenHandler"/>
<add verb="*" path="*.asp" type="System.Web.HttpForbiddenHandler"/>
<add verb="*" path="*.licx" type="System.Web.HttpForbiddenHandler"/>
<add verb="*" path="*.resx" type="System.Web.HttpForbiddenHandler"/>
<add verb="*" path="*.resources" type="System.Web.HttpForbiddenHandler"/>
<add verb="GET,HEAD" path="*" type="System.Web.StaticFileHandler"/>
<add verb="*" path="*" type="System.Web.HttpMethodNotAllowedHandler"/>
```

Notice that source code and project file extensions such as .vjsproj and .java are assigned to the appropriately named *System.Web.HttpForbiddenHandler*. Pages that should be processed, such as .aspx files, are handled by *System.Web. UI.PageHandlerFactory*. Near the end of the code, the line `<add verb="GET,HEAD" path="*" type="System.Web.StaticFileHandler"/>` catches any processing requests submitted using either the HTTP *GET* or *HEAD* commands that have not yet been processed, and processes them using the *System.Web.StaticFileHandler* handler. This default handler allows you to configure IIS to send any file extensions to ASP.NET to protect the files with ASP.NET authentication, while still allowing Web browsers to retrieve the files normally. The final line of this code, `<add verb="*" path="*" type="System.Web.HttpMethodNotAllowedHandler"/>`, catches any request using HTTP verbs that has not yet been handled and throws an exception.

If your application has files that simply should be transferred by IIS without being processed but should still be protected by ASP.NET authentication, specify the *System.Web.StaticFileHandler* handler. If your application has files that have other extensions with your ASP.NET Web application, configure IIS to use ASP.NET to process those file extensions. If those files should never be processed by ASP.NET or downloaded by users, add sections to the `<httpHandlers>` section to enable *System.Web.HttpForbiddenHandler* to handle those file extensions, as shown in this example:

```
<add verb="*" path="*.passwords" type="System.Web.HttpForbiddenHandler"/>
```

How to Reduce the Attack Surface of ASP.NET Web Services

ASP.NET Web services enable applications to exchange XML information using standard Web protocols. This is a simple concept with significant implications— Web services enable information traditionally exchanged between a Web server and a Web browser to be accessed by different types of clients. Instead of just running a Web site, businesses can exchange data with partners and customers programmatically, enabling incredible improvements to automation and efficiency.

ASP.NET Web services, such as those that expose application functionality using Simple Object Access Protocol (SOAP), are based on ASP.NET and, as such, have most of the same security considerations as other ASP.NET Web applications. Even though the client is no longer a Web browser, the primary protocols are still HTTP and HTTPS. Firewalls, .config files, authorization, encryption, file permissions, extension mappings, impersonation, and trust are all virtually identical for ASP.NET Web applications and Web services. However, security designers also need to understand several configuration issues that are unique to ASP.NET Web services.

One aspect of the default behavior of ASP.NET Web services that has security implications is the Documentation protocol, which automatically generates a browser-friendly interface when a user navigates to a .asmx file. As shown in Figure 12-14, this interface provides detailed information about the Web service methods available and the information these methods require as parameters, and it even allows someone to call these methods manually without writing a client application. Although Web services are designed to be simple to connect to, you might not want the details of Web services exposed to anyone with a browser.

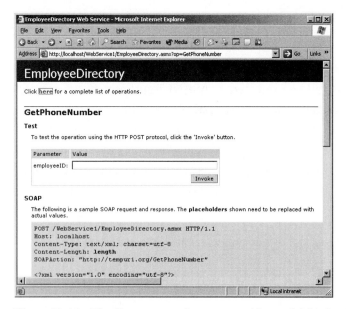

Figure 12-14   The Documentation protocol is useful for both developers writing a client-side application and attackers identifying potential entry points.

The behavior of the Documentation protocol is defined in the `<webServices>` section of the Machine.config file. By default, the Machine.config file contains the following:

```
<webServices>
     <protocols>
          <add name="HttpSoap"/>
          <add name="HttpPost"/>
          <add name="HttpGet"/>
          <add name="Documentation"/>
     </protocols>
</webServices>
```

Therefore, to disable the Documentation protocol, edit the Web.config file for the application and add the following section to the `<system.web>` section:

```
<webServices>
     <protocols>
          <remove name="Documentation"/>
     </protocols>
</webServices>
```

In addition, to reduce an application's attack surface, remove any protocols that the application does not specifically remove.

DESIGNING A WEB CONTENT MANAGEMENT STRATEGY

Many IIS security issues are not caused by misconfigurations or missing updates. Rather, human error causes them when users update content. For example, a member of your public relations organization might publish your organization's quarterly financial results to your Web site a day early, giving unscrupulous stock traders the opportunity to profit from the advance knowledge. On the other hand, a member of your documentation team might publish an online manual that contains an exaggerated description of a product's safety, exposing your organization to greater liability in the event of an accident when a customer uses your product.

Developers can abuse content management by adding malicious code to a Web application. Such malicious code might do the following:

- Record the user names and passwords of authenticated users for later abuse by the developer.

- Store private information processed by the Web application.

- Grant a developer elevated privileges to the application by creating a back door.

The sections that follow discuss how you can mitigate these risks by implementing a content management process, designing your networks for content management, and using content management software.

The Content Management Process

Many organizations use a very informal process for updating content on a Web site. For example, if the organization decides to market a new product, they might open a shared folder on the Web server and directly edit the HTML file by using an editor such as FrontPage. Organizations rarely use an informal process for long, however, because it is only a matter of time until someone makes a critical mistake while updating content.

Common content management errors include making confidential information publicly accessible, releasing news updates too early, and adding a security vulnerability when updating a Web application. You can greatly reduce the risk of these types of mistakes by implementing a content management policy. Environments that use a strict content management policy typically maintain three separate environments:

- **Test environment**   The test environment is a lab environment optimized for developing and rigorously testing new content. Quality assurance (QA) verifies that the content is functional, complies with content standards, and does not contain any significant bugs or security vulnerabilities.

- **Staging environment**   After rigorous testing in the test environment, content can be pushed to the staging environment. The staging environment is designed to closely simulate the production environment. The servers in the staging environment should closely match those used in production, including using the same hardware and software versions. QA should test the content in the staging environment to verify that it is functional and does not affect the performance or security of the site. The staging environment is partially redundant to the test environment; however, some bugs and vulnerabilities can be discovered only in the staging environment because it more closely matches the production environment.

- **Production environment**   The production environment serves content to end users. Push content to the production environment only after it has been tested in both the test and staging environments. Content typically is not tested in the production environment to avoid affecting end users. However, monitor the production environment to detect any performance or security impact introduced by new changes.

A typical content management process includes the following steps:

1. Determine that a change is required and identify the user who will make the change.

2. Develop the change in a test environment.

3. If you are adding application code, have a QA team test and validate the change in the test environment.

4. Publish the change to the staging environment.

5. If you are adding application code, have a QA team test and validate the change in the staging environment, paying particular attention to security vulnerabilities and performance impact.

6. Have public relations validate that the new content meets your organization's content standards, which might include layout, color, and font policies. Have the legal team approve the content.

7. Schedule the change. If the change is not likely to affect critical services, publish it to the production site during working hours. If the change might affect critical services, schedule the change after-hours. Notify any groups ahead of time who might be affected by the change.

8. Make the change, and then document that the change has been made.

9. Review the impact of the change. If you are adding application code, verify that it does not affect the security or performance of the site.

10. If necessary, plan the end of life for the content. For example, if you are publishing documentation for a product that your company sells, you might have to remove the content after you have discontinued support for the product. Although you might not know when support will discontinue, ensure that the process is in place to remove the content once support is discontinued.

Designing Networks for Content Management

When possible, use a separate network segment for content management. As discussed in Chapter 4, "Designing a Management Infrastructure," creating separate networks for public services and internal management communications enables you to block all management requests initiated from the Internet. As shown in Figure 12-15, using a dedicated management network provides defense-in-depth for public Web servers because network and host-based firewalls can block content management requests. If staff personnel need to update content from the Internet, they can initiate a VPN connection to the internal network.

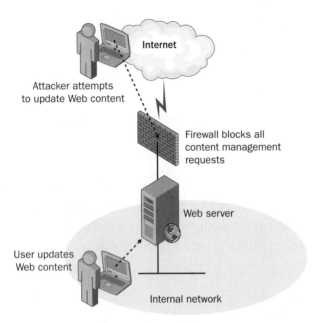

Figure 12-15   When possible, limit content management requests to a separate network.

Content Management Software

Although there are many content management solutions available, two of the most common are Microsoft Content Management Server and Microsoft Visual SourceSafe (VSS).

- **Content Management Server**   Content Management Server makes it easy for nontechnical users to publish Web content while providing an approved workflow with multiple levels, automatic content scheduling and archiving, and content indexing. Developers can create centrally managed templates and publishing processes that ensure consistency across the site, making it easy to ensure adherence to corporate publishing standards and branding without diminishing the flexibility of the publishing environment.

- **VSS**   VSS provides content management for Web applications. Although the most significant benefit to using VSS is improved productivity, VSS also provides significant security features. It will audit all changes to Web applications, audit which users made a particular change to an application and when they made that change, and enable you to roll back undesired changes quickly. Publishing changes can be restricted so that a manager approves all code. VSS provides accountability for development environments and reduces the likelihood that developers will attempt to insert malicious code into an application.

MONITORING IIS

IIS servers need the following types of monitoring:

- **Performance monitoring** Monitoring the time it takes for the Web server to process incoming requests, and the total load on the server. Use performance monitoring to verify that your Web server is functioning properly, that Web applications operate efficiently, and that your servers can scale to meet peak demand. Because performance monitoring is not primarily a security concern, it will not be discussed further in this chapter.

- **Fault monitoring** Monitoring the number of errors generated by the Web server, and verifying that the server is successfully fulfilling requests.

  > **MORE INFO** **Fault Monitoring** For more information about fault monitoring, refer to Chapter 4.

- **Security auditing** Recording important security events such as successful and unsuccessful authentication attempts, and users accessing protected files.

The sections that follow discuss Web application security auditing in more detail and provide an overview of the IIS monitoring capabilities provided by Microsoft Operations Manager (MOM).

Web Application Security Auditing

Like most Windows services, you can use Windows security auditing to monitor specific aspects of IIS usage. In particular, you can do the following:

- **Track when specific Web pages are accessed** When you enable NTFS success file auditing on a file, Windows will add an event to the Security event log each time the page is accessed. Enable success auditing for important files such as Web pages that administrators use to modify Web application security configuration settings, add user accounts, or change user permissions.

- **Track when IIS successfully authenticates users**   When IIS successfully authenticates a user, Windows adds an event to the Security event log if you have enabled success event logging for logon events. You cannot use security auditing to log Passport or ASP.NET Forms authentication, however, because these authentication types do not leverage the Windows user database. Instead, require your application developers to build auditing capabilities into the applications.

- **Record password-guessing attacks**   Because Web servers often give attackers on the Internet the opportunity to authenticate, attackers might use password-guessing attacks to identify a valid set of credentials. You can use failure auditing for logon events to add events to the Security event log for each authentication attempt, just as you could if someone were performing a password-guessing attack by sitting at the keyboard of a computer. As when auditing success events, you cannot use failure security auditing to log Passport or ASP.NET Forms authentication attempts.

In addition to the standard Windows security auditing, you can also gather information from IIS usage logs. By default, IIS logs information about each incoming request to a text-based log file located within %Systemroot%\System32\LogFiles\W3SVC*x*. These log files are completely separate from the logs viewable in Event Viewer. Each Web site creates a separate log file that includes information such as the source IP address, the number of bytes sent and received, the user name (if provided by the browser), and the type of browser used to make the request.

The following is an example of a single log entry created when the Administrator user requested the page /autoupdate/administration/default.asp:

```
2003-07-28 13:38:34 127.0.0.1 GET /autoupdate/administration/
default.asp - 80 DOMAIN1\Administrator 127.0.0.1 Mozilla/
4.0+(compatible;+MSIE+6.0;+Windows+NT+5.2;+.NET+CLR+1.1.4322) 200 0 0
```

The information in this log file is intended primarily for non-security-related analysis of Web site traffic. For example, members of the marketing team could use this information to determine which partner Web site was directing the highest number of users to the site. Become familiar with IIS log files, however, because Web sites are a frequent point of entry for attackers, and analyzing IIS log files can reveal that you were attacked by a malicious user, the method the attacker used, and information about the attacker's identity.

NOTE   Working with Law Enforcement   If you host a public Web site, you are going to be attacked. In fact, you are probably going to be attacked dozens of times per day. Thousands of systems infected with worms perform automated attacks against random Web servers, and many of those worms are specifically seeking out earlier, unpatched versions of IIS. Because of this, review your IIS logs regularly. If you do not have software specifically designed to analyze IIS logs and notify you about attacks, you can browse through the log files manually looking for unusual patterns. Look for requests for files that do not exist and requests that repeat on a regular basis.

If you discovered that someone had been coming to your home and trying to enter your house several times a day, you would probably call the police. On the Internet, however, there are far too many attacks to notify the authorities about every single one. If you do find traces of a Web-based attack, you don't need to panic. First, examine the requests from that user's IP address to determine whether the attack originated from a worm. If it did, just make sure your system is not vulnerable to attacks from that worm and continue with your day. You will never be able to chase down every worm-infected host on the Internet.

If you determine that an attack originated from an actual attacker targeting your computer systems, such as an ex-employee or a competitor, follow up on the attack. If you decide that the attacker should be punished, report the attack to an appropriate law enforcement agency. The Department of Justice's "How to Report Internet-Related Crime" page is a useful reference, located at *http://www.cybercrime.gov/reporting.htm*. Depending on your local laws, you might even be required to report such an attack.

If an attack is not serious enough to report to law enforcement, but you'd like to report it to the user's Internet service provider (ISP), find the user's IP address in the IIS log file and look it up at *http://whois.arin.net*. The American Registry for Internet Numbers (ARIN) site will tell you the ISP or organization that owns that IP address range, and usually provides an e-mail address and phone number for reporting abuse. It is up to the ISP whether, and how, it will deal with your complaint. It might choose to send the user a warning letter, ban the user completely, or simply do nothing.

IIS usage log information also can be sent directly to a database. This is useful if you manage multiple Web servers. In addition, this improves the security of the log files. If an attacker compromises your Web server, the attacker will have to gain access to a second system, the database server, to erase traces of the attack present in the log file. Furthermore, logs can be written to a remote share over a network using a full Universal Naming Convention (UNC) path. Remote logging allows administrators to set up centralized log file storage and backup. However, writing the log file over the network could negatively affect server performance.

Using Microsoft Operations Manager

MOM with the IIS Management Pack is one of the most effective ways to monitor your IIS servers. MOM is a management and monitoring framework that is a separate product from the Windows operating systems. The IIS Management Pack is a free download for MOM users that performs availability, health, and configuration monitoring of IIS and its related services. By monitoring the applications and Web sites running on IIS, the IIS Management Pack highlights issues that cause downtime or poor performance, such as broken links, unavailable sites, and security breaches.

The most useful security feature of the IIS Management Pack is the automatic IP address blocking. The IIS Management Pack can add the IP address of an Internet site attacker to the IP Deny list for all Web sites on the local computer. The attacker is added to this list based on the number of HTTP 401 (Access Denied) errors that are generated within a threshold period. By default, when a computer requesting a site generates more than 100 HTTP 401 (Access Denied) errors within 120 seconds, it exceeds the lockout threshold. This will greatly reduce the risk of brute-force attacks against IIS.

Similar to the way the IIS Management Pack implements automatic IP address blocking, you can trigger alerts based on other types of repeated events. For example, you could notify systems administrators if a server is repeatedly generating HTTP 500 (Server Error) events, which could indicate a failed server or a successful denial-of-service attack. You could also generate an alarm if a client repeatedly attempts to authenticate to an FTP server, indicating a password-guessing attack.

> **MORE INFO   IIS Management Pack**   For more information about the IIS Management Pack, read the IIS Management Pack Guide at http://www.microsoft.com/technet/prodtechnol/mom/mom2005/maintain/iismpguide.mspx.

SUMMARY

- Whenever possible, upgrade earlier versions of Windows to Windows Server 2003 to limit the risk of compromise while running IIS. Install only the components your Web application absolutely requires and configure Web site permissions as restrictively as possible.

- If your Web site requires authentication, you have several options: Basic, Digest, Integrated Windows, Passport, and client certificates. If you must use Basic authentication, protect communications by using an SSL certificate and requiring HTTPS. Use client certificates for extranet scenarios.

- ASP.NET Web applications require a separate security design effort. All ASP.NET authentication and authorization settings are configured by using XML-based .config files.

- To reduce the risk of publishing confidential information or running Web applications with security vulnerabilities, implement a content management policy.

- Monitor IIS to detect failures and security incidents. Proper monitoring can reduce downtime by notifying administrators of a problem and enabling them to resolve it quickly.

REVIEW QUESTIONS

1. Which of the following security features is supported by IIS 5.0?

    a. IIS runs with restrictive privileges.

    b. ASP is disabled by default.

    c. ISAPI extensions are disabled by default.

    d. You can authenticate users with client certificates.

2. You are configuring the application server role on a computer running Windows Server 2003 to run an ASP.NET application. Which of the following components should you install? (Choose all that apply.)

    a. Active Server Pages

    b. ASP.NET

    c. Common Files

    d. Enable Network DTC Access

    e. FTP Service

    f. FrontPage 2002 Server Extensions

    g. Internet Data Connector

    h. Message Queuing

    i. NNTP Service

    j. SMTP Service

    k. World Wide Web Service

3. You are configuring the application server role on a computer running Windows Server 2003 to host several static HTML pages that members of your public relations team have created. They want to use FTP to upload the files. Which of the following components should you install? (Choose all that apply.)

    a. Active Server Pages

    b. ASP.NET

    c. Common Files

    d. Enable Network DTC Access

    e. FTP Service

    f. FrontPage 2002 Server Extensions

    g. Internet Data Connector

    h. Message Queuing

    i. NNTP Service

    j. SMTP Service

    k. World Wide Web Service

4. You need to configure IIS authentication for an ASP.NET application that uses Forms authentication. Which IIS authentication method do you choose?

    a. Anonymous

    b. Windows

    c. Passport

    d. Client-side certificates

5. Which of the following IIS authentication methods does not provide encryption for the user credentials?

    a. Basic

    b. Integrated Windows

    c. Digest

    d. Client-side certificates

6. How would you configure the Web.config file for an ASP.NET application to grant access to users named Shaun and Anna, but deny access to all other users?

CASE SCENARIOS

Case Scenario 12-1: Designing Authentication for Extranet Web Access

You are a security designer for Consolidated Messenger, a small software development company. Recently, product management decided to outsource the development of a new software product to a development firm called Litware, Inc. The Litware developers need access to several internal resources, including a password-protected Web site containing your organization's development standards and methodologies stored in static HTML files. This is the first time you have needed to grant access to internal resources to external users.

You are concerned that the contractors might attempt to abuse any privileges that you grant them. Therefore, while you need to grant the contractors access to your intranet site, you do not want to create user accounts for them in the Web server's local user database, nor in your Active Directory domain.

You meet with the IT manager at Consolidated Messenger and suggest creating a new domain to store the contractor credentials, but the IT manager refused to take responsibility for managing an additional domain. In fact, the IT manager refuses to manage any type of user account for the contractors. In particular, your IT manager is concerned that if a developer leaves Litware, Litware won't notify Consolidated Messenger that the developer's user account needs to be removed. The IT manager would prefer that Litware manage its own user accounts.

You meet with the Litware IT manager to discuss the possibilities. They currently have an Active Directory domain with user accounts for all contractors, a Windows Server 2003 certification authority, an ISA Server 2004 firewall, and a Windows Server 2003 VPN server that authenticates by using RADIUS running on an IAS server. The Litware IT manager is happy to manage the company's own user accounts, but you need to identify a way to grant access to the Web site based on user credentials stored in its Active Directory.

1. What techniques can you use to grant access to your Web site while enabling Litware to manage its own user accounts?

2. What is the simplest way to grant access to your Web site while enabling Litware to manage its own user accounts?

3. What configuration steps do you need to go through to enable users with client certificates issued by the Litware CA to authenticate to your Web server?

Case Scenario 12-2: Designing Security for an ASP.NET Application

You are the principal security designer for Fourth Coffee, a nationwide, prestigious coffee retailer. Product management has been studying customer satisfaction to identify ways to improve the performance of your retail outlets. Customers have voiced complaints about how long it takes to move through the checkout line. After further analysis, product management determined that one of the ways they would streamline the checkout process is to offer Fourth Coffee debit cards that allow customers to prepay for coffee so they don't have to exchange cash or wait for change.

As part of the debit card strategy, product management has determined that the company needs a Web site that a projected 25 percent of the 2 million Fourth Coffee customers can use to manage their Fourth Coffee debit card accounts. Your Web development team has chosen ASP.NET as their development environment, and your Web hosting team requires all Web servers to run Windows Server 2003. The Web hosting team also supports Microsoft SQL Server running on Windows Server 2003. Internally, an Active Directory domain environment manages user accounts.

You have been asked to provide a Web site design that can meet the scalability and security requirements of the new Web applications. Based on this information, answer the following questions.

1. Should the Web developers store customer account information in the Active Directory domain or in a SQL Server database?

2. Which IIS and ASP.NET authentication types do you recommend?

3. The Web servers will require which of the following components? (Choose all that apply.)

    a. Active Server Pages

    b. ASP.NET

    c. Common Files

    d. Enable Network DTC Access

    e. FTP Service

    f. FrontPage 2002 Server Extensions

    g. Internet Data Connector

    h. Message Queuing

    i. NNTP Service

    j. SMTP Service

    k. World Wide Web Service

CHAPTER 13

CREATING A DISASTER RECOVERY PLAN

Upon completion of this chapter, you will be able to:

- Design a backup process.

- Choose a backup facility.

- Design a disaster recovery process.

Disaster might never strike; the odds of a disaster happening that makes your office unusable are very low. The risk is still significant, though, because the potential damage could be extreme. Fires, earthquakes, tornados, floods, and acts of war can all devastate a business. In the past, many businesses have been totally unprepared for such incidents, and have had to close their doors permanently after a disaster.

As a security designer, it is your responsibility to make sure that your organization is prepared for the worst. Even if you never experience a true disaster, disaster recovery planning is useful for more-common types of incidents such as hard-drive failure and theft. This chapter teaches you the fundamentals of planning enterprise backup and disaster recovery procedures.

DESIGNING A BACKUP PROCESS

The disaster recovery process must start when things are going smoothly. First, determine your backup requirements based on acceptable downtime, data loss, and your data retention requirements. Then, choose the backup media you will use and identify a strategy for off-site backups. Although your high-level backup design can apply equally well to Microsoft Windows, UNIX, and almost any other type of operating system that you have, computers running Windows have several backup-related technologies that you must understand to design backup strategies for Windows networks. The sections that follow discuss these topics.

Determining Backup Requirements

Before you begin thinking about the technical details of backing up and restoring computers, determine your requirements. Consult with your legal department about these requirements because many types of organizations have to meet legal or contractual agreements. Generate two sets of requirements: one set that applies to disk failures in which backups can be restored from locally available media, and another set that applies to disasters in which data needs to be recovered from off-site media.

Consider the following criteria:

- **Maximum acceptable downtime**   How long can critical services be offline? Keep in mind that shorter downtime requirements increase costs significantly. The maximum acceptable downtime that you determine will guide your choices for backup facilities.

- **Maximum acceptable data loss**   In the event of a disaster, are you willing to tolerate the loss of a week's worth of updates, a day's worth of updates, or only an hour's worth of updates? The lower your acceptable data loss, the more frequently you have to perform backups. To protect against disasters that destroy a facility, ship backups off-site or replicate them across a network to a remote facility at least as frequently as your maximum acceptable data loss for a disaster.

- **Data retention requirements**   How far back do you need to archive data? Although it is common to store backups for three months so that you can restore data to any point in time during that period, the law requires many types of organizations to store data for several years. Longer data retention requirements increase your cost by requiring you to store more data, and to test those backups continually to ensure that data can still be recovered. In the United States, these regulations include the following:

    - Securities and Exchange (SEC) Act Rules 17a-3 and 4 for the financial services industry

    - The Sarbanes-Oxley Act for public corporations

    - Health Insurance Portability and Accountability Act (HIPAA) for the medical industry

Choosing Backup Media

When choosing backup media for enterprises, you have four main choices: hard disk, tape, writable CDs and DVDs, and other optical media. Most likely, you will need to use a combination of hard disks, tapes, and writable DVDs. The sections that follow discuss each of these types of media and offer guidelines on how to choose the right combination for your environment.

Hard Disks

Hard disks are the backup media of choice when restoring files quickly is a priority. Hard disks can be read from much faster than tapes because you can instantly read from any point in the disk, whereas tapes need to fast-forward or rewind to find a file that needs to be restored. This means that restoration happens quicker when you back up to disk.

Hard disks are also very durable for repeated reuse. Hard disks are designed for continuous writing and rewriting, so you can reuse the same set of disks almost indefinitely. This makes hard disks an excellent choice for daily backups.

Whereas you can purchase very expensive enterprise disk backup solutions, you do not necessarily need to purchase a special server for doing disk backups because any server with sufficient storage will work. When designing a dedicated disk backup server, save money by choosing inexpensive processors and smaller quantities of memory. Instead, optimize the computer for network throughput and disk reliability. Network backups will saturate your network connection, so it is important to use a high-performance network, as described in the section titled, "Designing Backup Networks" later in this chapter. Protecting the backup server's storage subsystem with redundant array of independent disks (RAID) will reduce the damage caused by a single failed disk. When possible, choose RAID 5 to provide disk redundancy while optimizing read and write performance.

Although enterprises typically require a centralized backup solution in which computers are backed up across the network to a central backup server, external hard disks can also be used as a distributed backup solution for computers that are not connected to the corporate network. For example, if you have employees who work from home and need to back up their home computers, they could perform these backups directly to an external hard disk. They would still need to perform regular off-site backups, however.

In addition to physically protecting your backup server, hard disks can be protected by both access control lists (ACLs) and encryption. ACLs are more important for protecting hard disks than encryption is, because hard disks will remain online continuously, where they, potentially, can be accessed across the network. Encryption is primarily useful when you cannot provide sufficient physical security, such as when the backup media are shipped off-site or you are using external hard disks to protect mobile computers.

Tapes

Tapes are less expensive per gigabyte than hard disks and are much easier to archive. Tapes typically are not any slower during backups than hard disks; however, if you have to restore data from tapes, it will take significantly longer than it would if you were restoring data from disk. This means that downtime, and the associated costs, would increase. The lifetime of a tape varies, but you can expect a tape to be usable for 15 to 30 years if it is archived. You can reuse tapes, but only for a limited number of times. Tapes typically are rated for a specific number of uses, but you can count on rewriting an entire tape between 50 and 300 times.

If you use tapes for daily backups, implement a tape rotation schedule to minimize the risk of losing data because of faulty media. For example, if you perform full backups every day to a single tape and change tapes once per week, a single bad tape could cause you to lose a full week of data. However, if you use different tapes for each day of the week, a single bad tape would cause you to lose only one day of data.

In the two-week rotation schedule, as illustrated in Table 13-1, a different backup tape is used each weekday for two weeks. The first tape (M-1) is used again at the beginning of a new rotation cycle every third week.

Table 13-1   A Two-Week Tape Rotation Schedule for a Month

	Monday	Tuesday	Wednesday	Thursday	Friday
Week 1	M-1	T-1	W-1	T-1	F-1
Week 2	M-2	T-2	W-2	T-2	F-2
Week 3	M-1	T-1	W-1	T-1	F-1
Week 4	M-2	T-2	W-2	T-2	F-2

This two-week plan does not account for off-site storage. The best way to accommodate off-site storage with a two-week tape rotation schedule is to copy a set of full backup tapes and ship the copy to off-site storage. Using a four-week tape rotation schedule, as shown in Table 13-2, provides more flexibility for off-site storage because you have the option of always storing the previous week's tapes off-site. Therefore, if you need to restore a file, you would always have the current week's tapes available. However, if disaster struck and you needed to use tapes stored off-site, the tapes would be (at most) a week old. You could retrieve the tapes before they were required for the rotation while always keeping at least one week's worth of tapes off-site.

Table 13-2   A Four-Week Tape Rotation Schedule for a Month

	Monday	Tuesday	Wednesday	Thursday	Friday
Week 1	M-1	T-1	W-1	T-1	F-1
Week 2	M-2	T-2	W-2	T-2	F-2
Week 3	M-3	T-3	W-3	T-3	F-3
Week 4	M-4	T-4	W-4	T-4	F-4

Small organizations often use a backup unit that supports a single tape. In this type of environment, systems administrators need to change the tape daily and must keep track of the rotation schedule manually. Enterprises typically invest in tape changers (also called tape jukeboxes), which store anywhere from six to hundreds of tapes, and can access any tape without human intervention. If you use a tape changer, the backup software you use will allow you to program a tape rotation schedule. Of course, a systems administrator will still need to remove tapes for off-site storage.

Protect tapes with both encryption and ACLs. Encryption is vital because tapes are a common target of theft, and encryption is the best way to protect media for which you cannot guarantee physical security. Tapes are more likely to be stolen than hard disks because they are commonly sent to off-site storage and may not receive a consistent level of physical security during transit and storage. If you do use encryption, be sure to protect your private keys. You must have a copy of the decryption keys stored off-site so that you can restore files in the event of a disaster; however, storing your decryption keys with the backup tapes themselves would give an attacker everything he or she needed to restore your backups.

You cannot protect tapes with traditional NTFS ACLs; however, all backup software provides for some level of authorization control. Take advantage of this capability to limit who can restore backup data because an attacker who can restore files can access any of your confidential data.

> **NOTE Windows Backup** You will never use Windows Backup in an enterprise environment. Windows Backup was designed for backing up a single computer. It supports a very limited number of media types, backs up a single computer at a time, doesn't support compression, and lacks many other important backup features.

Writable CDs and DVDs

Whether you choose disk, tape, or optical media, invest in backup equipment at the outset. Backup equipment is one of the most significant investments IT departments make. Many small businesses cannot justify the large initial expense of disk- or tape-based backup solutions. To provide backups for small businesses, choose media formats that consumers have adopted, such as writable CDs and DVDs. Although these media do not have as high a capacity as disks or tapes, the cost per gigabyte is very low, and DVD-burning drives are extremely inexpensive compared to typical enterprise backup solutions.

Writable CDs and DVDs are also excellent solutions for creating off-site backups for traveling laptop computers. Laptops are a backup challenge because they are often not connected to a network that would enable you to back them up using traditional techniques. Most laptop hardware vendors offer DVD-burning drives as accessories, and traveling employees can load blank DVD media into their computers and initiate a backup manually. They can then ship the media to your offices or to your off-site backup facility.

Optical Media

High-capacity optical media are replacing tape backups in many enterprises. Optical media typically are rated for a much longer archive lifetime than tapes, and can last hundreds of years when stored in the proper conditions. Optical media currently are more expensive than tapes. However, optical media costs might fall faster than tape costs, which might make optical media a better option. To protect data stored on optical media, follow the same guidelines provided for protecting tapes.

Combining Media Types

To take advantage of the benefits of both disks and tapes, perform on-site backups to hard disks, and then archive those backups to tape for off-site storage. For example, you might perform daily backups to disks across the network. You would need to have sufficient disk storage capacity to store a copy of every critical file and database on your network; however, you could reuse those disks continuously for many years. Every weekend, make a copy of the backed-up data to backup tapes and ship those tapes to an off-site storage facility. For daily file recoveries caused by users accidentally deleting files and failures of individual servers, you can quickly restore files from your backup disks. For disaster recovery, you can restore from your off-site tapes.

Choosing Backup Methods

You might already be familiar with the three major types of backups:

- **Full (also known as Normal)**   Backs up all files and turns off the **archive bit** on the files. The archive bit is a per-file setting that indicates whether a file has been changed since it was last backed up. When a file is modified after a backup, the operating system sets the archive bit, so that the file will be backed up during the next incremental or differential backup. If you need to restore a computer immediately after performing a full backup, you need to restore only a single backup because the full backup contains all of the computer's files.

- **Incremental**   Backs up files that have changed since the last full or incremental backup and turns off the archive bit on all files. Because incremental backups only back up files that have changed since the last backup, the number of files being backed up is smaller. If an organization performs a full backup on Sunday, and then performs incremental backups every other day of the week, restoring a computer on Friday would require restoring Sunday's full backup, Monday's incremental backup, Tuesday's incremental backup, Wednesday's incremental backup, and, finally, Thursday's incremental backup. Therefore, incremental backups are quick during the backup process, but can lead to very long restore times.

- **Differential** Backs up files that have changed since the last full or incremental backup, but does not change the archive bit on files. Differential backups are slightly less efficient than incremental backups, but they make restoring computers much easier because you need to restore only the last full backup and the most recent differential backup. If an organization performs a full backup on Sunday, and then performs differential backups every other day of the week, restoring a computer on Friday would require restoring only Sunday's full backup and Thursday's differential backup. In theory, incremental daily backups are smaller differential daily backups. In practice, the same files tend to change day after day. For example, if you download your e-mail every day, your e-mail client updates your mail file daily. Therefore, it would be backed up every day regardless of whether you used an incremental or differential backup. Because differential backups provide easier restores and incremental backups are only minimally more efficient during the backup process, choose a combination of full and differential backups when designing a backup strategy.

Windows Backup also supports two less-frequently used backup types:

- **Copy** Like a full backup, a copy backup backs up all files. However, copy backup does not change the archive bit on files. Therefore, you can use a copy backup to back up a computer without affecting future incremental or differential backups.

- **Daily** Daily backups back up only those files that have changed in the last day. There's no good reason to use a daily backup. Even if you perform backups every day, it is better to use differential or incremental backups because they are less likely to miss backing up files if a backup error occurs.

Table 13-3 summarizes the trade-offs evaluated for three primary backup types and rotation schedules you can use to back up Exchange data.

Table 13-3 **Evaluating Trade-Offs for Backup Types and Schedules**

Trade-offs	Full Daily Backup	Full Weekly and Incremental Daily Backup	Full Weekly and Differential Daily Backup
Availability	A complete copy of the data can easily be made available for recovery.	The full backup copy and all subsequent sets of incremental backups are required.	A full backup and the last differential backup are required.

Table 13-3   **Evaluating Trade-Offs for Backup Types and Schedules**

Trade-offs	Full Daily Backup	Full Weekly and Incremental Daily Backup	Full Weekly and Differential Daily Backup
Restore performance	Best. Full backups include all data; only one backup set is required.	Decreased. Data is spread over multiple backup sets since the last full backup.	Differential back-ups are faster to restore than incremental backups because only two backup sets are required.
Backup performance	Lowest. A complete set of data is backed up each time.	Best. Only changed files are backed up.	Slightly less than incremental. A complete set of data that has changed since the last full backup is backed up.
Management	Lower due to single backup set.	Increased due to additional backup sets.	Increased due to additional backup sets.
Costs	Highest due to storage and infrastructure requirements.	Lower than full backups. However, cost is increased because of the need to manage multiple backup sets.	Lower than full backups because of reduced storage requirements.

Designing Backup Networks

Server performance impact is another important consideration for backups. If you back up files across a network, the backup will most likely consume all available network bandwidth. Although this will not necessarily cause other services to be completely unavailable, it will negatively affect their performance. There are three ways to reduce this impact: scheduling backups after-hours, adding a dedicated backup network, and performing backups across a storage area network (SAN).

Most organizations that perform network backups schedule them after-hours to minimize user impact. This has significant disadvantages, however.

- If a backup fails, there might not be a systems administrator available to detect and resolve the problem. If administrators need to restore a file the next day, the backup would not be available.

- Environments with large amounts of data might not be able to complete a backup after-hours. For 100-megabit-per-second (Mbps) networks, you can back up about 350 gigabytes (GB) in 12 hours. For gigabit networks, you can back up about 3.5 terabytes (TB) in that same time. Organizations with multiple terabytes of data might need more than 24 hours to complete a full backup.

- Environments that operate 24 hours a day do not have off-hours during which users will not be affected.

- Finally, users with laptop computers are likely to take their computers home with them at night, meaning the computers will not be available for the network backup.

Chapter 4, "Designing a Management Infrastructure," discussed the benefits of using a separate network for management tasks. You can also use this network for backups, as shown in Figure 13-1, or even add a third network for backups. This is particularly important in environments where backups take too long to complete during off-hours. For example, a server with 10 terabytes of storage would take more than 30 hours to back up across a gigabit Ethernet network. If the server is busy every day, it would be impossible to perform a full backup during off-hours, and the backup would definitely affect the performance of connections on the user network if you did not design a separate backup network.

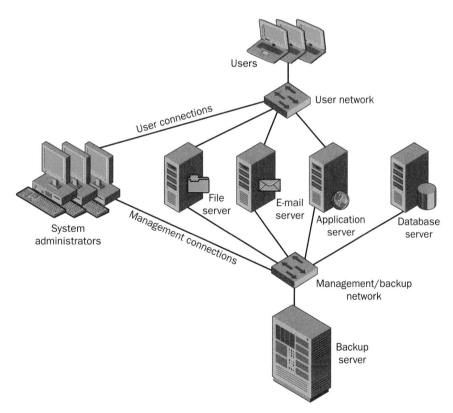

Figure 13-1   Using a separate network for backups reduces the bandwidth impact.

Another alternative is SAN backups. A SAN is a type of high-speed network opti-mized for accessing storage. With a SAN, you can connect one or more servers to one or more external storage devices. You can also connect backup servers directly to the SAN, enabling the backup server to communicate directly with the storage device. Therefore, the servers would not need to run a backup client at all because files could be transferred directly from the hard disks to the backup server. Figure 13-2 illustrates this configuration.

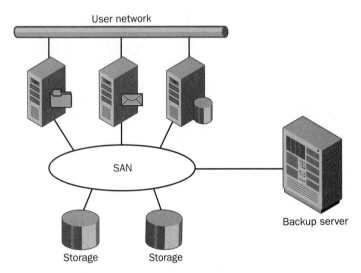

Figure 13-2   SANs enable backup servers to communicate directly with storage devices.

Finally, you can choose a decentralized backup model in which backup devices are connected to each server. This works well in small environments where each computer can be configured with a DVD burner and administrators can manually change backup media at each computer. However, in enterprises, maintaining separate backup devices for each server is extremely costly and time-consuming. Therefore, large environments should back up servers across a network or SAN.

Backing Up Windows Servers

Whereas understanding the difference between full, incremental, and differential backups is typically sufficient for backing up client computers, servers are much more complicated. Servers usually run 24 hours per day and keep files open that entire time. In addition, servers are continually updating files and databases, and might update files during the time span that it takes to back up the computer. This can lead to inconsistent backups. For example, if a server with large hard disks takes 8 hours to perform a full backup and the backup starts at midnight, the first file to be backed up would reflect only changes performed before midnight. However, the last file to be backed up might have changes made at 7:55 A.M. If the first file to be backed up was a list of orders, and the last file was a list of customers, after completing the recovery process you might discover orders in which the customer information does not exist.

To address these problems, Microsoft Windows Server 2003 provides the Volume Shadow Copy capability, as described in the next section. In addition, factor in both network and server performance into your network architecture, and make application-specific accommodations where necessary.

Volume Shadow Copy

The Volume Shadow Copy service is a feature of Windows Server 2003 that enables snapshot backups. Snapshot backups enable a backup process to back up all files, even open files, without any file changes taking effect during the backup process. Volume Shadow Copy allows server processes to continue reading and writing to files, but the changes are temporarily recorded in a shadow copy so that the backup process reflects the state of the files as they were the moment the backup began. The amount of disk space consumed depends on the amount of data that changes on the volume during the backup. After the backup is completed, the shadow copy of the volume is deleted because it is no longer needed.

In the event that a shadow copy is unsuccessful, for example, when there is not enough temporary disk space available on the volume, Windows Backup continues without using shadow-copy techniques and, as in previous versions of Windows, reads files from the original volume and does not back up any open files. Not all backup software takes advantage of volume shadow copies, however, so ensure that your backup software supports it or provides its own, similar functionality.

Assigning Backup Permissions

You must carefully plan how you assign backup operator privileges because backup operator privileges can have significant risk potential. If you are a member of the Administrators or Backup Operators local groups, you can back up any file and folder on the local computer to which the local group applies. Likewise, if you are an administrator or backup operator on a domain controller, you can back up any file and folder locally on any computer in the domain or any computer on a domain with which you have a two-way trust relationship. However, if you are not an administrator or a backup operator, you must be the owner of the files and folders you want to back up or you must have one or more of the following permissions for the files and folders you want to back up: Read, Read And Execute, Modify, or Full Control.

Be cautious when assigning Backup Operator privileges. Although these privileges are required for users running backups, the user has access to read any file they have permissions to back up. Enterprise backup software typically has functionality to provide some protection by enabling the backup software to run in the context of a backup operator while not granting the user managing the backups those same permissions.

Backing up Windows Server Applications

Many server applications have special backup requirements. For example, whereas you can perform a simple file backup on a SQL Server computer, you would need to stop the computer first, and it might not leave you with a usable backup. In a similar way, Active Directory domain controllers constantly replicate their data and you must consider that replication when performing a restoration. Any application might have special backup requirements, but some of the most important Windows services to understand are the following:

- **Active Directory** Active Directory directory service is backed up as part of System State and is, therefore, very straightforward. Restoration is more complicated. During the restore process, choose whether to perform a primary, non-authoritative, or authoritative restore. Perform a primary restore when all domain controllers have been lost and you are rebuilding the domain. Choose non-authoritative when at least one other domain controller is still active, because this enables the restored domain controller to receive a replicated copy of the Active Directory domain database from the remaining domain controller. You will not use the authoritative restore option in disaster recovery scenarios typically; it should be used only when you have deleted critical Active Directory data and those changes have been replicated to other domain controllers. Authoritative restores replicate the restored Active Directory database to all other domain controllers, overwriting recent changes.

- **DNS Server** If you have Active Directory–integrated Domain Name System (DNS), the zone data will be backed up as part of the Active Directory database. If you do not have Active Directory–integrated DNS, the zone files will have to be backed up explicitly as part of a file backup. If you back up the system disk along with the System State, this data will be backed up as part of the system disk.

- **IIS** Be sure to back up and restore the Internet Information Server (IIS) metabase, which happens automatically when you back up System State. File system backups do not work well for the metabase because the metabase depends on other components that are missed during a file backup. You can also manually back up the metabase by using the

Internet Services Manager. Remember, however, that relying on manual processes introduces the potential for human error, increasing the likelihood that you will not be able to restore the computer successfully.

■ **Certificate services** Certificate services are backed up as part of the System State. If your certificate server issues certificates and then fails before the computer is backed up, the certificate server will not have a record of those certificates once the computer is restored. However, because the certificates are signed properly with the certificate server's private key, the certificates will still be valid.

■ **Microsoft SQL Server 2000** SQL Server databases cannot be backed up like other files. You have two choices for backing up SQL Server computers in an automated fashion:

   ❑ Use backup software that specifically supports backing up live SQL Server databases, and configure that software to back up your critical tables.

   ❑ Use SQL Enterprise Manager to configure automatic backups to a file on the server's hard disk, as shown in Figure 13-3. Then, back up this file using a standard file backup. Database backup software can be very expensive, and using this technique for database backups can save you a significant amount of money.

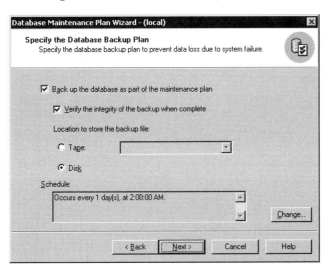

Figure 13-3 You can configure automatic SQL database backups to a file, and then back up that file.

Alternatively, you can manually back up SQL Server by using the SQL Enterprise Manager tool. Regardless of the method you choose, you must keep in mind that new databases added to a server will not be backed up automatically. Therefore, have a process in place to either detect new databases or ensure that database administrators inform backup administrators that a new database requires backing up.

Depending on your needs, you might choose to back up SQL Server data more often than other types of data because most enterprises use databases to store the most critical, rapidly changing data, such as customer orders. If you do need to back up a database frequently, you can choose to back up just the transaction log when performing incremental backups. The transaction log contains only changes made to the database, and can be reapplied after restoring a full database backup to bring the database up to date. Consult with your database administrators about the most efficient way to back up your database frequently.

- **Cluster services**   Cluster services are backed up as part of the System State.

- **Microsoft Exchange Server 2003**   Microsoft Exchange 2000 Server and Exchange Server 2003 store some information in the metabase on the local computer. Therefore, like IIS, be sure to back it up by backing up System State. Exchange Server 2003 supports Windows Server 2003 Volume Shadow Copy, which simplifies backup.

> **MORE INFO**   **Exchange Server Disaster Recovery**   For more information about disaster recovery planning for Exchange Server 2003, read the Exchange Server 2003 Disaster Recovery Planning Guide at *http://www.microsoft.com/downloads/details.aspx?FamilyId=784BBEA2-28DD-409A-8368-F9914E993B28.*

> **NOTE**   **System State Backups**   System State backups include a great deal of data that is not included in standard file backups, including the following:
>
> - System startup files and protected operating system files
> - System registry
> - COM+ Class registration database
> - IIS metabase
> - Certificate Services database
> - Cluster service
> - SYSVOL
> - Active Directory

Automated System Recovery

Automated System Recovery (ASR) is a tool to help you automatically restore a computer running Windows Server 2003 or Windows XP. You can boot the computer from the operating system CD, and then use an ASR floppy disk to recover the system directly from a backup. ASR works with Windows Setup to rebuild the storage configuration of the physical disks and writes the critical operating system files to the boot and system partitions to allow the system to boot successfully. After an ASR restore completes, you can restore any needed user or application files.

> **NOTE   ASR versus Emergency Repair Disk**   ASR behaves differently from the Emergency Repair Disk feature in Windows 2000 Server, which ASR replaces. Emergency Repair Disk replaces missing or corrupt system files without formatting drives or reconfiguring storage. ASR, by contrast, always formats the boot volume and might format the system volume.

ASR works with Windows Backup and requires you to run the ASR Wizard. Non-Microsoft backup software typically provides similar functionality, but may have different configuration requirements. ASR, unfortunately, requires the replacement computer's hardware to be very similar to the original computer's hardware. Variations in hard disks, video cards, and network adapters should be automatically detected, but different processor types or motherboards might cause problems.

CHOOSING A BACKUP FACILITY

Floods, fires, earthquakes, tornados, power outages, and acts of war can leave you without usable office space. These disasters don't have to mean that all employees get a week off while contractors complete repairs, as tempting as that might sound. Just as you should keep replacement server hardware on hand to bring a failed computer back online quickly, have a plan to replace your facilities temporarily.

There are five main approaches to designing a backup facility: **hot site**, **warm site**, **cold site**, **mobile site**, and **reciprocal agreement**.

Hot Site

The hot site is a true backup facility from which your employees can work at a moment's notice. Hot sites typically have desktop computers for the staff, actively running servers with recent copies of your applications and data, and a working, continuously monitored network. Hot sites are very expensive to maintain because your organization needs to lease the building space, pay for desktop and server hardware that will go unused the vast majority of the time, and maintain that equipment in the event it is needed in a disaster.

> **NOTE   Laptop Computers and Disaster Recovery**   You might not need to keep duplicates of all client hardware in a hot site. Many employees with laptops will still have their laptops available to them.

Hot sites generally make the following sacrifices compared to the production facility:

- Interior decorations are nonexistent.

- They are typically an open space with no private offices.

- Luxuries such as a cafeteria are missing.

- Server performance might be slower because applications are consolidated onto fewer computers and running on less-expensive hardware.

- Noncritical services such as internal Web sites might not be duplicated.

In the event of a disaster, administrators typically acquire the backup media from off-site storage and use it to bring the servers at the hot site online. Depending on your off-site backup schedule, this might cause you to lose between a day and a week of data and transactions. If this loss is not acceptable to you (as it would not be for high-volume distributors or financial organizations), you need to keep your backup servers online and configure replication between your production servers and the backup servers at the hot site. To protect Active Directory data, you could place a domain controller at the hot site. To protect data stored in a database, configure automatic database replication.

To ensure that a hot site is functional, arrange annual tests. It is important that you use the equipment at the hot site to restore files from backup, because it's possible that the backups could be read by your production backup equipment, but not by the equipment at the hot site. Include critical, non-security staff in the test to ensure that staff are properly trained and have the resources they need to do their jobs.

Warm Site

Warm sites provide many of the benefits of a hot site, but rather than having all critical computers and network infrastructure duplicated, warm sites duplicate only the least expensive infrastructure components. These components might include server racks, desks, and telephone lines. In the event of a disaster that made the production facility unusable but did not destroy it (such as an extended power outage), staff would need to transport production equipment to the warm-site facility and connect it. Depending on the size of the production facility, this could take anywhere from a day to a week.

> **NOTE** **Software Licenses** Enterprises that participate in the Microsoft Software Assurance plan typically do not need to purchase additional licenses for warm or cold sites because they are eligible for complimentary cold backup server licenses and related client access licenses. The primary requirement is that your backup servers must be

turned off except during period disaster recovery testing or during an actual disaster.

If a disaster destroys the production facility, staff will need to order new computer hardware and network equipment, and wait for vendors to deliver that equipment before configuring it and restoring backups. This process can take anywhere from a week to a month. Even if you are accustomed to getting new equipment delivered overnight, keep in mind that your vendor might be affected by the same disaster that affected you. In addition, the disaster might affect the communications and transport infrastructure, which would slow your ability to place the orders for new equipment and receive them in a timely manner.

> **NOTE Buying New Equipment**   Buying new equipment takes a long time, but if the production facility is really destroyed, you are going to need to buy new equipment anyway. In addition, insurance will probably cover a large portion of the equipment costs.

It is more difficult to perform testing with a warm site, unfortunately, because you cannot unplug your production servers and move them to a new facility. In most circumstances, such a test would not only cause downtime, but the hardware might be damaged in transit.

Cold Site

Besides walls and a roof, cold sites have only the most basic infrastructure: electricity, lighting, plumbing, and heat. Plan to spend several weeks bringing a cold-site facility into an operational state after a disaster. The primary benefit of using a cold site is the low cost. Disaster-recovery-service organizations can offer leases on cold-site facilities at a very low price because many different organizations can share the same cold-site facility, provided they won't be affected by the same disaster. Because no equipment is stored at a cold-site facility, any organization can use it equally well.

> **NOTE Mobile Phones and Disaster Recovery**   If you lose your phone service or must move to a cold site without telecommunications equipment, you can use employee mobile phones for communications. Wireless networks have proven valuable in many recent disasters.

Mobile Site

A mobile site is, essentially, a trailer that can function as office space during an emergency. The mobile site typically will have a generator to provide electricity, and some telecommunications capabilities such as a satellite uplink for phone and Internet services. Mobile sites can be configured as hot, warm, or cold sites, depending on how much equipment you want to store in the trailer.

Because a mobile site can be driven to different locations, it is highly flexible. A mobile site can protect multiple offices within several hours' driving time. In the event of an extremely localized emergency such as a fire, you can even park a mobile site in your production facility's parking lot. Such an arrangement simplifies moving production equipment to the site and makes it easy for employees to find.

Reciprocal Agreement

With a reciprocal agreement, you make plans with a partner organization to use part of each other's facilities in the event of a disaster. The partner organization must have facilities that are not likely to be affected by the same disaster. Employees can temporarily relocate to the partner organization's facilities and make use of existing telephone and Internet connections for communications. IT staff will still need to bring server equipment online at the partner facilities, just as they would at a warm or cold site.

Reciprocal agreements carry the significant risk that the partnering company will not allow you to use its facilities in the event of an actual disaster. Most businesses use close to 100 percent of the capacity of their facilities, and trying to run a second business from the same facility would cause a great deal of stress to employees of both organizations. This arrangement would also introduce significant security risks because employees from both organizations would be working in the same area. Even if they are contractually obligated to share their facilities with you, they might decide it is more beneficial to challenge the contract than to help you. When considering a reciprocal agreement, compare this risk against the lower cost.

If you do decide to create a reciprocal agreement with another organization, you must address the following issues:

- What infrastructure will you share? You might choose to share telephone and Internet access, but not enable the partnering company to use your server and client computers.

- How many partnering employees will be allowed to use your facilities? Your local building codes might restrict the number of people allowed.

- How long will the partnering company be allowed to use your facilities?

- Who is responsible for creating the temporary workspace and configuring the network and server infrastructure?

- How much notice do you need to give before moving into the partner's facility?

- Can the partner owning the unaffected offices have some employees work from home to reduce issues with overcrowding?

- Can one of the partners shift its operations to earlier in the morning or later at night to reduce issues with overcrowding?

- Knowing that it affects your partner's organization, how frequently can you test the disaster recovery process?

- Where network infrastructure is shared, do you use the same standards? If not, how will you resolve the interoperability issues? For example, if your partner uses an 802.11a wireless network infrastructure, but you use 802.11b, your clients will not be able to connect to their wireless network.

Backup Facility Advantages and Disadvantages

Table 13-4 highlights the advantages and disadvantages of each, and the sections that follow describe them in more detail.

Table 13-4   **Advantages of Various Backup Facilities**

Backup Facility Type	Advantages	Disadvantages
Hot site	Quickest recovery time: might be less than a day. Easiest to test.	Highest cost.
Warm site	Lower cost than a hot site.	Longer recovery time: several days. If the production facility is destroyed, recovery time could be weeks. Higher cost.
Cold site	Very low cost.	Long recovery time: might take several weeks.
Mobile site	Low cost. Location can change depending on the disaster. Can provide backup for multiple locations.	Limited space.
Reciprocal agreement	Lowest cost.	Significant risk that the facility will not be available during a disaster.

Typically, you would lease space from a disaster-recovery-service organization for a hot, warm, or cold site. Such service organizations might lease the same space to multiple customers, with some assurance that all customers will not need the facility at the same time. For example, if Organization A is 50 miles from the backup facility and Organization B is also 50 miles from the backup facility, but 75 miles away from Organization A, there is little chance that both Organization A and Organization B would be affected by the same disaster. Therefore, the service organization could lease the facility to both customers and reduce both companies' costs.

> **NOTE** **Disaster Recovery When Outsourcing** If you outsource any aspect of your IT infrastructure, such as Web hosting or e-mail, ask your service provider about its disaster recovery plans and make sure it meets your requirements.

DESIGNING A DISASTER RECOVERY PROCESS

You do not need to design the disaster recovery process separate from the standard security risk management process. The security risk management process treats disasters like any other types of attacks. All of the same methodologies and formulas apply equally well to disaster recovery.

However, many organizations do approach disaster recovery as a separate process because it is often budgeted separately from standard security planning and the countermeasures are very different. For example, you cannot really implement preventive countermeasures for all types of disasters because you can't stop hurricanes, floods, and acts of war. Instead, you must focus on transferring the risk with insurance and using reactive countermeasures such as moving to backup facilities.

The following steps outline a traditional disaster recovery design process and show how each step maps to the security risk management process.

1. **Do risk analysis and business impact analysis** Risk analysis (RA) and **business impact analysis (BIA)** are processes that assess the damage that would be caused by different types of disasters. In essence, you perform this step as part of steps 1 through 4 of Phase 1 of the overall security risk management process (described in Chapter 2, "Analyzing Risk"). When disaster recovery professionals use the term BIA, they refer to a process like the security risk management process that focuses on different types of disasters. This phase provides you with the information you need to determine your disaster recovery priorities.

2. **Develop the plan** During this phase, determine the most effective way to limit your exposure to different types of disasters. This phase maps directly to step 5 of Phase 1 of the security risk management process.

3. **Implement the policies and procedures**   During this phase, you implement your ongoing disaster recovery policies and procedures, including performing backups of critical data, acquiring backup facilities, and training users. This phase maps directly to Phase 2, steps 1 and 3 of the security risk management process.

4. **Test the process**   The purpose of disaster recovery is to limit your risk. If you don't test your disaster recovery plans, you are exposing yourself to a great deal of risk. Therefore, proper testing is essential. During this phase, have staff go through the same process they would use in the event of an actual disaster. You must verify that critical business tasks, such as processing customer orders, can continue in a reasonable amount of time after the simulated disaster begins. This phase maps directly to Phase 2, step 2 of the security risk management process.

5. **Maintain the process (tracking changes and so on)**   Directly related to Phase 3 of the security risk management process, during this phase you strive to maintain your ability to recover from a disaster as your IT infrastructure goes through normal changes. It is critical that you track new servers brought online and plan to recover those computers in the event of a failure.

The sections that follow provide information about responding to and recovering from a disaster.

The Disaster Response Process

Follow these six steps when you respond to incidents ranging from virus attacks to disasters:

1. **Protect human life and people's safety**   Safety must always be your first priority. For example, part of your disaster recovery process might include systems administrators retrieving last night's backup tapes from a safe before leaving the building. This will work well in the event of an extended power outage or flooding. However, your systems administrators must be instructed to abandon the tapes if their lives are in danger because the building is on fire. Further, your disaster recovery plans must be flexible enough to accommodate making the preservation of human life the top priority.

2. **Contain the damage**   In the event of a compromise, containing the attack limits additional damage. In general, this means disconnecting attacked computers from the network immediately. Keeping systems

up during an attack might reduce downtime, but can result in greater and more widespread problems in the end. For example, if you contract a worm in your environment, try to limit the damage by disconnecting servers from the network. Containment should begin as quickly as possible by disconnecting from the network the systems known to be affected during a security incident.

3. **Assess the damage**   Determine the extent of the damage that the attack caused as soon as possible, immediately after you contain the situation. This is important so that you can restore the organization's operations as soon as possible. If it is not possible to assess the damage in a timely manner, implement a contingency plan so that normal business operations and productivity can continue. It is at this point that you might engage legal authorities regarding the incident if you believe someone has broken the law, such as in cases of theft or arson.

4. **Determine the cause of the damage**   The cause of damage in a disaster is typically obvious. However, for non-disastrous security events, it is necessary to understand the resources at which the attack was aimed and what vulnerabilities were exploited to gain access or disrupt services. Review the system configuration, patch level, system logs, audit logs, and audit trails on both the systems that were directly affected and the network devices that route traffic to them. These reviews often help you to discover where the attack originated in the system and what other resources were affected.

5. **Repair the damage**   In most cases, it is very important to repair the damage as quickly as possible to restore normal business operations and recover data lost during the attack. In the event of a disaster, this step might include moving operations to a backup facility. If, after a non-disastrous security event, you determine that you were maliciously attacked, take care to verify that worms, viruses, or other malicious software do not infect computers before returning the computers to service.

6. **Review response and update policies**   After the documentation and recovery phases are complete, review the process thoroughly. Determine which steps were executed successfully and what mistakes the incident response made. In almost all cases, you will find that your processes need to be modified to allow you to handle incidents better in the future. You will inevitably find weaknesses in your incident-response plan. The point of this after-the-fact exercise is to identify opportunities for improvement. Any flaws should prompt another

round of the incident-response planning process so that you can handle future incidents more smoothly.

Server Recovery Strategies

You must choose a strategy for bringing services back online after a server has been destroyed. You have the following three options:

- **Restore the server**   Restore application data, system files, and System State data all at once. This provides the quickest restore when you are restoring data to server hardware that exactly matches the damaged server. However, if your replacement server hardware is different at all from the production hardware, the operating system and applications might fail to load properly. In addition, performing this type of restore requires you to back up all computer files, including the operating system and application executable files, so backup storage requirements will be higher than if you plan on rebuilding failed servers. If your server hardware varies significantly, you are better off rebuilding your server.

- **Rebuild the server**   You can rebuild the server entirely by reinstalling Windows, reinstalling all applications, restoring your configuration settings, and then reapplying all patches. This process can take many hours, but is more likely to succeed when the backup server hardware is different from the production server hardware. You usually end up with a cleaner, more stable operating system environment with better performance than if you restored a server from full computer backups. This is because full computer backup sets back up every file on a disk drive, including any damaged files or mismatched DLLs. However, if your server hardware varies too much (in particular, if disk configurations are different), you still might run into problems after restoring application settings. In this case, you would need to reconfigure applications manually.

- **Use a standby server**   You can also use a standby recovery server, also known as a hot backup server. This involves keeping recovery servers available with the operating system and applications installed. Having standby recovery servers available reduces the amount of time it takes to rebuild a damaged server. However, you must monitor, patch, and maintain standby servers, so they have a significant ongoing cost. To reduce downtime even further, you can set up replication between your production servers and your standby server, enabling you to bring the standby server online without restoring data from backups. Standby servers protect against hardware failures, but do not offer protection from attacks that modify your data or install malicious software.

Table 13-5 summarizes the three recovery strategies, including the advantages and disadvantages for each method.

Table 13-5   Requirements and Restore Procedures for Each Server Recovery Method

	Restoring the Server	Rebuilding the Server	Standby Recovery Server
Requirements	Full computer backup set.	Windows operating system and application setup files. Backups of documents and data. Documented configuration settings.	Standby recovery server with identical hardware, operating system, and applications. Backups of documents and data.
Restore Procedures	Replace damaged hardware. Perform a full restore. Restore the System State. Restore databases.	Replace damaged hardware. Reinstall operating system and applications. Restore application data. Reconfigure operating system and applications.	Start the standby recovery server. Restore application data.
Advantages	Faster than rebuilding a server. Easier to restore applications and configuration information.	Uses less disk or tape space for the backups. Resulting operating environment is usually more stable and provides better performance.	Resulting operating environment is usually more stable and provides better performance. Faster than both restoring and rebuilding a server.

Table 13-5   **Requirements and Restore Procedures for Each Server Recovery Method**

	Restoring the Server	**Rebuilding the Server**	**Standby Recovery Server**
Disadvantages	Requires more disk space or tapes for the backup. Backup jobs take longer to keep your backups current. Backups may be incompatible if your replacement hardware is not identical. Operating system environment and other elements might not be installed as cleanly as with other strategies.	Takes longer to recover a server than it does using either of the other two strategies. Backups may be incompatible if you replace the damaged hardware with hardware that has different specifications.	Requires extra hardware that you do not use until a disaster. Does not totally eliminate the risk of hardware incompatibility with your backups. Perform a test restore to ensure that your backups are compatible with the hardware on your standby recovery server.

Server Recovery Problems

It's critical to test your server recovery strategy because problems during restores are common, but can be extremely costly. To help you anticipate and plan for these situations, here are the most common problems:

- When restoring to a new server with different hardware—for example, if the original server used Small Computer System Interface (SCSI) storage and the server where you restore the data uses Integrated Device Electronics (IDE) storage—you might need to filter files such as Boot.ini from the restore job. If the restored data replaces the Boot.ini file, the system might not be able to boot following the restore, and the parameters in the restored Boot.ini file would need to be modified.

- When restoring to a new server with different hardware, you might need different drivers, such as drivers for the network adapter or display adapter. Make sure that these drivers are available during the restore.

- The time required to restore data might exceed the time allotted in your recovery plan, which means you must change your backup schedule, your process, or your equipment to improve the speed of the restoration.

- Backup media might be corrupt. Your disaster recovery plan should specify preventive measures (such as redundant backups), and indicate the procedures to follow in the event of corrupt media (such as the location of any redundant backups, or whether out-of-date backups are to be used).

Creating Testing Scripts

After you restore your network and computers, whether at your primary facility or a backup facility, you must have a way to test the network to ensure that critical services are functioning properly. Do not wait until disaster strikes to determine how best to test your systems—design a testing plan ahead of time. Automate this testing as much as possible. Create scripts and batch files that query Web servers, databases, and Active Directory domain controllers for information you know should be present.

For example, imagine that you are responsible for planning a disaster recovery process for a critical application consisting of a Windows Server 2003–based Web server front end, a SQL Server 2000 database also running on Windows Server 2003, and an Active Directory domain controller. After administrators have configured the recovery network, connected the backup computers to the recovery network, and restored the data, you must be able to verify that all application functionality is available. Simply connecting to the Web server front end isn't sufficient because it might not query the database or Active Directory servers until a user attempts to use a specific feature of the application. Even if you did detect that the application was not functioning, you would not have an easy way to identify the source of the problem.

A developer or an administrator with scripting skills can create scripts to test all aspects of the application and the back-end servers the application depends on. The following simplified pseudo-code illustrates how this might work:

```
if ( test.database.customers == success )

    print "Passed: Query database table 'customers'"

else

    print "FAILED: Query database table 'customers'"

if ( test.database.inventory == success )

    print "Passed: Update database table 'inventory'"

else
```

```
    print "FAILED: Update database table 'inventory'"


if ( test.domainController.userQuery == success )

    print "Passed: Test that domain user exists"

else

    print "FAILED: Test that domain user exists"


if ( test.web.page1 == success )

    print "Passed: Retrieve Web page 1"

else

    print "FAILED: Retrieve Web page 1"
```

Of course, you would need to write a great deal more code to actually submit database, Web, and Active Directory queries. However, all development environments, including Microsoft .NET Framework and Perl, have this capability built in and can execute queries with only a few lines of code. When internal development groups create new applications, participate in the development process and have developers set aside time to create such testing scripts. Your quality assurance (QA) group might even be creating the scripts to use during their testing, but might not be aware of the usefulness of the scripts for disaster recovery purposes.

When you run a well-designed test script, the output would quickly identify the source of any failures, speeding the troubleshooting process. For example, the following output from a slightly more complex script clearly shows that the database is up and running, but there is a problem with the domain controller database:

```
Passed: Establish database connection

Passed: Query database table 'customers'

Passed: Query database table 'inventory'

Passed: Connect to domain controller

FAILED: Test that domain user exists

Passed: Retrieve Web page 1
```

Developing testing scripts before a disaster enables you to quickly identify and resolve any problems during recovery, which reduces the downtime caused by the disaster. This, in turn, reduces the risk posed by the disaster.

Guidelines for Designing a Recovery Process

Follow these guidelines when designing a disaster recovery process:

- **Plan for business continuance**   You can lessen the impact of some disasters without going through a full recovery process. Gasoline-powered generators can provide offices and data centers with power during extended outages. Cross-training employees can enable one office to take over some responsibilities if another office is temporarily unavailable.

- **Maintain hardware records**   To limit the amount of time you spend troubleshooting hardware configuration problems during a disaster recovery, maintain current hardware configuration records, including:

  - ❑ A list of your hardware vendor's contact information, such as support phone numbers, e-mail addresses, and Web pages for online support.

  - ❑ A list of the hardware in each server, with firmware update versions and hardware driver versions. (This hardware information can be found in Windows Server 2003 Device Manager.)

  - ❑ A list of the basic input/output system (BIOS) information, interrupt request (IRQ) settings, hard-disk configuration information, and jumper settings on your server's hardware.

- **Maintain software records**   To limit the amount of time you spend troubleshooting software-related problems during a disaster recovery, maintain current software records, including the following:

  - ❑ A list of your software vendor's contact information, such as support phone numbers, e-mail addresses, and Web pages for online support.

  - ❑ A list, organized by date, of software upgrades (such as service packs) and software patches that are installed on your servers.

- **Divide systems by computer role on the network, and create separate backup and recovery policies for each role**   What a computer is used for dictates what type of backup and restore plan needs to be developed for it. Databases, for example, might contain extremely sensitive data, large amounts of data, require special backup software, and take a long time to back up and restore. Desktop computers, on the other hand, might not store any data locally and might simply require a fresh imaging or replacement if they fail.

- **Have written procedures for each computer role**   Don't trust any one person's knowledge of how computers must be backed up or how they can be restored. This person might not be available when needed. Written plans are critical.

- **Practice recovery steps**   Provide test systems and require IT personnel who recover systems to practice the recovery steps. Keep records of which IT personnel have completed practicing the recovery steps. Provide a drill. Simulate the loss of critical systems and data, and require IT personnel to recover the system. Provide feedback and analysis on the results of the drill.

- **Audit backup processes**   There should be processes in place—including logging—to monitor backups. The people responsible for performing backups might not be willing to notify others when problems occur, so it's vital that an outside group monitors the critical task of performing backups.

- **Back up software and licenses, not just data**   In the event of a disaster, you must be able to rebuild your computers from scratch. Backups typically include only data, so you must have operating system and application media backed up. In addition, you need software licenses and application codes. This must be available at both on- and off-site backup locations. If you need to rebuild computers, keep operating system and application CDs available, preferably slipstreamed with the latest updates. For more information about slipstreaming, refer to Chapter 3, "Reducing the Risk of Software Vulnerabilities."

- **Ensure that your insurance policy is adequate**   Insure your company against the cost of recovering, replacing, or reconstructing the lost data in the event of critical data loss. Consult your insurance provider for more information about the coverage options that would suit your company best.

SUMMARY

- To design a backup process, determine your backup requirements, choose backup media, choose backup methods, design a backup network, and then identify special backup requirements for your applications.

- To minimize downtime, configure a hot backup facility. As an alternative, you can lease a warm or cold site for lower cost, but at the expense of having more downtime in the event of a disaster. Mobile sites provide an excellent alternative for organizations that need to provide recovery services for multiple facilities. Reciprocal agreements provide backup facilities while minimizing up-front costs, but are extremely risky.

- The disaster recovery planning process, like the security risk management process, requires you to identify different threats and determine the most cost-effective countermeasures. Disasters require special planning, however, because you might need to rebuild multiple servers from replacement computers.

REVIEW QUESTIONS

1. Which of the following types of backup facilities has the lowest cost?

    a. Hot site

    b. Warm site

    c. Cold site

    d. Mobile site

    e. Reciprocal agreement

2. Which of the following types of backup facilities provides the lowest downtime in the event of a disaster that destroys your primary facilities?

    a. Hot site

    b. Warm site

    c. Cold site

    d. Mobile site

    e. Reciprocal agreement

3. Over dinner, a friend who is a systems administrator at a medium-sized business asks you for advice regarding disaster recovery. At present, he

backs up servers across the network to other servers that have available disk space. Recently, the legal team has informed him that he needs to use off-site backups. What media type would you recommend?

    a. Hard disks

    b. Tapes

    c. Optical media

    d. Writable DVDs

4. During the security risk management process, you identify an extremely critical server. The cost of downtime for the server is so high that you should spare no expense to recover the failed server in a timely manner. Which backup method should you use?

    a. Daily full backups

    b. Weekly full backups, daily incremental backups

    c. Weekly full backups, daily differential backups

5. You are configuring a mobile backup site with standby hardware. Several different offices might use the mobile backup site in the event of a disaster, so you decide to wait for a disaster to occur before you configure the software. Because the backup server hardware will go unused the vast majority of the time, you have chosen lower-cost hardware than you typically use for production servers. When a disaster occurs, should you restore it from backup or rebuild it?

6. Which of the following steps of the incident-response process must happen first?

    a. Determine the cause of the damage.

    b. Contain the damage.

    c. Review response and update policies.

    d. Protect human lives and safety.

    e. Repair the damage.

    f. Assess the damage.

CASE SCENARIOS

Case Scenario 13-1: Designing a Backup Strategy

You are a newly hired security designer at Trey Research. Approximately 200 employees work in a single office near the Atlantic Ocean coastline in Daytona Beach, Florida. A total of 90 percent of the employees use laptop computers so that they can work from home by using a virtual private network (VPN). All critical data is stored on servers.

Recently, Florida suffered a devastating series of hurricanes—four severe hurricanes in two months. The roads to the Trey Research offices were closed because of severe flooding, so employees were instructed to work from home. This worked well for the first day. However, on the second day, the Trey Research basement developed a leak and flooded. Unfortunately, the company had been using the basement as a data center. All computers were submerged in about 5 feet of water and were destroyed.

Trey Research was devastated. Not only did the flood cause the entire organization to lose about a week of productive work, but its computers, data, and even their on-site backup tapes were destroyed. Flood insurance covered part of the cost of replacing the servers; however, the Trey Research systems administrators were forced to revert to the last off-site backup they had stored. This backup was approximately a month old. The tape existed only because a systems administrator had read an article about disaster recovery and decided to bring a copy of the backup tapes to his home. Employees had copies of some data stored on their laptops; however, several weeks of productive work would need to be re-created.

As your first assignment, your manager has asked you to design a backup plan that would prevent such a devastating loss of data in the future. At most, your manager would not want to lose more than a week of data. Ideally, you can design a strategy for minimizing loss in the event of another flood, an event your insurance agency considers very likely. Your boss has asked you to meet these requirements while minimizing costs. Based on this information, answer the questions that follow.

1. How often will you perform backups, and what types of backups (full, incremental, or differential) will you perform?

2. What type of media will you use for the daily backups?

3. How often will you move backups off-site?

4. How can you minimize the risk of damage to the on-site backup tapes by future flooding?

5. How can you minimize the risk of damage to the servers by future flooding?

Case Scenario 13-2: Designing a Disaster Recovery Strategy

It's been nine months since you designed Trey Research's backup strategy, and it has worked perfectly. You have not had any major disasters, fortunately. Then, your boss calls you into her office. She's holding a copy of the *Farmer's Almanac* in her hand.

"I know it's old-fashioned, but I think these *Farmer's Almanac* writers know what they're talking about. They're predicting that the hurricanes blowing in from the Atlantic are going to be much worse than last year. I love being here on the coast, but looking at this building, I'm not so sure it's going to hold up to a series of serious hurricanes. I'd like to put together a plan to keep our business functioning even if the building is severely damaged. I don't care if we miss a few days of work, but I don't want us to be offline for weeks at a time. We should be able to keep working for, say, the six weeks it would take us to identify a new facility and move our servers in."

Based on your boss's requirements and the background information provided in Case Scenario 13-1, answer the questions that follow.

1. What type of backup facility should you use, and why?

2. You contact a disaster-recovery-service organization that provides backup facilities. They have locations in Jacksonville, Tampa, and Miami that would meet your requirements. Figure 13-4 shows these cities on a map.

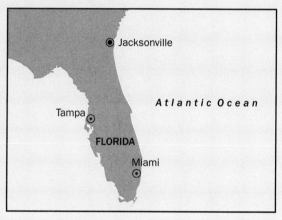

Figure 13-4   Backup facilities are available in Jacksonville, Tampa, and Miami.

Which city should you choose?

   a. Jacksonville

   b. Tampa

   c. Miami

3. Once you bring your backup site online, where will the Trey Research employees work? What technology will you need to configure at the backup facility to enable this?

GLOSSARY

access control entry (ACE)   An entry in an object's access control list (ACL) that grants permissions to a user or group.

ACE   *See* access control entry (ACE).

ACL   *See* discretionary access control list (DACL).

AH   *See* Authentication Header (AH).

ALE   *See* annual loss expectancy (ALE).

annual loss expectancy (ALE)   The average amount of money that your organization will lose in one year if nothing is done to mitigate a risk. The ALE is determined by the equation

$$ALE = SLE \times ARO$$

where SLE represents single-loss expectancy and ARO represents annual rate of occurrence.

annual rate of occurrence (ARO)   The chance of a security compromise in any given year. ARO is expressed as a percentage, from 0 percent (could not happen) to 100 percent (will definitely happen).

answer file   A file that provides information—without prompting the user—that all recent versions of Microsoft Windows Setup use to configure the system.

archive bit   A per-file setting that indicates whether a file has been changed since it was last backed up.

ARO   *See* annual rate of occurrence (ARO).

asset   Anything within an organization's environment that might require some level of protection. This could include items that were purchased outright, such as software, hardware, and facili-

ties. Assets can also be data, people, and information.

asset valuation   *See* asset value (AV).

asset value (AV)   The amount it costs to maintain an asset, what it would cost if the asset were lost or destroyed, and what benefit would be gained if another party obtained this asset.

asymmetric key encryption   *See* public key encryption.

Authentication Header (AH)   An Internet Protocol Security (IPSec) protocol that provides data origin authentication, data integrity, and antireplay protection for the entire packet, including the IP header and the data payload carried in the packet.

authorization store   A database that defines which users and groups can access an application's features.

autoenrollment   A process whereby the certification authority (CA) issues certificates to users automatically by authenticating the user with the user's domain credentials.

autostatic updates   A method of automatically adding static routes to the routing table after establishing a demand-dial connection.

AV   *See* asset value (AV).

availability   Keeping systems and information accessible to users, even during catastrophic events and security attacks.

Background Intelligent Transfer Service (BITS)   A service that transfers data from the Software Update Services (SUS) or Windows Update server to the Automatic Updates client with minimal impact to other network services.

base certificate revocation list (CRL) A complete list of revoked certificates.

Basic authentication An unencrypted Microsoft Internet Information Services (IIS) authentication mechanism supported by every common browser. User credentials are Base64-encoded, which does not provide any privacy.

BIA *See* business impact analysis (BIA).

BITS *See* Background Intelligent Transfer Service (BITS).

business impact analysis (BIA) A process that assesses the damage that would be caused by different types of disasters.

CA *See* certification authority (CA).

CAS *See* code access security (CAS).

certificate A tool for using public key encryption for authentication and encryption.

certificate enrollment The process of requesting and installing certificates for a user, computer, or service.

certificate policy A set of rules for issuing certificates.

certificate revocation list (CRL) A list of certificates no longer considered valid, but not yet expired.

certificate templates The sets of rules and settings that define the format and content of a certificate based on the certificate's intended use.

certificate trust list (CTL) A list of certificates, defined in advance, that are signed by a trusted entity.

certification authority (CA) A server trusted to issue certificates to an individual, a computer, or a service.

cipher text Data that has been encrypted and cannot easily be decrypted without an encryption key; resembles random data.

code access security (CAS) A security system that allows administrators and developers to control application authorization. With CAS, you can allow one application to read and write to the registry, while restricting access for a different application.

code review A type of procedure that requires a manager to review and approve all code written by a developer. Code review procedures reduce the risk of a developer injecting malicious code, such as a back door, into internal software.

cold site A backup facility that has only the most basic infrastructure: electricity, lighting, plumbing, and heat.

compromise The successful exploitation of a vulnerability by a threat.

confidentiality Protecting the privacy of information so that no one except authorized users can access it.

contingency plan A process that can be activated in case efforts to prevent an attack fail.

cookie A piece of data, issued by the Web server application, that the Web browser submits in subsequent requests to prove that the requests originated from the same user to whom the original cookie was issued.

countermeasure Software, hardware, or a procedure that, when deployed, counteracts a threat and protects a vulnerability to reduce risk in a computer environment.

critical update A broadly released fix addressing a critical nonsecurity-related bug for a specific problem.

CRL *See* certificate revocation list (CRL).

cross-certificates Special certificates used to establish complete or qualified one-way trusts between otherwise unrelated CAs.

CTL *See* certificate trust list (CTL).

DACL   *See* discretionary access control list (DACL).

data recovery   A process by which data is encrypted in such a way that more than one person can retrieve the data in plaintext form.

dedicated forest root domain   A domain that is created specifically to function as the forest root. It does not contain any user accounts other than the service administrator accounts for the forest root domain, and it does not represent any region in your domain structure.

defense-in-depth   A security design technique that uses multiple levels of countermeasures to overcome unpredictable vulnerabilities and human errors.

delayed signing   A two-part application-signing process that separates the public and private strong-name keys, enabling enterprises to centralize application signing and restrict the distribution of private keys. The fewer people who have access to a private key, the lower the risk of the key's being abused.

delta CRL   A list of certificates revoked after the last base or delta CRL was published.

demand-dial routing   A virtual private network (VPN) connection that is established only when traffic needs to be sent to the remote network. Demand-dial routing is used for VPN connections across dial-up links.

demilitarized zone (DMZ)   *See* perimeter network.

detective countermeasure   A countermeasure that enables you to detect a compromise. Examples of detective countermeasures include intrusion-detection systems, fault-monitoring software, and file-integrity checking.

dial-up networking   A remote-access method that enables a remote-access client to establish a temporary dial-up connection to a physical port on a remote-access server by a circuit such as analog phone lines, Integrated Services Digital Network (ISDN), or X.25.

Digest authentication   A hashed IIS authentication mechanism that allows the Web browser to submit the user's password in a Message Digest 5 algorithm (MD5) hash. If digest authentication traffic is intercepted, an attacker would not be able to easily determine the user's password. Digest authentication provides higher security than Basic authentication and can pass through firewalls.

discretionary access control list (DACL)   A mechanism for tracking the privileges users have to resources. DACLs, also known simply as ACLs, identify the users and groups that are assigned or denied access permissions on an object. If a DACL does not explicitly identify a user, or any groups that a user is a member of, the user will be denied access to that object.

DMZ   *See* perimeter network.

domain   A partition in an Active Directory directory service forest. In contrast to a forest, a domain is not a security boundary because within a forest it is not possible for administrators from one domain to prevent a malicious administrator from another domain from accessing data in their domain.

EF   *See* exposure factor (EF).

EFS   *See* Encrypting File System (EFS).

Emergency Management Services (EMS)   A new feature in Microsoft Windows Server 2003 that provides command-line access to a server when the server is not accessible across the network or by using a keyboard.

EMS   *See* Emergency Management Services (EMS).

Encapsulating Security Payload (ESP)   An Internet Protocol Security (IPSec) protocol that provides data origin authentication, data integrity, antireplay protection, and the option of privacy.

Encrypting File System (EFS)   A transparent file encryption service provided by the Microsoft Windows 2000, Windows XP Professional (not Windows XP Home Edition), and Windows Server 2003 family for files on NTFS volumes. EFS provides what file permissions cannot: protection when the operating system is bypassed.

ESP   *See* Encapsulating Security Payload (ESP).

explicit permission   A permission that is assigned directly to an object, rather than being inherited from a parent container.

exploit   When used as a noun, a threat that has the potential to compromise a vulnerability. A worm, virus, Trojan horse, or other tool that can be used by an attacker to compromise a vulnerable computer is an exploit. When used as a verb, this term is synonymous with compromise.

exposure factor (EF)   The percentage of an asset's total value that a threat could potentially damage.

firewall   A system that creates a boundary between a public and a private network.

forest   A collection of one or more Active Directory directory service domains that share a common logical structure, global catalog, directory schema, and directory configuration, as well as automatic two-way transitive trust relationships. Each forest is a single instance of the directory and defines a security boundary.

forest trust   A type of trust in which every domain trusts every other domain in the other forests. Forest

trusts are Kerberos version 5 authentication style and can be one-way or two-way trusts. Forest trusts between domains in both forests are transitive, but the forest trust itself is not.

Forms authentication   An ASP.NET authentication type that redirects unauthenticated requests to a Hypertext Markup Language (HTML) form that prompts the user for credentials. ASP.NET can authenticate the credentials against a list of names stored in a configuration file, a database, or any custom mechanism created by the application developer.

fully trusted application   An application that is exempt from code access security (CAS) security checks, just like an unmanaged application.

group nesting   The process of placing security groups into other security groups. Group nesting is an effective way to scale the groups in an organization.

honeypot   Software that impersonates an entire network and waits for an attacker to launch an attack.

host-based firewall   A software firewall installed on an individual computer to protect communications regardless of the network to which the computer connects.

hot site   A true backup facility from which your employees can work at a moment's notice. Hot sites typically have desktop computers for the staff, actively running servers with recent copies of your applications and data, and a working, continuously monitored network.

hotfix   A package consisting of one or many files that provides a fix for a product problem. A hotfix addresses a specific customer problem and is available only through a support relationship with Microsoft. Other terms that have been used in the past are quick-fix engineering (QFE) update, patch, and update.

IDS   *See* intrusion-detection system (IDS).

in-band connection   A connection that uses traditional network communications, such as a Telnet or Secure Shell (SSH) connection to a terminal concentrator.

incident response   The process that defines what happens when an attack or suspected attack occurs.

inherited permission   A permission that is not assigned directly to a child object, but rather is assigned to a parent in which the child is contained, and inherited by the child object. Most objects in Microsoft Windows environments have only inherited permissions.

Integrated Windows Authentication   An encrypted IIS authentication mechanism that provides either Microsoft Windows NT LAN Manager (NTLM) or Kerberos v5 authentication between a Web client and server. This allows the Web browser to send the user's password in the form of a hash without requiring the user's password to be stored using reversible encryption.

integrity   Preventing unauthorized users from creating or modifying data, and ensuring that you know which authorized users have created and modified data.

Internet Protocol Security (IPSec)   A protocol suite that works with Transmission Control Protocol/Internet Protocol (TCP/IP) to verify the integrity of communications, authenticate computers, and encrypt traffic.

Intrusion-detection system (IDS)   Software that uses algorithms to detect a potential attack from the thousands of legitimate events, and then alerts administrative staff to the attack so that they can analyze it further and respond if necessary.

IPSec   *See* Internet Protocol Security (IPSec).

IPSec negotiation   The process by which two Internet Protocol Security (IPSec) hosts identify the most secure set of protocols they can use to communicate.

Kerberos   A network authentication protocol designed to provide strong authentication for client/server applications by using secret-key cryptography.

key recovery   A process that allows a trusted agent to gain access to users' private keys.

latency   The time it takes a packet to travel between two points, usually measured in milliseconds.

legacy system   Any infrastructure component such as hardware, operating system software, network device, or application that is technically outdated and cannot be upgraded. For example, Microsoft Windows 2000–based computers that cannot be upgraded might be defined as legacy systems because they do not support Windows Firewall.

LM hash   A hashed version of a password, used for storing and transmitting passwords when using the original LM authentication protocol. LM Hash versions of passwords are extremely vulnerable to cracking attacks because of weaknesses in the hashing algorithm.

long-term key   In Kerberos authentication, a secret key that only the key distribution center (KDC) and the client know. They use the long-term key to prove their identity in future communications.

MAC address filtering   A wireless security technique that filters traffic from wireless network adapters that do not have an approved media access control (MAC) address.

managed application An application based on the Microsoft .NET Framework.

many-to-one certificate mapping Maps one or more certificates to an Active Directory directory service user account by comparing information contained in client certificates to administrator-specified criteria. When a user holding a matching certificate authenticates to Microsoft Internet Information Services (IIS), IIS will use the mapped Active Directory user account to access resources. This enables you to restrict the user's access by using NTFS file permissions.

Microsoft Passport A Microsoft authentication service that enables users to use a single set of credentials to authenticate to multiple Web sites on the Internet. Both Microsoft Internet Information Services (IIS) and ASP.NET support Passport authentication.

Microsoft Security Response Center (MSRC) severity rating A system that applies a rating to an announced vulnerability.

mobile site A trailer that can function as office space during an emergency. The mobile site typically has a generator to provide electricity, and some telecommunications capabilities, such as a satellite uplink for phone and Internet services.

NAT-T *See* NAT Traversal (NAT-T).

NAT Traversal (NAT-T) A feature that enables Internet Protocol Security (IPSec) traffic to pass through compatible network-address translation (NAT) servers.

Network Load Balancing (NLB) A Microsoft clustering technology that spreads requests for a single Internet Protocol (IP) address among several Microsoft Windows servers. It can also provide load balancing in addition to scalability and redundancy. If a VPN server that is using NLB fails, client sessions will also fail and the user will be prompted to log on again. The user's new session will be managed by one of the other virtual private network (VPN) servers in the cluster.

NLB *See* Network Load Balancing (NLB).

nonce A 16-byte random-character string used to encrypt a password hash in NTLM authentication communications.

nonrepudiation A security concept that ensures that a user actually performed an action, such as sending an e-mail.

nontransitive trust relationship Where multiple trust relationships exist, trust does not extend from trust to trust. That is, if domains A and B trust each other and domains B and C trust each other, domains A and C do not trust each other. Microsoft Windows NT 4.0–style trusts are nontransitive.

NT Hash A hashed version of a password used for storing and transmitting passwords when using the NTLMv1 authentication protocol. NT Hashes are much less vulnerable to cracking attacks than LM Hashes.

one-to-one certificate mapping Maps a single exported certificate to an Active Directory directory service user account. When the user holding the certificate authenticates to Microsoft Internet Information Services (IIS), IIS will use the Active Directory user account to access resources. This enables you to restrict the user's access by using NTFS file permissions.

one-way trust A trust relationship that extends in one direction. All Microsoft Windows trusts can be created in a single direction. However a bidirectional trust can be created by creating two trust relationships, one in each direction.

open relay Mail servers that accept messages from anyone and attempt to forward the message on to its final destination.

out-of-band connection A connection, such as a serial port, that uses a nontraditional medium for communications. A common example of an out-of-band connection is the link from a terminal concentrator to an Emergency Management Services (EMS) management port.

packet filtering A basic function of firewalls that examines incoming and outgoing packets and drops packets based on predefined criteria, such as port numbers, source Internet Protocol (IP) address, and destination IP address.

partially trusted application An application that must undergo code access security (CAS) permission checks whenever it accesses a protected resource.

passphrase A very long password that is composed of multiple words, numbers, and symbols, such as IWasBornInNYOnJanuary3.

password dictionary A text file that contains commonly used passwords. Attackers use password dictionaries to guess user passwords because it is more efficient than trying every possible password combination.

patch A broadly released fix for a specific problem. Addresses a noncritical, nonsecurity-related bug.

perimeter network A small network that is set up separately from an organization's private network and the Internet. A perimeter network provides a layer of protection for internal systems in the event of compromise of a system offering services to the Internet. Also known as a demilitarized zone (DMZ) or a screened subnet.

PKI *See* public key infrastructure (PKI).

preventive countermeasure A countermeasure that is designed to prevent a threat from exploiting a vulnerability. Examples of preventive countermeasures include firewalls, security updates, antivirus software, and physical locks.

private key encryption Encryption that requires both the sender and the recipient of an encrypted message to have a shared secret. Also known as shared key encryption or symmetric key encryption.

privileged groups User groups that have more access and authority than ordinary users, such as the local Administrators group or the Domain Admins group.

public key certificate *See* certificate.

public key encryption Encryption that uses one key to encrypt a message and a second, related key to decrypt the message.

public key infrastructure (PKI) A set of policies, standards, and software for managing certificates and public key pairs.

qualified subordination Microsoft Windows Server 2003 restrictions placed on a cross-certification.

quarantine control A remote-access server feature that provides phased network access for remote clients by limiting their communications to a quarantine network until the security configuration of the client computer is verified.

RBS *See* role-based security (RBS).

reactive countermeasure A countermeasure that enables you to respond to and recover from a compromise. Examples of reactive countermeasures include backups, disaster recovery plans, and archiving of security event logs.

reciprocal agreement   Plans with a partner organization to share facilities in the event disaster strikes one or the other organization.

reduce the attack surface   A security principle that says the fewer avenues of attack that are available, the less there is to protect and the less chance there is of the network being compromised. For example, to decrease the number of avenues of attack, disable unneeded services, refrain from installing unnecessary services or applications, and protect sensitive data with encryption.

role-based security (RBS)   The traditional security mechanism, by which rights are granted to users and groups.

routing protocol   A technology that enables routers to share information about neighboring networks.

routing table   A list of remote networks and the neighboring routers that can forward traffic to each network.

SACL   *See* security access control list (SACL).

screened subnet   An area that defines a network that is neither part of an organization's internal network nor part of the external network but is under the control of the organization. Provides users on the Internet with limited access to some internal servers, while providing protection for users and servers on the private network. See also perimeter network.

security access control list (SACL)   A usage-event logging mechanism that determines how file or folder access is audited. Unlike a discretionary access control list (DACL), an SACL cannot restrict access to a file or folder. However, an SACL can cause an event to be recorded in the Security event log when a user accesses a file or folder. This auditing can be used to troubleshoot access problems or identify intrusions.

security boundary   A logical division that separates users outside the boundary from resources inside the boundary. Unless an administrator inside the security boundary explicitly allows it, users outside the boundary have no access.

security-by-obscurity   Relying only on a threat agent's ignorance to protect an asset.

security identifier filtering   A process that prevents users from outside the forest from using their security identifiers (SIDs) to access resources within the forest.

security rollup package (SRP)   A collection of security updates, critical updates, other updates, and hotfixes released as a cumulative offering or targeted at a single product component such as Microsoft Internet Information Services (IIS) or Microsoft Internet Explorer. Allows for easier deployment of multiple software updates.

security template   A physical file representation of a security configuration applied to a local computer or imported to a Group Policy object (GPO) in Active Directory directory service. When you import a security template to a GPO, Group Policy processes the template and makes the corresponding changes to the members of that GPO, which can be users or computers.

security update   A released fix that addresses a vulnerability in a specific product.

security update processes   The ways in which security changes can be made.

selective authentication   The ability to limit authentication across an external or forest trust.

service pack   A cumulative set of hot-fixes, security updates, critical updates, and other updates that have been released since the release of the product, including many resolved problems that have not been made available through any other software updates. Service packs might also contain a limited number of customer-requested design changes or features. Service packs are broadly distributed and are more thoroughly tested by Microsoft than any other software updates.

service processor   A hardware component built into some computers that allows for out-of-band management of the computer when the operating system is unavailable.

shared secret   A password used to encrypt and decrypt a message.

SID filtering   A process that does not allow the use of security identifiers (SIDs) from outside the forest to be used to access resources within the forest. When a user attempts to access resources across forest boundaries, SIDs are dropped from the user's access credentials if they do not come from the forest in which the user's account resides.

SID spoofing   An attack in which a domain administrator from a trusted domain attaches a well-known security principal to the SID of a normal user account to gain elevated privileges to the trusting domain.

Simple Network Management Protocol (SNMP)   The communications protocol used by most network management software to collect data from servers, clients, and network equipment.

single-loss expectancy (SLE)   The total amount of revenue that is lost from a single security compromise. The SLE is determined by the equation

$$SLE = AV \times EF$$

SLE   *See* single-loss expectancy (SLE).

slipstreaming   The process of integrating a service pack into operating system setup files so that new computers immediately have the service pack installed.

sniffing   Capturing communications as packets pass across a network.

SNMP   *See* Simple Network Management Protocol (SNMP).

SNMP agent   A computer or network device that is capable of responding to Simple Network Management Protocol (SNMP) queries.

SNMP community name   A simple credential that acts as both a user name and a simple password for Simple Network Management Protocol (SNMP) agents' and servers' use to identify themselves.

SNMP trap   Simple Network Management Protocol (SNMP) messages sent from an SNMP agent to a server after a specific event occurs. Can be used for limited security checking.

social engineering   An attack that tricks people into revealing their passwords or some form of security information.

split tunneling   A technique for allowing virtual private network (VPN) clients to communicate with a private network and the Internet simultaneously.

spyware A component of some free software that tracks your Web-browsing habits.

SQL injection attack A threat agent that inserts database commands into user input to modify commands sent from an application to a back-end database.

SRP *See* security rollup package (SRP).

stateful inspection A firewall feature that enables the firewall to keep track of all valid connections and drop all packets that are not part of an existing session.

symmetric key encryption *See* private key encryption.

Telnet A simple protocol for command-line management of network computers.

terminal concentrator A network device that accepts Telnet or Secure Shell (SSH) connections from administrators and communicates with serial or modem ports on computers. The terminal concentrator also may be able to connect directly to a modem to allow for dial-in access to Emergency Management Services (EMS).

threat The method of attack used by a threat agent.

threat agent A person, place, or thing that has the potential to access resources without proper authorization and thereby cause harm.

threat modeling The process of brainstorming all possible risks to a system so that countermeasures can be developed.

transitive trust relationship Where multiple trust relationships exist, trust extends between all trusted and trusting domains. Microsoft Windows 2000 Server and Windows Server 2003 domains within a forest are in a transitive trust relationship, so all domains trust all other domains.

transport mode An Internet Protocol Security (IPSec) mode for protecting host-to-host communications in which IPSec tunnels traffic at the Transport Layer, also known as Layer 4.

trust A conjoining of domains that allows authentication and access across domain boundaries, forest boundaries, or both.

trust chaining The ability for public key infrastructure (PKI) clients to trust certificates issued by a subordinate certification authority (CA) when the client has been configured to trust only the root CA.

trust model The number and arrangement of trusts within and between forests and the way in which these trusts are restricted.

trusted In a one-way trust, the trusted domain is the domain whose accounts can be given access to resources in the trusting domain.

trusting In a one-way trust, the trusting domain is the domain whose resources can be accessed by accounts in the trusted domain.

tunnel mode An Internet Protocol Security (IPSec) mode for protecting network-to-network or host-to-network communications in which IPSec tunnels traffic at the Internet Layer, also known as Layer 3.

unilateral cross-certification A trust in which one certification authority (CA) cross-certifies another CA, but not the reverse.

unmanaged application An application that is not based on the .NET Framework, such as Microsoft Win32® applications.

vulnerability An opportunity for an attacker to launch a successful attack. Also commonly known as a weakness or a security compromise.

warm site A backup facility that duplicates the least expensive infrastructure components: server racks, desks, and telephone lines.

Web.config files Per-folder configuration settings for ASP.NET applications.

Wireless Provisioning Services (WPS) Software that simplifies the process of connecting to a wireless hotspot by providing a standardized procedure for authenticating and authorizing a user and configuring wireless security.

WPS *See* Wireless Provisioning Services (WPS).

INDEX

A

acceptable use policies, 67
accept (risk response), 59
access control
    MMC snap-ins, 154
    Network Load Balancing, 171
    restricting physical access to servers, 365
    as security domain, 11
    wireless networks, 554, 556–57
access control entries. *See* ACEs (access control entries)
access controller, WPS, 554
access control lists. *See* ACLs (access control lists)
access points. *See* APs (access points)
Account Group/ACL authorization, 272, 338
Account Group/Resource Group authorization, 272–73
account lockout
    Account Management events, 323
    avoiding for remote-access, 596
    IAS servers, 382–83
    kiosks, 436
    LM authentication, 196
    logon events, 319
    overview of, 211–13
    password cracking threats and, 210
    security templates, 349
Account Management events, 322–23
Account Operators group, 263
Account Policies node, 348–49
accounts
    auditing, 320–23
    mapping, 245
ACEs (access control entries)
    CAS permissions and, 441–43
    minimizing number of, 294
    overview of, 257–58
ACLs (access control lists)
    Active Directory permissions and, 294
    backup tapes protected with, 681
    hard backup disks protected with, 679
    listing security groups in, 260
    overview of, 257–58
    SID filtering and, 238–39
    special permissions configuring, 280
    standard permissions configuring, 280
    User/ACL authorization method, 271–72
Active Directory, 191–254
    to ADAMSync, 611
    backup, 688
    case scenarios, 250–54
    database protection, 368
    groups, 259–60
    IPSec and, 531–32, 538
    overview of, 219–22
    permissions, 284–87
    review questions, 247–50
    security templates deployed with, 355–62
    security templates deployed without, 362–63
    summary, 247

UNIX interoperating with, 244–46
updates deployed with GPOs and, 103
wireless networking and, 539–40
Active Directory Application Mode (ADAM), 366, 609–10
Active Directory, authentication
    anonymous, 242–43
    Kerberos, 200–205
    LM, 195–99
    multifactor, 215–18
    overview of, 192–95
    protocol support, 194
Active Directory, forests, 218–42
    creating trusts between, 236, 237
    hardening trusts, 236–42
    identifying domain model, 231–33
    identifying forest model, 226–30
    need for isolation, 222–26
    overview of, 218–19
    role of, 219–20
    selecting forest root domain, 233–35
Active Directory, passwords, 205–15
    account lockout policy, 211–13
    long passwords and interoperability, 213–14
    risk of attempts to crack, 209–10, 212
    risk of reset tools, 210–11
    strong passwords, 206–9
    technical controls enforcing, 214–15
ADAM (Active Directory Application Mode), 366, 609–10
ADAMSync (ADAM Synchronizer), 611, 613
Add/Remove Programs
    advantages and disadvantages, 98
    deploying updates, 103–4
    removing updates, 112
Add/Remove Windows Components, 623
administrators. *See also* delegation of administration
    after-hours network backups, 684–85
    authenticating, 178–82
    backup permissions, 687–88
    dedicated forest root domains, 234
    forest design risk of, 223–24
    remote access for, 176–78
    Remote Desktop security, 156
    SharePoint Team Services, 171–72
    smart cards, 218
    software inventory, 91
Administrators group, 263
ADSI Edit
    Active Directory permissions and, 286–87
    ADAM version of, 610
    IPSec and, 531
AES (Advanced Encryption System), 549
AH (Authentication Header), 530
A (host) resource records, 376–77
AirSnort, 543
ALE (annual loss expectancy), 55, 60, 77
alerts, security, 106
ALT keys, 199
American Registry for Internet Numbers (ARIN), 669

C